INTRODUCTION TO
ARISTOTLE

INTRODUCTION
TO
ARISTOTLE

Second edition, revised and enlarged
With a New General Introduction and
New Introductions to the Particular Works

by RICHARD McKEON

The University of Chicago Press
Chicago and London

The University of Chicago Press, Chicago 60637
The University of Chicago Press, Ltd., London

Copyright, 1947, by Random House, Inc.
© 1973 by Richard P. McKeon

All rights reserved. Published 1973
Printed in the United States of America

82 81 80 79 78   6 5 4 3 2

International Standard Book Number: 0-226-56032-5
Library of Congress Catalog Card Number: 73-87305

Contents

Preface

Aristotle is himself the best introduction to what Aristotle thought and meant. Reading and rereading is, indeed, the only introduction to the writings of a philosopher, or a poet, or a scientist, whose influence on the vision, thought, and comprehension of mankind has been long and complex. In attentive reading, each line, each argument, and each structured part serves in turn as introduction to what is read next, and each reconsideration deepens and enriches the conception and interpretation of what is successively or recurrently encountered and fitted into place. Aristotle's influence on men's thought has been variegated. There have been many interpretations of his philosophy in the past, and many are current today. This introduction to Aristotle is not an interpretation. It is a selection from the writings of Aristotle, in which Aristotle speaks for himself about philosophical problems and basic ideas, methods, and distinctions used in treating them. It is left to the reader to judge for himself whether Aristotle has made use of what he has said about methods to relate the various parts of his work to each other. The reader is given the means and the matter to form his own interpretation and the opportunity to use that interpretation as a basis for speculating and for inquiring further into philosophic problems and into Aristotle's influence on their formulation and treatment.

Nine selections are presented in their entirety, unaltered, and uncut: four complete treatises, the *Posterior Analytics*, *On the Soul*, the *Nicomachean Ethics*, and the *Poetics*; complete books from three other treatises, one book from the *Physics*, two from the *Metaphysics*, and two from the *Politics*; and selected chapters from two treatises, the first chapter of Book I of *On the Parts of Animals* and the first four chapters of Book I and Chapters 18–22 of Book II of the *Rhetoric*. The nine introductions which precede these nine selections from Aristotle's work place them in their contexts by using Aristotle's distinctions to relate the ideas treated in one work to their meanings and applications in others, to distinguish the method used on a particular subject from methods proper to other subjects, and to locate the works themselves within the structure that Aristotle forms for the arts and sciences and for experience and knowledge. The General Introduction sets forth basic ideas, methods, and distinctions which Aristotle expounds and applies in the course of his philosophic inquiry and presentation, and places Aristotle's work in his times, relates it to the work of his predecessors as Aristotle interpreted them, and sketches the shifting forms of later Aristotelianism and anti-Aristotelianism.

Grateful acknowledgement is hereby extended to the Oxford University Press for permission to reprint the translation of the works of Aristotle prepared under the editorship of W. D. Ross.

R. McKeon

General Introduction

by Richard McKeon

1. The Life and Times of Aristotle

The stages of the career of Aristotle and of the formation of his school reflect the stages in which the kingdom of Macedonia extended its hegemony to Athens and Greece and the culture, polity, and military establishment of Greece to the world. This dynastic unification terminated abruptly, on the death of Alexander, and disintegrated into a network of commercial and dynastic communications and rivalries among the Hellenistic kingdoms. Stagira, in which Aristotle was born in 384/3, was a city in the Hellenic part of Thrace. Ancient biographies of Aristotle place his birth in Thrace. Stagira was destroyed in the wars of Philip, but was restored on the petition of Aristotle, who, when his request had been granted, drew up a code of laws for its inhabitants. Later biographies make him a native of Macedonia. His father, Nicomachus, was court physician to Amyntas II, father of Philip II, or Philip the Great. His father was descended, according to an ancient life of Aristotle, from Nicomachus, son of Machaon, the physician in the *Iliad*, who in turn was son of Asclepius, the god of medicine. In 368/7, Aristotle was sent to Athens, where he remained in close association with the Academy of Plato for twenty years, from his eighteenth to his thirty-seventh year, until the death of Plato in 348/7. After Plato's death, Aristotle left Athens and, together with Xenocrates, visited the court of Hermias, who had studied at the Academy before he became tyrant of Atar-

neus and Assos in Mysia in Asia Minor. Aristotle married
Hermias's niece (or daughter or concubine), Pythias, and
he may have taught at a kind of Academic center in Assos.
He left Assos, before Hermias's betrayal to, and execution
by, the Persians, for Mitylene in Lesbos, where he engaged
in biological observation and research. In 343/2, on the
invitation of Philip of Macedon, he returned to Pella, the
capitol of Macedonia, to become tutor to Alexander, who
was then thirteen years old. The instruction probably
lasted only two years, until 340, when Alexander was appointed regent for his father. Aristotle remained in the
north; he may have gone from Pella to his native Stagira;
and he returned to Athens in 335/4, a year after the death
of Philip.

Aristotle devoted the next twelve years at Athens with
extraordinary industry and concentration to the establishment of a school, the Lyceum; to the institution and execution of a program of empirical research; to historical,
theoretic, and systematic speculation; to teaching, exoteric
and esoteric, that is, lectures addressed to the general public and inquiries conducted with research groups of scholars, in almost every branch of knowledge; and to the
composition of all, or most, or at least the most scientific
portions, of those of his writings which are still extant.
When Alexander died in 323, the Athenians revolted
against Macedonian domination, and their revulsion extended to all reminders of Macedonian presence or influence. Aristotle left Athens lest, he is said to have remarked,
the Athenians sin twice against philosophy. The charges
on which Socrates had been condemned and executed,
and which were echoed in the accusations which led to
the exile of Anaxagoras and Protagoras, were aired in
rumors and allegations of impious attachment to strange
gods, treasonable plots against the institutions of the state,
and immoral relations with youths. One charge was that
he had instituted a private cult in the memory of his friend
Hermias, since he had erected a statue to him at Delphi

and had composed a poem, in the manner of a paean, in his honor. This took on the character of impiety, even in a religion in which men often became gods, since Hermias was a eunuch. Aristotle took refuge under the protection of his old friend Antipater, viceroy to Alexander, at Chalcis in Euboea, where he died in 322, less than a year after Alexander and a few months before Demosthenes, whose impassioned efforts to persuade Athenians to treat Macedonian advances as military aggression rather than cultural unification has made the word "philippic" a common noun. The three deaths mark the close of an age. The Hellenistic Age began, and Hellenistic Aristotelianism was the first of the varied forms of Aristotle's influence.

Scholars have sought suggestions for the interpretation of Aristotle's philosophy and its development in the influence of his circumstances, and critics and opponents have used alleged occurrences to explain its deficiencies and errors. Nonetheless, the causes put forth for Aristotle's achievements or vagaries, his insights or misconceptions, though sometimes circumstantially plausible or narratively beguiling, cannot be connected unambiguously with any idea, any argument, or any doctrine in the works of Aristotle. It is plausible to suppose that he received the training of a physician from his father; but we do not know how old Aristotle was when his father died, or how a physician would train his son, apart from the education specified by Galen for an Aesclepiad—reading, writing, and "anatomy." It is plausible to suppose that the boy would have been influenced in his youth by Macedonian court life, but we do not know whether Aristotle accompanied his father from Stagira to Pella. Twenty years of study and research at the Academy seem to argue for a profound impress of Plato's dialectic and ideas on his thought; but, on the one side, we do not know what contacts Aristotle had with Plato in the Academy—Plato was not at the Academy at the time of Aristotle's arrival and was absent on frequent and long trips, to Syracuse and possibly to other foreign lands, during Aristotle's stay —and, on the other side, the references to Plato's dialectic and ideas in Aristotle's later works are highly critical and, according to Platonists, inaccurate and false. We do not know how Aristotle spent his time at the Academy. There is an ancient tradition that he undertook the teaching of rhetoric in opposition to the flourishing school of Isocrates, who is praised by Plato through Socrates in the *Phaedrus*; and an ancient rumor that he planned to establish a school of philosophy in rivalry to the Academy. It is probable that he participated in the biological research which was flourishing at the Academy, and the fragments of his early dialogues treat Platonic problems using the Platonic literary form and adapting the Platonic dialectic. He left Athens immediately after the death of Plato: possibly because his friendship for Plato was the only bond which kept him in Athens; possibly because he had been passed over when Plato's nephew Speusippus was chosen to succeed him; possibly because of the basic importance which Speusippus and his followers put on mathematics rather than metaphysics.

The relationship between Aristotle and Alexander has been elaborated by philosophers from Plutarch to Hegel as a model of how philosophy may contribute to the formation of policy and institution and of how political power and financial support might encourage and advance scientific research and theoretic system-formation. The theme has been given factual and imaginative elaboration in histories and novels of the life of Alexander. Plato's ambition to influence kings through the study of philosophy has been used as an analogy to supply missing details concerning Aristotle's teaching, but we have no evidence that Aristotle had any influence on the moral ideals or political ambitions or intellectual habits of his royal pupil. He is reputed to have written two works for Alexander, *On Monarchy* and *On Colonies*, and to have revised the text of the *Iliad* for him, but we have no information concerning the contents of the essays or the purport of the edition. Aristotle did not inspire Alexander's ideal of world conquest or his conception of the brotherhood of man to be institutionalized in a world state. Brotherhood and universal community were ideas conceived by the Cynics and given systematic grounds and extensions, after Alexander's death, by the Stoics. The structure of Aristotle's *Politics* was built on the small unit, the city-state, and, far from speculating on the possibilities of larger political organization, based on other models than the Persian empire and the Greek leagues, Aristotle shows no awareness of the implications of his pupil's actions and ideas for political science. Alexander is said to have sent biological specimens to his master during his campaigns in the East and to have provided other means, including funds, to support his researches: but whereas the results of Aristotle's observations in Lesbos are apparent in the descriptions of animals and fishes in his biological works, and whereas he might have secured information from royal hunters or herdsmen in Pella, he mentions no species concerning which his information would depend on royal shipments of animals. Research was costly in antiquity, as it is still today, but no plausible connection can be made between any of Aristotle's research projects and a royal grant for its support. Aristotle's nephew, Callisthenes, who accompanied Alexander on his campaigns, was executed for treason: there were those who accused Aristotle of complicity in the plot.

Aristotle presents himself as virtually the originator of politics as a science (preceded only by Socrates and Plato), a creative function which he claimed in many other sciences; but in spite of his close association with men on whom the development of the Macedonian empire depended he did not himself participate in those movements, and he had little or no direct political experience, as a citizen or as an official. During his residence in Athens he was a "metic," a resident alien who had some rights of citizenship. His first stay of twenty years in the Academy coincided with Philip's alternating cold and hot war against Athens. Greek orators debated issues of policy and fundamental political philosophy: Demosthenes opposed Philip in defense of the constitutional tradition of a democratic city-state; Aeschines advocated peace with Philip and contributed to the success of his campaign; Isocrates advocated a reconception of the scope of political unity in a cultural concept of panhellenism. Aristotle did not participate in these political movements and debates and doubtless lived subject to suspicions and hostilities as a Macedonian; no echo of the problems of divisive city-state nationalisms advocated in the name of freedom and of tendencies to unify all Greeks or all men in an empire based on conquest and inclined to totalitarianism appears in Aristotle's political writings. It is probable that Hermias, Aristotle's host at Assos, served as an advance agent of Philip against the Persian empire, but Aristotle had no active part in that movement apart from leaving Assos for Lesbos. The period of his service as Alexander's tutor came to an end with the defeat of Athens at Chaeronea and the nonviolent occupation of Athens. Aristotle's second residence of twelve years in Athens coincided with the reign of Alexander and came to an end with Aristotle's flight from Athens to the protection of Antipater. Theophrastus remained to substitute for him in the teaching at the Lyceum. In his will Aristotle named Theophrastus his successor and bequeathed his library to him. As a "metic" Aristotle did not have the rights needed to acquire property in Athens, and therefore the school he opened, unlike Plato's Academy, did not have buildings, property, or endowment, but carried on its work in the Lyceum, a gymnasium open to the public. Under Theophrastus the Lyceum acquired institutional and property rights during the rule of Demetrius of Phalerum, a student of Theophrastus, who was appointed by Antipater to take charge of the government of Athens (317–307) and who, after having been exiled by the Athenians, fled to Egypt where he contributed to the foundation of the Alexandrian Library. After the defeat of the Athenians by Antipater, the Athenians condemned Demosthenes to death, and Demosthenes took his own life by poison.

We do not know what relation the works of Aristotle that have survived had to his teaching and research. They are sometimes treated as lecture notes prepared by Aristotle, sometimes as notes of lectures or of research taken by students, sometimes as a mixture of the two. Since they refer to each other, they are sometimes thought to be records of work in progress, available for consultation and alteration at the Lyceum, in which new inquiries and new conclusions were inserted in the science appropriate to them and referred to in related sciences. In the tradition that Aristotle gave public lectures as well as graduate work for experts, his surviving works are research or, as they have been called, "esoteric" works, while his public or "exoteric" works, with the exception of some fragments of his early dialogues, have been lost. In the comparison of his philosophy with that of his master, if his works are conceived in this fashion, we are in the curious position of comparing the esoteric works of Aristotle with the exoteric works of Plato, for none of Plato's lectures, not even the famous *Lecture on the Good*, has survived, while the large mass of his dialogues has.

Scholars have differed concerning the authenticity, order, and relation of Aristotle's works: some have found a unity in them so precise and well articulated that every science and art, and every body of conclusions, and even the meanings, applications, and functions of every word can be accounted for and justified; others have found masses of contradictions and collections of clichés, half-truths, and palpable errors; still others have found stages of development which require the reordering of the works and their parts into those which are Platonic, those which mark a skeptical doubt and tentative transition, and those which develop a characteristic mature empirical method and philosophy. There have been many interpretations of Aristotle, and grounds have been found in his writings and in his times for each of them. It is unlikely that a single authoritative interpretation will be discovered which will secure consensus and establish a coherent doctrine. The only way to resolve problems in the interpretation of Aristotle is by reading and rereading his works. Many contradictions encountered in a first reading are removed by rereading a text in the context of what he says elsewhere. The virtue of removal of contradictions is not that it vindicates an image of the master as a shrewd observer, a keen analyst, and a systematic thinker who remembers what he has said before in different connections and in relation to different problems, but that it brings the reader into contact with meanings, applications, implications, and doctrines rather than with dubious, incoherent, and meaningless statements. It is that rightness and suggestivity which accounts for the long, diversified influence of Aristotle's works and for the no less persistent, strenuous, and fruitful oppositions which they have aroused. A new reader coming to those works for the first time need not be abashed by the complexity of the works or the intricacy of the tradition: he need not seek to learn the philosophy of Aristotle, but he cannot avoid contact with philosophic problems which become significant and develop philosophic implications as he comes to perceive the consequences and perspectives which open up in the consideration and resolutions of problems. Such an introduction to Aristotle is an introduction to philosophy and to science, art, action, and life.

2. Science and Art in the Philosophy of Aristotle

Aristotle's philosophy is not a theory, or phenomenology, or logic of science, art, history, or action, nor is it a body of knowledge or doctrine related to other speculations or constructions. The parts of Aristotle's philosophy are sciences and arts; apart from the sciences and arts which he distinguishes and originates and constructs, there are no parts of his philosophy. This conception of philosophy was one of Aristotle's most radical departures from the teaching of Plato. Dialectic—one method and one hierarchically graded subject-matter—was the whole of philosophy for Plato. Dialectic is the method of the dialogues, and in them it is adapted to the discussion of all problems —problems of being and becoming, of knowledge and opinion, of will and desire, and of natural and conventional modes of expression in language. Dialectic is also the supreme method by which the contradictions, antinomies, and paralogisms developed in less inclusive and more divisive uses of dialectic may be resolved: the contradictions of becoming are resolved in the unchanging Ideas of Being, and the kinds of things, faculties of thought, virtues of action, and modes of formulation are related to each other. Instead of merging them into a single method, Aristotle distinguished scientific methods of inquiry from technical arts of formulation, statement, and inference. He used the word "method," *methodos*, in a strict scientific sense to apply to ways of investigating the problems encountered in a particular subject-matter, and he used words like "hunting," "looking for," and "examining" to describe the devices of inquiry. Inquiry in a particular science, like physics or politics, pursued in accordance with its specific method, may in turn be divided into parts by methods appropriate to different problems in those fields, and the parts of scientific treatises are referred to as methods. Once substantive scientific problems have been resolved by the discovery of causes, the conclusions may be stated, warranted, and tested in arguments which have common structures applicable in the formulation of results obtained by methods as different as those of physics, mathematics, and politics. Aristotle is fond of repeating that every science has its own subject-matter, its own method, and its own principles. The universal arts, on the other hand, have no subject-matter, and in the degree to which they are particularized to special problems and specified principles they lose their universality and approximate one of the sciences.

There are three kinds of science—theoretic, practical, and productive or poetic—differentiated by their respective objectives—knowing, doing, and making. There are three kinds of theoretic sciences—metaphysics, mathematics, and physics—differentiated by their respective objects—being, quantity, and change or motion. There are three universal arts of argumentation—dialectic, rhetoric, and analytic. Aristotle applies the word "logic" or "logical" loosely to any of these universal arts, and what is called logic today is a historical outgrowth of Aristotle's universal art developed and systematized as analytic, dialectic, rhetoric, sophistic, mathematic, or syntactic. The *Organon* or "Instrument" is a collection of six logical treatises brought together by Aristotle's first editor, Andronicus of Rhodes, in the first century B.C. Many scholars and commentators, from antiquity to the present, have argued that it is a haphazard collection, without plan and replete with inconsistencies and contradictions. These are questions which the reader and rereader of the logical treatises, and of the sciences to which their arts are applied, must judge for himself.

The central treatises of the six are two "analytics," a *Prior Analytics* and a *Posterior Analytics*—not, it should be noted, an Analytic and a Synthetic. The *Prior Analytics* analyzes arguments into terms—the three terms of the syllogism—from which more complex arguments may be constructed; the forms of completed syllogisms and the valid and invalid modes of inference in each figure are examined and formalized, and a schematism is constructed to organize individual terms applied to experience and to construct syllogisms from their relations. The term in a syllogism is a "variable" symbolized by a letter of the alphabet; it is not an arbitrary symbol devoid of significa-

tion, relation, application, or reference. The two treatises
that precede the *Prior Analytics* also are concerned with
the properties—the meanings and references—of terms and
with their relations to each other: the *Categories* treats
individual terms, the kinds of terms in isolation and the
relations and oppositions of pairs of terms; the *On Interpretation* treats pairs of terms predicated one of another
in propositions, their quantification (universal or particular, positive or negative), and the relations among their
modalities (assertoric, possible, necessary, and impossible).
The proposition is not a synthesis of simple terms or
categories, nor is the inference a synthesis of simple propositions or judgments. The three treatises treat different
aspects of the term—the significative denotative symbol—
which constitute it, in its use, as predicate, as predicable,
and as variable.

The first analytic examines the conditions of valid
inference in which the truth or falsity of the conclusion
depends on the unspecified truth-values of the premisses;
the second analytic, the *Posterior Analytics*, analyzes the
properties of terms in valid syllogisms with examined
premisses that establish true, necessary, probable, or impossible conclusions and the properties that lead to opposite results. There are three kinds of valid and invalid
syllogisms, differentiated by the kinds of premisses on
which the conclusion is or seems to be based: demonstrative or scientific syllogisms, based on premisses which are
or are derived from true and primary principles warranted
by the nature of things investigated; dialectical syllogisms,
based on opinions warranted as common opinions or as
opinions of experts; and sophistical, contentious, or eristic
syllogisms, based on opinions which seem to be generally
accepted but are not, or consisting of apparent reasoning
rather than valid reasoning from opinions generally accepted or apparently accepted. A fourth kind of inference,
in addition to these three kinds of syllogism, "misreason-
ing," differs from them in its material applications rather

than in its form. The *Posterior Analytics* takes up demonstrative arguments or syllogisms used in transmitting what
is already known and in investigating what is not yet
known, for both teaching and inquiry depend upon pre-
existent knowledge. Dialectical arguments or syllogisms
used in formulation of problems for inquiry and in disputation between positions asserted and questioned, are
examined in the *Topics* to distinguish places or topics,
topoi, to be used to secure agreement with, or refutation
of, common opinions or expert opinions. The *Posterior
Analytics* adjusts the terms of arguments to things; the
Topics adjusts them to thoughts; the errors which arise
from distortions due to thought or word are treated in the
On Sophistical Refutations.

Dialectic has a place in the logical treatises of the
Organon, displaced from the function Plato gave it as the
method of knowledge and science to become the method
of opinion and at best a propaedeutic to inquiry. Aristotle
wrote a separate treatise on rhetoric, which he calls the
counterpart of dialectic, in which places or topics are used
to adjust arguments of opinion not to the requirements of
terms as predicables used by all men but to the use of
means of persuasion available in the passions, characters,
and circumstances of particular audiences. The contribution of his *Rhetoric*, according to Aristotle, was to introduce the consideration of arguments, which had been
neglected by all his predecessors. In the *Rhetoric*, rhetorical
syllogism is the enthymeme, a form of argument in which
the convictions of the hearer affect the selection of premisses, and rhetorical induction becomes example by which
the hearer is made to see the reference of a statement by a
vivid instance of its application; and the three dimensions
of a term—symbol, significance, and reference—are separated. The references or subject-matters of discussions are
differentiated on the basis of the interests of audiences in
Book I; the emotive significances or credibilities of statements are treated in terms of the characters and passions

of speaker and hearer in Book II; and the contribution of symbols and words is analyzed in the characteristics and uses of styles and arrangements of speeches in Book III

In the final paragraph of On Sophistical Refutations, Aristotle remarks that in this inquiry, unlike those in other arts, in which he could build on and correct the work of predecessors, he had found no investigation of syllogisms or arguments. There had been progress in the art of rhetorical speeches, but no one had considered the arguments of dialectic or rhetoric. Since the lack is of examination of syllogizing, the generalization should apply not only to rhetoric and to the inquiry of the On Sophistical Refutations and of the Topics, of which it may be considered a part, but to the two Analytics, which also treat syllogisms or arguments, but with the difference that dialectic is an inquiry or methodos, since it takes into account opinions, whereas analytic proceeds solely on the basis of terms and their relations in arguments. Aristotle, in these words, claims to be the originator of logic in the large sense, a claim which has been questioned by disciples and opponents, by logicians, and by historians. The Organon, whatever its authenticity, coherence, or originality, became, with omissions, compressions, and misinterpretations, the "traditional" or "Aristotelian" logic. In the long history of its development and modification, it has rarely been structured about two analytics as Aristotle organized it, but has usually been improved or rectified by substituting for the devices and objectives of analytic those of dialectic, rhetoric, sophistic, mathematic, or syntactic.

3. Experience, Art, and Science

Aristotle's departure from Plato's conception of the nature of reality and of the relation of the structures of knowledge to the sequences of phenomena was no less radical than his reduction of dialectic from a method of knowledge to a method of opinion. All knowledge takes its origin in

sense perception and experience, for Plato no less than for
Aristotle, but Plato sought the "principle" or origin of
true knowledge in Ideas which come to mind or are
"recalled" in, and because of, the experience. Aristotle
elaborates even more arguments against the existence of
such "separated" Ideas than he does against the heuristic
fruitfulness and demonstrative cogency of the dialectical
method of division. In their place Aristotle sought connections between knowledge and what knowledge is about
in "causes," which are discovered in inquiry to be principles or origins of processes and things under investigation,
and which can therefore be formulated as principles or
grounds for scientific proofs and demonstrative truths. As
he had separated methods of inquiry concerning problems
encountered in subject-matters from analyses of arguments
formulated to prove or test the results of such inquiries,
or to secure agreement among experts or acceptance
among men without specialized knowledge, in opposition
to a unified dialectic which confused proof and persuasion,
so he separated the causes which provide principles for
scientific knowledge from the positions asserted or postulated in controversy, debate, discussion, and dialogue, in
opposition to apriorisms, reductionisms, relativisms, and
skepticisms which confused causes and suppositions,
axioms and postulates. We think that we know, Aristotle
says from time to time, when we have found a cause. As
the methods (*methodos*) of inquiry are ways (*hodos*) of
examining problems encountered in experience, the principles or grounds of the resolution of problems and the
establishment of truths are causes.

Aristotle frequently expounded his position concerning
the derivation of knowledge from experience and the relation of knowledge to things in opposition to the errors of
reducing things to thoughts and of reducing thoughts to
things. Plato made all things and all thoughts imitations of
Ideas, which unite thoughts and things and ground knowledge and existence in Being. Democritus made all things

compositions of simple things or atoms (which he also called "ideas") and all thoughts motions of atoms. At prominent points in his works, in the first chapter of the *Metaphysics* and the last chapter of the *Posterior Analytics*, Aristotle traces stages in the development of knowledge from the perceptions of the senses, which disclose differences among things, through the retentions and connections of memory based on sensation, through the articulations of experience developed from repeated memories, through the formations of art based on recognition and use of causes, to the accumulations and orderings of science and wisdom by the investigation of causes. He argues that there is no need to go beyond this sequence to introduce unexperienced principles from without—from above or below experience, from supreme beings supposed to transcend understanding, or from least beings supposed to underlie sensations and occurrences. Most animals live by sense alone; the more intelligent animals by sense and memory; experience guides men in action; art and technology use causes found in experience to develop skills and to make things; science and wisdom investigate causes for an understanding of things and their properties and functions. Only individual things exist and are encountered in sense experience. That they are is warranted by sensation, but what they are, and how they function and why, are questions which go beyond the functions of sensation and the sensibilia perceived in individual things, and lead to inquiry into the properties and operations which they share with other individual things. Sensation is of individual things and occurrences; experience is of related particulars; art and science are of universals.

The sequence from sensation to knowledge provides distinctions which are used to differentiate the subject matters of sciences, the faculties of psychology, the virtues of ethics, and the principles and organizations of the sciences. The matters organized and the organizing universals of the sciences are differentiated and related in that sequence. Inanimate objects move by natural powers and causes; animals other than man live by locomotion, sensation, and memory; men order their motions and experiences by arts and sciences. The faculties of the mind investigated in the science of psychology range from faculties which provide powers for locomotion, shared by all natural things; for reproduction, nutrition, and growth, shared by all living things; for sensation, memory, and imagination—the external senses and the common senses —shared by animals; and for thought, shared by rational animals. Natural powers are increased and supplemented by acquired powers, or virtues, studied in ethics, among which are intellectual virtues: art and prudence, powers of thought adapted, for making and doing, to changing things; science, intuition, and wisdom, powers of thought adapted, for knowing, to unchanging things. Sciences are also products, bodies of truths discovered by inquiry and certified by demonstration; and particular sciences are differentiated by their principles, methods, and subject-matters, and by their distinctive formulations in separate treatises which afford instances of the use of the arts of argument as well as of the methods and principles of inquiry. The sciences which investigate the nature and powers of man and of other things which share his nature and powers are differentiated by their subject-matters into physical, psychological, and biological, and by the psychological functions they distinguish, study, and develop, into practical sciences about deliberation concerning actions to be taken and theoretic sciences about inquiry into causes of things. Scientific knowledge of the causes of things is distinct from scientific knowledge of the affairs of men and from scientific knowledge of the products of art; practical science is distinct from virtue and prudence; poetic science is distinct from art; and all varieties of scientific knowledge are distinct from technical skills and from expert information and common opinion. Aristotle uses the word "science" to designate fields, faculties,

virtues, and truths, and he created one science, metaphysics, to relate the meanings of "science," the varieties
of things, and the organizations of sciences.

Existent individual things are perceived only by the
external or proper senses, but the sequence from sensation
to knowledge is a sequence of awareness of kinds of
things, not a sequence from things to constructs or inventions of the mind. The mind in its experiences, arts, and
sciences becomes all things. For man, perceived, experienced, made, and known things are the only things which
are. The definitions and arguments (*logos*) of arts and
sciences are essences (*logos*) of things made, done, and
known. For human action, experience is not inferior to
art, and men of experience succeed even better than those
who have theory without experience, since experience is
knowledge of individuals, art of universals; and actions and
productions are concerned with the individual. The man
of experience knows only the fact, however, while art and
science supply and take into account the causes—art
causes for the processes of production and action, science
causes for the essence and properties of being and of what
is and for the nature and processes of change and of what
changes. The universal, which is first isolated in the
recognition of the one in the many in experience, is thus
the basis of both the skill of the artist and the knowledge
of the scientist. The sequence from sensation to thought
is a transition, as Aristotle likes to put it, from things
prior and better known to us to things prior and better
known in nature. Our reason is like the eyes of bats in
the blaze of the day with respect to things best known in
nature. We do not perceive first principles immediately,
nor are they innate in our souls, but we proceed from
the half-light of sensation to the principles of science,
which, once grasped, are better known than the conclusions which flow from them or the experiences from which
they were derived.

We get to know first principles by induction, abstraction, and analogy, but they are apprehended as principles by intuition. In an inchoate sense they are present in sensation, for though the act of sensation is of the individual, its content is universal, as for example "man" rather than any of the particular "men" encountered in experience or any of the individuals, "Socrates" or "Plato," perceived in sensation. Principles, perceived without discrimination in sensation, are isolated in the repetitions of experience and in the manipulations of art, and are identified and established by induction, abstraction, and analogy, and are finally perceived as principles in intuition. Moreover, just as the universal is present and is fixed in the experience of particulars and the perception of individuals, so too particulars emerge at each point at which perception and thought deal with ultimates—not only in sense perception of individuals of existence and in imagination of particulars of experience, but in judgment, understanding, and practical wisdom or prudence which operate on the particulars of practical decisions, and finally in intuitive reason which is concerned with the ultimates in both directions, with first terms and with last, for the intuitive reason presupposed in demonstrations grasps unchangeable and first terms, while the intuitive reason involved in practical judgments grasps last and variable facts.

4. The Theoretic Sciences

The theoretic sciences are formed for the pursuit of knowledge. As knowledge of something, they are adapted to the investigation and study of subject-matters. Not any random collection of things or haphazard association of experiences, however, constitutes a subject-matter for scientific inquiry. The data of existence and the facts of experience are made into subjects of inquiry by recognizing in them and deriving from them common properties and functions. Such universals are not given as data or encountered as facts ready-made in sensation or experience. The subject-matter of a science is inseparable from methods and principles; it is a product of method and a consequence of principles. The progress of science is a concomitant development of subject-matter, method, and principles. The advancement of knowledge, even within a single science, depends on devising new methods which determine and define new subject-matters within which new principles of inquiry and proof are uncovered, established, and proved. The proliferation of subject-matters leads to the differentiation of sciences and kinds of science. Science originates in experience, and experience provides the matter for scientific inquiry, but the connections and sequences investigated by scientific method depend on formal distinction and definitions used to discover and delimit material relations. Method is employed to constitute subject-matters composed of form and matter and to establish formal principles to serve as origins or grounds of connections.

The subject-matter of physics is bodies in change or motion. Physics does not investigate all motions but only those which can be traced back to a principle of motion internal to the bodies in motion. That internal principle is called Nature. There are other principles of motion—chance, fortune, art, and intelligence—which are distinguished from nature as external, or accidental, or incidental principles of change. The inquiries of physics are into natural interconnections of things and processes and not into chance coincidences, fortunate or unfortunate concurrences, artful contrivances, or prudential provisions. The subdivisions of physics are determined by the kinds of motion and the kinds of things in motion. Motions are divided into four kinds by the categories of things which undergo motion—changes of substance, or generation and corruption; changes of quantity, or increase and decrease; changes of quality, or alteration; and changes of place, or locomotion. Kinds of things or substances are not the same as kinds of natures or principles: substances "have natures," internal principles of motion and rest. Physics includes many kinds of things in its investigation and many principles adapted to their distinctive motions—the changes of inorganic bodies and their parts, of souls and their faculties, and of animate bodies and their parts. The method used to establish the definitions of natural things and the principles of natural motions is induction: physical definitions are of matter as well as form, and principles of motion are forms which appear in succession in a matter which persists through the change.

The subject-matter of mathematics is quantities, continuous and discrete—surfaces, volumes, and lines; points and numbers—which are perceived in experience as properties of physical bodies and are treated as physical inductions rather than as mathematical abstractions in various branches of physics. Mathematical definitions are formed by abstraction of forms from matter and motion. Aristotle illustrates the difference between mathematical and physical definitions several times in his work by the example of "curve," which specifies no matter other than a continuous quantity, a line, and "snub," which specifies the curved matter, a nose. Since the objects of mathematics are abstract and devoid of physical matter, the method of mathematics consists in constructing proportions and relations for which discrete quantities provide forms for delimitation or definition, and continuous quantities serve as matter for differentiation and connection. Numbers and points can be ordered in an endless variety of continua, and their properties are revealed and examined in series. Lines, surfaces, and volumes can be cut into discontinuous parts which can then be used to construct discrete figures and to discover and examine their properties and relations. The possibility of mathematics depends on this peculiarity of quantity which adapts it alone among the properties of things to abstraction in thought and separate treatment in science, as the possibility of physics depends on the peculiarity of substance which makes possible the induction by which universal definitions of second substances are derived from particular experiences of first substances, and the properties and motions of things which persist through the change may be investigated. The definitions and principles of both kinds of science are kinds of form and matter.

The subject-matter of metaphysics, which Aristotle called first philosophy, or wisdom, or theology, and which received the name by which we know it from its place in the edition of Andronicus of Rhodes after the books on physics, ta meta ta physica, is "that which is most truly" or "being qua being," which Aristotle shows to be substance. Aristotle begins his investigation of substances with the natural things studied in physics, and he grants that if these were the only beings, there would be no need for a separate science of metaphysics, since the inquiry concerning first principles would be a branch of physics. The substances of physics are sensible substances, which are divided into two kinds, the perishable substances of the sublunary world which move in finite, straight lines and the eternal substances of the heavens which move in endless circles. The first causes or first movers, which are principles of motion and of order, are evidence for a third kind of substance, and the characteristic mark of both the metaphysics and the physics of Aristotle is the central place occupied in both by a nonsensible substance. There are forms which can not only be known apart but also exist apart from matter and motion. The concern of metaphysics with being as such, therefore, involves inquiry not only into the ultimate principles of knowledge and the ultimate causes of existence and change, but also into the principles of order, the first movers, which determine the interrelations of the universe and of the processes of change and knowledge in the universe. God is the supreme and unmoved mover of these first movers, exempt from the mutability of which he is the source.

The differentiation of forms according to their existence and intelligibility, in matter or apart from matter, determines the three theoretic sciences, physics, mathematics, and metaphysics. The methods—induction, abstraction, and intuition—by which they discover and establish definitions, demonstrations, and principles are different, but they agree in the logical structure and analysis of arguments formulated to establish their conclusions: the illustrations of demonstration in the *Posterior Analytics* are from both physics and mathematics. Form and matter, actuality and potentiality, provide the bases for method. The three sciences treat three kinds of actuality—enmattered form, abstract form, and unmattered form—and three kinds of potentiality—one which passes from potentiality to actuality, one which is never fully actualized, and one which is always actual. Physical matter is actualized in motion and generation. Mathematical continua may be divided in a fixed ratio, endlessly, as a line may be divided into half and the remainder halved continuously, and numbering the steps actually taken in that process generates a series of numbers, or discrete quantities, which has no last step. The actualities are finite; the potentialities generate two kinds of infinity, one proceeding toward the infinitely small, the other toward the infinitely large. Divine potentiality is never unactualized.

Fundamental truths and definitions are stated in universal propositions which are convertible into universal propositions, that is, the scope or denotation of the predicate is coextensive with that of the subject. There are self-evident truths, that is, truths known by intuition, in physics about the functions of things, in mathematics about the equality of things, and in metaphysics about the essence or identity of things. All three sciences treat of necessary, not of contingent, things; and scientific propositions are therefore necessary, not merely probable. Metaphysics investigates absolute or simple necessity based on essence and stated in essential definition: it is the necessity by which a thing is, and continues to be, what it is. The necessities studied and used in mathematics and physics are hypothetical necessities. In mathematics, if the premisses are granted or are established as true, the conclusions derived from them by valid demonstrations are necessarily true, but the premisses are not necessarily true if the conclusion derived from them is true, for true conclusions may be drawn from false premisses. In physics, if a process or motion has been completed, it can be shown that the antecedent steps to that completion must have occurred, but the existence of antecedent stages in a process is not grounds for concluding that the final effect or product will follow necessarily, for natural processes are often cut short before they complete their normal course, and physics is the study of what happens frequently or for the most part. Necessity in metaphysics is sought in essence, in mathematics in postulates, and in physics in products. In all three the discovery of the necessary depends on definition and on demonstration used to fix on and determine essences and causes.

By far the greatest part of the surviving works of Aristotle is on physics. Four treatises are devoted to inquiries concerning the motions of inanimate bodies: the *Physics* establishes privation, form, and matter as the principles of motion, nature as the internal cause of natural motion, and the first causes of nature and of natural motions; the *On the Heavens* investigates the local motion and elements of bodies, the four elements of earthly bodies and their motions in straight lines, and the fifth "primary element" of heavenly bodies and their circular motions; the *On Generation and Corruption* investigates the causes of other changes of terrestrial bodies—generation and corruption (or changes of substances coming to be or ceasing to be), alteration (or change in their qualities), and growth and diminution (or change in their quantity or size); the *Meteorology* investigates the composition and interaction of elements, mixtures, and compounds—seeking the causes of comets, rain, snow, dew, winds, earthquakes, thunder, lightning, storms; studying the processes which affect mixed bodies, water, metals, clays, oils, wines; and finally making a transition from inorganic to organic bodies by differentiating (1) elements, (2) "homogeneous bodies" (like metals among inanimate things, or the wood and bark of plants, or the tissues and bones of animals), which possess different qualities than the elements of which they are compounded, and (3) "heterogeneous bodies" (like organs and parts, hands and faces), which possess functions and purposes distinct from those of the homogeneous bodies of which they are compounded.

Organic bodies have a form and cause distinct from those of inorganic bodies; the soul is the form of natural bodies which have life potentially in them. The functions of the soul, enumerated and treated in On the Soul, therefore, include nutrition, growth, and reproduction (which animals share with plants), sensation, emotion, and local motion (which men share with other animals), and thought (which is peculiar to man among animals, although God shares, in a sense, in thinking). The investigation of higher activities of human living in On the Soul is supplemented by inquiry, in the Short Natural Treatises, into the common characteristics of animal bodies and into the similar objects of animal activity, in sense and sensibles, memory and reminiscence, length and brevity of life, youth and old age, life and death, and respiration. The lower activities of the soul, which are touched on briefly in the On the Soul, are investigated in Aristotle's four biological treatises. Bodily organs and psychic functions of animals are examined in the context of the study of human functions, and the On the Soul provides the principles of biology as well as of psychology, partly because, as men, we are more familiar with man than with any other animal, partly because man is more rounded and complete than other animals and the qualities and capacities investigated in biology are found in their perfection in him (cf. the *History of Animals* i. 6. 491ª19–23 and ix. 1. 608ª4–8). The *History of Animals* is a lengthy classification of animals on the basis of similarities and differences in their parts, organs, and functions—the processes of reproduction, the factors of heredity, differences in the development of the embryo, in diet, diseases, the effects of environment on the activities of animals, and of the struggle for scarce means of subsistence on their survival, differences in sensitivity, response, and intelligence. The *On the Parts of Animals* treats of biological phenomena that are explained by the material parts and organs of animals. The *On the Progression of Animals* differentiates their modes of locomotion. The *On the Generation of Animals* treats of modes of reproduction in terms of efficient causes.

The book *On Mathematics*, listed in ancient catalogues of Aristotle's works, has not survived, but we can reconstruct something of his conception of mathematics from what he says about mathematical demonstration in the *Organon*, from the contrasts between mathematical and physical inquiries and definitions which he points out in the physical treatises, and from the differentiation of the subject-matters and principles of the sciences in the *Metaphysics*. After the ten books of physics, the *Metaphysics* treats essences and first causes. The two parts of practical science are organized and expounded in the *Nicomachean Ethics* and the *Politics*. The *Poetics* is a fragment of productive science employed in the investigation of tragedy. The universal arts are expounded and analyzed in the *Rhetoric* and in the logical treatises of the *Organon*.

Many of the treatises on the sciences begin with a dialectical survey of other men's theories and conjectures and even of common opinion, and new problems are likewise introduced in the course of a treatise by the dialectical statement of alternative hypotheses each of which employs a distinctive method, marking off a subject-matter or part of the science. Such dialectical examination of accepted scientific opinions is preliminary and preparatory for scientific inquiry, and Aristotle frequently marks the transition from argument to inquiry, from analysis to method, by indicating a fresh start. The first book of the *Physics* examines and evaluates proposed principles of motion sufficiently to establish that there are principles, and what they are, and how many they are: "Now let us make a fresh start and proceed." The first book of the *On the Soul* enumerates and disposes of theories of the soul, and the call for a fresh start is the opening sentence of the second book. The first book of the *On the Parts of Animals* examines the scientific methods of various sciences, and the second book begins with the statement that the parts of animals have been described in the *History of Animals* and the inquiry is now into the causes of the composition of parts in different animals. The first book of the *Metaphysics* enumerates and adjusts theories of causes and kinds of causes, and the inquiry into the principles and causes of the things that are begins in the sixth book, Book Epsilon, and the fresh start is made in Book Eta.

The scientific methods in physics and in the productive sciences begin with an idea of the end or product and then reason back through necessary antecedents to a starting point, whereas the mathematical sciences proceed deductively from axioms and principles to conclusions. The physical treatises are not systematic deductive systems, as mathematical treatises, if we had any composed by Aristotle, would in all likelihood be, but methodical inquiries. The demonstration of the existence of the First Mover, God, in Book VIII of the *Physics* establishes him as the first efficient cause of the universe; the demonstration of the existence of the First Mover in the twelfth book of the *Metaphysics*, Book Lambda, establishes God as the consummate final cause of all being. Book II of the *Politics* examines the political theories of Socrates and Plato, ideal commonwealths, and the best existent states, Sparta, Crete, and Carthage; the inquiry into kinds of governments begins in Book III after this examination of constitutions which actually exist or have been devised by theorists. Chapters 4 and 5 of the *Poetics* contain a résumé, not of theories, but of the history of poetry, of tragedy, comedy, and epic, and chapter 6 begins by gathering up the definition of tragedy from what has been said. The methods of the sciences vary with variations in subject-matter and principles, and the dialectical examination of what is already known and available as preparation for inquiry varies with variations in the uses of science: for knowing, the examination of theories; for doing, the examination of institutions and habits; for making, the examination of artificial or made objects.

5. The Practical and Productive Sciences

The practical sciences are differentiated from the theoretical sciences by their purposes or ends, but differences may also be detected in subject-matters and in methods consequent on this difference in principles. The end of the theoretic sciences is knowledge, and the subject-matters which are investigated and the truths which are sought do not depend on our action or our volition. The end of the practical sciences, on the other hand, is not merely to know, but rather to act in the light of knowledge: it is not the purpose of political science, for example, to know the good, but to make men good. Aristotle sometimes isolates the practical sciences in general by this contrast to the theoretic sciences; he sometimes couples the physical sciences with the productive sciences or arts in contrast to mathematics because they use ends as principles or causes of inquiry—the completed process, the fully developed animal, or the artificial or made object; he sometimes treats the productive sciences as one variety of the practical sciences, and he sometimes differentiates among the ends of human purposes and operations, contrasting the processes of making, which use an external matter and produce an artificial object, to the processes of doing, which use internal potentialities as matter to develop moral virtues, artistic skills, and prudential reasons, and separating the arts and their products from virtues and institutions and their actions.

The differences between the subject-matter and the methods of the practical sciences and those of the theoretic sciences may all be related to this difference of purposes. Since the end of the practical sciences is action, they have to do with potentialities, situations, and things which may be modified by human intelligence and volition. Their subject-matter is things which may be other than they are, that is, contingent things as contrasted to necessary connections and things which cannot be otherwise than they are found to be in the theoretic sciences. The inquirer in the practical sciences will therefore not seek the precision which is appropriate to mathematics or other theoretic sciences. His definitions will be different, for his inquiries are not concerned with a "nature" or a "substance." The fashion in which a man grows, reproduces, nourishes himself, moves, perceives, or thinks may be studied as functions of his nature; but his virtues, the social and political institutions under which he lives, and the objects of art and technology which he produces, uses, and appreciates depend on the habits induced by actions he has performed, on the influences he has undergone from external circumstances or from the example of other men, and on the ideas and ideals he has conceived.

Yet each science is concerned with one class or genus of things, and the practical and productive sciences may be related to their appropriate subject-matters by contrasting their concern with action and production, or with doing and making, to the manner in which motions and changes are investigated in physics. The physical sciences are confined to the study of substances which have the principles of their motion and rest present within themselves. The principles of action, on the other hand, are in the doer acting to change himself and others, and the principles of production are in the producer changing materials to make things. Although the external principles of practical and productive sciences are thus contrasted to the internal principles of the physical sciences, they are also comparable, since the physicist, like the practical man and the artist and artisan, conceives his principle as an end to be achieved in a process and directs his inquiry to discovering the conditions, materials, and causes necessary for its achievement. Moreover, even when all three are viewed as external causes, there is a difference in the ways in which the cause may, or may not, lead to the external result in the three cases, for the cause of motion is a nature or a power or faculty in an inorganic or organic mover; the cause of production is reason or an art in a producer; the cause of action is will or a desire in the doer. Power is therefore more important as a cause in motion than in art or in action; reason is more important in producing art than in starting natural motions or in inducing moral actions; and the character of the agent is of crucial importance in the judgment of actions but irrelevant in physical science or artistic making. The end of natural motions studied in the physical and biological sciences is found in the nature studied, fully actualized in the exercise of its powers; the end of the practical sciences is found in the actions themselves and the states of character produced by them; the end of the productive sciences is found in the objects produced and in the qualities discerned in those objects.

There are no sharp separations among the practical sciences. Ethics is a part of politics, and human conduct is studied in both parts— in ethics from the point of view of individual morality but with the recognition that the conduct of the individual is influenced and formed by the communities in which he grows up; in politics from the point of view of the associations and institutions of men but with the recognition that the character and operation of communal institutions are determined by the tendencies and preferences of the men who compose them and exercise offices under them. The single political science of Aristotle has been the source of the division of the two, and indeed of their increase into three, practical sciences, for the treatment of the household and household management, *oikonomia*, in the first book of the *Politics* led to the differentiation of ethics, economics, and politics. In both parts of political science, a natural foundation is sought for the ends of action and association. Ethics is concerned with the study of virtues, which are not natures or natural powers but habits; a natural basis is found for habits in the potentialities of man which are influenced in their actualization by repeated actions and passions. Politics is concerned with the study of constitutions or forms of human association, which likewise have no natural definitions or species; a natural basis is found for communities in the needs and interdependences of men; the ends of mere living are satisfied in the household and village, the ends of living well require the state. The family, the village, and the state are in this sense natural, and man is by nature a political animal.

The arts are differentiated according to their products, and there are no sharply defined lines to separate the arts or to classify the kinds of artificial things. The Greeks did not differentiate the fine arts from the mechanical arts in the fashion which has been customary since the Renaissance, when the expressions *beaux arts* and *belles lettres* were invented, although they did differentiate banausic arts, which depend on extensive physical exertion and which are sometimes translated "mechanical arts," from the arts of free men, and Aristotle argued that employment in the banausic arts was incompatible with the exercise of the functions of citizenship. The Greeks have therefore been criticized by humanists, who based their rebirth of the arts on imitating and borrowing from Greek art, for confusing arts and trades, and they have been criticized by pragmatists, who borrowed their name and their criterion of successful operation from the Greeks, for separating art and science, thereby reducing productive operations and mechanical contrivances to a servile level. The arts as conceived by Aristotle include not only painting, music, and poetry, but medicine, architecture, cobbling, and rhetoric. Since the arts imitate nature, they may be differentiated by consideration of the object, means, and manner of their imitation, and therefore, although he has no word for fine arts, Aristotle is able, in the opening chapters of the *Poetics*, to assemble the arts we call fine by isolating their means of imitation and to differentiate tragedy from the other arts. He did have a word to differentiate the liberal arts from the banausic or mechanical, and he sought the marks of their differentiation in the educative influence of the arts in the formation of men for freedom.

The interrelations among the theoretic, practical, and productive sciences are complex and flexible: each kind may be differentiated from the others by means of subject-matter, method, and end or principle, yet each science is pertinent to all the others: the subject-matter of each may be treated incidentally from the point of view of the others, and the principles of each may be employed incidentally in the others. The theoretic sciences are distinct from the practical and the productive by their end or purpose or principle. Yet the theoretic sciences, the pursuit and transmission of knowledge and its presentation and acceptance, are subjects treated by the practical and the productive sciences: scientific knowledge is examined among the intellectual virtues in ethics, and the problems of promoting scientific research and of improving or limiting the teaching of science are political problems; devices of invention, discovery, and creation, forms of presentation and organization of the results of inquiry, and persuasive means of securing acceptance are artistic or poetic problems. Conversely, the principles of the arts and of ethics and politics are studied and certified in metaphysics; the proportions treated in mathematics provide schemata for treating relations in arts, virtues, and constitutions; and music is a mathematical and a cosmological, that is, physical, science as well as a poetic or productive science; and the psychological and intellectual faculties and processes used in inquiry and proof in all the sciences are studied in the science of psychology, which is a branch of physics. The practical sciences, in like fashion, are distinct from both the theoretic and the productive sciences; yet the theoretic and productive sciences figure among the problems of ethics and politics, not because of the problems they treat but because of their practical implications. The practical sciences, in turn, derive basic distinctions and underlying facts from the theoretic sciences, and problems of action are so inextricably involved in problems of art that practical thinkers, like the Sophists who taught the arts of politics, confuse politics with rhetoric, just policy with consensus and persuasion. The productive sciences, finally, are directed wholly to the artificial objects produced by art and they make their own materials, yet knowledge of the potentialities and possibilities of materials, of the sensibilities and reactions of audiences, and of the organizations and proportions of forms, may come from the theoretic and the practical sciences; and the arts may in turn contribute to the construction of sciences, to the formation of virtues, and to the constitution of states.

The clarity, subtlety, and adaptability of the Aristotelian organization of the sciences depends on basic discriminations used throughout his development and differentiation of the arts and sciences which constitute his philosophy. The distinction between the objective method of scientific inquiry and the formal analysis of artful argument, the relations between matter, form, and cause, and the stages of potentiality, actuality, and actualization, at once permit artistic, moral, and theoretic considerations to be kept unambiguously distinct, and yet make it possible for the scrutiny of each mode of inquiry to fall on the same objects and processes in their various circumstances and characteristics. The problem of the interrelations of the arts and sciences has continued to be discussed through the ages since Aristotle in terms suggested by or borrowed from his philosophy, but without the functional variations he employed, and the history of the frozen schematisms that have resulted has been in the main a record of efforts to reduce all knowledge to theory or practice or art.

6. The Influence of Aristotle

Aristotle has been presented, in the age-long discussion of his influence on later thought, as the originator of philosophical inquiry and of scientific method and as the inspirer of dogmatism and the stifler of originality. During the Middle Ages he was referred to as the Philosopher. In some periods of some Western cultures commentaries on his works were an important part of philosophical inquiry and disputation, and they have been the lifework of some philosophers. One of the Greek commentators, Alexander of Aphrodisias, was referred to simply as the Exegete or as the second Aristotle. One of the greatest of the Arabic philosophers, Averroës, made his contribution to philosophy in three series of commentaries (Great, Middle, and Short) on the works of Aristotle and was referred to as the Commentator without need of further specification of what or of whom. For other periods Aristotle's works were not read or commented on, sometimes because they were not available, sometimes in spite of the fact that they were available. There were "Aristotelians" during those periods, as Peter Abailard was called the "Peripatetic," although his acquaintance with Aristotle's works was limited to a few short treatises of logic. Nonetheless we still repeat the pronouncement of the Humanists that Aristotle enslaved the minds of men for two thousand years, and that the spell was broken only when men began to examine nature rather than quote physical and biological laws and principles, to look at art rather than recite rules and seek unities, and to examine the methods of scientific inquiry rather than the figures and moods of the syllogism.

Aristotle's philosophy, or what passed for his philosophy, was influential, positively and negatively, during all periods in the West from the time of his death to the present, but his influence took no uniform guise and followed no single direction. His influence on the vocabulary of philosophy may be taken as typical of his influence in general and as central to the more specific lines of influence attributed to him, for the technical terminology of later philosophical discussion is taken largely from his distinctions, but the terms to which he gave prominence were for the most part used in other senses than he gave them and in other contexts of arguments and suppositions than his. He distinguished fields of inquiry, organized what had previously been discovered in those fields, and set up new sciences. Later philosophers and historians have argued that he misunderstood the subject matter of metaphysics, physics, psychology, and other fields of philosophy; that he misrepresented his predecessors and distorted their positions to make them conform with his; and that he did not originate the sciences he claimed as his inventions. He applied technical names to things and processes and gave existing words technical definitions, laying the foundations of scientific and philosophical vocabulary in basic terms and distinctions. Many of the terms have persisted and have generated cognate terms, have been modified and ordered in different systems, and have opened up new directions of inquiry in which they have acquired new meanings or have returned to the old meanings of opponents whose uses and applications Aristotle criticized. Refuting or denying Aristotelian distinctions is a well-trodden path to philosophical originality.

During the first phase of Aristotle's influence, during the Hellenistic period, Aristotelianism was a method, not a doctrine. His immediate successors, those who had heard him and had worked with him, used his problematic method in the investigation of problems and sciences which Aristotle had not treated, in the reexamination of problems he had treated, in defense or in criticism of his solutions, in political council of princes and statesmen, in the organization of the Library of Alexandria, in empirical investigations, and in tracing the history of the sciences. Theophrastus, his successor as head of the Lyceum, extended Aristotelian inquiry from zoology to botany in his *History of Plants* and *On the Causes of Plants*. His *Metaphysics* raises questions concerning Aristotle's treatment of first principles, the Prime Mover, and teleological explanation, and defends other Aristotelian positions against critics. Theophrastus and his fellow disciple Eudemus made major modifications in Aristotelian logic. They transformed Aristotle's practice of reviewing the doctrines of his predecessors in the opening books of a scientific work into the beginning of the history of ideas or doctrines, the tradition of doxology—Theophrastus in his *Doctrines of the Natural Sciences* of which we have the portion on the development of the psychology of sensation, Eudemis in his three books on the *History of Mathematics*, the first on the history of geometry, the second on the history of arithmetic, and the third on the history of astronomy. We have fragments of their departures from the physics of Aristotle, and it is supposed that the *Eudemian Ethics* of Aristotle (which departs from the doctrine of the *Nicomachean Ethics* in spite of the fact tha the two *Ethics* have three books in common) was so called because it was edited by Eudemus. Theophrastus's *Characters*, for all its dependence on the *Rhetoric* and the *Ethics*, established a new and influential genre of literature and probably influenced the initiation and development

of the New Comedy. Aristoxenus used Aristotle's problematic method on materials borrowed from the Pythagoreans to construct a theory of music in his *Elements of
Harmony* and *Elements of Rhythm*, and he wrote a *Life
of Pythagoras and His Companions* and a *Life of Archytas*.
Dicaearchus seems to have used Pythagoreanism and the
Aristotelian method in geography in his *Travels on the
Earth*, in psychology in *On the Soul*, in political theory in
his *Tripolitikos*, which defends the mixed constitution and
presents it as the constitution of Sparta. Demetrius of
Phaleron, a disciple of Theophrastus, often called the
"Peripatetic," was installed in power by the Macedonians
after the democratic revolt against the pro-Macedonian
aristocratic party and organized the government of Athens
along Aristotelian lines for ten years, from 317 to 307.
During this period the Lyceum acquired the right to own
property and buildings. Demetrius fled to Egypt in 307
where he influenced the political policy of Ptolemy and
probably contributed to the organization and establishment of the Library at Alexandria. It is likely that Aristotle's organization of the arts and sciences was adopted
in the recorded classifications of books in the Library, and
that his scientific method influenced the empirical research
in the Museum. Strato of Lampsacus, the Physicist, the
third head of the Lyceum, was tutor to Ptolemy's son in
Alexandria, where he might have met Euclid the geometer.
Like Aristoxenus and Dicaearchus, he was a materialist
and shared many of the doctrines of his contemporary
Epicurus, although he rejected atomism.

During the first phase of Aristotle's influence, Peri-
patetics were scholars and empirical inquirers rather than
speculative thinkers and theoretical scientists, and the
subject of their chief interest was morality and letters:
Hellenistic philosophers were engrossed in controversies
concerning the sovereign good and concerning poetics,
rhetoric, grammar, and language. Successive heads of the
Lyceum shared positions with Academics, Platonists, Py-

thagoreans, Stoics, and Epicureans. The influence of Aristotle entered into a second phase when Andronicus of Rhodes, the tenth (or eleventh) head of the Lyceum edited his works. He arranged them in an order which has persisted almost unchanged to the present, and it was doubtless he who brought the logical treatises together under the title *Organon* and gave the name *Metaphysics* to the treatises which come "after the works on physics" in the sequence of books in his edition. In the first phase Aristotelianism was a method of inquiry; during the second phase it became an organized body of doctrines. According to Strabo, the geographer, Theophrastus had bequeathed his own works and those of Aristotle to one of his disciples, Neleus of Skepsis (in order, it has been conjectured, to prevent their falling into the hands of Strato, his successor), who took them to Asia Minor, where, to protect them from the Attalides kings who had ambitions to make the Library of Pergamum excel the Library of Alexandria, he buried them in a cellar. They were later exhumed, badly damaged by worms and damp, and sold to an Athenian book collector, and Sulla brought them to Rome as part of the bounty after he took Athens in 86 B.C. It is improbable that these were the only copies of the works of Aristotle—there must have been copies in the Alexandrian Library and elsewhere—but it is probable that philosophers, peripatetic or antiperipatetic, seldom felt the impulse or need to consult them. Andronicus himself wrote commentaries and paraphrases and initiated a long line of interpretations and controversies concerning the interpretation of Aristotle's doctrines. Even philosophers and scientists who were not primarily commentators, like Plotinus, Ptolemy, and Galen, paused in their treatment of logical, scientific, and philosophical questions to set forth the differences between the Platonic, Aristotelian, and Stoic positions on those questions.

Paradoxically, in the course of this learned study of the text and doctrines of Aristotle, spurious texts were included in the corpus of his writings and the genuine works were interpreted from other philosophical standpoints than his own. During the Middle Ages the *De Mundo*, the *Theology of Aristotle*, and the *Liber de Causis* helped shape the accepted notions of Aristotelian philosophy. The *De Mundo*, or *On the World*, composed probably in the first century A.D. with marked Stoic admixtures, was translated into Latin by Apuleius, the Platonist. The *Theology of Aristotle* is a collection of excerpts from Plotinus. The *Liber de Causis*, or *On Causes*, is largely excerpted from the *Elementatio Theologica*, or *Elements of Theology*, of Proclus. The line of Peripatetic commentators reached its culmination and end in the third century with Alexander of Aphrodisias, the Exegete, who in addition to his commentaries wrote treatises in which he opposed Stoic doctrines and Platonic Ideas. Themistius, who taught in Constantinople in the fourth century, elevated the "paraphrase" to the status of a genre of philosophic literature. In the fourth century began the long line of Neoplatonic commentators, the remains of whose works occupy eighteen of the twenty-three volumes of the Berlin edition of the Greek Commentators. In addition to commentaries they wrote introductions or prolegomena to the study of Aristotle, like Porphyry's *Isagoge*, or *Introduction* to the *Categories*, which finds the introductory ideas in Aristotle's *Topics*, on the supposition that the predicables, which he increased from Aristotle's four to five, are essential to the understanding of the categories, and so gives priority to dialectic over demonstrative proof.

Judaism, Christianity, and Islam provided contexts in the Middle Ages in which the influence of Aristotle was shaped in four distinct and paradoxically related phases. In each of the great monotheistic traditions of religion a continuing controversy evolved between those who saw a contradiction between religion and the pagan arts and sciences and those who found in human literature, science, and philosophy modes by which to present, and arguments by which to support, divine truths and wisdom. The influence of Aristotle in Latin Christianity was fixed, in part, by the works available in Latin. Boethius translated only the *Categories* and the *On Interpretation*, and possibly the *Prior Analytics* (but if he did, its discernible influence was slight before the twelfth century), and he placed them in the context of a translation of, and two commentaries on, the *Isagoge* of Porphyry and a treatise on the *Topics*, based on Cicero and Themistius rather than the *Topics* of Aristotle. The logic of Aristotle was dominated by dialectic until the *Posterior Analytics* was translated in the twelfth century in the context of a Christian theology which had been given Platonic form by Augustine. Aristotle's scientific doctrines were known only at second hand in similarly Platonized doxologies until they were introduced in specific details by the translation of Arabic summaries in the twelfth century.

The influence of Aristotle in Greek Christianity faced no problem in translation, but was fixed in the battle of literature and theology. When Julian the Apostate turned from Christianity to paganism, it was with the confidence that education based on the study of literature, rhetoric, and poetry provides a better basis for the community and the state than the interpretation of biblical revelations; the study of mathematics and of Plato and Aristotle has its place in the study of the classics. Themistius likewise recommends, in one of his *Orations*, a return to the humanities, to *philanthropia*, and the abandonment of religious superstition as a means of restoring and strengthening the empire. The *Bibliotheca* of Photius and the *Lexicon* of Suidas are handbooks of literature and history.

The influence of Aristotle in Islam was fixed by the fact that Syriac Christians had made Syriac translations of Greek science, including the works of Aristotle, as well as of the New Testament. Muslim scholars made translations of those Syriac translations, prepared new translations from the Greek, wrote commentaries on the works of Aristotle, at first with an Epicurean coloring which they had learned from the Greek Commentators, and made additions to the sciences, such as the arabic numerals, which they borrowed from India, and algebra. In the ninth century Al-Kindi wrote an *Introduction to the Study of Aristotle* which was probably based on a lost work of the Neoplatonist Simplicius, and Arabic philosophy culminated in the works of Avicenna and of Averroës, the Commentator.

Judaism had been hellenized in Alexandria to such an extent that the Greek translation of the Old Testament, the Septuagint, had been prepared for Jews who could read no Hebrew or Aramaic, and Philo Judaeus had borrowed from Greek rhetoric and philosophy a method of biblical interpretation and hermeneutics. Maimonides, who like many of his Muslim predecessors was a physician and lawyer as well as a theologian and philosopher, sought to renew the Talmud, which was a renewal of the Torah, by the hermeneutic method developed from Greek arts of interpretation, and borrowed from Aristotle, in his *Guide for the Perplexed*, setting forth twenty-five propositions from Aristotle's *Physics* as a basis for the demonstration of the existence of God. Crescas thereafter demonstrated that all twenty-five propositions are false.

Latin philosophers learned about Greek and Aristotelian science when the works of Arabic scientists and philosophers were translated, beginning with Arabic medical works in the eleventh century, and going on to résumés of Arabic doctrines and sciences, like those of Adelard of Bath and Gundissalinus in the twelfth century, and finally translations of Aristotle's works, from the Arabic and then from the Greek, and of the Arabic commentators in the twelfth and thirteenth centuries. The effect of the new translations was revolutionary: they made available vast new subject-matters and new methods to investigate new problems. It was not, however, a triumph of Aristotle in any simple sense, for it was difficult to determine what Aristotle had said or what he had meant, what positions he held and what positions he opposed, and therefore how his philosophy reinforced and how it endangered Christian truths. Some philosophers, like Bonaventura, argued that Aristotle spoke the language of science, Plato spoke the language of wisdom, and Augustine combined the two; others, like Albertus Magnus and Thomas Aquinas, strove in their commentaries to separate the method and doctrines of Aristotle from alien accretions and perversions, and in their commentaries on the *Sentences* of Peter Lombard to separate natural theology, which derived its principles from experience, from revealed theology. They sometimes opposed and sometimes followed Arabic interpretations. Both enterprises were endangered by the teaching of the Latin Averroists which were condemned at the Universities of Paris and Oxford, because, it was alleged, they taught a doctrine of two truths, one derived from Aristotle, the other from revelation, which were frequently in contradiction, as they were on the eternity or the creation of the world and personal immortality. Intellectual communication between East and West was at a higher point in the thirteenth century than it has been before or since: Western philosophers read the works of Arabic and Jewish philosophers, quoted them accurately, and discussed the same or related questions of interpretation of Aristotle. But the intercultural communication did not bring with it tolerance: books of Aristotle and doctrines of Averroës and Maimonides were condemned and prohibited by academic faculties and ecclesiastical councils.

The influence of Aristotle entered a new phase when his works and the commentaries on his works became available in the West. The scope of science and philosophy was broadened, but the method and doctrines of Aristotle continued to be mixed with those of other philosophers. The logic taught at Paris and Oxford was terministic logic, the *logica moderna*, which derived as much from rhetoric and grammar as from the logic of Aristotle. The interpretation of Aristotle by theologians continued to have a Neoplatonic cast which became more pronounced the further the analysis moved from phenomena and human actions to the attributes and works of God, but the *Commentaries on the Sentences* took up new questions which were to become parts of the new physics, like the nature of motion and the velocity of free falling bodies; and in literary criticism, even before Petrarch, and in science even after Galileo, questions of style, motion, and the soul were disputed by contemporary followers of ancient commentators, frequently named for them, as the question of the immortality of the soul, during the Renaissance, pitted the Alexandrians against the Averroists, that is, the adherents of a third-century Greek commentator, the Exegete, against those of a twelfth-century Arabic philosopher, the Commentator. The Renaissance interest in Method applied techniques of invention and discovery derived from Ciceronian rhetoric and Platonic dialectic as well as techniques of proof derived from Aristotle's logic to scientific problems but with little trace of Aristotle's conception of Method as distinguished from Analytic. The Renaissance commentaries on the *Poetics* mixed Aristotle with Horace to make literary criticism a branch of rhetoric rather than a poetic science. In this phase Aristotle laid out a subject-matter, but the principles and methods of the new physics, the new metaphysics, the new philology, and the new history merged Aristotle with Plato, or Epicurus, or Cicero, or with the paradoxes of the Sophists with whom he had been associated in commentaries. Yet new editions and new translations of Aristotle's works were prepared, and new commentaries on them were written.

With the beginnings of modern philosophy in the seventeenth century, the influence of Aristotle entered a new phase. In philosophy, references to him were primarily to adduce instances of errors attributed to him in humanistic criticisms and commentaries, although his works were occasionally used for positive purposes, as Hobbes prepared an abstract of Aristotle's *Rhetoric*. Modern biologists, on the other hand, found much in his works that was trustworthy and suggestive of new inquiries —but for the most part the study of Aristotle moved into philology, the preparation of new editions and the study of the structure of the works and their relation to each other. The great modern edition of his works published in five volumes by the Berlin Academy between 1831 and 1870, the *Supplementum Aristotelicum* in three volumes between 1885 and 1903, and the edition of the Greek Commentators published in twenty-three volumes between 1882 and 1909 were the basis and beginning of a vast array of philological studies of the Aristotelian corpus, its backgrounds, and tradition. The numbers in the margin of the translations in this edition, like 82^{b}29 in the *Posterior Analytics*, are the page, column, and line numbers of the Berlin edition, that is, page 82, second column, line 29. The Greek Commentators who appear in the collected edition range from the second century A.D., when Aspasius flourished, to the fourteenth century, when Sophonias flourished, and include Alexander (third century), Themistius (fourth century), Philoponus and Simplicius (sixth century). We have only scattered editions of the Syriac commentators who wrote from the fifth to the twelfth century and of the Arabic commentators, although previously unpublished works of Alfarabi are appearing and a collected edition of the commentaries of Averroës in Arabic, Hebrew, and Latin is in process.

Aristotle's influence entered into a new phase in the twentieth century. When his name and doctrines are referred to in current philosophical discussions, the references often do nothing more than reopen old disputes and repeat old accusations and refutations, but the citation is sometimes part of a recognition that Aristotle's terms and distinctions are embedded in our past intellectual traditions and our present habits of thought, and is sometimes part of an effort to understand Aristotle in order to shed light on the history of the problems we treat and to suggest alternatives to solutions that have become fashionable or dubious in modern philosophical positions. The beginnings of neo-Thomism and the revival of the study of medieval philosophy brought with them a renewed historical and philosophical interest in Aristotle; Polish logicians returned to the study of the Aristotelian syllogistic; English analytical philosophers uncovered hidden traces of the treatment of words in new translations and interpretations of the Organon; and the Chicago school of literary criticism distinguished the method of the Poetics from the method of rhetoric, and published examples of practical Aristotelian criticism of poems and novels. Such purposes—the understanding of strands of continuity in Western civilization and the clarification of basic problems in philosophy—rather than the pursuit of historical or antiquarian curiosity, have led to new efforts to uncover the thought behind Aristotle's reputation, and they provide reasons to return from what are alleged to have been his errors and his deleterious dogmatic influences to an Introduction to Aristotle.

Logic

INTRODUCTION

Aristotle distinguished the scientfic *methods* of inquiry adapted to the investigation of the problems and the subject-matters of the different sciences from the logical *arts* of constructing arguments to demonstrate the conclusions discovered concerning the subject-matters and to test them against counterclaims of other solutions to the problems. The two central books among the logical treatises assembled under the name *Organon* or *Instrument* (probably so named by Andronicus of Rhodes) are called *Analytics*—a *Prior* or *First Analytics*, and a *Posterior* or *Second Analytics*. The *Prior Analytics*, coming after two books in which the characteristics of simple terms and of simple propositions (composed of one subject and one predicate) are set forth, analyzes simple inference in syllogisms constructed of three terms, treated as undefined variables and symbolized by letters of the alphabet, classifies them in figures and moods, and establishes the conditions of their validity and of their transformations, qualifications, and modalities. The *Posterior Analytics* examines scientific or demonstrative inference in syllogisms constructed of propositions taken from the sciences as instances of true premisses and true conclusions connected in valid inferential relations. The examination of demonstrative reasoning is followed by two books, the *Topics*, in which dialectical reasoning about the opinions of men rather than the propositions of sciences is examined, and the *On Sophistical Refutations*, in which eristic reasoning based on misconceived premisses or invalid inferences, on errors of thought and of statement, is treated. Dialectic and rhetoric are "methods" as well as arts because their use depends on knowledge of opinions, the opinions of all or most men, or the opinions of groups of men envisaged as the particular audiences or recipients of forms of communication. The two *Analytics* are not methods, because the only subject-matter knowledge they are concerned with is stated in propositions warranted by the sciences among which they construct and examine inferential relations.

The relation between the two books of the *Posterior Analytics* is indicated by the first sentence of the treatise: "All instruction given or received by way of argument proceeds from pre-existent knowledge," or, rendered more literally, "all dianoetic [i.e., intellectual or discursive] instruction and inquiry proceeds from pre-existent knowledge." The two books are concerned respectively with teaching or instruction and with learning or inquiry, and they proceed in opposite and supplementary directions. The pre-existent knowledge in instruction, as treated in the first book, is the knowledge which the instructor has of scientific truths already established and assembled in the sciences. The course of instruction proceeds from the statement of definitions, principles, axioms, and theses through the differentiation of knowledge of fact and knowledge of reasoned fact, that is, of "knowledge that" and "knowledge why," through the processes by which knowledge is warranted and established, to conclude with some instruction concerning the processes by which middle terms are discovered for the construction of such demonstrations. The pre-existent knowledge in inquiry, as treated in the second book, is the knowledge which the inquirer has when he turns to the solution of new problems raised by that existing knowledge. The course of inquiry proceeds from the differentiation of four kinds of scientific questions to the differentiation of definition and demonstration, through the examination of knowledge of existence and knowledge of cause, the establishment of basic "reflexive" premisses, known to be true because they are "self-caused," and the use of middle terms in the establishment of first principles which are the source of scientific knowledge and demonstration.

Since instruction by reason or by discursive arguments is for the purpose of conveying scientific knowledge which already exists and which can be acquired, the first book of the *Posterior Analytics* begins with an examination of the nature of scientific knowledge and of the conditions of demonstration. A basic truth can be recognized in the proposition in which it is stated, for the predicate which is asserted of the subject must be true in every instance, essential and not accidental, and commensurately universal, that is, the subject and the predicate must have the same scope of application, as "equal to two right angles" is a commensurately universal attribute of "triangle" and not of "geometric figure" or "isosceles triangle." The premisses of demonstration must be necessary and essential, and each science must have its own basic premisses. Scientific demonstration connects knowledge of existence or knowledge of fact with knowledge of cause or knowledge of reasoned fact, and the growth of a science consists in the apposition of new extreme terms, not in the interposition of new middle terms. In inference from principles to conclusions, the first figure is the true type of scientific syllogism, since it alone will provide grounds for a universal affirmative conclusion, and ignorance is either the result of erroneous inference or the negation of knowledge, such as might result from the lack of a sense. Since demonstration is impossible if there is an infinite regress of principles, there are first principles for demonstration and first principles for each of the subject-matters examined in the sciences. Therefore there is a finite number of ultimate subjects of scientific propositions and a finite number of primary attributes, that is, a finite number of categories; in each of the categories, for each subject and predicate, the process of predication must terminate upward, in a universal category, like "substance" or "quantity," and downward, in the existent particular or individual, like "this body" or "this number"; and there must be a finite number of steps between the top and the bottom. The various kinds of demonstration and the various kinds of sciences are distinguished from each other and ordered relative to each other, and the marks of the unity of a science are found in its subject-matter, methods, and principles. The final subject of instruction concerning scientific demonstration, the discovery of middle terms, like genius in art, cannot itself be learned for it depends on quick wit, the faculty of instantaneously hitting upon the middle term.

Learning or inquiry, on the other hand, is for the purpose of going beyond what is already known in search for new knowledge in the unknown. The second book of the *Posterior Analytics* begins therefore by distinguishing kinds of questions that can be raised in science. With respect to anything, one may ask what properties it has or how it is qualified and then go on to the question why it has those properties. One can also raise the question whether there are such things and then go on to the question of what they are. The answers to these pairs of questions provide knowledge of reasoned fact, or why, and knowledge of fact, or how, which were distinguished in differentiating among the propositions and principles of science in the first book. They differentiate two aspects of scientific knowledge, knowledge of existence and knowledge of cause. These differentiations were made in the first book in terms of true propositions used as premisses, principles, and conclusions. In the second book, since inquiry begins with data, unassembled and unconnected, they are made by distinguishing the terms which are to be connected in propositions and proofs. Definitions and demonstrations may be constructed from the same terms or data, differently ordered and connected. Definitions identify subjects and their properties. They do not establish existence and they do not demonstrate, but they may figure as principles, conclusions, or connecting links in demonstrations. Demonstrations prove existence, reveal the essential nature of things that have causes other than themselves, and con-

nect existing things and their causes. These are all questions of middle terms, which are of many kinds and have
many uses in definition and demonstration. One middle
term may prove several connections, and different causes
may have the same effect in things which are not specifically identical. Causes and effects may be traced in time
or be found in simultaneity, and causes may be chosen
close to the effect, or proximate, or further removed from
the effect, or more universal, the true cause being the
proximate cause.

Since scientific knowledge through demonstration is impossible without knowledge of primary immediate premisses, they must be acquired and known. They cannot be
demonstrated; they are not innate in explicit and fully
formed knowledge; and they cannot be acquired or learned
without a basis of pre-existent knowledge. They must exist
in potentiality, not actuality. They are formed from sense
perceptions, which are retained in memory, and from
memories, which joined together constitute experience.
From experience universals are formed, and art and science
—art by the use of causes in the realm of becoming, and
science by the knowledge of causes in the realm of being.
Knowledge of first principles is formed by induction from
experience. Since they cannot be demonstrated, and since
demonstration depends on them, they are perceived immediately by intuition of their reflexively ascertained truth.
Intuition and scientific knowing are the two forms of true
thinking. Intuition of original basic premisses is the source
of science, and science in turn is the source of the whole
body of facts.

The first book of the *Posterior Analytics* has left its impress on subsequent logic in the central place it gives to
axioms, principles, and propositions. Later theories of inference, implication, and entailment, however, are not
always framed in ways that require a defense of first principles, eternal truths, causes, existence, or categories, finite
in number or finite in inferential steps between a top and

a bottom. The emphasis on the function of middle terms in the construction of proof and of sciences usually disappears, its place being taken by forms, or models, or sets, or paradigms. The influence of the second book of the *Posterior Analytics*, which centers on middle terms, has therefore been limited in logic, and there is little discussion of the distinction between definition and demonstration, between fact and cause, or between existence and essence, as logical problems, apart from continuing disputes between formalism and intuitionism. The four kinds of scientific question have, however, been influential in other fields. They entered into rhetoric to provide the distinction between four "constitutions" or issues or conflicts of causes: questions of fact or the conjectural issue, questions of name or the definitional issue, questions of sorts of thing or the general or qualitative issue, and questions of legal procedures and jurisdictions or the translative issue. From rhetoric the issues moved into speculations concerning methods of invention or discovery in other fields, including the field of scientific method, as in the theories of Francis Bacon. Taken as a whole, however, the *Posterior Analytics* and its scientific demonstration have had little effect on logic, even on what is called "Aristotelian logic." Its place is taken by dialectic in logics in which the unit is the idea rather than the term and in which propositions become judgments; by paradoxes, sophistries, and tautologies in logics in which the unit is the word and the propositions become sentences; by model structures of things in logistic logics in which arguments are mapped to underlying facts. The Port Royal Logic reduced the last three books of the *Organon* to a single book on Method, and later textbooks of Aristotelian logic follow that lead and devote much of the consideration of method to the examination of fallacies. Recently, however, increasing attention has been given to problems treated in the large portions of the *Organon* omitted in the textbooks.

ANALYTICA POSTERIORA

CONTENTS

BOOK I

Analytica Posteriora
Posterior Analytics

Translated by G. R. G. Mure

பபப

BOOK I

1 All instruction given or received by way of argument proceeds from pre-existent knowledge. This becomes evident upon a survey of all the species of such instruction. The mathematical sciences and all other speculative disciplines are acquired in this way, and so are the two 5 forms of dialectical reasoning, syllogistic and inductive; for each of these latter makes use of old knowledge to impart new, the syllogism assuming an audience that accepts its premisses, induction exhibiting the universal as implicit in the clearly known particular. Again, the persuasion exerted by rhetorical arguments is in principle the same, since they use either example, a kind of induction, or en- 10 thymeme, a form of syllogism.

The pre-existent knowledge required is of two kinds. In some cases admission of the fact must be assumed, in others comprehension of the meaning of the term used, and sometimes both assumptions are essential. Thus, we assume that every predicate can be either truly affirmed or truly denied of any subject, and that 'triangle' means so and so, as regards 'unit' we have to make the double assumption of the meaning of the word and the existence of 15 the thing. The reason is that these several objects are not equally obvious to us. Recognition of a truth may in some

cases contain as factors both previous knowledge and also
knowledge acquired simultaneously with that recognition
—knowledge, this latter, of the particulars actually falling
under the universal and therein already virtually known.
20 For example, the student knew beforehand that the angles
of every triangle are equal to two right angles; but it was
only at the actual moment at which he was being led on
to recognize this as true in the instance before him that he
came to know 'this figure inscribed in the semicircle' to
be a triangle. For some things (viz. the singulars finally
reached which are not predicable of anything else as subject) are only learnt in this way, i. e. there is here no recognition through a middle of a minor term as subject to a
major. Before he was led on to recognition or before he
actually drew a conclusion, we should perhaps say that in
25 a manner he knew, in a manner not.

If he did not in an unqualified sense of the term *know*
the existence of this triangle, how could he *know* without
qualification that its angles were equal to two right angles?
No: clearly he *knows* not without qualification but only
in the sense that he *knows* universally. If this distinction is
not drawn, we are faced with the dilemma in the *Meno*: [1]
either a man will learn nothing or what he already knows;
for we cannot accept the solution which some people of-
30 fer. A man is asked, 'Do you, or do you not, know that
every pair is even?' He says he does know it. The ques-
tioner then produces a particular pair, of the existence,
and so a *fortiori* of the evenness, of which he was unaware. The solution which some people offer is to assert
that they do not know that every pair is even, but only
that everything which they know to be a pair is even: yet
71ᵇ what they know to be even is that of which they have
demonstrated evenness, i. e. what they made the subject
of their premiss, viz. not merely every triangle or number
which they know to be such, but any and every number
or triangle without reservation. For no premiss is ever

[1] Plato, *Meno*, 80 E.

couched in the form 'every number which you know to
be such', or 'every rectilinear figure which you know to be
such': the predicate is always construed as applicable to
any and every instance of the thing. On the other hand,
I imagine there is nothing to prevent a man in one sense 5
knowing what he is learning, in another not knowing it.
The strange thing would be, not if in some sense he knew
what he was learning, but if he were to know it in that
precise sense and manner in which he was learning it.[2]

2 We suppose ourselves to possess unqualified scientific knowledge of a thing, as opposed to knowing it
in the accidental way in which the sophist knows, when
we think that we know the cause on which the fact de- 10
pends, as the cause of that fact and of no other, and, further, that the fact could not be other than it is. Now that
scientific knowing is something of this sort is evident—
witness both those who falsely claim it and those who
actually possess it, since the former merely imagine themselves to be, while the latter are also actually, in the condition described. Consequently the proper object of unqualified scientific knowledge is something which cannot
be other than it is.   15

There may be another manner of knowing as well—that
will be discussed later.[3] What I now assert is that at all
events we do know by demonstration. By demonstration
I mean a syllogism productive of scientific knowledge, a
syllogism, that is, the grasp of which is *eo ipso* such knowledge. Assuming then that my thesis as to the nature of sci- 20
entific knowing is correct, the premisses of demonstrated
knowledge must be true, primary, immediate, better
known than and prior to the conclusion, which is further
related to them as effect to cause. Unless these conditions
are satisfied, the basic truths will not be 'appropriate' to
the conclusion. Syllogism there may indeed be without

[2] Cf. *An. Pr.* ii, ch. 21.
[3] Cf. the following chapter and more particularly ii, ch. 19.

these conditions, but such syllogism, not being productive
of scientific knowledge, will not be demonstration. The
25 premisses must be true: for that which is non-existent cannot be known—we cannot know, e. g., that the diagonal of a
square is commensurate with its side. The premisses must be
primary and indemonstrable; otherwise they will require
demonstration in order to be known, since to have knowledge, if it be not accidental knowledge, of things which are
demonstrable, means precisely to have a demonstration of
them. The premisses must be the causes of the conclusion,
30 better known than it, and prior to it; its causes, since we possess scientific knowledge of a thing only when we know its
cause; prior, in order to be causes; antecedently known,
this antecedent knowledge being not our mere understanding of the meaning, but knowledge of the fact as well.
Now 'prior' and 'better known' are ambiguous terms, for
there is a difference between what is prior and better known
72ᵃ in the order of being and what is prior and better known
to man. I mean that objects nearer to sense are prior and
better known to man; objects without qualification prior
and better known are those further from sense. Now the
most universal causes are furthest from sense and particular
5 causes are nearest to sense, and they are thus exactly opposed to one another. In saying that the premisses of demonstrated knowledge must be primary, I mean that they
must be the 'appropriate' basic truths, for I identify primary
premiss and basic truth. A 'basic truth' in a demonstration
is an immediate proposition. An immediate proposition is
one which has no other proposition prior to it. A proposition is either part of an enunciation, i. e. it predicates a
single attribute of a single subject. If a proposition is dia-
10 lectical, it assumes either part indifferently; if it is demonstrative, it lays down one part to the definite exclusion of
the other because that part is true. The term 'enunciation'
denotes either part of a contradiction indifferently. A contradiction is an opposition which of its own nature excludes
a middle. The part of a contradiction which conjoins a

predicate with a subject is an affirmation; the part disjoin-
ing them is a negation. I call an immediate basic truth of ₁₅
syllogism a 'thesis' when, though it is not susceptible of
proof by the teacher, yet ignorance of it does not constitute
a total bar to progress on the part of the pupil: one which
the pupil must know if he is to learn anything whatever
is an axiom. I call it an axiom because there are such truths
and we give them the name of axioms *par excellence*. If a
thesis assumes one part or the other of an enunciation, i. e.
asserts either the existence or the non-existence of a sub- ₂₀
ject, it is a hypothesis; if it does not so assert, it is a definition. Definition is a 'thesis' or a 'laying something down',
since the arithmetician lays it down that to be a unit is to
be quantitatively indivisible; but it is not a hypothesis, for
to define what a unit is is not the same as to affirm its
existence.

Now since the required ground of our knowledge—i. e.
of our conviction—of a fact is the possession of such a syl- ₂₅
logism as we call demonstration, and the ground of the
syllogism is the facts constituting its premisses, we must
not only know the primary premisses—some if not all of
them—beforehand, but know them better than the conclusion: for the cause of an attribute's inherence in a subject always itself inheres in the subject more firmly than
that attribute; e. g. the cause of our loving anything is dearer
to us than the object of our love. So since the primary
premisses are the cause of our knowledge—i. e. of our con- ₃₀
viction—it follows that we know them better—that is, are
more convinced of them—than their consequences, precisely because our knowledge of the latter is the effect of
our knowledge of the premisses. Now a man cannot believe
in anything more than in the things he knows, unless he
has either actual knowledge of it or something better than
actual knowledge. But we are faced with this paradox if a
student whose belief rests on demonstration has not prior ₃₅
knowledge; a man must believe in some, if not in all, of the
basic truths more than in the conclusion. Moreover, if a

man sets out to acquire the scientific knowledge that comes
through demonstration, he must not only have a better
knowledge of the basic truths and a firmer conviction of
them than of the connexion which is being demonstrated:
72ᵇ more than this, nothing must be more certain or better
known to him than these basic truths in their character as
contradicting the fundamental premisses which lead to the
opposed and erroneous conclusion. For indeed the conviction of pure science must be unshakable.

3   Some hold that, owing to the necessity of knowing the
5   primary premisses, there is no scientific knowledge.
Others think there is, but that all truths are demonstrable.
Neither doctrine is either true or a necessary deduction
from the premisses. The first school, assuming that there is
no way of knowing other than by demonstration, maintain
that an infinite regress is involved, on the ground that if
behind the prior stands no primary, we could not know the
10 posterior through the prior (wherein they are right, for one
cannot traverse an infinite series): if on the other hand—
they say—the series terminates and there are primary premisses, yet these are unknowable because incapable of demonstration, which according to them is the only form of
knowledge. And since thus one cannot know the primary
premisses, knowledge of the conclusions which follow from
them is not pure scientific knowledge nor properly knowing
at all, but rests on the mere supposition that the premisses
15 are true. The other party agree with them as regards knowing, holding that it is only possible by demonstration, but
they see no difficulty in holding that all truths are demonstrated, on the ground that demonstration may be circular
and reciprocal.

Our own doctrine is that not all knowledge is demonstrative: on the contrary, knowledge of the immediate prem-
20 isses is independent of demonstration. (The necessity of this
is obvious; for since we must know the prior premisses from

which the demonstration is drawn, and since the regress must end in immediate truths, those truths must be indemonstrable.) Such, then, is our doctrine, and in addition we maintain that besides scientific knowledge there is its originative source which enables us to recognize the definitions.

Now demonstration must be based on premisses prior to 25 and better known than the conclusion; and the same things cannot simultaneously be both prior and posterior to one another: so circular demonstration is clearly not possible in the unqualified sense of 'demonstration', but only possible if 'demonstration' be extended to include that other method of argument which rests on a distinction between truths prior to us and truths without qualification prior, i. e. the method by which induction produces knowl- 30 edge. But if we accept this extension of its meaning, our definition of unqualified knowledge will prove faulty; for there seem to be two kinds of it. Perhaps, however, the second form of demonstration, that which proceeds from truths better known to us, is not demonstration in the unqualified sense of the term.

The advocates of circular demonstration are not only faced with the difficulty we have just stated: in addition their theory reduces to the mere statement that if a thing exists, then it does exist—an easy way of proving anything. 35 That this is so can be clearly shown by taking three terms, for to constitute the circle it makes no difference whether many terms or few or even only two are taken. Thus by direct proof, if A is, B must be; if B is, C must be; therefore if A is, C must be. Since then—by the circular proof—if A is, B must be, and if B is, A must be, A may be substituted **73ᵃ** for C above. Then 'if B is, A must be' = 'if B is, C must be' which above gave the conclusion 'if A is, C must be': but C and A have been identified. Consequently the upholders of circular demonstration are in the position of saying that if A is, A must be—a simple way of proving anything. 5

Moreover, even such circular demonstration is impossible except in the case of attributes that imply one another, viz. 'peculiar' properties.

Now, it has been shown that the positing of one thing— be it one term or one premiss—never involves a necessary consequent: [4] two premisses constitute the first and small-
10 est foundation for drawing a conclusion at all and therefore a *fortiori* for the demonstrative syllogism of science. If, then, A is implied in B and C, and B and C are reciprocally implied in one another and in A, it is possible, as has been shown in my writings on the syllogism,[5] to prove all the assumptions on which the original conclusion rested, by circular demonstration in the first figure. But it has also
15 been shown that in the other figures either no conclusion is possible, or at least none which proves both the original premisses.[6] Propositions the terms of which are not convertible cannot be circularly demonstrated at all, and since convertible terms occur rarely in actual demonstrations, it is clearly frivolous and impossible to say that demonstration is reciprocal and that therefore everything can be dem-
20 onstrated.

4   Since the object of pure scientific knowledge cannot be other than it is, the truth obtained by demonstrative knowledge will be necessary. And since demonstrative knowledge is only present when we have a demonstration, it follows that demonstration is an inference from necessary premisses. So we must consider what are the premisses
25 of demonstration—i. e. what is their character: and as a preliminary, let us define what we mean by an attribute 'true in every instance of its subject', an 'essential' attribute, and a 'commensurate and universal' attribute. I call 'true in every instance' what is truly predicable of all instances—not of one to the exclusion of others—and at all times, not at

[4] An. Pr. i, ch. 25.
[5] Ibid. ii, ch. 5.
[6] Ibid. ii, cc. 5 and 6.

this or that time only; e. g. if animal is truly predicable of
every instance of man, then if it be true to say 'this is a 30
man', 'this is an animal' is also true, and if the one be true
now the other is true now. A corresponding account holds
if point is in every instance predicable as contained in line.
There is evidence for this in the fact that the objection we
raise against a proposition put to us as true in every instance
is either an instance in which, or an occasion on which, it is
not true. Essential attributes are (1) such as belong to their 35
subject as elements in its essential nature (e. g. line thus belongs to triangle, point to line; for the very being or 'substance' of triangle and line is composed of these elements,
which are contained in the formulae defining triangle and
line): (2) such that, while they belong to certain subjects,
the subjects to which they belong are contained in the
attribute's own defining formula. Thus straight and curved-
belong to line, odd and even, prime and compound, square 40
and oblong, to number; and also the formula defining any 73ᵇ
one of these attributes contains its subject—e. g. line or
number as the case may be.

Extending this classification to all other attributes, I
distinguish those that answer the above description as belonging essentially to their respective subjects; whereas attributes related in neither of these two ways to their subjects I call accidents or 'coincidents'; e. g. musical or white
is a 'coincident' of animal.

Further (a) that is essential which is not predicated of a 5
subject other than itself: e. g. 'the walking [thing]' walks
and is white in virtue of being something else besides;
whereas substance, in the sense of whatever signifies a 'this
somewhat', is not what it is in virtue of being something
else besides. Things, then, not predicated of a subject I
call essential; things predicated of a subject I call accidental or 'coincidental'.

In another sense again (b) a thing consequentially con- 10
nected with anything is essential; one not so connected is
'coincidental'. An example of the latter is 'While he was

walking it lightened': the lightning was not due to his
walking; it was, we should say, a coincidence. If, on the
other hand, there is a consequential connexion, the predication is essential; e. g. if a beast dies when its throat is being
cut, then its death is also essentially connected with the
15 cutting, because the cutting was the cause of death, not
death a 'coincident' of the cutting.

So far then as concerns the sphere of connexions scientifically known in the unqualified sense of that term, all
attributes which (within that sphere) are essential either in
the sense that their subjects are contained in them, or in
the sense that they are contained in their subjects, are
necessary as well as consequentially connected with their
subjects. For it is impossible for them not to inhere in
their subjects—either simply or in the qualified sense that
20 one or other of a pair of opposites must inhere in the subject; e. g. in line must be either straightness or curvature, in
number either oddness or evenness. For within a single
identical genus the contrary of a given attribute is either
its privative or its contradictory; e. g. within number what
is not odd is even, inasmuch as within this sphere even is a
necessary consequent of not-odd. So, since any given predicate must be either affirmed or denied of any subject, essential attributes must inhere in their subjects of necessity.

Thus, then, we have established the distinction between
25 the attribute which is 'true in every instance' and the 'essential' attribute.

I term 'commensurately universal' an attribute which belongs to every instance of its subject, and to every instance
essentially and as such; from which it clearly follows that all
commensurate universals inhere necessarily in their subjects. The essential attribute, and the attribute that belongs
to its subject as such, are identical. E. g. point and straight
30 belong to line essentially, for they belong to line as such;
and triangle as such has two right angles, for it is essentially
equal to two right angles.

An attribute belongs commensurately and universally to

a subject when it can be shown to belong to any random instance of that subject and when the subject is the first thing to which it can be shown to belong. Thus, e. g., (1) the equality of its angles to two right angles is not a commensurately universal attribute of figure. For though it is possible to show that a figure has its angles equal to two right angles, this attribute cannot be demonstrated of any 35 figure selected at haphazard, nor in demonstrating does one take a figure at random—a square is a figure but its angles are not equal to two right angles. On the other hand, any isosceles triangle has its angles equal to two right angles, yet isosceles triangle is not the primary subject of this attribute but triangle is prior. So whatever can be shown to have its angles equal to two right angles, or to possess any other attribute, in any random instance of itself and pri- 40 marily—that is the first subject to which the predicate in question belongs commensurately and universally, and the 74ᵇ demonstration, in the essential sense, of any predicate is the proof of it as belonging to this first subject commensurately and universally: while the proof of it as belonging to the other subjects to which it attaches is demonstration only in a secondary and unessential sense. Nor again (2) is equality to two right angles a commensurately universal attribute of isosceles; it is of wider application.

5 We must not fail to observe that we often fall into error because our conclusion is not in fact primary and commensurately universal in the sense in which we think 5 we prove it so. We make this mistake (1) when the subject is an individual or individuals above which there is no universal to be found: (2) when the subjects belong to different species and there is a higher universal, but it has no name: (3) when the subject which the demonstrator takes as a whole is really only a part of a larger whole; for then the demonstration will be true of the individual instances 10 within the part and will hold in every instance of it, yet the

demonstration will not be true of this subject primarily and commensurately and universally. When a demonstration is true of a subject primarily and commensurately and universally, that is to be taken to mean that it is true of a given subject primarily and as such. Case (3) may be thus exemplified. If a proof were given that perpendiculars to the same line are parallel, it might be supposed that *lines thus perpendicular* were the proper subject of the demonstration
15 because being parallel is true of every instance of them. But it is not so, for the parallelism depends not on these angles being equal to one another because each is a right angle, but simply on their being equal to one another. An example of (1) would be as follows: if isosceles were the only triangle, it would be thought to have its angles equal to two right angles qua isosceles. An instance of (2) would be the law that proportionals alternate. Alternation used to be demonstrated separately of numbers, lines, solids,
20 and durations, though it could have been proved of them all by a single demonstration. Because there was no single name to denote that in which numbers, lengths, durations, and solids are identical, and because they differed specifically from one another, this property was proved of each of them separately. To-day, however, the proof is commensurately universal, for they do not possess this attribute qua lines or qua numbers, but qua manifesting this generic
25 character which they are postulated as possessing universally. Hence, even if one prove of each kind of triangle that its angles are equal to two right angles, whether by means of the same or different proofs; still, as long as one treats separately equilateral, scalene, and isosceles, one does not yet know, except sophistically, that triangle has its angles equal to two right angles, nor does one yet know that triangle has this property commensurately and universally,
30 even if there is no other species of triangle but these. For one does not know that triangle as such has this property, nor even that 'all' triangles have it—unless 'all' means 'each taken singly': if 'all' means 'as a whole class', then, though

there be none in which one does not recognize this property, one does not know it of 'all triangles'.

When, then, does our knowledge fail of commensurate
universality, and when is it unqualified knowledge? If triangle be identical in essence with equilateral, i. e. with each
or all equilaterals, then clearly we have unqualified knowledge: if on the other hand it be not, and the attribute belongs to equilateral qua triangle; then our knowledge fails
of commensurate universality. 'But', it will be asked, 'does 35
this attribute belong to the subject of which it has been
demonstrated qua triangle or qua isosceles? What is the
point at which the subject to which it belongs is primary?
(i. e. to what subject can it be demonstrated as belonging
commensurately and universally?)' Clearly this point is the
first term in which it is found to inhere as the elimination
of inferior *differentiae* proceeds. Thus the angles of a brazen
isosceles triangle are equal to two right angles: but eliminate brazen and isosceles and the attribute remains. 'But'
—you may say—'eliminate figure or limit, and the attribute 74ᵇ
vanishes'. True, but figure and limit are not the first *differentiae* whose elimination destroys the attribute. 'Then
what is the first?' If it is triangle, it will be in virtue of
triangle that the attribute belongs to all the other subjects
of which it is predicable, and triangle is the subject to which
it can be demonstrated as belonging commensurately and
universally.

6 Demonstrative knowledge must rest on necessary basic
truths; for the object of scientific knowledge cannot be 5
other than it is. Now attributes attaching essentially to their
subjects attach necessarily to them: for essential attributes
are either elements in the essential nature of their subjects,
or contain their subjects as elements in their own essential
nature. (The pairs of opposites which the latter class includes are necessary because one member or the other necessarily inheres.) It follows from this that premisses of the
demonstrative syllogism must be connexions essential in 10

the sense explained: for all attributes must inhere essentially or else be accidental, and accidental attributes are not necessary to their subjects.

We must either state the case thus, or else premise that the conclusion of demonstration is necessary and that a demonstrated conclusion cannot be other than it is, and
15 then infer that the conclusion must be developed from necessary premises. For though you may reason from true premises without demonstrating, yet if your premises are necessary you will assuredly demonstrate—in such necessity you have at once a distinctive character of demonstration. That demonstration proceeds from necessary premises is also indicated by the fact that the objection we raise against a professed demonstration is that a premiss of it is not a
20 necessary truth—whether we think it altogether devoid of necessity, or at any rate so far as our opponent's previous argument goes. This shows how naïve it is to suppose one's basic truths rightly chosen if one starts with a proposition which is (1) popularly accepted and (2) true, such as the sophists' assumption that to know is the same as to possess knowledge.[7] For (1) popular acceptance or rejection is no criterion of a basic truth, which can only be the primary
25 law of the genus constituting the subject matter of the demonstration; and (2) not all truth is 'appropriate'.

A further proof that the conclusion must be the development of necessary premises is as follows. Where demonstration is possible, one who can give no account which includes the cause has no scientific knowledge. If, then, we suppose a syllogism in which, though A necessarily inheres in C, yet B, the middle term of the demonstration, is not necessarily connected with A and C, then the man who
30 argues thus has no reasoned knowledge of the conclusion, since this conclusion does not owe its necessity to the middle term; for though the conclusion is necessary, the mediating link is a contingent fact. Or again, if a man is without knowledge now, though he still retains the steps of the ar-

[7] Plato, *Euthydemus*, 277 B.

gument, though there is no change in himself or in the fact and no lapse of memory on his part; then neither had he knowledge previously. But the mediating link, not being necessary, may have perished in the interval; and if so, 35 though there be no change in him nor in the fact, and though he will still retain the steps of the argument, yet he has not knowledge, and therefore had not knowledge before. Even if the link has not actually perished but is liable to perish, this situation is possible and might occur. But such a condition cannot be knowledge.

When the conclusion is necessary, the middle through 75ᵃ which it was proved may yet quite easily be non-necessary. You can in fact infer the necessary even from a non-necessary premiss, just as you can infer the true from the not true. On the other hand, when the middle is necessary the 5 conclusion must be necessary; just as true premisses always give a true conclusion. Thus, if A is necessarily predicated of B and B of C, then A is necessarily predicated of C. But when the conclusion is non-necessary the middle cannot be necessary either. Thus: let A be predicated non-neces- 10 sarily of C but necessarily of B, and let B be a necessary predicate of C; then A too will be a necessary predicate of C, which by hypothesis it is not.

To sum up, then: demonstrative knowledge must be knowledge of a necessary nexus, and therefore must clearly be obtained through a necessary middle term; otherwise its possessor will know neither the cause nor the fact that his 15 conclusion is a necessary connexion. Either he will mistake the non-necessary for the necessary and believe the necessity of the conclusion without knowing it, or else he will not even believe it—in which case he will be equally ignorant, whether he actually infers the mere fact through middle terms or the reasoned fact and from immediate premisses.

Of accidents that are not essential according to our definition of essential there is no demonstrative knowledge; for since an accident, in the sense in which I here speak of it, may also not inhere, it is impossible to prove its in- 20

herence as a necessary conclusion. A difficulty, however,
might be raised as to why in dialectic, if the conclusion is
not a necessary connexion, such and such determinate
premisses should be proposed in order to deal with such
and such determinate problems. Would not the result be
the same if one asked any questions whatever and then
merely stated one's conclusion? The solution is that de-
25 terminate questions have to be put, not because the replies
to them affirm facts which necessitate facts affirmed by
the conclusion, but because these answers are propositions
which if the answerer affirm, he must affirm the conclusion
—and affirm it with truth if they are true

Since it is just those attributes within every genus which
are essential and possessed by their respective subjects as
such that are necessary, it is clear that both the conclusions
and the premisses of demonstrations which produce scien-
30 tific knowledge are essential. For accidents are not necessary: and, further, since accidents are not necessary one does
not necessarily have reasoned knowledge of a conclusion
drawn from them (this is so even if the accidental premisses are invariable but not essential, as in proofs through
signs; for though the conclusion be actually essential, one
will not know it as essential nor know its reason); but to
35 have reasoned knowledge of a conclusion is to know it
through its cause. We may conclude that the middle must
be consequentially connected with the minor, and the
major with the middle.

7   It follows that we cannot in demonstrating pass from
        one genus to another. We cannot, for instance, prove
geometrical truths by arithmetic. For there are three elements in demonstration: (1) what is proved, the conclu-
40 sion—an attribute inhering essentially in a genus; (2)
the axioms, i. e. axioms which are premisses of demonstra-
75ᵇ tion; (3) the subject-genus whose attributes, i. e. essential
properties, are revealed by the demonstration. The axioms
which are premisses of demonstration may be identical in

two or more sciences: but in the case of two different genera such as arithmetic and geometry you cannot apply arithmetical demonstration to the properties of magnitudes 5 unless the magnitudes in question are numbers.[8] How in certain cases transference is possible I will explain later.[9]

Arithmetical demonstration and the other sciences likewise possess, each of them, their own genera; so that if the demonstration is to pass from one sphere to another, the genus must be either absolutely or to some extent the same. 10 If this is not so, transference is clearly impossible, because the extreme and the middle terms must be drawn from the same genus: otherwise, as predicated, they will not be essential and will thus be accidents. That is why it cannot be proved by geometry that opposites fall under one science, nor even that the product of two cubes is a cube. Nor can the theorem of any one science be demonstrated by 15 means of another science, unless these theorems are related as subordinate to superior (e. g. as optical theorems to geometry or harmonic theorems to arithmetic). Geometry again cannot prove of lines any property which they do not possess qua lines, i. e. in virtue of the fundamental truths of their peculiar genus: it cannot show, for example, that the straight line is the most beautiful of lines or the contrary of the circle; for these qualities do not belong to lines in virtue of their peculiar genus, but through some property 20 which it shares with other genera.

8 It is also clear that if the premisses from which the syllogism proceeds are commensurately universal, the conclusion of such demonstration—demonstration, i. e., in the unqualified sense—must also be eternal. Therefore no attribute can be demonstrated nor known by strictly scientific knowledge to inhere in perishable things. The proof can only be accidental, because the attribute's connexion 25 with its perishable subject is not commensurately universal

---

[8] Cf. *Met.* 1039ᵃ 9.
[9] Cf. i, cc. 9 and 13.

but temporary and special. If such a demonstration is made, one premiss must be perishable and not commensurately universal (perishable because only if it is perishable will the conclusion be perishable; not commensurately universal, because the predicate will be predicable of some instances of the subject and not of others); so that the conclusion can only be that a fact is true at the moment—not com-
30 mensurately and universally. The same is true of defini-tions, since a definition is either a primary premiss or a con-clusion of a demonstration, or else only differs from a dem-onstration in the order of its terms. Demonstration and science of merely frequent occurrences—e. g. of eclipse as happening to the moon—are, as such, clearly eternal: whereas so far as they are not eternal they are not fully com-mensurate. Other subjects too have properties attaching to
35 them in the same way as eclipse attaches to the moon.

9   It is clear that if the conclusion is to show an attribute inhering as such, nothing can be demonstrated except from its 'appropriate' basic truths. Consequently a proof even from true, indemonstrable, and immediate premisses
40 does not constitute knowledge. Such proofs are like Bry-son's method of squaring the circle; for they operate by taking as their middle a common character—a character, therefore, which the subject may share with another—and
76ᵃ consequently they apply equally to subjects different in kind. They therefore afford knowlege of an attribute only as inhering accidentally, not as belonging to its subject as such: otherwise they would not have been applicable to an-other genus.

Our knowledge of any attribute's connexion with a sub-ject is accidental unless we know that connexion through the middle term in virtue of which it inheres, and as an
5 inference from basic premisses essential and 'appropriate' to the subject—unless we know, e. g., the property of pos-sessing angles equal to two right angles as belonging to that

subject in which it inheres essentially, and as inferred from basic premises essential and 'appropriate' to that subject: so that if that middle term also belongs essentially to the minor, the middle must belong to the same kind as the major and minor terms. The only exceptions to this rule are such cases as theorems in harmonics which are demonstrable by arithmetic. Such theorems are proved by the 10 same middle terms as arithmetical properties, but with a qualification—the fact falls under a separate science (for the subject genus is separate), but the reasoned fact concerns the superior science, to which the attributes essentially belong. Thus, even these apparent exceptions show that no attribute is strictly demonstrable except from its 'appropriate' basic truths, which, however, in the case of these sciences have the requisite identity of character. 15

It is no less evident that the peculiar basic truths of each inhering attribute are indemonstrable; for basic truths from which they might be deduced would be basic truths of all that is, and the science to which they belonged would possess universal sovereignty. This is so because he knows better whose knowledge is deduced from higher causes, for his knowledge is from prior premisses when it derives from 20 causes themselves uncaused: hence, if he knows better than others or best of all, his knowledge would be science in a higher or the highest degree. But, as things are, demonstration is not transferable to another genus, with such exceptions as we have mentioned of the application of geometrical demonstrations to theorems in mechanics or optics, or 25 of arithmetical demonstrations to those of harmonics.

It is hard to be sure whether one knows or not; for it is hard to be sure whether one's knowledge is based on the basic truths appropriate to each attribute—the differentia of true knowledge. We think we have scientific knowledge if we have reasoned from true and primary premisses. But that is not so: the conclusion must be homogeneous with 30 the basic facts of the science.

10 I call the basic truths of every genus those elements in
it the existence of which cannot be proved. As regards
both these primary truths and the attributes dependent on
them the meaning of the name is assumed. The fact of their
existence as regards the primary truths must be assumed;
but it has to be proved of the remainder, the attributes.
Thus we assume the meaning alike of unity, straight, and
35 triangular; but while as regards unity and magnitude we
assume also the fact of their existence, in the case of the
remainder proof is required.

Of the basic truths used in the demonstrative sciences
some are peculiar to each science, and some are common,
but common only in the sense of analogous, being of use
only in so far as they fall within the genus constituting the
province of the science in question.

40   Peculiar truths are, e. g., the definitions of line and
straight; common truths are such as 'take equals from
equals and equals remain'. Only so much of these common
76ᵇ truths is required as falls within the genus in question:
for a truth of this kind will have the same force even if
not used generally but applied by the geometer only to
magnitudes, or by the arithmetician only to numbers. Also
peculiar to a science are the subjects the existence as well
as the meaning of which it assumes, and the essential attri-
5 butes of which it investigates, e. g. in arithmetic units, in
geometry points and lines. Both the existence and the
meaning of the subjects are assumed by these sciences; but
of their essential attributes only the meaning is assumed.
For example arithmetic assumes the meaning of odd and
even, square and cube, geometry that of incommensurable,
or of deflection or verging of lines, whereas the existence of
10 these attributes is demonstrated by means of the axioms
and from previous conclusions as premisses. Astronomy too
proceeds in the same way. For indeed every demonstrative
science has three elements: (1) that which it posits, the
subject genus whose essential attributes it examines; (2)
15 the so-called axioms, which are primary premisses of its

demonstration; (3) the attributes, the meaning of which it assumes. Yet some sciences may very well pass over some of these elements; e. g. we might not expressly posit the existence of the genus if its existence were obvious (for instance, the existence of hot and cold is more evident than that of number); or we might omit to assume expressly the meaning of the attributes if it were well understood. In the same way the meaning of axioms, such as 'Take equals from 20 equals and equals remain', is well known and so not expressly assumed. Nevertheless in the nature of the case the essential elements of demonstration are three: the subject, the attributes, and the basic premisses.

That which expresses necessary self-grounded fact, and which we must necessarily believe,[10] is distinct both from the hypotheses of a science and from illegitimate postulate —I say 'must believe', because all syllogism, and therefore a fortiori demonstration, is addressed not to the spoken word, but to the discourse within the soul,[11] and though we can 25 always raise objections to the spoken word, to the inward discourse we cannot always object. That which is capable of proof but assumed by the teacher without proof is, if the pupil believes and accepts it, hypothesis, though only in a limited sense hypothesis—that is, relatively to the pupil; if the pupil has no opinion or a contrary opinion on the 30 matter, the same assumption is an illegitimate postulate. Therein lies the distinction between hypothesis and illegitimate postulate: the latter is the contrary of the pupil's opinion, demonstrable, but assumed and used without demonstration.

The definitions—viz. those which are not expressed as statements that anything is or is not—are not hypotheses: 35 but it is in the premisses of a science that its hypotheses are contained. Definitions require only to be understood, and this is not hypothesis—unless it be contended that the pupil's hearing is also an hypothesis required by the teacher.

---

[10] sc. axioms.
[11] Cf. Plato, *Theaetetus*, 189 E ff.

Hypotheses, on the contrary, postulate facts on the being of which depends the being of the fact inferred. Nor are the geometer's hypotheses false, as some have held, urging that 40 one must not employ falsehood and that the geometer is uttering falsehood in stating that the line which he draws is a foot long or straight, when it is actually neither. The 77ᵃ truth is that the geometer does not draw any conclusion from the being of the particular line of which he speaks, but from what his diagrams symbolize. A further distinction is that all hypotheses and illegitimate postulates are either universal or particular, whereas a definition is neither.

11 So demonstration does not necessarily imply the be-
5   ing of Forms nor a One beside a Many, but it does necessarily imply the possibility of truly predicating one of many; since without this possibility we cannot save the universal, and if the universal goes, the middle term goes with it, and so demonstration becomes impossible. We conclude, then, that there must be a single identical term unequivocally predicable of a number of individuals.
10   The law that it is impossible to affirm and deny simultaneously the same predicate of the same subject is not expressly posited by any demonstration except when the conclusion also has to be expressed in that form; in which case the proof lays down as its major premiss that the major is truly affirmed of the middle but falsely denied. It makes no difference, however, if we add to the middle, or again to the minor term, the corresponding negative. For grant a 15 minor term of which it is true to predicate man—even if it be also true to predicate not-man of it—still grant simply that man is animal and not not-animal, and the conclusion follows: for it will still be true to say that Callias—even if it be also true to say that not-Callias—is animal and not not-animal. The reason is that the major term is predicable not only of the middle, but of something other than the 20 middle as well, being of wider application; so that the conclusion is not affected even if the middle is extended to

cover the original middle term and also what is not the original middle term.[12]

The law that every predicate can be either truly affirmed or truly denied of every subject is posited by such demonstration as uses *reductio ad impossibile*, and then not always universally, but so far as it is requisite; within the limits, that is, of the genus—the genus, I mean (as I have already 25 explained [13]), to which the man of science applies his demonstrations. In virtue of the common elements of demonstration—I mean the common axioms which are used as premisses of demonstration, not the subjects or the attributes demonstrated as belonging to them—all the sciences have communion with one another, and in communion with them all is dialectic and any science which might attempt a universal proof of axioms such as the law of ex- 30 cluded middle, the law that the subtraction of equals from equals leaves equal remainders, or other axioms of the same kind. Dialectic has no definite sphere of this kind, not being confined to a single genus. Otherwise its method would not be interrogative; for the interrogative method is barred to the demonstrator, who cannot use the opposite facts to prove the same *nexus*. This was shown in my work on the syllogism.[14]
35

12 If a syllogistic question [15] is equivalent to a proposition embodying one of the two sides of a contradiction, and if each science has its peculiar propositions from which its peculiar conclusion is developed, then there is such a thing as a distinctively scientific question, and it is the interrogative form of the premisses from which the 'appropriate'

---

[12] Lit. 'even if the middle is itself and also what is not itself'; i. e. you may pass from the middle term man to include not-man without affecting the conclusion.

[13] Cf. 75ᵃ 42 ff. and 76ᵇ 13.

[14] *An. Pr.* i. 1. The 'opposite facts' are those which would be expressed in the alternatively possible answers to the dialectical question, the dialectician's aim being to refute his interlocutor whether the latter answers the question put to him affirmatively or in the negative.

[15] i. e. a premiss put in the form of a question.

40 conclusion of each science is developed. Hence it is clear
that not every question will be relevant to geometry, nor to
medicine, nor to any other science: only those questions
will be geometrical which form premises for the proof of
77ᵇ the theorems of geometry or of any other science, such as
optics, which uses the same basic truths as geometry. Of the
other sciences the like is true. Of these questions the geometer is bound to give his account, using the basic truths of
geometry in conjunction with his previous conclusions; of
the basic truths the geometer, as such, is not bound to give
5 any account. The like is true of the other sciences. There
is a limit, then, to the questions which we may put to each
man of science; nor is each man of science bound to answer
all inquiries on each several subject, but only such as fall
within the defined field of his own science. If, then, in controversy with a geometer qua geometer the disputant confines himself to geometry and proves anything from geometrical premises, he is clearly to be applauded; if he goes
10 outside these he will be at fault, and obviously cannot even
refute the geometer except accidentally. One should therefore not discuss geometry among those who are not geometers, for in such a company an unsound argument will pass
15 unnoticed. This is correspondingly true in the other sciences.

Since there are 'geometrical' questions, does it follow
that there are also distinctively 'ungeometrical' questions?
Further, in each special science—geometry for instance—
what kind of error is it that may vitiate questions, and yet
not exclude them from that science? Again, is the erroneous
conclusion one constructed from premises opposite to the
20 true premises, or is it formal fallacy though drawn from
geometrical premises? Or, perhaps, the erroneous conclusion is due to the drawing of premises from another science; e. g. in a geometrical controversy a musical question is
distinctively ungeometrical, whereas the notion that parallels meet is in one sense geometrical, being ungeometrical
in a different fashion: the reason being that 'ungeometri-

cal', like 'unrhythmical,' is equivocal, meaning in the one
case not geometry at all, in the other bad geometry? It is 25
this error, i. e. error based on premisses of this kind—'of' the
science but false—that is the contrary of science. In mathematics the formal fallacy is not so common, because it is the
middle term in which the ambiguity lies, since the major is
predicated of the whole of the middle and the middle of 30
the whole of the minor (the *predicate* of course never has
the prefix 'all'); and in mathematics one can, so to speak,
see these middle terms with an intellectual vision, while in
dialectic the ambiguity may escape detection. E. g. 'Is every
circle a figure?' A diagram shows that this is so, but the
minor premiss 'Are epics circles?' is shown by the diagram
to be false.

If a proof has an inductive minor premiss, one should not
bring an 'objection' against it. For since every premiss must 35
be applicable to a number of cases (otherwise it will not be
true in every instance, which, since the syllogism proceeds
from universals, it must be), then assuredly the same is true
of an 'objection'; since premisses and 'objections' are so far
the same that anything which can be validly advanced as an
'objection' must be such that it could take the form of a 40
premiss, either demonstrative or dialectical. On the other
hand arguments formally illogical do sometimes occur
through taking as middles mere attributes of the major and
minor terms. An instance of this is Caeneus' proof that fire 78ᵇ
increases in geometrical proportion: 'Fire', he argues, 'increases rapidly, and so does geometrical proportion'. There
is no syllogism so, but there is a syllogism if the most
rapidly increasing proportion is geometrical and the most
rapidly increasing proportion is attributable to fire in its 5
motion. Sometimes, no doubt, it is impossible to reason
from premisses predicating mere attributes: but sometimes
it is possible, though the possibility is overlooked. If false
premisses could never give true conclusions 'resolution'
would be easy, for premisses and conclusion would in that
case inevitably reciprocate. I might then argue thus: let A

be an existing fact; let the existence of A imply such and
such facts actually known to me to exist, which we may call
B. I can now, since they reciprocate, infer A from B.

10   Reciprocation of premisses and conclusion is more frequent in mathematics, because mathematics takes definitions, but never an accident, for its premisses—a second
characteristic distinguishing mathematical reasoning from
dialectical disputations.

A science expands not by the interposition of fresh middle terms, but by the apposition of fresh extreme terms.
E. g. A is predicated of B, B of C, C of D, and so indefi-
15 nitely. Or the expansion may be lateral: e. g. one major, A,
may be proved of two minors, C and E. Thus let A represent number—a number or *number* taken indeterminately;
B determinate odd number; C any particular odd number.
We can then predicate A of C. Next let D represent deter-
20 minate even number, and E even number. Then A is predicable of E.

13   Knowledge of the fact differs from knowledge of the
reasoned fact. To begin with, they differ within the
same science and in two ways: (1) when the premisses of
the syllogism are not immediate (for then the proximate
25 cause is not contained in them—a necessary condition of
knowledge of the reasoned fact): (2) when the premisses
are immediate, but instead of the cause the better known
of the two reciprocals is taken as the middle; for of two reciprocally predicable terms the one which is not the cause
may quite easily be the better known and so become the
middle term of the demonstration. Thus (2) (a) you might
30 prove as follows that the planets are near because they do not
twinkle: let C be the planets, B not twinkling, A proximity.
Then B is predicable of C; for the planets do not twinkle.
But A is also predicable of B, since that which does not
twinkle is near—we must take this truth as having been
reached by induction or sense-perception. Therefore A is a
35 necessary predicate of C; so that we have demonstrated that

the planets are near. This syllogism, then, proves not the reasoned fact but only the fact; since they are not near be-cause they do not twinkle, but, because they are near, do not twinkle. The major and middle of the proof, however, may be reversed, and then the demonstration will be of the reasoned fact. Thus: let C be the planets, B proximity, A 40 not twinkling. Then B is an attribute of C, and A—not 78ᵇ twinkling—of B. Consequently A is predicable of C, and the syllogism proves the reasoned fact, since its middle term is the proximate cause. Another example is the inference that the moon is spherical from its manner of waxing. Thus: since that which so waxes is spherical, and since the moon so waxes, clearly the moon is spherical. Put in this 5 form, the syllogism turns out to be proof of the fact, but if the middle and major be reversed it is proof of the reasoned fact; since the moon is not spherical because it waxes in a certain manner, but waxes in such a manner because it is spherical. (Let C be the moon, B spherical, and A waxing.) Again (b), in cases where the cause and the effect are not 10 reciprocal and the effect is the better known, the fact is demonstrated but not the reasoned fact. This also occurs (1) when the middle falls outside the major and minor, for here too the strict cause is not given, and so the demonstra-tion is of the fact, not of the reasoned fact. For example, 15 the question 'Why does not a wall breathe?' might be an-swered, 'Because it is not an animal'; but that answer would not give the strict cause, because if not being an ani-mal causes the absence of respiration, then being an animal should be the cause of respiration, according to the rule that if the negation of x causes the non-inherence of y, the 20 affirmation of x causes the inherence of y; e. g. if the dispro-portion of the hot and cold elements is the cause of ill health, their proportion is the cause of health; and con-versely, if the assertion of x causes the inherence of y, the negation of x must cause y's non-inherence. But in the case given this consequence does not result; for not every animal breathes. A syllogism with this kind of cause takes place

in the second figure. Thus: let A be animal, B respiration,
25 C wall. Then A is predicable of all B (for all that breathes
is animal), but of no C; and consequently B is predicable
of no C; that is, the wall does not breathe. Such causes are
like far-fetched explanations, which precisely consist in
30 making the cause too remote, as in Anacharsis' account of
why the Scythians have no flute-players; namely because
they have no vines.

Thus, then, do the syllogism of the fact and the syllogism
of the reasoned fact differ within one science and according
to the position of the middle terms. But there is another
way too in which the fact and the reasoned fact differ, and
35 that is when they are investigated respectively by different
sciences. This occurs in the case of problems related to one
another as subordinate and superior, as when optical prob-
40 lems are subordinated to geometry, mechanical problems
to stereometry, harmonic problems to arithmetic, the data
79ᵃ of observation to astronomy. (Some of these sciences bear
almost the same name; e. g. mathematical and nautical
astronomy, mathematical and acoustical harmonics.) Here
it is the business of the empirical observers to know the
fact, of the mathematicians to know the reasoned fact; for
the latter are in possession of the demonstrations giving
5 the causes, and are often ignorant of the fact: just as we
have often a clear insight into a universal, but through lack
of observation are ignorant of some of its particular instances. These connexions ¹⁶ have a perceptible existence
though they are manifestations of forms. For the mathematical sciences concern forms: they do not demonstrate
properties of a substratum, since, even though the geometrical subjects are predicable as properties of a perceptible
substratum, it is not as thus predicable that the mathematician demonstrates properties of them. As optics is related
10 to geometry, so another science is related to optics, namely
the theory of the rainbow. Here knowledge of the fact is
within the province of the natural philosopher, knowledge

¹⁶ sc. 'which require two sciences for their proof.' Cf. 78ᵇ 35.

of the reasoned fact within that of the optician, either qua optician or qua mathematical optician. Many sciences not standing in this mutual relation enter into it at points; e. g. medicine and geometry: it is the physician's business to know that circular wounds heal more slowly, the geometer's to know the reason why.   15

14 Of all the figures the most scientific is the first. Thus, it is the vehicle of the demonstrations of all the mathematical sciences, such as arithmetic, geometry, and optics, and practically of all sciences that investigate causes: for the 20 syllogism of the reasoned fact is either exclusively or generally speaking and in most cases in this figure—a second proof that this figure is the most scientific; for grasp of a reasoned conclusion is the primary condition of knowledge. Thirdly, the first is the only figure which enables us to pursue knowledge of the essence of a thing. In the second figure no affirmative conclusion is possible, and knowledge 25 of a thing's essence must be affirmative; while in the third figure the conclusion can be affirmative, but cannot be universal, and essence must have a universal character: e. g. man is not two-footed animal in any qualified sense, but universally. Finally, the first figure has no need of the others, while it is by means of the first that the other two 30 figures are developed, and have their intervals close-packed until immediate premisses are reached. Clearly, therefore, the first figure is the primary condition of knowledge.

15 Just as an attribute A may (as we saw) be atomically connected with a subject B, so its disconnexion may be atomic. I call 'atomic' connexions or disconnexions which involve no intermediate term; since in that case the connexion or disconnexion will not be mediated by something 35 other than the terms themselves. It follows that if either A or B, or both A and B, have a genus, their disconnexion cannot be primary. Thus: let C be the genus of A. Then, if C is not the genus of B—for A may well have a genus which is

40 not the genus of *B*—there will be a syllogism proving *A*'s disconnexion from *B* thus:

79ᵇ

all *A* is *C*,

no *B* is *C*,

∴ no *B* is *A*.

Or if it is *B* which has a genus *D*, we have

all *B* is *D*,

no *D* is *A*,

∴ no *B* is *A*, by syllogism;

5 and the proof will be similar if both *A* and *B* have a genus. That the genus of *A* need not be the genus of *B* and vice versa, is shown by the existence of mutually exclusive co-ordinate series of predication. If no term in the series *ACD* . . . is predicable of any term in the series *BEF*. . . , and 10 if *G*—a term in the former series—is the genus of *A*, clearly *G* will not be the genus of *B*; since, if it were, the series would not be mutually exclusive. So also if *B* has a genus, it will not be the genus of *A*. If, on the other hand, neither *A* nor *B* has a genus and *A* does not inhere in *B*, this dis-connexion must be atomic. If there be a middle term, one 15 or other of them is bound to have a genus, for the syllogism will be either in the first or the second figure. If it is in the first, *B* will have a genus—for the premiss containing it must be affirmative;[17] if in the second, either *A* or *B* indif-ferently, since syllogism is possible if either is contained in 20 a negative premiss,[18] but not if both premisses are negative.

Hence it is clear that one thing may be atomically dis-connected from another, and we have stated when and how this is possible.

16   Ignorance—defined not as the negation of knowledge but as a positive state of mind—is error produced by inference.

[17] i.e. in Celarent.

[18] i.e. in Cesare or Camestres.

(1) Let us first consider propositions asserting a pred- 25
icate's immediate connexion with or disconnexion from
a subject. Here, it is true, positive error may befall one in
alternative ways; for it may arise where one directly believes
a connexion or disconnexion as well as where one's belief
is acquired by inference. The error, however, that consists
in a direct belief is without complication; but the error
resulting from inference—which here concerns us—takes
many forms. Thus, let A be atomically disconnected from
all B: then the conclusion inferred through a middle term 30
C, that all B is A, will be a case of error produced by syllogism. Now, two cases are possible. Either (a) both premisses, or (b) one premiss only, may be false. (a) If neither
A is an attribute of any C nor C of any B, whereas the
contrary was posited in both cases, both premisses will be
false. (C may quite well be so related to A and B that C is 35
neither subordinate to A nor a universal attribute of B: for
B, since A was said to be primarily disconnected from B,
cannot have a genus, and A need not necessarily be a universal attribute of all things. Consequently both premisses
may be false.) On the other hand, (b) one of the premisses 40
may be true, though not either indifferently but only the
major A–C; since, B having no genus, the premiss C–B
will always be false, while A–C may be true. This is the 80ᵃ
case if, for example, A is related atomically to both C and
B; because when the same term is related atomically to
more terms than one, neither of those terms will belong to
the other. It is, of course, equally the case if A–C is not
atomic.   5

Error of attribution, then, occurs through these causes
and in this form only—for we found that no syllogism of
universal attribution was possible in any figure but the first.
On the other hand, an error of non-attribution may occur
either in the first or in the second figure. Let us therefore
first explain the various forms it takes in the first figure and
the character of the premisses in each case.   10

(c) It may occur when both premisses are false; e. g.

supposing A atomically connected with both C and B, if it
be then assumed that no C is A, and all B is C, both premisses are false.

(d) It is also possible when one is false. This may be
either premiss indifferently. A–C may be true, C–B false
15 —A–C true because A is not an attribute of all things, C–B
false because C, which never has the attribute A, cannot be
an attribute of B; for if C–B were true, the premiss A–C
would no longer be true, and besides if both premisses were
true, the conclusion would be true. Or again, C–B may be
20 true and A–C false; e. g. both C and A contain B as genera,
one of them must be subordinate to the other, so that if the
premiss takes the form No C is A, it will be false. This
25 makes it clear that whether either or both premisses are
false, the conclusion will equally be false.

In the second figure the premisses cannot both be wholly
false; for if all B is A, no middle term can be with truth
universally affirmed of one extreme and universally denied
30 of the other: but premisses in which the middle is affirmed
of one extreme and denied of the other are the necessary
condition if one is to get a valid inference at all. Therefore
if, taken in this way, they are wholly false, their contraries
conversely should be wholly true. But this is impossible.
On the other hand, there is nothing to prevent both premisses being partially false; e. g. if actually some A is C and
35 some B is C, then if it is premised that all A is C and no
B is C, both premisses are false, yet partially, not wholly,
false. The same is true if the major is made negative instead
of the minor. Or one premiss may be wholly false, and it
may be either of them. Thus, supposing that actually an
40 attribute of all A must also be an attribute of all B,
80ᵇ then if. C is yet taken to be a universal attribute of all A
but universally non-attributable to B, C–A will be true
but C–B false. Again, actually that which is an attribute
of no B will not be an attribute of all A either; for if
it be an attribute of all A, it will also be an attribute of
all B, which is contrary to supposition; but if C be never-

theless assumed to be a universal attribute of A, but 5
an attribute of no B, then the premiss C–B is true but the
major is false. The case is similar if the major is made the
negative premiss. For in fact what is an attribute of no A
will not be an attribute of any B either; and if it be yet
assumed that C is universally non-attributable to A, but a
universal attribute of B, the premiss C–A is true but the 10
minor wholly false. Again, in fact it is false to assume that
that which is an attribute of all B is an attribute of no A,
for if it be an attribute of all B, it must be an attribute
of some A. If then C is nevertheless assumed to be an attribute of all B but of no A, C–B will be true but C–A false.

It is thus clear that in the case of atomic propositions
erroneous inference will be possible not only when both 15
premisses are false but also when only one is false.

17 (2) In the case of attributes not atomically connected with or disconnected from their subjects, (a)
(i) as long as the false conclusion is inferred through the
'appropriate' middle, only the major and not both prem- 20
isses can be false. By 'appropriate middle' I mean the
middle term through which the contradictory—i. e. the
true—conclusion is inferrible. Thus, let A be attributable
to B through a middle term C: then, since to produce a
conclusion the premiss C–B must be taken affirmatively,
it is clear that this premiss must always be true, for its 25
quality is not changed. But the major A–C is false, for it is
by a change in the quality of A–C that the conclusion becomes its contradictory—i. e. true. Similarly (ii) if the middle is taken from another series of predication; e. g. suppose
D to be not only contained within A as a part within its whole
but also predicable of all B. Then the premiss D–B must remain unchanged, but the quality of A–D must be changed; 30
so that D–B is always true, A–D always false. Such error
is practically identical with that which is inferred through
the 'appropriate' middle. On the other hand, (b) if the
conclusion is not inferred through the 'appropriate' middle

—(i) when the middle is subordinate to A but is predicable
35 of no B, both premisses must be false, because if there is to
be a conclusion both must be posited as asserting the contrary of what is actually the fact, and so posited both
become false: e. g. suppose that actually all D is A
but no B is D; then if these premisses are changed in
quality, a conclusion will follow and both of the new
40 premisses will be false. When, however, (ii) the mid-
81ᵃ dle D is not subordinate to A, A–D will be true, D–B
false—A–D true because A was not subordinate to D, D–B
false because if it had been true, the conclusion too would
have been true; but it is ex *hypothesi* false.

When the erroneous inference is in the second figure,
5 both premisses cannot be entirely false; since if B is subordinate to A, there can be no middle predicable of all of
one extreme and of none of the other as was stated before.[19]
One premiss, however, may be false, and it may be either
of them. Thus, if C is actually an attribute of both A and
10 B, but is assumed to be an attribute of A only and not of
B, C–A will be true, C–B false: or again if C be assumed
to be attributable to B but to no A, C–B will be true, C–A
false.

We have stated when and through what kinds of prem-
15 isses error will result in cases where the erroneous conclusion is negative. If the conclusion is affirmative, (a) (i)
it may be inferred through the 'appropriate' middle term.
In this case both premisses cannot be false since, as we
said before,[20] C–B must remain unchanged if there is to be
a conclusion, and consequently A–C, the quality of which
is changed, will always be false. This is equally true if (ii)
20 the middle is taken from another series of predication, as
was stated to be the case also with regard to negative
error;[21] for D–B must remain unchanged, while the quality

[19] Cf. 80ᵃ 29.
[20] Cf. 80ᵇ 17–26.
[21] Cf. 80ᵇ 26–32.

of A–D must be converted, and the type of error is the same as before.

(b) The middle may be inappropriate. Then (i) if D is subordinate to A, A–D will be true, but D–B false; since A may quite well be predicable of several terms no one of which can be subordinated to another. If, however, (ii) D is not subordinate to A, obviously A–D, since it is affirmed, will always be false, while D–B may be either true or false; for A may very well be an attribute of no D, whereas all B is D, e. g. no science is animal, all music is science. Equally well A may be an attribute of no D, and D of no B. It emerges, then, that if the middle term is not subordinate to the major, not only both premisses but either singly may be false.

Thus we have made it clear how many varieties of erroneous inference are liable to happen and through what kinds of premisses they occur, in the case both of immediate and of demonstrable truths.

18 It is also clear that the loss of any one of the senses entails the loss of a corresponding portion of knowledge, and that, since we learn either by induction or by demonstration, this knowledge cannot be acquired. Thus demonstation develops from universals, induction from particulars; but since it is possible to familiarize the pupil with even the so-called mathematical abstractions only through induction—i. e. only because each subject genus possesses, in virtue of a determinate mathematical character, certain properties which can be treated as separate even though they do not exist in isolation—it is consequently impossible to come to grasp universals except through induction. But induction is impossible for those who have not sense-perception. For it is sense-perception alone which is adequate for grasping the particulars: they cannot be objects of scientific knowledge, because neither can universals give us knowledge of them without induction, nor can we get it through induction without sense-perception.

10 **19** Every syllogism is effected by means of three terms. One kind of syllogism serves to prove that A inheres in C by showing that A inheres in B and B in C; the other is negative and one of its premisses asserts one term of another, while the other denies one term of another. It is 15 clear, then, that these are the fundamentals and so-called hypotheses of syllogism. Assume them as they have been stated, and proof is bound to follow—proof that A inheres in C through B, and again that A inheres in B through some other middle term, and similarly that B inheres in C. If our reasoning aims at gaining credence and so is merely dialectical, it is obvious that we have only to see that our 20 inference is based on premisses as credible as possible: so that if a middle term between A and B is credible though not real, one can reason through it and complete a dialectical syllogism. If, however, one is aiming at truth, one must be guided by the real connexions of subjects and attributes. Thus: since there are attributes which are predi-25 cated of a subject essentially or naturally and not coincidentally—not, that is, in a sense in which we say 'That white (thing) is a man', which is not the same mode of predication as when we say The man is white : the man is white not because he is something else but because he is man, but the white is man because 'being white' coincides with 'humanity' within one substratum—therefore there 30 are terms such as are naturally subjects of predicates. Suppose, then, C such a term not itself attributable to anything else as to a subject, but the proximate subject of the attribute B—i. e. so that B–C is immediate; suppose further E related immediately to F, and F to B. The first question is, must this series terminate, or can it proceed to infinity? The second question is as follows: Suppose nothing is essentially predicated of A, but A is predicated 35 primarily of H and of no intermediate prior term, and sup-

pose *H* similarly related to *G* and *G* to *B*; then must this series also terminate, or can it too proceed to infinity? There is this much difference between the questions: the first is, is it possible to start from that which is not itself attributable to anything else but is the subject of attributes, and ascend to infinity? The second is the problem whether one can start from that which is a predicate but not itself a subject of predicates, and descend to infinity? A third question is, if the extreme terms are fixed, can there be an infinity of middles? I mean this: suppose for example that *A* inheres in *C* and *B* is intermediate between them, but between *B* and *A* there are other middles, and between these again fresh middles; can these proceed to infinity or can they not? This is the equivalent of inquiring, do demonstrations proceed to infinity, i. e. is everything demonstrable? Or do ultimate subject and primary attribute limit one another?

I hold that the same questions arise with regard to negative conclusions and premisses: viz. if *A* is attributable to no *B*, then either this predication will be primary, or there will be an intermediate term prior to *B* to which *A* is not attributable—*G*, let us say, which is attributable to all *B*—and there may still be another term *H* prior to *G*, which is attributable to all *G*. The same questions arise, I say, because in these cases too either the series of prior terms to which *A* is not attributable is infinite or it terminates.

One cannot ask the same questions in the case of reciprocating terms, since when subject and predicate are convertible there is neither primary nor ultimate subject, seeing that all the reciprocals qua subjects stand in the same relation to one another, whether we say that the subject has an infinity of attributes or that both subjects and attributes—and we raised the question in both cases—are infinite in number. These questions then cannot be asked—unless, indeed, the terms can reciprocate by two different modes, by accidental predication in one relation and natural predication in the other.

20 Now, it is clear that if the predications terminate in
both the upward and the downward direction (by
'upward' I mean the ascent to the more universal, by
'downward' the descent to the more particular), the middle terms cannot be infinite in number. For suppose that
25 A is predicated of F, and that the intermediates—call them
BB' B" . . . —are infinite, then clearly you might descend
from A and find one term predicated of another ad infinitum, since you have an infinity of terms between you
and F; and equally, if you ascend from F, there are infinite terms between you and A. It follows that if these
processes are impossible there cannot be an infinity of inter-
30 mediates between A and F. Nor is it of any effect to urge
that some terms of the series AB . . . F are contiguous so
as to exclude intermediates, while others cannot be taken
into the argument at all: whichever terms of the series B
. . . I take, the number of intermediates in the direction
either of A or of F must be finite or infinite: where the
infinite series starts, whether from the first term or from a
35 later one, is of no moment, for the succeeding terms in any
case are infinite in number.

21 Further, if in affirmative demonstration the series
terminates in both directions, clearly it will terminate
too in negative demonstration. Let us assume that we cannot proceed to infinity either by ascending from the ulti-
82ᵇ mate term (by 'ultimate term' I mean a term such as F
was, not itself attributable to a subject but itself the subject of attributes), or by descending towards an ultimate
from the primary term (by 'primary term' I mean a term
predicable of a subject but not itself a subject [22]). If this
assumption is justified, the series will also terminate in the
5 case of negation. For a negative conclusion can be proved
in all three figures. In the first figure it is proved thus: no B
is A, all C is B. In packing the interval B–C we must reach

[22] sc. a predicate above which is no wider universal.

immediate propositions—as-is always the case with the minor premiss—since *B–C* is affirmative. As regards the other premiss it is plain that if the major term is denied of a term *D* prior to *B*, *D* will have to be predicable of all *B*, 10 and if the major is denied of yet another term prior to *D*, this term must be predicable of all *D*. Consequently, since the ascending series is finite, the descent will also terminate and there will be a subject of which *A* is primarily non-predicable. In the second figure the syllogism is, all *A* is *B*, no *C* is *B*, ∴ no *C* is *A*. If proof of this [23] is required, plainly it may be shown either in the first figure as above, 15 in the second as here, or in the third. The first figure has been discussed, and we will proceed to display the second, proof by which will be as follows: all *B* is *D*, no *C* is *D* . . . , since it is required that *B* should be a subject of which a predicate is affirmed. Next, since *D* is to be proved not to belong to *C*, then *D* has a further predicate which is denied of *C*. Therefore, since the succession of predicates affirmed of an ever higher universal terminates,[24] the suc- 20 cession of predicates denied terminates too.[25]

The third figure shows it as follows: all *B* is *A*, some *B* is not *C*, ∴ some *A* is not *C*. This premiss, 1. e. *C–B*, will be proved either in the same figure or in one of the two figures discussed above. In the first and second figures the series 25 terminates. If we use the third figure, we shall take as premisses, all *E* is *B*, some *E* is not *C*, and this premiss

---

[23] sc. 'that no *C* is *B*'.

[24] i. e. each of the successive prosyllogisms required to prove the negative minors contains an affirmative major in which the middle is affirmed of a subject successively 'higher' or more universal than the subject of the first syllogism. Thus:

Syllogism:	All *B* is *D*	Prosyllogisms: All *D* is *E*	All *E* is *F*
	No *C* is *D*	No *C* is *E*	No *C* is *F*
	∴ No *C* is *B*	∴ No *C* is *D*	∴ No *C* is *E*

B, D, E, &c., are successively more universal subjects; and the series of affirmative majors containing them must *ex hypothesi* terminate.

[25] Since the series of affirmative majors terminates and since an affirmative major is required for each prosyllogism, we shall eventually reach a minor incapable of proof and therefore immediate.

again will be proved by a similar prosyllogism. But since it is assumed that the series of descending subjects also terminates, plainly the series of more universal non-predicables will terminate also. Even supposing that the proof is not confined to one method, but employs them all and is 30 now in the first figure, now in the second or third—even so the regress will terminate, for the methods are finite in number, and if finite things are combined in a finite number of ways, the result must be finite.

Thus it is plain that the regress of middles terminates in the case of negative demonstration, if it does so also in the case of affirmative demonstration. That in fact the regress terminates in both these cases may be made clear by the 35 following dialectical considerations.

22 In the case of predicates constituting the essential nature of a thing, it clearly terminates, seeing that if definition is possible, or in other words, if essential form is knowable, and an infinite series cannot be traversed, predicates constituting a thing's essential nature must be finite 83ᵃ in number.[26] But as regards predicates generally we have the following prefatory remarks to make. (1) We can affirm without falsehood 'the white (thing) is walking', and 'that big (thing) is a log'; or again, 'the log is big', and 'the man walks'. But the affirmation differs in the two cases. When I 5 affirm 'the white is a log', I mean that something which happens to be white is a log—not that white is the substratum in which log inheres, for it was not qua white or qua a species of white that the white (thing) came to be a log, and the white (thing) is consequently not a log except incidentally. On the other hand, when I affirm 'the log is white', I do not mean that something else, which 10 happens also to be a log, is white (as I should if I said 'the musician is white', which would mean 'the man who hap-

---

[26] If the attributes in a series of predication such as we are discussing are substantial, they must be finite in number, because they are then the elements constituting the definition of a substance.

pens also to be a musician is white'); on the contrary, log is here the substratum—the substratum which actually came to be white, and did so qua wood or qua a species of wood and qua nothing else.

If we must lay down a rule, let us entitle the latter kind of statement predication, and the former not predication at all, or not strict but accidental predication. 'White' and 'log' will thus serve as types respectively of predicate and subject.

We shall assume, then, that the predicate is invariably predicated strictly and not accidentally of the subject, for on such predication demonstrations depend for their force. It follows from this that when a single attribute is predicated of a single subject, the predicate must affirm of the subject either some element constituting its essential nature, or that it is in some way qualified, quantified, essentially related, active, passive, placed, or dated.[27]

(2) Predicates which signify substance signify that the subject is identical with the predicate or with a species of the predicate. Predicates not signifying substance which are predicated of a subject not identical with themselves or with a species of themselves are accidental or coincidental; e. g. white is a coincident of man, seeing that man is not identical with white or a species of white, but rather with animal, since man *is* identical with a species of animal. These predicates which do not signify substance must be predicates of some other subject, and nothing can be white which is not also other than white. The Forms we can dispense with, for they are mere sound without sense; and even if there are such things, they are not relevant

---

[27] The first of three statements preliminary to a proof that predicates which are accidental—other than substantial—cannot be unlimited in number: Accidental is to be distinguished from essential or natural predication [cf. i, ch. 4, 73ᵇ 5 ff. and *An. Pr.* i, ch. 25, 43ᵃ 25–6]. The former is alien to demonstration: hence, provided that a single attribute is predicated of a single subject, all genuine predicates fall either under the category of substance or under one of the adjectival categories.

to our discussion, since demonstrations are concerned with
35 predicates such as we have defined.[28]

(3) If A is a quality of B, B cannot be a quality of A—
a quality of a quality. Therefore A and B cannot be predicated reciprocally of one another in strict predication: they
can be affirmed without falsehood of one another, but not
genuinely predicated of each other.[29] For one alternative
is that they should be substantially predicated of one another, i. e. B would become the genus or differentia of A—
83ᵇ the predicate now become subject. But it has been shown
that in these substantial predications neither the ascending predicates nor the descending subjects form an infinite
series; e. g. neither the series, man is biped, biped is animal, &c., nor the series predicating animal of man, man of
Callias, Callias of a further subject as an element of its essential nature, is infinite. For all such substance is definable,
5 and an infinite series cannot be traversed in thought: consequently neither the ascent nor the descent is infinite,
since a substance whose predicates were infinite would not
be definable. Hence they will not be predicated each as the
genus of the other; for this would equate a genus with one
10 of its own species. Nor (the other alternative) can a *quale*
be reciprocally predicated of a *quale*, nor any term belonging to an adjectival category of another such term, except
by accidental predication; for all such predicates are coincidents and are predicated of substances.[30] On the other

---

[28] Second preliminary statement: The precise distinction of substantive from adjectival predication makes clear (implicitly) the two
distinctions, (a) that between natural and accidental predication, (b)
that between substantival and adjectival predication, which falls
within natural predication. This enables us to reject the Platonic
Forms.

[29] Third preliminary statement merging into the beginning of the
proof proper: Reciprocal predication cannot produce an indefinite
regress because it is not natural predication.

[30] Expansion of third preliminary statement: Reciprocals A and B
might be predicated of one another (a) substantially; but it has been
proved already that because a definition cannot contain an infinity of
elements substantial predication cannot generate infinity; and it would
disturb the relation of genus and species: (b) as *qualia* or *quanta* &c.;
but this would be unnatural predication, because all such predicates
are adjectival, i.e. accidents, or coincidents, of substances.

hand—in proof of the impossibility of an infinite ascending series—every predication displays the subject as somehow qualified or quantified or as characterized under one
of the other adjectival categories, or else is an element in
its substantial nature: these latter are limited in number, 15
and the number of the widest kinds under which predications fall is also limited, for every predication must exhibit
its subject as somehow qualified, quantified, essentially related, acting or suffering, or in some place or at some time.[31]

I assume first that predication implies a single subject
and a single attribute, and secondly that predicates which
are not substantial are not predicated of one another. We
assume this because such predicates are all coincidents,
and though some are essential coincidents, others of a dif- 20
ferent type, yet we maintain that all of them alike are
predicated of some substratum and that a coincident is
never a substratum—since we do not class as a coincident
anything which does not owe its designation to its being
something other than itself, but always hold that any
coincident is predicated of some substratum other than
itself, and that another group of coincidents may have a
different substratum. Subject to these assumptions then,
neither the ascending nor the descending series of predica- 25
tion in which a single attribute is predicated of a single
subject is infinite.[32] For the subjects of which coincidents
are predicated are as many as the constitutive elements of

[31] The ascent of predicates is also finite; because all predicates fall
under one or other of the categories, and (a) the series of predicates
under each category terminates when the category is reached, and (b)
the number of the categories is limited. [(a) seems to mean that an
attribute as well as a substance is definable by genus and differentia,
and the elements in its definition must terminate in an upward direction at the category, and can therefore no more form an infinite series
than can the elements constituting the definition of a substance.]

[32] To reinforce this brief proof that descent and ascent are both
finite we may repeat the premisses on which it depends. These are (1)
the assumption that predication means the predication of one attribute
of one subject, and (2) our proof that accidents cannot be reciprocally
predicated of one another, because that would be unnatural predication. It follows from these premisses that both ascent and descent are
finite. [Actually (2) only reinforces the proof that the descent terminates.]

each individual substance, and these we have seen are not
infinite in number, while in the ascending series are contained those constitutive elements with their coincidents
—both of which are finite.[33] We conclude that there is a
given subject <D> of which some attribute <C> is
primarily predicable; that there must be an attribute <B>
30 primarily predicable of the first attribute, and that the
series must end with a term <A> not predicable of any
term prior to the last subject of which it was predicated
<B>, and of which no term prior to it is predicable.[34]

[33] To repeat again the proof that both ascent and descent are finite:
The subjects cannot be more in number than the constituents of a
definable form, and these, we know, are not infinite in number: hence
the descent is finite. The series regarded as an ascent contains subjects
and ever more universal accidents, and neither subjects nor accidents
are infinite in number.

[34] Formal restatement of the last conclusion. [This is obscure: apparently Aristotle here contemplates a hybrid series: category, accident,
further specified accident . . . substantial genus, subgenus . . .
infima species, individual substance.

If this interpretation of the first portion of the chapter is at all correct, Aristotle's first proof that the first two questions of ch. 19 must
be answered in the negative is roughly as follows: The ultimate subject
of all judgement is an individual substance, a concrete singular. Of
such concrete singulars you can predicate substantially only the elements constituting their infima species. These are limited in number
because they form an intelligible synthesis. So far, then, as substantial
predicates are concerned, the questions are answered. But these elements are also the subjects of which accidents, or coincidents, are
predicated, and therefore as regards accidental predicates, at any rate,
the descending series of subjects terminates. The ascending series of
attributes also terminates, (1) because each higher attribute in the
series can only be a higher genus of the accident predicated of the ultimate subject of its genus, and therefore an element in the accident's
definition; (2) because the number of the categories is limited.

We may note that the first argument seems to envisage a series
which, viewed as an ascent, starts with a concrete individual of which
the elements of its definition are predicated successively, specific differentia being followed by proximate genus, which latter is the starting-
point of a succession of ever more universal attributes terminating in a
category; and that the second argument extends the scope of the dispute to the sum total of all the trains of accidental predication which
one concrete singular substance can beget. It is, as so often in Aristotle, difficult to be sure whether he is regarding the infima species or
the concrete singular as the ultimate subject of judgement. I have assumed that he means the latter.]

The argument we have given is one of the so-called proofs; an alternative proof follows. Predicates so related to their subjects that there are other predicates prior to them predicable of those subjects are demonstrable; but of demonstrable propositions one cannot have something better than knowledge, nor can one know them without dem- 35 onstration. Secondly, if a consequent is only known through an antecedent (viz. premisses prior to it) and we neither know this antecedent nor have something better than knowledge of it, then we shall not have scientific knowledge of the consequent. Therefore, if it is possible through demonstration to know anything without quali-fication and not merely as dependent on the acceptance of certain premisses—i. e. hypothetically—the series of in-termediate predications must terminate. If it does not ter-minate, and beyond any predicate taken as higher than 84ᵇ another there remains another still higher, then every predi-cate is demonstrable. Consequently, since these demonstra-ble predicates are infinite in number and therefore cannot be traversed, we shall not know them by demonstration. If, therefore, we have not something better than knowl-edge of them, we cannot through demonstration have un- 5 qualified but only hypothetical science of anything.[35]

As dialectical proofs of our contention these may carry conviction, but an analytic process will show more briefly that neither the ascent nor the descent of predication can be infinite in the demonstrative sciences which are the ob- 10 ject of our investigation. Demonstration proves the inher-ence of essential attributes in things. Now attributes may be

[35] The former proof was dialectical. So is that which follows in this paragraph. If a predicate inheres in a subject but is subordinate to a higher predicate also predicable of that subject [i. e. not to a wider predicate but to a middle term giving logically prior premisses and in that sense higher], then the inherence can be known by demonstration and only by demonstration. But that means that it is known as the consequent of an antecedent. Therefore, if demonstration gives genu-ine knowledge, the series must terminate; i. e. every predicate is de-monstrable and known only as a consequent and therefore hypothet-ically, unless an antecedent known *per se* is reached.

essential for two reasons: either because they are elements
in the essential nature of their subjects, or because their
subjects are elements in their essential nature. An example
15 of the latter is odd as an attribute of number—though it
is number's attribute, yet number itself is an element in
the definition of odd; of the former, multiplicity or the
indivisible, which are elements in the definition of number. In neither kind of attribution can the terms be infinite. They are not infinite where each is related to the
term below it as odd is to number, for this would mean the
20 inherence in odd of another attribute of odd in whose nature odd was an essential element: but then number will
be an ultimate subject of the whole infinite chain of attributes, and be an element in the definition of each of
them. Hence, since an infinity of attributes such as contain their subject in their definition cannot inhere in a
single thing, the ascending series is equally finite.[36] Note,
moreover, that all such attributes must so inhere in the
ultimate subject—e. g. its attributes in number and number in them—as to be commensurate with the subject and
25 not of wider extent. Attributes which are essential elements
in the nature of their subjects are equally finite: otherwise definition would be impossible. Hence, if all the attributes predicated are essential and these cannot be
infinite, the ascending series will terminate, and consequently the descending series too.[37]

[36] As regards type (2) [the opening of the chapter has disposed of
type (1)]: in any series of such predicates any given term will contain
in its definition all the lower terms, and the series will therefore
terminate at the bottom in the ultimate subject. But since every term
down to and including the ultimate subject is contained in the definition of any given term, if the series ascend infinitely there must be a
term containing an infinity of terms in its definition. But this is impossible, and therefore the ascent terminates.

[37] Note too that either type of essential attribute must be commensurate with its subject, because the first defines, the second is
defined by, its subject; and consequently no subject can possess an
infinite number of essential predicates of either type, or definition
would be impossible. Hence if the attributes predicated are all essential, the series terminates in both directions. [This passage merely

If this is so, it follows that the intermediates between any two terms are also always limited in number.[38] An immediately obvious consequence of this is that demonstrations necessarily involve basic truths, and that the contention of some—referred to at the outset—that all truths are demonstrable is mistaken. For if there are basic truths, (a) not all truths are demonstrable, and (b) an infinite regress is impossible; since if either (a) or (b) were not a fact, it would mean that no interval was immediate and indivisible, but that all intervals were divisible. This is true because a conclusion is demonstrated by the interposition, not the apposition, of a fresh term. If such interposition could continue to infinity there might be an infinite number of terms between any two terms; but this is impossible if both the ascending and descending series of predication terminate; and of this fact, which before was shown dialectically, analytic proof has now been given.[39]

23   It is an evident corollary of these conclusions that if the same attribute A inheres in two terms C and D predicable either not at all, or not of all instances, of one another, it does not always belong to them in virtue of a common middle term. Isosceles and scalene possess the attribute of having their angles equal to two right angles in virtue of a common middle; for they possess it in so far as they are both a certain kind of figure, and not in so far as they differ from one another. But this is not always the case; for, were it so, if we take B as the common middle in

displays the ground underlying the previous argument that the ascent of attributes of type (2) is finite, and notes in passing its more obvious and already stated application to attributes of type (1).]

[38] It follows that the intermediates between a given subject and a given attribute must also be limited in number.

[39] Corollary: (a) demonstrations necessarily involve basic truths, and therefore (b) not all truths, as we saw [84ᵃ 32] that some maintain, are demonstrable [cf. 72ᵇ 6]. If either (a) or (b) were not a fact, since conclusions are demonstrated by the interposition of a middle and not by the apposition of an extreme term [cf. note on 78ᵃ 15], no premiss would be an immediate indivisible interval. This closes the analytic argument.

10 virtue of which A inheres in C and D, clearly B would inhere in C and D through a second common middle, and
this in turn would inhere in C and D through a third, so
that between two terms an infinity of intermediates would
fall—an impossibility. Thus it need not always be in virtue
of a common middle term that a single attribute inheres
15 in several subjects, since there must be immediate intervals. Yet if the attribute to be proved common to two subjects is to be one of their essential attributes, the middle
terms involved must be within one subject genus and be
derived from the same group of immediate premisses; for
we have seen that processes of proof cannot pass from one
genus to another.[40]

It is also clear that when A inheres in B, this can be dem-
20 onstrated if there is a middle term. Further, the 'elements'
of such a conclusion are the premisses containing the middle in question, and they are identical in number with the
middle terms, seeing that the immediate propositions—or
at least such immediate propositions as are universal—are
the 'elements'. If, on the other hand, there is no middle
term, demonstration ceases to be possible: we are on the
way to the basic truths. Similarly if A does not inhere in
25 B, this can be demonstrated if there is a middle term or a
term prior to B in which A does not inhere: otherwise
there is no demonstration and a basic truth is reached.
There are, moreover, as many 'elements' of the demonstrated conclusion as there are middle terms, since it is
propositions containing these middle terms that are the
basic premisses on which the demonstration rests; and as
there are some indemonstrable basic truths asserting that
30 'this is that' or that 'this inheres in that', so there are others
denying that 'this is that' or that 'this inheres in that'—in
fact some basic truths will affirm and some will deny being.

When we are to prove a conclusion, we must take a
primary essential predicate—suppose it C—of the subject
B, and then suppose A similarly predicable of C. If we pro-

[40] i, ch. 7.

ceed in this manner, no proposition or attribute which falls beyond A is admitted in the proof: the interval is constantly condensed until subject and predicate become indivisible, i. e. one. We have our unit when the premiss becomes immediate, since the immediate premiss alone is a single premiss in the unqualified sense of 'single'. And as in other spheres the basic element is simple but not identical in all—in a system of weight it is the mina, in music the quarter-tone, and so on—so in syllogism the unit is an immediate premiss, and in the knowledge that demonstration gives it is an intuition. In syllogisms, then, which prove the inherence of an attribute, nothing falls outside the major term. In the case of negative syllogisms on the other hand, (1) in the first figure nothing falls outside the major term whose inherence is in question; e. g. to prove through a middle C that A does not inhere in B the premisses required are, all B is C, no C is A. Then if it has to be proved that no C is A, a middle must be found between A and C; and this procedure will never vary.

(2) If we have to show that E is not D by means of the premisses, all D is C; no E, or not all E,[41] is C; then the middle will never fall beyond E, and E is the subject of which D is to be denied in the conclusion.

(3) In the third figure the middle will never fall beyond the limits of the subject and the attribute denied of it.

24 Since demonstrations may be either commensurately universal or particular,[42] and either affirmative or negative; the question arises, which form is the better? And the same question may be put in regard to so-called 'direct' demonstration and *reductio ad impossibile*. Let us first examine the commensurately universal and the particular forms, and when we have cleared up this problem proceed to discuss 'direct' demonstration and *reductio ad impossibile*.

---

[41] Second figure, Camestres or Baroco.
[42] The distinction is that of whole and part, genus and species; not that of universal and singular.

The following considerations might lead some minds
20 to prefer particular demonstration.

(1) The superior demonstration is the demonstration
which gives us greater knowledge (for this is the ideal of
demonstration), and we have greater knowledge of a particular individual when we know it in itself than when we
know it through something else; e. g. we know Coriscus
25 the musician better when we know that Coriscus is musical
than when we know only that man is musical, and a like argument holds in all other cases. But commensurately universal demonstration, instead of proving that the subject
itself actually is x, proves only that something else is x—e. g.
in attempting to prove that isosceles is x, it proves not that
isosceles but only that triangle is x—whereas particular
demonstration proves that the subject itself is x. The demonstration, then, that a subject, as such, possesses an attribute is superior. If this is so, and if the particular rather
than the commensurately universal form so demonstrates,
30 particular demonstration is superior.

(2) The universal has not a separate being over against
groups of singulars. Demonstration nevertheless creates the
opinion that its function is conditioned by something like
this—some separate entity belonging to the real world;
35 that, for instance, of triangle or of figure or number, over
against particular triangles, figures, and numbers. But demonstration which touches the real and will not mislead is
superior to that which moves among unrealities and is delu-
sory. Now commensurately universal demonstration is of
the latter kind: if we engage in it we find ourselves reasoning after a fashion well illustrated by the argument that
the proportionate is what answers to the definition of some
85ᵇ entity which is neither line, number, solid, nor plane, but
a proportionate apart from all these. Since, then, such a
proof is characteristically commensurate and universal,
and less touches reality than does particular demonstration,
and creates a false opinion, it will follow that commensurate and universal is inferior to particular demonstration.

We may retort thus. (1) The first argument applies no more to commensurate and universal than to particular demonstration. If equality to two right angles is attributa- 5 ble to its subject not *qua* isosceles but *qua* triangle, he who knows that isosceles possesses that attribute knows the subject as *qua* itself possessing the attribute, to a less degree than he who knows that triangle has that attribute. To sum up the whole matter: if a subject is proved to possess *qua* triangle an attribute which it does not in fact possess *qua* triangle, that is not demonstration: but if it does possess it *qua* triangle, the rule applies that the greater knowledge is his who knows the subject as possessing its attribute *qua* that in virtue of which it actually does possess it. Since, 10 then, triangle is the wider term, and there is one identical definition of triangle—i. e. the term is not equivocal—and since equality to two right angles belongs to all triangles, it is isosceles *qua* triangle and not triangle *qua* isosceles which has its angles so related. It follows that he who knows a connexion universally has greater knowledge of it as it in fact is than he who knows the particular; and the inference is that commensurate and universal is superior 15 to particular demonstration. (2) If there is a single identical definition—i. e. if the commensurate universal is unequivocal—then the universal will possess being not less but more than some of the particulars, inasmuch as it is universals which comprise the imperishable, particulars that tend to perish.

(3) Because the universal has a single meaning, we are not therefore compelled to suppose that in these examples it has being as a substance apart from its particulars—any more than we need make a similar supposition in the other cases of unequivocal universal predication, viz. where the predicate signifies not substance but quality, essential relatedness, or action. If such a supposition is entertained, 20 the blame rests not with the demonstration but with the hearer.

(4) Demonstration is syllogism that proves the cause,

i. e. the reasoned fact, and it is rather the commensurate universal than the particular which is causative (as may be shown thus: that which possesses an attribute through its
25 own essential nature is itself the cause of the inherence, and the commensurate universal is primary; [43] hence the commensurate universal is the cause). Consequently commensurately universal demonstration is superior as more especially proving the cause, that is the reasoned fact.

(5) Our search for the reason ceases, and we think that we know, when the coming to be or existence of the fact before us is not due to the coming to be or existence of some other fact, for the last step of a search thus conducted is eo
30 *ipso* the end and limit of the problem. Thus: 'Why did he come?' 'To get the money—wherewith to pay a debt—that he might thereby do what was right.' When in this regress we can no longer find an efficient or final cause, we regard the last step of it as the end of the coming—or being or coming to be—and we regard ourselves as then only having full knowledge of the reason why he came.

If, then, all causes and reasons are alike in this respect,
35 and if this is the means to full knowledge in the case of final causes such as we have exemplified, it follows that in the case of the other causes also full knowledge is attained when an attribute no longer inheres because of something else. Thus, when we learn that exterior angles are equal to four right angles because they are the exterior angles of an isosceles, there still remains the question 'Why has isosceles this attribute?' and its answer 'Because it is a
86ᵃ triangle, and a triangle has it because a triangle is a rectilinear figure.' If rectilinear figure possesses the property for no further reason, [44] at this point we have full knowledge— but at this point our knowledge has become commensurately universal, and so we conclude that commensurately universal demonstration is superior.

(6) The more demonstration becomes particular the

---

[43] And therefore also essential; cf. i, ch. 4, 73ᵇ 26 ff.
[44] i. e. for no reason other than its own nature.

more it sinks into an indeterminate manifold, while universal demonstration tends to the simple and determinate. But objects so far as they are an indeterminate manifold are unintelligible, so far as they are determinate, intelligible: they are therefore intelligible rather in so far as they are universal than in so far as they are particular. From this it follows that universals are more demonstrable: but since relative and correlative increase concomitantly, of the more demonstrable there will be fuller demonstration. Hence the commensurate and universal form, being more truly demonstration, is the superior.

(7) Demonstration which teaches two things is preferable to demonstration which teaches only one. He who possesses commensurately universal demonstration knows the particular as well, but he who possesses particular demonstration does not know the universal. So that this is an additional reason for preferring commensurately universal demonstration. And there is yet this further argument:

(8) Proof becomes more and more proof of the commensurate universal as its middle term approaches nearer to the basic truth, and nothing is so near as the immediate premiss which is itself the basic truth. If, then, proof from the basic truth is more accurate than proof not so derived, demonstration which depends more closely on it is more accurate than demonstration which is less closely dependent. But commensurately universal demonstration is characterized by this closer dependence, and is therefore superior. Thus, if A had to be proved to inhere in D, and the middles were B and C, B being the higher term would render the demonstration which it mediated the more universal.

Some of these arguments, however, are dialectical. The clearest indication of the precedence of commensurately universal demonstration is as follows: if of two propositions, a prior and a posterior, we have a grasp of the prior, we have a kind of knowledge—a potential grasp—of the posterior as well. For example, if one knows that the angles

of all triangles are equal to two right angles, one knows in a sense—potentially—that the isosceles' angles also are equal to two right angles, even if one does not know that the isosceles is a triangle; but to grasp this posterior proposition is by no means to know the commensurate universal either potentially or actually. Moreover, commensurately
30 universal demonstration is through and through intelligible; particular demonstration issues in sense-perception.

25 The preceding arguments constitute our defence of the superiority of commensurately universal to particular demonstration. That affirmative demonstration excels negative may be shown as follows.

(1) We may assume the superiority *ceteris paribus* of the demonstration which derives from fewer postulates or
35 hypotheses—in short from fewer premisses; for, given that all these are equally well known, where they are fewer knowledge will be more speedily acquired, and that is a desideratum. The argument implied in our contention that demonstration from fewer assumptions is superior may be set out in universal form as follows. Assuming that in both cases alike the middle terms are known, and that middles which are prior are better known than such as are posterior, we may suppose two demonstrations of the in-
86ᵇ herence of A in E, the one proving it through the middles B, C and D, the other through F and G. Then A–D is known to the same degree as A–E (in the second proof), but A–D is better known than and prior to A–E (in the first proof); since A–E is proved through A–D, and the ground is more certain than the conclusion.

Hence demonstration by fewer premisses is *ceteris pari-*
5 *bus* superior. Now both affirmative and negative demonstration operate through three terms and two premisses, but whereas the former assumes only that something is, the latter assumes both that something is and that something else is not, and thus operating through more kinds of premiss is inferior.

(2) It has been proved [45] that no conclusion follows if both premisses are negative, but that one must be negative, the other affirmative. So we are compelled to lay down the following additional rule: as the demonstration expands, the affirmative premisses must increase in number, but there cannot be more than one negative premiss in each complete proof.[46] Thus, suppose no *B* is *A*, and all *C* is *B*. Then, if both the premisses are to be again expanded, a middle must be interposed. Let us interpose *D* between *A* and *B*, and *E* between *B* and *C*. Then clearly *E* is affirmatively related to *B* and *C*, while *D* is affirmatively related to *B* but negatively to *A*; for all *B* is *D*, but there must be no *D* which is *A*. Thus there proves to be a single negative premiss, *A–D*. In the further prosyllogisms too it is the same, because in the terms of an affirmative syllogism the middle is always related affirmatively to both extremes; in a negative syllogism it must be negatively related only to one of them, and so this negation comes to be a single negative premiss, the other premisses being affirmative. If, then, that through which a truth is proved is a better known and more certain truth, and if the negative proposition is proved through the affirmative and not vice versa, affirmative demonstration, being prior and better known and more certain, will be superior.

(3) The basic truth of demonstrative syllogism is the universal immediate premiss, and the universal premiss asserts in affirmative demonstration and in negative denies: and the affirmative proposition is prior to and better known than the negative (since affirmation explains denial and is prior to denial, just as being is prior to not-being). It follows that the basic premiss of affirmative demonstration is superior to that of negative demonstration, and the demonstration which uses superior basic premisses is superior.

(4) Affirmative demonstration is more of the nature of

---

[45] *An. Pr.* i, ch. 7.
[46] i. e. in one syllogism and two prosyllogisms proving its premisses.

a basic form of proof, because it is a *sine qua non* of negative demonstration.

87ᵃ 26   Since affirmative demonstration is superior to negative, it is clearly superior also to *reductio ad impossibile*. We must first make certain what is the difference between negative demonstration and *reductio ad impossibile*. Let us
5   suppose that no B is A, and that all C is B: the conclusion necessarily follows that no C is A. If these premisses are assumed, therefore, the negative demonstration that no C is A is direct. *Reductio ad impossibile*, on the other hand, proceeds as follows: Supposing we are to prove that A does not inhere in B, we have to assume that it does inhere, and further that B inheres in C, with the resulting inference
10   that A inheres in C. This we have to suppose a known and admitted impossibility; and we then infer that A cannot inhere in B. Thus if the inherence of B in C is not questioned, A's inherence in B is impossible.

The order of the terms is the same in both proofs: they differ according to which of the negative propositions is the better known, the one denying A of B or the one denying
15   A of C. When the falsity of the conclusion [47] is the better known, we use *reductio ad impossibile*; when the major premiss of the syllogism is the more obvious, we use direct demonstration. All the same the proposition denying A of B is, in the order of being, prior to that denying A of C; for premisses are prior to the conclusion which follows from them, and 'no C is A' is the conclusion, 'no B is A' one of its
20   premisses. For the destructive result of *reductio ad impossibile* is not a proper conclusion, nor are its antecedents proper premisses. On the contrary: the constituents of syllogism are premisses related to one another as whole to part or part to whole, whereas the premisses A–C and A–B are
25   not thus related to one another. Now the superior demonstration is that which proceeds from better known and prior

[47] i.e. the impossibility of A–C, the conclusion of the hypothetical syllogism.

premisses, and while both these forms depend for credence on the not-being of something, yet the source of the one is prior to that of the other. Therefore negative demonstration will have an unqualified superiority to *reductio ad impossibile*, and affirmative demonstration, being superior to negative, will consequently be superior also to *reductio ad* 30 *impossibile*.

27 The science which is knowledge at once of the fact and of the reasoned fact, not of the fact by itself without the reasoned fact, is the more exact and the prior science.

A science such as arithmetic, which is not a science of properties *qua* inhering in a substratum, is more exact than and prior to a science like harmonics, which is a science of properties inhering in a substratum; and similarly a science like arithmetic, which is constituted of fewer basic elements, is more exact than and prior to geometry, which requires additional elements. What I mean by 'additional elements' is this: a unit is substance without position, while 35 a point is substance with position; the latter contains an additional element.

28 A single science is one whose domain is a single genus, viz. all the subjects constituted out of the primary entities of the genus—i. e. the parts of this total subject—and their essential properties.

One science differs from another when their basic truths have neither a common source nor are derived those of the one science from those of the other. This is verified when we reach the indemonstrable premisses of a science, for 87ᵇ they must be within one genus with its conclusions: and this again is verified if the conclusions proved by means of them fall within one genus—i. e. are homogeneous.

29 One can have several demonstrations of the same con- 5 nexion not only by taking from the same series of predication middles which are other than the immediately co-

hering term—e. g. by taking C, D, and F severally to prove
A–B—but also by taking a middle from another series.
Thus let A be change, D alteration of a property, B feeling
pleasure, and G relaxation. We can then without falsehood predicate D of B and A of D, for he who is pleased
10 suffers alteration of a property, and that which alters a
property changes. Again, we can predicate A of G without
falsehood, and G of B; for to feel pleasure is to relax, and to
relax is to change. So the conclusion can be drawn through
middles which are different, i. e. not in the same series—
yet not so that neither of these middles is predicable of the
other, for they must both be attributable to some one sub-
15 ject.

A further point worth investigating is how many ways of
proving the same conclusion can be obtained by varying
the figure.

30 There is no knowledge by demonstration of chance
conjunctions; for chance conjunctions exist neither
20 by necessity nor as general connexions but comprise what
comes to be as something distinct from these. Now demonstration is concerned only with one or other of these two;
for all reasoning proceeds from necessary or general premisses, the conclusion being necessary if the premisses are
25 necessary and general if the premisses are general. Consequently, if chance conjunctions are neither general nor
necessary, they are not demonstrable.

31 Scientific knowledge is not possible through the act
of perception. Even if perception as a faculty is of
'the such' and not merely of a 'this somewhat', yet one must
30 at any rate actually perceive a 'this somewhat', and at a
definite present place and time: but that which is commensurately universal and true in all cases one cannot perceive, since it is not 'this' and it is not 'now'; if it were, it
would not be commensurately universal—the term we ap-

ply to what is always and everywhere. Seeing, therefore, that demonstrations are commensurately universal and universals imperceptible, we clearly cannot obtain scientific knowledge by the act of perception: nay, it is obvious that 35 even if it were possible to perceive that a triangle has its angles equal to two right angles, we should still be looking for a demonstration—we should not (as some [48] say) possess knowledge of it; for perception must be of a particular, whereas scientific knowledge involves the recognition of the commensurate universal. So if we were on the moon, and saw the earth shutting out the sun's light, we 40 should not know the cause of the eclipse: we should perceive the present fact of the eclipse, but not the reasoned 88ᵃ fact at all, since the act of perception is not of the commensurate universal. I do not, of course, deny that by watching the frequent recurrence of this event we might, after tracking the commensurate universal, possess a demonstration, for the commensurate universal is elicited from the several groups of singulars.

The commensurate universal is precious because it makes 5 clear the cause; so that in the case of facts like these which have a cause other than themselves universal knowledge [49] is more precious than sense-perceptions and than intuition. (As regards primary truths there is of course a different account to be given.[50]) Hence it is clear that knowledge of things demonstrable cannot be acquired by perception, un- 10 less the term perception is applied to the possession of scientific knowledge through demonstration. Nevertheless certain points do arise with regard to connexions to be proved which are referred for their explanation to a failure in sense-perception: there are cases when an act of vision would terminate our inquiry, not because in seeing we should be knowing, but because we should have elicited the universal from seeing; if, for example, we saw the pores

[48] Protagoras is perhaps referred to.
[49] i. e. demonstration through the commensurate universal.
[50] Cf. e. g. 100ᵇ 12.

in the glass and the light passing through, the reason of the
15 kindling would be clear to us [51] because we should at the
same time see it in each instance and intuit that it must be
so in all instances.

32 All syllogisms cannot have the same basic truths. This
may be shown first of all by the following dialectical
considerations. (1) Some syllogisms are true and some
20 false: for though a true inference is possible from false
premisses, yet this occurs once only—I mean if A, for instance, is truly predicable of C, but B, the middle, is false,
both A–B and B–C being false; nevertheless, if middles are
taken to prove these premisses, they will be false because
every conclusion which is a falsehood has false premisses,
25 while true conclusions have true premisses, and false and
true differ in kind. Then again, (2) falsehoods are not all
derived from a single identical set of principles: there are
falsehoods which are the contraries of one another and
cannot coexist, e. g. 'justice is injustice', and 'justice is cowardice'; 'man is horse', and 'man is ox'; 'the equal is greater',
and 'the equal is less'. From our established principles we
30 may argue the case as follows, confining ourselves · therefore to true conclusions. Not even all these are inferred
from the same basic truths; many of them in fact have
basic truths which differ generically and are not transferable; units, for instance, which are without position,
cannot take the place of points, which have position. The
transferred terms could only fit in as middle terms or as
35 major or minor terms, or else have some of the other terms
between them, others outside them.

Nor can any of the common axioms—such, I mean, as
the law of excluded middle—serve as premisses for the
proof of all conclusions. For the kinds of being are dif-
88ᵇ ferent, and some attributes attach to *quanta* and some to
qualia only; and proof is achieved by means of the common

[51] A theory of the concentration of rays through a burning-glass
which was not Aristotle's.

axioms taken in conjunction with these several kinds and their attributes.

Again, it is not true that the basic truths are much fewer than the conclusions, for the basic truths are the premisses, and the premisses are formed by the apposition of a fresh 5 extreme term or the interposition of a fresh middle. Moreover, the number of conclusions is indefinite, though the number of middle terms is finite; and lastly some of the basic truths are necessary, others variable.

Looking at it in this way we see that, since the number of conclusions is indefinite, the basic truth cannot be identical or limited in number. If, on the other hand, 10 identity is used in another sense, and it is said, e. g., 'these and no other are the fundamental truths of geometry, these the fundamentals of calculation, these again of medicine'; would the statement mean anything except that the sciences have basic truths? To call them identical because they are self-identical is absurd, since everything can be identified with everything in that sense of identity. Nor 15 again can the contention that all conclusions have the same basic truths mean that from the mass of all possible premisses any conclusion may be drawn. That would be exceedingly naïve, for it is not the case in the clearly evident mathematical sciences, nor is it possible in analysis, since it is the immediate premisses which are the basic truths, and a fresh conclusion is only formed by the addition of a new 20 immediate premiss: but if it be admitted that it is these primary immediate premisses which are basic truths, each subject-genus will provide one basic truth. If, however, it is not argued that from the mass of all possible premisses any conclusion may be proved, nor yet admitted that basic truths differ so as to be generically different for each science, it remains to consider the possibility that, while the basic truths of all knowledge are within one genus, special premisses are required to prove special conclusions. But that this cannot be the case has been shown by our 25 proof that the basic truths of things generically different

themselves differ generically. For fundamental truths are
of two kinds, those which are premisses of demonstration
and the subject-genus; and though the former are common,
the latter—number, for instance, and magnitude—are peculiar.

30 **33**   Scientific knowledge and its object differ from opinion
and the object of opinion in that scientific knowledge
is commensurately universal and proceeds by necessary
connexions, and that which is necessary cannot be otherwise. So though there are things which are true and real
and yet can be otherwise, *scientific knowledge* clearly does
not concern them: if it did, things which can be otherwise
35 would be incapable of being otherwise. Nor are they any
concern of *rational intuition*—by rational intuition I mean
an originative source of scientific knowledge—nor of in-
89ᵃ demonstrable knowledge, which is the grasping of the immediate premiss. Since then rational intuition, science, and
opinion, and what is revealed by these terms, are the only
things that can be 'true', it follows that it is *opinion* that
is concerned with that which may be true or false, and can
be otherwise: opinion in fact is the grasp of a premiss which
is immediate but not necessary. This view also fits the ob-
5 served facts, for opinion is unstable, and so is the kind of
being we have described as its object. Besides, when a man.
thinks a truth incapable of being otherwise he always thinks
that he knows it, never that he opines it. He thinks that
he opines when he thinks that a connexion, though actually
so, may quite easily be otherwise; for he believes that such
is the proper object of opinion, while the necessary is the
10 object of knowledge.

In what sense, then, can the same thing be the object of
both opinion and knowledge? And if any one chooses to
maintain that all that he knows he can also opine, why
should not opinion be knowledge? For he that knows and
he that opines will follow the same train of thought
through the same middle terms until the immediate premisses are reached; because it is possible to opine not only

the fact but also the reasoned fact, and the reason is the 15
middle term; so that, since the former knows, he that
opines also has knowledge.

The truth perhaps is that if a man grasp truths that cannot be other than they are, in the way in which he grasps
the definitions through which demonstrations take place,
he will have not opinion but knowledge: if on the other
hand he apprehends these attributes as inhering in their
subjects, but not in virtue of the subjects' substance and essential nature, he possesses opinion and not genuine knowl- 20
edge; and his opinion, if obtained through immediate
premisses, will be both of the fact and of the reasoned
fact; if not so obtained, of the fact alone. The object of
opinion and knowledge is not quite identical; it is only in a
sense identical, just as the object of true and false opinion
is in a sense identical. The sense in which some maintain 25
that true and false opinion can have the same object leads
them to embrace many strange doctrines, particularly the
doctrine that what a man opines falsely he does not opine
at all. There are really many senses of 'identical', and in one
sense the object of true and false opinion can be the same,
in another it cannot. Thus, to have a true opinion that the
diagonal is commensurate with the side would be absurd: 30
but because the diagonal with which they are both concerned is the same, the two opinions have objects so far the
same: on the other hand, as regards their essential definable
nature these objects differ. The identity of the objects of
knowledge and opinion is similar. Knowledge is the apprehension of, e. g. the attribute 'animal' as incapable of being
otherwise, opinion the apprehension of 'animal' as capable
of being otherwise—e. g. the apprehension that animal is 35
an element in the essential nature of man is knowledge; the
apprehension of animal as predicable of man but not as an
element in man's essential nature is opinion: man is the
subject in both judgments, but the mode of inherence
differs.

This also shows that one cannot opine and know the
same thing simultaneously; for then one would apprehend

the same thing as both capable and incapable of being
89ᵇ otherwise—an impossibility. Knowledge and opinion of
the same thing can coexist in two different people in the
sense we have explained, but not simultaneously in the
same person. That would involve a man's simultaneously
apprehending, e. g., (1·) that man is essentially animal—
i. e. cannot be other than animal—and (2) that man is not
5 essentially animal, that is, we may assume, may be other
than animal.

Further consideration of modes of thinking and their distribution under the heads of discursive thought, intuition,
science, art, practical wisdom, and metaphysical thinking,
belongs rather partly to natural science, partly to moral philosophy.

10 **34** Quick wit is a faculty of hitting upon the middle term
instantaneously. It would be exemplified by a man
who saw that the moon has her bright side always turned
towards the sun, and quickly grasped the cause of this,
namely that she borrows her light from him; or observed
somebody in conversation with a man of wealth and
divined that he was borrowing money, or that the friendship of these people sprang from a common enmity. In all
15 these instances he has seen the major and minor terms and
then grasped the causes, the middle terms.

Let A represent 'bright side turned sunward', B 'lighted
from the sun', C the moon. Then B, 'lighted from the sun',
is predicable of C, the moon, and A, 'having her bright side
20 towards the source of her light', is predicable of B. So A is
predicable of C through B.

BOOK II

1 The kinds of question we ask are as many as the kinds
of things which we know. They are in fact four:—(1)
whether the connexion of an attribute with a thing is a fact,
25 (2) what is the reason of the connexion, (3) whether a

thing exists; (4) what is the nature of the thing. Thus, when our question concerns a complex of thing and attribute and we ask whether the thing is thus or otherwise qualified—whether, e. g., the sun suffers eclipse or not—then we are asking as to the fact of a connexion. That our inquiry ceases with the discovery that the sun does suffer eclipse is an indication of this; and if we know from the start that the sun suffers eclipse, we do not inquire whether it does so or not. On the other hand, when we know the fact we ask the reason; as, for example, when we know that the sun is being eclipsed and that an earthquake is in progress, it is the reason of eclipse or earthquake into which we 30 inquire.

Where a complex is concerned, then, those are the two questions we ask; but for some objects of inquiry we have a different kind of question to ask, such as whether there is or is not a centaur or a God. (By 'is or is not' I mean 'is or is not, without further qualification'; as opposed to 'is or is not (e. g.) white'.) On the other hand, when we have ascertained the thing's existence, we inquire as to its nature, asking, for instance, 'what, then, is God?' or 'what is man?'. 35

2   These, then, are the four kinds of question we ask, and it is in the answers to these questions that our knowledge consists.

Now when we ask whether a connexion is a fact, or whether a thing without qualification *is*, we are really asking whether the connexion or the thing has a 'middle'; and when we have ascertained either that the connexion is a fact or that the thing *is*—i. e. ascertained either the partial or the unqualified being of the thing—and are proceeding 90ᵃ to ask the reason of the connexion or the nature of the thing, then we are asking what the 'middle' is.

(By distinguishing the fact of the connexion and the existence of the thing as respectively the partial and the unqualified being of the thing, I mean that if we ask 'does the moon suffer eclipse?', or 'does the moon wax?', the question concerns a part of the thing's being; for what we are asking in such questions is whether a thing is this or that, i. e. has or has not this or that attribute: whereas, if we ask whether the moon or night exists, the question concerns the unqualified being of a thing.)

We conclude that in all our inquiries we are asking
5 either whether there is a 'middle' or what the 'middle' is: for the 'middle' here is precisely the cause, and it is the cause that we seek in all our inquiries. Thus, 'Does the moon suffer eclipse?' means 'Is there or is there not a cause producing eclipse of the moon?', and when we have learnt that there is, our next question is, 'What, then, is this cause?'; for the cause through which a thing is—not is this or that, i. e. has this or that attribute, but without qualifica-
10 tion is—and the cause through which it is—not is without qualification, but is this or that as having some essential attribute or some accident—are both alike the 'middle'. By that which is without qualification I mean the subject, e. g. moon or earth or sun or triangle; by that which a subject is (in the partial sense) I mean a property, e. g. eclipse, equality or inequality, interposition or non-interposition.
15 For in all these examples it is clear that the nature of the thing and the reason of the fact are identical: the question 'What is eclipse?' and its answer 'The privation of the moon's light by the interposition of the earth' are identical with the question 'What is the reason of eclipse?' or 'Why does the moon suffer eclipse?' and the reply 'Because of the failure of light through the earth's shutting it out'. Again, for 'What is a concord? A commensurate numerical ratio
20 of a high and a low note', we may substitute 'What reason makes a high and a low note concordant? Their relation according to a commensurate numerical ratio.' 'Are the high and the low note concordant?' is equivalent to 'Is their ratio commensurate?'; and when we find that it is commensurate, we ask 'What, then, is their ratio?'.

Cases in which the 'middle' is sensible show that the ob-
25 ject of our inquiry is always the 'middle': we inquire, be-

cause we have not perceived it, whether there is or is not a 'middle' causing e. g. an eclipse. On the other hand, if we were on the moon we should not be inquiring either as to the fact or the reason, but both fact and reason would be obvious simultaneously. For the act of perception would have enabled us to know the universal too; since, the present fact of an eclipse being evident, perception would then at the same time give us the present fact of the earth's 30 screening the sun's light, and from this would arise the universal.

Thus, as we maintain, to know a thing's nature is to know the reason why it is; and this is equally true of things in so far as they are said without qualification to *be* as opposed to being possessed of some attribute, and in so far as they are said to be possessed of some attribute such as equal to two right angles, or greater or less.

3 It is clear, then, that all questions are a search for a 35 'middle'. Let us now state how essential nature is revealed, and in what way it can be reduced to demonstration;[1] what definition is, and what things are definable. And let us first discuss certain difficulties which these ques- 90ᵇ tions raise, beginning what we have to say with a point most intimately connected with our immediately preceding remarks, namely the doubt that might be felt as to whether or not it is possible to know the same thing in the same relation, both by definition and by demonstration. It might, I mean, be urged that definition is held to concern essential nature and is in every case universal and affirmative; where- 5 as, on the other hand, some conclusions are negative and some are not universal; e. g. all in the second figure are negative, none in the third are universal. And again, not even all affirmative conclusions in the first figure are definable, e. g. 'every triangle has its angles equal to two right angles'. An argument proving this difference between demonstration and definition is that to have scientific knowledge of

[1] Cf. 94ª 11–14.

10 the demonstrable is identical with possessing a demonstration of it: hence if demonstration of such conclusions as
these is possible, there clearly cannot also be definition of
them. If there could, one might know such a conclusion
also in virtue of its definition without possessing the demonstration of it; for there is nothing to stop our having the
one without the other.

Induction too will sufficiently convince us of this difference; for never yet by defining anything—essential attribute
15 or accident—did we get knowledge of it. Again, if to define
is to acquire knowledge of a substance, at any rate such attributes are not substances.

It is evident, then, that not everything demonstrable can
be defined. What then? Can everything definable be demonstrated, or not? There is one of our previous arguments
20 which covers this too. Of a single thing qua single there is
a single scientific knowledge. Hence, since to know the demonstrable scientifically is to possess the demonstration of
it, an impossible consequence will follow:—possession of
its definition without its demonstration will give knowledge
of the demonstrable.

Moreover, the basic premisses of demonstrations are definitions, and it has already been shown [2] that these will be
found indemonstrable; either the basic premisses will be
25 demonstrable and will depend on prior premisses, and the
regress will be endless; or the primary truths will be indemonstrable definitions.

But if the definable and the demonstrable are not wholly
the same, may they yet be partially the same? Or is that
impossible, because there can be no demonstration of the
definable? There can be none, because definition is of the
30 essential nature or being of something, and all demonstrations evidently posit and assume the essential nature—
mathematical demonstrations, for example, the nature of
unity and the odd, and all the other sciences likewise. Moreover, every demonstration proves a predicate of a subject

[2] Cf. 72[b] 18–25 and 84[a] 30–[b] 2.

as attaching or as not attaching to it, but in definition one thing is not predicated of another; we do not, e. g., predi- 35 cate animal of biped nor biped of animal, nor yet figure of plane—plane not being figure nor figure plane. Again, to prove essential nature is not the same as to prove the fact of a connexion. Now definition reveals essential nature, demonstration reveals that a given attribute attaches or does 91ᵇ not attach to a given subject; but different things require different demonstrations—unless the one demonstration is related to the other as part to whole. I add this because if all triangles have been proved to possess angles equal to two right angles, then this attribute has been proved to· attach to isosceles; for isosceles is a part of which all triangles constitute the whole. But in the case before us the fact and the 5 essential nature are not so related to one another, since the one is not a part of the other.

So it emerges that not all the definable is demonstrable nor all the demonstrable definable; and we may draw the general conclusion that there is no identical object of which it is possible to possess both a definition and a demonstra- 10 tion. It follows obviously that definition and demonstration are neither identical nor contained either within the other: if they were, their objects would be related either as identical or as whole and part.

4 So much, then, for the first stage of our problem. The next step is to raise the question whether syllogism— i. e. demonstration—of the definable nature is possible or, as our recent argument assumed, impossible.

We might argue it impossible on the following grounds: —(a) syllogism proves an attribute of a subject through the middle term; on the other hand (b) its definable na- 15 ture is both 'peculiar' to a subject and predicated of it as belonging to its essence. But in that case (1) the subject, its definition, and the middle term connecting them must be reciprocally predicable of one another; for if A is 'peculiar' to C, obviously A is 'peculiar' to B and B to C—in fact

all three terms are 'peculiar' to one another: and further
(2) if A inheres in the essence of all B and B is predicated
20 universally of all C as belonging to C's essence, A also must
be predicated of C as belonging to its essence.

If one does not take this relation as thus duplicated—if,
that is, A is predicated as being of the essence of B, but B
is not of the essence of the subjects of which it is predicated—A will not necessarily be predicated of C as belonging to its essence. So both premisses will predicate essence,
25 and consequently B also will be predicated of C as its essence. Since, therefore, both premisses do predicate essence
—i. e. definable form—C's definable form will appear in the
middle term before the conclusion is drawn.

We may generalize by supposing that it is possible to
prove the essential nature of man. Let C be man, A man's
essential nature—two-footed animal, or aught else it may
be. Then, if we are to syllogize, A must be predicated of all
B. But this premiss will be mediated by a fresh definition,
30 which consequently will also be the essential nature of
man.[3] Therefore the argument assumes what it has to
prove, since B too is the essential nature of man. It is, however, the case in which there are only the two premisses—
i. e. in which the premisses are primary and immediate—
which we ought to investigate, because it best illustrates
the point under discussion.

Thus they who prove the essential nature of soul or man
35 or anything else through reciprocating terms beg the question. It would be begging the question, for example, to con-
tend that the soul is that which causes its own life, and that
what causes its own life is a self-moving number; for one
would have to postulate that the soul is a self-moving
91ᵇ number in the sense of being identical with it. For if A is

[3] sc. 'and an indefinite regress occurs'. This argument is a corollary
of the proof in 91ª 15–26 that if the proposition predicating A—its
definition—of C can be a conclusion, there must be a middle term,
B, and since A, B, and C are reciprocally predicable, B too, as well as
A, will be a definition of C.

predicable as a mere consequent of *B* and *B* of *C*, *A* will not on that account be the definable form of *C*: *A* will merely be what it was true to say of *C*. Even if *A* is predicated of all *B* inasmuch as *B* is identical with-a species of *A*, still it will not follow: being an animal is predicated of being a man— since it is true that in all instances to be human is to be 5 animal, just as it is also true that every man is an animal— but not as identical with being man.

We conclude, then, that unless one takes both the prem- isses as predicating essence, one cannot infer that *A* is the definable form and essence of *C*: but if one does so take them, in assuming *B* one will have assumed, before drawing the conclusion, what the definable form of *C* is; so that there has been no inference, for one has begged the ques- 10 tion.

5 Nor, as was said in my formal logic, is the method of division a process of inference at all, since at no point does the characterization of the subject follow necessarily from the premising of certain other facts: division demon- strates as little as does induction. For in a genuine demon- 15 stration the conclusion must not be put as a question nor depend on a concession, but must follow necessarily from its premises, even if the respondent deny it. The definer asks 'Is man animal or inanimate?' and then assumes—he has not inferred—that man is animal. Next, when pre- sented with an exhaustive division of animal into terrestrial and aquatic, he assumes that man is terrestrial. Moreover, 20 that man is the complete formula, terrestrial-animal, does not follow necessarily from the premises: this too is an assumption, and equally an assumption whether the divi- sion comprises many differentiae or few. (Indeed as this method of division is used by those who proceed by it, even truths that can be inferred actually fail to appear as 25 such.) For why should not the whole of this formula be true of man, and yet not exhibit his essential nature or de-

finable form? Again, what guarantee is there against an unessential addition, or against the omission of the final or of
an intermediate determinant of the substantial being?

The champion of division might here urge that though
these lapses do occur, yet we can solve that difficulty if all
the attributes we assume are constituents of the definable
form, and if, postulating the genus, we produce by division
30 the requisite uninterrupted sequence of terms, and omit
nothing; and that indeed we cannot fail to fulfil these conditions if what is to be divided falls whole into the division
at each stage, and none of it is omitted; and that this—the
dividendum—must without further question be (ultimately) incapable of fresh specific division. Nevertheless,
we reply, division does not involve inference; if it gives
knowledge, it gives it in another way. Nor is there any absurdity in this: induction, perhaps, is not demonstration
any more than is division, yet it does make evident some
35 truth. Yet to state a definition reached by division is not
to state a conclusion: as, when conclusions are drawn without their appropriate middles, the alleged necessity by
which the inference follows from the premisses is open to
a question as to the reason for it, so definitions reached by
division invite the same question. Thus to the question
92ᵃ 'What is the essential nature of man?' the divider replies
'Animal, mortal, footed, biped, wingless'; and when at each
step he is asked 'Why?', he will say, and, as he thinks, prove
by division, that all animal is mortal or immortal: but such
a formula taken in its entirety is not definition; so that even
5 if division does demonstrate its formula, definition at any
rate does not turn out to be a conclusion of inference.

6   Can we nevertheless actually demonstrate what a thing
    essentially and substantially is, but hypothetically,
i. e. by premising (1) that its definable form is constituted
by the 'peculiar' attributes of its essential nature; (2) that
such and such are the only attributes of its essential nature,
and that the complete synthesis of them is peculiar to the

thing; and thus—since in this synthesis consists the being of the thing—obtaining our conclusion? Or is the truth that, since proof must be through the middle term, the 10 definable form is once more assumed in this minor premiss too?

Further, just as in syllogizing we do not premise what syllogistic inference is (since the premisses from which we conclude must be related as whole and part),[4] so the definable form must not fall within the syllogism but remain outside the premisses posited. It is only against a doubt as to its having been a syllogistic inference at all that we have 15 to defend our argument as conforming to the definition of syllogism. It is only when some one doubts whether the conclusion proved is the definable form that we have to defend it as conforming to the definition of definable form which we assumed. Hence syllogistic inference must be possible even without the express statement of what syllogism is or what definable form is.

The following type of hypothetical proof also begs the question. If evil is definable as the divisible, and the defini- 20 tion of a thing's contrary—if it has one—is the contrary of the thing's definition; then, if good is the contrary of evil and the indivisible of the divisible, we conclude that to be good is essentially to be indivisible. The question is begged because definable form is assumed as a premiss, and as a premiss which is to prove definable form. 'But not the same definable form', you may object. That I admit, for in demonstrations also we premise that 'this' is predicable of 'that'; 25 but in this premiss the term we assert of the minor is neither the major itself nor a term identical in definition, or convertible, with the major.

Again, both proof by division and the syllogism just described are open to the question why man should be animal-biped-terrestrial and not merely animal and terrestrial, since

---

[4] A reminder of a necessary condition of syllogism. If the definition of syllogism is premised the conclusion would have to affirm some subject to be of the nature of syllogism.

30 what they premise does not ensure that the predicates shall
constitute a genuine unity and not merely belong to a single
subject as do musical and grammatical when predicated of
the same man.

7   How- then by definition shall we prove substance or
essential nature? We cannot show it as a fresh fact
35 necessarily following from the assumption of premisses admitted to be facts—the method of demonstration: we may
not proceed as by induction to establish a universal on the
evidence of groups of particulars which offer no exception,
because induction proves not what the essential nature of
a thing is but that it has or has not some attribute. There-
92ᵇ fore, since presumably one cannot prove essential nature
by an appeal to sense perception or by pointing with the
finger, what other method remains?

To put it another way: how shall we by definition prove
essential nature? He who knows what human—or any other
5 —nature is, must know also that man exists; for no one
knows the nature of what does not exist—one can know the
meaning of the phrase or name 'goat-stag' but not what the
essential nature of a goat-stag is. But further, if definition
can prove what is the essential nature of a thing, can it also
prove that it exists? And how will it prove them both by
the same process, since definition exhibits one single thing
10 and demonstration another single thing, and what human
nature is and the fact that man exists are not the same
thing? Then too we hold that it is by *demonstration* that
the being of everything must be proved—unless indeed to
be were its essence; and, since being is not a genus, it is not
the essence of anything. Hence the being of anything as
15 fact is matter for demonstration; and this is the actual procedure of the sciences, for the geometer assumes the meaning of the word triangle, but that it is possessed of some attribute he proves. What is it, then, that we shall prove in
defining essential nature? Triangle? In that case a man will

know by definition what a thing's nature is without knowing whether it exists. But that is impossible.

Moreover it is clear, if we consider the methods of defining actually in use, that definition does not prove that the thing defined exists: since even if there does actually exist 20 something which is equidistant from a centre, yet why should the thing named in the definition exist? Why, in other words, should this be the formula defining circle? One might equally well call it the definition of mountain copper. For definitions do not carry a further guarantee that the thing defined can exist or that it is what they claim to 25 define: one can always ask why.

Since, therefore, to define is to prove either a thing's essential nature or the meaning of its name, we may conclude that definition, if it in no sense proves essential nature, is a set of words signifying precisely what a name signifies. But that were a strange consequence; for (1) both what is not substance and what does not exist at all would be definable, since even non-existents can be signified by 30 a name: (2) all sets of words or sentences would be definitions, since any kind of sentence could be given a name; so that we should all be talking in definitions, and even the *Iliad* would be a definition: (3) no demonstration can prove that any particular name means any particular thing: neither, therefore, do definitions, in addition to revealing the meaning of a name, also reveal that the name has *this* 35 meaning. It appears then from these considerations that neither definition and syllogism nor their objects are identical, and further that definition neither demonstrates nor proves anything, and that knowledge of essential nature is not to be obtained either by definition or by demonstration.

8 We must now start afresh and consider which of these conclusions are sound and which are not, and what 93ᵃ is the nature of definition, and whether essential nature is in any sense demonstrable and definable or in none.

Now to know its essential nature is, as we said, the same
as to know the cause of a thing's existence, and the proof of
5 this depends on the fact that a thing must have a cause.
Moreover, this cause is either identical with the essential
nature of the thing or distinct from it; [5] and if its cause is
distinct from it, the essential nature of the thing is either
demonstrable or indemonstrable. Consequently, if the
cause is distinct from the thing's essential nature and demonstration is possible, the cause must be the middle term,
and, the conclusion proved being universal and affirmative,
the proof is in the first figure. So the method just examined
of proving it through another essential nature would be one
10 way of proving essential nature, because a conclusion containing essential nature must be inferred through a middle
which is an essential nature just as a 'peculiar' property
must be inferred through a middle which is a 'peculiar'
property; so that of the two definable natures of a single
thing this method will prove one and not the other.[6]

Now it was said before [7] that this method could not
amount to demonstration of essential nature—it is actually
15 a dialectical proof of it—so let us begin again and explain
by what method it can be demonstrated. When we are
aware of a fact we seek its reason, and though sometimes
the fact and the reason dawn on us simultaneously, yet we
cannot apprehend the reason a moment sooner than the
fact; and clearly in just the same way we cannot apprehend
a thing's definable form without apprehending that it
exists, since while we are ignorant whether it exists we can-

---

[5] 'distinct from it'; i. e. in the case of properties, with the definition
of which Aristotle is alone concerned in this chapter. The being of a
property consists in its inherence in a substance through a middle
which defines it. Cf. the following chapter.

[6] Aristotle speaks of two moments of the definable form as two essential natures. His argument amounts to this: that if the conclusion
contains the whole definition, the question has been begged in the
premises (cf. ii, ch. 4). Hence syllogism—and even so merely dialectical syllogism—is only possible if premises and conclusion each contain a part of the definition.

[7] ii, ch. 2.

not know its essential nature. Moreover we are aware 20 whether a thing exists or not sometimes through apprehending an element in its character, and sometimes accidentally,[8] as, for example, when we are aware of thunder as a noise in the clouds, of eclipse as a privation of light, or of man as some species of animal, or of the soul as a self-moving thing. As often as we have accidental knowledge that the thing exists, we must be in a wholly negative state 25 as regards awareness of its essential nature; for we have not got genuine knowledge even of its existence, and to search for a thing's essential nature when we are unaware that it exists is to search for nothing. On the other hand, whenever we apprehend an element in the thing's character there is less difficulty. Thus it follows that the degree of our knowledge of a thing's essential nature is determined by the sense in which we are aware that it exists. Let us then take the following as our first instance of being aware of an element in the essential nature. Let A be eclipse, C the 30 moon, B the earth's acting as a screen. Now to ask whether the moon is eclipsed or not is to ask whether or not B has occurred. But that is precisely the same as asking whether A has a defining condition; and if this condition actually exists, we assert that A also actually exists. Or again we may ask which side of a contradiction the defining condition necessitates: does it make the angles of a triangle equal or not equal to two right angles? When we have found the answer, if the premisses are immediate, we know fact and 35 reason together; if they are not immediate, we know the fact without the reason, as in the following example: let C be the moon, A eclipse, B the fact that the moon fails to produce shadows [9] though she is full and though no visible body intervenes between us and her. Then if B, failure to produce shadows in spite of the absence of an intervening 93ᵇ

[8] The distinction is that between genuine knowledge of a connexion through its cause and accidental knowledge of it through a middle not the cause.

[9] i.e. that there is no moonlight casting shadows on the earth on a clear night at full moon.

body, is attributable to C, and A, eclipse, is attributable to
B, it is clear that the moon is eclipsed, but the reason
why is not yet clear, and we know that eclipse exists, but we
do not know what its essential nature is. But when it is clear
5 that A is attributable to C and we proceed to ask the reason
of this fact, we are inquiring what is the nature of B: is it
the earth's acting as a screen, or the moon's rotation or her
extinction? But B is the definition of the other term, viz.,
in these examples, of the major term A; for eclipse is constituted by the earth acting as a screen. Thus, (1) 'What is
thunder?' 'The quenching of fire in cloud', and (2) 'Why
does it thunder?' 'Because fire is quenched in the cloud',
are equivalent. Let C be cloud, A thunder, B the quench-
10 ing of fire. Then B is attributable to C, cloud, since fire is
quenched in it; and A, noise, is attributable to B; and B is
assuredly the definition of the major term A. If there be a
further mediating cause of B, it will be one of the remaining partial definitions of A.

We have stated then how essential nature is discovered
15 and becomes known, and we see that, while there is no
syllogism—i. e. no demonstrative syllogism—of essential
nature, yet it is through syllogism, viz. demonstrative syllogism, that essential nature is exhibited. So we conclude
that neither can the essential nature of anything which has
a cause distinct from itself be known without demonstration, nor can it be demonstrated; and this is what we con-
20 tended in our preliminary discussions.[10]

9 · Now while some things have a cause distinct from
themselves, others have not. Hence it is evident that
there are essential natures which are immediate, that is,
are basic premises; and of these not only *that* they are but
also *what* they are must be assumed or revealed in some
other way. This too is the actual procedure of the arithmetician, who assumes both the nature and the existence of

[10] ii, ch. 3.

unit. On the other hand, it is possible (in the manner ex- 25
plained) to exhibit through demonstration the essential
nature of things which have a 'middle',[11] i. e. a cause of
their substantial being other than that being itself; but we
do not thereby demonstrate it.

10 Since definition is said to be the statement of a thing's
nature, obviously one kind of definition will be a statement of the meaning of the name, or of an equivalent
nominal formula. A definition in this sense tells you, e. g. 30
the meaning of the phrase 'triangular character'.[12] When
we are aware that triangle exists, we inquire the reason why
it exists. But it is difficult thus to learn the definition of
things the existence of which we do not genuinely know—
the cause of this difficulty being, as we said before,[13] that we
only know accidentally whether or not the thing exists.
Moreover, a statement may be a unity in either of two ways, 35
by conjunction, like the *Iliad*, or because it exhibits a
single predicate as inhering not accidentally in a single
subject.[14]

That then is one way of defining definition. Another
kind of definition is a formula exhibiting the cause of a
thing's existence. Thus the former signifies without prov- 94ᵃ
ing, but the latter will clearly be a *quasi*-demonstration of
essential nature, differing from demonstration in the arrangement of its terms. For there is a difference between
stating why it thunders, and stating what is the essential
nature of thunder; since the first statement will be 'Because
fire is quenched in the clouds', while the statement of what
the nature of thunder is will be 'The noise of fire being 5
quenched in the clouds'. Thus the same statement takes a

---

[11] Cf., however, ii, ch. 2.

[12] i. e. as treated by geometry; that is, as abstracted a *materia* and
treated as a subject. Cf. 81ᵇ 25.

[13] Cf. 93ᵃ 16–27.

[14] Presumably a reason for there being a kind of definition other
than nominal. The reference is obviously to 92ᵇ 32.

different form: in one form it is continuous [15] demonstration, in the other definition. Again, thunder can be defined
as noise in the clouds, which is the conclusion of the dem-
10 onstration embodying essential nature. On the other hand
the definition of immediates is an indemonstrable positing
of essential nature. We conclude then that definition is (a)
an indemonstrable statement of essential nature, or (b) a
syllogism of essential nature differing from demonstration
in grammatical form, or (c) the conclusion of a demonstration giving essential nature.

Our discussion has therefore made plain (1) in what
sense and of what things the essential nature is demon-
15 strable, and in what sense and of what things it is not;
(2) what are the various meanings of the term definition,
and in what sense and of what things it proves the essential
nature, and in what sense and of what things it does not;
(3) what is the relation of definition to demonstration,
and how far the same thing is both definable and demonstrable and how far it is not.

20 **11** We think we have scientific knowledge when we know
the cause, and there are four causes: (1) the definable
form, (2) an antecedent which necessitates a consequent,[16]
(3) the efficient cause, (4) the final cause. Hence each of
these can be the middle term of a proof, for [17] (a) though
25 the inference from antecedent to necessary consequent
does not hold if only one premiss is assumed—two is the
minimum—still when there are two it holds on condition
that they have a single common middle term. So it is from
the assumption of this single middle term that the conclusion follows necessarily. The following example will also

[15] Demonstration, like a line, is continuous because its premisses are
parts which are conterminous (as linked by middle terms), and there
is a movement from premisses to conclusion. Definition resembles
rather the indivisible simplicity of a point.

[16] By this Aristotle appears to mean the material cause; cf. *Physics*
ii, 195ᵃ 18, 19, where the premisses of a syllogism are said to be the
material cause of the conclusion.

[17] sc. 'lest you should suppose that (2) could not be a middle'.

show this.[18] Why is the angle in a semicircle a right angle?
—or from what assumption does it follow that it is a right
angle? Thus, let A be right angle, B the half of two right
angles, C the angle in a semicircle. Then B is the cause in 30
virtue of which A, right angle, is attributable to C, the
angle in a semicircle, since B = A and the other, viz. C,
= B, for C is half of two right angles. Therefore it *is* the
assumption of B, the half of two right angles, from which
it follows that A is attributable to C, i. e. that the angle in
a semicircle is a right angle. Moreover, B is identical with
(b) the defining form of A, since it is what A's definition [19]
signifies. Moreover, the formal cause has already been
shown to be the middle.[20] (c) 'Why did the Athenians 35
become involved in the Persian war?' means 'What cause
originated the waging of war against the Athenians?' and
the answer is, 'Because they raided Sardis with the Eretri-
ans', since this originated the war. Let A be war, B un- 94ᵇ
provoked raiding, C the Athenians. Then B, unprovoked
raiding, is true of C, the Athenians, and A is true of B,
since men make war on the unjust aggressor. So A, having
war waged upon them, is true of B, the initial aggressors, 5
and B is true of C, the Athenians, who were the aggressors.
Hence here too the cause—in this case the efficient cause—
is the middle term. (d) This is no less true where the cause
is the final cause. E. g. why does one take a walk after
supper? For the sake of one's health. Why does a house
exist? For the preservation of one's goods. The end in view
is in the one case health, in the other preservation. To ask 10
the reason why one must walk after supper is precisely to
ask to what end one must do it. Let C be walking after
supper, B the non-regurgitation of food, A health. Then let

[18] *sc.* 'that (2) can appear as a middle'.
[19] Cf. Euclid, *Elem.* i, Def. x, but Aristotle may be referring to
some earlier definition. The proof here given that the angle in a semicircle is a right angle is not that of Euclid iii. 31; cf. Heath, *Greek
Mathematics*, i. pp. 339, 340.
[20] The reference is to 93ᵃ 3 ff., and other passages such as 94ᵇ 5 ff.,
where the middle is shown to define the major.

walking after supper possess the property of preventing
15 food from rising to the orifice of the stomach, and let
this condition be healthy; since it seems that B, the
non-regurgitation of food, is attributable to C, taking a
walk, and that A, health, is attributable to B. What, then,
is the cause through which A, the final cause, inheres in C?
It is B, the non-regurgitation of food; but B is a kind of
20 definition of A, for A will be explained by it. Why is B the
cause of A's belonging to C? Because to be in a condition
such as B is to be in health. The definitions must be trans-
posed, and then the detail will become clearer. Incidentally, here the order of coming to be is the reverse of what
it is in proof through the efficient cause: in the efficient
25 order the middle term must come to be first, whereas in the
teleological order the minor, C, must first take place, and
the end in view comes last in time.

The same thing may exist for an end and be necessitated
as well. For example, light shines through a lantern (1)
because that which consists of relatively small particles
30 necessarily passes through pores larger than those particles
—assuming that light does issue by penetration—and (2)
for an end, namely to save us from stumbling. If, then, a
thing can exist through two causes, can it come to be
through two causes—as for instance if thunder be a hiss and
a roar necessarily produced by the quenching of fire, and
also designed, as the Pythagoreans say, for a threat to terrify
35 those that lie in Tartarus? Indeed, there are very many such
cases, mostly among the processes and products of the
natural world; for nature, in different senses of the term
'nature', produces now for an end, now by necessity.

Necessity too is of two kinds. It may work in accordance
95ᵃ with a thing's natural tendency, or by constraint and in
opposition to it; as, for instance, by necessity a stone is
borne both upwards and downwards, but not by the same
necessity.

Of the products of man's intelligence some are never
due to chance or necessity but always to an end, as for

example a house or a statue; others, such as health or safety, 5
may result from chance as well.

It is mostly in cases where the issue is indeterminate
(though only where the production does not originate in
chance, and the end is consequently good), that a result is
due to an end, and this is true alike in nature or in art. By
chance, on the other hand, nothing comes to be for an end.

12 The effect may be still coming to be, or its occurrence 10
may be past or future, yet the cause will be the same
as when it is actually existent—for it is the middle which is
the cause—except that if the effect actually exists the cause
is actually existent, if it is coming to be so is the cause, if its
occurrence is past the cause is past, if future the cause is
future. For example, the moon was eclipsed because the
earth intervened, is becoming eclipsed because the earth is
in process of intervening, will be eclipsed because the earth 15
will intervene, is eclipsed because the earth intervenes.

To take a second example: assuming that the definition
of ice is solidified water, let *C* be water, *A* solidified, *B* the
middle, which is the cause, namely total failure of heat.
Then *B* is attributed to *C*, and *A*, solidification, to *B*: ice
forms when *B* is occurring, has formed when *B* has oc- 20
curred, and will form when *B* shall occur.

This sort of cause, then, and its effect come to be simultaneously when they are in process of becoming, and exist
simultaneously when they actually exist; and the same
holds good when they are past and when they are future.
But what of cases where they are not simultaneous? Can
causes and effects different from one another form, as they
seem to us to form, a continuous succession, a past effect
resulting from a past cause different from itself, a future 25
effect from a future cause different from it, and an effect
which is coming-to-be from a cause different from and prior
to it? Now on this theory it is from the posterior event that
we reason (and this though these later events actually have
their source of origin in previous events—a fact which

shows that also when the effect is coming-to-be we still
reason from the posterior event), and from the prior event
we cannot reason (we cannot argue that because an event
30 A has occurred, therefore an event B has occurred subsequently to A but still in the past—and the same holds good
if the occurrence is future)—cannot reason because, be the
time interval definite or indefinite, it will never be possible
to infer that because it is true to say that A occurred, therefore it is true to say that B, the subsequent event, occurred;
for in the interval between the events, though A has already
35 occurred, the latter statement will be false. And the same
argument applies also to future events; i. e. one cannot
infer from an event which occurred in the past that a future
event will occur. The reason of this is that the middle must
be homogeneous, past when the extremes are past, future
when they are future, coming to be when they are coming-
to-be, actually existent when they are actually existent; and
there cannot be a middle term homogeneous with extremes
respectively past and future. And it is a further difficulty
40 in this theory that the time interval can be neither indefi-
95ᵇ nite nor definite, since during it the inference will be false.
We have also to inquire what it is that holds events together so that the coming-to-be now occurring in actual
things follows upon a past event. It is evident, we may suggest, that a past event and a present process cannot be
'contiguous', for not even two past events can be 'contigu-
5 ous'. For past events are limits and atomic; so just as points
are not 'contiguous' neither are past events, since both are
indivisible. For the same reason a past event and a present
process cannot be 'contiguous', for the process is divisible,
the event indivisible. Thus the relation of present process
10 to past event is analogous to that of line to point, since a
process contains an infinity of past events. These questions,
however, must receive a more explicit treatment in our
general theory of change.²¹

The following must suffice as an account of the manner
in which the middle would be identical with the cause

²¹ Cf. *Physics* vi.

on the supposition that coming-to-be is a series of consecutive events: for [22] in the terms of such a series too the middle and major terms must form an immediate premiss; e. g. we argue that, since *C* has occurred, therefore *A* occurred: and *C*'s occurrence was posterior, *A*'s prior; but *C* is the source of the inference because it is nearer to the present moment, and the starting-point of time is the present. We next argue that, since *D* has occurred, therefore *C* occurred. Then we conclude that, since *D* has occurred, therefore *A* must have occurred; and the cause is *C*, for since *D* has occurred *C* must have occurred, and since *C* has occurred *A* must previously have occurred.

If we get our middle term in this way, will the series terminate in an immediate premiss, or since, as we said, no two events are 'contiguous', will a fresh term always intervene because there is an infinity of middles? No: though no two events are 'contiguous', yet we must start from a premiss consisting of a middle and the present event as major. The like is true of future events too, since if it is true to say that *D* will exist, it must be a prior truth to say that *A* will exist, and the cause of this conclusion is *C*; for if *D* will exist, *C* will exist prior to *D*, and if *C* will exist, *A* will exist prior to it. And here too the same infinite divisibility might be urged, since future events are not 'contiguous'. But here too an immediate basic premiss must be assumed. And in the world of fact this is so: if a house has been built, then blocks must have been quarried and shaped. The reason is that a house having been built necessitates a foundation having been laid, and if a foundation has been laid blocks must have been shaped beforehand. Again, if a house will be built, blocks will similarly be shaped beforehand; and proof is through the middle in the

[22] i. e. Aristotle has had in this chapter to explain (1) how syllogisms concerning a process of events can be brought into line with other demonstrations equally derivable from immediate primary premisses, and (2) in what sense the middle term contains the cause. He has in fact had (1) to show that in these syllogisms inference must find its primary premiss in the effect, and (2) to imply that the 'cause' which appears as middle when cause and effect are not simultaneous is a *causa cognoscendi* and not *essendi*.

same way, for the foundation will exist before the house.

Now we observe in Nature a certain kind of circular process of coming-to-be; and this is possible only if the middle and extreme terms are reciprocal, since conversion is
40 conditioned by reciprocity in the terms of the proof. This
96ᵇ—the convertibility of conclusions and premisses—has been proved in our early chapters,[23] and the circular process is an instance of this. In actual fact it is exemplified thus: when the earth had been moistened an exhalation was bound to rise, and when an exhalation had risen cloud was bound to form, and from the formation of cloud rain necessarily resulted, and by the fall of rain the earth was
5 necessarily moistened: but this was the starting-point, so that a circle is completed; for posit any one of the terms and another follows from it, and from that another, and from that again the first.

Some occurrences are universal (for they are, or come-to-be what they are, always and in every case); others again are not always what they are but only as a general rule: for
10 instance, not every man can grow a beard, but it is the general rule. In the case of such connexions the middle term too must be a general rule. For if A is predicted universally of B and B of C, A too must be predicted always and in every instance of C, since to hold in every instance and always is of the nature of the universal. But we have
15 assumed a connexion which is a general rule; consequently the middle term B must also be a general rule. So connexions which embody a general rule—i. e. which exist or come to be as a general rule—will also derive from immediate basic premisses.

13 [24] We have already explained how essential nature is set
20   out in the terms of a demonstration, and the sense in which it is or is not, demonstrable or definable; so let us now discuss the method to be adopted in tracing the elements predicated as constituting the definable form.

[23] i, ch. 3 and An. Pr. ii, cc. 3–5, 8–10.
[24] This chapter treats only the definition of substances.

Now of the attributes which inhere always in each several thing there are some which are wider in extent than it but not wider than its genus (by attributes of wider extent I 25 mean all such as are universal attributes of each several subject, but in their application are not confined to that subject). I. e. while an attribute may inhere in every triad, yet also in a subject not a triad—as being inheres in triad but also in subjects not numbers at all—odd on the other hand is an attribute inhering in every triad and of wider application (inhering as it does also in pentad), but which does not extend beyond the genus of triad; for pentad is a 30 number, but nothing outside number is odd. It is such attributes which we have to select, up to the exact point at which they are severally of wider extent than the subject but collectively coextensive with it; for this synthesis must be the substance of the thing. For example every triad possesses the attributes number, odd, and prime in both 35 senses, i. e. not only as possessing no divisors, but also as not being a sum of numbers. This, then, is precisely what triad is, viz. a number, odd, and prime in the former and also the latter sense of the term: for these attributes taken severally apply, the first two to all odd numbers, the last 96ᵇ to the dyad also as well as to the triad, but, taken collectively, to no other subject. Now since we have shown above [25] that attributes predicated as belonging to the essential nature are necessary and that universals are necessary, and since the attributes which we select as inhering in triad, or in any other subject whose attributes we select in this way, are predicated as belonging to its essential 5 nature, triad will thus possess these attributes necessarily. Further, that the synthesis of them constitutes the substance of triad is shown by the following argument. If it is not identical with the being of triad, it must be related to triad as a genus named or nameless. It will then be of wider extent than triad—assuming that wider potential extent is the character of a genus. If on the other hand this synthe- 10 sis is applicable to no subject other than the individual

[25] i, ch. 4.

triads, it will be identical with the being of triad, because
we make the further assumption that the substance of each
subject is the predication of elements in its essential nature
down to the last differentia characterizing the individuals. It
follows that any other synthesis thus exhibited will likewise
be identical with the being of the subject.

15 The author of a hand-book [26] on a subject that is a
generic whole should divide the genus into its first *infimae
species*—number e. g. into triad and dyad—and then endeavour to seize their definitions by the method we have
described—the definition, for example, of straight line or
circle or right angle. After that, having established what the
category is to which the subaltern genus belongs—quantity
20 or quality, for instance—he should examine the properties
'peculiar' to the species, working through the proximate
common differentiae. He should proceed thus because the
attributes of the genera compounded of the *infimae species*
will be clearly given by the definitions of the species; since
the basic element of them all [27] is the definition, i. e. the
simple *infima species*, and the attributes inhere essentially
in the simple *infimae species*, in the genera only in virtue
of these.

Divisions according to differentiae are a useful accessory
25 to this method. What force they have as proofs we did,
indeed, explain above,[28] but that merely towards collecting
the essential nature they may be of use we will proceed to
show. They might, indeed, seem to be of no use at all,
but rather to assume everything at the start and to be no
better than an initial assumption made without division.
30 But, in fact, the order in which the attributes are predicated
does make a difference—it matters whether we say animal
—tame—biped, or biped—animal—tame. For if every definable thing consists of two elements and 'animal-tame'
forms a unity, and again out of this and the further differ-

[26] With the remainder of the chapter compare *An. Pr.* i, ch. 25,
where the treatment covers all syllogism.
[27] sc. genera and species.
[28] ii, ch. 5 and *An. Pr.* i, ch. 31.

entia man (or whatever else is the unity under construction) is constituted, then the elements we assume have necessarily been reached by division. Again, division is the only possible method of avoiding the omission of any ele- 35 ment of the essential nature. Thus, if the primary genus is assumed and we then take one of the lower divisions, the dividendum will not fall whole into this division: e. g. it is not all animal which is either whole-winged or split-winged but all winged animal, for it is winged animal to which this differentiation belongs. The primary differentia- 97ᵃ tion of animal is that within which all animal falls. The like is true of every other genus, whether outside animal or a subaltern genus of animal; e. g. the primary differentiation of bird is that within which falls every bird, of fish that within which falls every fish. So, if we proceed in this way, we can be sure that nothing has been omitted: by any other 5 method one is bound to omit something without knowing it.

To define and divide one need not know the whole of existence. Yet some hold it impossible to know the differentiae distinguishing each thing from every single other thing without knowing every single other thing; and one cannot, they say, know each thing without knowing its differentiae, since everything is identical with that from 10 which it does not differ, and other than that from which it differs. Now first of all this is a fallacy: not every differentia precludes identity, since many differentiae inhere in things specifically identical, though not in the substance of these nor essentially. Secondly, when one has taken one's differing pair of opposites and assumed that the two sides exhaust the genus, and that the subject one seeks to define is present in one or other of them, and one 15 has further verified its presence in one of them; then it does not matter whether or not one knows all the other subjects of which the differentiae are also predicated. For it is obvious that when by this process one reaches subjects incapable of further differentiation one will possess the for-

mula defining the substance. Moreover, to postulate that
20 the division exhausts the genus is not illegitimate if the
opposites exclude a middle; since if it is the differentia
of that genus, anything contained in the genus must lie on
one of the two sides.

In establishing a definition by division one should keep
three objects in view: (1) the admission only of elements
in the definable form, (2) the arrangement of these in the
25 right order, (3) the omission of no such elements. The first
is feasible because one can establish genus and differentia
through the topic of the genus,[29] just as one can conclude
the inherence of an accident through the topic of the accident.[30] The right order will be achieved if the right term
is assumed as primary, and this will be ensured if the term
30 selected is predicable of all the others but not all they of it;
since there must be one such term. Having assumed this
we at once proceed in the same way with the lower terms;
for our second term will be the first of the remainder, our
third the first of those which follow the second in a 'contiguous' series, since when the higher term is excluded, that
term of the remainder which is 'contiguous' to it will be
primary, and so on. Our procedure makes it clear that no
35 elements in the definable form have been omitted: we have
taken the differentia that comes first in the order of division, pointing out that animal e. g. is divisible exhaustively
into A and B, and that the subject accepts one of the two
as its predicate. Next we have taken the differentia of the
whole thus reached, and shown that the whole we finally
reach is not further divisible—i. e. that as soon as we have
taken the last differentia to form the concrete totality,
97ᵇ this totality admits of no division into species. For it is
clear that there is no superfluous addition, since all these
terms we have selected are elements in the definable form;
and nothing lacking, since any omission would have to be
a genus or a differentia. Now the primary term is a genus,

---

[29] Cf. Topics iv.
[30] Cf. Topics ii.

and this term taken in conjunction with its differentiae is a genus: moreover the differentiae are all included, because there is now no further differentia; if there were, the 5 final concrete would admit of division into species, which, we said, is not the case.

To resume our account of the right method of investigation: We must start by observing a set of similar—i. e. specifically identical—individuals, and consider what element they have in common. We must then apply the same process to another set of individuals which belong to one species and are generically but not specifically identical with the former set. When we have established what the com- 10 mon element is in all members of this second species, and likewise in members of further species, we should again consider whether the results established possess any identity, and persevere until we reach a single formula, since this will be the definition of the thing. But if we reach not one formula but two or more, evidently the *definiendum* cannot be one thing but must be more than one. I may illustrate my meaning as follows. If we were inquiring 15 what the essential nature of pride is, we should examine instances of proud men we know of to see what, as such, they have in common; e. g. if Alcibiades was proud, or Achilles and Ajax were proud, we should find, on inquiring what they all had in common, that it was intolerance of insult; it was this which drove Alcibiades to war, Achilles to wrath, and Ajax to suicide. We should next examine other 20 cases, Lysander, for example, or Socrates, and then if these have in common indifference alike to good and ill fortune, I take these two results and inquire what common element have equanimity amid the vicissitudes of life and impatience of dishonour. If they have none, there will be two genera of pride. Besides, every definition is always uni- 25 versal and commensurate: the physician does not prescribe what is healthy for a single eye, but for all eyes or for a determinate species of eye. It is also easier by this method to define the single species than the universal,

and that is why our procedure should be from the several
species to the universal genera—this for the further reason
30 too that equivocation is less readily detected in genera than
in infimae species. Indeed, perspicuity is essential in definitions, just as inferential movement is the minimum required in demonstrations; and we shall attain perspicuity if
we can collect separately the definition of each species
through the group of singulars which we have established
—e. g. the definition of similarity not unqualified but re-
35 stricted to colours and to figures; the definition of acute-
ness, but only of sound—and so proceed to the common
universal with a careful avoidance of equivocation. We
may add that if dialectical disputation must not employ
metaphors, clearly metaphors and metaphorical expressions
are precluded in definition: otherwise dialectic would involve metaphors.

14   In order to formulate the connexions we wish to prove
98ᵃ   we have to select our analyses and divisions. The
method of selection consists in laying down the common
genus of all our subjects of investigation—if e. g. they are
animals, we lay down what the properties are which inhere
in every animal. These established, we next lay down the
properties essentially connected with the first of the re-
5 maining classes—e. g. if this first subgenus is bird, the essential properties of every bird—and so on, always characterizing the proximate subgenus. This will clearly at once
enable us to say in virtue of what character the subgenera
10 —man, e. g., or horse—possess their properties. Let A be
animal, B the properties of every animal, C, D, E, various
species of animal. Then it is clear in virtue of what character B inheres in D—namely A—and that it inheres in C
and E for the same reason: and throughout the remaining
subgenera always the same rule applies.

We are now taking our examples from the traditional
class-names, but we must not confine ourselves to con-
15 sidering these. We must collect any other common char-

acter which we observe, and then consider with what species it is connected and what properties belong to it. For example, as the common properties of horned animals we collect the possession of a third stomach and only one row of teeth. Then since it is clear in virtue of what character they possess these attributes—namely their horned character—the next question is, to what species does the possession of horns attach?

Yet a further method of selection is by analogy: for we cannot find a single identical name to give to a squid's pounce, a fish's spine, and an animal's bone, although these too possess common properties as if there were a single osseous nature.

15 Some connexions that require proof are identical in that they possess an identical 'middle'—e. g. a whole group might be proved through 'reciprocal replacement' —and of these one class are identical in genus, namely all those whose difference consists in their concerning different subjects or in their mode of manifestation. This latter class may be exemplified by the questions as to the causes respectively of echo, of reflection, and of the rainbow: the connexions to be proved which these questions embody are identical generically, because all three are forms of repercussion; but specifically they are different.

Other connexions that require proof only differ in that the 'middle' of the one is subordinate to the 'middle' of the other. For example: Why does the Nile rise towards the end of the month? Because towards its close the month is more stormy. Why is the month more stormy towards its close? Because the moon is waning. Here the one cause is subordinate to the other.

16 The question might be raised with regard to cause and effect whether when the effect is present the cause also is present; whether, for instance, if a plant sheds its leaves or the moon is eclipsed, there is present also the

cause of the eclipse or of the fall of the leaves—the possession of broad leaves, let us say, in the latter case, in
98ᵇ the former the earth's interposition. For, one might argue,
if this cause is not present, these phenomena will have some
other cause: if it *is* present, its effect will be at once implied
by it—the eclipse by the earth's interposition, the fall of the
leaves by the possession of broad leaves; but if so, they will
be logically coincident and each capable of proof through
5 the other. Let me illustrate: Let A be deciduous character,
B the possession of broad leaves, C vine. Now if A inheres
in B (for every broad-leaved plant is deciduous), and B in
C (every vine possessing broad leaves); then A inheres in C
(every vine is deciduous), and the middle term B is the
10 cause. But we can also demonstrate that the vine has broad
leaves because it is deciduous. Thus, let D be broad-leaved,
E deciduous, F vine. Then E inheres in F (since every vine
is deciduous), and D in E (for every deciduous plant has
15 broad leaves): therefore every vine has broad leaves, and
the cause is its deciduous character. If,[31] however, they cannot each be the cause of the other (for cause is prior to effect, and the earth's interposition is the cause of the moon's
eclipse and not the eclipse of the interposition)—if, then,
demonstration through the cause is of the reasoned fact
20 and demonstration not through the cause is of the bare
fact, one who knows it through the eclipse knows the fact
of the earth's interposition but not the reasoned fact.
Moreover, that the eclipse is not the cause of the interposition, but the interposition of the eclipse, is obvious because the interposition is an element in the definition of
eclipse, which shows that the eclipse is known through the
interposition and not vice versa.

On the other hand, can a single effect have more than
25 one cause? One might argue as follows: if the same attribute is predicable of more than one thing as its primary
subject, let B be a primary subject in which A inheres, and
C another primary subject of A, and D and E primary sub-

---

[31] Here begins Aristotle's answer.

jects of *B* and *C* respectively. *A* will then inhere in *D* and *E*, and *B* will be the cause of *A*'s inherence in *D*, *C* of *A*'s inherence in *E*. The presence of the cause thus necessitates that of the effect, but the presence of the effect necessitates the presence not of all that may cause it but only of a 30 cause which yet need not be the whole cause. We may, however, suggest [32] that if the connexion to be proved is always universal and commensurate, not only will the cause be a whole but also the effect will be universal and commensurate. For instance, deciduous character will belong exclusively to a subject which is a whole, and, if this whole has species, universally and commensurately to those species—i. e. either to all species of plant or to a single 35 species. So in these universal and commensurate connexions the 'middle' and its effect must reciprocate, i. e. be convertible. Supposing, for example, that the reason why trees are deciduous is the coagulation of sap, then if a tree is deciduous, coagulation must be present, and if coagulation is present—not in any subject but in a tree— then that tree must be deciduous.

17 Can the cause of an identical effect be not identical 99ᵃ in every instance of the effect but different? Or is that impossible? Perhaps it is impossible if the effect is demonstrated as essential and not as inhering in virtue of a symptom or an accident—because the middle is then the definition of the major term—though possible if the demonstration is not essential. Now it is possible to consider the effect and its subject as an accidental conjunction, though 5 such conjunctions would not be regarded as connexions demanding scientific proof. But if they are accepted as such, the middle will correspond to the extremes, and be equivocal if they are equivocal, generically one if they are generically one. Take the question why proportionals alternate. The cause when they are lines, and when they are numbers, is both different and identical; different in so far as lines are 30

[32] Here begins Aristotle's answer.

lines and not numbers, identical as involving a given determinate increment. In all proportionals this is so. Again, the
cause of likeness between colour and colour is other than
that between figure and figure; for likeness here is equivocal,
meaning perhaps in the latter case equality of the ratios of
the sides and equality of the angles, in the case of colours
15 identity of the act of perceiving them, or something else of
the sort. Again, connexions requiring proof which are
identical by analogy have middles also analogous.

The truth is that cause, effect, and subject are reciprocally predicable in the following way. If the species are
taken severally, the effect is wider than the subject (e. g.
the possession of external angles equal to four right angles
20 is an attribute wider than triangle or square), but it is coextensive with the species taken collectively (in this instance with all figures whose external angles are equal to
four right angles). And the middle likewise reciproc.\..,
for the middle is a definition of the major; which is incidentally the reason why all the sciences are built up through
definition.

We may illustrate as follows. Deciduous is a universal
attribute of vine, and is at the same time of wider extent
than vine; and of fig, and is of wider extent than fig: but it
25 is not wider than but coextensive with the totality of the
species. Then if you take the middle which is proximate, it
is a definition of deciduous. I say that, because you will
first reach a middle [33] next the subject,[34] and a premiss asserting it of the whole subject, and after that a middle—
the coagulation of sap or something of the sort—proving the
connexion of the first middle with the major:[35] but it is
the coagulation of sap at the junction of leaf-stalk and stem
which defines deciduous.[36]

[33] sc. broad-leaved.
[34] Vine, fig, &c.
[35] Broad-leaved with deciduous.
[36] Aristotle contemplates four terms: (1) deciduous, (2) coagulation, (3) broad-leaved, (4) vine, fig, &c.
If we get the middle proximate to (1) it is a definition of (1). But

If an explanation in formal terms of the inter-relation of cause and effect is demanded, we shall offer the follow-30 ing. Let *A* be an attribute of all *B*, and *B* of every species of *D*, but so that both *A* and *B* are wider than their respective subjects. Then *B* will be a universal attribute of each species of *D* (since I call such an attribute universal even if it is not commensurate, and I call an attribute primary universal if it is commensurate,[37] not with each species severally but with their totality), and it extends beyond each of them taken separately. Thus, *B* is the cause of *A*'s inherence in the species of *D*: consequently *A* must 35 be of wider extent than *B*; otherwise why should *B* be the cause of *A*'s inherence in *D* any more than *A* the cause of *B*'s inherence in *D*? Now if *A* is an attribute of all the species of *E*, all the species of *E* will be united by possessing some common cause other than *B*: otherwise how shall we be able to say that *A* is predicable of all of which *E* is predicable, while *E* is not predicable of all of which *A* can be predicated? I mean how can there fail to be some special cause of *A*'s inherence in *E*, as there was of *A*'s inherence in all the species of *D*? Then are the species of *E*, too, united by possessing some common cause? This cause we must look for. Let us call it *C*.[38]

in investigating vines, figs, &c. according to the method of chapter 13, we shall first find a common character of them in broad-leaved, and, taking this as a middle, we shall prove that vine, fig, &c., qua broad-leaved, are deciduous. But this proof is not demonstration, because broad-leaved is not a definition of deciduous. So our next step will be to find a middle—coagulation—mediating the major premiss of this proof, and demonstrate that broad-leaved plants, qua liable to coagulation, are deciduous. This is strict demonstration, because coagulation defines deciduous.

[37] But cf. i, ch. 4, 73ᵇ 21–74ᵃ 3.
[38] The schema of Aristotle's argument in this paragraph is:

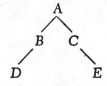

We conclude, then, that the same effect may have more than one cause, but not in subjects specifically identical. 5 For instance, the cause of longevity in quadrupeds is lack of bile, in birds a dry constitution—or certainly something different.

18 If immediate premises are not reached at once, and there is not merely one middle but several middles, i. e. several causes; is the cause of the property's inherence in 10 the several species the middle which is proximate to the primary universal,[39] or the middle which is proximate to the species? [40] Clearly the cause is that nearest to each species severally in which it is manifested, for that is the cause of the subject's falling under the universal. To illustrate formally: C is the cause of B's inherence in D; hence C is the cause of A's inherence in D, B of A's inherence in C, while the cause of A's inherence in B is B itself.

15 **19** As regards syllogism and demonstration, the definition of, and the conditions required to produce each of them, are now clear, and with that also the definition of, and the conditions required to produce, demonstrative knowledge, since it is the same as demonstration. As to the basic premises, how they become known and what is the developed state of knowledge of them is made clear by raising some preliminary problems.

20   We have already said [41] that scientific knowledge through demonstration is impossible unless a man knows the primary immediate premises. But there are questions which might be raised in respect of the apprehension of these immediate premises: one might not only ask whether it is of the same kind as the apprehension of the conclusions, but also whether there is or is not scientific knowledge of both; or scientific knowledge of the latter, and of the former a

[39] i. e. the property.
[40] the subject
[41] i, ch. 2.

different kind of knowledge; and, further, whether the developed states of knowledge are not innate but come 25 to be in us, or are innate but at first unnoticed. Now it is strange if we possess them from birth; for it means that we possess apprehensions more accurate than demonstration and fail to notice them. If on the other hand we acquire them and do not previously possess them, how could we apprehend and learn without a basis of pre-existent knowledge? For that is impossible, as we used to 30 find [42] in the case of demonstration. So it emerges that neither can we possess them from birth, nor can they come to be in us if we are without knowledge of them to the extent of having no such developed state at all. Therefore we must possess a capacity of some sort, but not such as to rank higher in accuracy than these developed states. And this at least is an obvious characteristic of all animals, for they possess a congenital discriminative capacity which 35 is called sense-perception. But though sense-perception is innate in all animals, in some the sense-impression comes to persist, in others it does not. So animals in which this persistence does not come to be have either no knowledge at all outside the act of perceiving, or no knowledge of objects of which no impression persists; animals in which it does come into being have perception and can continue to retain the sense-impression in the soul: and when such per- 100ª sistence is frequently repeated a further distinction at once arises between those which out of the persistence of such sense-impressions develop a power of systematizing them and those which do not. So out of sense-perception comes to be what we call memory, and out of frequently repeated memories of the same thing develops experience; for a num- 5 ber of memories constitute a single experience.[43] From experience again—i. e. from the universal now stabilized in its entirety within the soul, the one beside the many which

---

[42] i, ch. 1.
[43] Cf. *Met* A 980ª 28. *Met* A 1 should be compared with this chapter.

is a single identity within them all—originate the skill of
the craftsman and the knowledge of the man of science,
skill in the sphere of coming to be and science in the sphere
of being.

We conclude that these states of knowledge are neither
innate in a determinate form, nor developed from other
10 higher states of knowledge, but from sense-perception. It
is like a rout in battle stopped by first one man making a
stand and then another, until the original formation has
been restored. The soul is so constituted as to be capable
of this process.

Let us now restate the account given already, though
with insufficient clearness. When one of a number of
15 logically indiscriminable particulars has made a stand, the
earliest universal is present in the soul: for though the act
of sense-perception is of the particular, its content is uni-
100ᵇ versal—is man, for example, not the man Callias. A fresh
stand is made among these rudimentary universals, and
the process does not cease until the indivisible concepts,
the true universals, are established: e. g. such and such a
species of animal is a step towards the genus animal, which
by the same process is a step towards a further generalization.

Thus it is clear that we must get to know the primary
premisses by induction; for the method by which even
5 sense-perception implants the universal is inductive. Now
of the thinking states by which we grasp truth, some are
unfailingly true, others admit of error—opinion, for instance, and calculation, whereas scientific knowing and intuition are always true: further, no other kind of thought
except intuition is more accurate than scientific knowledge,
whereas primary premisses are more knowable than dem-
10 onstrations, and all scientific knowledge is discursive.
From these considerations it follows that there will be no
scientific knowledge of the primary premisses, and since except intuition nothing can be truer than scientific knowledge, it will be intuition that apprehends the primary

premisses—a result which also follows from the fact that demonstration cannot be the originative source of demonstration, nor, consequently, scientific knowledge of scientific knowledge. If, therefore, it is the only other kind of true thinking except scientific knowing, intuition will be 15 the originative source of scientific knowledge. And the originative source of science grasps the original basic premiss, while science as a whole is similarly related as originative source to the whole body of fact.

Physics

ⵎⵎⵎⵎⵎⵎⵎⵎⵎⵎⵎⵎⵎⵎⵎⵎⵎⵎⵎⵎⵎⵎ

INTRODUCTION

The three theoretic sciences are distinguished from each other by their subject-matters and their methods, but they use a common logic in the statement and proof of what is discovered concerning their subject-matters. Inquiry is planned and teaching is ordered in accordance with common analytical structures. Subject-matters and their principles, problems and their solutions are set forth or "demonstrated" by "teaching" what has been proved and on what assumptions, and by "learning" what must be found out and what problems must be solved. Since first principles cannot be demonstrated, all sciences—practical and poetic as well as theoretic—differ in their principles as well as in their methods and subject-matters, despite their use of a common analytic or arguments to state their distinctive problems and results. Physics is the science of moving things, mathematics the science of abstract quantity, and metaphysics the science of unqualified simple being. All arts and sciences originate in experience. Theoretic sciences derive their subject-matters and their principles, their facts and their causes from sense-perceptions, memories, and experience, but in different ways: physics by induction which separates forms from matter but not motion, to yield knowledge of motions and their causes; mathematics by abstraction of forms from motion as well as from matter, to yield knowledge of quantities and their measures, continuities, and limits; and metaphysics by intuition of simple forms, to yield knowledge of actualities as causes and to relate motions and separable forms to first movers and separate forms. Physics, mathematics, and metaphysics investigate different problems in different subject-matters, by different methods, according to different principles, but they originate in a common experience, use a common logic, and are interrelated by common principles.

The scope of physics, the science of motion, includes all motions and changes, inanimate and animate, elemental and cosmic, sensitive and intellectual. The greater part of Aristotle's extant works—ten treatises or collections of treatises—is concerned with physics in this broad sense: there are four books of physics of inanimate motions, four of biology, and two of psychology. In the *Physics*, which is the first of these ten books on natural change, Aristotle examines the principles, causes, and elements of motion, the basic concepts of physical science, and the kinds of motions it distinguishes. In the first book he reviews the positions taken by his predecessors in the science of motions and changes, and concludes from a dialectical consideration of the problems raised and the conclusions reached that nothing happens at random in nature, that there are three principles of coming-to-be, or change, or motion: a "matter" which persists unchanged, and two forms, an initial "privation" and a "form" acquired in the change. "Coming-to-be" or "change" may be used in a narrow sense limited to changes of substance or in a broad sense to include three kinds of motions as well, change of quality or "alteration," change of quantity or "increase and decrease," and change of place or "locomotion." In the physical science, principles are arrived at by induction and are stated in simple terms like "form," "matter," and "privation," rather than by propositions like the principle of contradiction in logic, "a proposition cannot be both true and false," or the principle of addition in mathematics, "equals added to equals yield equal results." The results of the dialectical examination of alternative approaches to the science of natural motions are judged, at the end of Book I of the *Physics*, to have been "sufficient to establish that there are principles and what they are and how they are." Aristotle announces, as he frequently does after such dialectical surveys of prior theories, that a "fresh start" must be taken, a departure from examination of opinions and a beginning of inquiry into problems.

The second book of the *Physics*, which is included in this collection of texts, makes that fresh start by turning to the consideration of causes of existent things and by distinguishing things that exist "by nature" from those that exist from other causes. Things that exist "by nature" include animals and their parts, plants and their parts, and simple bodies (earth, fire, air, water) and their "elements." These are substances, not natures. As substances they "have" natures or exist "by nature." Nature is an internal principle of motion and rest. Aristotle supplements the differentiation of the existent things which are the subject-matter of natural sciences from other nonphysical existent things, by differentiating the methods of the physicist from those of the mathematician and the metaphysician. All three kinds of science take their beginnings from physical bodies and their properties. The mathematician abstracts from matter and motion, and the differences between the objects of mathematics and those of physics may be exemplified in the difference between "curves" and "snub noses." The physicist is concerned with forms which are separable but do not exist apart from matter, whereas the metaphysician is concerned with the mode of existence of the separable. The differences between the objects of physics and those of metaphysics is summed up in the sentence, "Man is begotten by man and by the sun as well," for the being and coming-to-be of a man is explained by the generations of his progenitors and also by his place in an ongoing cosmos.

Causes, likewise, are distinguished in many ways, not only the four causes (material, formal, moving or efficient, and final) but the operation of causes (plurality of causes of the same thing, reciprocal causes, identity of causes of contrary results), and modes of causation (particular or generic, incidental attribute or its genus, separately or together, and all six modes either actual or potential). Changes and occurrences have other causes than nature: there are external as well as internal essential causes and also incidental or accidental causes, both internal and external. Art and intelligence are external principles of change in making (studied in the poetic or productive science) or of doing (studied in the practical sciences). There can be no sciences of incidental causes, of fortune and chance. Chance is a cause, similar to nature as a cause. It is observable in occurrences which take place without internal principle or external art (like a thrown tripod landing on its feet). Fortune is a cause, similar to art or intelligence as a cause. It is detectable in occurrences which might have been planned, but were not, for the purpose of achieving the results to which they happended to lead (like digging for potatoes and finding a treasure). The question "why" is answered in physics by the cause—the matter, the form, the moving cause, and that for the sake of which. Natural motions operate both for a purpose and in accordance with necessity. They are purposive since the sequences of natural processes are not at random. As in productive art or intelligent action, series of occurrences in nature have a completion, and the antecedent steps lead to and are for the sake of the end. The necessities of physics and of mathematics are hypothetical necessities as contrasted to the simple necessities of metaphysics. Simple necessity is the necessity that to be what it is, a thing must possess the properties that make it what it is. A mathematical hypothetical necessity takes its beginning from what is assumed and defined: if this is as posited, conclusions or consequences follow necessarily, but the reverse is not true: the conclusions may be established on other grounds. A physical hypothetical necessity takes its beginning from the product: if it exists, the steps antecedent to its production must have been completed, but the reverse is not true: after some antecedent steps the process may be interrupted without producing the product. Having set forth the principles, causes, and kinds of motions, Aristotle proceeds in the third and fourth books of the *Physics* to determine the nature of motion and to examine fundamental concepts, like infinity, place, void, and time, associated with motion. Inquiry into motions and changes in the last four books runs through motion and rest, the analysis of concepts related to succession, contiguity, and continuity, the investigation of mover and moved, and the demonstration of a First Mover.

The *Physics* sets forth the principles, causes, and elements of natural motion and lays down the grounds and structure of the physical sciences. It is followed by three treatises which investigate kinds of physical change and their principles and provide bases for the transition to the study of organic, or biological, physical change. In *On the Heavens* Aristotle turns to the study of the local motions of bodies. He divides his inquiry, as like inquiries have been divided by later theorists, into two parts, the locomotions of simple bodies, or elementary motions, and the locomotions of heavenly bodies, or cosmological motions. In *On Generation and Corruption* he investigates questions of generation and corruption, coming-to-be and passing-away, of simple bodies and of composite bodies. He considers and refutes the doctrine of simple indivisible bodies or atoms and void interspaces or pores, and the doctrine that simple bodies or elements are eternal and do not come to be or pass away. Earth, air, fire, and water are not "elements" of bodies but simple bodies. The elements of bodies are primary matter and four elementary qualities—hot, cold, dry or solid, moist or fluid—which constitute simple bodies. Simple bodies undergo reciprocal transformations by the interchange of elementary qualities. Composite bodies come to be and pass away by combination and separation of simple bodies. Finally in the *Meteorology* the interplay of natural simple bodies and of their mixtures and compounds is investigated, the causes of comets, rains, snow, dew, earthquakes, thunder, lightning, storms, and rainbows are sought, and the processes observed in mixed bodies like water, metals, clays, oils, and wines are examined. The final book of the *Meteorology* has been considered a starting point of the science of chemistry, but in the structure of Aristotle's sciences of natural motions it provides a transition from the motions of inorganic bodies to the investigation of the motions of organic bodies by differentiating (1) simple bodies or elements, (2) "homogeneous bodies" (like the metals among inanimate things, or the wood or bark of plants, or the tissues and bones of animals), which possess qualities different from the elements of which they are compounded, and (3) "heterogeneous bodies" (like organs and parts, hands and faces), which possess functions and purposes distinct from those of the homogeneous bodies of which they are compounded.

PHYSICA

CONTENTS

BOOK II

Physica[1]

Physics

Translated by R. P. Hardie and R. K. Gaye

⊓⊔⊓⊔

BOOK II

192ᵇ 1   Of things that exist, some exist by nature, some from
other causes. 'By nature' the animals and their parts
10 exist, and the plants and the simple bodies (earth, fire, air,
water)—for we say that these and the like exist 'by nature'.

All the things mentioned present a feature in which
they differ from things which are *not* constituted by nature.
15 Each of them has *within itself* a principle of motion and
of stationariness (in respect of place, or of growth and
decrease, or by way of alteration). On the other hand, a
bed and a coat and anything else of that sort, *qua* receiving
these designations—i. e. in so far as they are products of art
—have no innate impulse to change. But in so far as they
20 happen to be composed of stone or of earth or of a mixture of the two, they *do* have such an impulse, and just to
that extent—which seems to indicate that *nature is a source*

---

[1] The present treatise, usually called the *Physics*, deals with natural
body in general: the special kinds are discussed in Aristotle's other
physical works, the *De Caelo*, &c. The first book is concerned with
the elements of a natural body (matter and form): the second mainly
with the different types of cause studied by the physicist. Books III–
VII deal with movement, and the notions implied in it. The subject
of VIII is the prime mover, which, though not itself a natural body, is
the cause of movement in natural bodies.

or cause of being moved and of being at rest in that to
which it belongs primarily, in virtue of itself and not in
virtue of a concomitant attribute.

I say 'not in virtue of a concomitant attribute', because
(for instance) a man who is a doctor might cure himself.
Nevertheless it is not in so far as he is a patient that he 25
possesses the art of medicine: it merely has happened that
the same man is doctor and patient—and that is why these
attributes are not always found together. So it is with all
other artificial products. None of them has in itself the
source of its own production. But while in some cases (for
instance houses and the other products of manual labour)
that principle is in something else external to the thing, 30
in others—those which may cause a change in themselves
in virtue of a concomitant attribute—it lies in the things
themselves (but not in virtue of what they are).

'Nature' then is what has been stated. Things 'have a
nature' which have a principle of this kind. Each of them
is a substance; for it is a subject, and nature always implies
a subject in which it inheres.

The term 'according to nature' is applied to all these 35
things and also to the attributes which belong to them in
virtue of what they are, for instance the property of fire
to be carried upwards—which is not a 'nature' nor 'has a
nature' but is 'by nature' or 'according to nature'.

What nature is, then, and the meaning of the terms 'by
nature' and 'according to nature', has been stated. That 193ᵃ
nature exists, it would be absurd to try to prove; for it is
obvious that there are many things of this kind, and to
prove what is obvious by what is not is the mark of a man 5
who is unable to distinguish what is self-evident from what
is not. (This state of mind is clearly possible. A man blind
from birth might reason about colours. Presumably therefore such persons must be talking about words without any
thought to correspond.)

Some identify the nature or substance of a natural object with that immediate constituent of it which taken by

10 itself is without arrangement, e. g. the wood is the 'nature'
of the bed, and the bronze the 'nature' of the statue.

As an indication of this Antiphon points out that if you
planted a bed and the rotting wood acquired the power of
sending up a shoot, it would not be a bed that would
come up, but wood—which shows that the arrangement in
15 accordance with the rules of the art is merely an incidental
attribute, whereas the real nature is the other, which,
further, persists continuously through the process of making.

But if the material of each of these objects has itself the
same relation to something else, say bronze (or gold) to
water, bones (or wood) to earth and so on, that (they say)
20 would be their nature and essence. Consequently some assert earth, others fire or air or water or some or all of these,
to be the nature of the things that are. For whatever any
one of them supposed to have this character—whether one
thing or more than one thing—this or these he declared to
25 be the whole of substance, all else being its affections,
states, or dispositions. Every such thing they held to be
eternal (for it could not pass into anything else), but other
things to come into being and cease to be times without
number.

This then is one account of 'nature', namely that it is
the immediate material substratum of things which have in
themselves a principle of motion or change.

Another account is that 'nature' is the shape or form
30 which is specified in the definition of the thing.

For the word 'nature' is applied to what is according to
nature and the natural in the same way as 'art' is applied
to what is artistic or a work of art. We should not say in
the latter case that there is anything artistic about a thing,
35 if it is a bed only potentially, not yet having the form of a
bed; nor should we call it a work of art. The same is true of
natural compounds. What is potentially flesh or bone has
not yet its own 'nature', and does not exist 'by nature',
193ᵇ until it receives the form specified in the definition, which

we name in defining what flesh or bone is. Thus in the second sense of 'nature' it would be the shape or form (not separable except in statement) of things which have in 5 themselves a source of motion. (The combination of the two, e. g. man, is not 'nature' but 'by nature' or 'natural'.)

The form indeed is 'nature' rather than the matter; for a thing is more properly said to be what it is when it has attained to fulfilment than when it exists potentially. Again man is born from man, but not bed from bed. That is why people say that the figure is not the nature of a bed, 10 but the wood is—if the bed sprouted not a bed but wood would come up. But even if the figure is art, then on the same principle the shape of man is his nature. For man is born from man.

We also speak of a thing's nature as being exhibited in the process of growth by which its nature is attained. The 'nature' in this sense is not like 'doctoring', which leads not 15 to the art of doctoring but to health. Doctoring must start from the art, not lead to it. But it is not in this way that nature (in the one sense) is related to nature (in the other). What grows qua growing grows from something into something. Into what then does it grow? Not into that from which it arose but into that to which it tends. The shape then is nature.

'Shape' and 'nature', it should be added, are used in two senses. For the privation too is in a way form. But whether 20 in unqualified coming to be there is privation, i. e. a contrary to what comes to be, we must consider later.[2]

2   We have distinguished, then, the different ways in which the term 'nature' is used.

The next point to consider is how the mathematician differs from the physicist. Obviously physical bodies contain surfaces and volumes, lines and points, and these are the subject-matter of mathematics.

Further, is astronomy different from physics or a de- 25

[2] *De Gen. et Corr.* i. 3.

partment of it? It seems absurd that the physicist should be
supposed to know the nature of sun or moon, but not to
know any of their essential attributes, particularly as the
30 writers on physics obviously do discuss their shape also
and whether the earth and the world are spherical or not.

Now the mathematician, though he too treats of these
things, nevertheless does not treat of them as the limits of
a physical body; nor does he consider the attributes indicated as the attributes of such bodies. That is why he
separates them; for in thought they are separable from
motion, and it makes no difference, nor does any falsity result, if they are separated. The holders of the theory of
35 Forms do the same, though they are not aware of it; for
they separate the objects of physics, which are less separable
than those of mathematics. This becomes plain if one tries
194ᵃ to state in each of the two cases the definitions of the things
and of their attributes. 'Odd' and 'even', 'straight' and
'curved', and likewise 'number', 'line', and 'figure', do not
5 involve motion; not so 'flesh' and 'bone' and 'man'—these
are defined like 'snub nose', not like 'curved'.

Similar evidence is supplied by the more physical of the
branches of mathematics, such as optics, harmonics, and
astronomy. These are in a way the converse of geometry.
While geometry investigates physical lines but not qua
10 physical, optics investigates mathematical lines, but qua
physical, not qua mathematical.

Since 'nature' has two senses, the form and the matter,
we must investigate its objects as we would the essence
of snubness. That is, such things are neither independent
of matter nor can be defined in terms of matter only. Here
15 too indeed one might raise a difficulty. Since there are two
natures, with which is the physicist concerned? Or should
he investigate the combination of the two? But if the combination of the two, then also each severally. Does it belong
then to the same or to different sciences to know each
severally?

If we look at the ancients, physics would seem to be concerned with the *matter*. (It was only very slightly that Empedocles and Democritus touched on the forms and the es- 20
sence.)

But if on the other hand art imitates nature, and it is the
part of the same discipline to know the form and the matter
up to a point (e. g. the doctor has a knowledge of health
and also of bile and phlegm, in which health is realized, and
the builder both of the form of the house and of the
matter, namely that it is bricks and beams, and so forth): 25
if this is so, it would be the part of physics also to know
nature in both its senses.

Again, 'that for the sake of which', or the end, belongs
to the same department of knowledge as the means. But
the nature is the end or 'that for the sake of which'. For if
a thing undergoes a continuous change and there is a stage
which is last, this stage is the end or 'that for the sake of
which'. (That is why the poet was carried away into making 30
an absurd statement when he said 'he has the end [3] for the
sake of which he was born'. For not every stage that is last
claims to be an end, but only that which is best.)

For the arts make their material (some simply 'make' it,
others make it serviceable), and we use everything as if it
was there for our sake. (We also are in a sense an end. 'That 35
for the sake of which' has two senses: the distinction is
made in our work *On Philosophy*.[4]) The arts, therefore,
which govern the matter and have knowledge are two, **194ᵇ**
namely the art which uses the product and the art which
directs the production of it. That is why the using art
also is in a sense directive; but it differs in that it knows the
form, whereas the art which is directive as being concerned
with production knows the matter. For the helmsman 5
knows and prescribes what sort of form a helm should have,
the other from what wood it should be made and by means

---

[3] i. e. death.
[4] i. e. in the dialogue *De Philosophia*.

of what operations. In the products of art, however, we make the material with a view to the function, whereas in the products of nature the matter is there all along.

Again, matter is a relative term: to each form there cor-
10 responds a special matter. How far then must the physicist know the form or essence? Up to a point, perhaps, as the doctor must know sinew or the smith bronze (i. e. until he understands the purpose of each): and the physicist is concerned only with things whose forms are separable indeed, but do not exist apart from matter. Man is begotten by man and by the sun as well. The mode of existence and
15 essence of the separable it is the business of the primary type of philosophy to define.

3   Now that we have established these distinctions, we must proceed to consider causes, their character and number. Knowledge is the object of our inquiry, and men do
20 not think they know a thing till they have grasped the 'why' of it (which is to grasp its primary cause). So clearly we too must do this as regards both coming to be and passing away and every kind of physical change, in order that, knowing their principles, we may try to refer to these principles each of our problems.

In one sense, then, (1) that out of which a thing comes to be and which persists, is called 'cause', e. g. the bronze
25 of the statue, the silver of the bowl, and the genera of which the bronze and the silver are species.

In another sense (2) the form or the archetype, i. e. the statement of the essence, and its genera, are called 'causes' (e. g. of the octave the relation of 2 : 1, and generally number), and the parts in the definition.

Again (3) the primary source of the change or coming to rest; e. g. the man who gave advice is a cause, the father
30 is cause of the child, and generally what makes of what is made and what causes change of what is changed.

Again (4) in the sense of end or 'that for the sake of which' a thing is done, e. g. health is the cause of walking about. ('Why is he walking about?' we say, 'To be healthy', and, having said that, we think we have assigned the cause.) The same is true also of all the intermediate steps which are 35 brought about through the action of something else as means towards the end, e. g. reduction of flesh, purging, drugs, or surgical instruments are means towards health. All these things are 'for the sake of' the end, though they 195ᵃ differ from one another in that some are activities, others instruments.

This then perhaps exhausts the number of ways in which the term 'cause' is used.

As the word has several senses, it follows that there are several causes of the same thing (not merely in virtue of a concomitant attribute), e. g. both the art of the sculptor and the bronze are causes of the statue. These are causes 5 of the statue qua statue, not in virtue of anything else that it may be—only not in the same way; the one being the material cause, the other the cause whence the motion comes. Some things cause each other reciprocally, e. g. hard work causes fitness and vice versa, but again not in the same way, but the one as end, the other as the origin of change. 10 Further the same thing is the cause of contrary results. For that which by its presence brings about one result is sometimes blamed for bringing about the contrary by its absence. Thus we ascribe the wreck of a ship to the absence of the pilot whose presence was the cause of its safety.

All the causes now mentioned fall into four familiar divisions. The letters are the causes of syllables, the material 15 of artificial products, fire, &c., of bodies, the parts of the whole, and the premisses of the conclusion, in the sense of 'that from which'. Of these pairs the one set are causes in the sense of substratum, e. g. the parts, the other set in 20 the sense of essence—the whole and the combination and the form. But the seed and the doctor and the adviser, and generally the maker, are all sources whence the change or stationariness originates, while the others are causes in the sense of the end or the good of the rest; for 'that for the

sake of which' means what is best and the end of the things
25 that lead up to it. (Whether we say the 'good itself' or the
'apparent good' makes no difference.)

Such then is the number and nature of the kinds of
cause.

Now the modes of causation are many, though when
brought under heads they too can be reduced in number.
30 For 'cause' is used in many senses and even within the same
kind one may be prior to another (e. g. the doctor and the
expert are causes of health, the relation 2 : 1 and number of
the octave), and always what is inclusive to what is particular. Another mode of causation is the incidental and its
genera, e. g. in one way 'Polyclitus', in another 'sculptor'
35 is the cause of a statue, because 'being Polyclitus' and
'sculptor' are incidentally conjoined. Also the classes in
which the incidental attribute is included; thus 'a man'
195ᵇ could be said to be the cause of a statue or, generally, 'a
living creature'. An incidental attribute too may be more or
less remote, e. g. suppose that 'a pale man' or 'a musical
man' were said to be the cause of the statue.

All causes, both proper and incidental, may be spoken of
5 either as potential or as actual; e. g. the cause of a house
being built is either 'house-builder' or 'house-builder building'.

Similar distinctions can be made in the things of which
the causes are causes, e. g. of 'this statue' or of 'statue' or of
'image' generally, of 'this bronze' or of 'bronze' or of 'ma-
10 terial' generally. So too with the incidental attributes.
Again we may use a complex expression for either and say,
e. g., neither 'Polyclitus' nor 'sculptor' but 'Polyclitus,
sculptor'.

All these various uses, however, come to six in number,
under each of which again the usage is twofold. Cause
15 means either what is particular or a genus, or an incidental
attribute or a genus of that, and these either as a complex or
each by itself; and all six either as actual or as potential.
The difference is this much, that causes which are actually

at work and particular exist and cease to exist simultaneously with their effect, e.g. this healing person with this
being-healed person and that housebuilding man with that
being-built house; but this is not always true of potential 20
causes—the house and the housebuilder do not pass away
simultaneously.

In investigating the cause of each thing it is always necessary to seek what is most precise (as also in other
things): thus man builds because he is a builder, and a
builder builds in virtue of his art of building. This last
cause then is prior: and so generally.

Further, generic effects should be assigned to generic 25
causes, particular effects to particular causes, e.g. statue to
sculptor, this statue to this sculptor; and powers are relative to possible effects, actually operating causes to things
which are actually being effected.

This must suffice for our account of the number of
causes and the modes of causation.   30

4   But fortune also and chance are reckoned among
causes: many things are said both to be and to come to be
as a result of fortune and chance. We must inquire 15
therefore in what manner fortune and chance are present
among the causes enumerated, and whether they are the
same or different, and generally what fortune and chance
are.   35

Some people [5] even question whether they are real or
not. They say that nothing happens by fortune, but that
everything which we ascribe to fortune or chance has 196ᵃ
some definite cause, e.g. coming 'by fortune' into the
market and finding there a man whom one wanted but
did not expect to meet is due to one's wish to go and buy
in the market. Similarly in other cases of fortune it is 5
always possible, they maintain, to find something which
is the cause; but not fortune, for if fortune were real, it
would seem strange indeed, and the question might be

[5] Apparently Democritus is meant.

raised, why on earth none of the wise men of old in speaking of the causes of generation and decay took account of
10 fortune; whence it would seem that they too did not believe that anything is by fortune. But there is a further
circumstance that is surprising. Many things both come
to be and are by fortune and chance, and although all
know that each of them can be ascribed to some cause (as
15 the old argument said which denied fortune), nevertheless they speak of some of these things as happening by
fortune and others not. For this reason also they ought to
have at least referred to the matter in some way or other.

Certainly the early physicists found no place for fortune
among the causes which they recognized—love, strife,
mind, fire, or the like. This is strange, whether they supposed that there is no such thing as fortune or whether
20 they thought there is but omitted to mention it—and
that too when they sometimes used it, as Empedocles does
when he says that the air is not always separated into the
highest region, but 'fortuitously'. At any rate he says in his
cosmogony that 'it happened to run that way at that time,
but it often ran otherwise.' He tells us also that most of
the parts of animals came to be by fortune.

There are some [6] too who ascribe this heavenly sphere
25 and all the worlds to chance. They say that the vortex
arose by chance, i.e. the motion that separated and arranged in its present order all that exists. This statement
might well cause surprise. For they are asserting that
fortune is not responsible for the existence or generation
of animals and plants, nature or mind or something of the
30 kinds being the cause of them (for it is not any fortuitous
thing that comes from a given seed but an olive from one
kind and a man from another); and yet at the same time
they assert that the heavenly sphere and the divinest of
35 visible things arose by chance, having no such cause as is
assigned to animals and plants. Yet if this is so, it is a fact
which deserves to be dwelt upon, and something might

[6] Apparently Democritus is meant.

well have been said about it. For besides the other ab- 196ᵛ
surdities of the statement, it is the more absurd that people should make it when they see nothing coming to be
by chance in the heavens, but much happening fortuitously among the things which as they say are not due to
fortune; whereas we should have expected exactly the
opposite.

Others [7] there are who, indeed, believe that fortune is a 5
cause, but that it is inscrutable to human intelligence, as
being a divine thing and full of mystery.

Thus we must inquire what fortune and chance are,
whether they are the same or different, and how they fit
into our division of causes.

5   First then we observe that some things always come 10
to pass in the same way, and others for the most part. It
is clearly of neither of these that fortune is said to be the
cause, nor can the 'effect of fortune' be identified with
any of the things that come to pass by necessity and always, or for the most part. But as there is a third class of
events besides these two—events which all say are 'by
fortune'—it is plain that there is such a thing as fortune
and chance; for we know that things of this kind are due
to fortune and that things due to fortune are of this kind.

But, secondly, some events are for the sake of something, others not. Again, some of the former class are in
accordance with deliberate intention, others not, but both
are in the class of things which are for the sake of some- 20
thing. Hence it is clear that even among the things which
are outside the necessary and the normal, there are some
in connexion with which the phrase 'for the sake of something' is applicable. (Events that are for the sake of something' include whatever may be done as a result of
thought or of nature.) Things of this kind, then, when
they come to pass incidentally are said to be 'by fortune'.
For just as a thing is something either in virtue of itself 25

[7] Democritus.

or incidentally, so may it be a cause. For instance, the housebuilding faculty is in virtue of itself the cause of a house, whereas the pale or the musical [8] is the incidental cause. That which is *per se* cause of the effect is determinate, but the incidental cause is indeterminable, for the possible attributes of an individual are innumerable. To
30 resume then; when a thing of this kind comes to pass among events which are for the sake of something, it is said to be by chance or fortuitous. (The distinction between the two must be made later [9]—for the present it is sufficient if it is plain that both are in the sphere of things done for the sake of something.)

Example: A man is engaged in collecting subscriptions for a feast. He would have gone to such and such a place for the purpose of getting the money, if he had known.
35 He actually went there for another purpose, and it was only incidentally that he got his money by going there; and this was not due to the fact that he went there as a
197ᵃ rule or necessarily, nor is the end effected (getting the money) a cause present in himself—it belongs to the class of things that are intentional and the result of intelligent deliberation. It is when these conditions are satisfied that the man is said to have gone 'by fortune'. If he had gone of deliberate purpose and for the sake of this—if he always or normally went there when he was collecting payments—he would not be said to have gone 'by fortune'.

It is clear then that fortune is an incidental cause in the
5 sphere of those actions for the sake of something which involve purpose. Intelligent reflection, then, and fortune are in the same sphere, for purpose implies intelligent reflection.

It is necessary, no doubt, that the causes of what comes to pass by fortune be indefinite and that is why fortune is supposed to belong to the class of the indefinite and to be
10 inscrutable to man, and why it might be thought that, in

---

[8] Incidental attributes of the housebuilder.
[9] In ch. 6.

a way, nothing occurs by fortune. For all these statements
are correct, because they are well grounded. Things do, in
a way, occur by fortune, for they occur incidentally and
fortune is an *incidental cause*. But strictly it is not the
cause—without qualification—of anything; for instance, a
housebuilder is the cause of a house; incidentally, a flute-
player may be so.

And the causes of the man's coming and getting the
money (when he did not come for the sake of that) are 15
innumerable. He may have wished to see somebody or
been following somebody or avoiding somebody, or may
have gone to see a spectacle. Thus to say that fortune is a
thing contrary to rule is correct. For 'rule' applies to what
is always true or true for the most part, whereas fortune
belongs to a third type of event. Hence, to conclude,
since causes of this kind are indefinite, fortune too is in- 20
definite. (Yet in some cases one might raise the question
whether any incidental fact might be the cause of the
fortunate occurrence, e.g. of health the fresh air or the sun's
heat may be the cause, but having had one's hair cut
cannot; for some incidental causes are more relevant to
the effect than others.)

Fortune is called 'good' when the result is good, 'evil' 25
when it is evil. The terms 'good fortune' and 'ill fortune'
are used when either result is of considerable magnitude.
Thus one who comes within an ace of some great evil or
great good is said to be fortunate or unfortunate. The
mind affirms the presence of the attribute, ignoring the
hair's breadth of difference. Further, it is with reason that 30
good fortune is regarded as unstable; for chance is unstable, as none of the things which result from it can be
invariable or normal.

Both are then, as I have said, incidental causes—both
fortune and chance—in the sphere of things which are
capable of coming to pass not necessarily, nor normally,
and with reference to such of these as might come to pass 35
for the sake of something.

6   They differ in that 'chance' is the wider term. Every result of fortune is from what is by chance, but not everything that is from what is by chance is from fortune.

197ᵇ   Fortune and what results from fortune are appropriate to agents that are capable of good fortune and of moral action generally. Therefore necessarily fortune is in the sphere of moral actions. This is indicated by the fact that good fortune is thought to be the same, or nearly the same, as happiness, and happiness to be a kind of moral action,
5 since it is well-doing. Hence what is not capable of moral action cannot do anything by fortune Thus an inanimate thing or a lower animal or a child cannot do anything by fortune, because it is incapable of deliberate intention; nor can 'good fortune' or 'ill fortune' be ascribed to them, except metaphorically, as Protarchus for example, said that the stones of which altars are made are fortunate be-
10 cause they are held in honour, while their fellows are trodden under foot. Even these things, however, can in a way be affected by fortune, when one who is dealing with them does something to them by fortune, but not otherwise.

Chance on the other hand is found both in the lower
15 animals and in many inanimate objects. We say, for example, that the horse came 'by chance', because, though his coming saved him, he did not come for the sake of safety. Again, the tripod fell 'of itself', because, though when it fell it stood on its feet so as to serve for a seat, it did not fall for the sake of that.

Hence it is clear that events which (1) belong to the general class of things that may come to pass for the sake of something, (2) do not come to pass for the sake of what actually results, and (3) have an external cause,
20 may be described by the phrase 'from chance'. These 'chance' events are said to be 'from fortune' if they have the further characteristics of being the objects of deliberate intention and due to agents capable of that mode of action. This is indicated by the phrase 'in vain', which is

used when A, which is for the sake of B, does not result
in B. For instance, taking a walk is for the sake of evacua-
tion of the bowels; if this does not follow after walking,
we say that we have walked 'in vain' and that the walking
was 'vain'. This implies that what is naturally the means 25
to an end is 'in vain', when it does not effect the end
towards which it was the natural means—for it would be
absurd for a man to say that he had bathed in vain because the sun was not eclipsed, since the one was not
done with a view to the other. Thus chance is even according to its derivation the case in which the thing itself
happens in vain. The stone that struck the man did not 30
fall for the purpose of striking him; therefore it fell by
chance, because it might have fallen by the action of an
agent and for the purpose of striking. The difference between chance and what results by fortune is greatest in
things that come to be by nature; for when anything
comes to be contrary to nature, we do not say that it
came to be by fortune, but by chance. Yet strictly this too
is different from chance proper; for the cause of the latter 35
is external, that of the former internal.

We have now explained what fortune is and what
chance is, and in what they differ from each other. Both 198ª
belong to the mode of causation 'source of change', for
either some natural or some intelligent agent is always the
cause; but in this sort of causation the number of possible
causes is infinite.

Chance and fortune are causes of effects which, though
they might result from intelligence or nature, have in 5
fact been caused by something *incidentally*. Now since
nothing which is incidental is prior to what is *per se*, it is
clear that no incidental cause can be prior to a cause *per
se*. Chance and fortune, therefore, are posterior to intelligence and nature. Hence, however true it may be that the 10
heavens are due to chance, it will still be true that intelligence and nature will be prior causes of this All and
of many things in it besides.

7   It is clear then that there are causes, and that the
number of them is what we have stated. The number
15 is the same as that of the things comprehended under the
question 'why'. The 'why' is referred ultimately either (1),
in things which do not involve motion, e. g. in mathematics,
to the 'what' (to the definition of 'straight line' or 'commensurable', &c.), or (2) to what initiated a motion, e. g.
'why did they go to war?—because there had been a raid';
20 or (3) we are inquiring 'for the sake of what?'—'that they
may rule'; or (4), in the case of things that come into being,
we are looking for the matter. The causes, therefore, are
these and so many in number.

Now, the causes being four, it is the business of the
physicist to know about them all, and if he refers his problems back to all of them, he will assign the 'why' in the way
25 proper to his science—the matter, the form, the mover,
'that for the sake of which'. The last three often coincide;
for the 'what' and 'that for the sake of which' are one,
while the primary source of motion is the same in species as
these (for man generates man), and so too, in general, are
all things which cause movement by being themselves
moved; and such as are not of this kind are no longer inside
the province of physics, for they cause motion not by possessing motion or a source of motion in themselves, but
being themselves incapable of motion. Hence there are
30 three branches of study, one of things which are incapable
of motion, the second of things in motion, but indestruct-
ible, the third of destructible things.

The question 'why', then, is answered by reference to the
matter, to the form, and to the primary moving cause. For
in respect of coming to be it is mostly in this last way that
causes are investigated—'what comes to be after what? what
was the primary agent or patient?' and so at each step of the
series.

35   Now the principles which cause motion in a physical way
are two, of which one is not physical, as it has no principle
198ᵇ of motion in itself. Of this kind is whatever causes move-

ment, not being itself moved, such as (1) that which is completely unchangeable, the primary reality, and (2) the essence of that which is coming to be, i. e. the form; for this is the end or 'that for the sake of which'. Hence since nature is for the sake of something, we must know this cause also. We must explain the 'why' in all the senses of the 5 term, namely, (1) that from this that will necessarily result ('from this' either without qualification or in most cases); (2) that 'this must be so if that is to be so' (as the conclusion presupposes the premises); (3) that this was the essence of the thing; and (4) because it is better thus (not without qualification, but with reference to the essential nature in each case).

8 We must explain then (1) that Nature belongs to the class of causes which act for the sake of something; (2) 10 about the necessary and its place in physical problems, for all writers ascribe things to this cause, arguing that since the hot and the cold, &c., are of such and such a kind, therefore certain things *necessarily* are and come to be—and if they mention any other cause (one [10] his 'friendship and strife', 15 another [11] his 'mind'), it is only to touch on it, and then good-bye to it.

A difficulty presents itself: why should not nature work, not for the sake of something, nor because it is better so, but just as the sky rains, not in order to make the corn grow, but of necessity? What is drawn up must cool, and what has been cooled must become water and descend, the result 20 of this being that the corn grows. Similarly if a man's crop is spoiled on the threshing-floor, the rain did not fall for the sake of this—in order that the crop might be spoiled—but that result just followed. Why then should it not be the same with the parts in nature, e. g. that our teeth should come up *of necessity*—the front teeth sharp, fitted for tearing, the molars broad and useful for grinding down the food 25

[10] Empedocles.
[11] Anaxagoras.

—since they did not arise for this end, but it was merely a coincident result; and so with all other parts in which we suppose that there is purpose? Wherever then all the parts came about just what they would have been if they had
30 come to be for an end, such things survived, being organized spontaneously in a fitting way; whereas those which grew otherwise perished and continue to perish, as Empedocles says his 'man-faced ox-progeny' did.

Such are the arguments (and others of the kind) which may cause difficulty on this point. Yet it is impossible that this should be the true view. For teeth and all other natural
35 things either invariably or normally come about in a given way; but of not one of the results of chance or spontaneity is this true. We do not ascribe to chance or mere coincidence
199ᵃ the frequency of rain in winter, but frequent rain in summer we do; nor heat in the dog-days, but only if we have it in winter. If then, it is agreed that things are either the result of coincidence or for an end, and these cannot be the result of coincidence or spontaneity, it follows that they
5 must be for an end; and that such things are all due to nature even the champions of the theory which is before us would agree. Therefore action for an end is present in things which come to be and are by nature.

Further, where a series has a completion, all the preceding steps are for the sake of that. Now surely as in intelli-
10 gent action, so in nature; and as in nature, so it is in each action, if nothing interferes. Now intelligent action is for the sake of an end; therefore the nature of things also is so. Thus if a house, e. g., had been a thing made by nature, it would have been made in the same way as it is now by art; and if things made by nature were made also by art, they
15 would come to be in the same way as by nature. Each step then in the series is for the sake of the next; and generally art partly completes what nature cannot bring to a finish, and partly imitates her. If, therefore, artificial products are for the sake of an end, so clearly also are natural products.

The relation of the later to the earlier terms of the series is the same in both.

This is most obvious in the animals other than man: they 20 make things neither by art nor after inquiry or deliberation. Wherefore people discuss whether it is by intelligence or by some other faculty that these creatures work,—spiders, ants, and the like. By gradual advance in this direction we come to see clearly that in plants too that is produced which is 25 conducive to the end—leaves, e. g. grow to provide shade for the fruit. If then it is both by nature and for an end that the swallow makes its nest and the spider its web, and plants grow leaves for the sake of the fruit and send their roots down (not up) for the sake of nourishment, it is plain that this kind of cause is operative in things which come to be 30 and are by nature. And since 'nature' means two things, the matter and the form, of which the latter is the end, and since all the rest is for the sake of the end, the form must be the cause in the sense of 'that for the sake of which'.

Now mistakes come to pass even in the operations of art: the grammarian makes a mistake in writing and the doctor pours out the wrong dose. Hence clearly mistakes are pos- 35 sible in the operations of nature also. If then in art there 199ᵇ are cases in which what is rightly produced serves a purpose, and if where mistakes occur there was a purpose in what was attempted, only it was not attained, so must it be also in natural products, and monstrosities will be failures in the purposive effort. Thus in the original combinations the 'ox- 5 progeny' if they failed to reach a determinate end must have arisen through the corruption of some principle corresponding to what is now the seed.

Further, seed must have come into being first, and not straightway the animals: the words 'whole-natured first . . .'[12] must have meant seed.

Again, in plants too we find the relation of means to end, though the degree of organization is less. Were there then 10

[12] Empedocles, Fr. 62. 4.

in plants also 'olive-headed vine-progeny', like the 'man-headed ox-progeny', or not? An absurd suggestion; yet there must have been, if there were such things among animals.

Moreover, among the seeds anything must have come to be at random. But the person who asserts this entirely does away with 'nature' and what exists 'by nature'. For those 15 things are natural which, by a continuous movement originated from an internal principle, arrive at some completion: the same completion is not reached from every principle; nor any chance completion, but always the tendency in each is towards the same end, if there is no impediment.

The end and the means towards it may come about by chance. We say, for instance, that a stranger has come by 20 chance, paid the ransom, and gone away, when he does so as if he had come for that purpose, though it was not for that that he came. This is incidental, for chance is an incidental cause, as I remarked before.[13] But when an event takes place always or for the most part, it is not incidental 25 or by chance. In natural products the sequence is invariable, if there is no impediment.

It is absurd to suppose that purpose is not present because we do not observe the agent deliberating. Art does not deliberate. If the ship-building art were in the wood, it would produce the same results by nature. If, therefore, purpose is present in art, it is present also in nature. The 30 best illustration is a doctor doctoring himself: nature is like that.

It is plain then that nature is a cause, a cause that operates for a purpose.

9   As regards what is 'of necessity', we must ask whether the necessity is 'hypothetical', or 'simple' as well. The 35 current view places what is of necessity in the process of 200ᵃ production, just as if one were to suppose that the wall of a house necessarily comes to be because what is heavy is naturally carried downwards and what is light to the top,

¹³ 196ᵇ 23–7.

wherefore the stones and foundations take the lowest place,
with earth above because it is lighter, and wood at the top
of all as being the lightest. Whereas, though the wall does
not come to be *without* these, it is not *due* to these, except 5
as its material cause: it comes to be for the sake of shelter-
ing and guarding certain things. Similarly in all other things
which involve production for an end; the product cannot
come to be without things which have a necessary nature,
but it is not due to these (except as its material); it comes
to be for an end. For instance, why is a saw such as it is? 10
To effect so-and-so and for the sake of so-and-so. This end,
however, cannot be realized unless the saw is made of iron.
It is, therefore, necessary for it to be of iron, *if* we are to
have a saw and perform the operation of sawing. What is
necessary then, is necessary *on a hypothesis*; it is not a result
necessarily determined by antecedents. Necessity is in the
matter, while 'that for the sake of which' is in the definition.

Necessity in mathematics is in a way similar to necessity 15
in things which come to be through the operation of nature. Since a straight line is what it is, it is necessary that
the angles of a triangle should equal two right angles. But
not conversely; though if the angles are *not* equal to two
right angles, then the straight line is not what it is either.
But in things which come to be for an end, the reverse is
true. If the end is to exist or does exist, that also which pre- 20
cedes it will exist or does exist; otherwise just as there, if the
conclusion is not true, the premiss will not be true, so here
the end or 'that for the sake of which' will not exist. For this
too is itself a starting-point, but of the reasoning, not of the
action; while in mathematics the starting-point is the starting point of the reasoning only, as there is no action. If then
there is to be a house, such-and-such things must be made 25
or be there already or exist, or generally the matter relative
to the end, bricks and stones if it is a house. But the end is
not due to these except as the matter, nor will it come to
exist because of them. Yet if they do not exist at all, neither

will the house, or the saw—the former in the absence of
stones, the latter in the absence of iron—just as in the other
case the premisses will not be true, if the angles of the triangle are not equal to two right angles.

30   The necessary in nature, then, is plainly what we call by
the name of matter, and the changes in it. Both causes must
be stated by the physicist, but especially the end; for that is
the cause of the matter, not *vice versa*; and the end is 'that
35 for the sake of which', and the beginning starts from the
200ᵇ definition or essence; as in artificial products, since a house
is of such-and-such a kind, certain things must *necessarily*
come to be or be there already, or since health is this, these
things must necessarily come to be or be there already.
Similarly if man is this, then these; if these, then those.

5 Perhaps the necessary is present also in the definition. For
if one defines the operation of sawing as being a certain
kind of dividing, then this cannot come about unless the
saw has teeth of a certain kind; and these cannot be unless
it is of iron. For in the definition too there are some parts
that are, as it were, its matter.

Psychology

‿◻‿◻‿◻‿◻‿◻‿◻‿◻‿◻‿◻‿◻‿◻‿◻‿◻‿◻‿

INTRODUCTION

In the first book of the *De Anima,* or *On the Soul,* Aristotle reviews and criticizes earlier theories of the soul, or principles and causes of life and thought, as he presented and examined dialectically in the first book of the *Physics* earlier formulations of the principles and causes of motion. He gives reasons, at the beginning, for assigning to this science a special importance among the physical sciences: its precision and the dignity of its subject-matter. As the study of the principles of animal life, it contributes to the advance of truth in general and to our understanding of nature. It provides a key to the study of other living things based on self-observation and reflexively known first principles. The differentiation of methods of inquiry, adapted to particular subject-matters, from logical demonstrations, used to construct common forms of argument to warrant conclusions discovered by different methods, is applied to the problem of defining the soul. The definition should suggest and open ways to the discovery of derived properties and functions of the soul. It should take into account the operations and the objects on which they are exercised as well as the faculties, or powers, of the soul which are the sources of the function.

Aristotle differentiates three kinds among proposed definitions of the "soul" by analogy with the definition of a passion, like "anger," and the definition of an artificial object, like a "house": (1) a "dialectical" definition ("anger is an appetite to return pain for pain," "a house is a shelter against destruction by wind, rain, and heat"), (2) a "physical" definition ("anger is a boiling of the blood or warm substance surrounding the heart," "a house is stones, bricks, and timber"), and (3) a definition which he presents as a genuine physical definition since it combines the form and the matter which are separated in the formal and material definitions. Physics is concerned with all the active and passive properties of bodies defined as natural, and leaves other attributes to other disciplines, or arts, or sciences. Technical arts like carpentry and medicine treat forms which are produced or changed in bodies. Mathematics treats forms which are inseparable in fact but separable from any particular kind of body by abstraction. First philosophy or metaphysics treats forms which are separate both in fact and in thought from bodies. Earlier philosophers found two marks of the soul, movement and perception. Seeking the principles of movement, perception, and knowledge, they either distinguished or identified soul and mind. Aristotle argues that the soul is not related to the body as a body pushing a body or as a spirit imprisoned in a cage. It is not a movement or a harmony or a number. It is not composed of elements. It is not present in all things. It is not divisible into separate parts. All the parts of the soul are present in each part of the body and are homogeneous with each other and with the whole.

The second book of the *De Anima*, like the second book of the *Physics*, makes a fresh start by turning from the dialectical examination of other men's definitions to the construction of a physical definition of the soul. Such a definition must relate body and soul, form and matter, actuality and potentiality, not as logical relations, but according to physical functions. The soul is an *actuality* and a substance; it determines the *powers* or functions or faculties of living; and it initiates the *actions* by which those potentialities are actualized. The body also is an *actuality* and a substance; it is the *potentiality* or matter of motion and of life; and it provides the connection and continuity which persists through change, and it has a "nature," an internal principle of *motion*, which connects inner functions with outer objects. The soul is the form of a natural body having life potentially in it. The first form of the physical definition, in the first chapter of the second book of the *De Anima,* is built on the differentiation of heterogeneous organic bodies and their functions from simple homogeneous bodies and their motions made in the last book of the *Meteorology:* "the soul is the first actuality, or first grade of actuality, or entelechy, of a natural organic body." The presence and operation of the soul is recognized in the functions which a body exercises. If an organ, like the eye, had a soul, its soul would be the operation of seeing; if an artificial object, like an axe, had a soul, its soul would be the operation of cutting. The existence of the soul therefore does not need to be demonstrated. It is perceived in the difference between a living hand and a dead hand or the sculptured hand of a statue.

The soul is the potentiality or power to exercise such functions, and that power, even when unused, is the first actuality, or "first grade of actuality," for the actual exercise of those functions. The seeing and the cutting, and the moving and perceiving, are second actualities which actualize the potentialities of the first actuality. Aristotle is fond of repeating in the course of his physical works that inquiry proceeds from things of experience which are confused in nature and general, but more observable to us, to things known by science which are clear in themselves and particular and are in accordance with reason. The first definition of the soul is at the level of experience. It expresses the "what" but not the "why," the fact but not the reasoned fact; it is like the conclusion of a syllogism. Since we seek the principle by which to differentiate the living from the nonliving, the animate from the inanimate, which is not revealed by the difference between the organic and the inorganic, the different senses of "living" must be examined to discover the different functions of the soul. "Life" may mean thinking, or perception, or local motion and rest, or movement in the sense of nutrition, decay, and growth. The second definition of the soul, constructed in the second chapter, is such a formulation of the principle of living bodies exercised by the faculties of the soul: "the soul is the actuality or entelechy and form or *logos* of a body which has the potentiality of being besouled." With this definition the inquiry moves from the consideration of bodily organs which make life possible to the consideration of living operations consequent on principles or faculties or souls interrelated by a common principle or single soul.

These faculties of the soul—the nutritive, appetitive, sensory, locomotive, and thinking faculties—are considered in relation to the living things which exhibit them, and their definitions as souls are related to the common definition of the soul of which they are instances. Some living bodies have all these faculties; some have some; and some only one. A serial order is found among faculties when a single living body has more than one. Plants have only the nutritive power. Other living things have the nutritive power and the sensory power, and the appetitive always accompanies the sensory. All animals have at least one sense. Touch is the first or primary sense. It is the sense for food; the sensibles it apprehends are the elemental qualities—the dry or solid, the moist or fluid, the hot, the cold. Other sensible qualities—sounds, colours, odours, the proper sensibles of hearing, sight, and smell—contribute nothing to nutriment, while flavours, the proper sensibles of taste, fall within the field of tangible qualities. Some animals have locomotion; some have imagination; and man has the power of thinking or mind. A single definition of the soul can be given, comparable to the definition of "figure" in mathematics, which applies to all figures without expressing the peculiar nature of any one. As figures can be arranged in series, the square containing the triangle, the souls have a like serial order, the sensory power containing the self-nutritive. Consequently the way to give the most adequate definition of the soul is to seek for the most appropriate definition of each of its forms.

Functions are combined with functions to differentiate

kinds of animals in Aristotle's biological works. One treatise is devoted to the generation and corruption of animals, to the processes of genetics, survival, and death, and
another to the mechanisms and faculties of motion in
place, while the principles of nutrition and growth are
used in the course of consideration of problems of reproduction and survival. In the De Anima all faculties from
nutrition to thought are examined individually, and are
ordered relative to each other by use of the scientific
method. The method is stated and applied to the nutritive faculty in the fourth chapter, and the remaining
chapters of the second book apply the method to the
examination of the five exterior senses. Our consideration
of the problem of defining the soul has led us back from
the soul to individual faculties recognized in actions and
differentiated by objects on which they are exercised: the
sequence of methodical inquiry is the reverse, from (1)
the object, to (2) the activity, to (3) the faculty from
which it proceeds, to (4) the soul as common principle.
The soul is the cause and principle of the living body. The
body is the material cause; the soul is (a) the formal cause
of its being and essence, (b) the final cause of what is
done, both in the sense of determining the end of the action and the interest of the agent, and (c) the moving or
efficient cause not only of change of place but also of
change of quality and change of quantity. Nutrition and
reproduction are the same faculty, and the analysis of nutrition proceeds from its object, food, to the motion,
digestion, to the faculty, nutrition. Three factors are involved in nutrition: the body which is fed, the food with
which it is fed, and the soul which does the feeding. As
we found it necessary to examine the several senses of
"life," many of the other terms used to describe the process are ambiguous, including "food," which has contrary
meanings, "undigested" and "digested," at different stages
of the process. They are like and unlike, external and
internal, and the process is an internalization in the living

body of an external body. The examination of each of the
five senses proceeds in like fashion from sensible object,
to medium, to sense perception, to the sense faculty, in-
teriorizing the sensible in the perception.

The psychological faculties examined in the third book
of the De Anima are not exercised on existent external
objects, but on objects derived from sense-experience. The
contrarieties, activities, and passivities are all internalized
in the powers and processes of the soul. The book begins
with a demonstration, from consideration of touch or
contact, media, and elements, that there are no more than
five senses, and then differentiates sensings and imaginings from the perception of "proper sensibles." We are
aware thaat we are seeing or hearing, but not by sight or
hearing. When the sensible objects are no longer present,
the sensings and imaginings continue to exist in the sense-
organs. The activity of the sensible object and the percipient sense is a single activity, but the object and the
sensation are different in being. There is no special organ
for the perception of perception or for the perception of
"common sensibles" perceived by more than one sense—
movement, rest, figure, magnitude, number, unity. They
are all perceived by "common sense" in the perception of
movement. Thinking depends on imagination, which provides images derived from sense perception, and judgment, which operates on them to produce truths and
falsities. The mind, like its thoughts, is likewise passive
and active. In the process in which the forms, which exist actually and are potentially intelligible in the sensible,
are rendered actually intelligible in knowledge and
thought, the mind, which is actually a power of understanding but empty, is actualized by the knowledge
formed by thinking. Actual knowledge is identical with
its object. The logos which is the essence of things is the
logos which is the argument or the knowledge about
things, and the mind is potentially all things. After distinguishing practical mind from contemplative or the-

oretic mind, and comparing mind with sense and imagination, Aristotle turns to the faculty of motion in the
ninth chapter, observing that the soul of animals has two
faculties, the faculty of discrimination which is the work
of thought and sense, and the faculty of originating local
motion, and devotes the final two chapters of the book
to the unity of the faculties of the soul and their adapta-
tion to life.

The soul is the principle and cause of the living body,
and it orders the faculties and activities of living. It also
has characteristics which result from its interactions with
the operations of the body which are treated in the *Short
Natural Treatises*, involving problems of sense and the
sensible, memory and reminiscence, sleep and waking,
dreams, foresight in dreams, length and brevity of life,
life and death, and respiration.

DE ANIMA

CONTENTS

BOOK I

BOOK II

BOOK III

De Anima

On the Soul

Translated by J. A. Smith

ЛЛЛ

BOOK I

1   Holding as we do that, while knowledge of any kind is
a thing to be honoured and prized, one kind of it may, **402ᵃ**
either by reason of its greater exactness or of a higher dignity and greater wonderfulness in its objects, be more honourable and precious than another, on both accounts we
should naturally be led to place in the front rank the study
of the soul. The knowledge of the soul admittedly contributes greatly to the advance of truth in general, and, above
all, to our understanding of Nature, for the soul is in some 5
sense the principle of animal life. Our aim is to grasp and
understand, first its essential nature, and secondly its properties; of these some are thought to be affections proper to
the soul itself, while others are considered to attach to the
animal ¹ owing to the presence within it of soul.

   To attain any assured knowledge about the soul is one of
the most difficult things in the world. As the form of ques- 10
tion which here presents itself, viz. the question 'What is
it?', recurs in other fields, it might be supposed that there
was some single method of inquiry applicable to all objects
whose essential nature we are endeavouring to ascertain 15
(as there *is* for derived properties the single method of

---

¹ i. e. the complex of soul and body.

demonstration); in that case what we should have to seek
for would be this unique method. But if there is no such
single and general method for solving the question of essence, our task becomes still more difficult; in the case of
each different subject we shall have to determine the appropriate process of investigation. If to this there be a clear
answer, e. g. that the process is demonstration or division,
20 or some other known method, difficulties and hesitations
still beset us—with what facts shall we begin the inquiry?
For the facts which form the starting-points in different
subjects must be different, as e. g. in the case of numbers
and surfaces.

First, no doubt, it is necessary to determine in which
of the *summa genera* soul lies, what it *is*; is it 'a this-somewhat', a substance, or is it a quale or a quantum, or some
25 other of the remaining kinds of predicates which we have
distinguished? Further, does soul belong to the class of potential existents, or is it not rather an actuality? Our answer
to this question is of the greatest importance.

402ᵇ   We must consider also whether soul is divisible or is
without parts, and whether it is everywhere homogeneous
or not; and if not homogeneous, whether its various
forms are different specifically or generically: up to the
5 present time those who have discussed and investigated
soul seem to have confined themselves to the human soul.
We must be careful not to ignore the question whether
soul can be defined in a single unambiguous formula, as is
the case with animal, or whether we must not give a
separate formula for each sort of it, as we do for horse, dog,
man, god (in the latter case the 'universal' animal—and so
too every other 'common predicate'—being treated either
as nothing at all or as a later product [2]). Further, if what
exists is not a plurality of souls, but a plurality of parts of
10 one soul, which ought we to investigate first, the whole soul
or its parts? (It is also a difficult problem to decide which

[2] i. e. as presupposing the various sorts instead of being presupposed
by them.

of these parts are in nature distinct from one another.)
Again, which ought we to investigate first, these parts or
their functions, mind or thinking, the faculty or the act
of sensation, and so on? If the investigation of the functions
precedes that of the parts, the further question suggests
itself: ought we not before either to consider the cor- 15
relative objects, e. g. of sense or thought? It seems not only
useful for the discovery of the causes of the derived properties of substances to be acquainted with the essential nature
of those substances (as in mathematics it is useful for the
understanding of the property of the equality of the in-
terior angles of a triangle to two right angles to know the 20
essential nature of the straight and the curved or of the line
and the plane) but also conversely, for the knowledge of
the essential nature of a substance is largely promoted by
an acquaintance with its properties: for, when we are
able to give an account conformable to experience of all or
most of the properties of a substance, we shall be in the
most favourable position to say something worth saying
about the essential nature of that subject; in all demon- 25
stration a definition of the essence is required as a starting-
point, so that definitions which do not enable us to dis- **403ᵃ**
cover the derived properties, or which fail to facilitate
even a conjecture about them, must obviously, one and all,
be dialectical and futile.

A further problem presented by the affections of soul
is this: are they all affections of the complex of body and
soul, or is there any one among them peculiar to the soul
by itself? To determine this is indispensable but difficult.
If we consider the majority of them, there seems to be no 5
case in which the soul can act or be acted upon without
involving the body; e. g. anger, courage, appetite, and
sensation generally. Thinking seems the most probable
exception; but if this too proves to be a form of imagination or to be impossible without imagination, it too requires a body as a condition of its existence. If there is any 10
way of acting or being acted upon proper to soul, soul will

be capable of separate existence; if there is none, its separate existence is impossible. In the latter case, it will be like what is straight, which has many properties arising from the straightness in it, e. g. that of touching a bronze sphere at a point, though straightness divorced from the other constituents of the straight thing cannot touch it in this way; it cannot be so divorced at all, since it is always
15 found in a body. It therefore seems that all the affections of soul involve a body—passion, gentleness, fear, pity, courage, joy, loving, and hating; in all these there is a concurrent affection of the body. In support of this we may point to the fact that, while sometimes on the occasion of violent and striking occurrences there is no excitement or fear
20 felt, on others faint and feeble stimulations produce these emotions, viz. when the body is already in a state of tension resembling its condition when we are angry. Here is a still clearer case: in the absence of any external cause of terror we find ourselves experiencing the feelings of a man in terror. From all this it is obvious that the affections of soul are enmattered formulable essences.

Consequently their definitions ought to correspond, e. g.
25 anger should be defined as a certain mode of movement of such and such a body (or part or faculty of a body) by this or that cause and for this or that end. That is precisely why the study of the soul must fall within the science of Nature, at least so far as in its affections it manifests this double character. Hence a physicist would define an affection of soul differently from a dialectician; the latter
30 would define e. g. anger as the appetite for returning pain for pain, or something like that, while the former would define it as a boiling of the blood or warm substance sur-
403ᵇ rounding the heart. The latter assigns the material conditions, the former the form or formulable essence; for what he states is the formulable essence of the fact, though for its actual existence there must be embodiment of it in a material such as is described by the other. Thus the essence of a house is assigned in such a formula as 'a shelter against

destruction by wind, rain, and heat'; the physicist would 5
describe it as 'stones, bricks, and timbers'; but there is a
third possible description which would say that it was that
form in that material with that purpose or end. Which,
then, among these is entitled to be regarded as the genuine
physicist? The one who confines himself to the material,
or the one who restricts himself to the formulable essence
alone? Is it not rather the one who combines both in a
single formula? If this is so, how are we to characterize the
other two? Must we not say that there is no type of thinker
who concerns himself with those qualities or attributes of
the material which are in fact inseparable from the material, and without attempting even in thought to sep- 10
arate them? The physicist is he who concerns himself with
all the properties active and passive of bodies or materials
thus or thus defined; attributes not considered as being of
this character he leaves to others, in certain cases it may
be to a specialist, e. g. a carpenter or a physician, in others
(a) where they are inseparable in fact, but are separable
from any particular kind of body by an effort of abstrac- 15
tion, to the mathematician, (b) where they are separate
both in fact and in thought from body altogether, to the
First Philosopher or metaphysician. But we must return
from this digression, and repeat that the affections of soul
are inseparable from the material substratum of animal
life, to which we have seen that such affections, e. g. passion and fear, attach, and have not the same mode of being
as a line or a plane.

2   For our study of soul it is necessary, while formulating 20
the problems of which in our further advance we are
to find the solutions, to call into council the views of those
of our predecessors who have declared any opinion on
this subject, in order that we may profit by whatever is
sound in their suggestions and avoid their errors.

The starting-point of our inquiry is an exposition of those
characteristics which have chiefly been held to belong to

25 soul in its very nature. Two characteristic marks have above
all others been recognized as distinguishing that which has
soul in it from that which has not—movement and sensation: It may be said that these two are what our predecessors have fixed upon as characteristic of soul.

Some say that what originates movement is both pre-
eminently and primarily soul; believing that what is not
30 itself moved cannot originate movement in another, they
arrived at the view that soul belongs to the class of things in
404ª movement. This is what led Democritus to say that soul
is a sort of fire or hot substance; his 'forms' or atoms are infinite in number; those which are spherical he calls fire
and soul, and compares them to the motes in the air which
we see in shafts of light coming through windows; the mixture of seeds of all sorts he calls the elements of the whole
of Nature (Leucippus gives a similar account); the spher-
5 ical atoms are identified with soul because atoms of that
shape are most adapted to permeate everywhere, and to
set all the others moving by being themselves in movement.
This implies the view that soul is identical with what produces movement in animals. That is why, further, they regard respiration as the characteristic mark of life; as the
10 environment compresses the bodies of animals, and tends
to extrude those atoms which impart movement to them,
because they themselves are never at rest, there must be
a reinforcement of these by similar atoms coming in from
without in the act of respiration; for they prevent the
extrusion of those which are already within by counteracting the compressing and consolidating force of the environ-
15 ment; and animals continue to live only as long as they
are able to maintain this resistance.

The doctrine of the Pythagoreans seems to rest upon the
same ideas; some of them declared the motes in air, others
what moved them, to be soul. These motes were referred
to because they are seen always in movement, even in a
complete calm.

The same tendency is shown by those who define soul as

that which moves itself; all seem to hold the view that 20
movement is what is closest to the nature of soul, and that
while all else is moved by soul, it alone moves itself. This
belief arises from their never seeing anything originating
movement which is not first itself moved.

Similarly also Anaxagoras (and whoever agrees with him
in saying that mind set the whole in movement) declares 25
the moving cause of things to be soul. His position must,
however, be distinguished from that of Democritus. Democritus roundly identifies soul and mind, for he identifies
what appears with what is true—that is why he commends
Homer for the phrase 'Hector lay with thought dis-
traught' [3]; he does not employ mind as a special faculty
dealing with truth, but identifies soul and mind. What 30
Anaxagoras says about them is more obscure; in many 404ᵇ
places he tells us that the cause of beauty and order is
mind, elsewhere that it is soul; it is found, he says, in all
animals, great and small, high and low, but mind (in the
sense of intelligence) appears not to belong alike to all 5
animals, and indeed not even to all human beings.

All those, then, who had special regard to the fact that
what has soul in it is moved, adopted the view that soul is
to be identified with what is eminently originative of movement. All, on the other hand, who looked to the fact that
what has soul in it knows or perceives what is, identify
soul with the principle or principles of Nature, according 10
as they admit several such principles or one only. Thus
Empedocles declares that it is formed out of all his elements, each of them also being soul; his words are:

> For 'tis by Earth we see Earth, by Water Water,
> By Ether Ether divine, by Fire destructive Fire,
> By Love Love, and Hate by cruel Hate.　　15

In the same way Plato in the *Timaeus* [4] fashions the soul
out of his elements; for like, he holds, is known by like, and

[3] II. xxiii. 698.
[4] 35 A ff.

things are formed out of the principles or elements, so
20 that soul must be so too. Similarly also in his lectures 'On
Philosophy' it was set forth that the Animal-itself is compounded of the Idea itself of the One together with the
primary length, breadth, and depth, everything else, the
objects of its perception, being similarly constituted. Again
he puts his view in yet other terms: Mind is the monad,
science or knowledge the dyad (because [5] it goes undevi-
atingly from one point to another), opinion the number of
the plane,[6] sensation the number of the solid [7]; the numbers are by him expressly identified with the Forms themselves or principles, and are formed out of the elements;
25 now things are apprehended either by mind or science or
opinion or sensation, and these same numbers are the
Forms of things.

Some thinkers, accepting both premisses, viz. that the
soul is both originative of movement and cognitive, have
compounded it of both and declared the soul to be a self-
moving number.

30   As to the nature and number of the first principles
opinions differ. The difference is greatest between those
who regard them as corporeal and those who regard them
405ª as incorporeal, and from both dissent those who make a
blend and draw their principles from both sources. The
number of principles is also in dispute; some admit one
only, others assert several. There is a consequent diversity
in their several accounts of soul; they assume, naturally
5 enough, that what is in its own nature originative of movement must be among what is primordial. That has led
some to regard it as fire, for fire is the subtlest of the elements and nearest to incorporeality; further, in the most
primary sense, fire both is moved and originates movement
in all the others.

Democritus has expressed himself more ingeniously than

---

[5] Like the straight line, whose number is the dyad.
[6] The triad.
[7] The tetrad.

the rest on the grounds for ascribing each of these two characters to soul; soul and mind are, he says, one and the 10 same thing, and this thing must be one of the primary and indivisible bodies, and its power of originating movement must be due to its fineness of grain and the shape of its atoms; he says that of all the shapes the spherical is the most mobile, and that this is the shape of the particles of both fire and mind.

Anaxagoras, as we said above,[8] seems to distinguish between soul and mind, but in practice he treats them as a single substance, except that it is mind that he specially posits as the principle of all things; at any rate what he 15 says is that mind alone of all that is is simple, unmixed, and pure. He assigns both characteristics, knowing and origination of movement, to the same principle, when he says that it was mind that set the whole in movement.

Thales, too, to judge from what is recorded about him, seems to have held soul to be a motive force, since he said 20 that the magnet has a soul in it because it moves the iron.

Diogenes (and others) held the soul to be air because he believed air to be finest in grain and a first principle; therein lay the grounds of the soul's powers of knowing and originating movement. As the primordial principle from which all other things are derived, it is cognitive; as finest in grain, it has the power to originate movement.

Heraclitus too says that the first principle—the 'warm exhalation' of which, according to him, everything else is 25 composed—is soul; further, that this exhalation is most incorporeal and in ceaseless flux; that what is in movement requires that what knows it should be in movement; and that all that is has its being essentially in movement (herein agreeing with the majority).

Alcmaeon also seems to have held a similar view about soul; he says that it is immortal because it resembles 'the immortals', and that this immortality belongs to it in 30 virtue of its ceaseless movement; for all the 'things divine',

[8] 404[b] 1–6.

moon, sun, the planets, and the whole heavens, are in perpetual movement.

405ᵇ Of more superficial writers, some, e. g. Hippo, have pronounced it to be water; they seem to have argued from the
fact that the seed of all animals is fluid, for Hippo tries to
refute those who say that the soul is blood, on the ground
that the seed, which is the primordial soul, is not blood.

Another group (Critias, for example) did hold it to be
5 blood; they take perception to be the most characteristic
attribute of soul, and hold that perceptiveness is due to
the nature of blood.

Each of the elements has thus found its partisan, except
earth—earth has found no supporter unless we count as
such those who have declared soul to be, or to be com-
10 pounded of, *all* the elements. All, then, it may be said,
characterize the soul by three marks, Movement, Sensation, Incorporeality, and each of these is traced back to
the first principles. That is why (with one exception) all
those who define the soul by its power of knowing make it
either an element or constructed out of the elements. The
15 language they all use is similar; like, they say, is known by
like; as the soul knows everything, they construct it out of
all the principles. Hence all those who admit but one
cause or element, make the soul also one (e. g. fire or air),
while those who admit a multiplicity of principles make the
20 soul also multiple. The exception is Anaxagoras; he alone
says that mind is impassible and has nothing in common
with anything else. But, if this is so, how or in virtue of
what cause can it know? That Anaxagoras has not explained, nor can any answer be inferred from his words.
All who acknowledge pairs of opposites among their principles, construct the soul also out of these contraries, while
25 those who admit as principles only one contrary of each
pair, e. g. either hot or cold, likewise make the soul some
one of these. That is why, also, they allow themselves to be
guided by the names; those who identify soul with the hot
argue that *zen* (to live) is derived from *zein* (to boil),

while those who identify it with the cold say that soul
(*psyche*) is so called from the process of respiration and
refrigeration (*katapsyxis*).

Such are the traditional opinions concerning soul, to- 30
gether with the grounds on which they are maintained.

3　We must begin our examination with movement; for,
　doubtless, not only is it false that the essence of soul is
correctly described by those who say that it is what moves **406ª**
(or is capable of moving) itself, but it is an impossibility
that movement should be even an attribute of it.

We have already [9] pointed out that there is no necessity
that what originates movement should itself be moved.
There are two senses in which anything may be moved—
either (a) indirectly, owing to something other than itself, 5
or (b) directly, owing to itself. Things are 'indirectly
moved' which are moved as being contained in something
which is moved, e. g. sailors in a ship, for they are moved in
a different sense from that in which the ship is moved; the
ship is 'directly moved', they are 'indirectly moved', because
they are in a moving vessel. This is clear if we consider their
limbs; the movement proper to the legs (and so to man) is
walking, and in this case the sailors are not walking. Recog- 10
nizing the double sense of 'being moved', what we have to
consider now is whether the soul is 'directly moved' and
participates in such direct movement.

There are four species of movement—locomotion, alteration, diminution, growth; consequently if the soul is
moved, it must be moved with one or several or all of these
species of movement. Now if its movement is not incidental, there must be a movement natural to it, and, if so, 15
as all the species enumerated involve place, place must be
natural to it. But if the essence of soul be to move itself,
its being moved cannot be incidental to it, as it is to what
is white or three cubits long; they too can be moved, but
only incidentally—what is moved is that of which 'white'

[9] *Phys.* viii. 5, esp. 257ª 31–258ᵇ 9.

and 'three cubits long' are the attributes, the body in
20 which they inhere; hence *they* have no place: but if the
soul naturally partakes in movement, it follows that it
must have a place.

Further, if there be a movement natural to the soul,
there must be a counter-movement unnatural to it, and
conversely. The same applies to rest as well as to movement; for the *terminus ad quem* of a thing's natural move-
25 ment is the place of its natural rest, and similarly the
terminus ad quem of its enforced movement is the place of
its enforced rest. But what meaning can be attached to enforced movements or rests of the soul, it is difficult even to
imagine.

Further, if the natural movement of the soul be upward,
the soul must be fire; if downward, it must be earth; for upward and downward movements are the definitory characteristics of these bodies. The same reasoning applies to the
intermediate movements, *termini*, and bodies. Further,
30 since the soul is observed to originate movement in the
body, it is reasonable to suppose that it transmits to the
body the movements by which it itself is moved, and so,
reversing the order, we may infer from the movements of
the body back to similar movements of the soul. Now the
406ᵇ body is moved from place to place with movements of
locomotion. Hence it would follow that the soul too must
in accordance with the body change either its place as a
whole or the relative places of its parts. This carries with it
the possibility that the soul might even quit its body and re-
enter it, and with this would be involved the possibility of
a resurrection of animals from the dead. But, it may be con-
5 tended, the soul can be moved indirectly by something else;
for an animal can be pushed out of its course. Yes, but that
to whose *essence* belongs the power of being moved by
itself, cannot be moved by something else except incidentally,[10] just as what is good by or in itself cannot owe its

---

[10] i. e. so that what is moved is not it but something which 'goes
along with it', e.g. a vehicle in which it is contained.

goodness to something external to it or to some end to which it is a means.

If the soul *is* moved, the most probable view is that what moves it is sensible things.[11]

We must note also that, if the soul moves itself, it must be the mover itself that is moved, so that it follows that if movement is in every case a displacement of that which is in movement, in that respect in which it is said to be moved, the movement of the soul must be a departure from its essential nature, at least if its self-movement is essential to it, not incidental.

Some go so far as to hold that the movements which the soul imparts to the body in which it is are the same in kind as those with which it itself is moved. An example of this is Democritus, who uses language like that of the comic dramatist Philippus, who accounts for the movements that Daedalus imparted to his wooden Aphrodite by saying that he poured quicksilver into it; similarly Democritus says that the spherical atoms which according to him constitute soul, owing to their own ceaseless movements draw the whole body after them and so produce its movements. We must urge the question whether it is these very same atoms which produce rest also—how they could do so, it is difficult and even impossible to say. And, in general, we may object that it is not in this way that the soul appears to originate movement in animals—it is through intention or process of thinking.

It is in the same fashion that the *Timaeus* [12] also tries to give a physical account of how the soul moves its body; the soul, it is here said, is in movement, and so owing to their mutual implication moves the body also. After compounding the soul-substance out of the elements and dividing it in accordance with the harmonic numbers, in order that it may possess a connate sensibility for 'harmony'

[11] sc. in which case the movement can only be 'incidental'; for, as we shall see later, it is really the bodily organ of sensation that then is 'moved'.

[12] 35 A ff.

and that the whole may move in movements well attuned,
the Demiurge bent the straight line into a circle; this single
407ᵃ circle he divided into two circles united at two common
points; one of these he subdivided into seven circles. All
this implies that the movements of the soul are identified
with the local movements of the heavens.

Now, in the first place, it is a mistake to say that the
soul is a spatial magnitude. It is evident that Plato means
5 the soul of the whole to be like the sort of soul which is
called mind—not like the sensitive or the desiderative
soul, for the movements of neither of these are circular.
Now mind is one and continuous in the sense in which the
process of thinking is so, and thinking is identical with the
thoughts which are its parts; these have a serial unity like
that of number, not a unity like that of a spatial magnitude. Hence mind cannot have that kind of unity either;
mind is either without parts or is continuous in some other
way than that which characterizes a spatial magnitude.
How, indeed, if it were a spatial magnitude, could mind
10 possibly think? Will it think with any one indifferently
of its parts? In this case, the 'part' must be understood
either in the sense of a spatial magnitude or in the sense of
a point (if a point can be called a part of a spatial magnitude). If we accept the latter alternative, the points being
infinite in number, obviously the mind can never exhaustively traverse them; if the former, the mind must think
the same thing over and over again, indeed an infinite
number of times (whereas it is manifestly possible to think
15 a thing once only). If contact of any part whatsoever of
itself with the object is all that is required, why need mind
move in a circle, or indeed possess magnitude at all? On the
other hand, if contact with the whole circle is necessary,
what meaning can be given to the contact of the parts?
Further, how could what has no parts think what has parts,
or what has parts think what has none? [13] We must identify
the circle referred to with mind; for it is mind whose move-

[13] sc. but mind in fact thinks or cognizes both.

ment is thinking, and it is the circle whose movement is 20
revolution, so that if thinking is a movement of revolution,
the circle which has this characteristic movement must be
mind.

If the circular movement is eternal, there must be something which mind is always thinking—what can this be?
For all practical processes of thinking have limits—they
all go on for the sake of something outside the process,
and all theoretical processes come to a close in the same
way as the phrases in speech which express processes and
results of thinking. Every such linguistic phrase is either
definitory or demonstrative. Demonstration has both a 25
starting-point and may be said to end in a conclusion or
inferred result; even if the process never reaches final completion, at any rate it never returns upon itself again to its
starting-point, it goes on assuming a fresh middle term or
a fresh extreme, and moves straight forward, but circular
movement returns to its starting-point. Definitions, too,
are closed groups of terms.   30

Further, if the same revolution is repeated, mind must
repeatedly think the same object.

Further, thinking has more resemblance to a coming to
rest or arrest than to a movement; the same may be said of
inferring.

It might also be urged that what is difficult and enforced
is incompatible with blessedness; if the movement of the
soul is not of its essence, movement of the soul must be 407ᵇ
contrary to its nature.[14] It must also be painful for the soul
to be inextricably bound up with the body; nay more, if, as
is frequently said and widely accepted, it is better for mind
not to be embodied the union must be for it undesirable.

Further, the cause of the revolution of the heavens is 5
left obscure. It is not the essence of soul which is the cause
of this circular movement—that movement is only incidental to soul—nor is, *a fortiori*, the body its cause. Again,
it is not even asserted that it is better that soul should be so

[14] sc. 'and so a hindrance to its bliss'.

10 moved; and yet the reason for which God caused the soul
to move in a circle can only have been that movement was
better for it than rest, and movement of this kind better
than any other. But since this sort of consideration is more
appropriate to another field of speculation, let us dismiss
it for the present.

The view we have just been examining, in company
with most theories about the soul, involves the following
15 absurdity: they all join the soul to a body, or place it in a
body, without adding any specification of the reason of
their union, or of the bodily conditions required for it.
Yet such explanation can scarcely be omitted; for some
community of nature is presupposed by the fact that the
one acts and the other is acted upon, the one moves and
the other is moved; interaction always implies a *special* na-
20 ture in the two interagents. All, however, that these
thinkers do is to describe the specific characteristics of
the soul; they do not try to determine anything about the
body which is to contain it, as if it were possible, as in the
Pythagorean myths, that any soul could be clothed upon
with any body—an absurd view, for each body seems to
have a form and shape of its own. It is as absurd as to say
25 that the art of carpentry could embody itself in flutes; each
art must use its tools, each soul its body.

4   There is yet another theory about soul, which has
commended itself to many as no less probable than
30 any of those we have hitherto mentioned, and has rendered public account of itself in the court of popular
discussion. Its supporters say that the soul is a kind of
harmony, for (a) harmony is a blend or composition of
contraries, and (b) the body is compounded out of contraries. Harmony, however, is a certain proportion or composition of the constituents blended, and soul can be
neither the one nor the other of these. Further, the power
of originating movement cannot belong to a harmony,
while almost all concur in regarding this as a principal

attribute of soul. It is more appropriate to call health (or 408ᵃ generally one of the good states of the body) a harmony than to predicate it of the soul. The absurdity becomes most apparent when we try to attribute the active and passive affections of the soul to a harmony; the necessary readjustment of their conceptions is difficult. Further, in using the word 'harmony' we have one or other of two 5 cases in our mind; the most proper sense is in relation to spatial magnitudes which have motion and position, where harmony means the disposition and cohesion of their parts in such a manner as to prevent the introduction into the whole of anything homogeneous with it, and the secondary sense, derived from the former, is that in which it means the ratio between the constituents so blended; in neither of these senses is it plausible to predicate it of 10 soul. That soul is a harmony in the sense of the mode of composition of the parts of the body is a view easily refutable; for there are many composite parts and those variously compounded; of what bodily part is mind or the sensitive or the appetitive faculty the mode of composition? And what is the mode of composition which constitutes each of them? It is equally absurd to identify the soul with the ratio of the mixture; for the mixture which makes flesh has a different ratio between the elements from that 15 which makes bone. The consequence of this view will therefore be that distributed throughout the whole body there will be many souls, since every one of the bodily parts is a different mixture of the elements, and the ratio of mixture is in each case a harmony, i. e. a soul.

From Empedocles at any rate we might demand an answer to the following question—for he says that each of the parts of the body is what it is in virtue of a ratio between the elements: is the soul identical with this ratio, 20 or is it not rather something over and above this which is formed in the parts? Is love the cause of any and every mixture, or only of those that are in the right ratio? Is love this ratio itself, or is love something over and above this?

Such are the problems raised by this account. But, on the other hand, if the soul is different from the mixture, why
25 does it disappear at one and the same moment with that relation between the elements which constitutes flesh or the other parts of the animal body? Further, if the soul is not identical with the ratio of mixture, and it is consequently not the case that each of the parts has a soul, what is that which perishes when the soul quits the body?

That the soul cannot either be a harmony, or be moved in a circle, is clear from what we have said. Yet that it can
30 be moved incidentally is, as we said above,[15] possible, and even that in a sense it can move itself, i. e. in the sense that *the vehicle* in which it is can be moved, and moved by it; in no other sense can the soul be moved in space. More legitimate doubts might remain as to its movement in view
408ᵇ of the following facts. We speak of the soul as being pained or pleased, being bold or fearful, being angry, perceiving, thinking. All these are regarded as modes of movement, and hence it might be inferred that the soul is moved.
5 This, however, does not necessarily follow. We may admit to the full that being pained or pleased, or thinking, are movements (each of them a 'being moved'), and that the movement is originated by the soul. For example we may regard anger or fear as such and such movements of the heart, and thinking as such and such another movement of that organ, or of some other; these modifications may arise either from changes of place in certain parts or from
10 qualitative alterations (the special nature of the parts and the special modes of their changes being for our present purpose irrelevant). Yet to say that it is *the soul* which is angry is as inexact as it would be to say that it is the soul that weaves webs or builds houses. It is doubtless better to avoid saying that the soul pities or learns or thinks, and
15 rather to say that it is the man who does this with his soul. What we mean is not that the movement is in the soul, but that sometimes it terminates in the soul and sometimes

---

¹⁵ 406ᵃ 30 ff., ᵇ5–8.

starts from it, sensation e. g. coming from without inwards, and reminiscence starting from the soul and terminating with the movements, actual or residual, in the sense organs.

The case of mind is different; it seems to be an independent substance implanted within the soul and to be incapable of being destroyed. If it could be destroyed at all, it would be under the blunting influence of old age. What 20 really happens in respect of mind in old age is, however, exactly parallel to what happens in the case of the sense organs; if the old man could recover the proper kind of eye, he would see just as well as the young man. The incapacity of old age is due to an affection not of the soul but of its vehicle, as occurs in drunkenness or disease. Thus it is that in old age the activity of mind or intellectual apprehension declines only through the decay of some other inward 25 part; mind itself is impassible. Thinking, loving, and hating are affections not of mind, but of that which has mind, so far as it has it. That is why, when this vehicle decays, memory and love cease; they were activities not of mind, but of the composite which has perished; mind is, no doubt, something more divine and impassible. That the soul can- 30 not be moved is therefore clear from what we have said, and if it cannot be moved at all, manifestly it cannot be moved by itself.

Of all the opinions we have enumerated, by far the most unreasonable is that which declares the soul to be a self-moving number; it involves in the first place all the impossibilities which follow from regarding the soul as moved, and in the second special absurdities which follow from call- **409ª** ing it a number. How are we to imagine a unit being moved? By what agency? What sort of movement can be attributed to what is without parts or internal differences? If the unit is both originative of movement and itself capable of being moved, it must contain difference.[16]

Further, since they say a moving line generates a surface

[16] sc. 'and so, be no unit'.

and a moving point a line, the movements of the psychic
5 units must be lines (for a point is a unit having position,
and the number of the soul is, of course, somewhere and
has position).

Again, if from a number a number or a unit is subtracted,
the remainder is another number; but plants and many
animals when divided continue to live, and each segment
is thought to retain the same kind of soul.

It must be all the same whether we speak of units or
10 corpuscles; for if the spherical atoms of Democritus became
points, nothing being retained but their being a quantum,
there must remain in each a moving and a moved part,
just as there is in what is continuous; what happens has
nothing to do with the size of the atoms, it depends solely
upon their being a quantum. That is why there must
15 be something to originate movement in the units. If in the
animal what originates movement is the soul, so also must
it be in the case of the number, so that not the mover and
the moved together, but the mover only, will be the soul.
But how is it possible for one of the units to fulfil this
function of originating movement? There must be some
difference between such a unit and all the other units, and
20 what difference can there be between one placed unit and
another except a difference of position? If then, on the
other hand, these psychic units within the body are different from the points of the body, there will be two sets of
units both occupying the same place; for each unit will
occupy a point. And yet, if there can be two, why cannot
there be an infinite number? For if things can occupy an indivisible place, they must themselves be indivisible. If, on
25 the other hand, the points of the body are identical with
the units whose number is the soul, or if the number of the
points in the body is the soul, why have not all bodies
souls? For all bodies contain points or an infinity of points.

Further, how is it possible for these points to be isolated
or separated from their bodies, seeing that lines cannot be
30 resolved into points?

5   The result is, as we have said,[17] that this view, while on
the one side identical with that of those who maintain
that soul is a subtle kind of body,[18] is on the other entangled
in the absurdity peculiar to Democritus' way of describing 409ᵇ
the manner in which movement is originated by soul. For
if the soul is present throughout the whole percipient
body, there must, if the soul be a kind of body, be two
bodies in the same place; and for those who call it a number, there must be many points at one point, or every body 5
must have a soul, unless the soul be a different sort of number—other, that is, than the sum of the points existing in a
body. Another consequence that follows is that the animal
must be moved by its number precisely in the way that
Democritus explained its being moved by his spherical
psychic atoms. What difference does it make whether we
speak of small spheres or of large [19] units, or, quite simply,
of units in movement? One way or another, the move- 10
ments of the animal must be due to their movements.
Hence those who combine movement and number in the
same subject lay themselves open to these and many other
similar absurdities. It is impossible not only that these
characters should give the definition of soul—it is impossible that they should even be attributes of it. The point
is clear if the attempt be made to start from this as the ac- 15
count of soul and explain from it the affections and actions of the soul, e. g. reasoning, sensation, pleasure, pain,
&c. For, to repeat what we have said earlier,[20] movement
and number do not facilitate even conjecture about the
derivative properties of soul.

Such are the three ways in which soul has traditionally
been defined; one group of thinkers declared it to be that
which is most originative of movement because it moves 20
itself, another group to be the subtlest and most nearly
incorporeal of all kinds of body. We have now sufficiently

[17] 408ᵇ 33 ff.
[18] e. g. Heraclitus, and Diogenes of Apollonia.
[19] i. e. extended.
[20] 402ᵇ 25–403ᵃ 2.

set forth the difficulties and inconsistencies to which these theories are exposed. It remains now to examine the doctrine that soul is composed of the elements.

The reason assigned for this doctrine is that thus the soul may perceive or come to know everything that is, 25 but the theory necessarily involves itself in many impossibilities. Its upholders assume that like is known only by like, and imagine that by declaring the soul to be composed of the elements they succeed in identifying the soul with all the things it is capable of apprehending. But the elements are not the only things it knows; there are many others, or, more exactly, an infinite number of others, 30 formed out of the elements. Let us admit that the soul knows or perceives the elements out of which each of these composites is made up; but by what means will it know or perceive the composite whole, e. g. what God, man, flesh, bone (or any other compound) is? For each *is*, not 410ᵃ merely the elements of which it is composed, but those elements combined in a determinate mode or ratio, as Empedocles himself says of bone,

> The kindly Earth in its broad-bosomed moulds
> 5   Won of clear Water·two parts out of eight
> And four of Fire; and so white bones were formed.

Nothing, therefore, will be gained by the presence of the elements in the soul, unless there be also present there the various formulae of proportion and the various compositions in accordance with them. Each element will indeed know its fellow outside, but there will be no knowledge of bone or man, unless they too are present in the constitution of the soul. The impossibility of this needs no point- 10 ing out; for who would suggest that stone or man could enter into the constitution of the soul? The same applies to 'the good' and 'the not-good', and so on.

Further, the word 'is' has many meanings: it may be used of a 'this' or substance, or of a quantum, or of a quale, or of any other of the kinds of predicates we have distinguished. Does the soul consist of all of these or not? It does not appear that all have common elements. Is the soul formed 15 out of those elements alone which enter into substances? If so, how will it be able to know each of the other kinds of thing? Will it be said that each kind of thing has elements or principles of its own, and that the soul is formed out of the whole of these? In that case, the soul must be a quantum and a quale and a substance. But all that can be 20 made out of the elements of a quantum is a quantum, not a substance. These (and others like them) are the consequences of the view that the soul is composed of all the elements.

It is absurd, also, to say both (a) that like is not capable of being affected by like, and (b) that like is perceived or known by like, for perceiving, and also both thinking and knowing, are, on their own assumption, ways of being 25 affected or moved.

There are many puzzles and difficulties raised by saying, as Empedocles does, that each set of things is known by means of its corporeal elements and by reference to something in soul which is like them, and additional testimony is furnished by this new consideration; for all the parts of 30 the animal body which consist wholly of earth such as bones, sinews, and hair seem to be wholly insensitive and consequently not perceptive even of objects earthy like 410ᵇ themselves, as they ought to have been.

Further, each of the principles will have far more ignorance than knowledge, for though each of them will know one thing, there will be many of which it will be ignorant. Empedocles at any rate must conclude that his God is the 5 least intelligent of all beings, for of him alone is it true that there is one thing, Strife, which he does not know, while there is nothing which mortal beings do not know, for there is nothing which does not enter into their composition.

In general, we may ask, Why has not everything a soul,

since everything either is an element, or is formed out of
one or several or all of the elements? Each must certainly
know one or several or all.

10   The problem might also be raised, What is that which
unifies the elements into a soul? The elements correspond,
it would appear, to the matter; what unites them, whatever
it is, is the supremely important factor. But it is impossible
that there should be something superior to, and dominant
over, the soul (and a *fortiori* over the mind); it is reasonable
15 to hold that mind is by nature most primordial and dominant, while their statement is that it is the elements which
are first of all that is.

All, both those who assert that the soul, because of its
knowledge or perception of what is, is compounded out of
the elements, and those who assert that it is of all things
the most originative of movement, fail to take into consideration all kinds of soul. In fact (1) not all beings that per-
20 ceive can originate movement; there appear to be certain
animals which are stationary, and yet local movement is the
only one, so it seems, which the soul originates in animals.
And (2) the same objection holds against all those who
construct mind and the perceptive faculty out of the elements; for it appears that plants live, and yet are not endowed with locomotion or perception, while a large number
of animals are without discourse of reason. Even if these
points were waived and mind admitted to be a part of the
25 soul (and so too the perceptive faculty), still, even so, there
would be kinds and parts of soul of which they had failed
to give any account.

The same objection lies against the view expressed in the
'Orphic' poems: there it is said that the soul comes in from
30 the whole when breathing takes place, being borne in upon
the winds. Now this cannot take place in the case of plants,
411ᵃ nor indeed in the case of certain classes of animal, for not
all classes of animal breathe. This fact has escaped the
notice of the holders of this view.

If we must construct the soul out of the elements, there

is no necessity to suppose that *all* the elements enter into
its construction; one element in each pair of contraries will
suffice to enable it to know both that element itself and its
contrary. By means of the straight line we know both itself
and the curved—the carpenter's rule enables us to test 5
both—but what is curved does not enable us to distinguish
either itself or the straight.

Certain thinkers say that soul is intermingled in the
whole universe, and it is perhaps for that reason that Thales
came to the opinion that all things are full of gods. This
presents some difficulties: Why does the soul when it resides in air or fire not form an animal, while it does so 10
when it resides in mixtures of the elements, and that although it is held to be of higher quality when contained in
the former? (One might add the question, why the soul in
air is maintained to be higher and more immortal than that
in animals.) Both possible ways of replying to the former
question lead to absurdity or paradox; for it is beyond
paradox to say that fire or air is an animal, and it is absurd 15
to refuse the name of animal to what has soul in it. The
opinion that the elements have soul in them seems to have
arisen from the doctrine that a whole must be homogeneous with its parts. If it is true that animals become animate
by drawing into themselves a portion of what surrounds
them, the partisans of this view are bound to say that the
soul of the Whole too is homogeneous with all its parts.
If the air sucked in is homogeneous, but soul heterogeneous, clearly while some part of soul will exist in the in- 20
breathed air, some other part will not. The soul must either
be homogeneous, or such that there are some parts of the
Whole in which it is not to be found.

From what has been said it is now clear that knowing
as an attribute of soul cannot be explained by soul's being
composed of the elements, and that it is neither sound nor
true to speak of soul as moved. But since (a) knowing, 25
perceiving, opining, and further (b) desiring, wishing, and
generally all other modes of appetition, belong to soul, and

30 (c) the local movements of animals, and (d) growth, maturity, and decay are produced by the soul, we must ask
whether each of these is an attribute of the soul as a whole,
411ᵇ i. e. whether it is with the whole soul we think, perceive,
move ourselves, act or are acted upon, or whether each of
them requires a different part of the soul? So too with
regard to life. Does it depend on one of the parts of soul?
Or is it dependent on more than one? Or on all? Or has it
some quite other cause?

Some hold that the soul is divisible, and that one part
5 thinks, another desires. If, then, its nature admits of its
being divided, what can it be that holds the parts together?
Surely not the body; on the contrary it seems rather to be
the soul that holds the body together; at any rate when the
soul departs the body disintegrates and decays. If, then,
there is something else which makes the soul one, this uni-
10 fying agency would have the best right to the name of soul,
and we shall have to repeat for it the question: Is it one or
multipartite? If it is one, why not at once admit that 'the
soul' is one? If it has parts, once more the question must
be put: What holds its parts together, and so ad infinitum?

The question might also be raised about the parts of the
soul: What is the separate rôle of each in relation to the
15 body? For, if the whole soul holds together the whole body,
we should expect each part of the soul to hold together a
part of the body. But this seems an impossibility; it is
difficult even to imagine what sort of bodily part mind
will hold together, or how it will do this.

It is a fact of observation that plants and certain insects
20 go on living when divided into segments; this means that
each of the segments has a soul in it identical in species,
though not numerically identical in the different segments,
for both of the segments for a time possess the power of
sensation and local movement. That this does not last is
not surprising, for they no longer possess the organs necessary for self-maintenance. But, all the same, in each of the
25 bodily parts there are present all the parts of soul, and the.

souls so present are homogeneous with one another and
with the whole; this means that the several parts of the soul
are indisseverable from one another, although the whole
soul is [21] divisible. It seems also that the principle found in
plants is also a kind of soul; for this is the only principle
which is common to both animals and plants; and this
exists in isolation from the principle of sensation, though 30
there is nothing which has the latter without the former.

BOOK II

1　Let the foregoing suffice as our account of the views 412ᵃ
concerning the soul which have been handed on by our
predecessors; let us now dismiss them and make as it were
a completely fresh start, endeavouring to give a precise 5
answer to the question, What is soul? i. e. to formulate the
most general possible definition of it.

We are in the habit of recognizing, as one determinate
kind of what is, substance, and that in several senses, (a) in
the sense of matter or that which in itself is not 'a this', and
(b) in the sense of form or essence, which is that precisely
in virtue of which a thing is called 'a this', and thirdly (c)
in the sense of that which is compounded of both (a) and
(b). Now matter is potentiality, form actuality; of the latter 10
there are two grades related to one another as e. g. knowledge to the exercise of knowledge.

Among substances are by general consent reckoned
bodies and especially natural bodies; for they are the principles of all other bodies. Of natural bodies some have life
in them, others not; by life we mean self-nutrition and
growth (with its correlative decay). It follows that every 15
natural body which has life in it is a substance in the sense
of a composite.

But since it is also a *body* of such and such a kind, viz.
having life, the *body* cannot be soul; the body is the subject

---

[21] sc. 'in a sense, i. e. so as to preserve its homogeneity in even its
smallest part'.

or matter, not what is attributed to it. Hence the soul must
20 be a substance in the sense of the form of a natural body
having life potentially within it. But substance [1] is actuality,
and thus soul is the actuality of a body as above characterized. Now the word actuality has two senses corresponding
respectively to the possession of knowledge and the actual
exercise of knowledge. It is obvious that the soul is actuality
in the first sense, viz. that of knowledge as possessed, for
both sleeping and waking presuppose the existence of soul,
25 and of these waking corresponds to actual knowing, sleeping to knowledge possessed but not employed, and, in the
history of the individual, knowledge comes before its employment or exercise.

That is why the soul is the first grade of actuality of a
natural body having life potentially in it. The body so described is a body which is organized. The parts of plants in
412ᵇ spite of their extreme simplicity are 'organs'; e. g. the leaf
serves to shelter the pericarp, the pericarp to shelter the
fruit, while the roots of plants are analogous to the mouth
of animals, both serving for the absorption of food. If, then,
we have to give a general formula applicable to all kinds of
5 soul, we must describe it as the first grade of actuality of a
natural organized body. That is why we can wholly dismiss
as unnecessary the question whether the soul and the body
are one: it is as meaningless as to ask whether the wax and
the shape given to it by the stamp are one, or generally the
matter of a thing and that of which it is the matter.
Unity has many senses (as many as 'is' has), but the most
proper and fundamental sense of both is the relation of
an actuality to that of which it is the actuality.

We have now given an answer to the question, What is
10 soul?—an answer which applies to it in its full extent. It is
substance in the sense which corresponds to the definitive
formula of a thing's essence. That means that it is 'the essential whatness' of a body of the character just assigned.[2]

---

[1] sc. in the sense of form.
[2] viz. organized, or possessed potentially of life.

Suppose that what is literally an 'organ',[3] like an axe, were a *natural* body, its 'essential whatness', would have been its essence, and so its soul; if this disappeared from it, it would have ceased to be an axe, except in name. As it is,[4] it is just 15 an axe; it wants the character which is required to make its whatness or formulable essence a soul; for that, it would have had to be a *natural* body of a particular kind, viz. one having *in itself* the power of setting itself in movement and arresting itself. Next, apply this doctrine in the case of the 'parts' of the living body. Suppose that the eye were an animal—sight would have been its soul, for sight is the substance or essence of the eye which corresponds to the for- 20 mula,[5] the eye being merely the matter of seeing; when seeing is removed the eye is no longer an eye, except in name— it is no more a real eye than the eye of a statue or of a painted figure. We must now extend our consideration from the 'parts' to the whole living body; for what the departmental sense is to the bodily part which is its organ, that the whole faculty of sense is to the whole sensitive body as such.

We must not understand by that which is 'potentially 25 capable of living' what has lost the soul it had, but only what still retains it; but seeds and fruits are bodies which possess the qualification.[6] Consequently, while waking is actuality in a sense corresponding to the cutting and the 413ᵃ seeing,[7] the soul is actuality in the sense corresponding to the power of sight and the power in the tool;[8] the body corresponds to what exists in potentiality; as the pupil *plus* the power of sight constitutes the eye, so the soul *plus* the body constitutes the animal.

From this it indubitably follows that the soul is insepar-

---

[3] i. e. instrument.
[4] Being an artificial, not a natural, body.
[5] i. e. which states what it is to be an eye.
[6] Though only potentially, i. e. they are at a further remove from actuality than the fully formed and organized body.
[7] i. e. to the second grade of actuality.
[8] i. e. to the first grade of actuality.

able from its body, or at any rate that certain parts of it are
5 (if it has parts)—for the actuality of some of them is nothing but the actualities of their bodily parts. Yet some may
be separable because they are not the actualities of any body
at all. Further, we have no light on the problem whether
the soul may not be the actuality of its body in the sense
in which the sailor is the actuality [9] of the ship.

This must suffice as our sketch or outline determination
10 of the nature of soul.

2   Since what is clear or logically more evident emerges
from what in itself is confused but more observable by
us, we must reconsider our results from this point of view.
For it is not enough for a definitive formula to express as
15 most now do the mere fact; it must include and exhibit the
ground also. At present definitions are given in a form analogous to the conclusion of a syllogism; e. g. What is squaring? The construction of an equilateral rectangle equal to
a given oblong rectangle. Such a definition is in form
equivalent to a conclusion.[10] One that tells us that squaring
is the discovery of a line which is a mean proportional between the two unequal sides of the given rectangle discloses
the ground of what is defined.

We resume our inquiry from a fresh starting-point by
20 calling attention to the fact that what has soul in it differs
from what has not in that the former displays life. Now this
word has more than one sense, and provided any one alone
of these is found in a thing we say that thing is living.
Living, that is, may mean thinking or perception or local
movement and rest, or movement in the sense of nutrition,
25 decay and growth. Hence we think of plants also as living,
for they are observed to possess in themselves an originative
power through which they increase or decrease in all spatial
directions; they grow up and down, and everything that
grows increases its bulk alike in both directions or indeed

[9] i. e. actuator.
[10] i. e. it has nothing in it corresponding to a middle term.

in all, and continues to live so long as it can absorb nutriment. 30

This power of self-nutrition can be isolated from the other powers mentioned, but not they from it—in mortal beings at least. The fact is obvious in plants; for it is the only psychic power they possess.

This is the originative power the possession of which leads us to speak of things as *living* at all, but it is the pos- 413ᵇ session of sensation that leads us for the first time to speak of living things as animals; for even those beings which possess no power of local movement but do possess the power of sensation we call animals and not merely living things.

The primary form of sense is touch, which belongs to all animals. Just as the power of self-nutrition can be isolated from touch and sensation generally, so touch can be 5 isolated from all other forms of sense. (By the power of self-nutrition we mean that departmental power of the soul which is common to plants and animals: all animals whatsoever are observed to have the sense of touch.) What the explanation of these two facts is, we must discuss later.[11] At present we must confine ourselves to saying that soul is 10 the source of these phenomena and is characterized by them, viz. by the powers of self-nutrition, sensation, thinking, and motivity.

Is each of these a soul or a part of a soul? And if a part, a part in what sense? A part merely distinguishable by definition or a part distinct in local situation as well? In the case 15 of certain of these powers, the answers to these questions are easy, in the case of others we are puzzled what to say. Just as in the case of plants which when divided are observed to continue to live though removed to a distance from one another (thus showing that in *their* case the soul of each individual plant before division was actually one, potentially many), so we notice a similar result in other varieties of soul, i. e. in insects which have been cut in two; 20 each of the segments possesses both sensation and local

[11] iii. 12, esp. 434ᵃ 22–30, ᵇ10 ff.

movement; and if sensation, necessarily also imagination and appetition; for, where there is sensation, there is also pleasure and pain, and, where these, necessarily also desire.

We have no evidence as yet about mind or the power to think; it seems to be a widely different kind of soul, differing as what is eternal from what is perishable; it alone is capable of existence in isolation from all other psychic powers. All the other parts of soul, it is evident from what we have said, are, in spite of certain statements to the contrary, incapable of separate existence though, of course, distinguishable by definition. If opining is distinct from perceiving, to be capable of opining and to be capable of perceiving must be distinct, and so with all the other forms of living above enumerated. Further, some animals possess all these parts of soul, some certain of them only, others one only (this is what enables us to classify animals); the cause must be considered later.[12] A similar arrangement is found also within the field of the senses; some classes of animals have all the senses, some only certain of them, others only one, the most indispensable, touch.

Since the expression 'that whereby we live and perceive' has two meanings, just like the expression 'that whereby we know'—that may mean either (a) knowledge or (b) the soul, for we can speak of knowing by or with either, and similarly that whereby we are in health may be either (a) health or (b) the body or some part of the body; and since of the two terms thus contrasted knowledge or health is the name of a form, essence, or ratio, or if we so express it an actuality of a recipient matter—knowledge of what is capable of knowing, health of what is capable of being made healthy (for the operation of that which is capable of originating change terminates and has its seat in what is changed or altered); further, since it is the soul by or with which primarily we live, perceive, and think:—it follows that the soul must be a ratio or formulable essence, not a

[12] iii. 12, 13.

matter or subject. For, as we said,[13] the word substance has
three meanings—form, matter, and the complex of both—
and of these three what is called matter is potentiality, what 15
is called form actuality. Since then the complex here is the
living thing, the body cannot be the actuality of the soul;
it is the soul which is the actuality of a certain kind of
body. Hence the rightness of the view that the soul cannot
be without a body, while it cannot be a body; it is not a 20
body but something relative to a body. That is why it is in
a body, and a body of a definite kind. It was a mistake,
therefore, to do as former thinkers did, merely to fit it into
a body without adding a definite specification of the kind or
character of that body. Reflection confirms the observed
fact; the actuality of any given thing can only be realized 25
in what is already potentially that thing, i. e. in a matter of
its own appropriate to it. From all this it follows that soul is
an actuality or formulable essence of something that possesses a potentiality of being besouled.

3 Of the psychic powers above enumerated [14] some kinds
   of living things, as we have said,[15] possess all, some less
than all, others one only. Those we have mentioned are the
nutritive, the appetitive, the sensory, the locomotive, and 30
the power of thinking. Plants have none but the first, the
nutritive, while another order of living things has this *plus*
the sensory. If any order of living things has the sensory, it **414ᵇ**
must also have the appetitive; for appetite is the genus of
which desire, passion, and wish are the species; now all animals have one sense at least, viz. touch, and whatever has a
sense has the capacity for pleasure and pain and therefore
has pleasant and painful objects present to it, and wherever
these are present, there is desire, for desire is just appetition
of what is pleasant. Further, all animals have the sense for 5

[13] 412ᵃ 7.
[14] 413ᵃ 23–5, ᵇ11–13, 21–4.
[15] 413ᵇ 32–414ᵃ 1.

food (for touch is the sense for food); the food of all living things consists of what is dry, moist, hot, cold, and these are the qualities apprehended by touch; all other sensible qualities are apprehended by touch only indirectly. Sounds, 10·colours, and odours contribute nothing to nutriment; flavours fall within the field of tangible qualities. Hunger and thirst are forms of desire, hunger a desire for what is dry and hot, thirst a desire for what is cold and moist; flavour is a sort of seasoning added to both. We must later [16] clear up 15 these points, but at present it may be enough to say that all animals that possess the sense of touch have also appetition. The case of imagination is obscure; we must examine it later.[17] Certain kinds of animals possess in addition the power of locomotion, and still another order of animate be- 20 ings, i. e. man and possibly another order like man or superior to him, the power of thinking, i. e. mind. It is now evident that a single definition can be given of soul only in the same sense as one can be given of figure. For, as in that case there is no figure distinguishable and apart from triangle, &c., so here there is no soul apart from the forms of soul just enumerated. It is true that a highly general definition can be given for figure which will fit all figures without expressing the peculiar nature of any figure. So here in the 25 case of soul and its specific forms. Hence it is absurd in this and similar cases to demand an absolutely general definition, which will fail to express the peculiar nature of anything that *is*, or again, omitting this, to look for separate definitions corresponding to each *infima species*. The cases of figure and soul are exactly parallel; for the particulars sub- 30 sumed under the common name in both cases—figures and living beings—constitute a series, each successive term of which potentially contains its predecessor, e. g. the square the triangle, the sensory power the self-nutritive. Hence we must ask in the case of each order of living things, What is its soul, i. e. What is the soul of plant, animal, man? Why

---

[16] c. 11. iii. 12. 434ᵇ 18–21.
[17] iii. 3, 11. 433ᵇ 31–434ᵃ 7.

the terms are related in this serial way must form the sub- 415ᵃ
ject of later examination.[18] But the facts are that the power
of perception is never found apart from the power of self-
nutrition, while—in plants—the latter is found isolated
from the former. Again, no sense is found apart from that
of touch, while touch is found by itself; many animals have 5
neither sight, hearing, nor smell. Again, among living things
that possess sense some have the power of locomotion,
some not. Lastly, certain living beings—a small minority—
possess calculation and thought, for (among mortal beings)
those which possess calculation have all the other powers
above mentioned, while the converse does not hold—in- 10
deed some live by imagination alone, while others have not
even imagination. The mind that knows with immediate intuition presents a different problem.[19]

It is evident that the way to give the most adequate definition of soul is to seek in the case of each of its forms for
the most appropriate definition.

4   It is necessary for the student of these forms of soul
first to find a definition of each, expressive of what it 15
is, and then to investigate its derivative properties, &c. But
if we are to express what each is, viz. what the thinking
power is, or the perceptive, or the nutritive, we must go
farther back and first give an account of thinking or perceiving, for in the order of investigation the question of
what an agent does precedes the question, what enables it
to do what it does. If this is correct, we must on the same
ground go yet another step farther back and have some clear 20
view of the objects of each; thus we must start with these
objects, e. g. with food, with what is perceptible, or with
what is intelligible.

It follows that first of all we must treat of nutrition and
reproduction,[20] for the nutritive soul is found along with all

---

[18] iii. 12, 13.
[19] Cf. iii. 4–8.
[20] sc 'which we shall see to be inseparable from nutrition'.

the others and is the most primitive and widely distributed power of soul, being indeed that one in virtue of which all 25 are said to have life. The acts in which it manifests itself are reproduction and the use of food—reproduction, I say, because for any living thing that has reached its normal development and which is unmutilated, and whose mode of generation is not spontaneous, the most natural act is the production of another like itself, an animal producing an animal, a plant a plant, in order that, as far as its nature 415ᵇ allows, it may partake in the eternal and divine. That is the goal towards which all things strive, that for the sake of which they do whatsoever their nature renders possible. The phrase 'for the sake of which' is ambiguous; it may mean either (a) the end to achieve which, or (b) the being in whose interest, the act is done. Since then no living thing is able to partake in what is eternal and divine by un-interrupted continuance (for nothing perishable can for 5 ever remain one and the same), it tries to achieve that end in the only way possible to it, and success is possible in vary-ing degrees; so it remains not indeed as the self-same indi-vidual but continues its existence in something *like* itself —not numerically but specifically one.[21]

The soul is the cause or source of the living body. The terms cause and source have many senses. But the soul is the cause of its body alike in all three senses which we ex-10 plicitly recognize. It is (a) the source or origin of move-ment, it is (b) the end, it is (c) the essence of the whole living body.

That it is the last, is clear; for in everything the essence is identical with the ground of its being, and here, in the case of living things, their being is to live, and of their being and their living the soul in them is the cause or source. Further, the actuality of whatever is potential is identical with its formulable essence.

---

[21] There is an unbroken current of the same specific life flowing through a discontinuous series of individual beings of the same species united by descent.

It is manifest that the soul is also the final cause of its 15 body. For Nature, like mind, always does whatever it does for the sake of something, which something is its end. To that something corresponds in the case of animals the soul and in this it follows the order of nature; all natural bodies are organs of the soul. This is true of those that enter into the constitution of plants as well as of those which enter into that of animals. This shows that that for the sake of 20 which they are is soul. We must here recall the two senses of 'that for the sake of which', viz. (a) the end to achieve which, and (b) the being in whose interest, anything is or is done.

We must maintain, further, that the soul is also the cause of the living body as the original source of local movement. The power of locomotion is not found, however, in all living things. But change of quality and change of quantity are also due to the soul. Sensation is held to be a qualitative alteration, and nothing except what has soul in it is capable of sensation. The same holds of the 25 quantitative changes which constitute growth and decay; nothing grows or decays naturally [22] except what feeds itself, and nothing feeds itself except what has a share of soul in it.

Empedocles is wrong in adding that growth in plants is to be explained, the downward rooting by the natural tendency of earth to travel downwards, and the upward **416ᵃ** branching by the similar natural tendency of fire to travel upwards. For he misinterprets up and down; up and down are not for all things what they are for the whole Cosmos: if we are to distinguish and identify organs according to 5 their *functions*, the roots of plants are analogous to the head in animals. Further, we must ask what is the force that holds together the earth and the fire which tend to travel in contrary directions; if there is no counteracting force, they will be torn asunder; if there is, this must be the soul and the cause of nutrition and growth. By some the ele-

[22] i. e. of itself.

10 ment of fire is held to be the cause of nutrition and growth, for it alone of the primary bodies or elements is observed to feed and increase itself. Hence the suggestion that in both plants and animals it is it which is the operative force. A concurrent cause in a sense it certainly is, but not 15 the principal cause; that is rather the soul; for while the growth of fire goes on without limit so long as there is a supply of fuel, in the case of all complex wholes formed in the course of nature there is a limit or ratio which determines their size and increase, and limit and ratio are marks of soul but not of fire, and belong to the side of formulable essence rather than that of matter.

Nutrition and reproduction are due to one and the same psychic power. It is necessary first to give precision to our account of food, for it is by this function of absorbing 20 food that this psychic power is distinguished from all the others. The current view is that what serves as food to a living thing is what is contrary to it—not that in every pair of contraries each is food to the other: to be food a contrary must not only be transformable into the other and vice versa, it must also in so doing increase the bulk of the other. Many a contrary is transformed into its other and vice versa, where neither is even a quantum and so cannot 25 increase in bulk, e. g. an invalid into a healthy subject. It is clear that not even those contraries which satisfy both the conditions mentioned above are food to one another in precisely the same sense; water may be said to feed fire, but not fire water. Where the members of the pair are elementary bodies only one of the contraries, it would appear, can be said to feed the other. But there is a difficulty 30 here. One set of thinkers assert that like is fed, as well as increased in amount, by like. Another set, as we have said, maintain the very reverse, viz. that what feeds and what is fed are contrary to one another; like, they argue, is incapable of being affected by like; but food is changed in the process of digestion, and change is always to what is opposite or to what is intermediate. Further, food is acted

upon by what is nourished by it, not the other way round, 35
as timber is worked by a carpenter and not conversely; 416ᵛ
there is a change in the carpenter but it is merely a change
from not-working to working. In answering this problem
it makes all the difference whether we mean by 'the food'
the 'finished' or the 'raw' product. If we use the word food
of both, viz. of the completely undigested and the completely digested matter, we can justify both the rival accounts of it; taking food in the sense of undigested matter, 5
it is the contrary of what is fed by it, taking it as digested it
is like what is fed by it. Consequently it is clear that in a
certain sense we may say that both parties are right, both
wrong.

Since nothing except what is alive can be fed, what is fed
is the besouled body and just because it has soul in it.
Hence food is essentially related to what has soul in it. Food
has a power which is other than the power to increase the 10
bulk of what is fed by it; so far forth as what has soul in it
is a quantum, food may increase its quantity, but it is only
so far as what has soul in it is a 'this-somewhat' or substance
that food acts as food; in that case it maintains the being
of what is fed, and that continues to be what it is so long as
the process of nutrition continues. Further, it is the agent in
generation, i. e. not the generation of the individual fed 15
but the reproduction of another like it; the substance of the
individual fed is already in existence; the existence of no
substance is a self-generation but only a self-maintenance.

Hence the psychic power which we are now studying may
be described as that which tends to maintain whatever has
this power in it of continuing such as it was, and food helps
it to do its work. That is why, if deprived of food, it must
cease to be.

The process of nutrition involves three factors, (a) what 20
is fed, (b) that wherewith it is fed, (c) what does the feeding; of these (c) is the first soul,²³ (a) the body which has
that soul in it, (b) the food. But since it is right to call

²³ i. e. the earliest and most indispensable kind of soul.

things after the ends they realize, and the end of this soul is
25 to generate another being like that in which it is, the first
soul ought to be named the reproductive soul. The expression (b) 'wherewith it is fed' is ambiguous just as is
the expression 'wherewith the ship is steered'; that may
mean either (i) the hand or (ii) the rudder, i. e. either (i)
what is moved and sets in movement, or (ii) what is merely
moved. We can apply this analogy here if we recall that all
food must be capable of being digested, and that what produces digestion is warmth; that is why everything that has
soul in it possesses warmth.
30   We have now given an outline account of the nature of
food; further details must be given in the appropriate place.

5   Having made these distinctions let us now speak of
sensation in the widest sense. Sensation depends, as
we have said,[24] on a process of movement or affection from
35 without, for it is held to be some sort of change of quality.
417ª Now some thinkers assert that like is affected only by like;
in what sense this is possible and in what sense impossible,
we have explained in our general discussion of acting and
being acted upon.[25]

Here arises a problem: why do we not perceive the senses
themselves as well as the external objects of sense, or why
without the stimulation of external objects do they not pro-
5 duce sensation, seeing that they contain in themselves fire,
earth, and all the other elements, which are the direct or
indirect objects of sense? It is clear that what is sensitive is
so only potentially, not actually. The power of sense is
parallel to what is combustible, for that never ignites itself
spontaneously, but requires an agent which has the power
of starting ignition; otherwise it could have set itself on
fire, and would not have needed actual fire to set it ablaze.

In reply we must recall that we use the word 'perceive'
in two ways, for we say (a) that what has the power to hear

[24] 415ᵇ 24, cf. 410ª 25.
[25] De Gen. et Corr. 323ᵇ 18 ff.

or see, 'sees' or 'hears', even though it is at the moment 10 asleep, and also (b) that what is actually seeing or hearing, 'sees' or 'hears'. Hence 'sense' too must have two meanings, sense potential, and sense actual. Similarly 'to be a sentient' means either (a) to have a certain power or (b) to manifest a certain activity. To begin with, for a time, let us speak as if there were no difference between (i) being moved or affected, and (ii) being active, for movement is a kind of 15 activity—an imperfect kind, as has elsewhere been explained.[26] Everything that is acted upon or moved is acted upon by an agent which is actually at work. Hence it is that in one sense, as has already been stated,[27] what acts and what is acted upon are like, in another unlike, i. e. prior to and during the change the two factors are unlike, after 20 it like.

But we must now distinguish not only *between* what is potential and what is actual but also different senses in which things can be said to be potential or actual; up to now we have been speaking as if each of these phrases had only one sense. We can speak of something as 'a knower' either (a) as when we say that man is a knower, meaning that man falls within the class of beings that know or have knowledge, or (b) as when we are speaking of a man who possesses a knowledge of grammar; each of these is so 25 called as having in him a certain potentiality, but there is a difference between their respective potentialities, the one (a) being a potential knower, because his kind or matter is such and such, the other (b), because he can in the absence of any external counteracting cause realize his knowledge in actual knowing at will. This implies a third meaning of 'a knower' (c), one who is already realizing his knowledge—he is a knower in actuality and in the most proper sense is knowing, e. g. this A. Both the former are 30 potential knowers, who realize their respective potentialities, the one (a) by change of quality, i. e. repeated transi-

[26] Phys. 201[b] 31, 257[b] 8.
[27] 416[a] 29–[b]9.

tions from one state to its opposite [28] under instruction, the
other (b) by the transition from the inactive possession of
417ᵇ sense or grammar to their active exercise. The two kinds
of transition are distinct.

Also the expression 'to be acted upon' has more than one
meaning; it may mean either (a) the extinction of one of
two contraries by the other, or (b) the maintenance of
what is potential by the agency of what is actual and already
like what is acted upon, with such likeness as is compatible
5 with one's being actual and the other potential. For what
possesses knowledge becomes an actual knower by a transition which is either not an alteration of it at all (being in
reality a development into its true self or actuality) or at
least an alteration in a quite different sense from the usual
meaning.

Hence it is wrong to speak of a wise man as being 'altered'
when he uses his wisdom, just as it would be absurd to
speak of a builder as being altered when he is using his skill
in building a house.

10   What in the case of knowing or understanding leads
from potentiality to actuality ought not to be called teaching but something else. That which starting with the power
to know learns or acquires knowledge through the agency of
one who actually knows and has the power of teaching
15 either (a) ought not to be said 'to be acted upon' at all or
(b) we must recognize two senses of alteration, viz. (i) the
substitution of one quality for another, the first being the
contrary of the second, or (ii) the development of an
existent quality from potentiality in the direction of fixity
or nature.

In the case of what is to possess sense, the first transition
is due to the action of the male parent and takes place before birth so that at birth the living thing is, in respect of
sensation, at the stage which corresponds to the *possession*
of knowledge. Actual sensation corresponds to the stage of
20 the exercise of knowledge. But between the two cases com-

---

[28] viz. from ignorance or error to knowledge or truth.

pared there is a difference; the objects that excite the
sensory powers to activity, the seen, the heard, &c., are
outside. The ground of this difference is that what actual
sensation apprehends is individuals, while what knowledge
apprehends is universals, and these are in a sense within the
soul. That is why a man can exercise his knowledge when he
wishes, but his sensation does not depend upon himself— 25
a sensible object must be there. A similar statement must
be made about our *knowledge* of what is sensible—on the
same ground, viz. that the sensible objects are individual
and external.

A later more appropriate occasion may be found [29] thoroughly to clear up all this. At present it must be enough to 30
recognize the distinctions already drawn; a thing may be
said to be potential in either of two senses, (a) in the sense
in which we might say of a boy that he may become a general or (b) in the sense in which we might say the same of
an adult, and there are two corresponding senses of the 418ᵃ
term 'a potential sentient'. There are no separate names for
the two stages of potentiality; we have pointed out that they
are different and how they are different. We cannot help
using the incorrect terms 'being acted upon or altered' of
the two transitions involved. As we have said,[30] what has
the power of sensation is potentially like what the perceived object is actually; that is, while at the beginning of 5
the process of its being acted upon the two interacting
factors are dissimilar, at the end the one acted upon is assimilated to the other and is identical in quality with it.

6   In dealing with each of the senses we shall have first
to speak of the objects which are perceptible by each.
The term 'object of sense' covers three kinds of objects, two
kinds of which are, in our language, directly perceptible,
while the remaining one is only incidentally perceptible. Of
the first two kinds one (a) consists of what is perceptible

---

[29] iii. 4, 5.
[30] 417ᵃ 12–20.

by a single sense, the other (b) of what is perceptible by
10 any and all of the senses.[31] I call by the name of special
object of this or that sense that which cannot be perceived by any other sense than that one and in respect of
which no error is possible; in this sense colour is the special
object of sight, sound of hearing, flavour of taste. Touch,
indeed, discriminates more than one set of different qualities. Each sense has one kind of object which it discerns,
15 and never errs in reporting that what is before it is colour or
sound (though it may err as to what it is that is coloured
or where that is, or what it is that is sounding or where that
is). Such objects are what we propose to call the special
objects of this or that sense.

'Common sensibles' are movement, rest, number, figure,
magnitude; these are not peculiar to any one sense, but are
common to all. There are at any rate certain kinds of movement which are perceptible both by touch and by sight.

We speak of an incidental object of sense where e. g. the
20 white object which we see is the son of Diares; here because 'being the son of Diares' is incidental to the directly
visible white patch we speak of the son of Diares as being
(incidentally) perceived or seen by us. Because this is only
incidentally an object of sense, it in no way as such affects
the senses. Of the two former kinds, both of which are in
their own nature perceptible by sense, the first kind—that
of special objects of the several senses—constitute the
objects of sense in the strictest sense of the term and it is to
25 them that in the nature of things the structure of each
several sense is adapted.

7   The object of sight is the visible, and what is visible is
(a) colour and (b) a certain kind of object which can
be described in words but which has no single name; what
we mean by (b) will be abundantly clear as we proceed.
Whatever is visible is colour and colour is what lies upon
30 what is in its own nature visible; 'in its own nature' here

[31] Really, it is enough if it is perceptible by more than one sense.

means not that visibility is involved in the definition of what thus underlies colour, but that that substratum contains in itself the cause of visibility. Every colour has in it the power to set in movement what is actually transparent; **418ᵛ** that power constitutes its very nature. That is why it is not visible except with the help of light; it is only in light that the colour of a thing is seen. Hence our first task is to explain what light is.

Now there clearly is something which is transparent, and by 'transparent' I mean what is visible, and yet not visible 5 in itself, but rather owing its visibility to the colour of *something else*; of this character are air, water, and many solid bodies. Neither air nor water is transparent because it is air or water; they are transparent because each of them has contained in it a certain substance which is the same in both and is also found in the eternal body which constitutes the uppermost shell of the physical Cosmos. Of this substance light is the activity—the activity of what is transparent so far forth as it has in it the determinate power of becoming 10 transparent; where this power is present, there is also the potentiality of the contrary, viz. darkness. Light is as it were the proper colour of what is transparent, and exists whenever the potentially transparent is excited to actuality by the influence of fire or something resembling 'the uppermost body'; for fire too contains something which is one and the same with the substance in question.

We have now explained what the transparent is and what light is; light is neither fire nor any kind whatsoever of body nor an efflux from any kind of body (if it were, it 15 would again itself be a kind of body)—it is the presence of fire or something resembling fire in what is transparent. It is certainly not a body, for two bodies cannot be present in the same place. The opposite of light is darkness; darkness is the absence from what is transparent of the corresponding positive state above characterized; clearly therefore, light is just the presence of that.

Empedocles (and with him all others who used the same 20

forms of expression) was wrong in speaking of light as 'travelling' or being at a given moment between the earth and its envelope, its movement being unobservable by us; that view is contrary both to the clear evidence of argu-
25 ment and to the observed facts; if the distance traversed were short, the movement might have been unobservable, but where the distance is from extreme East to extreme West, the draught upon our powers of belief is too great.

What is capable of taking on colour is what in itself is colourless, as what can take on sound is what is soundless; what is colourless includes (a) what is transparent and (b)
30 what is invisible or scarcely visible, i. e. what is 'dark'. The latter (b) is the same as what is transparent, when it is potentially, not of course when it is actually transparent; it is the same substance which is now darkness, now light.

Not everything that is visible depends upon light for its
419ᵃ visibility. This is only true of the 'proper' colour of things. Some objects of sight which in light are invisible, in dark-ness stimulate the sense; that is, things that appear fiery or shining. This class of objects has no simple common name,
5 but instances of it are fungi, flesh, heads, scales, and eyes of fish. In none of these is what is seen their own 'proper' col-our. Why we see these at all is another question. At present what is obvious is that what is seen in light is always colour. That is why without the help of light colour remains in-visible. Its being colour at all means precisely its having in it
10 the power to set in movement what is already actually transparent, and, as we have seen, the actuality of what is transparent is just light.

The following experiment makes the necessity of a medium clear. If what has colour is placed in immediate contact with the eye, it cannot be seen. Colour sets in movement not the sense organ but what is transparent, e. g. the air, and that, extending continuously from the ob-
15 ject of the organ, sets the latter in movement. Democritus misrepresents the facts when he expresses the opinion that if the interspace were empty one could distinctly see an ant

on the vault of the sky; that is an impossibility. Seeing is
due to an affection or change of what has the perceptive
faculty, and it cannot be affected by the seen colour itself;
it remains that it must be affected by what comes between.
Hence it is indispensable that there be *something* in between—if there were nothing, so far from seeing with 20
greater distinctness, we should see nothing at all.

We have now explained the cause why colour cannot be
seen otherwise than in light. Fire on the other hand is seen
both in darkness and in light; this double possibility follows
necessarily from our theory, for it is just fire that makes
what is potentially transparent actually transparent.

The same account holds also of sound and smell; if the
object of either of these senses is in immediate contact with 25
the organ no sensation is produced. In both cases the object
sets in movement only what lies between, and this in turn
sets the organ in movement: if what sounds or smells is
brought into immediate contact with the organ, no sensation will be produced. The same, in spite of all appear- 30
ances, applies also to touch and taste; why there is this apparent difference will be clear later.[32] What comes between
in the case of sounds is air; the corresponding medium in
the case of smell has no name. But, corresponding to what
is transparent in the case of colour, there is a quality found
both in air and water, which serves as a medium for what 35
has smell—I say 'in water' because animals that live in water
as well as those that live on land seem to possess the sense
of smell, and 'in air' because man and all other land animals **419ᵇ**
that breathe, perceive smells only when they breathe air in.
The explanation of this too will be given later.[33]

8 Now let us, to begin with, make certain distinctions
about sound and hearing.

Sound may mean either of two things—(*a*) actual, and **5**
(*b*) potential, sound. There are certain things which, as we

[32] 422ᵇ 34 ff.
[33] 421ᵇ 13–422ᵃ 6.

say, 'have no sound', e. g. sponges or wool, others which
have, e. g. bronze and in general all things which are smooth
and solid—the latter are said to have a sound because they
can make a sound, i. e. can generate actual sound between
themselves and the organ of hearing.

Actual sound requires for its occurrence (i, ii) two such
10 bodies and (iii) a space between them; for it is generated
by an impact. Hence it is impossible for one body only to
generate a sound—there must be a body impinging and a
body impinged upon; what sounds does so by striking
against something else, and this is impossible without a
movement from place to place.

As we have said, not all bodies can by impact on one another produce sound; impact on wool makes no sound,
15 while the impact on bronze or any body which is smooth
and hollow does. Bronze gives out a sound when struck because it is smooth; bodies which are hollow owing to reflection repeat the original impact over and over again, the
body originally set in movement being unable to escape
from the concavity.

Further, we must remark that sound is heard both in air
and in water, though less distinctly in the latter. Yet neither
20 air nor water is the principal cause of sound. What is required for the production of sound is an impact of two
solids against one another and against the air. The latter
condition is satisfied when the air impinged upon does not
retreat before the blow, i. e. is not dissipated by it.

That is why it must be struck with a sudden sharp blow,
if it is to sound—the movement of the whip must outrun
the dispersion of the air, just as one might get in a stroke at
a heap or whirl of sand as it was travelling rapidly past.

25   An echo occurs, when, a mass of air having been unified,
bounded, and prevented from dissipation by the containing
walls of a vessel, the air originally struck by the impinging
body and set in movement by it rebounds from this mass
of air like a ball from a wall. It is probable that in all generation of sound echo takes place, though it is frequently

only indistinctly heard. What happens here must be analogous to what happens in the case of light; light is always
reflected—otherwise it would not be diffused and outside
what was directly illuminated by the sun there would be 30
blank darkness; but this reflected light is not always strong
enough, as it is when it is reflected from water, bronze, and
other smooth bodies, to cast a shadow, which is the distinguishing mark by which we recognize light.

It is rightly said that an empty space plays the chief part
in the production of hearing, for what people mean by 'the
vacuum' is the air, which is what causes hearing, when that
air is set in movement as one continuous mass; but owing
to its friability it emits no sound, being dissipated by im- 35
pinging upon any surface which is not smooth. When the 420ᵃ
surface on which it impinges is quite smooth, what is produced by the original impact is a united mass, a result due
to the smoothness of the surface with which the air is in
contact at the other end.

What has the power of producing sound is what has the
power of setting in movement a single mass of air which is
continuous from the impinging body up to the organ of
hearing. The organ of hearing is physically united with
air,[34] and because it is in air, the air inside is moved con-
currently with the air outside. Hence animals do not hear 5
with all parts of their bodies, nor do all parts admit of the
entrance of air; for even the part which can be moved and
can sound has not air everywhere in it. Air in itself is, owing
to its friability, quite soundless; only when its dissipation
is prevented is its movement sound. The air in the ear is
built into a chamber just to prevent this dissipating movement, in order that the animal may accurately apprehend 10
all varieties of the movements of the air outside. That is
why we hear also in water, viz. because the water cannot
get into the air chamber or even, owing to the spirals, into
the outer ear. If this does happen, hearing ceases, as it also
does if the tympanic membrane is damaged, just as sight

[34] i. e. it has air incorporated in its structure.

ceases if the membrane covering the pupil is damaged. It is
15 also a test of deafness whether the ear does or does not
reverberate like a horn; the air inside the ear has always a
movement of its own, but the sound we hear is always
the sounding of something else, not of the organ itself.
That is why we say that we hear with what is empty and
echoes, viz. because what we hear with is a chamber which
contains a bounded mass of air.

Which is it that 'sounds', the striking body or the struck?
Is not the answer 'it is both, but each in a different way'?
20 Sound is a movement of what can rebound from a smooth
surface when struck against it. As we have explained [35] not
everything sounds when it strikes or is struck, e. g. if one
25 needle is struck against another, neither emits any sound.
In order, therefore, that sound may be generated, what is
struck must be smooth, to enable the air to rebound and
be shaken off from it in one piece.

The distinctions between different sounding bodies show
themselves only in actual sound; [36] as without the help of
light colours remain invisible, so without the help of actual
sound the distinctions between acute and grave sounds remain inaudible. Acute and grave are here metaphors, trans-
30 ferred from their proper sphere, viz. that of touch, where
they mean respectively (a) what moves the sense much in
a short time, (b) what moves the sense little in a long time.
Not that what is sharp really moves fast, and what is grave,
slowly, but that the difference in the qualities of the one
420ᵇ and the other movement is due to their respective speeds.
There seems to be a sort of parallelism between what is
acute or grave to hearing and what is sharp or blunt to
touch; what is sharp as it were stabs, while what is blunt
pushes, the one producing its effect in a short, the other in
a long time, so that the one is quick, the other slow.
5   Let the foregoing suffice as an analysis of sound. Voice is

[35] 419ᵇ 6, 13.
[36] i. e. when these bodies, e. g. the strings of a lyre, are actually
sounding.

a kind of sound characteristic of what has soul in it; nothing
that is without soul utters voice, it being only by a metaphor that we speak of the voice of the flute or the lyre or
generally of what (being without soul) possesses the power
of producing a succession of notes which differ in length
and pitch and timbre. The metaphor is based on the fact
that all these differences are found also in voice. Many animals are voiceless, e. g. all non-sanguineous animals and
among sanguineous animals fish. This is just what we 10
should expect, since voice is a certain movement of air. The
fish, like those in the Achelous, which are said to have voice,
really make the sounds with their gills or some similar organ. Voice is the sound made by an animal, and that with
a special organ. As we saw, everything that makes a sound
does so by the impact of something (a) against something
else, (b) across a space, (c) filled with air; hence it is only 15
to be expected that no animals utter voice except those
which take in air. Once air is inbreathed, Nature uses it
for two different purposes, as the tongue is used both for
tasting and for articulating; in that case of the two functions tasting is necessary for the animal's existence (hence
it is found more widely distributed), while articulate speech
is a luxury subserving its possessor's well-being; similarly in
the former case Nature employs the breath both as an in- 20
dispensable means to the regulation of the inner temperature of the living body and also as the matter of articulate
voice, in the interests of its possessor's well-being. Why its
former use is indispensable must be discussed elsewhere.[37]

The organ of respiration is the windpipe, and the organ
to which this is related as means to end is the lungs. The
latter is the part of the body by which the temperature of
land animals is raised above that of all others. But what
primarily requires the air drawn in by respiration is not 25
only this but the region surrounding the heart. That is
why when animals breathe the air must penetrate inwards.

Voice then is the impact of the inbreathed air against

[37] De Resp. 478ᵃ 28; P. A. 642ᵃ 31–ᵇ4.

the 'windpipe', and the agent that produces the impact
is the soul resident in these parts of the body. Not every
30 sound, as we said, made by an animal is voice (even with
the tongue we may merely make a sound which is not
voice, or without the tongue as in coughing); what produces the impact must have soul in it and must be accompanied by an act of imagination, for voice is a sound
with a meaning, and is not merely the result of any impact
of the breath as in coughing; in voice the breath in the
windpipe is used as an instrument to knock with against
421ᵃ the walls of the windpipe. This is confirmed by our in-
ability to speak when we are breathing either out or in—we
can only do so by holding our breath; we make the movements with the breath so checked. It is clear also why fish
are voiceless; they have no windpipe. And they have no
5 windpipe because they do not breathe or take in air. Why
they do not is a question belonging to another inquiry.[38]

9   Smell and its object are much less easy to determine
than what we have hitherto discussed; the distinguishing characteristic of the object of smell is less obvious than
those of sound or colour. The ground of this is that our
power of smell is less discriminating and in general inferior
10 to that of many species of animals; men have a poor sense
of smell and our apprehension of its proper objects is inseparably bound up with and so confused by pleasure and
pain, which shows that in us the organ is inaccurate. It is
probable that there is a parallel failure in the perception of
colour by animals that have hard eyes: probably they
discriminate differences of colour only by the presence or
15 absence of what excites fear, and that it is thus that human
beings distinguish smells. It seems that there is an analogy
between smell and taste, and that the species of tastes run
parallel to those of smells—the only difference being that
our sense of taste is more discriminating than our sense of
smell, because the former is a modification of touch, which

38 Cf. *De Resp.* 474ᵇ 25–9, 476ᵃ 6–15; *P. A.* 669ᵃ 2–5

reaches in man the maximum of discriminative accuracy. 20
While in respect of all the other senses we fall below many
species of animals, in respect of touch we far excel all other
species in exactness of discrimination. That is why man is
the most intelligent of all animals. This is confirmed by
the fact that it is to differences in the organ of touch and to
nothing else that the differences between man and man in
respect of natural endowment are due; men whose flesh is 25
hard are ill-endowed by nature, men whose flesh is soft,
well-endowed.

As flavours may be divided into (*a*) sweet, (*b*) bitter, so
with smells. In some things the flavour and the smell
have the same quality, i. e. both are sweet or both bitter,
in others they diverge. Similarly a smell, like a flavour, may 30
be pungent, astringent, acid, or succulent. But, as we said,
because smells are much less easy to discriminate than
flavours, the names of these varieties are applied to smells
only metaphorically; for example 'sweet' is extended from **421ᵇ**
the taste to the smell of saffron or honey, 'pungent' to that
of thyme, and so on.[39]

In the same sense in which hearing has for its object both
the audible and the inaudible, sight both the visible and 5
the invisible, smell has for its object both the odorous
and the inodorous. 'Inodorous' may be either (*a*) what has
no smell at all, or (*b*) what has a small or feeble smell. The
same ambiguity lurks in the word 'tasteless'.

Smelling, like the operation of the senses previously examined, takes place through a medium, i. e. through air or
water—I add water, because water-animals too (both 10
sanguineous and non-sanguineous) seem to smell just as
much as land-animals; at any rate some of them make directly for their food from a distance if it has any scent. That
is why the following facts constitute a problem for us. All
animals smell in the same way, but man smells only when
he inhales; if he exhales or holds his breath, he ceases to 15

[39] Because of the felt likeness between the respective smells and the
really sweet or pungent tastes of the same herbs, &c.

smell, no difference being made whether the odorous object is distant or near, or even placed inside the nose and actually on the wall of the nostril; it is a disability common to all the senses not to perceive what is in immediate contact with the organ of sense, but our failure to apprehend what is odorous without the help of inhalation is peculiar (the fact is obvious on making the experiment). Now since bloodless animals do not breathe, they must, it might be
20 argued, have some novel sense not reckoned among the usual five. Our reply must be that this is impossible, since it is scent that is perceived; a sense that apprehends what is odorous and what has a good or bad odour cannot be anything but smell. Further, they are observed to be deleteriously affected by the same strong odours as man is, e. g.
25 bitumen, sulphur, and the like. These animals must be able to smell without being able to breathe. The probable explanation is that in man the organ of smell has a certain superiority over that in all other animals just as his eyes have over those of hard-eyed animals. Man's eyes have in the eyelids a kind of shelter or envelope, which must be shifted or drawn back in order that we may see, while
30 hard-eyed animals have nothing of the kind, but at once see whatever presents itself in the transparent medium. Similarly in certain species of animals the organ of smell is like the eye of hard-eyed animals, uncurtained, while in others
422ᵃ which take in air it probably has a curtain over it, which is drawn back in inhalation, owing to the dilating of the veins or pores. That explains also why such animals cannot smell
5 under water; to smell they must first inhale, and that they cannot do under water.

Smells come from what is dry as flavours from what is moist. Consequently the organ of smell is potentially dry.

10 What can be tasted is always something that can be touched, and just for that reason it cannot be perceived *through* an interposed foreign body, for touch means the
10 absence of any intervening body. Further, the flavoured

and tasteable body is suspended in a liquid matter, and this
is tangible. Hence, if we lived in water, we should perceive
a sweet object introduced into the water, but the water
would not be the medium *through* which we perceived; our
perception would be due to the solution of the sweet substance in what we imbibed, just as if it were mixed with
some drink. There is no parallel here to the perception of
colour, which is due neither to any blending of anything
with anything, nor to any efflux of anything from anything. In the case of taste, there is nothing corresponding to
the medium in the case of the senses previously discussed; 15
but as the object of sight is colour, so the object of taste is
flavour. But nothing excites a perception of flavour without
the help of liquid; what acts upon the sense of taste must be
either actually or potentially liquid like what is saline; it
must be both (a) itself easily dissolved, and (b) capable of
dissolving along with itself the tongue. Taste apprehends 20
both (a) what has taste and (b) what has no taste, if we
mean by (b) what has only a slight or feeble flavour or
what tends to destroy the sense of taste. In this it is
exactly parallel to sight, which apprehends both what is
visible and what is invisible (for darkness is invisible and
yet is discriminated by sight; so is, in a different way, what
is over-brilliant), and to hearing, which apprehends both
sound and silence, of which the one is audible and the other 25
inaudible, and also over-loud sound. This corresponds in
the case of hearing to over-bright light in the case of sight.
As a faint sound is 'inaudible', so in a sense is a loud or violent sound. The word 'invisible' and similar privative terms
cover not only (a) what is simply without some power, but
also (b) what is adapted by nature to have it but has not it
or has it only in a very low degree, as when we say that a
species of swallow is 'footless' or that a variety of fruit is
'stoneless'. So too taste has as its object both what can be
tasted and the tasteless—the latter in the sense of what has 30
little flavour or a bad flavour or one destructive of taste.
The difference between what is tasteless and what is not

seems to rest ultimately on that between what is drinkable and what is undrinkable—both are tasteable, but the latter is bad and tends to destroy taste, while the former is the normal stimulus of taste. What is drinkable is the common object of both touch and taste.

422ᵇ   Since what can be tasted is liquid, the organ for its perception cannot be either (a) actually liquid or (b) incapable of becoming liquid. Tasting means a being affected by [40] what can be tasted as such; hence the organ of taste must be liquefied, and so to start with must be non-liquid
5 but capable of liquefaction without loss of its distinctive nature. This is confirmed by the fact that the tongue cannot taste either when it is too dry or when it is too moist; in the latter case what occurs is due to a contact with the pre-existent moisture in the tongue itself, when after a fore-taste of some strong flavour we try to taste another flavour; it is in this way that sick persons find everything they taste bitter, viz. because, when they taste, their tongues are overflowing with bitter moisture.

10   The species of flavour are, as in the case of colour, (a) simple, i. e. the two contraries, the sweet and the bitter, (b) secondary, viz. (i) on the side of the sweet, the succulent, (ii) on the side of the bitter, the saline, (iii) between these come the pungent, the harsh, the astringent, and the acid;
15 these pretty well exhaust the varieties of flavour. It follows that what has the power of tasting is what is potentially of that kind, and that what is tasteable is what has the power of making it actually what it itself already is.

11   Whatever can be said of what is tangible, can be said of touch, and vice versa; if touch is not a single sense but a group of senses, there must be several kinds of what is tangible. It is a problem whether touch is a single sense or
20 a group of senses. It is also a problem, what is the organ of touch; is it or is it not the flesh (including what in certain animals is homologous with flesh)? On the second view,

[40] sc. 'and so, as we have seen, a being assimilated to'.

flesh is 'the medium' of touch, the real organ being situated
farther inward. The problem arises because the field of each
sense is according to the accepted view determined as the
range between a single pair of contraries, white and black
for sight, acute and grave for hearing, bitter and sweet for
taste; but in the field of what is tangible we find several 25
such pairs, hot cold, dry moist, hard soft, &c. This problem
finds a partial solution, when it is recalled that in the case
of the other senses more than one pair of contraries are to
be met with, e. g. in sound not only acute and grave but
loud and soft, smooth and rough, &c.; there are similar con- 30
trasts in the field of colour. Nevertheless we are unable
clearly to detect in the case of touch what the single subject
is which underlies the contrasted qualities and corresponds
to sound in the case of hearing.

To the question whether the organ of touch lies inward
or not (i. e. whether we need look any farther than the
flesh), no indication in favour of the second answer can be
drawn from the fact that if the object comes into contact 423ᵃ
with the flesh it is at once perceived. For even under present
conditions if the experiment is made of making a web and
stretching it tight over the flesh, as soon as this web is
touched the sensation is reported in the same manner as
before, yet it is clear that the organ is not in this membrane.
If the membrane could be grown on to the flesh, the report
would travel still quicker. The flesh plays in touch very 5
much the same part as would be played in the other senses
by an air-envelope growing round our body; had we such an
envelope attached to us we should have supposed that it
was by a single organ that we perceived sounds, colours,
and smells, and we should have taken sight, hearing, and
smell to be a single sense. But as it is, because that
through which the different movements are transmitted is 10
not naturally attached to our bodies, the difference of the
various sense-organs is too plain to miss. But in the case of
touch the obscurity remains.

There must be such a naturally attached 'medium' as

flesh, for no living body could be constructed of air or
water; it must be something solid. Consequently it must
be composed of earth along with these, which is just what
15 flesh and its analogue in animals which have no true flesh
tend to be. Hence of necessity the medium through which
are transmitted the manifoldly contrasted tactual qualities must be a body naturally attached to the organism.
That they are manifold is clear when we consider touching
with the tongue; we apprehend at the tongue all tangible
qualities as well as flavour. Suppose all the rest of our flesh
20 was, like the tongue, sensitive to flavour, we should have
identified the sense of taste and the sense of touch; what
saves us from this identification is the fact that touch and
taste are not always found together in the same part of the
body. The following problem might be raised. Let us assume that every body has depth, i. e. has three dimensions,
and that if two bodies have a third body between them
25 they cannot be in contact with one another; let us remember that what is liquid is a body and must be or contain
water, and that if two bodies touch one another under
water, their touching surfaces cannot be dry, but must have
water between, viz. the water which wets their bounding
surfaces; from all this it follows that in water two bodies
cannot be in contact with one another. The same holds of
two bodies in air—air being to bodies in air precisely what
30 water is to bodies in water—but the facts are not so evident
to our observation, because we live in air, just as animals
423ᵇ that live in water would not notice that the things which
touch one another in water have wet surfaces. The problem,
then, is: does the perception of all objects of sense take
place in the same way, or does it not, e. g. taste and touch
requiring contact (as they are commonly thought to do),
while all other senses perceive over a distance? The distinc-
5 tion is unsound; we perceive what is hard or soft, as well
as the objects of hearing, sight, and smell, through a 'medium', only that the latter are perceived over a greater
distance than the former; that is why the facts escape our

notice. For we do perceive everything through a medium; but in these cases the fact escapes us. Yet, to repeat what we said before, if the medium for touch were a membrane separating us from the object without our observing its existence, we should be relatively to it in the same condi- 10 tion as we are now to air or water in which we are immersed; in their case we fancy we can touch objects, nothing coming in between us and them. But there remains this difference between what can be touched and what can be seen or can sound; in the latter two cases we perceive because the medium produces a certain effect upon us, whereas in the perception of objects of touch we are affected not *by* but 15 *along with* the medium; it is as if a man were struck through his shield, where the shock is not first given to the shield and passed on to the man, but the concussion of both is simultaneous.

In general, flesh and the tongue are related to the real organs of touch and taste, as air and water are to those of sight, hearing, and smell. Hence in neither the one case nor the other can there be any perception of an object 20 if it is placed immediately upon the organ, e. g. if a white object is placed on the surface of the eye. This again shows that what has the power of perceiving the tangible is seated inside. Only so would there be a complete analogy with all the other senses. In their case if you place the object on the organ it is not perceived, here if you place it on the flesh it *is* perceived; therefore flesh is not the organ but the 25 *medium* of touch.

What can be touched are distinctive qualities of body as body; by such differences I mean those which characterize the elements, viz. hot cold, dry moist, of which we have spoken earlier in our treatise on the elements.[41] The organ for the perception of these is that of touch—that part of the 30 body in which primarily the sense of touch resides. This is that part which is potentially such as its object is actually: for all sense-perception is a process of being so affected; so

[41] *De Gen. et Corr.* ii. 2, 3.

that that which makes something such as it itself actually is
424ᵃ makes the other such because the other is already potentially such. That is why when an object of touch is equally
hot and cold or hard and soft we cannot perceive; what we
perceive must have a degree of the sensible quality lying
beyond the neutral point. This implies that the sense itself
is a 'mean' between any two opposite qualities which determine the field of that sense. It is to this that it owes
5 its power of discerning the objects in that field. What is
'in the middle' is fitted to discern; relatively to either extreme it can put itself in the place of the other. As what
is to perceive *both* white and black must, to begin with, be
actually neither but potentially either (and so with all the
other sense-organs), so the organ of touch must be neither
hot nor cold.

Further, as in a sense sight had [42] for its object both what
10 was visible and what was invisible (and there was a parallel
truth about all the other senses discussed),[43] so touch has
for its object both what is tangible and what is intangible.
Here by 'intangible' is meant (a) what like air possesses
some quality of tangible things in a very slight degree and
(b) what possesses it in an excessive degree, as destructive
things do.

We have now given an outline account of each of the
15 several senses.

12 The following results applying to any and every sense
may now be formulated.

(A) By a 'sense' is meant what has the power of receiving
into itself the sensible forms of things without the matter.
This must be conceived of as taking place in the way in
20 which a piece of wax takes on the impress of a signet-ring
without the iron or gold; we say that what produces the
impression is a signet of bronze or gold, but its particular
metallic constitution makes no difference: in a similar way

[42] 422ᵃ 20 ff.
[43] 421ᵇ 3–6, 422ᵃ 29.

the sense is affected by what is coloured or flavoured or sounding, but it is indifferent what in each case the *substance* is; what alone matters is what *quality* it has, i. e. in what *ratio* its constituents are combined.

(B) By 'an organ of sense' is meant that in which ultimately such a power is seated.

The sense and its organ are the same in fact, but their 25 essence is not the same. What perceives is, of course, a spatial magnitude, but we must not admit that either the having the power to perceive or the sense itself is a magnitude; what they are is a certain ratio or power in a magnitude. This enables us to explain why objects of sense which possess one of two opposite sensible qualities in a degree largely in excess of the other opposite destroy the organs of sense; if the movement set up by an object is too strong 30 for the organ, the equipoise of contrary qualities in the organ, which just is its sensory power, is disturbed; it is precisely as concord and tone are destroyed by too violently twanging the strings of a lyre. This explains also why plants cannot perceive, in spite of their having a portion of soul in them and obviously being affected by tangible objects themselves; for undoubtedly their temperature can be lowered or raised. The explanation is that they have no mean **424ᵇ** of contrary qualities, and so no principle in them capable of taking on the forms of sensible objects without their matter; in the case of plants the affection is an affection by form-and-matter together. The problem might be raised: Can what cannot smell be said to be affected by smells or what cannot see by colours, and so on? It might be said that 5 a smell is just what can be smelt, and if it produces any effect it can only be so as to make something smell it, and it might be argued that what cannot smell cannot be affected by smells and further that what can smell can be affected by it only in so far as it has in it the power to smell (similarly with the proper objects of all the other senses). Indeed that this is so is made quite evident as follows. Light or darkness, sounds and smells leave *bodies* quite un- 10

affected; what does affect bodies is not these but the bodies
which are their vehicles, e. g. what splits the trunk of a tree
is not the sound of the thunder but the air which accompanies thunder. Yes, but, it may be objected, bodies are
affected by what is tangible and by flavours. If not, by
what are things that are without soul affected, i. e. altered
in quality? Must we not, then, admit that the objects of the
other senses also may affect them? Is not the true account
this, that all bodies are capable of being affected by smells
15 and sounds, but that some on being acted upon, having no
boundaries of their own, disintegrate, as in the instance of
air, which does become odorous, showing that some effect
is produced on it by what is odorous? But smelling is more
than such an affection by what is odorous—what more?
Is not the answer that, while the air owing to the momen-
tary duration of the action upon it of what is odorous does
itself become perceptible to the sense of smell, smelling is
an observing of the result produced?

BOOK III

1 That there is no sixth sense in addition to the five
20   enumerated—sight, hearing, smell, taste, touch—may
be established by the following considerations:
If we have actually sensation of everything of which
touch can give us sensation (for all the qualities of the tan-
25 gible qua tangible are perceived by us through touch); and
if absence of a sense necessarily involves absence of a sense-
organ; and if (1) all objects that we perceive by immediate
contact with them are perceptible by touch, which sense we
actually possess, and (2) all objects that we perceive
through media, i. e. without immediate contact, are percep-
30 tible by or through the simple elements, e. g. air and water
(and this is so arranged that (a) if more than one kind of
sensible object is perceivable through a single medium, the
possessor of a sense-organ homogeneous with that medium
has the power of perceiving both kinds of objects; for ex-

ample, if the sense-organ is made of air, and air is a medium both for sound and for colour; and that (*b*) if more than one medium can transmit the same kind of sensible objects, as e. g. water as well as air can transmit colour, both **425ᵃ** being transparent, then the possessor of either alone will be able to perceive the kind of objects transmissible through both); and if of the simple elements two only, air and water, go to form sense-organs (for the pupil is made of water, the organ of hearing is made of air, and the organ of smell of one or other of these two, while fire is found either in none or in all—warmth being an essential condition of all sensibility—and earth either in none or, if 5 anywhere, specially mingled with the components of the organ of touch; wherefore it would remain that there can be no sense-organ formed of anything except water and air); and if these sense-organs are actually found in certain animals;—then all the possible senses are possessed by those animals that are not imperfect or mutilated (for even the 10 mole is observed to have eyes beneath its skin); so that, if there is no fifth element and no property other than those which belong to the four elements of our world, no sense can be wanting to such animals.

Further, there cannot be a special sense-organ for the common sensibles either, i. e. the objects which we per- 15 ceive incidentally through this or that special sense, e. g. movement, rest, figure, magnitude, number, unity; for all these we perceive by movement, e. g. magnitude by movement, and therefore also figure (for figure is a species of magnitude), what is at rest by the absence of movement: number is perceived by the negation of continuity, and by the special sensibles; for each sense perceives one class of sensible objects. So that it is clearly impossible that there 20 should be a special sense for any one of the common sensibles, e. g. movement; for, if that were so, our perception of it would be exactly parallel to our present perception of what is sweet by vision. That is so because we have a sense for each of the two qualities, in virtue of which

when they happen to meet in one sensible object we are
15 aware of both contemporaneously. If it were not like this
our perception of the common qualities would always be
incidental, i. e. as is the perception of Cleon's son, where
we perceive him not as Cleon's son but as white, and the
white thing which we really perceive happens to be Cleon's
son.

But in the case of the common sensibles there is already
in us a general sensibility which enables us to perceive them
directly; there is therefore no special sense required for
their perception: if there were, our perception of them
would have been exactly like what has been above described.

30   The senses perceive each other's special objects incidentally; not because the percipient sense is this or that
special sense, but because all form a unity: this incidental
perception takes place whenever sense is directed at one
425ᵇ and the same moment to two disparate qualities in one
and the same object, e. g. to the bitterness and the yellow-
ness of bile; the assertion of the identity of both cannot
be the act of either of the senses; hence the illusion of
sense, e. g. the belief that if a thing is yellow it is bile.

It might be asked why we have more senses than one. Is
5 it to prevent a failure to apprehend the common sensibles,
e. g. movement, magnitude, and number, which go along
with the special sensibles? Had we no sense but sight, and
that sense no object but white, they would have tended
to escape our notice and everything would have merged for
us into an indistinguishable identity because of the concomitance of colour and magnitude. As it is, the fact that
the common sensibles are given in the objects of more than
one sense reveals their distinction from each and all of
10 the special sensibles.

2   Since it is through sense that we are aware that we
are seeing or hearing, it must be either by sight that we
are aware of seeing, or by some sense other than sight. But

the sense that gives us this new sensation must perceive
both sight and its object, viz. colour: so that either (1)
there will be two senses both percipient of the same sensible object, or (2) the sense must be percipient of itself.
Further, even if the sense which perceives sight were dif- 15
ferent from sight, we must either fall into an infinite regress,
or we must somewhere assume a sense which is aware of
itself. If so, we ought to do this in the first case.

This presents a difficulty: if to perceive by sight is just to
see, and what is seen is colour (or the coloured), then if
we are to see that which sees, that which sees originally
must be coloured. It is clear therefore that 'to perceive by
sight' has more than one meaning; for even when we are 20
not seeing, it is by sight that we discriminate darkness from
light, though not in the same way as we distinguish one
colour from another. Further, in a sense even that which
sees is coloured; for in each case the sense-organ is capable
of receiving the sensible object without its matter. That is
why even when the sensible objects are gone the sensings
and imaginings continue to exist in the sense-organs.   25

The activity of the sensible object and that of the percipient sense is one and the same activity, and yet the distinction between their being remains. Take as illustration
actual sound and actual hearing: a man may have hearing
and yet not be hearing, and that which has a sound is not
always sounding. But when that which can hear is actively
hearing and that which can sound is sounding, then the 30
actual hearing and the actual sound are merged in one
(these one might call respectively hearkening and sound- 426ᵃ
ing).

If it is true that the movement, both the acting and the
being acted upon, is to be found in that which is acted
upon,[1] both the sound and the hearing so far as it is actual
must be found in that which has the faculty of hearing; for
it is in the passive factor that the actuality of the active
or motive factor is realized; that is why that which causes 5

[1] Cf. *Phys.* iii. 3.

movement may be at rest. Now the actuality of that which
can sound is just sound or sounding, and the actuality of
that which can hear is hearing or hearkening; 'sound' and
'hearing' are both ambiguous. The same account applies to
10 the other senses and their objects. For as the-acting-and-
being-acted-upon is to be found in the passive, not in the
active factor, so also the actuality of the sensible object and
that of the sensitive subject are both realized in the latter.
But while in some cases each aspect of the total actuality
has a distinct name, e. g. sounding and hearkening, in some
one or other is nameless, e. g. the actuality of sight is called
seeing, but the actuality of colour has no name: the actual-
15 ity of the faculty of taste is called tasting, but the actuality of flavour has no name. Since the actualities of the
sensible object and of the sensitive faculty are one actuality
in spite of the difference between their modes of being,
actual hearing and actual sounding appear and disappear
from existence at one and the same moment, and so actual
20 savour and actual tasting, &c., while as potentialities one of
them may exist without the other. The earlier students of
nature were mistaken in their view that without sight there
was no white or black, without taste no savour. This statement of theirs is partly true, partly false: 'sense' and 'the
sensible object' are ambiguous terms, i. e. may denote
25 either potentialities or actualities: the statement is true of
the latter, false of the former. This ambiguity they wholly
failed to notice.

If voice always implies a concord, and if the voice and
the hearing of it are in one sense one and the same, and if
concord always implies a ratio, hearing as well as what is
30 heard must be a ratio. That is why the excess of either the
sharp or the flat destroys the hearing. (So also in the case of
426ᵇ savours excess destroys the sense of taste, and in the case
of colours excessive brightness or darkness destroys the
sight, and in the case of smell excess of strength whether
in the direction of sweetness or bitterness is destructive.)
This shows that the sense is a ratio.

That is also why the objects of sense are (1) pleasant when the sensible extremes such as acid or sweet or salt being pure and unmixed are brought into the proper ratio; [2] then they are pleasant: and in general what is blended is 5 more pleasant than the sharp or the flat alone; or, to touch, that which is capable of being either warmed or chilled: the sense and the ratio are identical: while (2) in excess the sensible extremes are painful or destructive.

Each sense then is relative to its particular group of sensible qualities: it is found in a sense-organ as such [3] and discriminates the differences which exist within that group; e. g. sight discriminates white and black, taste sweet and bitter, and so in all cases. Since we also discriminate white 10 from sweet, and indeed each sensible quality from every other, with what do we perceive that they are different? It must be by sense; for what is before us is sensible objects. (Hence it is also obvious that the flesh cannot be the ultimate sense-organ: if it were, the discriminating power 15 could not do its work without immediate contact with the object.)

Therefore (1) discrimination between white and sweet cannot be effected by two agencies which remain separate; both the qualities discriminated must be present to something that is one and single. On any other supposition even if I perceived sweet and you perceived white, the difference between them would be apparent. What says that two 20 things are different must be one; for sweet is different from white. Therefore what asserts this difference must be self-identical, and as what asserts, so also what thinks or perceives. That it is not possible by means of two agencies which remain separate to discriminate two objects which are separate is therefore obvious; and that (2) it is not possible to do this in separate moments of time may be seen if we look at it as follows. For as what asserts the dif-

[2] i. e. that which is involved in the structure of the sense-organ.

[3] The qualification appears to mean that the sense-organ may in other respects have other qualities. Thus the tongue can touch as well as taste.

ference between the good and the bad is one and the same,
25 so also the time at which it asserts the one to be different
and the other to be different is not accidental to the assertion (as it is for instance when I now assert a difference
but do not assert that there is now a difference); it asserts
thus—both now and that the objects are different now;
the objects therefore must be present at one and the same
moment. Both the discriminating power and the time of its
exercise must be one and undivided.

But, it may be objected, it is impossible that what is self-
identical should be moved at one and the same time with
30 contrary movements in so far as it is undivided, and in an
undivided moment of time. For if what is sweet be the quality perceived, it moves the sense or thought in this de-
427ª terminate way, while what is bitter moves it in a contrary way, and what is white in a different way. Is it the
case then that what discriminates, though both numerically
one and indivisible, is at the same time divided in its being? In one sense, it is what is divided that perceives two
separate objects at once, but in another sense it does so
qua undivided; for it is divisible in its being, but spatially
and numerically undivided.·

5   But is not this impossible? For while it is true that what
is self-identical and undivided may be both contraries at
once potentially, it cannot be self-identical in its being—it
must lose its unity by being put into activity. It is not
possible to be at once white and black, and therefore it
must also be impossible for a thing to be affected at one
and the same moment by the forms of both, assuming it to
be the case that sensation and thinking are properly so described.[4]

10   The answer is that just as what is called a 'point' is, as
being at once one and two, properly said to be divisible, so
here, that which discriminates is qua undivided one, and
active in a single moment of time, while so far forth as it is
divisible it twice over uses the same dot at one and the

[4] i. e. as the being affected by the forms of sensible qualities.

same time. So far forth then as it takes the limit as two, it discriminates two separate objects with what in a sense is divided: while so far as it takes it as one, it does so with what is one and occupies in its activity a single moment of time.

About the principle in virtue of which we say that animals are percipient, let this discussion suffice.   15

3   There are two distinctive peculiarities by reference to which we characterize the soul—(1) local movement and (2) thinking, discriminating, and perceiving. Thinking, both speculative and practical, is regarded as akin to a form of perceiving; for in the one as well as the other the 20 soul discriminates and is cognizant of something which *is*. Indeed the ancients go so far as to identify thinking and perceiving; e. g. Empedocles says 'For 'tis in respect of what is present that man's wit is increased', and again 'whence it befalls them from time to time to think diverse thoughts', and Homer's phrase [5] 'For suchlike is man's 25 mind' means the same. They all look upon thinking as a bodily process like perceiving, and hold that like is *known* as well as *perceived* by like, as I explained at the beginning of our discussion.[6] Yet they ought at the same time to have accounted for error also; for it is more intimately 427^{b} connected with animal existence and the soul continues longer in the state of error than in that of truth. They cannot escape the dilemma: either (1) whatever seems is true (and there are some who accept this) or (2) error is contact with the unlike; for that is the opposite of the knowing of like by like.

But it is a received principle that error as well as knowl- 5 edge in respect to contraries is one and the same.

That perceiving and practical thinking are not identical is therefore obvious; for the former is universal in the animal world, the latter is found in only a small division of

[5] *Od.* xviii. 136.
[6] 404^{b} 8–18.

it. Further, speculative thinking is also distinct from perceiving—I mean that in which we find rightness and
10 wrongness—rightness in prudence, knowledge, true opinion, wrongness in their opposites; for perception of the
special objects of sense is always free from error, and is
found in all animals, while it is possible to think falsely as
well as truly, and thought is found only where there is
discourse of reason as well as sensibility. For imagination is
15 different from either perceiving or discursive thinking,
though it is not found without sensation, or judgement
without it. That this activity is not the same kind of
thinking as judgement is obvious. For imagining lies within
our own power whenever we wish (e. g. we can call up a
picture, as in the practice of mnemonics by the use of
20 mental images), but in forming opinions we are not free:
we cannot escape the alternative of falsehood or truth.
Further, when we think something to be fearful or threat-
ening, emotion is immediately produced, and so too with
what is encouraging; but when we merely imagine we remain as unaffected as persons who are looking at a painting
of some dreadful or encouraging scene. Again within the
field of judgement itself we find varieties—knowledge,
opinion, prudence, and their opposites; of the differences
between these I must speak elsewhere.[7]

Thinking is different from perceiving and is held to be
in part imagination, in part judgement: we must therefore
first mark off the sphere of imagination and then speak of
428ᵃ judgment. If then imagination is that in virtue of which an
image arises for us, excluding metaphorical uses of the term,
is it a single faculty or disposition relative to images, in
virtue of which we discriminate and are either in error or
not? The faculties in virtue of which we do this are sense,
opinion, science, intelligence.

That imagination is not sense is clear from the following
5 considerations: (1) Sense is either a faculty or an activity,
e. g. sight or seeing: imagination takes place in the ab-

[7] The reference is perhaps to E. N. 1139ᵇ 15 ff.

sence of both, as e. g. in dreams. (2) Again, sense is always present, imagination not If actual imagination and actual sensation were the same, imagination would be found in all the brutes: this is held not to be the case; e. g. it is not found in ants or bees or grubs. (3) Again, sensations are 10 always true, imaginations are for the most part false. (4) Once more, even in ordinary speech, we do not, when sense functions precisely with regard to its object, say that we imagine it to be a man, but rather when there is some failure of accuracy in its exercise. And (5), as we were 15 saying before, visions appear to us even when our eyes are shut. Neither is imagination any of the things that are never in error: e. g. knowledge or intelligence; for imagination may be false.

It remains therefore to see if it is opinion, for opinion may be either true or false.

But opinion involves belief (for without belief in what 20 we opine we cannot have an opinion), and in the brutes though we often find imagination we never find belief. Further, every opinion is accompanied by belief, belief by conviction, and conviction by discourse of reason: while there are some of the brutes in which we find imagination, without discourse of reason. It is clear then that imagination cannot, again, be (1) opinion *plus* sensation, or (2) 25 opinion mediated by sensation, or (3) a blend of opinion and sensation; [8] this is impossible both for these reasons and because the content of the supposed opinion cannot be different from that of the sensation (I mean that imagination must be the blending of the perception of white with 30 the opinion that it is white: it could scarcely be a blend of the opinion that it is good with the perception that it is white): to imagine is therefore (on this view) identical 428ᵇ with the thinking of exactly the same as what one in the strictest sense perceives. But what we imagine is sometimes false though our contemporaneous judgement about it is true; e. g. we imagine the sun to be a foot in diameter

[8] For these three views Cf. Pl. *Tim.* 52 A, *Soph.* A, B, *Phil.* 39 B.

though we are convinced that it is larger than the in-
habited part of the earth, and the following dilemma presents itself. Either (a) while the fact has not changed and
5 the observer has neither forgotten nor lost belief in the
true opinion which he had, that opinion has disappeared,
or (b) if he retains it then his opinion is at once true and
false. A true opinion, however, becomes false only when
the fact alters without being noticed.

Imagination is therefore neither any one of the states
enumerated, nor compounded out of them.

10   But since when one thing has been set in motion another
thing may be moved by it, and imagination is held to be a
movement and to be impossible without sensation, i. e.
to occur in beings that are percipient and to have for its
content what can be perceived, and since movement may
be produced by actual sensation and that movement is
necessarily similar in character to the sensation itself, this
15 movement must be (1) necessarily (a) incapable of existing apart from sensation, (b) incapable of existing except
when we perceive, (2) such that in virtue of its possession
that in which it is found may present various phenomena
both active and passive, and (3) such that it may be either
true or false.

The reason of the last characteristic is as follows. Perception (1) of the special objects of sense is never in error
or admits the least possible amount of falsehood. (2)
That of the concomitance of the objects concomitant with
20 the sensible qualities comes next: in this case certainly we
may be deceived; for while the perception that there is
white before us cannot be false, the perception that what
is white is this or that may be false. (3) Third comes the
perception of the universal attributes which accompany
the concomitant objects to which the special sensibles attach (I mean e. g. of movement and magnitude); it is in
respect of these that the greatest amount of sense-illusion
is possible.

The motion which is due to the activity of sense in these

three modes of its exercise will differ from the activity of 25 sense; (1) the first kind of derived motion is free from error while the sensation is present; (2) and (3) the others may be erroneous whether it is present or absent, especially when the object of perception is far off. If then imagina- 30 tion presents no other features than those enumerated and is what we have described, then imagination must be a movement resulting from an actual exercise of a power of 429ᵃ sense.

As sight is the most highly developed sense, the name *phantasia* (imagination) has been formed from *phaos* (light) because it is not possible to see without light.

And because imaginations remain in the organs of sense and resemble sensations, animals in their actions are largely guided by them, some (i. e. the brutes) because of the non- 5 existence in them of mind, others (i. e. men) because of the temporary eclipse in them of mind by feeling or disease or sleep.

About imagination, what it is and why it exists, let so much suffice.

4 Turning now to the part of the soul with which the soul knows and thinks (whether this is separable 10 from the others in definition only, or spatially as well) we have to inquire (1) what differentiates this part, and (2) how thinking can take place.

If thinking is like perceiving, it must be either a process in which the soul is acted upon by what is capable of being thought, or a process different from but analogous to that. The thinking part of the soul must therefore be, while im- passible, capable of receiving the form of an object; that is, 15 must be potentially identical in character with its object without being the object. Mind must be related to what is thinkable, as sense is to what is sensible.

Therefore, since everything is a possible object of thought, mind in order, as Anaxagoras says, to dominate, that is, to know, must be pure from all admixture; for the 20

co-presence of what is alien to its nature is a hindrance and a block: it follows that it too, like the sensitive part, can have no nature of its own, other than that of having a certain capacity. Thus that in the soul which is called mind (by mind I mean that whereby the soul thinks and judges) is, before it thinks, not actually any real thing. For this
25 reason it cannot reasonably be regarded as blended with the body: if so, it would acquire some quality, e. g. warmth or cold, or even have an organ like the sensitive faculty: as it is, it has none. It was a good idea to call the soul 'the place of forms', though (1) this description holds only of the intellective soul, and (2) even this is the forms only potentially, not actually.

Observation of the sense-organs and their employment
30 reveals a distinction between the impassibility of the sensitive and that of the intellective faculty. After strong
429ᵇ stimulation of a sense we are less able to exercise it than before, as e. g. in the case of a loud sound we cannot hear easily immediately after, or in the case of a bright colour or a powerful odour we cannot see or smell, but in the case of mind, thought about an object that is highly intelligible renders it more and not less able afterwards to think objects that are less intelligible: the reason is that while the faculty of sensation is dependent upon the body, mind is separable from it.

5   Once the mind has become each set of its possible objects, as a man of science has, when this phrase is used of one who is actually a man of science (this happens when he is now able to exercise the power on his own initiative), its condition is still one of potentiality, but in a different sense from the potentiality which preceded the acquisition of knowledge by learning or discovery: the mind too is then able to think *itself*.

10   Since we can distinguish between a spatial magnitude and what it is to be such, and between water and what it is to be water, and so in many other cases (though not in all; for in certain cases the thing and its form are identical),

flesh and what it is to be flesh are discriminated either by different faculties, or by the same faculty in two different states: for flesh necessarily involves matter and is like what is snub-nosed, a *this* in a *this*.⁹ Now it is by means of the sensitive faculty that we discriminate the hot and the cold, i. e. the factors which combined in a certain ratio 15 constitute flesh: the essential character of flesh is apprehended by something different either wholly separate from the sensitive faculty or related to it as a bent line to the same line when it has been straightened out.

Again in the case of abstract objects what is straight is analogous to what is snub-nosed; for it necessarily implies a continuum as its matter: its constitutive essence is different, if we may distinguish between straightness and what is straight: let us take it to be two-ness. It must be appre- 20 hended, therefore, by a different power or by the same power in a different state. To sum up, in so far as the realities it knows are capable of being separated from their matter, so it is also with the powers of mind.

The problem might be suggested: if thinking is a passive affection, then if mind is simple and impassible and has nothing in common with anything else, as Anaxagoras says, how can it come to think at all? For interaction between two factors is held to require a precedent community of nature between the factors. Again it might be asked, is mind a possible object of thought to itself? For if mind is thinkable per se and what is thinkable is in kind one and the same, then either (a) mind will belong to everything, or (b) mind will contain some element common to it with all other realities which makes them all thinkable.

(1) Have not we already disposed of the difficulty about interaction involving a common element, when we said ¹⁰ that mind is in a sense potentially whatever is thinkable, 30 though actually it is nothing until it has thought? What it thinks must be in it just as characters may be said to be on a

---

⁹ i. e. a particular form in a particular matter.
¹⁰ ᵃ15–24.

430ᵃ writing-tablet on which as yet nothing actually stands written: this is exactly what happens with mind.

(2) Mind is itself thinkable in exactly the same way as its objects are. For (*a*) in the case of objects which involve no matter, what thinks and what is thought are identical; for speculative knowledge and its object are identical.
5 (Why mind is not always thinking we must consider later.) [11] (*b*) In the case of those which contain matter each of the objects of thought is only potentially present. It follows that while they will not have mind in them (for mind is a potentiality of them only in so far as they are capable of being disengaged from matter) mind may yet be thinkable.

5 Since in every class of things, as in nature as a whole,
10 we find two factors involved, (1) a matter which is potentially all the particulars included in the class, (2) a cause which is productive in the sense that it makes them all (the latter standing to the former, as e. g. an art to its material), these distinct elements must likewise be found within the soul.

And in fact mind as we have described it [12] is what it is
15 by virtue of becoming all things, while there is another which is what it is by virtue of making all things: this is a sort of positive state like light; for in a sense light makes potential colours into actual colours.

Mind in this sense of it is separable, impassible, unmixed, since it is in its essential nature activity (for always the active is superior to the passive factor, the originating force to the matter which it forms).
20 Actual knowledge is identical with its object: in the individual, potential knowledge is in time prior to actual knowledge, but in the universe as a whole it is not prior even in time. Mind is not at one time knowing and at another not. When mind is set free from its present con-

[11] Ch. 5.
[12] In ch. 4.

ditions it appears as just what it is and nothing more: this alone is immortal and eternal (we do not, however, remember its former activity because, while mind in this sense is impassible, mind as passive is destructible), and 25 without it nothing thinks.

6　The thinking then of the simple objects of thought is found in those cases where falsehood is impossible: where the alternative of true or false applies, there we always find a putting together of objects of thought in a quasi-unity. As Empedocles said that 'where heads of many a creature sprouted without necks' they afterwards by 30 Love's power were combined, so here too objects of thought which were given separate are combined, e. g. 'incommensurate' and 'diagonal': if the combination be of objects past or future the combination of thought includes in its content the date. For falsehood always involves a synthesis; for **430ᵇ** even if you assert that what is white is not white you have included not-white in a synthesis. It is possible also to call all these cases division as well as combination. However that may be, there is not only the true or false assertion that Cleon is white but also the true or false assertion that he *was* or *will be* white. In each and every case that which 5 unifies is mind.

Since the word 'simple' has two senses, i. e. may mean either (a) 'not capable of being divided' or (b) 'not actually divided', there is nothing to prevent mind from knowing what is undivided, e. g. when it apprehends a length (which is actually undivided) and that in an undivided time; for the time is divided or undivided in the same manner as the line. It is not possible, then, to tell 10 what part of the line it was apprehending in each half of the time: the object has no actual parts until it has been divided: if in thought you think each half separately, then by the same act you divide the time also, the half-lines becoming as it were new wholes of length. But if you think it as a whole consisting of these two possible parts, then also

you think it in a time which corresponds to both parts
together. (But what is not quantitatively but qualitatively
15 simple is thought in a simple time and by a simple act of
the soul.)

But that which mind thinks and the time in which it
thinks are in this case divisible only incidentally and not
as such. For in them too there is something indivisible
(though, it may be, not isolable) which gives unity to
the time and the whole of length; and this is found
equally in every continuum whether temporal or spatial.

Points and similar instances of things that divide, them-
20 selves being indivisible, are realized in consciousness in
the same manner as privations.

A similar account may be given of all other cases, e. g.
how evil or black is cognized; they are cognized, in a
sense, by means of their contraries. That which cognizes
must have an element of potentiality in its being, and one
of the contraries must be in it.[13] But if there is anything
25 that has no contrary, then it knows itself and is actually and
possesses independent existence.

Assertion is the saying of something concerning something, e. g. affirmation, and is in every case either true or
false: this is not always the case with mind: the thinking of
the definition in the sense of the constitutive essence is
never in error nor is it the assertion of something concerning something, but, just as while the seeing of the special
object of sight can never be in error, the belief that the
white object seen is a man may be mistaken, so too in the
30 case of objects which are without matter.

7   Actual knowledge is identical with its object: potential
431ᵃ   knowledge in the individual is in time prior to actual
knowledge but in the universe it has no priority even in
time; for all things that come into being arise from what

---

[13] i. e. it must be characterized actually by one and potentially by
the other of the contraries.

actually is. In the case of sense clearly the sensitive faculty already was potentially what the object makes it to be actu- 5 ally; the faculty is not affected or altered. This must therefore be a different kind from movement; for movement is, as we saw,[14] an activity of what is imperfect, activity in the unqualified sense, i. e. that of what has been perfected, is different from movement.

To perceive then is like bare asserting or knowing; but when the object is pleasant or painful, the soul makes a quasi-affirmation or negation, and pursues or avoids the object. To feel pleasure or pain is to act with the sensitive 10 mean towards what is good or bad as such. Both avoidance and appetite when actual are identical with this: the faculty of appetite and avoidance are not different, either from one another or from the faculty of sense-perception; but their being *is* different.

To the thinking soul images serve as if they were contents of perception (and when it asserts or denies them to be 15 good or bad it avoids or pursues them). That is why the soul never thinks without an image. The process is like that in which the air modifies the pupil in this or that way and the pupil transmits the modification to some third thing (and similarly in hearing), while the ultimate point of arrival is one, a single mean, with different manners of being.

With what part of itself the soul discriminates sweet 20 from hot [15] I have explained before [16] and must now describe again as follows: That with which it does so is a sort of unity, but in the way just mentioned,[17] i. e. as a connecting term. And the two faculties it connects,[18] being one by analogy and numerically, are each to each as the qualities

---

[14] Cf. 417^b 2–16.
[15] i. e. the sweetness and the heat in a sweet-hot object.
[16] 426^b 12–427^a 14.
[17] i. e. as one thing with two aspects; cf. l. 19.
[18] i. e. the faculty by which we discern sweet and that by which we discern hot.

discerned are to one another (for what difference does it make whether we raise the problem of discrimination be-
25 tween disparates or between contraries, e. g. white and black?). Let then C be to D as A is to B: [19] it follows *alternando* that C:A::D:B. If then C and D belong to one subject, the case will be the same with them as with A and B;
431ᵇ A and B form a single identity with different modes of being; so too will the former pair. The same reasoning holds if A be sweet and B white.

The faculty of thinking then thinks the forms in the images, and as in the former case [20] what is to be pursued or avoided is marked out for it, so where there is no sensation
5 and it is engaged upon the images it is moved to pursuit or avoidance. E. g. perceiving by sense that the beacon is fire, it recognizes in virtue of the general faculty of sense that it signifies an enemy, because it sees it moving; but sometimes by means of the images or thoughts which are within the soul, just as if it were seeing, it calculates and deliberates what is to come by reference to what is present; and when it makes a pronouncement, as in the case of sensation it pronounces the object to be pleasant or painful, in this case it avoids or pursues; and so generally in cases of action.

That too which involves no action, i. e. that which is true
10 or false, is in the same province with what is good or bad: yet they differ in this, that the one set imply and the other do not a reference to a particular person.

The so-called abstract objects the mind thinks just as, if one had thought of the snub-nosed not as snub-nosed but as hollow, one would have thought of an actuality without
15 the flesh in which it is embodied: it is thus that the mind when it is thinking the objects of Mathematics thinks as separate, elements which do not exist separate. In every case the mind which is actively thinking is the objects

---

[19] i. e. let the faculty that discerns sweet be to that which discerns hot as sweet is to hot.
[20] i. e. that of sense-data.

which it thinks. Whether it is possible for it while not existing separate from spatial conditions to think anything that
is separate, or not, we must consider later.[21]

8   Let us now summarize our results about soul, and re-
      peat that the soul is in a way all existing things; for 20
existing things are either sensible or thinkable, and knowledge is in a way what is knowable, and sensation is in a way
what is sensible: in *what* way we must inquire.

Knowledge and sensation are divided to correspond with
the realities, potential knowledge and sensation answering
to potentialities, actual knowledge and sensation to actuali- 25
ties. Within the soul the faculties of knowledge and sensation are *potentially* these objects, the one what is knowable,
the other what is sensible. They must be either the things
themselves or their forms. The former alternative is of
course impossible: it is not the stone which is present in
the soul but its form.

It follows that the soul is analogous to the hand; for as
the hand is a tool of tools,[22] so the mind is the form of 432ᵃ
forms and sense the form of sensible things.

Since according to common agreement there is nothing
outside and separate in existence from sensible spatial magnitudes, the objects of thought are in the sensible forms,
viz both the abstract objects and all the states and affec- 5
tions of sensible things. Hence (1) no one can learn or
understand anything in the absence of sense, and (2)
when the mind is actively aware of anything it is necessarily
aware of it along with an image; for images are like sensuous contents except in that they contain no matter.

Imagination is different from assertion and denial; for
what is true or false involves a synthesis of concepts. In
what will the primary concepts differ from images? Must 10
we not say that neither these nor even our other concepts
are images, though they necessarily involve them?

[21] This promise does not seem to have been fulfilled.
[22] i. e. a tool for using tools.

15 **9**   The soul of animals is characterized by two faculties,
(a) the faculty of discrimination which is the work of
thought and sense, and (b) the faculty of originating local
movement. Sense and mind we have now sufficiently examined. Let us next consider what it is in the soul which
20 originates movement. Is it a single part of the soul separate
either spatially or·in definition? Or is it the soul as a whole?
If it is a part, is that part different from those usually
distinguished or already mentioned by us, or is it one of
them? The problem at once presents itself, in what sense
we are to speak of parts of the soul, or how many we
25 should distinguish. For in a sense there is an infinity of
parts: it is not enough to distinguish, with some thinkers,[23]
the calculative, the passionate, and the desiderative, or with
others [24] the rational and the irrational; for if we take the
dividing lines followed by these thinkers we shall find
parts far more distinctly separated from one another than
these, namely those we have just mentioned: (1) the nu-
30 tritive, which belongs both to plants and to all animals, and
(2) the sensitive, which cannot easily be classed as either
irrational or rational; further (3) the imaginative, which is,
432ᵇ in its being, different from all, while it is very hard to say
with which of the others it is the same or not the same, supposing we determine to posit *separate* parts in the soul; and
lastly (4) the appetitive, which would seem to be distinct
both in definition and in power from all hitherto enumerated.

5   It is absurd to break up the last-mentioned faculty: as
these thinkers do, for wish is found in the calculative part
and desire and passion in the irrational; [25] and if the soul is
tripartite appetite will be found in all three parts. Turning
our attention to the present object of discussion, let us ask
what that is which originates local movement of the animal.
The movement of growth and decay, being found in all

---

[23] Pl. Rep. 435–41.
[24] A popular view, Cf. E. N. 1102ᵃ 26–8.
[25] All three being forms of appetite.

living things, must be attributed to the faculty of repro- 10
duction and nutrition, which is common to all: inspiration
and expiration, sleep and waking, we must consider later: [26]
these too present much difficulty: at present we must consider local movement, asking what it is that originates forward movement in the animal.

That it is not the nutritive faculty is obvious; for this
kind of movement is always for an end and is accompanied 15
either by imagination or by appetite; for no animal moves
except by compulsion unless it has an impulse towards or
away from an object. Further, if it were the nutritive
faculty, even plants would have been capable of originating
such movement and would have possessed the organs
necessary to carry it out. Similarly it cannot be the
sensitive faculty either; for there are many animals which
have sensibility but remain fast and immovable throughout
their lives.   20

If then Nature never makes anything without a purpose
and never leaves out what is necessary (except in the case
of mutilated or imperfect growths; and that here we have
neither mutilation nor imperfection may be argued from
the facts that such animals (a) can reproduce their species
and (b) rise to completeness of nature and decay to an
end), it follows that, had they been capable of originating 25
forward movement, they would have possessed the organs
necessary for that purpose. Further, neither can the calculative faculty or what is called 'mind' be the cause of such
movement; for mind as speculative never thinks what is
practicable, it never says anything about an object to be
avoided or pursued, while this movement is always in something which is avoiding or pursuing an object. No, not even
when it is aware of such an object does it at once enjoin
pursuit or avoidance of it; e. g. the mind often thinks of 30
something terrifying or pleasant without enjoying the emotion of fear. It is the heart that is moved (or in the case of a
pleasant object some other part). Further, even when the 433[r]

[26] Cf. *De Respiratione, De Somno.*

mind does command and thought bids us pursue or avoid
something, sometimes no movement is produced; we act
in accordance with desire, as in the case of moral weakness.
And, generally, we observe that the possessor of medical
knowledge is not necessarily healing, which shows that
something else is required to produce action in accordance
5 with knowledge; the knowledge alone is not the cause.
Lastly, appetite too is incompetent to account fully for
movement; for those who successfully resist temptation
have appetite and desire and yet follow mind and refuse to
enact that for which they have appetite.

10   These two at all events appear to be sources of movement: appetite and mind (if one may venture to re-
10 gard imagination as a kind of thinking; for many men
follow their imaginations contrary to knowledge, and in all
animals other than man there is no thinking or calculation
but only imagination).

Both of these then are capable of originating local movement, mind and appetite: (1) mind, that is, which calcu-
15 lates means to an end, i. e. mind practical (it differs from
mind speculative in the character of its end); while (2)
appetite is in every form of it relative to an end: for that
which is the object of appetite is the stimulant of mind
practical; and that which is last in the process of thinking
is the beginning of the action. It follows that there is a
justification for regarding these two as the sources of movement, i. e. appetite and practical thought; for the object of
appetite starts a movement and as a result of that thought
20 gives rise to movement, the object of appetite being to
it a source of stimulation. So too when imagination originates movement, it necessarily involves appetite.

That which moves therefore is a single faculty and the
faculty of appetite; for if there had been two sources of
movement—mind and appetite—they would have produced movement in virtue of some common character.
As it is, mind is never found producing movement without

appetite (for wish is a form of appetite; and when movement is produced according to calculation it is also according to wish), but appetite can originate movement con- 25
trary to calculation, for desire is a form of appetite. Now
mind is always right, but appetite and imagination may be
either right or wrong. That is why, though in any case it is
the object of appetite which originates movement, this object may be either the real or the apparent good. To produce movement the object must be more than this: it must
be good that can be brought into being by action; and only
what can be otherwise than as it is can thus be brought 30
into being. That then such a power in the soul as has been
described, i. e. that called appetite, originates movement 433ᵇ
is clear. Those who distinguish parts in the soul, if they
distinguish and divide in accordance with differences of
power, find themselves with a very large number of parts,
a nutritive, a sensitive, an intellective, a deliberative, and
now an appetitive part; for these are more different from
one another than the faculties of desire and passion.

Since appetites run counter to one another, which happens when a principle of reason and a desire are contrary
and is possible only in beings with a sense of time (for
while mind bids us hold back because of what is future, desire is influenced by what is just at hand: a pleasant object
which is just at hand presents itself as both pleasant and
good, without condition in either case, because of want
of foresight into what is farther away in time), it follows 10
that while that which originates movement must be specifically one, viz. the faculty of appetite as such (or rather
farthest back of all the object of that faculty; for it is it
that itself remaining unmoved originates the movement by
being apprehended in thought or imagination), the things
that originate movement are numerically many.

All movement involves three factors, (1) that which
originates the movement, (2) that by means of which it
originates it, and (3) that which is moved. The expression
'that which originates the movement' is ambiguous: it may

mean either (a) something which itself is unmoved or (b)
15 that which at once moves and is moved. Here that which
moves without itself being moved is the realizable good,
that which at once moves and is moved is the faculty of
appetite (for that which is influenced by appetite so far
as it is actually so influenced is set in movement, and appetite in the sense of actual appetite is a kind of movement),
while that which is in motion is the animal. The instrument
which appetite employs to produce movement is no longer
20 psychical but bodily: hence the examination of it falls
within the province of the functions common to body and
soul.²⁷ To state the matter summarily at present, that which
is the instrument in the production of movement is to be
found where a beginning and an end coincide as e. g. in a
ball and socket joint; for there the convex and the concave
sides are respectively an end and a beginning (that is why
while the one remains at rest, the other is moved): they are
separate in definition but not separable spatially. For every-
25 thing is moved by pushing and pulling. Hence just as in the
case of a wheel, so here there must be a point which remains at rest, and from that point the movement must
originate.

To sum up, then, and repeat what I have said, inasmuch
as an animal is capable of appetite it is capable of self-
movement; it is not capable of appetite without possessing
imagination; and all imagination is either (1) calculative
30 or (2) sensitive. In the latter all animals, and not only man,
partake.

11 We must consider also in the case of imperfect animals, sc. those which have no sense but touch, what
it is that in them originates movement. Can they have
434ᵃ imagination or not? or desire? Clearly they have feelings
of pleasure and pain, and if they have these they must have
desire. But how can they have imagination? Must not we
say that, as their movements are indefinite, they have
imagination and desire, but indefinitely?

²⁷ Cf. *De Motu An.* 702ᵃ 21–703ᵃ 22.

Sensitive imagination, as we have said,[28] is found in all animals, deliberative imagination only in those that are 5 calculative: for whether this or that shall be enacted is already a task requiring calculation; and there must be a single standard to measure by, for that is pursued which is greater. It follows that what acts in this way must be able to make a unity out of several images.

This is the reason why imagination is held not to involve 10 opinion, in that it does not involve opinion based on inference, though opinion involves imagination. Hence appetite contains no deliberative element. Sometimes it overpowers wish and sets it in movement: at times wish acts thus upon appetite, like one sphere imparting its movement to another, or appetite acts thus upon appetite, i. e. in the condition of moral weakness (though by *nature* the higher faculty is *always* more authoritative and gives rise to move- ment). Thus *three* modes of movement are possible.   15

The faculty of knowing is never moved but remains at rest. Since the one premiss or judgment is universal and the other deals with the particular (for the first tells us that such and such a kind of man should do such and such a kind of act, and the second that *this* is an act of the kind meant, and I a person of the type intended), it is the latter 20 opinion that really originates movement, not the universal; or rather it is both, but the one does so while it remains in a state more like rest, while the other partakes in move- ment.

12 The nutritive soul then must be possessed by every- thing that is alive, and every such thing is endowed with soul from its birth to its death. For what has been born must grow, reach maturity, and decay—all of which 25 are impossible without nutrition. Therefore the nutritive faculty must be found in everything that grows and decays.

But sensation need not be found in all things that live. For it is impossible for touch to belong either (1) to those whose body is uncompounded or (2) to those which are

[28] 433ᵇ 29.

incapable of taking in the forms without their matter.
30 But animals must be endowed with sensation, since
Nature does nothing in vain. For all things that exist by
Nature are means to an end, or will be concomitants of
means to an end. Every body capable of forward movement
434ᵇ would, if unendowed with sensation, perish and fail to
reach its end, which is the aim of Nature; for how could
it obtain nutriment? Stationary living things, it is true,
have as their nutriment that from which they have arisen;
but it is not possible that a body which is not stationary
but produced by generation should have a soul and a discerning mind without also having sensation. (Nor yet even
if it were not produced by generation. Why should it not
5 have sensation? Because it were better so either for the
body or for the soul? But clearly it would not be better for
either: the absence of sensation will not enable the one to
think better or the other to exist better.) Therefore no
body which is not stationary has soul without sensation.

But if a body *has* sensation, it must be either simple or
compound. And simple it cannot be; for then it could not
10 have touch, which is indispensable. This is clear from what
follows. An animal is a body with soul in it: every body is
tangible, i. e. perceptible by touch; hence necessarily, if an
animal is to survive, its body must have tactual sensation.
15 All the other senses, e. g. smell, sight, hearing, apprehend
through media; but where there is immediate contact the
animal, if it has no sensation, will be unable to avoid some
things and take others, and so will find it impossible to survive. That is why taste also is a sort of touch; it is relative
to nutriment, which is just tangible body; whereas sound,
colour, and odour are innutritious, and further neither grow
20 nor decay. Hence it is that taste also must be a sort of
touch, because it is the sense for what is tangible and nutri-
tious.

Both these senses, then, are indispensable to the animal,
and it is clear that without touch it is impossible for an
animal to be. All the other senses subserve well-being and

for that very reason belong not to any and every kind of animal, but only to some, e. g. those capable of forward 25 movement must have them; for, if they are to survive, they must perceive not only by immediate contact but also at a distance from the object. This will be possible if they can perceive through a medium, the medium being affected and moved by the perceptible object, and the animal by the medium. Just as that which produces local movement causes a change extending to a certain point, and that 30 which gave an impulse causes another to produce a new impulse so that the movement traverses a medium—the first mover impelling without being impelled, the last moved being impelled without impelling, while the medium (or media, for there are many) is both—so is it also in the case of alteration, except that the agent produces it 435ᵃ without the patient's changing its place. Thus if an object is dipped into wax, the movement goes on until submersion has taken place, and in stone it goes no distance at all, while in water the disturbance goes far beyond the object dipped: in air the disturbance is propagated farthest of all, the air acting and being acted upon, so long as it maintains an unbroken unity. That is why in the case of reflection it is 5 better, instead of saying that the sight issues from the eye and is reflected, to say that the air, so long as it remains one, is affected by the shape and colour. On a smooth surface the air possesses unity; hence it is that it in turn sets the sight in motion, just as if the impression on the wax 10 were transmitted as far as the wax extends.

13   It is clear that the body of an animal cannot be simple, i. e. consist of one element such as fire or air. For without touch it is impossible to have any other sense; for every body that has soul in it must, as we have said,[29] be capable of touch. All the other elements with the exception of earth 15 can constitute organs of sense, but all of them bring about perception only through something else, viz. through the

[29] 434ᵇ 10–24.

media. Touch takes place by direct contact with its objects, whence also its name. All the other organs of sense, no doubt, perceive by contact, only the contact is mediate: touch alone perceives by immediate contact. Consequently no animal body can consist of these other elements.

20   Nor can it consist solely of earth. For touch is as it were a mean between all tangible qualities, and its organ is capable of receiving not only all the specific qualities which characterize earth, but also the hot and the cold and all 25 other tangible qualities whatsoever. That is why we have no 435ᵇ sensation by means of bones, hair, &c., because they consist of earth. So too plants, because they consist of earth, have no sensation. Without touch there can be no other sense, and the organ of touch cannot consist of earth or of any other single element.

It is evident, therefore, that the loss of this one sense 5 alone must bring about the death of an animal. For as on the one hand nothing which is not an animal can have this sense, so on the other it is the only one which is indispensably necessary to what is an animal. This explains, further, the following difference between the other senses and touch. In the case of all the others excess of intensity in the qualities which they apprehend, i. e. excess of intensity in colour, sound, and smell, destroys not the animal but only 10 the organs of the sense (except incidentally, as when the sound is accompanied by an impact or shock, or where through the objects of sight or of smell certain other things are set in motion, which destroy by contact); flavour also destroys only in so far as it is at the same time tangible. But excess of intensity in tangible qualities, e. g. heat, cold, 15 or hardness, destroys the animal itself. As in the case of every sensible quality excess destroys the organ, so here what is tangible destroys touch, which is the essential mark of life; for it has been shown that without touch it is impossible for an animal to be. That is why excess in intensity of tangible qualities destroys not merely the organ, but the animal itself, because this is the only sense which it must have.

All the other senses are necessary to animals, as we have said,[30] not for their being, but for their well-being. Such, e. g., is sight, which, since it lives in air or water, or generally in what is pellucid, it must have in order to see, and taste because of what is pleasant or painful to it, in order that it may perceive these qualities in its nutriment and so may desire to be set in motion, and hearing that it may have communication made to it, and a tongue that it may communicate with its fellows.

[30] 434ᵇ 24.

Biology

ᴸᴸᴸᴸᴸᴸᴸᴸᴸᴸᴸᴸᴸᴸᴸᴸᴸᴸᴸᴸᴸᴸ

INTRODUCTION

The four biological works of Aristotle use the same
method, the "physical method," as the four physical
treatises, adapting the method and the sequence of problems to the introduction of organic as well as simple or
elemental parts. The *History of Animals* in nine books
(in the course of the history of the text it acquired a tenth
book now generally judged spurious) is a lengthy classification of animals on the basis of similarities and differences of their parts, organs, and functions, including
reproduction, heredity, the development of the embryo,
diet, disease, the effects of environment and the struggle
for means of subsistence, psychological differences, and
intelligence. In the *History of Animals*, Aristotle repeats
the reasons for using the human psychic functions expounded and ordered in the *De Anima* as a foundation
for the investigation of processes of bodily organs and
psychic functions in animals. We are more familiar with
man than with any other animal, and as in finance we calculate other monetary values in terms of our own currency, so to understand the functions of other animals we
translate them into like operations and faculties which
we observe in ourselves. Moreover, man is more rounded
and complete than other animals, and the qualities and
capacities investigated in biology are found in their perfection in him (*History of Animals* i. 6. 491ᵃ19–23 and ix.
1. 608ᵇ4–8). The first book of the *History of Animals*
starts with the distinction of simple parts, which divide
into parts uniform with themselves, as flesh into flesh,
from composite parts, which divide into parts not uniform
with themselves, as the hand does not divide into hands
or the face into faces. Some composite parts are also limbs
or members, which, entire in themselves, have other parts
within themselves, as the head, foot, hand, arm, chest. All

composite parts are composed of simple parts, as the hand is composed of flesh, sinews, and bones.

After the examination of the physical characteristics of animals and their methods of generation, and after the determination of their habits and modes of living which vary according to their character and their food, the investigation turns, in the eighth book, to inquiry concerning psychical qualities or attitudes which are found in the great majority of animals but which are more markedly differentiated in human beings. There is a continuity in nature. "Nature proceeds little by little from things lifeless to animal life in such a way that it is impossible to determine the exact line of demarcation, nor on which side thereof an intermediate form should lie" (*History of Animals* viii. 1. 588^{b}4–7). The same is true of the habits of life and the faculties of the soul, which range from reproduction through sensibility to intelligence and memory, the latter of which are in turn the bases for familial and social living. The life of animals may be divided into two acts—procreation and feeding. The *History of Animals*, which provides a methodological and factual basis for biological inquiry, was written during the period of Aristotle's residence in Athens as head of the Lyceum when he also produced a collection of the constitutions of 158 states, which serves as a basis for political inquiry. The manuscript of one of those constitutions, *The Constitution of Athens*, and the manuscript of the *History of Animals* were recovered and published at the end of the nineteenth century.

On the basis of this organization of the whole range of animal life by the formal causes which differentiate and interrelate parts, functions, and faculties, the investigation turns in the *On the Parts of Animals* to the consideration of the ends of animal life, to the purposes and necessities which order the processes of actualization of the potentialities of the living body. Tht first chapter of the first book, which is included in this collection, returns to the

consideration of "physical method." There are two ways
.(*tropos*, that is, a trope, or a turn, or a direction) in which
one may become competent in any theory or method.
One is the scientific method of inquiry into the unknown,
or "learning," the other is the educational method of
organizing what is already known and established, or
"teaching." Aristotle calls the one science (*episteme*) and
the other education (*paideia*). The "cycle of education"
was to become a single word, "encyclopaedia," which
originally meant the program of interrelated arts, the liberal arts, which constitute a "general education" or "universal education." Such education provides the ability to
be critical in all branches of knowledge, that is, to judge
the method of a professed exposition apart from consideration of the truth or falsity of what is said to be the case.
Should such a method of education begin with general
characters and go to individuals or begin with the concrete and go to the generic; should it begin with facts or
causes, with the "what" or the "why"; should it begin
with final causes or with moving causes? Should it begin
with the process of formation of each animal or with the
character of the animal already formed?

The true method, Aristotle decides, is to state the
definitive characters that distinguish the animal as a
whole and explain the animal, as substance and form, and
its several organs in the same way, as substance and form,
but then the problem of whether to begin with the soul
or a part of the soul arises once more. The physical
method in the *On the Parts of Animals* continues the
method used in the *Physics* to examine natures and material motions. The definition of the soul as a form is sought
by examination of the functions and parts of the soul.
The inquiry begins with the formed character, or end,
works back to the operation that effects that end, determines the function or faculty, and relates it to the form
of the soul. Once more Aristotle decides that there are
two causes relevant to the inquiry, the motor cause and

the final end. Biological processes are purposive because they are adapted to ends. The generative power of a seed generates a plant or an animal of a particular kind. That generative power is closely related to the nutritive power which provides for the continuance of the living body by nourishing and to the power of growth which provides for developing it to maturity. Once again, he distinguishes hypothetical physical necessity from hypothetical mathematical necessity, absolute metaphysical necessity, which connects substances and their inherent properties, and coercive necessity of external causes. Animal nature, like inanimate nature, again is a cause similar to and distinct from art, chance, and fortune. Aristotle gives a brief history of the development of this scientific method: his predecessors had not combined the dialectical examination of form with the physical examination of matter, although Democritus was led close to using the true physical method by his fidelity to the facts of empirical observation. Socrates first speculated on method (in the *Metaphysics* Aristotle specifies that he was the first to examine induction and definition), but he and his contemporaries had turned their attention from the works of nature to political science and ethics.

The kinds of local motion, on land, in air, and in water, are differentiated and related, and the problems of the animate mechanics of limbs, or number of limbs, and of joints are investigated in the *On the Progression of Animals* (*De Incessu Animalium*). In that work Aristotle uses the distinction between what were later called homologies and analogies. Homologies are found in similarities of structure without a similarity of function: wings of birds and forelegs of animals are homologies. Analogies are found in similarities of function even when the structure is different: wings of birds and wings of butterflies are analogies. The *On the Movement of Animals* (*De Motu Animalium*) shows a strong analogizing tendency, and has sometimes been judged inauthentic. It may be argued, however, that it differs from the *De Incessu* as the *Short Natural Treatises* differ from the *De Anima* by considering functions common to the body and the soul rather than the functions of the soul as actuality of the body.

In the opening chapter of *On the Generation of Animals* Aristotle recapitulates the problems already treated and those that remain to be investigated in terms of the four causes. The parts of animals have been discussed both generally and with reference to the peculiarities of each kind, using three of the four causes—the final cause or end, the formal cause or definition, and the material cause or the nonhomogeneous parts of the whole animal, the homogeneous parts of the nonhomogeneous parts, and the material elements of the homogeneous parts. The remaining problem, which is treated in this final treatise, is the generation of animals or the moving or efficient cause.

DE PARTIBUS ANIMALIUM

CONTENTS

BOOK I

De Partibus Animalium

(On the Parts of Animals)

Translated by William Ogle

ᒣᒧᒣᒧ

BOOK I

1 Every systematic science, the humblest and the 639ᵃ
noblest alike, seems to admit of two distinct kinds of pro-
ficiency; one of which may be properly called scientific
knowledge of the subject, while the other is a kind of
educational acquaintance with it. For an educated man 5
should be able to form a fair off-hand judgement as to the
goodness or badness of the method used by a professor in
his exposition. To be educated is in fact to be able to do
this; and even the man of universal education we deem
to be such in virtue of his having this ability. It will, however, of course, be understood that we only ascribe universal education to one who in his own individual person 10
is thus critical in all or nearly all branches of knowledge,
and not to one who has a like ability merely in some special subject. For it is possible for a man to have this com-
petence in some one branch of knowledge without having
it in all.

It is plain then that, as in other sciences, so in that
which inquires into nature, there must be certain canons,
by reference to which a hearer shall be able to criticize the
method of a professed exposition, quite independently of
the question whether the statements made be true or
false. Ought we, for instance (to give an illustration of 15

what I mean), to begin by discussing each separate species—man, lion, ox, and the like—taking each kind in
hand independently of the rest, or ought we rather to deal
first with the attributes which they have in common in
virtue of some common element of their nature, and proceed from this as a basis for the consideration of them
20 separately? For genera that are quite distinct yet often-
times present many identical phenomena, sleep, for instance, respiration, growth, decay, death, and other similar affections and conditions, which may be passed over
for the present, as we are not yet prepared to treat of them
with clearness and precision. Now it is plain that if we
deal with each species independently of the rest, we shall
frequently be obliged to repeat the same statements over
25 and over again; for horse and dog and man present, each
and all, every one of the phenomena just enumerated. A
discussion therefore of the attributes of each such species
separately would necessarily involve frequent repetitions
30 as to characters, themselves identical but recurring in
animals specifically distinct. (Very possibly also there
may be other characters which, though they present spe-
639ᵇ cific differences, yet come under one and the same category. For instance, flying, swimming, walking, creeping,
are plainly specifically distinct, but yet are all forms of
animal progression.) We must, then, have some clear
understanding as to the manner in which our investiga-
5 tion is to be conducted; whether, I mean, we are first to
deal with the common or generic characters, and afterwards to take into consideration special peculiarities; or
whether we are to start straight off with the ultimate
species. For as yet no definite rule has been laid down in
this matter. So also there is a like uncertainty as to another point now to be mentioned. Ought the writer who
deals with the works of nature to follow the plan adopted
by the mathematicians in their astronomical demonstra-
10 tions, and after considering the phenomena presented by
animals, and their several parts, proceed subsequently to

treat of the causes and the reason why; or ought he to follow some other method? And when these questions are
answered, there yet remains another. The causes concerned in the generation of the works of nature are, as we
see, more than one. There is the final cause and there is the
motor cause. Now we must decide which of these two
causes comes first, which second. Plainly, however, that
cause is the first which we call the final one. For this is 15
the Reason, and the Reason forms the starting-point, alike
in the works of art and in works of nature. For consider
how the physician or how the builder sets about his work.
He starts by forming for himself a definite picture, in the
one case perceptible to mind, in the other to sense, of his
end—the physician of health, the builder of a house—and
this he holds foward as the reason and explanation of each
subsequent step that he takes, and of his action in this or
that way as the case may be. Now in the works of nature 20
the good end and the final cause is still more dominant
than in works of art such as these, nor is necessity a factor
with the same significance in them all; though almost all
writers, while they try to refer their origin to this cause,
do so without distinguishing the various senses in which
the term necessity is used. For there is absolute necessity,
manifested in eternal phenomena; and there is hypothet- 25
ical necessity, manifested in everything that is generated
by nature as in everything that is produced by art, be it a
house or what it may. For if a house or other such final
object is to be realized, it is necessary that such and such
material shall exist; and it is necessary that first this and
then that shall be produced, and first this and then that
set in motion, and so on in continuous succession, until 30
the end and final result is reached, for the sake of which
each prior thing is produced and exists. As with these
productions of art, so also is it with the productions of
nature. The mode of necessity, however, and the mode of
ratiocination are different in natural science from what 640ᵃ
they are in the theoretical sciences; of which we have

spoken elsewhere. For in the latter the starting-point is
that which is; in the former that which is to be. For
5 it is that which is yet to be—health, let us say, or a man—
that, owing to its being of such and such characters, necessitates the pre-existence or previous production of this
and that antecedent; and not this or that antecedent
which, because it exists or has been generated, makes
it necessary that health or a man is in, or shall come
into, existence. Nor is it possible to trace back the series
of necessary antecedents to a starting-point, of which you
can say that, existing itself from eternity, it has determined their existence as its consequent. These however,
10 again, are matters that have been dealt with in another
treatise. There too it was stated in what cases absolute
and hypothetical necessity exist; in what cases also the
proposition expressing hypothetical necessity is simply convertible, and what cause it is that determines this convertibility.

Another matter which must not be passed over without
consideration is, whether the proper subject of our exposition is that with which the ancient writers concerned
themselves, namely, what is the process of formation of
each animal; or whether it is not rather, what are the characters of a given creature when formed. For there is no
small difference between these two views. The best course
appears to be that we should follow the method already
mentioned, and begin with the phenomena presented by
15 each group of animals, and, when this is done, proceed
afterwards to state the causes of those phenomena, and
to deal with their evolution. For elsewhere, as for instance
in house building, this is the true sequence. The plan of
the house, or the house, has this and that form; and because it has this and that form, therefore is its construction carried out in this or that manner. For the process of
evolution is for the sake of the thing finally evolved, and
not this for the sake of the process. Empedocles, then,
20 was in error when he said that many of the characters

presented by animals were merely the results of incidental occurrences during their development; for instance, that the backbone was divided as it is into vertebrae, because it happened to be broken owing to the contorted position of the foetus in the womb. In so saying he overlooked the fact that propagation implies a creative seed endowed with certain formative properties. Secondly, he neglected another fact, namely, that the parent animal pre-exists, not 25 only in idea, but actually in time. For man is generated from man; and thus it is the possession of certain characters by the parent that determines the development of like characters in the child. The same statement holds good also for the operations of art, and even for those which are apparently by chance. For the same result as is produced by art may occur by chance. Chance, for instance, may bring about the restoration of health. The 30 products of art, however, require the pre-existence of an efficient cause homogeneous with themselves, such as the statuary's art, which must necessarily precede the statue; for this cannot possibly be produced by chance. Art indeed consists in the conception of the result to be produced before its realization in the material. As with chance, so with fortune; for this also produces the same result as art, and by the same process.

The fittest mode, then, of treatment is to say, a man has such and such parts, because the conception of a man includes their presence, and because they are necessary conditions of his existence, or, if we cannot quite say 35 this, which would be best of all, then the next thing to it, namely, that it is either quite impossible for him to exist without them, or, at any rate, that it is better for him that they should be there; and their existence involves the existence of other antecedents. Thus we should say, be- 640ᵇ cause man is an animal with such and such characters, therefore is the process of his development necessarily such as it is; and therefore is it accomplished in such and such an order, this part being formed first, that next, and so on in succession; and after a like fashion should we explain the evolution of all other works of nature.

5   Now that with which the ancient writers, who first philosophized about Nature, busied themselves, was the material principle and the material cause. They inquired what this is, and what its character; how the universe is generated out of it, and by what motor influence, whether, for instance, by antagonism or friendship, whether by intelligence or chance action, the substratum of matter being assumed to have certain inseparable properties; fire,
10   for instance, to have a hot nature, earth a cold one; the former to be light, the latter heavy. For even the genesis of the universe is thus explained by them. After a like fashion do they deal also with the development of plants and of animals. They say, for instance, that the water contained in the body causes by its currents the formation of the stomach and the other receptacles of food or of ex-
15   cretion; and that the breath by its passage breaks open the outlets of the nostrils; air and water being the materials of which bodies are made; for all represent nature as composed of such or similar substances.

But if men and animals and their several parts are natural phenomena, then the natural philosopher must take into consideration not merely the ultimate substances of which they are made, but also flesh, bone, blood, and
20   all the other homogeneous parts; not only these, but also the heterogeneous parts, such as face, hand, foot; and must examine how each of these comes to be what it is, and in virtue of what force. For to say what are the ultimate substances out of which an animal is formed, to state, for instance, that it is made of fire or earth, is no more sufficient than would be a similar account in the case of a couch or the like. For we should not be content with saying that the couch was made of bronze or wood
25   or whatever it might be, but should try to describe its design or mode of composition in preference to the material; or, if we did deal with the material, it would at

any rate be with the concretion of material and form. For a couch is such and such a form embodied in this or that matter, or such and such a matter with this or that form; so that its shape and structure must be included in our description. For the formal nature is of greater importance than the material nature.

Does, then, configuration and colour constitute the essence of the various animals and of their several parts? For if so, what Democritus says will be strictly correct. For such appears to have been his notion. At any rate he says that it is evident to every one what form it is that makes the man, seeing that he is recognizable by his shape and colour. And yet a dead body has exactly the same configuration as a living one; but for all that is not a man. So also no hand of bronze or wood or constituted in any but the appropriate way can possibly be a hand in more than name. For like a physician in a painting, or like a flute in a sculpture, in spite of its name it will be unable to do the office which that name implies. Precisely in the same way no part of a dead body, such I mean as its eye or its hand, is really an eye or a hand. To say, then, that shape and colour constitute the animal is an inadequate statement, and is much the same as if a woodcarver were to insist that the hand he had cut out was really a hand. Yet the physiologists, when they give an account of the development and causes of the animal form, speak very much like such a craftsman. What, however, I would ask, are the forces by which the hand or the body was fashioned into its shape? The woodcarver will perhaps say, by the axe or the auger; the physiologist, by air and by earth. Of these two answers the artificer's is the better, but it is neverthless insufficient. For it is not enough for him to say that by the stroke of his tool that part was formed into a concavity, that into a flat surface; but he must state the reasons why he struck his blow in such a way as to effect this, and what his final object was; namely, that the piece of wood should develop eventually into

this or that shape. It is plain, then, that the teaching of
15 the old physiologists is inadequate, and that the true
method is to state what the definitive characters are that
distinguish the animal as a whole; to explain what it is
both in substance and in form, and to deal after the same
fashion with its several organs; in fact, to proceed in
exactly the same way as we should do, were we giving a
complete description of a couch.

If now this something that constitutes the form of the
living being be the soul, or part of the soul, or something
that without the soul cannot exist; as would seem to be
the case, seeing at any rate that when the soul departs,
what is left is no longer a living animal, and that none of
20 the parts remain what they were before, excepting in
mere configuration, like the animals that in the fable are
turned into stone; if, I say, this be so, then it will come
within the province of the natural philosopher to inform
himself concerning the soul, and to treat of it, either in
its entirety, or, at any rate, of that part of it which constitutes the essential character of an animal; and it will
be his duty to say what this soul or this part of a soul is;
25 and to discuss the attributes that attach to this essential
character, especially as nature is spoken of in two senses,
and the nature of a thing is either its matter or its essence;
nature as essence including both the motor cause and the
final cause. Now it is in the latter of these two senses that
either the whole soul or some part of it constitutes that
nature of an animal; and inasmuch as it is the presence
of the soul that enables matter to constitute the animal
nature, much more than it is the presence of matter which
30 so enables the soul, the inquirer into nature is bound on
every ground to treat of the soul rather than of the matter.
· For though the wood of which they are made constitutes
the couch and the tripod, it only does so because it is
capable of receiving such and such a form.

What has been said suggests the question, whether it is
the whole soul or only some part of it, the consideration

of which comes within the province of natural science. 35
Now if it be of the whole soul that this should treat, then
there is no place for any other philosophy beside it. For 641ᵇ
as it belongs in all cases to one and the same science to
deal with correlated subjects—one and the same science,
for instance, deals with sensation and with the objects of
sense—and as therefore the intelligent soul and the objects of intellect, being correlated, must belong to one and
the same science, it follows that natural science will have
to include the whole universe in its province. But per- 5
haps it is not the whole soul, nor all its parts collectively,
that constitutes the source of motion; but there may be
one part, identical with that in plants, which is the source
of growth, another, namely the sensory part, which is the
source of change of quality, while still another, and this
not the intellectual part, is the source of locomotion. I
say not the intellectual part; for other animals than man
have the power of locomotion, but in none but him is
there intellect. Thus then it is plain that it is not of the
whole soul that we have to treat. For it is not the whole
soul that constitutes the animal nature, but only some 10
part or parts of it. Moreover, it is impossible that any
abstraction can form a subject of natural science, seeing
that everything that Nature makes is means to an end. For
just as human creations are the products of art, so living
objects are manifestly the products of an analogous cause
or principle, not external but internal, derived like the hot 15
and the cold from the environing universe. And that the
heaven, if it had an origin, was evolved and is maintained
by such a cause, there is therefore even more reason to
believe, than that mortal animals so originated. For order
and definiteness are much more plainly manifest in the
celestial bodies than in our own frame; while change and 20
fortune are characteristic of the perishable things of earth.
Yet there are some who, while they allow that every animal exists and was generated by nature, nevertheless hold
that the heaven was constructed to be what it is by

fortune and chance; the heaven, in which not the faintest
sign of hap-hazard or of disorder is discernible! Again,
whenever there is plainly some final end, to which a mo-
25 tion tends should nothing stand in the way, we always say
that such final end is the aim or purpose of the motion;
and from this it is evident that there must be a something or other really existing, corresponding to what we
call by the name of Nature. For a given germ does not
give rise to any fortuitous living being, nor spring from
any fortuitous one; but each germ springs from a definite
parent and gives rise to a definite progeny. And thus it is
the germ that is the ruling influence and fabricator of the
30 offspring. For these it is by nature, the offspring being at
any rate that which in nature will spring from it. At the
same time the offspring is anterior to the germ; for germ
and perfected progeny are related as the developmental
process and the result. Anterior, however, to both germ
and product is the organism from which the germ was derived. For every germ implies two organisms, the parent
and the progeny. For germ or seed is both the seed of the
35 organism from which it came, of the horse, for instance,
from which it was derived, and the seed of the organism
that will eventually arise from it, of the mule, or example,
which is developed from the seed of the horse. The same
seed then is the seed both of the horse and of the mule,
though in different ways as here set forth. Moreover, the
seed is potentially that which will spring from it, and the
relation of potentiality to actuality we know.

642[a]   There are then two causes, namely, necessity and the
final end. For many things are produced, simply as the
results of necessity. It may, however, be asked, of what
mode of necessity are we speaking when we say this. For
5 it can be of neither of those two modes which are set
forth in the philosophical treatises. There is, however, the
third mode, in such things at any rate as are generated.
For instance, we say that food is necessary; because an
animal cannot possibly do without it. This third mode is

what may be called hypothetical necessity. Here is another example of it. If a piece of wood is to be split with an axe, the axe must of necessity be hard; and, if hard, must of necessity be made of bronze or iron. Now exactly in the same way the body, which like the axe is an instrument—for both the body as a whole and its several parts individually have definite operations for which they are made—just in the same way, I say, the body, if it is to do its work, must of necessity be of such and such a character, and made of such and such materials.

It is plain then that there are two modes of causation, and that both of these must, so far as possible, be taken into account in explaining the works of nature, or that at any rate an attempt must be made to include them both; and that those who fail in this tell us in reality nothing about nature. For primary cause constitutes the nature of an animal much more than does its matter. There are indeed passages in which even Empedocles hits upon this, and following the guidance of fact, finds himself constrained to speak of the ratio as constituting the essence and real nature of things. Such, for instance, is the case when he explains what is a bone. For he does not merely describe its material, and say it is this one element, or those two or three elements, or a compound of all the elements, but states the ratio of their combination. As with a bone, so manifestly is it with the flesh and all other similar parts.

The reason why our predecessors failed in hitting upon this method of treatment was, that they were not in possession of the notion of essence, nor of any definition of substance. The first who came near it was Democritus, and he was far from adopting it as a necessary method in natural science, but was merely brought to it, spite of himself, by constraint of facts. In the time of Socrates a nearer approach was made to the method. But at this period men gave up inquiring into the works of nature, and philosophers diverted their attention to political science and to the virtues which benefit mankind.

Of the method itself the following is an example. In dealing with respiration we must show that it takes place for such or such a final object; and we must also show that this and that part of the process is necessitated by this and that other stage of it. By necessity we shall sometimes mean hypothetical necessity, the necessity, that is, that the requisite antecedents shall be there, if the final end is to be reached; and sometimes absolute necessity, such necessity as that which connects substances and their 35 inherent properties and characters. For the alternate discharge and re-entrance of heat and the inflow of air are necessary if we are to live. Here we have at once a neces-642ᵇ sity in the former of the two senses. But the alternation of heat and refrigeration produces of necessity an alternate admission and discharge of the outer air, and this is a necessity of the second kind.

In the foregoing we have an example of the method which we must adopt, and also an example of the kind of phenomena, the causes of which we have to investigate.

Metaphysics

⊓⊔⊓⊔⊓⊔⊓⊔⊓⊔⊓⊔⊓⊔⊓⊔⊓⊔⊓⊔⊓⊔⊓⊔⊓⊔

INTRODUCTION

The theoretic science which Aristotle refers to as "first philosophy" or "theology" or "wisdom" came to be called "metaphysics," not because of its subject-matter but because of its place in the edition of Aristotle's works by Andronicus of Rhodes—*ta meta ta physika*— "the books that come after the books on physics." In modern editions it still comes after the ten treatises on physical science and before the two treatises on practical science, the ethics and politics. The first book of the *Metaphysics*, Book Alpha, which is included in this collection, examines the need for, and the subject-matter of, such a science. Beginning with the observation that all men by nature desire to know, Aristotle inquires into the nature of the science we seek as "wisdom" by placing it in the sequence of faculties and purposive operations of animals—sense, memory, experience, art, and science— and by examining what the wise man knows. He concludes that wisdom is concerned with causes as such, and is the science of first principles and causes, which is architectonic or most authoritative among the sciences. The examination of earlier conceptions of cause, like the examination of theories of the soul as principles of motion and of life in the opening books of the *Physics* and the *De Anima*, turns on distinctions of matter and form. The earliest philosophers limited their attention to material causes and explained things by the matter or the elements of which they are composed. Later philosophers turned to formal causes or essences, which they separated from matter and constituted into independent and self-subsistent Forms. The moving or efficient cause, which initiates the change, and the final cause or end, in which it eventuates, which have a prominent place in the inquiries of Aristotle's physical treatises, were touched on only sporadically by a few philosophers like Empedocles and Anaxagoras. After criticisms and adaptations of earlier conceptions of cause, the book ends with a demonstration that there are no more than the four causes.

The examination of first causes is inquiry into being. Knowledge of being-in-itself, or simple being, presents difficulties, since any statement about simple being departs from its simplicity by attributing to it properties or predicates. The next four books, together with the first book, present an introduction preparatory to the inquiry into being. The second book, Book Little Alpha, states, in three chapters, three preconditions of the science with respect to thought, things, and methods. (1) With respect to thought, there is a paradox in the investigation of truth: it is in one way hard, in another way easy. It is easy because truth is like the proverbial door, which no one can fail to hit, but it is hard because we can have a whole truth and not the particular part at which we aim. (2) With respect to things, there is a precondition to the discovery of first causes: to have first causes, processes must have beginnings, and an infinite regress must be shown to be impossible with respect to all four kinds of causes. (3) With respect to method and discourse, there is a variability with habits of thought and properties of subject-matter: the formation of a science of first causes requires consideration of how arguments are taken and how the method required differs from the methods of physics and mathematics. The third book, Book Beta, is a dialectical statement and enumeration of problems, in general, in this science, and with respect to things, to intelligibility, to numbers and forms. The fourth book, Book Gamma, is an examination of the principles of inquiry and method, the logical and verbal preconditions of inquiry into first causes, including refutations of attacks on primary axioms, like the law of contradiction, the law of identity, and the law of excluded middle. The fifth book, Book Delta, is a lexicon of thirty terms used in ordinary language in the exploration of metaphysical issues, setting forth the range of their meanings. The list begins with 'principle,' runs through 'cause,' 'element,' 'nature,' 'necessity,' to end with 'genus,' 'false,' and 'accident.'

In the physical sciences the dialectical examination of what men have said prepared for a new start in inquiry, based on definition, concerning kinds of motions and vital processes. In the science of first causes and principles, the dialectical examination of what men have said is part of a dialectical examination of how thinking, changing, and stating are and affect concepts of cause and being. The sixth book, Book Epsilon, prepares for a new start by stating the problem of the science of being: "We are seeking the principles and the causes of the things that are, and obviously of things *qua* being," and by differentiating metaphysical problems from the problems of the other theoretical sciences, physics and mathematics, and those of the practical and productive sciences. As the varying meanings of "motion" and of "life" had been examined for distinctions of kinds of processes, now the various meanings of "being" provide the initial distinctions of kinds of being. Four meanings had been differentiated in chapter 7 of Book Delta: (1) an accidental sense (in which two properties are joined in one subject, as when a man happens *to be* musical and also a builder), and three essential senses, (2) a predicational sense (in which a predicate in any of the categories of predication is joined to, and *is*, a subject, as, "the man *is* musical"), (3) an assertoric sense (in which 'being' or 'is' means that the statement is true and 'non-being' that it is false, as, "the man is musical *is true*"), and (4) an ontic sense (in which that which is is related to being potentially or actually, as, "the man *is actually* musical"), In Book Epsilon two of these senses, the first and the third, accidental being and true being, are eliminated since they involve combinations and separations of terms and thoughts, and our concern is with the principles and causes of being itself, qua being apart from coincident occurrences or asserted thoughts.

The seventh book, Book Zeta, returns to the distinction between 'what is' and 'how it is qualified' which underlies the third kind of being, predicational being. The primary sense of the 'being of a thing' is 'what it is,' its substance, and not what qualities or quantities it has. Various senses of 'substance,' 'definition,' 'is,' and 'unity' are distinguished, and finally, in the last chapter of Zeta, the time has come for a "new start." "Let us state what should be said to be the genus and the differentia of substance, taking another starting point; for perhaps from this we shall get a clear view also of that substance which exists apart from sensible substances. Since, then, substance is a principle and a cause, let us attack it from this standpoint." The "why" is always sought in this form— "Why does an attribute attach to a subject? The examination of the four senses of being has lead us through the four scientific questions distinguished at the beginning of the second book of the *Posterior Analytics*: (1) Is it? Does it happen to have several attributes? (2) What is it? How is it defined? (3) Of what sort is it? By what attributes is it qualified? (4) Why? Why does that attribute attach to that subject?

The eighth book, Book Eta, begins by summing up the results thus far achieved in order "to put the finishing touches to our inquiry." The summary includes (a) a list of "generally recognized substances," similar to the list of "things that exist by nature" in the second book of the Physics, (1) the simple bodies, (2) plants and their parts, animals and their parts, (3) the heavens and the parts of the heavens, and (b) substances advocated by particular schools, including Ideas and mathematical objects. The ninth book, Book Theta, makes the new start by turning to the fourth sense of being, actual and potential being. Being may be divided, as it is in predicational being, into substance and the categories of attributes predicated of it. It may also be distinguished with respect to potency and actuality. The inquiry has led us through the plurality of attributes used to know, discuss, and act on things that are, to the simplicity of being, differentiated only by the functions which are manifested in being. The inquiry is based therefore on a differentiation of meanings of 'potency' and of 'can.' Form and matter are now viewed as actuality and potency, what is and its substrate. The ninth and tenth books, Books Iota and Kappa, turn to the consideration of the problems of metaphysics in this new structure of actuality and potency, of "what is" and "what it can be," of substance and function. Iota is concerned with the first step of that inquiry, how being is one as a functioning structure, what constitutes its unity as individual and measure, beginning with a differentiation of the senses of 'unity' and going on to the consideration of the relation of unity to essence and essences, substance and plurality. Kappa goes on to a consideration of the *substrata* of actuality in functioning substances. The authenticity and function of Book Kappa have been subject to puzzled and adverse scholarly criticism because it is a collection of recapitulations and extracts from the *Metaphysics* and the *Physics*. Yet in the structure of the argument, a review of the nature and kinds of matters, potentialities, and substrates is needed, and Kappa provides them from Books Beta, Gamma, and Epsilon of the *Metaphysics* and from Books II, III, IV, and V of the *Physics*. Iota and Kappa raise the question "Why?" with respect to essences and substrates preliminary to the treatment of functioning substances in terms of actuality and potency in Book Lambda.

The twelfth book, Book Lambda, which is included in this collection, turns to that question "Why?" "Substance is the subject of our inquiry; for the principles and causes we are seeking are those of substances. For if the universe is of the nature of a whole, substance is its first part; and if it coheres merely by virtue of serial succession, on this view also substance is first, and is succeeded by quality, and then by quantity." The list of three kinds of substance of Book Eta is restated and reorganized: (1) perishable (plants and animals), (2) eternal (the elements, whether one or many), (3) immovable. The first two kinds are the subject of physics; the third belongs to another science if there is no principle common to it and the other kinds. Neither matter nor form comes into being or ceases to be, for everything that changes is something and is changed by something and into something. Each substance comes into being out of something that shares its name in art, nature, chance, and fortune. The sequence is infinite, for motion and time, as well as matter, have no beginning or end. There must be a principle whose very essence is actuality, an unmoved mover. The *Physics* closed the discussion of natures and motions with the demonstration of an unmoved mover. The demonstration of the unmoved mover on the basis of the examination of being and substances is as a final rather than a moving cause. "The final cause, then, produces motion by being loved, and by that which it moves, it moves all other things." Whereas knowledge, perception, opinion, and understanding always have something else as their object, divine thought has itself for its object. Good is discernible in the universe in matter and as principle, as order in material parts and as principle manifesting a ruler. The thirteenth and fourteenth books, Books Mu and Nu, return to the consideration of immaterial substance, the refutation of mathematical objects and Ideas, and the criticism of characteristics and causal properties attributed to separated substances.

METAPHYSICA

CONTENTS

A. (I)

Λ. (XII)

mover, and one whose essence is actuality (actuality being prior to potency). To account for the uniform change in the universe, there must be one principle which acts always alike, and one whose action varies/ 315

Metaphysica

Metaphysics

Translated by W. D. Ross

ⅬⅬⅬ

BOOK A (I)

1　All men by nature desire to know. An indication of
this is the delight we take in our senses; for even apart 980ᵃ
from their usefulness they are loved for themselves; and
above all others the sense of sight. For not only with a view
to action, but even when we are not going to do anything, 25
we prefer seeing (one might say) to everything else. The
reason is that this, most of all the senses, makes us know
and brings to light many differences between things.

By nature animals are born with the faculty of sensation,
and from sensation memory is produced in some of them,
though not in others. And therefore the former are more
intelligent and apt at learning than those which cannot 980ᵇ
remember; those which are incapable of hearing sounds are
intelligent though they cannot be taught, e. g. the bee, and
any other race of animals that may be like it; and those
which besides memory have this sense of hearing can be
taught.

The animals other than man live by appearances and
memories, and have but little of connected experience; 25
but the human race lives also by art and reasonings. Now
from memory experience is produced in men; for the several
memories of the same thing produce finally the capacity for

981ᵃa single experience. And experience seems pretty much like science and art, but really science and art come to men *through* experience; for 'experience made art', as Polus says,[1] 'but inexperience luck'. Now art arises when from 5 many notions gained by experience one universal judgement about a class of objects is produced. For to have a judgement that when Callias was ill of this disease this did him good, and similarly in the case of Socrates and in many individual cases, is a matter of experience; but to judge that it has done good to all persons of a certain constitution, 10 marked off in one class, when they were ill of this disease, e. g. to phlegmatic or bilious people when burning with fever—this is a matter of art.

With a view to action experience seems in no respect inferior to art, and men of experience succeed even better 15 than those who have theory without experience. (The reason is that experience is knowledge of individuals, art of universals, and actions and productions are all concerned with the individual; for the physician does not cure *man*, except in an incidental way, but Callias or Socrates or some other called by some such individual name, who happens to 20 be a man. If, then, a man has the theory without the experience, and recognizes the universal but does not know the individual included in this, he will often fail to cure; for it is the individual that is to be cured.) But yet we think that 25 *knowledge* and *understanding* belong to art rather than to experience, and we suppose artists to be wiser than men of experience (which implies that Wisdom depends in all cases rather on knowledge); and this because the former know the cause, but the latter do not. For men of experi-30 ence know that the thing is so, but do not know why, while the others know the 'why' and the cause. Hence we think also that the master-workers in each craft are more honour-981ᵇable and know in a truer sense and are wiser than the manual workers, because they know the causes of the things that are done (we think the manual workers are like certain

[1] Cf. Pl. *Gorg.* 448 c, 462 bc.

lifeless things which act indeed, but act without knowing
what they do, as fire burns—but while the lifeless things
perform each of their functions by a natural tendency, the 5
labourers perform them through habit); thus we view them
as being wiser not in virtue of being able to act, but of
having the theory for themselves and knowing the causes.
And in general it is a sign of the man who knows and of the
man who does not know, that the former can teach, and
therefore we think art more truly knowledge than experience is; for artists can teach, and men of mere experience
cannot.

Again, we do not regard any of the senses as Wisdom; 10
yet surely these give the most authoritative knowledge of
particulars. But they do not tell us the 'why' of anything—
e. g. why fire is hot; they only say *that* it is hot.

At first he who invented any art whatever that went beyond the common perceptions of man was naturally admired by men, not only because there was something useful 15
in the inventions, but because he was thought wise and
superior to the rest. But as more arts were invented, and
some were directed to the necessities of life, others to
recreation, the inventors of the latter were naturally always
regarded as wiser than the inventors of the former, because
their branches of knowledge did not aim at utility. Hence
when all such inventions were already established, the sci- 20
ences which do not aim at giving pleasure or at the necessities of life were discovered, and first in the places where
men first began to have leisure. This is why the mathematical arts were founded in Egypt; for there the priestly caste
was allowed to be at leisure.

We have said in the *Ethics* [2] what the difference is between art and science and the other kindred faculties; but 25
the point of our present discussion is this, that all men suppose what is called Wisdom to deal with the first causes
and the principles of things; so that, as has been said before,
the man of experience is thought to be wiser than the pos- 30

[2] 1139ᵇ 14–1141ᵇ 8.

sessors of any sense-perception whatever, the artist wiser than the men of experience, the master-worker than the mechanic, and the theoretical kinds of knowledge to be more of the nature of Wisdom than the productive. Clearly
982ª then Wisdom is knowledge about certain principles and causes.

2   Since we are seeking this knowledge, we must inquire
5   of what kind are the causes and the principles, the knowledge of which is Wisdom. If one were to take the notions we have about the wise man, this might perhaps make the answer more evident. We suppose first, then, that the wise man knows all things, as far as possible, although
10 he has not knowledge of each of them in detail; secondly, that he who can learn things that are difficult, and not easy for man to know, is wise (sense-perception is common to all, and therefore easy and no mark of Wisdom); again, that he who is more exact and more capable of teaching the causes is wiser, in every branch of knowledge; and that of
15 the sciences, also, that which is desirable on its own account and for the sake of knowing it is more of the nature of Wisdom than that which is desirable on account of its results, and the superior science is more of the nature of Wisdom than the ancillary; for the wise man must not be ordered but must order, and he must not obey another, but the less wise must obey *him*.
    Such and so many are the notions, then, which we have
20 about Wisdom and the wise. Now of these characteristics that of knowing all things must belong to him who has in the highest degree universal knowledge; for he knows in a sense all the instances that fall under the universal. And these things, the most universal, are on the whole the hardest for men to know; for they are farthest from the senses.
25 And the most exact of the sciences are those which deal most with first principles; for those which involve fewer principles are more exact than those which involve additional principles, e. g. arithmetic than geometry. But the

science which investigates causes is also *instructive*, in a
higher degree, for the people who instruct us are those who
tell the causes of each thing. And understanding and knowl- 30
edge pursued for their own sake are found most in the
knowledge of that which is most knowable (for he who
chooses to know for the sake of knowing will choose most
readily that which is most truly knowledge, and such is the 982ᵇ
knowledge of that which is most knowable); and the first
principles and the causes are most knowable; for by reason
of these, and from these, all other things come to be known,
and not these by means of the things subordinate to them.
And the science which knows to what end each thing must
be done is the most authoritative of the sciences, and more 5
authoritative than any ancillary science; and this end is the
good of that thing, and in general the supreme good in the
whole of nature. Judged by all the tests we have mentioned,
then, the name in question falls to the same science; this
must be a science that investigates the first principles and 10
causes; for the good, i. e. the end, is one of the causes.

   That it is not a science of production is clear even from
the history of the earliest philosophers. For it is owing to
their wonder that men both now begin and at first began
to philosophize; they wondered originally at the obvious
difficulties, then advanced little by little and stated diffi- 15
culties about the greater matters, e. g. about the phenomena
of the moon and those of the sun and of the stars, and
about the genesis of the universe. And a man who is
puzzled and wonders thinks himself ignorant (whence even
the lover of myth is in a sense a lover of Wisdom, for the
myth is composed of wonders); therefore since they phi- 20
losophized in order to escape from ignorance, evidently
they were pursuing science in order to know, and not for
any utilitarian end. And this is confirmed by the facts; for
it was when almost all the necessities of life and the things
that make for comfort and recreation had been secured,
that such knowledge began to be sought. Evidently then
we do not seek it for the sake of any other advantage; but 25

as the man is free, we say, who exists for his own sake and not for another's, so we pursue this as the only free science, for it alone exists for its own sake.

Hence also the possession of it might be justly regarded as beyond human power; for in many ways human nature 30 is in bondage, so that according to Simonides 'God alone can have this privilege', and it is unfitting that man should not be content to seek the knowledge that is suited to him. 983ª If, then, there is something in what the poets say, and jealousy is natural to the divine power, it would probably occur in this case above all, and all who excelled in this knowledge would be unfortunate. But the divine power cannot be jealous (nay, according to the proverb, 'bards 5 tell many a lie'), nor should any other science be thought more honourable than one of this sort. For the most divine science is also most honourable; and this science alone must be, in two ways, most divine. For the science which it would be most meet for God to have is a divine science, and so is any science that deals with divine objects; and this science alone has both these qualities; for (1) God is thought to be among the causes of all things and to be a first principle, and (2) such a science either God alone 10 can have, or God above all others. All the sciences, indeed, are more necessary than this, but none is better.

Yet the acquisition of it must in a sense end in something which is the opposite of our original inquiries. For all men begin, as we said, by wondering that things are as 15 they are, as they do about self-moving marionettes, or about the solstices or the incommensurability of the diagonal of a square with the side; for it seems wonderful to all who have not yet seen the reason, that there is a thing which cannot be measured even by the smallest unit. But we must end in the contrary and, according to the proverb, the better state, as is the case in these instances too when men learn the cause; for there is nothing which would surprise a geometer so much as if the diagonal 20 turned out to be commensurable.

We have stated, then, what is the nature of the science we are searching for, and what is the mark which our search and our whole investigation must reach.

3   Evidently we have to acquire knowledge of the original causes (for we say we know each thing only when we think we recognize its first cause), and causes are 25 spoken of in four senses. In one of these we mean the substance, i. e. the essence (for the 'why' is reducible finally to the definition, and the ultimate 'why' is a cause and principle); in another the matter or substratum, in a third the source of the change, and in a fourth the cause 30 opposed to this, the purpose and the good (for this is the end of all generation and change). We have studied these 983ᵇ causes sufficiently in our work on nature,[3] but yet let us call to our aid those who have attacked the investigation of being and philosophized about reality before us. For obviously they too speak of certain principles and causes; to go over their views, then, will be of profit to the present inquiry, for we shall either find another kind of cause, or 5 be more convinced of the correctness of those which we now maintain.

Of the first philosophers, then, most thought the principles which were of the nature of matter were the only principles of all things. That of which all things that are consist, the first from which they come to be, the last into which they are resolved (the substance remaining, but 10 changing in its modifications), this they say is the element and this the principle of things, and therefore they think nothing is either generated or destroyed, since this sort of entity is always conserved, as we say Socrates neither comes to be absolutely when he comes to be beautiful or musical, nor ceases to be when he loses these character- 15 istics, because the substratum, Socrates himself, remains. Just so they say nothing else comes to be or ceases to be; for there must be some entity—either one or more than

[3] *Phys.* ii. 3, 7.

one—from which all other things come to be, it being conserved.

Yet they do not all agree as to the number and the
20 nature of these principles. Thales, the founder of this type
of philosophy, says the principle is water (for which
reason he declared that the earth rests on water), getting
the notion perhaps from seeing that the nutriment of
all things is moist, and that heat itself is generated from
the moist and kept alive by it (and that from which
25 they come to be is a principle of all things). He got his
notion from this fact, and from the fact that the seeds of
all things have a moist nature, and that water is the origin
of the nature of moist things.

Some[4] think that even the ancients who lived long
before the present generation, and first framed accounts of
30 the gods, had a similar view of nature; for they made
Ocean and Tethys the parents of creation,[5] and described
the oath of the gods as being by water,[6] to which they give
the name of Styx; for what is oldest is most honourable,
and the most honourable thing is that by which one
984ᵃ swears. It may perhaps be uncertain whether this opinion
about nature is primitive and ancient, but Thales at any
rate is said to have declared himself thus about the first
cause. Hippo no one would think fit to include among these
thinkers, because of the paltriness of his thought.

5 Anaximenes and Diogenes make air prior to water, and
the most primary of the simple bodies, while Hippasus of
Metapontium and Heraclitus of Ephesus say this of fire,
and Empedocles says it of the four elements (adding a
fourth—earth—to those which have been named); for
10 these, he says, always remain and do not come to be, except
that they come to be more or fewer, being aggregated into
one and segregated out of one.

Anaxagoras of Clazomenae, who, though older than

---

[4] The reference is probably to Plato (Crat. 402 ʙ, Theaet. 152 ᴇ, 162 ᴅ, 180 ᴄ).
[5] Hom. Il. xiv, 201, 246.
[6] Ibid. ii. 755, xiv. 271, xv. 37.

Empedocles, was later in his philosophical activity, says the principles are infinite in number; for he says almost all the things that are made of parts like themselves, in the manner of water or fire, are generated and destroyed in this way, only by aggregation and segregation, and are not in 15 any other sense generated or destroyed, but remain eternally.

From these facts one might think that the only cause is the so-called material cause; but as men thus advanced, the very facts opened the way for them and joined in forcing them to investigate the subject. However true it may be that all generation and destruction proceed from some one 20 or (for that matter) from more elements, why does this happen and what is the cause? For at least the substratum itself does not make itself change; e. g. neither the wood nor the bronze causes the change of either of them, nor does the wood manufacture a bed and the bronze a statue, but something else is the cause of the change. And to seek 25 this is to seek the second cause, as we should say—that from which comes the beginning of the movement. Now those who at the very beginning set themselves to this kind of inquiry, and said the substratum was one,[7] were not at all dissatisfied with themselves; but some at least of those who maintained it to be one [8]—as though defeated by this search for the second cause—say the one and 30 nature as a whole is unchangeable not only in respect of generation and destruction (for this is a primitive belief, and all agreed in it), but also of all other change; and this view is peculiar to them. Of those who said the universe was one, then, none succeeded in discovering a cause of 984[b] this sort, except perhaps Parmenides, and he only inasmuch as he supposes that there is not only one but also in some sense two causes. But for those who make more elements [9] it is more possible to state the second cause, e. g. for those 5

---

[7] Thales, Anaximenes, and Heraclitus.
[8] The Eleatics.
[9] The reference is probably to Empedocles.

who make hot and cold, or fire and earth, the elements; for they treat fire as having a nature which fits it to move things, and water and earth and such things they treat in the contrary way.

When these men and the principles of this kind had had their day, as the latter were found inadequate to generate the nature of things men were again forced by the truth
10 itself, as we said,[10] to inquire into the next kind of cause. For it is not likely either that fire or earth or any such element should be the reason why things manifest goodness and beauty both in their being and in their coming to be, or that those thinkers should have supposed it was; nor again could it be right to entrust so great a matter to spontaneity and chance. When one man [11] said, then, that
15 reason was present—as in animals, so throughout nature— as the cause of order and of all arrangement, he seemed like a sober man in contrast with the random talk of his predecessors. We know that Anaxagoras certainly adopted these views, but Hermotimus of Clazomenae is credited
20 with expressing them earlier. Those who thought thus stated that there is a principle of things which is at the same time the cause of beauty, and that sort of cause from which things acquire movement.

4   One might suspect that Hesiod was the first to look for such a thing—or some one else who put love or
25 desire among existing things as a principle, as Parmenides, too, does; for he, in constructing the genesis of the universe, says:—

Love first of all the Gods she planned.

And Hesiod says:—

First of all things was chaos made, and then
Broad-breasted earth, . . .
And love, 'mid all the gods pre-eminent,

[10] a18.
[11] Anaxagoras.

which implies that among existing things there must be 30
from the first a cause which will move things and bring
them together. How these thinkers should be arranged
with regard to priority of discovery let us be allowed to
decide later; [12] but since the contraries of the various forms
of good were also perceived to be present in nature—not
only order and the beautiful, but also disorder and the
ugly, and bad things in greater number than good, and 985ᵃ
ignoble things than beautiful—therefore another thinker
introduced friendship and strife, each of the two the cause
of one of these two sets of qualities. For if we were to
follow out the view of Empedocles, and interpret it accord- 5
ing to its meaning and not to its lisping expression, we
should find that friendship is the cause of good things, and
strife of bad. Therefore, if we said that Empedocles in a
sense both mentions, and is the first to mention, the bad
and the good as principles, we should perhaps be right,
since the cause of all goods is the good itself.

These thinkers, as we say, evidently grasped, and to this 10
extent, two of the causes which we distinguished in our
work on nature [13]—the matter and the source of the movement—vaguely, however, and with no clearness, but as
untrained men behave in fights; for they go round their 15
opponents and often strike fine blows, but they do not fight
on scientific principles, and so too these thinkers do not
seem to know what they say; for it is evident that, as a rule,
they make no use of their causes except to a small extent.
For Anaxagoras uses reason as a *deus ex machina* for the
making of the world, and when he is at a loss to tell from
what cause something necessarily is, then he drags reason 20
in, but in all other cases ascribes events to anything rather
than to reason. [14] And Empedocles, though he uses the
causes to a greater extent than this, neither does so sufficiently nor attains consistency in their use. At least, in

[12] The promise is not fulfilled.
[13] *Phys.* ii. 3, 7.
[14] Cf. Pl. *Phaedo*, 98 ʙᴄ, *Laws*, 967 ʙ–ᴅ.

many cases he makes love segregate things, and strife aggre-
25 gate them. For whenever the universe is dissolved into its
elements by strife, fire is aggregated into one, and so is each
of the other elements; but whenever again under the influence of love they come together into one, the parts must
again be segregated out of each element.

Empedocles, then, in contrast with his predecessors,
was the first to introduce the dividing of this cause, not
30 positing one source of movement, but different and contrary sources. Again, he was the first to speak of four
985ᵇ material elements; yet he does not use four, but treats them
as two only; he treats fire by itself, and its opposites—earth,
air, and water—as one kind of thing. We may learn this by
study of his verses.

This philosopher then, as we say, has spoken of the
principles in this way, and made them of this number.
Leucippus and his associate Democritus say that the full
5 and the empty are the elements, calling the one being and
the other non-being—the full and solid being being, the
empty non-being (whence they say being no more is than
non-being, because the solid no more is than the empty);
and they make these the material causes of things. And as
10 those who make the underlying substance one generate all
other things by its modifications, supposing the rare and
the dense to be the sources of the modifications, in the
same way these philosophers say the differences in the elements are the causes of all other qualities. These differences, they say, are three—shape and order and position.
15 For they say the real is differentiated only by 'rhythm'
and 'inter-contact' and 'turning'; and of these rhythm is
shape, inter-contact is order, and turning is position; for
A differs from N in shape, AN from NA in order, H from
H in position. The question of movement—whence or
how it is to belong to things—these thinkers, like the
others, lazily neglected.

Regarding the two causes, then, as we say, the inquiry

seems to have been pushed thus far by the early philos- 20
ophers.

5　Contemporaneously with these philosophers and before them, the so-called Pythagoreans, who were the
first to take up mathematics, not only advanced this study, 25
but also having been brought up in it they thought its
principles were the principles of all things. Since of these
principles numbers are by nature the first, and in numbers
they seemed to see many resemblances to the things that
exist and come into being—more than in fire and earth
and water (such and such a modification of numbers being
justice, another being soul and reason, another being op- 30
portunity—and similarly almost all other things being
numerically expressible); since, again, they saw that the
modifications and the ratios of the musical scales were expressible in numbers;—since, then, all other things seemed
in their whole nature to be modelled on numbers, and
numbers seemed to be the first things in the whole of 986ᵃ
nature, they supposed the elements of numbers to be the
elements of all things, and the whole heaven to be a
musical scale and a number. And all the properties of numbers and scales which they could show to agree with the
attributes and parts and the whole arrangement of the 5
heavens, they collected and fitted into their scheme; and if
there was a gap anywhere, they readily made additions so
as to make their whole theory coherent. E. g. as the number
10 is thought to be perfect and to comprise the whole nature of numbers, they say that the bodies which move 10
through the heavens are ten, but as the visible bodies are
only nine, to meet this they invent a tenth—the 'counter-
earth'. We have discussed these matters more exactly elsewhere.[15]

But the object of our review is that we may learn from
these philosophers also what they suppose to be the principles and how these fall under the causes we have named. 15

[15] *De Caelo*, ii. 13.

Evidently, then, these thinkers also consider that number is the principle both as matter for things and as forming both their modifications and their permanent states, and hold that the elements of number are the even and the odd, and that of these the latter is limited, and the former unlimited; and that the One proceeds from both of these 20 (for it is both even and odd), and number from the One; and that the whole heaven, as has been said, is numbers.

Other members of this same school say there are ten principles, which they arrange in two columns of cognates 25 —limit and unlimited, odd and even, one and plurality, right and left, male and female, resting and moving, straight and curved, light and darkness, good and bad, square and oblong. In this way Alcmaeon of Croton seems also to have conceived the matter, and either he got this view from them or they got it from him; for he expressed 30 himself similarly to them. For he says most human affairs go in pairs, meaning not definite contrarieties such as the Pythagoreans speak of, but any chance contrarieties, e. g. white and black, sweet and bitter, good and bad, great and small. He threw out indefinite suggestions about the other contrarieties, but the Pythagoreans declared both how 986ᵇ many and which their contrarieties are.

From both these schools, then, we can learn this much, that the contraries are the principles of things; and how many these principles are and which they are, we can learn from one of the two schools. But how these principles can 5 be brought together under the causes we have named has not been clearly and articulately stated by them; they seem, however, to range the elements under the head of matter; for out of these as immanent parts they say substance is composed and moulded.

From these facts we may sufficiently perceive the meaning of the ancients who said the elements of nature were more than one; but there are some who spoke of the uni- 10 verse as if it were one entity, though they were not all alike either in the excellence of their statement or in its

conformity to the facts of nature. The discussion of them
is in no way appropriate to our present investigation of
causes, for they do not, like some of the natural philosophers, assume being to be one and yet generate it out of
the one as out of matter, but they speak in another way; 15
those others add change, since they generate the universe,
but these thinkers say the universe is unchangeable. Yet
this much is germane to the present inquiry: Parmenides
seems to fasten on that which is one in definition, Melissus
on that which is one in matter, for which reason the former
says that it is limited, the latter that it is unlimited; while 20
Xenophanes, the first of these partisans of the One (for
Parmenides is said to have been his pupil), gave no clear
statement, nor does he seem to have grasped the nature of
either of these causes, but with reference to the whole
material universe he says the One is God. Now these thinkers, as we said, must be neglected for the purposes of the 25
present inquiry—two of them entirely, as being a little too
naïve, viz. Xenophanes and Melissus; but Parmenides
seems in places to speak with more insight. For, claiming
that, besides the existent, nothing non-existent exists, he
thinks that of necessity one thing exists, viz. the existent
and nothing else (on this we have spoken more clearly in
our work on nature),[16] but being forced to follow the ob- 30
served facts, and supposing the existence of that which is
one in definition, but more than one according to our sensations, he now posits two causes and two principles, calling them hot and cold, i. e. fire and earth; and of these
he ranges the hot with the existent, and the other with the 987ᵃ
non-existent.

From what has been said, then, and from the wise men
who have now sat in council with us, we have got thus
much—on the one hand from the earliest philosophers,
who regard the first principle as corporeal (for water and 5
fire and such things are bodies), and of whom some suppose
that there is one corporeal principle, others that there are

[16] *Phys.* i. 3

more than one, but both put these under the head of matter; and on the other hand from some who posit both this cause and besides this the source of movement, which we have got from some as single and from others as twofold.

Down to the Italian school, then, and apart from it, 10 philosophers have treated these subjects rather obscurely, except that, as we said, they have in fact used two kinds of cause, and one of these—the source of movement—some treat as one and others as two. But the Pythagoreans have 15 said in the same way that there are two principles, but added this much, which is peculiar to them, that they thought that finitude and infinity were not attributes of certain other things, e. g. of fire or earth or anything else of this kind, but that infinity itself and unity itself were the substance of the things of which they are predicated. 20 This is why number was the substance of all things. On this subject, then, they expressed themselves thus; and regarding the question of essence they began to make statements and definitions, but treated the matter too simply. For they both defined superficially and thought that the first subject of which a given definition was predicable was the substance of the thing defined, as if one supposed 25 that 'double' and '2' were the same, because 2 is the first thing of which 'double' is predicable. But surely to be double and to be 2 are not the same; if they are, one thing will be many [17]—a consequence which they actually drew.[18] From the earlier philosophers, then, and from their successors we can learn thus much.

6   After the systems we have named came the philos-
30   ophy of Plato, which in most respects followed these thinkers, but had peculiarities that distinguished it from the philosophy of the Italians. For, having in his youth first become familiar with Cratylus and with the Heraclitean doctrines (that all sensible things are ever in a state of flux

[17] i. e. 2 will be each of several things whose definition is predicable of it.
[18] e. g. 2 was identified both with opinion and with daring.

and there is no knowledge about them), these views he held even in later years. Socrates, however, was busying 987ᵇ himself about ethical matters and neglecting the world of nature as a whole but seeking the universal in these ethical matters, and fixed thought for the first time on definitions; Plato accepted his teaching, but held that the problem applied not to sensible things but to entities of another kind 5 —for this reason, that the common definition could not be a definition of any sensible thing, as they were always changing. Things of this other sort, then, he called Ideas, and sensible things, he said, were all named after these, and in virtue of a relation to these; for the many existed by participation in the Ideas that have the same name as they. Only the name 'participation' was new; for the Pythago- 10 reans say that things exist by 'imitation' of numbers, and Plato says they exist by participation, changing the name. But what the participation or the imitation of the Forms could be they left an open question.

Further, besides sensible things and Forms he says there are the objects of mathematics, which occupy an intermediate position, differing from sensible things in being eternal 15 and unchangeable, from Forms in that there are many alike, while the Form itself is in each case unique.

Since the Forms were the causes of all other things, he thought their elements were the elements of all things. As matter, the great and the small were principles; as essential 20 reality, the One; for from the great and the small, by participation in the One, come the Numbers.

But he agreed with the Pythagoreans in saying that the One is substance and not a predicate of something else; and in saying that the Numbers are the causes of the reality of other things he agreed with them; but positing a dyad 25 and constructing the infinite out of great and small, instead of treating the infinite as one, is peculiar to him; and so is his view that the Numbers exist apart from sensible things, while *they* say that the things themselves are Numbers, and do not place the objects of mathematics

between Forms and sensible things. His divergence from
30 the Pythagoreans in making the One and the Numbers
separate from things, and his introduction of the Forms,
were due to his inquiries in the region of definitions (for
the earlier thinkers had no tincture of dialectic), and his
making the other entity besides the One a dyad was due to
the belief that the numbers, except those which were
prime, could be neatly produced out of the dyad as out of
some plastic material.

Yet what *happens* is the contrary; the theory is not a
988ª reasonable one. For they make many things out of the matter, and the form generates only once, but what we observe
is that one table is made from one ̄matter, while the man
5 who applies the form, though he is one, makes many tables.
And the relation of the male to the female is similar; for
the latter is impregnated by one copulation, but the male
impregnates many females; yet these are analogues of those
first principles.

Plato, then, declared himself thus on the points in question; it is evident from what has been said that he has used
only two causes, that of the essence and the material cause
10 (for the Forms are the causes of the essence of all other
things, and the One is the cause of the essence of the
Forms); and it is evident what the underlying matter is,
of which the Forms are predicated in the case of sensible
things, and the One in the case of Forms, viz. that this is
a dyad, the great and the small. Further, he has assigned
the cause of good and that of evil to the elements, one to
15 each of the two, as we say [19] some of his predecessors sought
to do, e. g. Empedocles and Anaxagoras.

7 Our review of those who have spoken about first principles and reality and of the way in which they have
20 spoken, has been concise and summary; but yet we have
learnt *this* much from them, that of those who speak about
'principle' and 'cause' no one has mentioned any principle

[19] Cf. 984ᵇ 15–19, 32–ᵇ 10.

except those which have been distinguished in our work on nature,[20] but all evidently have some inkling of them, though only vaguely. For some speak of the first principle as matter, whether they suppose one or more first principles, and whether they suppose this to be a body or to be incorporeal; e. g. Plato spoke of the great and the small, the Italians of the infinite, Empedocles of fire, earth, water, and air, Anaxagoras of the infinity of things composed of similar parts. These, then, have all had a notion of this kind of cause, and so have all who speak of air or fire or water, or something denser than fire and rarer than air; for some have said the prime element is of this kind.

These thinkers grasped this cause only; but certain others have mentioned the source of movement, e. g. those who make friendship and strife, or reason, or love, a principle.

The essence, i. e. the substantial reality, no one has expressed distinctly. It is hinted at chiefly by those who believe in the Forms; for they do not suppose either that the Forms are the matter of sensible things, and the One the matter of the Forms, or that they are the source of movement (for they say these are causes rather of immobility and of being at rest), but they furnish the Forms as the essence of every other thing, and the One as the essence of the Forms.

That for whose sake actions and changes and movements take place, they assert to be a cause in a way, but not in this way, i. e. not in the way in which it is its nature to be a cause. For those who speak of reason or friendship class these causes as goods; they do not speak, however, as if anything that exists either existed or came into being for the sake of these, but as if movements started from these. In the same way those who say the One or the existent is the good, say that it is the cause of substance, but not that substance either is or comes to be for the sake of this. Therefore it turns out that in a sense they both say and do

[20] Phys. ii. 3, 7.

15 not say the good is a cause; for they do not call it a cause qua good but only incidentally.

All these thinkers, then, as they cannot pitch on another cause, seem to testify that we have determined rightly both how many and of what sort the causes are. Besides this it is plain that when the causes are being looked for, either all four must be sought thus or they must be sought in one 20 of these four ways. Let us next discuss the possible difficulties with regard to the way in which each of these thinkers has spoken, and with regard to his situation relatively to the first principles.

8 Those, then, who say the universe is one and posit one kind of thing as matter, and as corporeal matter which has spatial magnitude, evidently go astray in many ways. For they posit the elements of bodies only, not of in25 corporeal things, though there are also incorporeal things. And in trying to state the causes of generation and destruction, and in giving a physical account of all things, they do away with the cause of movement. Further, they err in not positing the substance, i. e. the essence, as the cause of anything, and besides this in lightly calling any of the 30 simple bodies except earth the first principle, without inquiring how they are produced out of one another,—I mean fire, water, earth, and air. For some things are produced out of each other by combination, others by separation, and this makes the greatest difference to their priority and posteriority. For (1) in a way the property of being 35 most elementary of all would seem to belong to the first thing from which they are produced by combination, and 989ᵃ this property would belong to the most fine-grained and subtle of bodies. For this reason those who make fire the principle would be most in agreement with this argument. But each of the other thinkers agrees that the ele5 ment of corporeal things is of this sort. At least none of those who named one element claimed that earth was the element, evidently because of the coarseness of its grain.

(Of the other three elements each has found some judge on its side; for some maintain that fire, others that water, others that air is the element. Yet why, after all, do they not name earth also, as most men do? For people say all things are earth. And Hesiod says earth was produced first 10 of corporeal things; so primitive and popular has the opinion been.) According to this argument, then, no one would be right who either says the first principle is any of the elements other than fire, or supposes it to be denser than air but rarer than water. But (2) if that which is 15 later in generation is prior in nature, and that which is concocted and compounded is later in generation, the contrary of what we have been saying must be true— water must be prior to air, and earth to water.

So much, then, for those who posit one cause such as we mentioned; but the same is true if one supposes more of 20 these, as Empedocles says the matter of things is four bodies. For he too is confronted by consequences some of which are the same as have been mentioned, while others are peculiar to him. For we see these bodies produced from one another, which implies that the same body does not always remain fire or earth (we have spoken about this in our works on nature [21]); and regarding the cause of movement 25 and the question whether we must posit one or two, he must be thought to have spoken neither correctly nor altogether plausibly. And in general, change of quality is necessarily done away with for those who speak thus, for on their view cold will not come from hot nor hot from cold. For if it did there would be something that accepted the contraries themselves, and there would be some one entity that became fire and water, which Empedocles denies.

As regards Anaxagoras, if one were to suppose that he 30 said there were two elements, the supposition would accord thoroughly with an argument which Anaxagoras himself did not state articulately, but which he must have ac-

[21] *De Caelo*, iii. 7.

cepted if any one had led him on to it. True, to say that
in the beginning all things were mixed is absurd both on
other grounds and because it follows that they must have
989ᵇ existed before in an unmixed form, and because nature
does not allow any chance thing to be mixed with any
chance thing, and also because on this view modifications
and accidents could be separated from substances (for the
same things which are mixed can be separated); yet if one
5 were to follow him up, piecing together what he means, he
would perhaps be seen to be somewhat modern in his
views. For when nothing was separated out, evidently nothing could be truly asserted of the substance that then existed. I mean, e. g., that it was neither white nor black,
nor grey nor any other colour, but of necessity colourless;
for if it had been coloured, it would have had one of these
10 colours. And similarly, by this same argument, it was fla-
vourless, nor had it any similar attribute; for it could not
be either of any quality or of any size, nor could it be any
definite kind of thing. For if it were, one of the particular
forms would have belonged to it, and this is impossible,
since all were mixed together; for the particular form would
necessarily have been already separated out, but he says
15 all were mixed except reason, and this alone was unmixed
and pure. From this it follows, then, that he must say the
principles are the One (for this is simple and unmixed)
and the Other, which is of such a nature as we suppose
the indefinite to be before it is defined and partakes of
some form. Therefore, while expressing himself neither
rightly nor clearly, he means something like what the
later thinkers say and what is now more clearly seen to be
20 the case.

But these thinkers are, after all, at home only in arguments about generation and destruction and movement;
for it is practically only of this sort of substance that they
seek the principles and the causes. But those who extend
25 their vision to all things that exist, and of existing things
suppose some to be perceptible and others not perceptible

evidently study both classes, which is all the more reason why one should devote some time to seeing what is good in their views and what bad from the standpoint of the inquiry we have now before us.

The 'Pythagoreans' treat of principles and elements stranger than those of the physical philosophers (the reason is that they got the principles from non-sensible 30 things, for the objects of mathematics, except those of astronomy, are of the class of things without movement); yet their discussions and investigations are all about nature; for they generate the heavens, and with regard to their parts and attributes and functions they observe the 990ᵃ phenomena, and use up the principles and the causes in explaining these, which implies that they agree with the others, the physical philosophers, that the *real* is just all that which is perceptible and contained by the so-called 'heavens'. But the causes and the principles which they 5 mention are, as we said, sufficient to act as steps even up to the higher realms of reality, and are more suited to these than to theories about nature. They do not tell us at all, however, how there can be movement if limit and un-limited and odd and even are the only things assumed, or how without movement and change there can be genera- 10 tion and destruction, or the bodies that move through the heavens can do what they do.

Further, if one either granted them that spatial magni-tude consists of these elements, or this were proved, still how would some bodies be light and others have weight? To judge from what they assume and maintain they are 15 speaking no more of mathematical bodies than of per-ceptible; hence they have said nothing whatever about fire or earth or the other bodies of this sort, I suppose because they have nothing to say which applies *peculiarly* to perceptible things.

Further, how are we to combine the beliefs that the at-tributes of number, and number itself, are causes of what 20 exists and happens in the heavens both from the beginning

and now, and that there is no other number than this
number out of which the world is composed? When in
one particular region they place opinion and opportunity,
and, a little above or below, injustice and decision or
mixture, and allege, as proof, that each of these is a number,
25 and that there happens to be already in this place a plurality
of the extended bodies composed of numbers, because
these attributes of number attach to the various places—
this being so, is this number, which we must suppose each
of these abstractions to be, the same number which is
exhibited in the material universe, or is it another than
30 this? Plato says it is different; yet even he thinks that both
these bodies and their causes are numbers, but that the
intelligible numbers are causes, while the others are *sensible*.

9 Let us leave the Pythagoreans for the present; for it is
enough to have touched on them as much as we have
990ᵇ done. But as for those who posit the Ideas as causes, firstly,
in seeking to grasp the causes of the things around us, they
introduced others equal in number to these, as if a man
who wanted to count things thought he would not be able
to do it while they were few, but tried to count them when
he had added to their number. For the Forms are prac-
5 tically equal to—or not fewer than—the things, in trying
to explain which these thinkers proceeded from them to
the Forms. For to each thing there answers an entity
which has the same name and exists apart from the substances, and so also in the case of all other groups there is a
one over many, whether the many are in this world or are
eternal.

Further, of the ways in which we prove that the Forms
10 exist, none is convincing; for from some no inference
necessarily follows, and from some arise Forms even of
things of which we think there are no Forms. For according to the arguments from the existence of the sciences
there will be Forms of all things of which there are sciences,

and according to the 'one over many' argument there will
be Forms even of negations, and according to the argument that there is an object for thought even when the
thing has perished, there will be Forms of perishable things;
for we have an image of these. Further, of the more ac- 15
curate arguments, some lead to Ideas of relations, of which
we say there is no independent class, and others introduce
the 'third man'.

And in general the arguments for the Forms destroy the
things for whose existence we are more zealous than for
the existence of the Ideas; for it follows that not the dyad
but number is first, i. e. that the relative is prior to the absolute—besides all the other points on which certain people 20
by following out the opinions held about the Ideas have
come into conflict with the principles of the theory.

Further, according to the assumption on which our belief in the Ideas rests, there will be Forms not only of
substances but also of many other things (for the concept
is single not only in the case of substances but also in the 25
other cases, and there are sciences not only of substance but
also of other things, and a thousand other such difficulties
confront them). But according to the necessities of the
case and the opinions held about the Forms, if Forms can
be shared in there must be Ideas of substances only. For
they are not shared in incidentally, but a thing must share
in its Form as in something not predicated of a subject 30
(by 'being shared in incidentally' I mean that e. g. if a
thing shares in 'double itself', it shares also in 'eternal', but
incidentally; for 'eternal' happens to be predicable of the
'double'). Therefore the Forms will be substance; but the
same terms indicate substance in this and in the ideal
world (or what will be the meaning of saying that there
is something apart from the particulars—the one over 991ᵃ
many?). And if the Ideas and the particulars that share
in them have the same form, there will be something common to these; for why should '2' be one and the same in
the perishable 2's or in those which are many but eternal,

and not the same in the '2 itself' as in the particular 2?
5 But if they have not the same form, they must have only
the name in common, and it is as if one were to call both
Callias and a wooden image a 'man', without observing
any community between them.[22]

Above all one might discuss the question what on earth
the Forms contribute to sensible things, either to those
that are eternal or to those that come into being and
10 cease to be. For they cause neither movement nor any
change in them. But again they help in no wise either
towards the knowledge of the other things (for they are
not even the substance of these, else they would have been
in them), or towards their being, if they are not in the particulars which share in them; though if they were, they
might be thought to be causes, as white causes whiteness
15 in a white object by entering into its composition. But
this argument, which first Anaxagoras and later Eudoxus
and certain others used, is very easily upset; for it is not
difficult to collect many insuperable objections to such a
view.

But, further, all other things cannot come from the
20 Forms in any of the usual senses of 'from'. And to say that
they are patterns and the other things share in them is to
use empty words and poetical metaphors. For what is it
that works, looking to the Ideas? And anything can either
be, or become, like another without being copied from it,
25 so that whether Socrates exists or not a man like Socrates
might come to be; and evidently this might be so even if
Socrates were eternal. And there will be several patterns of
the same thing, and therefore several Forms; e. g. 'animal'
and 'two-footed' and also 'man himself' will be Forms of
30 man. Again, the Forms are patterns not only of sensible
things, but of Forms themselves also; i. e. the genus, as
genus of various species, will be so; therefore the same
thing will be pattern and copy.

991ᵇ   Again, it would seem impossible that the substance and

[22] With 990ᵇ 2–991ᵃ 8 Cf. xiii. 1078ᵇ 34–1079ᵇ 3.

that of which it is the substance should exist apart; how, therefore, could the Ideas, being the substances of things, exist apart? In the *Phaedo* [23] the case is stated in this way—that the Forms are causes both of being and of becoming; yet when the Forms exist, still the things that 5 share in them do not come into being, unless there is something to originate movement; and many other things come into being (e. g. a house or a ring) of which we say there are no Forms. Clearly, therefore, even the other things can both be and come into being owing to such causes as produce the things just mentioned.[24]

Again, if the Forms are numbers, how can they be causes? Is it because existing things are other numbers, 10 e. g. one number is man, another is Socrates, another Callias? Why then are the one set of numbers causes of the other set? It will not make any difference even if the former are eternal and the latter are not. But if it is because things in this sensible world (e. g. harmony) are ratios of numbers, evidently the things between which they are ratios are some one class of things. If, then, this—the matter—is 15 some definite thing, evidently the numbers themselves too will be ratios of something to something else. E. g. if Callias is a numerical ratio between fire and earth and water and air, his Idea also will be a number of certain other underlying things; and man-himself, whether it is a number in a sense or not, will still be a numerical ratio of certain things and not a number proper, nor will it be a kind of number 20 merely because it is a numerical ratio.

Again, from many numbers one number is produced, but how can one Form come from many Forms? And if the number comes not from the many numbers themselves but from the units in them, e. g. in 10,000, how is it with the units? If they are specifically alike, numerous absurdities will follow, and also if they are not alike (neither the 25 units in one number being themselves like one another nor

[23] 100 c–e.
[24] With 991ᵃ 8–ᵇ 9 Cf. xiii. 1079ᵇ 12–1080ᵃ 8.

those in other numbers being all like to all); for in what will they differ, as they are without quality? This is not a plausible view, nor is it consistent with our thought on the matter.

Further, they must set up a second kind of number (with which arithmetic deals), and all the objects which are called 'intermediate' by some thinkers; and how do these exist or from what principles do they proceed? Or why 30 must they be intermediate between the things in this sensible world and the things-themselves?

Further, the units in 2 must each come from a prior 2; but this is impossible.

992ᵃ Further, why is a number, when taken all together, one?

Again, besides what has been said, if the units are *diverse* the Platonists should have spoken like those who say there are four, or two, elements; for each of these thinkers gives the name of element not to that which is common, e. g. 5 to body, but to fire and earth, whether there is something common to them, viz. body, or not. But in fact the Platonists speak as if the One were *homogeneous* like fire or water; and if this is so, the numbers will not be substances. Evidently, if there is a One-itself and this is a first principle, 'one' is being used in more than one sense; for otherwise the theory is impossible.

When we wish to reduce substances to their principles, 10 we state that lines come from the short and long (i. e. from a kind of small and great), and the plane from the broad and narrow, and body from the deep and shallow. Yet how then can either the plane contain a line, or the solid a line or a plane? For the broad and narrow is a different class 15 from the deep and shallow. Therefore, just as number is not present in these, because the many and few are different from these, evidently no other of the higher classes will be present in the lower. But again the broad is not a genus which includes the deep, for then the solid would have been a species of plane.[25] Further, from what principle will

[25] With 992ᵃ 10–19 Cf. xiii. 1085ᵃ 9–19.

the presence of the *points* in the line be derived? Plato even used to object to this class of things as being a geo- 20 metrical fiction. He gave the name of principle of the line —and this he often posited—to the indivisible lines. Yet these must have a limit; therefore the argument from which the existence of the line follows proves also the existence of the point.

In general, though philosophy seeks the cause of perceptible things, we have given this up (for we say nothing 25 of the cause from which change takes its start), but while we fancy we are stating the substance of perceptible things, we assert the existence of a second class of substances, while our account of the way in which they are the substances of perceptible things is empty talk; for 'sharing', as we said before,[26] means nothing.

Nor have the Forms any connexion with what we see to be the cause in the case of the arts, that for whose sake 30 both all mind and the whole of nature are operative [27]— with this cause which we assert to be one of the first principles; but mathematics has come to be identical with philosophy for modern thinkers, though they say that it should be studied for the sake of other things.[28]

Further, one might suppose that the substance which according to them underlies as matter is too mathematical, 992ᵇ and is a predicate and differentia of the substance, i. e. of the matter, rather than the matter itself; i. e. the great and the small are like the rare and the dense which the 5 physical philosophers speak of, calling these the primary differentiae of the substratum; for these are a kind of excess and defect. And regarding movement, if the great and the small are to be movement, evidently the Forms will be moved; but if they are not to be movement, whence did movement come? The whole study of nature has been annihilated.

[26] 991ᵃ 20–22.
[27] sc. the final cause.
[28] Cf. Plato, *Rep.* vii. 531 D, 533 B–E.

And what is thought to be easy—to show that all things
10 are one—is not done; for what is proved by the method
of setting out instances [29] is not that all things are one but
that there is a One-itself,—if we grant all the assumptions.
And not even this follows, if we do not grant that the universal is a genus; and this in some cases it cannot be.

Nor can it be explained either how the lines and planes
and solids that come after the numbers exist or can exist,
15 or what significance they have; for these can neither be
Forms (for they are not numbers), nor the intermediates
(for those are the objects of mathematics), nor the perishable things. This is evidently a distinct fourth class.

In general, if we search for the elements of existing
things without distinguishing the many senses in which
things are said to exist, we cannot find them, especially if
the search for the elements of which things are made is
20 conducted in this manner. For it is surely impossible to
discover what 'acting' or 'being acted on', or 'the straight',
is made of, but if elements can be discovered at all, it is
only the elements of substances; therefore either to seek
the elements of all existing things or to think one has
them is incorrect.

And how could we learn the elements of all things? Evidently we cannot start by knowing anything before. For as
25 he who is learning geometry, though he may know other
things before, knows none of the things with which the
science deals and about which he is to learn, so is it in all
other cases. Therefore if there is a science of all things, such
as some assert to exist, he who is learning this will know
nothing before. Yet all learning is by means of premisses
30 which are (either all or some of them) known before—
whether the learning be by demonstration or by definitions; for the elements of the definition must be known before and be familiar; and learning by induction proceeds
993ª similarly. But again, if the science were actually innate, it

[29] For this Platonic method Cf. vii. 1031ᵇ 21, xiii. 1086ᵇ 9, xiv.
1090ª 17.

were strange that we are unaware of our possession of the greatest of sciences.

Again, how is one to come to know what all things are made of, and how is this to be made *evident?* This also affords a difficulty; for there might be a conflict of opinion, as there is about certain syllables; some say *za* is made out 5 of *s* and *d* and *a*, while others say it is a distinct sound and none of those that are familiar.

Further, how could we know the objects of sense without having the sense in question? Yet we ought to, if the elements of which all things consist, as complex sounds consist of the elements proper to sound, are the same.   10

10 It is evident, then, even from what we have said before, that all men seem to seek the causes named in the *Physics,*[30] and that we cannot name any beyond these; but they seek these vaguely; and though in a sense they have all been described before, in a sense they have not been described at all. For the earliest philosophy is, on all 15 subjects, like one who lisps, since it is young and in its beginnings. For even Empedocles says bone exists by virtue of the ratio in it. Now this is the essence and the substance of the thing. But it is similarly necessary that flesh and each of the other tissues should be the ratio of its elements, or that not one of them should; for it is on account of this that both flesh and bone and everything 20 else will exist, and not on account of the matter, which *he* names—fire and earth and water and air. But while he would necessarily have agreed if another had said this, he has not said it clearly.

On these questions our views have been expressed before; but let us return to enumerate the difficulties that 25 might be raised on these same points; [31] for perhaps we may get from them some help toward our later difficulties.

[30] ii. 3, 7.
[31] The reference is to Bk. iii.

BOOK Λ (XII)

1069ᵃ 1 The subject of our inquiry is substance; for the principles and the causes we are seeking are those of sub-
20 stances. For if the universe is of the nature of a whole,
substance is its first part; and if it coheres merely by virtue
of serial succession, on this view also substance is first,
and is succeeded by quality, and then by quantity. At the
same time these latter are not even being in the full sense,
but are qualities and movements of it—or else even the
not-white and the not-straight would be being; at least we
25 say even these are, e. g. 'there is a not-white'.¹ Further, none
of the categories other than substance can exist apart. And
the early philosophers also in practice testify to the pri-
macy of substance; for it was of substance that they
sought the principles and elements and causes. The thinkers of the present² day tend to rank universals as substances (for genera are universals, and these they tend to
describe as principles and substances, owing to the abstract nature of their inquiry); but the thinkers of old
ranked particular things as substances, e. g. fire and earth,
not what is common to both, body.

30 There are three kinds of substance—one that is sensible
(of which one subdivision is eternal and another is perishable; the latter is recognized by all men, and includes e. g.
plants and animals), of which we must grasp the elements,
whether one or many; and another that is immovable, and
35 this certain thinkers assert to be capable of existing apart,
some dividing it into two, others identifying the Forms and
the objects of mathematics, and others positing, of these
two, only the objects of mathematics.³ The former two

---

¹ This is an implication of the ordinary type of judgement, 'x is
not white'.
² The Platonists.
³ The three views appear to have been held respectively by Plato,
Xenocrates, and Speusippus.

kinds of substance are the subject of physics (for they 1069ᵇ
imply movement); but the third kind belongs to another
science, if there is no principle common to it and to the
other kinds.

2   Sensible substance is changeable. Now if change pro-
    ceeds from opposites or from intermediates, and not
from all opposites (for the voice is not-white [but it does 5
not therefore change to white]), but from the contrary,
there must be something underlying which changes into
the contrary state; for the *contraries* do not change.
Further, something persists, but the contrary does not
persist; there is, then, some third thing besides the contraries, viz. the matter. Now since changes are of four
kinds—either in respect of the 'what' or of the quality or
of the quantity or of the place, and change in respect of 10
'thisness' is simple generation and destruction, and change
in quantity is increase and diminution, and change in respect of an affection is alteration, and change of place is
motion, changes will be from given states into those contrary to them in these several respects. The matter, then,
which changes must be capable of both states. And since
that which 'is' has two senses, we must say that everything 15
changes from that which is potentially to that which is
actually, e. g. from potentially white to actually white,
and similarly in the case of increase and diminution. Therefore not only can a thing come to be, incidentally, out of
that which is not, but also all things come to be out of
that which is, but is potentially, and is not actually. And
this is the 'One' of Anaxagoras; for instead of 'all things 20
were together'—and the 'Mixture' of Empedocles and
Anaximander and the account given by Democritus—it is
better to say 'all things were together potentially but not
actually'. Therefore these thinkers seem to have had some
notion of matter. Now all things that change have matter,
but different matter; and of eternal things those which are 25

not generable but are movable in space have matter—not matter for generation, however, but for motion from one place to another.

One might raise the question from what sort of non-being generation proceeds; for 'non-being' has three senses. If, then, one form of non-being exists potentially, still it is not by virtue of a potentiality for any and every thing, but different things come from different things; nor is it satisfactory to say that 'all things were together'; for they differ in their matter, since otherwise why did an infinity of things come to be, and not one thing? For 'reason' is one, so that if matter also were one, that must have come to be in actuality which the matter was in potency.[4] The causes and the principles, then, are three, two being the pair of contraries of which one is definition and form and the other is privation, and the third being the matter.

3   Note, next, that neither the matter nor the form comes to be—and I mean the last matter and form. For everything that changes is something and is changed by something and into something. That by which it is changed is the immediate mover; that which is changed, the matter; that into which it is changed, the form. The process, then, will go on to infinity, if not only the bronze comes to be round but also the round or the bronze comes to be; therefore there must be a stop.

Note, next, that each substance comes into being out of something that shares its name. (Natural objects and other things both rank as substances.) For things come into being either by art or by nature or by fortune or by chance. Now art is a principle of movement in something other than the thing moved, nature is a principle in the thing itself (for man begets man), and the other causes are privations of these two.

There are three kinds of substance—the matter, which is a 'this' in appearance (for all things that are characterized

---

[4] *sc.* an undifferentiated unity.

by contact and not by organic unity are matter and sub- 19
stratum, e. g. fire, flesh, head; for these are all matter, and
the last matter is the matter of that which is in the full 11
sense substance); the nature, which is a 'this' or positive
state towards which movement takes place; and again,
thirdly, the particular substance which is composed of these
two, e. g. Socrates or Callias. Now in some cases the 'this'
does not exist apart from the composite substance, e. g. the
form of house does not so exist, unless the art of building 15
exists apart (nor is there generation and destruction of
these forms, but it is in another way that the house apart
from its matter, and health, and all ideals of art, exist and
do not exist); but if the 'this' exists apart from the concrete
thing, it is only in the case of natural objects. And so
Plato was not far wrong when he said that there are as
many Forms as there are kinds of natural object (if there
are Forms distinct from the things of this earth). The 21
moving causes exist as things preceding the effects, but
causes in the sense of definitions are simultaneous with
their effects. For when a man is healthy, then health also
exists; and the shape of a bronze sphere exists at the same
time as the bronze sphere. (But we must examine whether 25
any form also survives afterwards. For in some cases there
is nothing to prevent this; e. g. the soul may be of this sort
—not all soul but the reason; for presumably it is impossible that *all* soul should survive.) Evidently then there is
no necessity, on this ground at least, for the existence of the
Ideas. For man is begotten by man, a given man by an
individual father; and similarly in the arts; for the medical 30
art is the formal cause of health.

4   The causes and the principles of different things are
      in a sense different, but in a sense, if one speaks
universally and analogically, they are the same for all. For
one might raise the question whether the principles and
elements are different or the same for substances and for 35
relative terms, and similarly in the case of each of the cate-

gories. But it would be paradoxical if they were the same
for all. For then from the same elements will proceed rela-
1070ᵃ tive terms and substances. What then will this common
element be? For (1) (a) there is nothing common to and
distinct from substance and the other categories, viz. those
which are predicated; but an element is prior to the things
of which it is an element. But again (b) substance is not
an element in relative terms, nor is any of these an element
in substance. Further, (2) how can all things have the
same elements? For none of the elements can be the same
5 as that which is composed of elements, e. g. b or a cannot
be the same as ba. (None, therefore, of the intelligibles,
e. g. being or unity, is an element; for these are predicable
of each of the compounds as well.) None of the elements,
then, will be either a substance or a relative term; but it
must be one or other. All things, then, have not the same
elements.

Or, as we are wont to put it, in a sense they have and
10 in a sense they have not; e. g. perhaps the elements of
perceptible bodies are, as *form*, the hot, and in another
sense the cold, which is the *privation*; and, as *matter*, that
which directly and of itself potentially has these attributes;
and substances comprise both these and the things composed of these, of which these are the principles, or any
unity which is produced out of the hot and the cold, e. g.
15 flesh or bone; for the product must be different from the
elements. These things then have the same elements and
principles (though specifically different things have specifically different elements); but *all* things have not the
same elements in this sense, but only analogically; i. e. one
might say that there are three principles—the form, the
privation, and the matter. But each of these is different
20 for each class; e. g. in colour they are white, black, and
surface, and in day and night they are light, darkness, and
air.

Since not only the elements present in a thing are causes,
but also something external, i. e. the moving cause, clearly

while 'principle' and 'element' are different both are causes, and 'principle' is divided into these two kinds [5] and that which acts as producing movement or rest is a principle and a substance. Therefore analogically there are three ele- 25 ments, and four causes and principles; but the elements are different in different things, and the proximate moving cause is different for different things. Health, disease, body; the moving cause is the medical art. Form, disorder of a particular kind, bricks; the moving cause is the building art. And since the moving cause in the case of natural 30 things is—for man, for instance, man, and in the products of thought the form or its contrary, there will be in a sense three causes, while in a sense there are four. For the medical art is in some sense health, and the building art is the form of the house, and man begets man; [6] further, besides these there is that which as first of all things moves all things. 35

5   Some things can exist apart and some cannot, and it is the former that are substances. And therefore all **1071ᵃ** things have the same causes,[7] because, without substances, modifications and movements do not exist. Further, these causes will probably be soul and body, or reason and desire and body.

And in yet another way, analogically identical things 5 are principles, i. e. actuality and potency; but these also are not only different for different things but also apply in different ways to them. For in some cases the same thing exists at one time actually and at another potentially, e. g. wine or flesh or man does so. (And these two fall under the above-named causes.[8] For the form exists actually, if it can exist apart, and so does the complex of form and 10 matter, and the privation, e. g. darkness or disease; but the matter exists potentially; for this is that which can become qualified either by the form or by the privation.) But the

[5] i. e. the principles which are elements and those which are not.
[6] i. e. the efficient cause is identical with the formal.
[7] i. e. the causes of substance are the causes of all things.
[8] i. e. the division into potency and actuality stands in a definite relation to the previous division into matter, form, and privation.

distinction of actuality and potentiality applies in another way to cases where the matter of cause and of effect is not the same, in some of which cases the form is not the same but different; e. g. the cause of man is (1) the elements in 15 man (viz. fire and earth as matter, and the peculiar form), and further (2) something else outside, i. e. the father, and (3) besides these the sun and its oblique course, which are neither matter nor form nor privation of man nor of the same species with him, but moving causes.

Further, one must observe that some causes can be expressed in universal terms, and some cannot. The proximate principles of all things are the 'this' which is proximate in actuality, and another which is proximate in 20 potentiality.[9] The universal causes, then, of which we spoke [10] do not exist. For it is the individual that is the originative principle of the individuals. For while man is the originative principle of man universally, there is no universal man, but Peleus is the originative principle of Achilles, and your father of you, and this particular b of this particular ba, though b in general is the originative principle of ba taken without qualification.

Further, if the causes of substances are the causes of all things, yet different things have different causes and ele-25 ments, as was said [11]; the causes of things that are not in the same class, e. g. of colours and sounds, of substances and quantities, are different except in an analogical sense; and those of things in the same species are different, not in species, but in the sense that the causes of different individuals are different, your matter and form and moving cause being different from mine, while in their universal definition they are the same. And if we inquire what are 30 the principles or elements of substances and relations and

[9] e. g. the proximate causes of a child are the individual father (who on Aristotle's view is the efficient and contains the formal cause) and the germ contained in the individual mother (which is the material cause).

[10] In l. 17.
[11] In 1070ᵇ 17.

qualities—whether they are the same or different—clearly when the names of the causes are used in several senses the causes of each are the same, but when the senses are distinguished the causes are not the same but different, except that in the following senses the causes of all are the same. They are (1) the same or analogous in this sense, that matter, form, privation, and the moving cause are common to all things; and (2) the causes of substances may be treated as causes of all things in this sense, that when substances are removed all things are removed; further, (3) that which is first in respect of complete reality is the cause **35** of all things. But in another sense there are different first causes, viz. all the contraries which are neither generic nor ambiguous terms; and, further, the matters of different things are different. We have stated, then, what are the **1071ᵇ** principles of sensible things and how many they are, and in what sense they are the same and in what sense different.

6   Since there were [12] three kinds of substance, two of them physical and one unmovable, regarding the latter we must assert that it is necessary that there should be an eternal unmovable substance. For substances are the first of existing things, and if they are all destructible, **5** all things are destructible. But it is impossible that movement should either have come into being or cease to be (for it must always have existed), or that time should. For there could not be a before and an after if time did not exist. Movement also is continuous, then, in the sense in which time is; for time is either the same thing as movement or an attribute of movement. And there is no continuous movement except movement in place, and of **10** this only that which is circular is continuous.

But if there is something which is capable of moving things or acting on them, but is not actually doing so, there will not necessarily be movement; for that which

[12] Cf. 1069ᵃ 30.

has a potency need not exercise it. Nothing, then, is gained even if we suppose eternal substances, as the believers in the Forms do, unless there is to be in them
15 some principle which can cause change; nay, even this is not enough, nor is another substance besides the Forms enough; for if it is not to act, there will be no movement. Further, even if it acts, this will not be enough, if its essence is potency; for there will not be eternal movement, since that which is potentially may possibly not be. There
20 must, then, be such a principle, whose very essence is actuality. Further, then, these substances must be without matter; for they must be eternal, if anything is eternal. Therefore they must be actuality.

Yet there is a difficulty; for it is thought that everything that acts is able to act, but that not everything that is able
25 to act acts, so that the potency is prior. But if this is so, nothing that is need be; for it is possible for all things to be capable of existing but not yet to exist.

Yet if we follow the theologians who generate the world from night, or the natural philosophers who say that 'all things were together',[13] the same impossible result ensues. For how will there be movement, if there is no actually
30 existing cause? Wood will surely not move itself—the carpenter's art must act on it; nor will the menstrual blood nor the earth set themselves in motion, but the seeds must act on the earth and the semen on the menstrual blood.

This is why some suppose eternal actuality—e. g. Leucippus [14] and Plato [15]; for they say there is always movement. But why and what this movement is they do not say, nor, if the world moves in this way or that, do they tell us the cause of its doing so. Now nothing is moved at random, but there must always be something present to

---

[13] Anaxagoras.
[14] Cf. De Caelo, iii. 300[b] 8.
[15] Cf. Timaeus, 30 A.

move it; e. g. as a matter of fact a thing moves in one way 35 by nature, and in another by force or through the influence of reason or something else. (Further, what sort of movement is primary? This makes a vast difference.) But again for Plato, at least, it is not permissible to name here that 1072ᵃ which he sometimes supposes to be the source of movement—that which moves itself; [16] for the soul is later, and coeval with the heavens, according to his account.[17] To suppose potency prior to actuality, then, is in a sense right, and in a sense not; and we have specified these senses.[18] That actuality is prior is testified by Anaxagoras 5 (for his 'reason' is actuality) and by Empedocles in his doctrine of love and strife, and by those who say that there is always movement, e. g. Leucippus. Therefore chaos or night did not exist for an infinite time, but the same things have always existed (either passing through a cycle of changes or obeying some other law), since actuality is prior to potency. If, then, there is a constant cycle, something must always remain,[19] acting in the same way. And 10 if there is to be generation and destruction, there must be something else [20] which is always acting in different ways. This must, then, act in one way in virtue of itself, and in another in virtue of something else—either of a third agent, therefore, or of the first. Now it must be in virtue of the first. For otherwise this again causes the motion both of the second agent and of the third. Therefore it is better to say 'the first'. For it was the cause of eternal uni- 15 formity; and something else is the cause of variety, and evidently both together are the cause of eternal variety. This, accordingly, is the character which the motions actually exhibit. What need then is there to seek for other principles?

[16] Cf. *Phaedrus*, 245 c; *Laws*, 894 E.
[17] Cf. *Timaeus*, 34 B.
[18] Cf. 1071ᵇ 22–26.
[19] i. e. the sphere of the fixed stars.
[20] i. e. the sun. Cf. *De Gen. et Corr.* ii. 336ᵃ 23 ff.

7   Since (1) this is a possible account of the matter, and
(2) if it were not true, the world would have proceeded out of night and 'all things together' and out of
20 non-being, these difficulties may be taken as solved. There
is, then, something which is always moved with an un-
ceasing motion, which is motion in a circle; and this is
plain not in theory only but in fact. Therefore the first
heaven [21] must be eternal. There is therefore also something which moves it. And since that which is moved and
moves is intermediate, there is something which moves
25 without being moved, being eternal, substance, and actuality. And the object of desire and the object of thought
move in this way; they move without being moved. The
primary objects of desire and of thought are the same. For
the apparent good is the object of appetite, and the real
good is the primary object of rational wish. But desire is
consequent on opinion rather than opinion on desire; for
30 the thinking is the starting-point. And thought is moved
by the object of thought, and one of the two columns of
opposites is in itself the object of thought; and in this,
substance is first, and in substance, that which is simple
and exists actually. (The one and the simple are not the
same; for 'one' means a measure, but 'simple' means that
the thing itself has a certain nature.) But the beautiful,
also, and that which is in itself desirable are in the same
35 column; and the first in any class is always best, or analogous to the best.

That a final cause may exist among unchangeable en-
1072ᵇ tities is shown by the distinction of its meanings. For the
final cause is (a) some being for whose good an action is
done, and (b) something at which the action aims; and of
these the latter exists among unchangeable entities though
the former does not. The final cause, then, produces motion as being loved, but all other things move by being
moved.

[21] i. e. the outer sphere of the universe, that in which the fixed stars
are set.

Now if something is moved it is capable of being otherwise than as it is. Therefore if its actuality is the primary form of spatial motion, then in so far as it is subject to change, in this respect it is capable of being otherwise—in place, even if not in substance. But since there is something which moves while itself unmoved, existing actually, this can in no way be otherwise than as it is. For motion in space is the first of the kinds of change, and motion in a circle the first kind of spatial motion; and this the first mover produces.[22] The first mover, then, exists of necessity; and in so far as it exists by necessity, its mode of being is good, and it is in this sense a first principle. For the necessary has all these senses—that which is necessary perforce because it is contrary to the natural impulse, that without which the good is impossible, and that which cannot be otherwise but can exist only in a single way.

On such a principle, then, depend the heavens and the world of nature. And it is a life such as the best which we enjoy, and enjoy for but a short time (for it is ever in this state, which we cannot be), since its actuality is also pleasure. (And for this reason [23] are waking, perception, and thinking most pleasant, and hopes and memories are so on account of these.) And thinking in itself deals with that which is best in itself, and that which is thinking in the fullest sense with that which is best in the fullest sense. And thought thinks on itself because it shares the nature of the object of thought; for it becomes an object of thought in coming into contact with and thinking its objects, so that thought and object of thought are the same. For that which is capable of receiving the object of thought, i. e. the essence, is thought. But it is active when it possesses this object. Therefore the possession rather than the receptivity is the divine element which thought

[22] If it had any movement, it would have the first. But it produces this and therefore cannot share in it; for if it did, we should have to look for something that is prior to the first mover and imparts this motion to it.
[23] sc. because they are activities or actualities.

seems to contain, and the act of contemplation is what
is most pleasant and best. If, then, God is always in that
good state in which we sometimes are, this compels our
25 wonder; and if in a better this compels it yet more. And
God *is* in a better state. And life also belongs to God;
for the actuality of thought is life, and God is that actuality; and God's self-dependent actuality is life most good
and eternal. We say therefore that God is a living being,
eternal, most good, so that life and duration continuous
and eternal belong to God; for this *is* God.

Those who suppose, as the Pythagoreans [24] and Speusip-
30 pus [25] do, that supreme beauty and goodness are not present in the beginning, because the beginnings both of plants
and of animals are *causes*, but beauty and completeness
are in the *effects* of these,[26] are wrong in their opinion.
35 For the seed comes from other individuals which are prior
and complete, and the first thing is not seed but the complete being; e. g. we must say that before the seed there is
1073ᵃ a man—not the man produced from the seed, but another from whom the seed comes.

It is clear then from what has been said that there is a
substance which is eternal and unmovable and separate
from sensible things. It has been shown also that this
5 substance cannot have any magnitude, but is without part
and indivisible (for it produces movement through infinite
time, but nothing finite has infinite power; and, while every
magnitude is either infinite or finite, it cannot, for the
above reason, have finite magnitude, and it cannot have
10 infinite magnitude because there is no infinite magnitude
at all). But it has also been shown that it is impassive and
unalterable; for all the other changes are posterior to [27]
change of place.

---

[24] Cf. 1075ᵃ 36.
[25] Cf. vii. 1028ᵇ 21, xiv. 1091ᵃ 34, 1092ᵃ 11.
[26] i. e. the animal or plant is more beautiful and perfect than the seed.
[27] i. e. impossible without.

8   It is clear, then, why these things are as they are.

But we must not ignore the question whether we have to suppose one such substance or more than one, and if the latter, how many; we must also mention, re- 15 garding the opinions expressed by others, that they have said nothing about the number of the substances that can even be clearly stated. For the theory of Ideas has no special discussion of the subject; for those who speak of Ideas say the Ideas are numbers, and they speak of numbers now as unlimited, now [28] as limited by the number 10; but as for the reason why there should be just so many num- 20 bers, nothing is said with any demonstrative exactness. We however must discuss the subject, starting from the presuppositions and distinctions we have mentioned. The first principle or primary being is not movable either in itself or accidentally, but produces the primary eternal and 25 single movement. But since that which is moved must be moved by something, and the first mover must be in itself unmovable, and eternal movement must be produced by something eternal and a single movement by a single thing, and since we see that besides the simple spatial movement of the universe, which we say the first and un- 30 movable substance produces, there are other spatial movements—those of the planets—which are eternal (for a body which moves in a circle is eternal and unresting; we have proved these points in the physical treatises [29]), each of these᾽ movements also must be caused by a substance both unmovable in itself and eternal. For the nature of the stars [30] is eternal just because it is a certain kind of substance, and the mover is eternal and prior to the moved, 35 and then which is prior to a substance must be a substance. Evidently, then, there must be substances which are of the

[28] The reference is to Plato (Cf. *Phys.* 206ᵇ 32).
[29] Cf. *Phys.* viii. 8, 9; *De Caelo*, i. 2, ii. 3–8.
[30] This is to be understood as a general term including both fixed stars and planets.

same number as the movements of the stars, and in their
nature eternal, and in themselves unmovable, and without
magnitude, for the reason before mentioned.[31]

1073ᵇ That the movers are substances, then, and that one of
these is first and another second according to the same
order as the movements of the stars, is evident. But in the
number of the movements we reach a problem which must
be treated from the standpoint of that one of the mathematical sciences which is most akin to philosophy—viz. of
5 astronomy; for this science speculates about substance
which is perceptible but eternal, but the other mathematical sciences, i. e. arithmetic and geometry, treat of no
substance. That the movements are more numerous than
the bodies that are moved is evident to those who have
given even moderate attention to the matter; for each of
10 the planets has more than one movement. But as to the
actual number of these movements, we now—to give some
notion of the subject—quote what some of the mathematicians say, that our thought may have some definite num-
15 ber to grasp; but, for the rest, we must partly investigate for
ourselves, partly learn from other investigators, and if those
who study this subject form an opinion contrary to what
we have now stated, we must esteem both parties indeed,
but follow the more accurate.

Eudoxus supposed that the motion of the sun or of the
moon involves, in either case, three spheres, of which the
first is the sphere of the fixed stars, and the second moves
20 in the circle which runs along the middle of the zodiac,
and the third in the circle which is inclined across the
breadth of the zodiac; but the circle in which the moon
moves is inclined at a greater angle than that in which the
sun moves. And the motion of the planets involves, in each
case, four spheres, and of these also the first and second
25 are the same as the first two mentioned above (for the
sphere of the fixed stars is that which moves all the other
spheres, and that which is placed beneath this and has its

[31] Cf. ll. 5–11.

movement in the circle which bisects the zodiac is common to all), but the *poles* of the third sphere of each planet are in the circle which bisects the zodiac, and the motion of the fourth sphere is in the circle which is inclined at an angle to the equator of the third sphere; and the poles of the third sphere are different for each of the other planets, 30 but those of Venus and Mercury are the same.

Callippus made the position of the spheres the same as Eudoxus did, but while he assigned the same number as Eudoxus did to Jupiter and to Saturn, he thought two more spheres should be added to the sun and two to the 35 moon, if one is to explain the observed facts; and one more to each of the other planets.

But it is necessary, if all the spheres combined are to explain the observed facts, that for each of the planets there should be other spheres (one fewer than those hith- **1074ᵃ** erto assigned) which counteract those already mentioned and bring back to the same position the outermost sphere of the star which in each case is situated below [32] the star in question; for only thus can all the forces at work produce 5 the observed motion of the planets. Since, then, the spheres involved in the movement of the planets themselves are— eight for Saturn and Jupiter and twenty-five for the others, and of these only those involved in the movement of the lowest-situated planet need not be counteracted, the spheres which counteract those of the outermost two planets will be six in number, and the spheres which counteract those of the next four planets will be sixteen; therefore the number of all the spheres—both those which 10 move the planets and those which counteract these—will be fifty-five. And if one were not to add to the moon and to the sun the movements we mentioned,[33] the whole set of spheres will be forty-seven in number.

Let this, then, be taken as the number of the spheres,

[32] i. e. inwards from, the universe being thought of as a system of concentric spheres encircling the earth.
[33] In 1073ᵇ 35, 38–1074ᵃ 4.

so that the unmovable substances and principles also may
15 probably be taken as just so many; the assertion of necessity
must be left to more powerful thinkers. But if there can
be no spatial movement which does not conduce to the
moving of a star, and if further every being and every substance which is immune from change and in virtue of
itself has attained to the best must be considered an end,
there can be no other being apart from these we have
20 named, but this must be the number of the substances.
For if there are others, they will cause change as being a
final cause of movement; but there cannot be other movements besides those mentioned. And it is reasonable to
25 infer this from a consideration of the bodies that are
moved; for if everything that moves is for the sake of that
which is moved, and every movement belongs to something that is moved, no movement can be for the sake
of itself or of another movement, but all the movements
must be for the sake of the stars. For if there is to be a
movement for the sake of a movement, this latter also will
30 have to be for the sake of something else; so that since
there cannot be an infinite regress, the end of every movement will be one of the divine bodies which move through
the heaven.

(Evidently there is but one heaven. For if there are
many heavens as there are many men, the moving principles, of which each heaven will have one, will be one in
form but in number many. But all things that are many in
35 number have matter; for one and the same definition, e. g.
that of man, applies to many things, while Socrates is one.
But the primary essence has not matter; for it is complete
reality. So the unmovable first mover is one both in definition and in number; so too, therefore, is that which is
moved always and continuously; therefore there is one
heaven alone.)

1074ᵇ Our forefathers in the most remote ages have handed
down to their posterity a tradition, in the form of a myth,

that these bodies are gods and that the divine encloses the whole of nature. The rest of the tradition has been added later in mythical form with a view to the persuasion of the 5 multitude and to its legal and utilitarian expediency; they say these gods are in the form of men or like some of the other animals, and they say other things consequent on and similar to these which we have mentioned. But if one were to separate the first point from these additions and take it alone—that they thought the first substances to be 10 gods, one must regard this as an inspired utterance, and reflect that, while probably each art and each science has often been developed as far as possible and has again perished, these opinions, with others, have been preserved until the present like relics of the ancient treasure. Only thus far, then, is the opinion of our ancestors and of our earliest predecessors clear to us.

9   The nature of the divine thought involves certain 15 problems; for while thought is held to be the most divine of things observed by us, the question how it must be situated in order to have that character involves difficulties. For if it thinks of nothing, what is there here of dignity? It is just like one who sleeps. And if it thinks, but this depends on something else, then (since that which is its substance is not the act of thinking, but a potency) it cannot be the best substance; for it is through thinking 20 that its value belongs to it. Further, whether its substance is the faculty of thought or the act of thinking, what does it think of? Either of itself or of something else; and if of something else, either of the same thing always or of something different. Does it matter, then, or not, whether it thinks of the good or of any chance thing? Are there not some things about which it is incredible that it should 25 think? Evidently, then, it thinks of that which is most divine and precious, and it does not change; for change would be change for the worse, and this would be already a movement. First, then, if 'thought' is not the act of thinking but a potency, it would be reasonable to suppose that the continuity of its thinking is wearisome to it. Secondly, there would evidently be something else more precious than thought, viz. that which is thought of. For 30 both thinking and the act of thought will belong even to one who thinks of the worst thing in the world, so that if this ought to be avoided (and it ought, for there are even some things which it is better not to see than to see), the act of thinking cannot be the best of things. Therefore it must be of itself that the divine thought thinks (since it is the most excellent of things), and its thinking is a thinking on thinking.

But evidently knowledge and perception and opinion 35 and understanding have always something else as their object, and themselves only by the way. Further, if thinking and being thought of are different, in respect of which does goodness belong to thought? For to be an act of thinking and to be an object of thought are not the same thing. We answer that in some cases the knowledge is the 1075ᵃ object. In the productive sciences it is the substance or essence of the object, matter omitted, and in the theoretical sciences the definition or the act of thinking is the object. Since, then, thought and the object of thought are not different in the case of things that have not matter, the divine thought and its object will be the same, i. e. the thinking will be one with the object of its thought.

A further question is left—whether the object of the 5 divine thought is composite; for if it were, thought would change in passing from part to part of the whole. We answer that everything which has not matter is indivisible— as human thought, or rather the thought of composite beings, is in a certain period of time (for it does not possess the good at this moment or at that, but its best, being something *different* from it, is attained only in a whole 10 period of time), so throughout eternity is the thought which has *itself* for its object.

10 We must consider also in which of two ways the nature of the universe contains the good and the highest good, whether as something separate and by itself, or as the order of the parts. Probably in both ways, as an army does; for its good is found both in its order and in its 15 leader, and more in the latter; for he does not depend on the order but it depends on him. And all things are ordered together somehow, but not all alike—both fishes and fowls and plants; and the world is not such that one thing has nothing to do with another, but they are connected. For all are ordered together to one end, but it is as in a house, 20 where the freemen are least at liberty to act at random, but all things or most things are already ordained for them, while the slaves and the animals do little for the common good, and for the most part live at random; for this is the sort of principle that constitutes the nature of each. I mean, for instance, that all must at least come to be dissolved into their elements,[34] and there are other functions similarly in which all share for the good of the whole.

We must not fail to observe how many impossible or 25 paradoxical results confront those who hold different views from our own, and what are the views of the subtler thinkers, and which views are attended by fewest difficulties. All make all things out of contraries. But neither 'all things' nor 'out of contraries' is right; nor do these thinkers tell us how all the things in which the contraries are present can be made out of the contraries; for contraries are not 30 affected by one another. Now for us this difficulty is solved naturally by the fact that there is a third element.[35] These thinkers however make one of the two contraries matter; this is done for instance by those who make the unequal matter for the equal, or the many matter for the one.[36] But this also is refuted in the same way; for the one matter

[34] sc. in order that higher forms of being may be produced by new combinations of the elements.
[35] i. e. the substratum.
[36] The reference is to Platonists.

which underlies any pair of contraries is contrary to
nothing. Further, all things, except the one, will, on the
35 view we are criticizing, partake of evil; for the bad itself is
one of the two elements. But the other school [87] does not
treat the good and the bad even as principles; yet in all
things the good is in the highest degree a principle. The
school we first mentioned is right in saying that it is a
principle, but how the good is a principle they do not say—
whether as end or as mover or as form.

1075[b]   Empedocles [88] also has a paradoxical view; for he identifies the good with love, but this is a principle both as mover
(for it brings things together) and as matter (for it is part
5 of the mixture). Now even if it happens that the same
thing is a principle both as matter and as mover, still the
being, at least, of the two is not ·the same. In which
respect then is love a principle? It is paradoxical also that
strife should be imperishable; the nature of his 'evil' is
just strife.

Anaxagoras makes the good a motive principle; for his
'reason' moves things. But it moves them for an end, which
must be something other than it, except according to our
way of stating the case; for, on our view, the medical art is
10 in a sense health. It is paradoxical also not to suppose a
contrary to the good, i. e. to reason. But all who speak of
the contraries make no use of the contraries, unless we
bring their views into shape. And why some things are
perishable and others imperishable, no one tells us; for they
make all existing things out of the same principles. Further,
15 some make existing things out of the non-existent; and
others to avoid the necessity of this make all things one.

Further, why should there always be becoming, and
what is the cause of becoming?—this no one tells us.
And those who suppose two principles must suppose another, a superior principle, and so must those who believe

[87] The reference is to the Pythagoreans and Speusippus; Cf. xii.
1072[b] 31.

[88] Cf. i. 985[a] 4.

in the Forms; for why did things come to participate, or why do they participate, in the Forms? And all other think- 20 ers [39] are confronted by the necessary consequence that there is something contrary to Wisdom, i. e. to the highest knowledge; but we are not. For there is nothing contrary to that which is primary; for all contraries have matter, and things that have matter exist only potentially; and the ignorance which is contrary to any knowledge leads to an object contrary to the object of the knowledge; but what is primary has no contrary.

Again, if besides sensible things no others exist, there will be no first principle, no order, no becoming, no 25 heavenly bodies, but each principle will have a principle before it, as in the accounts of the theologians and all the natural philosophers. But if the Forms or the numbers are to exist, they will be causes of nothing; or if not that, at least not of movement. Further, how is extension, i. e. a *continuum*, to be produced out of unextended parts? For number will not, either as mover or as form, produce a *continuum*. But again there cannot be any *contrary* that is 30 also essentially a productive or moving principle; or it would be possible not to be.[40] Or at least its action would be posterior to its potency. The world, then, would not be eternal. But it is; one of these premises, then, must be denied. And we have said how this must be done.[41] Further, in virtue of what the numbers, or the soul and the body, or 35 in general the form and the thing, are one—of this no one tells us anything; nor can any one tell, unless he says, as we do, that the mover makes them one. And those who say [42] mathematical number is first and go on to generate one kind of substance after another and give different principles for each, make the substance of the universe a 1076ᵃ mere series of episodes (for one substance has no influence

[39] The special reference is to Plato; Cf. *Rep.* 477.
[40] Since contraries must contain matter, and matter implies potentiality and contingency.
[41] Cf. 1071ᵇ 19, 20.
[42] Speusippus is meant; Cf. vii. 1028ᵇ 21, xiv. 1090ᵇ 13–20.

on another by its existence or non-existence), and they give us many governing principles; but the world refuses to be governed badly.

'The rule of many is not good; one ruler let there be.' [43]

[43] Cf. *Iliad*, ii. 204.

Ethics

INTRODUCTION

Practical science, or political science, is a single science with two parts. Ethics and politics are concerned respectively with the interrelated subjects of human behavior and human associations. The opening sentences of the treatises which Aristotle wrote on the two parts of political science lay bases and beginnings of the methods of inquiry into the problems of those two subjects. "Every art and every inquiry, and similarly every action and pursuit, is thought to be aimed at some good; and for this reason the good has rightly been declared to be that at which all things aim." Human associations, like human behavior, are also directed to some good. "Every state is a community of some kind, and every community is established with a view to some good; for mankind always act in order to obtain that which they think to be good." What is thought to be good depends, however, on the character of the individual and the customs of communities. One of the recurrent questions of the *Politics* is whether the good man and the good citizen are the same, since the judgment of the individual is frequently at variance with the opinion of the community or the law of the state. The good man and the good citizen would be the same only in a perfect state, and the nature of the good is not discovered apart from the actions and preferences of men in communities.

The fourth chapter of the first book of the *Nicomachean Ethics* makes a new beginning, after the preliminary consideration of the nature of ethics and its relation to ends, to examine the good. It is apparent on analysis of what men say that there is no agreement about the "good" among experts or among ordinary men, and "happiness" is an ambiguous substitute for "good" as an end. The good must be sought therefore in actions of men, not any action, but those in accordance with virtue, and virtue is found to be a habit which is acquired by performing actions of the same kind as those which it in turn produces once the habit has been formed. The first book closes with an examination of the faculties of man which are subject to habituation in order to distinguish two kinds of virtues, moral and intellectual. The soul is the first actuality of a body capable of living; the psychological method of investigation of the faculties of the soul began with objects in order to differentiate actions and define faculties. The virtues of man studied in ethics are "second natures" formed by actions which are stabilized in man's character to become principles of moral action. The beginning point of the study of moral behavior is the study of virtues, or habits, relative to individual men and their powers and desires which differentiate moral actions and goods.

The second book begins by contrasting virtue to nature, which is innate, and comparing virtues to arts, which can also be learned. The definition of moral virtue is constructed by assembling the four characteristics which are essential to it: it is (1) a habit or state of character, (2) concerned with choice, (3) lying in a mean relative to us, and (4) determined by a rational principle, or the principle by which a man of practical reason or prudence would determine it. In the third book, voluntary, choice, deliberation, and wish are subjected to further analysis, for virtuous action must be an exercise of free choice based on *deliberation* of means to attain ends *wished*. Means are chosen, ends are wished, not selected at random or by whim. Virtues are based on freedom and on firmly implanted dispositions of character. Actions are virtuous when they are both free *and* caused. Examination of the actions and passions subject to habituation yields eleven virtues which are examined in groups— courage, temperance; liberality, magnificence; pride, ambition; good temper; friendliness, truthfulness, ready wit; shame.

The fifth book broadens the consideration of virtue as a mean between two extremes, of excess and deficiency relative to the individual, to the consideration of justice as a connecting link between individuals and communities. 'Justice' is an ambiguous word: there are two kinds of justice, one a universal virtue, the other a particular virtue, the twelfth moral virtue. Justice as a universal virtue is the "lawful," for men are formed in all virtues by conformity with the laws and customs of communities which inculcate virtues and proscribe vices. Justice as a particular virtue is the "equal" or the "fair." As the moral virtues of individuals are formed by justice as lawfulness, so communities come to be and operate by justice as equality. Men are not by nature equal in all respects, but political equalities are instituted to operate in the state in distributions of functions and offices and in retributions for injuries done. Distributive justice determines in the constitution of a state who shall perform what functions for what rewards and honors; rectificatory justices rectifies injustices or injuries done in transactions between man and man, voluntary, as in the transaction of business, and involuntary, as in crimes, with or without violence. In the investigation of laws and constitutions and states in the *Politics* justice is again a connecting link: there are as many kinds of justice as there are kinds of constitutions: democratic justices, oligarchical justices, despotic justices, which differ from each other but respond in common to the need for some proportionality of distribution and rectification in any association, which is called 'natural justice.'

The sixth book of the *Nicomachean Ethics* broadens the perspective again by examining the intellectual virtues which are implicit principles of the moral virtues. Moral virtue is defined as in accordance with the rule of right reason or as a prudent man would choose. To have the moral virtue of courage or temperance, however, it is not necessary to have the intellectual virtue of prudence or practical wisdom, but it is necessary to have been habituated to acting courageously or temperately by living justly in a community whose laws embody prudence. There are two kinds of intellectual virtues, calculative and scientific. The calculative intellectual virtues are two: prudence or practical wisdom, concerned with action or doing, and art, concerned with production or making. The scientific or contemplative intellectual virtues are three: science or the virtue of discursive inference, intuition or the virtue of perception of principles, and wisdom or the virtue which combines discursive process with intuitive insight. The relation among the virtues is not one of identity and the relation between the moral and the intellectual virtues is not direct or immediate. Socrates was wrong in thinking that virtue is knowledge, but the moral virtues do depend on prudence which in turn depends on wisdom. The justice of individuals is different from the justice of states, but the two justices are connected, and prudence and wisdom provide the connecting links.

The seventh book makes a fresh beginning. The inquiry into the good in human actions and arts has thus far been limited to the morality of habitual or virtuous action. Habit, however, is not the only means by which the good can be achieved, and the alternatives to habit are not limited to nature, chance, or fortune. Some men are continent and have no need for virtue since their actions are guided directly by rational principles without the intervention of habituation. Some men are not constrained by the normal contraries of excess and deficiency since their actions are governed by heroic powers which can withstand the evil effects of the excesses of other men. A man may act according to the rule of right reason and avoid excess by temperate habituation, continent self-restraint, or by heroic virtue. The last four books of the *Nicomachean Ethics* explore these and like concepts which are relevant to good in human activity and behavior which are beyond the bounds of moral behavior or different in principle from virtuous behavior. Pleasure, thus, is an accompaniment of well-performed actions but does not mark pleasurable good actions off from pleasurable bad actions, despite the theories of hedonists like Protagoras and Democritus. Love or friendship (*philia*), in like fashion, renders virtues and states, morality and politics unnecessary, since true friends are true equals and have all things in common, which is the basis of the theories of communists, like Plato.

ETHICA NICOMACHEA

CONTENTS

BOOK I. THE GOOD FOR MAN

A. Subject of our inquiry.

B. Nature of the science.

C. What is the good for man?

D. *Kinds of virtue.*

BOOKS II–V. MORAL VIRTUE
II. 1—III. 5. GENERAL ACCOUNT

A. *Moral virtue, how produced, in what materials and in what manner exhibited.*

B. *Definition of moral virtue.*

C. *Characteristics of the extreme and mean states: practical corollaries.*

D. *Inner side of moral virtue: conditions of responsibility for action.*

B. Pleasure.

BOOKS VIII, IX. FRIENDSHIP

A. Kinds of friendship.

BOOK X. PLEASURE. HAPPINESS

A. Pleasure.

B. Happiness.

Ethica Nicomachea

Nicomachean Ethics

Translated by W. D. Ross

⎍⎍⎍

BOOK I

1 Every art and every inquiry, and similarly every action
1094ᵃ and pursuit, is thought to aim at some good; and for
this reason the good has rightly been declared ¹ to be that
at which all things aim. But a certain difference is found
among ends; some are activities, others are products apart
5 from the activities that produce them. Where there are
ends apart from the actions, it is the nature of the products
to be better than the activities. Now, as there are many
actions, arts, and sciences, their ends also are many; the
end of the medical art is health, that of shipbuilding a
vessel, that of strategy victory, that of economics wealth.
10 But where such arts fall under a single capacity—as bridle-
making and the other arts concerned with the equipment
of horses fall under the art of riding, and this and every
military action under strategy, in the same way other arts
fall under yet others—in all of these the ends of the
master arts are to be preferred to all the subordinate ends;
15 for it is for the sake of the former that the latter are pursued. It makes no difference whether the activities themselves are the ends of the actions, or something else apart
from the activities, as in the case of the sciences just
mentioned.

¹ Perhaps by Eudoxus; Cf. 1172ᵇ 9.

2   If, then, there is some end of the things we do, which
we desire for its own sake (everything else being desired for the sake of this), and if we do not choose everything for the sake of something else (for at that rate the
process would go on to infinity, so that our desire would 20
be empty and vain), clearly this must be the good and the
chief good. Will not the knowledge of it, then, have a
great influence on life? Shall we not, like archers who have
a mark to aim at, be more likely to hit upon what is right?
If so, we must try, in outline at least to determine what 25
it is, and of which of the sciences or capacities it is the
object. It would seem to belong to the most authoritative
art and that which is most truly the master art. And politics appears to be of this nature; for it is this that ordains
which of the sciences should be studied in a state, and 1094ᵇ
which each class of citizens should learn and up to what
point they should learn them; and we see even the most
highly esteemed of capacities to fall under this, e. g.
strategy, economics, rhetoric; now, since politics uses the 5
rest of the sciences, and since, again, it legislates as to what
we are to do and what we are to abstain from, the end of
this science must include those of the others, so that this
end must be the good for man. For even if the end is the
same for a single man and for a state, that of the state
seems at all events something greater and more complete
whether to attain or to preserve; though it is worth while
to attain the end merely for one man, it is finer and more
godlike to attain it for a nation or for city-states. These, 10
then, are the ends at which our inquiry aims, since it is
political science, in one sense of that term.

3   Our discussion will be adequate if it has as much clearness as the subject-matter admits of, for precision is
not to be sought for alike in all discussions, any more than
in all the products of the crafts. Now fine and just actions, 15
which political science investigates, admit of much variety

and fluctuation of opinion, so that they may be thought to exist only by convention, and not by nature. And goods also give rise to a similar fluctuation because they bring harm to many people; for before now men have been undone by reason of their wealth, and others by reason of
20 their courage. We must be content, then, in speaking of such subjects and with such premises to indicate the truth roughly and in outline, and in speaking about things which are only for the most part true and with premises of the same kind to reach conclusions that are no better. In the same spirit, therefore, should each type of statement be
25 received; for it is the mark of an educated man to look for precision in each class of things just so far as the nature of the subject admits; it is evidently equally foolish to accept probable reasoning from a mathematician and to demand from a rhetorician scientific proofs.

Now each man judges well the things he knows, and of these he is a good judge. And so the man who has been
1095ᵃ educated in a subject is a good judge of that subject, and the man who has received an all-round education is a good judge in general. Hence a young man is not a proper hearer of lectures on political science; for he is inexperienced in the actions that occur in life, but its discussions start from these and are about these; and, further, since he tends to follow his passions, his study will be vain and unprofitable, because the end aimed at is not knowledge but action.
5 And it makes no difference whether he is young in years or youthful in character; the defect does not depend on time, but on his living, and pursuing each successive object, as passion directs. For to such persons, as to the incontinent, knowledge brings no profit; but to those who
10 desire and act in accordance with a rational principle knowledge about such matters will be of great benefit.

These remarks about the student, the sort of treatment to be expected, and the purpose of the inquiry, may be taken as our preface.

4   Let us resume our inquiry and state, in view of the
fact that all knowledge and every pursuit aims at some
good, what it is that we say political science aims at and
what is the highest of all goods achievable by action. 15
Verbally there is very general agreement; for both the general run of men and people of superior refinement say that
it is happiness, and identify living well and doing well with
being happy; but with regard to what happiness is they
differ, and the many do not give the same account as the 20
wise. For the former think it is some plain and obvious
thing, like pleasure, wealth, or honour; they differ, however,
from one another—and often even the same man identifies
it with different things, with health when he is ill, with
wealth when he is poor; but, conscious of their ignorance, 25
they admire those who proclaim some great ideal that is
above their comprehension. Now some [2] thought that
apart from these many goods there is another which is self-
subsistent and causes the goodness of all these as well. To
examine all the opinions that have been held were perhaps
somewhat fruitless; enough to examine those that are most
prevalent or that seem to be arguable.

Let us not fail to notice, however, that there is a difference between arguments from and those to the first prin- 30
ciples. For Plato, too, was right in raising this question and
asking, as he used to do, 'are we on the way from or to the
first principles?' [3] There is a difference, as there is in a
race-course between the course from the judges to the
turning-point and the way back. For, while we must begin
with what is known, things are objects of knowledge in 1095ᵇ
two senses—some to us, some without qualification. Presumably, then, we must begin with things known to us.
Hence any one who is to listen intelligently to lectures
about what is noble and just and, generally, about the
subjects of political science must have been brought up 5

[2] The Platonic School; Cf. ch. 6.
[3] Cf. *Rep.* 511 B.

in good habits. For the fact is the starting-point, and if this is sufficiently plain to him, he will not at the start need the reason as well; and the man who has been well brought up has or can easily get starting-points. And as for him who neither has nor can get them, let him hear the words of Hesiod:

10   Far best is he who knows all things himself;
Good, he that hearkens when men counsel right;
But he who neither knows, nor lays to heart
Another's wisdom, is a useless wight.

5   Let us, however, resume our discussion from the point at which we digressed. To judge from the lives that 15 men lead, most men, and men of the most vulgar type, seem (not without some ground) to identify the good, or happiness, with pleasure; which is the reason why they love the life of enjoyment. For there are, we may say, three prominent types of life—that just mentioned, the political, and thirdly the contemplative life. Now the mass of man-20 kind are evidently quite slavish in their tastes, preferring a life suitable to beasts, but they get some ground for their view from the fact that many of those in high places share the tastes of Sardanapallus. A consideration of the prominent types of life shows that people of superior refinement and of active disposition identify happiness with honour; for this is, roughly speaking, the end of the political life. But it seems too superficial to be what we are looking for, 25 since it is thought to depend on those who bestow honour rather than on him who receives it, but the good we divine to be something proper to a man and not easily taken from him. Further, men seem to pursue honour in order that they may be assured of their goodness; at least it is by men of practical wisdom that they seek to be honoured, and among those who know them, and on the ground of their virtue; clearly, then, according to them, at any rate, virtue 30 is better. And perhaps one might even suppose this to be,

rather than honour, the end of the political life. But even
this appears somewhat incomplete; for possession of virtue
seems actually compatible with being asleep, or with life-
long inactivity, and, further, with the greatest sufferings 1096ᵇ
and misfortunes; but a man who was living so no one would
call happy, unless he were maintaining a thesis at all costs.
But enough of this; for the subject has been sufficiently
treated even in the current discussions. Third comes the
contemplative life, which we shall consider later.[4]

The life of money-making is one undertaken under compulsion, and wealth is evidently not the good we are seek- 5
ing; for it is merely useful and for the sake of something
else. And so one might rather take the aforenamed objects to be ends; for they are loved for themselves. But it is
evident that not even these are ends; yet many arguments
have been thrown away in support of them. Let us leave
this subject, then.   10

6   We had perhaps better consider the universal good
     and discuss thoroughly what is meant by it, although
such an inquiry is made an uphill one by the fact that the
Forms have been introduced by friends of our own. Yet it
would perhaps be thought to be better, indeed to be our
duty, for the sake of maintaining the truth even to destroy
what touches us closely, especially as we are philosophers
or lovers of wisdom; for, while both are dear, piety requires 15
us to honour truth above our friends.

The men who introduced this doctrine did not posit
Ideas of classes within which they recognized priority and
posteriority (which is the reason why they did not maintain the existence of an Idea embracing all numbers);
but the term 'good' is used both in the category of substance and in that of quality and in that of relation, and
that which is *per se*, i. e. substance, is prior in nature to the 20
relative (for the latter is like an offshoot and accident of
being); so that there could not be a common Idea set over

[4] 1177ᵃ 12–1178ᵃ 8, 1178ᵃ 22–1179ᵃ 32.

all these goods. Further, since 'good' has as many senses as 'being' (for it is predicated both in the category of sub-
25 stance, as of God and of reason, and in quality, i. e. of the virtues, and in quantity, i. e. of that which is moderate, and in relation, i. e. of the useful, and in time, i. e. of the right opportunity, and in place, i. e. of the right locality and the like), clearly it cannot be something universally present in all cases and single; for then it could not have been predicated in all the categories but in one only. Further, since of the things answering to one Idea there is one
30 science, there would have been one science of all the goods; but as it is there are many sciences even of the things that fall under one category, e. g. of opportunity, for opportunity in war is studied by strategics and in disease by medicine, and the moderate in food is studied by medicine and in exercise by the science of gymnastics. And one might ask the question, what in the world they mean by 'a thing itself', if (as is the case) in 'man himself' and in a
35 particular man the account of man is one and the same.
096ᵇ For in so far as they are man, they will in no respect differ; and if this is so, neither will 'good itself' and particular goods, in so far as they are good. But again it will not be good any the more for being eternal, since that which lasts
5 long is no whiter than that which perishes in a day. The Pythagoreans seem to give a more plausible account of the good, when they place the one in the column of goods; and it is they that Speusippus seems to have followed.

But let us discuss these matters elsewhere ⁵; an objection to what we have said, however, may be discerned in the
10 fact that the Platonists have not been speaking about all goods, and that the goods that are pursued and loved for themselves are called good by reference to a single Form, while those which tend to produce or to preserve these somehow or to prevent their contraries are called so by reference to these, and in a secondary sense. Clearly, then,

⁵ Cf. Met. 986ᵃ 22–6, 1028ᵇ 21–4, 1072ᵇ 30–1073ᵃ 3, 1091ᵃ 29–ᵇ 3, ᵇ 13–1092ᵃ 17.

goods must be spoken of in two ways, and some must be good in themselves, the others by reason of these. Let us separate, then, things good in themselves from things use- 15 ful, and consider whether the former are called good by reference to a single Idea. What sort of goods would one call good in themselves? Is it those that are pursued even when isolated from others, such as intelligence, sight, and certain pleasures and honours? Certainly, if we pursue these also for the sake of something else, yet one would place them among things good in themselves. Or is nothing other 20 than the Idea of good good in itself? In that case the Form will be empty. But if the things we have named are also things good in themselves, the account of the good will have to appear as something identical in them all, as that of whiteness is identical in snow and in white lead. But of honour, wisdom, and pleasure, just in respect of their good- 25 ness, the accounts are distinct and diverse. The good, therefore, is not some common element answering to one Idea.

But what then do we mean by the good? It is surely not like the things that only chance to have the same name. Are goods one, then, by being derived from one good or by all contributing to one good, or are they rather one by analogy? Certainly as sight is in the body, so is 30 reason in the soul, and so on in other cases. But perhaps these subjects had better be dismissed for the present; for perfect precision about them would be more appropriate to another branch of philosophy.[6] And similarly with re-gard to the Idea; even if there is some one good which is universally predicable of goods or is capable of separate and independent existence, clearly it could not be achieved or attained by man; but we are now seeking something attainable. Perhaps, however, some one might think it 35 worth while to recognize this with a view to the goods that are attainable and achievable; for having this as a sort of pattern we shall know better the goods that are good for 1097ᵃ

[6] Cf. *Met.* iv. 2.

us, and if we know them shall attain them. This argument
has some plausibility, but seems to clash with the procedure of the sciences; for all of these, though they aim at
5 some good and seek to supply the deficiency of it, leave on
one side the knowledge of the good. Yet that all the exponents of the arts should be ignorant of, and should not
even seek, so great an aid is not probable. It is hard, too,
to see how a weaver or a carpenter will be benefited in
regard to his own craft by knowing this 'good itself', or how
10 the man who has viewed the Idea itself will be a better
doctor or general thereby. For a doctor seems not even to
study health in this way, but the health of man, or perhaps rather the health of a particular man; it is individuals
that he is healing. But enough of these topics.

7   Let us again return to the good we are seeking, and ask
15   what it can be. It seems different in different actions
and arts; it is different in medicine, in strategy, and in the
other arts likewise. What then is the good of each? Surely
that for whose sake everything else is done. In medicine
20 this is health, in strategy victory, in architecture a house,
in any other sphere something else, and in every action
and pursuit the end; for it is for the sake of this that all
men do whatever else they do. Therefore, if there is an end
for all that we do, this will be the good achievable by
action, and if there are more than one, these will be the
goods achievable by action.

So the argument has by a different course reached the
same point; but we must try to state this even more clearly.
Since there are evidently more than one end, and we choose
25 some of these (e. g. wealth, flutes, and in general instruments) for the sake of something else, clearly not all ends
are final ends; but the chief good is evidently something
final. Therefore, if there is only one final end, this will be
what we are seeking, and if there are more than one, the
most final of these will be what we are seeking. Now we
30 call that which is in itself worthy of pursuit more final

than that which is worthy of pursuit for the sake of something else, and that which is never desirable for the sake of something else more final than the things that are desirable both in themselves and for the sake of that other thing, and therefore we call final without qualification that which is always desirable in itself and never for the sake of something else.

Now such a thing happiness, above all else, is held to be; for this we choose always for itself and never for the sake of something else, but honour, pleasure, reason, and every 1097ᵇ virtue we choose indeed for themselves (for if nothing resulted from them we should still choose each of them), but we choose them also for the sake of happiness, judging 5 that by means of them we shall be happy. Happiness, on the other hand, no one chooses for the sake of these, nor, in general, for anything other than itself.

From the point of view of self-sufficiency the same result seems to follow; for the final good is thought to be self-sufficient. Now by self-sufficient we do not mean that which is sufficient for a man by himself, for one who lives 10 a solitary life, but also for parents, children, wife, and in general for his friends and fellow citizens, since man is born for citizenship. But some limit must be set to this; for if we extend our requirement to ancestors and descendants and friends' friends we are in for an infinite series. Let us examine this question, however, on another occasion; [7] the self-sufficient we now define as that which when iso- 15 lated makes life desirable and lacking in nothing; and such we think happiness to be; and further we think it most desirable of all things, without being counted as one good thing among others—if it were so counted it would clearly be made more desirable by the addition of even the least of goods; for that which is added becomes an 20 excess of goods, and of goods the greater is always more desirable. Happiness, then, is something final and self-sufficient, and is the end of action.

[7] i. 10, 11, ix. 10.

Presumably, however, to say that happiness is the chief good seems a platitude, and a clearer account of what it is
25 is still desired. This might perhaps be given, if we could first ascertain the function of man. For just as for a flute-player, a sculptor, or any artist, and, in general, for all things that have a function or activity, the good and the 'well' is thought to reside in the function, so would it seem to be for man, if he has a function. Have the carpenter,
30 then, and the tanner certain functions or activities, and has man none? Is he born without a function? Or as eye, hand, foot, and in general each of the parts evidently has a function, may one lay it down that man similarly has a function apart from all these? What then can this be? Life seems to be common even to plants, but we are seeking
1098ª what is peculiar to man. Let us exclude, therefore, the life of nutrition and growth. Next there would be a life of perception, but *it* also seems to be common even to the horse, the ox, and every animal. There remains, then, an active life of the element that has a rational principle; of this, one part has such a principle in the sense of being
5 obedient to one, the other in the sense of possessing one and exercising thought. And, as 'life of the rational element' also has two meanings, we must state that life in the sense of activity is what we mean; for this seems to be the more proper sense of the term. Now if the function of man is an activity of soul which follows or implies a rational principle, and if we say 'a so-and-so' and 'a good so-and-so' have a function which is the same in kind, e. g. a lyre-player and a good lyre-player, and so without qualification in all cases, eminence in respect of goodness being added
10 to the name of the function (for the function of a lyre-player is to play the lyre, and that of a good lyre-player is to do so well) : if this is the case, [and we state the function of man to be a certain kind of life, and this to be an activity or actions of the soul implying a rational principle, and the function of a good man to be the good and noble perform-ance of these, and if any action is well performed when it

is performed in accordance with the appropriate excellence: 15 if this is the case,] human good turns out to be activity of soul in accordance with virtue, and if there are more than one virtue, in accordance with the best and most complete.

But we must add 'in a complete life'. For one swallow does not make a summer, nor does one day; and so too one day, or a short time, does not make a man blessed and happy.

Let this serve as an outline of the good; for we must presumably first sketch it roughly, and then later fill in the 20 details. But it would seem that any one is capable of carrying on and articulating what has once been well outlined, and that time is a good discoverer or partner in such a work; to which facts the advances of the arts are due; for any one can add what is lacking. And we must also remember what has been said before,[8] and not look for precision in 25 all things alike, but in each class of things such precision as accords with the subject-matter, and so much as is appropriate to the inquiry. For a carpenter and a geometer investigate the right angle in different ways; the former does so in so far as the right angle is useful for his work, while the 30 latter inquires what it is or what sort of thing it is; for he is a spectator of the truth. We must act in the same way, then, in all other matters as well, that our main task may not be subordinated to minor questions. Nor must we demand the cause in all matters alike; it is enough in some cases that the *fact* be well established, as in the case of the **1098ᵇ** first principles; the fact is the primary thing or first principle. Now of first principles we see some by induction, some by perception, some by a certain habituation, and others too in other ways. But each set of principles we must try to investigate in the natural way, and we must take pains to state them definitely, since they have a great in- 5 fluence on what follows. For the beginning is thought to be more than half of the whole, and many of the questions we ask are cleared up by it.

[8] 1094ᵇ 11–27.

8   We must consider it, however, in the light not only
10   of our conclusion and our premisses, but also of what
is commonly said about it; for with a true view all the data
harmonize, but with a false one the facts soon clash. Now
goods have been divided into three classes,[9] and some are
described as external, others as relating to soul or to body;
we call those that relate to soul most properly and truly
15 goods, and physical actions and activities we class as relating to soul. Therefore our account must be sound, at
least according to this view, which is an old one and agreed
on by philosophers. It is correct also in that we identify the
end with certain actions and activities; for thus it falls
among goods of the soul and not among external goods.
20 Another belief which harmonizes with our account is
that the happy man lives well and does well; for we have
practically defined happiness as a sort of good life and
good action. The characteristics that are looked for in happiness seem also, all of them, to belong to what we have
defined happiness as being. For some identify happiness
with virtue, some with practical wisdom, others with a kind
25 of philosophic wisdom, others with these, or one of these,
accompanied by pleasure or not without pleasure; while
others include also external prosperity. Now some of these
views have been held by many men and men of old, others
by a few eminent persons; and it is not probable that either
of these should be entirely mistaken, but rather that they
should be right in at least some one respect or even in most
respects.
30   With those who identify happiness with virtue or some
one virtue our account is in harmony; for to virtue belongs
virtuous activity. But it makes, perhaps, no small difference
whether we place the chief good in possession or in use, in
1099ᵃ state of mind or in activity. For the state of mind may exist
without producing any good result, as in a man who is
asleep or in some other way quite inactive, but the activity
cannot; for one who has the activity will of necessity be

[9] Pl. *Euthyd.* 279 ᴀʙ, *Phil.* 48 ᴇ, *Laws*, 743 ᴇ.

acting, and acting well. And as in the Olympic Games it is not the most beautiful and the strongest that are crowned but those who compete (for it is some of these that are 5 victorious), so those who act win, and rightly win, the noble and good things in life.

Their life is also in itself pleasant. For pleasure is a state of *soul*, and to each man that which he is said to be a lover of is pleasant; e. g. not only is a horse pleasant to the lover of horses, and a spectacle to the lover of sights, but also in 10 the same way just acts are pleasant to the lover of justice and in general virtuous acts to the lover of virtue. Now for most men their pleasures are in conflict with one another because these are not by nature pleasant, but the lovers of what is noble find pleasant the things that are by nature pleasant; and virtuous actions are such, so that these are pleasant for such men as well as in their own nature. Their life, therefore, has no further need of pleasure as a sort of 15 adventitious charm, but has its pleasure in itself. For, besides what we have said, the man who does not rejoice in noble actions is not even good; since no one would call a man just who did not enjoy acting justly, nor any man liberal who did not enjoy liberal actions; and similarly in all other cases. If this is so, virtuous actions must be in them- 20 selves pleasant. But they are also *good* and *noble*, and have each of these attributes in the highest degree, since the good man judges well about these attributes; his judgement is such as we have described.[10] Happiness then is the best, noblest, and most pleasant thing in the world, and these attributes are not severed as in the inscription at Delos— 25

> Most noble is that which is justest, and best is health;
> But pleasantest is it to win what we love.

For all these properties belong to the best activities; and these, or one—the best—of these, we identify with happiness. 30

[10] i. e., he judges that virtuous actions are good and noble in the highest degree.

Yet evidently, as we said,[11] it needs the external goods as well; for it is impossible, or not easy, to do noble acts 1099[b] without the proper equipment. In many actions we use friends and riches and political power as instruments; and there are some things the lack of which takes the lustre from happiness, as good birth, goodly children, beauty; for the man who is very ugly in appearance or ill-born or solitary and childless is not very likely to be happy, and perhaps 5 a man would be still less likely if he had thoroughly bad children or friends or had lost good children or friends by death. As we said,[11] then, happiness seems to need this sort of prosperity in addition; for which reason· some identify happiness with good fortune, though others identify it with virtue.

9   For this reason also the question is asked, whether happiness is to be acquired by learning or by habituation or some other sort of training, or comes in virtue of 10 some divine providence or again by chance. Now if there is any gift of the gods to men, it is reasonable that happiness should be god-given, and most surely god-given of all human things inasmuch as it is the best. But this question would perhaps be more appropriate to another inquiry; hap- 15 piness seems, however, even if it is not god-sent but comes as a result of virtue and some process of learning or training, to be among the most god-like things; for that which is the prize and end of virtue seems to be the best thing in the world, and something godlike and blessed.

It will also on this view be very generally shared; for all who are not maimed as regards their potentiality for 20 virtue may win it by a certain kind of study and care. But if it is better to be happy thus than by chance, it is reason· able that the facts should be so, since everything that depends on the action of nature is by nature as good as it can be, and similarly everything that depends on art or any rational cause, and especially if it depends on the best of

[11] 1098[b] 26–9.

all causes. To entrust to chance what is greatest and most noble would be a very defective arrangement.

The answer to the question we are asking is plain also 25 from the definition of happiness; for it has been said [12] to be a virtuous activity of soul, of a certain kind. Of the remaining goods, some must necessarily pre-exist as conditions of happiness, and others are naturally co-operative and useful as instruments. And this will be found to agree with what we said at the outset; [13] for we stated the end of political science to be the best end, and political science 30 spends most of its pains on making the citizens to be of a certain character, viz. good and capable of noble acts.

It is natural, then, that we call neither ox nor horse nor any other of the animals happy; for none of them is capable of sharing in such activity. For this reason also a boy is not **1100ᵃ** happy; for he is not yet capable of such acts, owing to his age; and boys who are called happy are being congratulated by reason of the hopes we have for them. For there is required, as we said,[14] not only complete virtue but also a complete life, since many changes occur in life, and all 5 manner of chances, and the most prosperous may fall into great misfortunes in old age, as is told of Priam in the Trojan Cycle; and one who has experienced such chances and has ended wretchedly no one calls happy.

10 Must no one at all, then, be called happy while he 10 lives; must we, as Solon says, see the end? Even if we are to lay down this doctrine, is it also the case that a man *is* happy when he is *dead*? Or is not this quite absurd, especially for us who say that happiness is an activity? But if we 15 do not call the dead man happy, and if Solon does not mean this, but that one can then safely *call* a man blessed as being at last beyond evils and misfortunes, this also affords matter for discussion; for both evil and good are

----

[12] 1098ᵃ 16.
[13] 1094ᵃ 27.
[14] 1098ᵃ 16–18.

thought to exist for a dead man, as much as for one who
20 is alive but not aware of them; e. g. honours and dishonours
and the good or bad fortunes of children and in general of
descendants. And this also presents a problem; for though
a man has lived happily up to old age and has had a death
worthy of his life, many reverses may befall his descendants
—some of them may be good and attain the life they de-
25 serve, while with others the opposite may be the case; and
clearly too the degrees of relationship between them and
their ancestors may vary indefinitely. It would be odd, then,
if the dead man were to share in these changes and become
at one time happy, at another wretched; while it would
also be odd if the fortunes of the descendants did not for
30 some time have some effect on the happiness of their ancestors.

But we must return to our first difficulty; for perhaps by
a consideration of it our present problem might be solved.
Now if we must see the end and only then call a man
happy, not as being happy but as having been so before,
35 surely this is a paradox, that when he is happy the attribute
that belongs to him is not to be truly predicated of him
because we do not wish to call living men happy, on ac-
1100ᵇ count of the changes that may befall them, and because
we have assumed happiness to be something permanent
and by no means easily changed, while a single man may
suffer many turns of fortune's wheel. For clearly if we were
5 to keep pace with his fortunes, we should often call the
same man happy and again wretched, making the happy
man out to be a 'chameleon and insecurely based'. Or is
this keeping pace with his fortunes quite wrong? Success or
failure in life does not depend on these, but human life,
as we said,[15] needs these as mere additions, while virtuous
activities or their opposites are what constitute happiness
10 or the reverse.

The question we have now discussed confirms our defini-

15 1099ᵃ 31–ᵇ 7.

tion. For no function of man has so much permanence as
virtuous activities (these are thought to be more durable
even than knowledge of the sciences), and of these themselves the most valuable are more durable because those 15
who are happy spend their life most readily and most continuously in these; for this seems to be the reason why we
do not forget them. The attribute in question,[16] then, will
belong to the happy man, and he will be happy throughout
his life; for always, or by preference to everything else, he
will be engaged in virtuous action and contemplation, and
he will bear the chances of life most nobly and altogether 20
decorously, if he is 'truly good' and 'foursquare beyond
reproach'.[17]

Now many events happen by chance, and events differing in importance; small pieces of good fortune or of its
opposite clearly do not weigh down the scales of life one
way or the other, but a multitude of great events if they 25
turn out well will make life happier (for not only are they
themselves such as to add beauty to life, but the way a man
deals with them may be noble and good), while if they
turn out ill they crush and maim happiness; for they both
bring pain with them and hinder many activities. Yet even 30
in these nobility shines through, when a man bears with
resignation many great misfortunes, not through insensibility to pain but through nobility and greatness of soul.

If activities are, as we said,[18] what gives life its character,
no happy man can become miserable; for he will never do
the acts that are hateful and mean. For the man who is 35
truly good and wise, we think, bears all the chances of life **1101ª**
becomingly and always makes the best of circumstances,
as a good general makes the best military use of the army
at his command and a good shoemaker makes the best
shoes out of the hides that are given him; and so with all 5

---

[16] Durability.
[17] Simonides.
[18] l. 9.

other craftsmen. And if this is the case, the happy man can never become miserable—though he will not reach *blessedness*, if he meet with fortunes like those of Priam.

Nor, again, is he many-coloured and changeable; for
10 neither will he be moved from his happy state easily or by any ordinary misadventures, but only by many great ones, nor, if he has had many great misadventures, will he recover his happiness in a short time, but if at all, only in a long and complete one in which he has attained many splendid successes.

Why then should we not say that he is happy who is
15 active in accordance with complete virtue and is sufficiently equipped with external goods, not for some chance period but throughout a complete life? Or must we add 'and who is destined to live thus and die as befits his life'? Certainly the future is obscure to us, while happiness, we claim, is an end and something in every way final. If so, we shall call happy those among living men in whom these conditions
20 are, and are to be, fulfilled—but happy *men*. So much for these questions.

11 [19]That the fortunes of descendants and of all a man's friends should not affect his happiness at all seems a very unfriendly doctrine, and one opposed to the opinions
25 men hold; but since the events that happen are numerous and admit of all sorts of difference, and some come more near to us and others less so, it seems a long—nay, an infinite—task to discuss each in detail; a general outline will perhaps suffice. If, then, as some of a man's own misadventures have a certain weight and influence on life while others are, as it were, lighter, so too there are differences
30 among the misadventures of our friends taken as a whole, and it makes a difference whether the various sufferings befall the living or the dead (much more even than whether lawless and terrible deeds are presupposed in a tragedy or done on the stage), this difference also must be taken into

[19] Aristotle now returns to the question stated in 1100[a] 18–30.

account; or rather, perhaps, the fact that doubt is felt
whether the dead share in any good or evil. For it seems, 35
from these considerations, that even if anything whether **1101ᵇ**
good or evil penetrates to them, it must be something weak
and negligible, either in itself or for them, or if not, at least
it must be such in degree and kind as not to make happy
those who are not happy nor to take away their blessedness
from those who are. The good or bad fortunes of friends,
then, seem to have some effects on the dead, but effects 5
of such a kind and degree as neither to make the happy
unhappy nor to produce any other change of the kind.

12 These questions having been definitely answered, let
      us consider whether happiness is among the things 10
that are praised or rather among the things that are prized;
for clearly it is not to be placed among *potentialities*.²⁰
Everything that is praised seems to be praised because it
is of a certain kind and is related somehow to something
else; for we praise the just or brave man and in general both
the good man and virtue itself because of the actions and
functions involved, and we praise the strong man, the good 15
runner, and so on, because he is of a certain kind and is
related in a certain way to something good and important.
This is clear also from the praises of the gods; for it seems
absurd that the gods should be referred to our standard,
but this *is* done because praise involves a reference, as we
said, to something else. But if praise is for things such as 20
we have described, clearly what applies to the best things is
not praise, but something greater and better, as is indeed
obvious; for what we do to the gods and the most godlike
of men is to call them blessed and happy. And so too with
good *things*; no one praises happiness as he does justice, 25
but rather calls it blessed, as being something more divine
and better.
      Eudoxus also seems to have been right in his method of
advocating the supremacy of pleasure; he thought that the

²⁰ Cf. *Top.* 126ᵇ 4; *M. M.* 1183ᵇ 20.

fact that, though a good, it is not praised indicated it to be
better than the things that are praised, and that this is what
30 God and the good are; for by reference to these all other
things are judged. *Praise* is appropriate to virtue, for as a
result of virtue men tend to do noble deeds; but *encomia*
are bestowed on acts, whether of the body or of the soul.
35 But perhaps nicety in these matters is more proper to those
who have made a study of encomia; to us it is clear from
1102ᵃ what has been said that happiness is among the things that
are prized and perfect. It seems to be so also from the fact
that it is a first principle; for it is for the sake of this that we
all do all that we do, and the first principle and cause of
goods is, we claim, something prized and divine.

5 **13** Since happiness is an activity of soul in accordance
with perfect virtue, we must consider the nature of
virtue; for perhaps we shall thus see better the nature of
happiness. The true student of politics, too, is thought to
have studied virtue above all things; for he wishes to make
10 his fellow citizens good and obedient to the laws. As an
example of this we have the lawgivers of the Cretans and
the Spartans, and any others of the kind that there may
have been. And if this inquiry belongs to political science,
clearly the pursuit of it will be in accordance with our
original plan. But clearly the virtue we must study is human
virtue; for the good we were seeking was human good and
15 the happiness human happiness. By human virtue we mean
not that of the body but that of the soul; and happiness
also we call an activity of soul. But if this is so, clearly the
student of politics must know somehow the facts about
soul, as the man who is to heal the eyes or the body as a
whole must know about the eyes or the body; and all the
20 more since politics is more prized and better than medicine; but even among doctors the best educated spend
much labour on acquiring knowledge of the body. The
student of politics, then, must study the soul, and must
study it with these objects in view, and do so just to the

extent which is sufficient for the questions we are discussing; for further precision is perhaps something more 25
laborious than our purposes require.

Some things are said about it, adequately enough, even
in the discussions outside our school, and we must use
these; e. g. that one element in the soul is irrational and
one has a rational principle. Whether these are separated 30
as the parts of the body or of anything divisible are, or are
distinct by definition but by nature inseparable, like convex and concave in the circumference of a circle, does not
affect the present question.

Of the irrational element one division seems to be widely
distributed, and vegetative in its nature, I mean that which
causes nutrition and growth; for it is this kind of power of
the soul that one must assign to all nurslings and to em-1102ᵇ
bryos, and this same power to full-grown creatures; this is
more reasonable than to assign some different power to
them. Now the excellence of this seems to be common to
all species and not specifically human; for this part or
faculty seems to function most in sleep, while goodness and 5
badness are least manifest in sleep (whence comes the saying that the happy are no better off than the wretched for
half their lives; and this happens naturally enough, since
sleep is an inactivity of the soul in that respect in which it
is called good or bad), unless perhaps to a small extent
some of the movements actually penetrate to the soul, and 10
in this respect the dreams of good men are better than
those of ordinary people. Enough of this subject, however;
let us leave the nutritive faculty alone, since it has by its
nature no share in human excellence.

There seems to be also another irrational element in the
soul—one which in a sense, however, shares in a rational
principle. For we praise the rational principle of the continent man and of the incontinent, and the part of their soul 15
that has such a principle, since it urges them aright and towards the best objects; but there is found in them also another element naturally opposed to the rational principle,

which fights against and resists that principle. For exactly
as paralysed limbs when we intend to move them to the
20 right turn on the contrary to the left, so is it with the soul;
the impulses of incontinent people move in contrary directions. But while in the body we see that which moves
astray, in the soul we do not. No doubt, however, we must
none the less suppose that in the soul too there is some-
25 thing contrary to the rational principle, resisting and opposing it. In what sense it is distinct from the other elements does not concern us. Now even this seems to have a
share in a rational principle, as we said; [21] at any rate in the
continent man it obeys the rational principle—and presumably in the temperate and brave man it is still more
obedient; for in him it speaks, on all matters, with the same
voice as the rational principle.

Therefore the irrational element also appears to be twofold. For the vegetative element in no way shares in a ra-
30 tional principle, but the appetitive, and in general the desiring element in a sense shares in it, in so far as it listens to
and obeys it; this is the sense in which we speak of 'taking
account' of one's father or one's friends, not that in which
we speak of 'accounting' for a mathematical property. That
the irrational element is in some sense persuaded by a rational principle is indicated also by the giving of advice and
1103ª by all reproof and exhortation. And if this element also
must be said to have a rational principle, that which has a
rational principle (as well as that which has not) will be
twofold, one subdivision having it in the strict sense and in
itself, and the other having a tendency to obey as one does
one's father.

Virtue too is distinguished into kinds in accordance with
this difference; for we say that some of the virtues are intel-
5 lectual and others moral, philosophic wisdom and understanding and practical wisdom being intellectual, liberality
and temperance moral. For in speaking about a man's character we do not say that he is wise or has understanding

[21] l. 13.

but that he is good-tempered or temperate; yet we praise
the wise man also with respect to his state of mind; and of
states of mind we call those which merit praise virtues.   10

BOOK II

1   Virtue, then, being of two kinds, intellectual and
moral, intellectual virtue in the main owes both its 15
birth and its growth to teaching (for which reason it requires experience and time), while moral virtue comes
about as a result of habit, whence also its name *ethike* is
one that is formed by a slight variation from the word *ethos*
(habit). From this it is also plain that none of the moral
virtues arises in us by nature; for nothing that exists by 20
nature can form a habit contrary to its nature. For instance
the stone which by nature moves downwards cannot be
habituated to move upwards, not even if one tries to train
it by throwing it up ten thousand times; nor can fire be
habituated to move downwards, nor can anything else that
by nature behaves in one way be trained to behave in another. Neither by nature, then, nor contrary to nature do
the virtues arise in us; rather we are adapted by nature to
receive them, and are made perfect by habit.   25

Again, of all the things that come to us by nature we first
acquire the potentiality and later exhibit the activity (this
is plain in the case of the senses; for it was not by often 30
seeing or often hearing that we got these senses, but on the
contrary we had them before we used them, and did not
come to have them by using them); but the virtues we get
by first exercising them, as also happens in the case of the
arts as well. For the things we have to learn before we can
do them, we learn by doing them, e. g. men become builders by building and lyre-players by playing the lyre; so too **1103ᵇ**
we become just by doing just acts, temperate by doing
temperate acts, brave by doing brave acts.

This is confirmed by what happens in states; for legislators make the citizens good by forming habits in them,

5 and this is the wish of every legislator, and those who do not effect it miss their mark, and it is in this that a good constitution differs from a bad one.

Again, it is from the same causes and by the same means that every virtue is both produced and destroyed, and similarly every art; for it is from playing the lyre that both good and bad lyre-players are produced. And the corresponding statement is true of builders and of all the rest; men will 10 be good or bad builders as a result of building well or badly. For if this were not so, there would have been no need of a teacher, but all men would have been born good or bad at their craft. This, then, is the case with the virtues also; by doing the acts that we do in our transactions with 15 other men we become just or unjust, and by doing the acts that we do in the presence of danger, and being habituated to feel fear or confidence, we become brave or cowardly. The same is true of appetites and feelings of anger; some men become temperate and good-tempered, others self-indulgent and irascible, by behaving in one way or the 20 other in the appropriate circumstances. Thus, in one word, states of character arise out of like activities. This is why the activities we exhibit must be of a certain kind; it is because the states of character correspond to the differences between these. It makes no small difference, then, whether we form habits of one kind or of another from our very 25 youth; it make a very great difference, or rather all the difference.

2   Since, then, the present inquiry does not aim at theoretical knowledge like the others (for we are inquiring not in order to know what virtue is, but in order to become good, since otherwise our inquiry would have been of no use), we must examine the nature of actions, namely how 30 we ought to do them; for these determine also the nature of the states of character that are produced, as we have said.[1] Now, that we must act according to the right rule

¹ ᵃ 31–ᵇ 25.

is a common principle and must be assumed—it will be discussed later,[2] i. e. both what the right rule is, and how it is related to the other virtues. But this must be agreed upon **1104ᵃ** beforehand, that the whole account of matters of conduct must be given in outline and not precisely, as we said at the very beginning [3] that the accounts we demand must be in accordance with the subject-matter; matters concerned with conduct and questions of what is good for us have no fixity, any more than matters of health. The general ac- 5 count being of this nature, the account of particular cases is yet more lacking in exactness; for they do not fall under any art or precept but the agents themselves must in each case consider what is appropriate to the occasion, as happens also in the art of medicine or of navigation.

But though our present account is of this nature we must give what help we can. First, then, let us consider 10 this, that it is the nature of such things to be destroyed by defect and excess, as we see in the case of strength and of health (for to gain light on things imperceptible we must use the evidence of sensible things); both excessive and defective exercise destroys the strength, and similarly drink 15 or food which is above or below a certain amount destroys the health, while that which is proportionate both produces and increases and preserves it. So too is it, then, in the case 20 of temperance and courage and the other virtues. For the man who flies from and fears everything and does not stand his ground against anything becomes a coward, and the man who fears nothing at all but goes to meet every danger becomes rash; and similarly the man who indulges in every pleasure and abstains from none becomes self-indulgent, while the man who shuns every pleasure, as boors do, be- 25 comes in a way insensible; temperance and courage, then, are destroyed by excess and defect, and preserved by the mean.

But not only are the sources and causes of their origina-

[2] vi. 13.
[3] 1094ᵇ 11–27.

tion and growth the same as those of their destruction,
but also the sphere of their actualization will be the same;
30 for this is also true of the things which are more evident
to sense, e. g. of strength; it is produced by taking much
food and undergoing much exertion, and it is the strong
man that will be most able to do these things. So too is it
with the virtues; by abstaining from pleasures we become
35 temperate, and it is when we have become so that we are
1104^b most able to abstain from them; and similarly too in the
case of courage; for by being habituated to despise things
that are terrible and to stand our ground against them we
become brave, and it is when we have become so that we
shall be most able to stand our ground against them.

3   We must take as a sign of states of character the
5   pleasure or pain that ensues on acts; for the man who
abstains from bodily pleasures and delights in this very
fact is temperate, while the man who is annoyed at it is
self-indulgent, and he who stands his ground against things
that are terrible and delights in this or at least is not pained
is brave, while the man who is pained is a coward. For
moral excellence is concerned with pleasures and pains; it
10 is on account of the pleasure that we do bad things, and on
account of the pain that we abstain from noble ones.
Hence we ought to have been brought up in a particular
way from our very youth, as Plato says,[4] so as both to delight in and to be pained by the things that we ought; for
this is the right education.

Again, if the virtues are concerned with actions and passions, and every passion and every action is accompanied
15 by pleasure and pain, for this reason also virtue will be
concerned with pleasures and pains. This is indicated also
by the fact that punishment is inflicted by these means; for
it is a kind of cure, and it is the nature of cures to be effected by contraries.

[4] *Laws*, 653 A ff., *Rep.* 401 E–402 A.

Again, as we said but lately,[5] every state of soul has a nature relative to and concerned with the kind of things by which it tends to be made worse or better; but it is by 20 reason of pleasures and pains that men become bad, by pursuing and avoiding these—either the pleasures and pains they ought not or when they ought not or as they ought not, or by going wrong in one of the other similar ways that may be distinguished. Hence men [6] even define the virtues as certain states of impassivity and rest; not well, 25 however, because they speak absolutely, and do not say 'as one ought' and 'as one ought not' and 'when one ought or ought not', and the other things that may be added. We assume, then, that this kind of excellence tends to do what is best with regard to pleasures and pains, and vice does the contrary.

The following facts also may show us that virtue and vice are concerned with these same things. There being three objects of choice and three of avoidance, the noble, 30 the advantageous, the pleasant, and their contraries, the base, the injurious, the painful, about all of these the good man tends to go right and the bad man to go wrong, and especially about pleasure; for this is common to the animals, and also it accompanies all objects of choice; for even the noble and the advantageous appear pleasant.   35

Again, it has grown up with us all from our infancy; this is why it is difficult to rub off this passion, engrained as it 1105ᵃ is in our life. And we measure even our actions, some of us more and others less, by the rule of pleasure and pain. 5 For this reason, then, our whole inquiry must be about these; for to feel delight and pain rightly or wrongly has no small effect on our actions.

Again, it is harder to fight with pleasure than with anger, to use Heraclitus' phrase, but both art and virtue are always concerned with what is harder; for even the good is better

---

[5] ᵃ 27–ᵇ 3.
[6] Probably Speusippus is referred to.

10 when it is harder. Therefore for this reason also the whole concern both of virtue and of political science is with pleasures and pains; for the man who uses these well will be good, he who uses them badly bad.

That virtue, then, is concerned with pleasures and pains, and that by the acts from which it arises it is both increased and, if they are done differently, destroyed, and that the 15 acts from which it arose are those in which it actualizes itself—let this be taken as said.

4   The question might be asked, what we mean by saying [7] that we must become just by doing just acts, and temperate by doing temperate acts; for if men do just and 20 temperate acts, they are already just and temperate, exactly as, if they do what is in accordance with the laws of grammar and of music, they are grammarians and musicians.

Or is this not true even of the arts? It is possible to do something that is in accordance with the laws of grammar, either by chance or at the suggestion of another. A man 25 will be a grammarian, then, only when he has both done something grammatical and done it grammatically; and this means doing it in accordance with the grammatical knowledge in himself.

Again, the case of the arts and that of the virtues are not similar; for the products of the arts have their goodness in themselves, so that it is enough that they should have a certain character, but if the acts that are in accordance with 30 the virtues have themselves a certain character it does not follow that they are done justly or temperately. The agent also must be in a certain condition when he does them; in the first place he must have knowledge, secondly he must choose the acts, and choose them for their own sakes, and thirdly his action must proceed from a firm and unchangeable character. These are not reckoned in as condi-
1105ᵇ tions of the possession of the arts, except the bare knowledge; but as a condition of the possession of the virtues

[7] 1103ᵃ 31–ᵇ 25, 1104ᵃ 27–ᵇ 3.

knowledge has little or no weight, while the other conditions count not for a little but for everything, i. e. the very conditions which result from often doing just and temperate acts.

Actions, then, are called just and temperate when they 5 are such as the just or the temperate man would do; but it is not the man who does these that is just and temperate, but the man who also does them as just and temperate men do them. It is well said, then, that it is by doing just acts 10 that the just man is produced, and by doing temperate acts the temperate man; without doing these no one would have even a prospect of becoming good.

But most people do not do these, but take refuge in theory and think they are being philosophers and will become good in this way, behaving somewhat like patients 15 who listen attentively to their doctors, but do none of the things they are ordered to do. As the latter will not be made well in body by such a course of treatment, the former will not be made well in soul by such a course of philosophy.

5   Next we must consider what virtue is. Since things that are found in the soul are of three kinds—passions, 20 faculties, states of character, virtue must be one of these. By passions I mean appetite, anger, fear, confidence, envy, joy, friendly feeling, hatred, longing, emulation, pity, and in general the feelings that are accompanied by pleasure or pain; by faculties the things in virtue of which we are said to be capable of feeling these, e. g. of becoming angry or being pained or feeling pity; by states of character the things in virtue of which we stand well or badly with refer- 25 ence to the passions, e. g. with reference to anger we stand badly if we feel it violently or too weakly, and well if we feel it moderately; and similarly with reference to the other passions.

Now neither the virtues nor the vices are *passions*, because we are not called good or bad on the ground of our

30 passions, but are so called on the ground of our virtues and
our vices, and because we are neither praised nor blamed
for our passions (for the man who feels fear or anger is not
praised, nor is the man who simply feels anger blamed,
but the man who feels it in a certain way), but for our
1106ᵃ virtues and our vices we are praised or blamed.

Again, we feel anger and fear without choice, but the
virtues are modes of choice or involve choice. Further, in
respect of the passions we are said to be moved, but in
5 respect of the virtues and the vices we are said not to be
moved but to be disposed in a particular way.

For these reasons also they are not *faculties*; for we are
neither called good nor bad, nor praised nor blamed, for
the simple capacity of feeling the passions; again, we have
the faculties by nature, but we are not made good or bad by
nature; we have spoken of this before.[8]

If, then, the virtues are neither passions nor faculties,
10 all that remains is that they should be *states of character*.

Thus we have stated what virtue is in respect of its genus.

6   We must, however, not only describe virtue as a state
of character, but also say what sort of state it is. We
15 may remark, then, that every virtue or excellence both
brings into good condition the thing of which it is the
excellence and makes the work of that thing be done well;
e. g. the excellence of the eye makes both the eye and its
work good; for it is by the excellence of the eye that we see
well. Similarly the excellence of the horse makes a horse
20 both good in itself and good at running and at carrying its
rider and at awaiting the attack of the enemy. Therefore,
if this is true in every case, the virtue of man also will be
the state of character which makes a man good and which
makes him do his own work well.

How this is to happen we have stated already,[9] but it will
be made plain also by the following consideration of the

[8] 1103ᵃ 18–ᵇ 2.
[9] 1104ᵃ 11–27.

specific nature of virtue. In everything that is continuous 25 and divisible it is possible to take more, less, or an equal amount, and that either in terms of the thing itself or relatively to us; and the equal is an intermediate between excess and defect. By the intermediate in the object I mean that which is equidistant from each of the extremes, which 30 is one and the same for all men; by the intermediate relatively to us that which is neither too much nor too little— and this is not one, nor the same for all. For instance, if ten is many and two is few, six is the intermediate, taken in terms of the object; for it exceeds and is exceeded by an equal amount; this is intermediate according to arithmeti- 35 cal proportion. But the intermediate relatively to us is not to be taken so; if ten pounds are too much for a particular **1106ᵇ** person to eat and two too little, it does not follow that the trainer will order six pounds; for this also is perhaps too much for the person who is to take it, or too little—too little for Milo,[10] too much for the beginner in athletic 5 exercises. The same is true of running and wrestling. Thus a master of any art avoids excess and defect, but seeks the intermediate and chooses this—the intermediate not in the object but relatively to us.

If it is thus, then, that every art does its work well—by looking to the intermediate and judging its works by this standard (so that we often say of good works of art that it 10 is not possible either to take away or to add anything, implying that excess and defect destroy the goodness of works of art, while the mean preserves it; and good artists, as we say, look to this in their work), and if, further, virtue is more exact and better than any art, as nature also is, then virtue must have the quality of aiming at the intermediate. 15 I mean moral virtue; for it is this that is concerned with passions and actions, and in these there is excess, defect, and the intermediate. For instance, both fear and confidence and appetite and anger and pity and in general pleasure and pain may be felt both too much and too little, and

---

[10] A famous wrestler.

20 in both cases not well; but to feel them at the right times, with reference to the right objects, towards the right people, with the right motive, and in the right way, is what is both intermediate and best, and this is characteristic of virtue. Similarly with regard to actions also there is excess, defect, and the intermediate. Now virtue is concerned with 25 passions and actions, in which excess is a form of failure, and so is defect, while the intermediate is praised and is a form of success; and being praised and being successful are both characteristics of virtue. Therefore virtue is a kind of mean, since, as we have seen, it aims at what is intermediate.

Again, it is possible to fail in many ways (for evil belongs to the class of the unlimited, as the Pythagoreans con- 30 jectured, and good to that of the limited), while to succeed is possible only in one way (for which reason also one is easy and the other difficult—to miss the mark easy, to hit it difficult); for these reasons also, then, excess and defect are characteristic of vice, and the mean of virtue;

35   For men are good in but one way, but bad in many.

Virtue, then, is a state of character concerned with choice, lying in a mean, i. e. the mean relative to us, this 1107ᵃ being determined by a rational principle, and by that principle by which the man of practical wisdom would determine it. Now it is a mean between two vices, that which depends on excess and that which depends on defect; and again it is a mean because the vices respectively fall short of or exceed what is right in both passions and actions, 5 while virtue both finds and chooses that which is intermediate. Hence in respect of its substance and the definition which states its essence virtue is a mean, with regard to what is best and right an extreme.

But not every action nor every passion admits of a mean; for some have names that already imply badness, e. g. spite, 10 shamelessness, envy, and in the case of actions adultery, theft, murder; for all of these and suchlike things imply by their names that they are themselves bad, and not the excesses or deficiencies of them. It is not possible, then, ever to be right with regard to them; one must always be wrong. Nor does goodness or badness with regard to such things depend on committing adultery with the right 15 woman, at the right time, and in the right way, but simply to do any of them is to go wrong. It would be equally absurd, then, to expect that in unjust, cowardly, and voluptuous action there should be a mean, an excess, and a deficiency; for at that rate there would be a mean of excess 20 and of deficiency, an excess of excess, and a deficiency of deficiency. But as there is no excess and deficiency of temperance and courage because what is intermediate is in a sense an extreme, so too of the actions we have mentioned there is no mean nor any excess and deficiency, but however they are done they are wrong; for in general there is neither a mean of excess and deficiency, nor excess and 25 deficiency of a mean.

7   We must, however, not only make this general statement, but also apply it to the individual facts. For among statements about conduct those which are general apply more widely, but those which are particular are more genuine, since conduct has to do with individual cases, and 30 our statements must harmonize with the facts in these cases. We may take these cases from our table. With regard to feelings of fear and confidence courage is the mean; of the people who exceed, he who exceeds in fearlessness has **1107ᵇ** no name (many of the states have no name), while the man who exceeds in confidence is rash, and he who exceeds in fear and falls short in confidence is a coward. With regard to pleasures and pains—not all of them, and not so much with regard to the pains—the mean is temperance, 5 the excess self-indulgence. Persons deficient with regard to the pleasures are not often found; hence such persons also have received no name. But let us call them 'insensible'.

With regard to giving and taking of money the mean is
10 liberality, the excess and the defect prodigality and meanness. In these actions people exceed and fall short in contrary ways; the prodigal exceeds in spending and falls short
in taking, while the mean man exceeds in taking and falls
short in spending. (At present we are giving a mere outline
15 or summary, and are satisfied with this; later these states
will be more exactly determined.[11]) With regard to money
there are also other dispositions—a mean, magnificence
(for the magnificent man differs from the liberal man;
the former deals with large sums, the latter with small
ones), and excess, tastelessness and vulgarity, and a defi-
20 ciency, niggardliness; these differ from the states opposed
to liberality, and the mode of their difference will be
stated later.[12]

With regard to honour and dishonour the mean is
proper pride, the excess is known as a sort of 'empty
vanity', and the deficiency is undue humility; and as we
25 said [13] liberality was related to magnificence, differing from
it by dealing with small sums, so there is a state similarly
related to proper pride, being concerned with small honours while that is concerned with great. For it is possible
to desire honour as one ought, and more than one ought,
and less, and the man who exceeds in his desires is called
30 ambitious, the man who falls short unambitious, while the
intermediate person has no name. The dispositions also are
nameless, except that that of the ambitious man is called
ambition. Hence the people who are at the extremes lay
claim to the middle place; and we ourselves sometimes call
the intermediate person ambitious and sometimes unambi-
1108ᵃ tious, and sometimes praise the ambitious man and sometimes the unambitious. The reason of our doing this will
be stated in what follows; [14] but now let us speak of the

---

[11] iv. 1.
[12] 1122ᵃ 20–9, ᵇ 10–18.
[13] ll. 17–19.
[14] ᵇ 11–26, 1125ᵇ 14–18.

remaining states according to the method which has been indicated.

With regard to anger also there is an excess, a deficiency, and a mean. Although they can scarcely be said to have 5 names, yet since we call the intermediate person good-tempered let us call the mean good temper; of the persons at the extremes let the one who exceeds be called irascible, and his vice irascibility, and the man who falls short an inirascible sort of person, and the deficiency inirascibility.

There are also three other means, which have a certain likeness to one another, but differ from one another: for they are all concerned with intercourse in words and ac- 10 tions, but differ in that one is concerned with truth in this sphere, the other two with pleasantness; and of this one kind is exhibited in giving amusement, the other in all the circumstances of life. We must therefore speak of these too, that we may the better see that in all things the mean is praiseworthy, and the extremes neither praiseworthy nor 15 right, but worthy of blame. Now most of these states also have no names, but we must try, as in the other cases, to invent names ourselves so that we may be clear and easy to follow. With regard to truth, then, the intermediate is a truthful sort of person and the mean may be called truth- 20 fulness, while the pretence which exaggerates is boastfulness and the person characterized by it a boaster, and that which understates is mock modesty and the person characterized by it mock-modest. With regard to pleasantness in the giving of amusement the intermediate person is ready-witted and the disposition ready wit, the excess is buffoonery and the person characterized by it a buffoon, while the man who falls short is a sort of boor and his 25 state is boorishness. With regard to the remaining kind of pleasantness, that which is exhibited in life in general, the man who is pleasant in the right way is friendly and the mean is friendliness, while the man who exceeds is an obsequious person if he has no end in view, a flatterer if he is aiming at his own advantage, and the man who falls short

and is unpleasant in all circumstances is a quarrelsome and
surly sort of person.

There are also means in the passions and concerned with
30 the passions; since shame is not a virtue, and yet praise is
extended to the modest man. For even in these matters
one man is said to be intermediate, and another to exceed,
as for instance the bashful man who is ashamed of everything; while he who falls short or is not ashamed of anything at all is shameless, and the intermediate person is
modest. Righteous indignation is a mean between envy
35 and spite, and these states are concerned with the pain and
1108ᵇ pleasures that are felt at the fortunes of our neighbours;
the man who is characterized by righteous indignation is
pained at undeserved good fortune, the envious man,
going beyond him, is pained at all good fortune, and the
5 spiteful man falls so far short of being pained that he even
rejoices. But these states there will be an opportunity of
describing elsewhere; ¹⁵ with regard to justice, since it has
not one simple meaning, we shall, after describing the
other states, distinguish its two kinds and say how each of
10 them is a mean; ¹⁶ and similarly we shall treat also of the
rational virtues.¹⁷

8   There are three kinds of disposition, then, two of
them vices, involving excess and deficiency respectively, and one a virtue, viz. the mean, and all are in a
sense opposed to all; for the extreme states are contrary
both to the intermediate state and to each other, and the
15 intermediate to the extremes; as the equal is greater relatively to the less, less relatively to the greater, so the middle
states are excessive relatively to the deficiencies, deficient

---

¹⁵ The reference may be to the whole treatment of the moral virtues
in iii. 6–iv. 9, or to the discussion of shame in iv. 9 and an intended
corresponding discussion of righteous indignation, or to the discussion
of these two states in Rhet. ii. 6, 9, 10.
¹⁶ 1129ᵃ 26–ᵇ 1, 1130ᵃ 14–ᵇ 5, 1131ᵇ 9–15, 1132ᵃ 24–30, 1133ᵇ
30–1134ᵃ 1.
¹⁷ Bk. vi.

relatively to the excesses, both in passions and in actions. For the brave man appears rash relatively to the coward, 20 and cowardly relatively to the rash man; and similarly the temperate man appears self-indulgent relatively to the insensible man, insensible relatively to the self-indulgent, and the liberal man prodigal relatively to the mean man, mean relatively to the prodigal. Hence also the people at the extremes push the intermediate man each over to the other, and the brave man is called rash by the coward, cowardly by 25 the rash man, and correspondingly in the other cases.

These states being thus opposed to one another, the greatest contrariety is that of the extremes to each other, rather than to the intermediate; for these are further from each other than from the intermediate, as the great is further from the small and the small from the great than 30 both are from the equal. Again, to the intermediate some extremes show a certain likeness, as that of rashness to courage and that of prodigality to liberality; but the extremes show the greatest unlikeness to each other; now contraries are defined as the things that are furthest from each other, so that things that are further apart are more 35 contrary.

To the mean in some cases the deficiency, in some the 1109ᵃ excess is more opposed; e. g. it is not rashness, which is an excess, but cowardice, which is a deficiency, that is more opposed to courage, and not insensibility, which is a deficiency, but self-indulgence, which is an excess, that is 5 more opposed to temperance. This happens from two reasons, one being drawn from the thing itself; for because one extreme is nearer and liker to the intermediate, we oppose not this but rather its contrary to the intermediate. E. g., since rashness is thought liker and nearer to courage, and cowardice more unlike, we oppose rather the latter to 10 courage; for things that are further from the intermediate are thought more contrary to it. This, then, is one cause, drawn from the thing itself; another is drawn from ourselves; for the things to which we ourselves more naturally

tend seem more contrary to the intermediate. For instance,
15 we ourselves tend more naturally to pleasures, and hence
are more easily carried away towards self-indulgence than
towards propriety. We describe as contrary to the mean,
then, rather the directions in which we more often go to
great lengths; and therefore self-indulgence, which is an
excess, is the more contrary to temperance.

9   That moral virtue is a mean, then, and in what sense
20   it is so, and that it is a mean between two vices, the
one involving excess, the other deficiency, and that it is
such because its character is to aim at what is intermediate
in passions and in actions, has been sufficiently stated.
Hence also it is no easy task to be good. For in everything
it is no easy task to find the middle, e. g. to find the
25 middle of a circle is not for every one but for him who
knows; so, too, any one can get angry—that is easy—or give
or spend money; but to do this to the right person, to the
right extent, at the right time, with the right motive, and in
the right way, that is not for every one, nor is it easy; wherefore goodness is both rare and laudable and noble.

Hence he who aims at the intermediate must first de-
30 part from what is the more contrary to it, as Calypso advises—

Hold the ship out beyond that surf and spray.[18]

For of the extremes one is more erroneous, one less so;
therefore, since to hit the mean is hard in the extreme, we
must as a second best, as people say, take the least of the
35 evils; and this will be done best in the way we describe.

But we must consider the things towards which we our-
1109ᵇ selves also are easily carried away; for some of us tend to
one thing, some to another; and this will be recognizable
from the pleasure and the pain we feel. We must drag

---

[18] *Od.* xii. 219 f. (Mackail's trans.). But it was Circe who gave the
advice (xii. 108), and the actual quotation is from Odysseus' orders
to his steersman.

ourselves away to the contrary extreme; for we shall get 5
into the intermediate state by drawing well away from error,
as people do in straightening sticks that are bent.

Now in everything the pleasant or pleasure is most to be
guarded against; for we do not judge it impartially. We
ought, then, to feel towards pleasure as the elders of the
people felt towards Helen, and in all circumstances repeat
their saying; [19] for if we dismiss pleasure thus we are less 10
likely to go astray. It is by doing this, then, (to sum the
matter up) that we shall best be able to hit the mean.

But this is no doubt difficult, and especially in individual
cases; for it is not easy to determine both how and with 15
whom and on what provocation and how long one should
be angry; for we too sometimes praise those who fall short
and call them good-tempered, but sometimes we praise
those who get angry and call them manly. The man, however, who deviates little from goodness is not blamed,
whether he do so in the direction of the more or of the
less, but only the man who deviates more widely; for *he*
does not fail to be noticed. But up to what point and to 20
what extent a man must deviate before he becomes blameworthy it is not easy to determine by reasoning, any more
than anything else that is perceived by the senses; such
things depend on particular facts, and the decision rests
with perception. So much, then, is plain, that the intermediate state is in all things to be praised, but that we must 25
incline sometimes towards the excess, sometimes towards
the deficiency; for so shall we most easily hit the mean and
what is right.

BOOK III

1   Since virtue is concerned with passions and actions, 30
and on voluntary passions and actions praise and
blame are bestowed, on those that are involuntary pardon,
and sometimes also pity, to distinguish the voluntary and

[19] *Il.* iii. 156–60.

the involuntary is presumably necessary for those who are studying the nature of virtue, and useful also for legislators with a view to the assigning both of honours and of punishments.

35   Those things, then, are thought involuntary, which take
1110ᵃ place under compulsion or owing to ignorance; and that is compulsory of which the moving principle is outside, being a principle in which nothing is contributed by the person who is acting or is feeling the passion, e. g. if he were to be carried somewhere by a wind, or by men who had him in their power.

But with regard to the things that are done from fear of
5 greater evils or for some noble object (e. g. if a tyrant were to order one to do something base, having one's parents and children in his power, and if one did the action they were to be saved, but otherwise would be put to death), it may be debated whether such actions are involuntary or voluntary. Something of the sort happens also with regard to the throwing of goods overboard in a
10 storm; for in the abstract no one throws goods away voluntarily, but on condition of its securing the safety of himself and his crew any sensible man does so. Such actions, then, are mixed, but are more like voluntary actions; for they are worthy of choice at the time when they are done, and the end of an action is relative to the occasion. Both the terms, then, 'voluntary' and 'involuntary', must be used with reference to the moment of action. Now the man acts
15 voluntarily; for the principle that moves the instrumental parts of the body in such actions is in him, and the things of which the moving principle is in a man himself are in his power to do or not to do. Such actions, therefore, are voluntary, but in the abstract perhaps involuntary; for no one would choose any such act in itself.

For such actions men are sometimes even praised, when
20 they endure something base or painful in return for great and noble objects gained; in the opposite case they are blamed, since to endure the greatest indignities for no

noble end or for a trifling end is the mark of an inferior person. On some actions praise indeed is not bestowed, but pardon is, when one does what he ought not under pressure which overstrains human nature and which no one 25 could withstand. But some acts, perhaps, we cannot be forced to do, but ought rather to face death after the most fearful sufferings; for the things that 'forced' Euripides' Alcmaeon to slay his mother seem absurd. It is difficult sometimes to determine what should be chosen at what cost, and what should be endured in return for what gain, and yet more difficult to abide by our decisions; for as a 30 rule what is expected is painful, and what we are forced to do is base, whence praise and blame are bestowed on those who have been compelled or have not.

What sort of acts, then, should be called compulsory? We answer that without qualification actions are so when **1110ᵇ** the cause is in the external circumstances and the agent contributes nothing. But the things that in themselves are involuntary, but now and in return for these gains are worthy of choice, and whose moving principle is in the agent, are in themselves involuntary, but now and in return 5 for these gains voluntary. They are more like voluntary acts; for actions are in the class of particulars, and the particular acts here are voluntary. What sort of things are to be chosen, and in return for what, it is not easy to state; for there are many differences in the particular cases.

But if some one were to say that pleasant and noble objects have a compelling power, forcing us from without, all acts would be for him compulsory; for it is for these objects that all men do everything they do. And those who 10 act under compulsion and unwillingly act with pain, but those who do acts for their pleasantness and nobility do them with pleasure; it is absurd to make external circumstances responsible, and not oneself, as being easily caught by such attractions, and to make oneself responsible for noble acts but the pleasant objects responsible for base acts. 15 The compulsory, then, seems to be that whose moving principle is outside, the person compelled contributing nothing.

Everything that is done by reason of ignorance is *not* voluntary; it is only what produces pain and repentance that is *in*voluntary. For the man who has done something
20 owing to ignorance, and feels not the least vexation at his action, has not acted voluntarily, since he did not know what he was doing, nor yet involuntarily, since he is not pained. Of people, then, who act by reason of ignorance he who repents is thought an involuntary agent, and the man who does not repent may, since he is different, be called a not voluntary agent; for, since he differs from the other, it is better that he should have a name of his own.

Acting by reason of ignorance seems also to be different
25 from acting *in* ignorance; for the man who is drunk or in a rage is thought to act as a result not of ignorance but of one of the causes mentioned, yet not knowingly but in ignorance.

Now every wicked man is ignorant of what he ought to do and what he ought to abstain from, and it is by reason of error of this kind that men become unjust and in general
30 bad; but the term 'involuntary' tends to be used not if a man is ignorant of what is to his advantage—for it is not mistaken purpose that causes involuntary action (it leads rather to wickedness), nor ignorance of the universal (for *that* men are *blamed*), but ignorance of particulars, i. e. of the circumstances of the action and the objects with
1111ᵃ which it is concerned. For it is on these that both pity and pardon depend, since the person who is ignorant of any of these acts involuntarily.

Perhaps it is just as well, therefore, to determine their nature and number. A man may be ignorant, then, of who he is, what he is doing, what or whom he is acting on, and
5 sometimes also what (e. g. what instrument) he is doing it with, and to what end (e. g. he may think his act will con- duce to some one's safety), and how he is doing it (e. g. whether gently or violently). Now of all of these no one

could be ignorant unless he were mad, and evidently also
he could not be ignorant of the agent; for how could he not
know himself? But of what he is doing a man might be
ignorant, as for instance people say 'it slipped out of their
mouths as they were speaking', or 'they did not know it 10
was a secret', as Aeschylus said of the mysteries, or a man
might say he 'let it go off when he merely wanted to
show its working', as the man did with the catapult. Again,
one might think one's son was an enemy, as Merope did,
or that a pointed spear had a button on it, or that a stone
was pumice-stone; or one might give a man a draught to
save him, and really kill him; or one might want to touch a
man, as people do in sparring, and really wound him. The 15
ignorance may relate, then, to any of these things, i. e. of
the circumstances of the action, and the man who was
ignorant of any of these is thought to have acted involuntarily, and especially if he was ignorant on the most important points; and these are thought to be the circumstances of the action and its end. Further, the doing of an
act that is called involuntary in virtue of ignorance of this
sort must be painful and involve repentance.   20

Since that which is done under compulsion or by
reason of ignorance is involuntary, the voluntary would
seem to be that of which the moving principle is in the
agent himself, he being aware of the particular circumstances of the action. Presumably acts done by reason of
anger or appetite are not rightly called involuntary.[1] For in
the first place, on that showing none of the other animals 25
will act voluntarily, nor will children; and secondly, is it
meant that we do not do voluntarily any of the acts that
are due to appetite or anger, or that we do the noble acts
voluntarily and the base acts involuntarily? Is not this absurd, when one and the same thing is the cause? But it
would surely be odd to describe as involuntary the things
one ought to desire; and we ought both to be angry at 30

[1] A reference to Pl. *Laws* 863 B, ff., where anger and appetite are
coupled with ignorance as sources of wrong action.

certain things and to have an appetite for certain things,
e. g. for health and for learning. Also what is involuntary is
thought to be painful, but what is in accordance with appetite is thought to be pleasant. Again, what is the difference
in respect of involuntariness between errors committed
upon calculation and those committed in anger? Both are
1111ᵇ to be avoided, but the irrational passions are thought not
less human than reason is, and therefore also the actions
which proceed from anger or appetite are the man's actions.
It would be odd, then, to treat them as involuntary.

2   Both the voluntary and the involuntary having been
delimited, we must next discuss choice; for it is
5 thought to be most closely bound up with virtue and to
discriminate characters better than actions do.

Choice, then, seems to be voluntary, but not the same
thing as the voluntary; the latter extends more widely. For
both children and the lower animals share in voluntary
action, but not in choice, and acts done on the spur of the
moment we describe as voluntary, but not as chosen.

10   Those who say it is appetite or anger or wish or a kind of
opinion do not seem to be right. For choice is not common
to irrational creatures as well, but appetite and anger are.
Again, the incontinent man acts with appetite, but not
15 with choice; while the continent man on the contrary acts
with choice, but not with appetite. Again, appetite is contrary to choice, but not appetite to appetite. Again, appetite
relates to the pleasant and the painful, choice neither to
the painful nor to the pleasant.

Still less is it anger; for acts due to anger are thought to
be less than any others objects of choice.

20   But neither is it wish, though it seems near to it; for
choice cannot relate to impossibles, and if any one said he
chose them he would be thought silly; but there may be a
wish even for impossibles, e. g. for immortality. And wish
may relate to things that could in no way be brought about
25 by one's own efforts, e. g. that a particular actor or athlete

should win in a competition; but no one chooses such things, but only the things that he thinks could be brought about by his own efforts. Again, wish relates rather to the end, choice to the means; for instance, we wish to be healthy, but we choose the acts which will make us healthy, and we wish to be happy and say we do, but we cannot well say we choose to be so; for, in general, choice seems to relate to the things that are in our own power.

For this reason, too, it cannot be opinion; for opinion 30 is thought to relate to all kinds of things, no less to eternal things and impossible things than to things in our own power; and it is distinguished by its falsity or truth, not by its badness or goodness, while choice is distinguished rather by these.

Now with opinion in general perhaps no one even says it is identical. But it is not identical even with any kind of 1112ᵃ opinion; for by choosing what is good or bad we are men of a certain character, which we are not by holding certain opinions. And we choose to get or avoid something good or bad, but we have opinions about what a thing is or whom it is good for or how it is good for him; we can hardly be said to opine to get or avoid anything. And choice is 5 praised for being related to the right object rather than for being rightly related to it, opinion for being truly related to its object. And we choose what we best know to be good, but we opine what we do not quite know; and it is not the same people that are thought to make the best choices and to have the best opinions, but some are thought to have fairly good opinions, but by reason of vice to choose what they should not. If opinion precedes choice or accompanies 10 it, that makes no difference; for it is not this that we are considering, but whether it is *identical* with some kind of opinion.

What, then, or what kind of thing is it, since it is none of the things we have mentioned? It seems to be voluntary, but not all that is voluntary to be an object of choice. Is it, then, what has been decided on by previous deliberation? 15

At any rate choice involves a rational principle and thought.
Even the name seems to suggest that it is what is chosen
before other things.

3 Do we deliberate about everything, and is everything
a possible subject of deliberation, or is deliberation
20 impossible about some things? We ought presumably to
call not what a fool or a madman would deliberate about,
but what a sensible man would deliberate about, a subject
of deliberation. Now about eternal things no one deliberates, e. g. about the material universe or the incommensurability of the diagonal and the side of a square. But
no more do we deliberate about the things that involve
movement but always happen in the same way, whether of
25 necessity or by nature or from any other cause, e. g. the
solstices and the risings of the stars; nor about things that
happen now in one way, now in another, e. g. droughts and
rains; nor about chance events, like the finding of treasure.
But we do not deliberate even about all human affairs; for
instance, no Spartan deliberates about the best constitution
for the Scythians. For none of these things can be brought
about by our own efforts.

We deliberate about things that are in our power and can
30 be done; and these are in fact what is left. For nature,
necessity, and chance are thought to be causes, and also
reason and everything that depends on man. Now every
class of men deliberates about the things that can be done
by their own efforts. And in the case of exact and self-con-
tained sciences there is no deliberation, e. g. about the let-
1112ᵇ ters of the alphabet (for we have no doubt how they
should be written); but the things that are brought about
by our own efforts, but not always in the same way, are
the things about which we deliberate, e. g. questions of
medical treatment or of money-making. And we do so more
5 in the case of the art of navigation than in that of gymnastics, inasmuch as it has been less exactly worked out,
and again about other things in the same ratio, and more

also in the case of the arts than in that of the sciences; for we have more doubt about the former. Deliberation is concerned with things that happen in a certain way for the most part, but in which the event is obscure, and with things in which it is indeterminate. We call in others to aid us in deliberation on important questions, distrusting ourselves as not being equal to deciding.

We deliberate not about ends but about means. For a doctor does not deliberate whether he shall heal, nor an orator whether he shall persuade, nor a statesman whether he shall produce law and order, nor does any one else deliberate about his end. They assume the end and consider how and by what means it is to be attained; and if it seems to be produced by several means they consider by which it is most easily and best produced, while if it is achieved by one only they consider how it will be achieved by this and by what means *this* will be achieved, till they come to the first cause, which in the order of discovery is last. For the person who deliberates seems to investigate and analyse in the way described as though he were analysing a geometrical construction [2] (not all investigation appears to be deliberation—for instance mathematical investigations —but all deliberation is investigation), and what is last in the order of analysis seems to be first in the order of becoming. And if we come on an impossibility, we give up the search, e. g. if we need money and this cannot be got; but if a thing appears possible we try to do it. By 'possible' things I mean things that might be brought about by our own efforts, and these in a sense include things that can be brought about by the efforts of our friends, since the moving principle is in ourselves. The subject of investigation is sometimes the instruments, sometimes the use of

[2] Aristotle has in mind the method of discovering the solution of a geometrical problem. The problem being to construct a figure of a certain kind, we suppose it constructed and then analyse it to see if there is some figure by constructing which we can construct the required figure, and so on till we come to a figure which our existing knowledge enables us to construct.

30 them; and similarly in the other cases—sometimes the
means, sometimes the mode of using it or the means of
bringing it about. It seems, then, as has been said, that man
is a moving principle of actions; now deliberation is about
the things to be done by the agent himself, and actions are
for the sake of things other than themselves. For the end
cannot be a subject of deliberation, but only the means;
1113ᵃ nor indeed can the particular facts be a subject of it, as
whether this is bread or has been baked as it should; for
these are matters of perception. If we are to be always deliberating, we shall have to go on to infinity.

The same thing is deliberated upon and is chosen, except that the object of choice is already determinate, since
5 it is that which has been decided upon as a result of deliberation that is the object of choice. For every one ceases
to inquire how he is to act when he has brought the moving
principle back to himself and to the ruling part of himself;
for this is what chooses. This is plain also from the ancient
constitutions, which Homer represented; for the kings announced their choices to the people. The object of choice
10 being one of the things in our own power which is desired
after deliberation, choice will be deliberate desire of things
in our own power; for when we have decided as a result of
deliberation, we desire in accordance with our deliberation.

We may take it, then, that we have described choice in
outline, and stated the nature of its objects and the fact
that it is concerned with means.

4   That wish is for the end has already been stated; [3]
15   some think it is for the good, others for the apparent
good. Now those who say that the good is the object of
wish must admit in consequence that that which the man
who does not choose aright wishes for is not an object of
wish (for if it is to be so, it must also be good; but it was, if
it so happened, bad); while those who say the apparent
20 good is the object of wish must admit that there is no

[3] 1111ᵇ 26.

natural object of wish, but only what seems good to each man. Now different things appear good to different people, and, if it so happens, even contrary things.

If these consequences are unpleasing, are we to say that absolutely and in truth the good is the object of wish, but for each person the apparent good; that that which is in 25 truth an object of wish is an object of wish to the good man, while any chance thing may be so to the bad man, as in the case of bodies also the things that are in truth wholesome are wholesome for bodies which are in good condition, while for those that are diseased other things are wholesome—or bitter or sweet or hot or heavy, and so on; since the good man judges each class of things rightly, and in each the truth appears to him? For each state of char- 30 acter has its own ideas of the noble and the pleasant, and perhaps the good man differs from others most by seeing the truth in each class of things, being as it were the norm and measure of them. In most things the error seems to be due to pleasure; for it appears a good when it is not. We therefore choose the pleasant as a good, and avoid pain as **1113ᵇ** an evil.

5   The end, then, being what we wish for, the means
       what we deliberate about and choose, actions concerning means must be according to choice and voluntary. Now the exercise of the virtues is concerned with means. 5 Therefore virtue also is in our own power, and so too vice. For where it is in our power to act it is also in our power not to act, and *vice versa*; so that, if to act, where this is noble, is in our power, not to act, which will be base, will also be in our power, and if not to act, where this is noble, 10 is in our power, to act, which will be base, will also be in our power. Now if it is in our power to do noble or base acts, and likewise in our power not to do them, and this was what being good or bad meant,[4] then it is in our power to be virtuous or vicious.

⁴ 1112ᵃ 1 f.

The saying that 'no one is voluntarily wicked nor in-
15 voluntarily happy' seems to be partly false and partly true;
for no one is involuntarily happy, but wickedness *is* voluntary. Or else we shall have to dispute what has just been
said, at any rate, and deny that man is a moving principle
or begetter of his actions as of children. But if these facts
are evident and we cannot refer actions to moving prin-
20 ciples other than those in ourselves, the acts whose moving
principles are in us must themselves also be in our power
and voluntary.

Witness seems to be borne to this both by individuals
in their private capacity and by legislators themselves; for
these punish and take vengeance on those who do wicked
acts (unless they have acted under compulsion or as a re-
25 sult of ignorance for which they are not themselves responsible), while they honour those who do noble acts, as
though they meant to encourage the latter and deter the
former. But no one is encouraged to do the things that are
neither in our power nor voluntary; it is assumed that
there is no gain in being persuaded not to be hot or in
30 pain or hungry or the like, since we shall experience these
feelings none the less. Indeed, we punish a man for his
very ignorance, if he is thought responsible for the ignorance, as when penalties are doubled in the case of
drunkenness; for the moving principle is in the man himself, since he had the power of not getting drunk and his
getting drunk was the cause of his ignorance. And we
punish those who are ignorant of anything in the laws that
1114ᵃ they ought to know and that is not difficult, and so too in
the case of anything else that they are thought to be ignorant of through carelessness; we assume that it is in
their power not to be ignorant, since they have the power
of taking care.

But perhaps a man is the kind of man not to take care.
Still they are themselves by their slack lives responsible for
5 becoming men of that kind, and men make themselves
responsible for being unjust or self-indulgent, in the one

case by cheating and in the other by spending their time in drinking bouts and the like; for it is activities exercised on particular objects that make the corresponding character. This is plain from the case of people training for any contest or action; they practice the activity the whole time. Now not to know that it is from the exercise of activities on particular objects that states of character 10 are produced is the mark of a thoroughly senseless person. Again, it is irrational to suppose that a man who acts unjustly does not wish to be unjust or a man who acts self-indulgently to be self-indulgent. But if *without* being ignorant a man does the things which will make him unjust, he will be unjust voluntarily. Yet it does not follow that if he wishes he will cease to be unjust and will be just. For neither does the man who is ill become well on those terms. We may suppose a case in which he is ill volun- 15 tarily, through living incontinently and disobeying his doctors. In that case it was *then* open to him not to be ill, but not now, when he has thrown away his chance, just as when you have let a stone go it is too late to recover it; but yet it was in your power to throw it, since the moving principle was in you. So, too, to the unjust and to the self-indulgent man it was open at the beginning not to be- 20 come men of this kind, and so they are unjust and self-indulgent voluntarily; but now that they have become so it is not possible for them not to be so.

But not only are the vices of the soul voluntary, but those of the body also for some men, whom we accordingly blame; while no one blames those who are ugly by nature, we blame those who are so owing to want of exercise and care. So it is, too, with respect to weakness and infirmity; 25 no one would reproach a man blind from birth or by disease or from a blow, but rather pity him, while every one would blame a man who was blind from drunkenness or some other form of self-indulgence. Of vices of the body, then, those in our own power are blamed, those not in our power are not. And if this be so, in the other cases 30 also the vices that are blamed must be in our own power.

Now some one may say that all men desire the apparent good, but have no control over the appearance, but the end appears to each man in a form answering to his **1114ᵇ** character. We reply that if each man is somehow responsible for his state of mind, he will also be himself somehow responsible for the appearance; but if not, no one is responsible for his own evildoing, but every one does evil acts through ignorance of the end, thinking that by these 5 he will get what is best, and the aiming at the end is not self-chosen but one must be born with an eye, as it were, by which to judge rightly and choose what is truly good, and he is well endowed by nature who is well endowed with this. For it is what is greatest and most noble, and 10 what we cannot get or learn from another, but must have just such as it was when given us at birth, and to be well and nobly endowed with this will be perfect and true excellence of natural endowment. If this is true, then, how will virtue be more voluntary than vice? To both men 15 alike, the good and the bad, the end appears and is fixed by nature or however it may be, and it is by referring everything else to this that men do whatever they do.

Whether, then, it is not by nature that the end appears to each man such as it does appear, but something also depends on him, or the end is natural but because the good 20 man adopts the means voluntarily virtue is voluntary, vice also will be none the less voluntary; for in the case of the bad man there is equally present that which depends on himself in his actions even if not in his end. If, then, as is asserted, the virtues are voluntary (for we are ourselves somehow partly responsible for our states of character, and it is by being persons of a certain kind that we assume the end to be so and so), the vices also will be voluntary; 25 for the same is true of them.

With regard to the virtues in general we have stated their genus in outline, viz. that they are means and that they are states of character, and that they tend, and by their own nature, to the doing of the acts by which they are produced, and that they are in our power and volun- 30 tary, and act as the right rule prescribes. But actions and states of character are not voluntary in the same way; for we are masters of our actions from the beginning right to the end, if we know the particular facts, but though we control the beginning of our states of character the gradual 1115ᵃ progress is not obvious, any more than it is in illnesses; because it was in our power, however, to act in this way or not in this way, therefore the states are voluntary.

Let us take up the several virtues, however, and say which they are and what sort of things they are concerned with and how they are concerned with them; at the same 5 time it will become plain how many they are. And first let us speak of courage.

6 That it is a mean with regard to feelings of fear and confidence has already been made evident;⁵ and plainly the things we fear are terrible things, and these are, to speak without qualification, evils; for which reason 10 people even define fear as expectation of evil. Now we fear all evils, e. g. disgrace, poverty, disease, friendliness, death, but the brave man is not thought to be concerned with all; for to fear some things is even right and noble, and it is base not to fear them—e. g. disgrace; he who fears this is good and modest, and he who does not is shameless. He is, however, by some people called brave, by a transference of the word to a new meaning; for he has in him something which is like the brave man, since the brave man also is a 15 fearless person. Poverty and disease we perhaps ought not to fear, nor in general the things that do not proceed from vice and are not due to a man himself. But not even the man who is fearless of these is brave. Yet we apply the word to him also in virtue of a similarity; for some who in 20 the dangers of war are cowards are liberal and are confident in face of the loss of money. Nor is a man a coward if

⁵ 1107ᵃ 33–ᵇ 4.

he fears insult to his wife and children or envy or anything of the kind; nor brave if he is confident when he is about to be flogged. With what sort of terrible things, then, is the brave man concerned? Surely with the greatest; for no 25 one is more likely than he to stand his ground against what is awe-inspiring. Now death is the most terrible of all things; for it is the end, and nothing is thought to be any longer either good or bad for the dead. But the brave man would not seem to be concerned even with death in *all* circumstances, e. g. at sea or in disease. In what circumstances, then? Surely in the noblest. Now such deaths are 30 those in battle; for these take place in the greatest and noblest danger. And these are correspondingly honoured in city-states and at the courts of monarchs. Properly, then, he will be called brave who is fearless in face of a noble death, and of all emergencies that involve death; and the emergencies of war are in the highest degree of this kind. 35 Yet at sea also, and in disease; the brave man is fearless, 1115ᵇ but not in the same way as the seamen; for he has given up hope of safety, and is disliking the thought of death in this shape, while they are hopeful because of their experience. At the same time, we show courage in situations where 5 there is the opportunity of showing prowess or where death is noble; but in these forms of death neither of these conditions is fulfilled.

7   What is terrible is not the same for all men; but we say there are things terrible even beyond human strength. These, then, are terrible to every one—at least to every sensible man; but the terrible things that are *not* beyond human strength differ in magnitude and degree, and so too do the things that inspire confidence. Now the 10 brave man is as dauntless as man may be. Therefore, while he will fear even the things that are not beyond human strength, he will face them as he ought and as the rule directs, for honour's sake; for this is the end of virtue. But it is possible to fear these more, or less, and again to fear 15 things that are not terrible as if they were. Of the faults that are committed one consists in fearing what one should not, another in fearing as we should not, another in fearing when we should not, and so on; and so too with respect to the things that inspire confidence. The man, then, who faces and who fears the right things and from the right motive, in the right way and at the right time, and who feels confidence under the corresponding conditions, is brave; for the brave man feels and acts according to the merits of the case and in whatever way the rule directs. Now the end 20 of every activity is conformity to the corresponding state of character. This is true, therefore, of the brave man as well as of others. But courage is noble. Therefore the end also is noble; for each thing is defined by its end. Therefore it is for a noble end that the brave man endures and acts as courage directs.

Of those who go to excess he who exceeds in fearlessness has no name (we have said previously that many states of 25 character have no names [6]), but he would be a sort of madman or insensible person if he feared nothing, neither earthquakes nor the waves, as they say the Celts do not; while the man who exceeds in confidence about what really is terrible is rash. The rash man, however, is also thought to be boastful and only a pretender to courage; at all events, 30 as the brave man *is* with regard to what is terrible, so the rash man wishes to *appear*; and so he imitates him in situations where he can. Hence also most of them are a mixture of rashness and cowardice; for, while in these situations they display confidence, they do not hold their ground against what is really terrible. The man who exceeds in fear is a coward; for he fears both what he ought not and as he 35 ought not, and all the similar characterizations attach to 1116ᵃ him. He is lacking also in confidence; but he is more conspicuous for his excess of fear in painful situations. The coward, then, is a despairing sort of person; for he fears everything. The brave man, on the other hand, has the opposite disposition; for confidence is the mark of a hopeful disposition. The coward, the rash man, and the brave man,

[6] 1107ᵇ 2, Cf. 1107ᵇ 29, 1108ᵃ 5.

5 then, are concerned with the same objects but are differently disposed towards them; for the first two exceed and
fall short, while the third holds the middle, which is the
right, position; and rash men are precipitate, and wish for
dangers beforehand but draw back when they are in them,
while brave men are keen in the moment of action, but
quiet beforehand.

10   As we have said, then, courage is a mean with respect
to things that inspire confidence or fear, in the circumstances that have been stated;[7] and it chooses or endures
things because it is noble to do so, or because it is base not
to do so.[8] But to die to escape from poverty or love or anything painful is not the mark of a brave man, but rather of
a coward; for it is softness to fly from what is troublesome,
and such a man endures death not because it is noble but
to fly from evil.

8   Courage, then, is something of this sort, but the name
15   is also applied to five other kinds. (1) First comes the
courage of the citizen-soldier; for this is most like true courage. Citizen-soldiers seem to face dangers because of the
penalties imposed by the laws and the reproaches they
would otherwise incur, and because of the honours they
win by such action; and therefore those peoples seem to
20 be bravest among whom cowards are held in dishonour and
brave men in honour. This is the kind of courage that
Homer depicts, e. g. in Diomede and in Hector:

First will Polydamas be to heap reproach on me then;[9]

and

25   For Hector one day 'mid the Trojans shall utter his vault-
ing harangue:
"Afraid was Tydeides, and fled from my face"[10]

[7] Ch. 6.
[8] 1115^b 11–24.
[9] Il. xxii. 100.
[10] Il. viii. 148, 149.

This kind of courage is most like to that which we described earlier,[11] because it is due to virtue; for it is due to shame and to desire of a nobel object (i. e. honour) and avoidance of disgrace, which is ignoble. One might rank in the same class even those who are compelled by their 30 rulers; but they are inferior, inasmuch as they do what they do not from shame but from fear, and to avoid not what is disgraceful but what is painful; for their masters compel them, as Hector [12] does:

But if I shall spy any dastard that cowers far from the fight,
Vainly will such an one hope to escape from the dogs.   35

And those who give them their posts, and beat them if they retreat, do the same, and so do those who draw them up with trenches or something of the sort behind them; all 1116ᵇ of these apply compulsion. But one ought to be brave not under compulsion but because it is noble to be so.

(2) Experience with regard to particular facts is also thought to be courage; this is indeed the reason why Socrates thought courage was knowledge. Other people exhibit this quality in other dangers, and professional sol- 5 diers exhibit it in the dangers of war; for there seem to be many empty alarms in war, of which these have had the most comprehensive experience; therefore they seem brave, because the others do not know the nature of the facts. Again, their experience makes them most capable in attack 10 and in defence, since they can use their arms and have the kind that are likely to be best both for attack and for defence; therefore they fight like armed men against unarmed or like trained athletes against amateurs; for in such contests too it is not the bravest men that fight best, but those who are strongest and have their bodies in the best condi- 15 tion. Professional soldiers turn cowards, however, when the

---

[11] Chs. 6, 7.
[12] Aristotle's quotation is more like *Il.* ii. 391–3, where Agamemnon speaks, than xv. 348–51, where Hector speaks.

danger puts too great a strain on them and they are inferior in numbers and equipment; for they are the first to
fly, while citizen-forces die at their posts, as in fact happened at the temple of Hermes.[13] For to the latter flight is
20 disgraceful and death is preferable to safety on those terms;
while the former from the very beginning faced the danger
on the assumption that they were stronger, and when they
know the facts they fly, fearing death more than disgrace;
but the brave man is not that sort of person.

(3) Passion also is sometimes reckoned as courage; those
who act from passion, like wild beasts rushing at those who
25 have wounded them, are thought to be brave, because brave
men also are passionate; for passion above all things is eager
to rush on danger, and hence Homer's 'put strength into his
passion' [14] and 'aroused their spirit and passion' [15] and 'hard
he breathed panting' [16] and 'his blood boiled'.[17] For all
such expressions seem to indicate the stirring and onset of
30 passion. Now brave men act for honour's sake, but passion
aids them; while wild beasts act under the influence of pain;
for they attack because they have been wounded or because
they are afraid, since if they are in a forest they do not come
near one. Thus they are not brave because, driven by pain
35 and passion, they rush on danger without foreseeing any of
the perils, since at that rate even asses would be brave when
1117ᵃ they are hungry; for blows will not drive them from their
food; and lust also makes adulterers do many daring things.
[Those creatures are not brave, then, which are driven on
to danger by pain or passion.] The 'courage' that is due to
passion seems to be the most natural, and to be courage if
choice and motive be added.

5   Men, then, as well as beasts, suffer pain when they are

13 The reference is to a battle at Coronea in the Sacred War, c.
353 B. C., in which the Phocians defeated the citizens of Coronea and
some Boeotian regulars.
14 This is a conflation of Il. xi. 11 or xiv. 151 and xvi. 529.
15 Cf. Il. v. 470, xv. 232, 594.
16 Cf. Od. xxiv. 318 f.
17 The phrase does not occur in Homer; it is found in Theocr. xx. 15.

angry, and are pleased when they exact their revenge; those who fight for these reasons, however, are pugnacious but not brave; for they do not act for honour's sake nor as the rule directs, but from strength of feeling; they have, however, something akin to courage.

(4) Nor are sanguine people brave; for they are confident in danger only because they have conquered often and 10 against many foes. Yet they closely resemble brave men, because both are confident; but brave men are confident for the reasons stated earlier,[18] while these are so because they think they are the strongest and can suffer nothing. (Drunken men also behave in this way; they become sanguine.) When their adventures do not succeed, however, they run away; but it was [18] the mark of a brave man to face 15 things that are, and seem, terrible for a man, because it is noble to do so and disgraceful not to do so. Hence also it is thought the mark of a braver man to be fearless and undisturbed in sudden alarms than to be so in those that are foreseen; for it must have proceeded more from a state of character, because less from preparation; acts that are foreseen may be chosen by calculation and rule, but sudden 20 actions must be in accordance with one's state of character.

(5) People who are ignorant of the danger also appear brave, and they are not far removed from those of a sanguine temper, but are inferior inasmuch as they have no self-reliance while these have. Hence also the sanguine hold their ground for a time; but those who have been deceived 25 about the facts fly if they know or suspect that these are different from what they supposed, as happened to the Argives when they fell in with the Spartans and took them for Sicyonians.[19]

9　We have, then, described the character both of brave men and of those who are thought to be brave.

Though courage is concerned with feelings of confidence

---

[18] 1115^{b} 11–24.
[19] At the Long Walls of Corinth, 392 B. C. Cf. Xen. *Hell.* iv. 4. 10.

and of fear, it is not concerned with both alike, but more
with the things that inspire fear; for he who is undisturbed
30 in face of these and bears himself as he should towards
these is more truly brave than the man who does so towards
the things that inspire confidence. It is for facing what is
painful, then, as has been said,[20] that men are called brave.
Hence also courage involves pain, and is justly praised; for
it is harder to face what is painful than to abstain from what
is pleasant. Yet the end which courage sets before it would
35 seem to be pleasant, but to be concealed by the attending
1117ᵇ circumstances, as happens also in athletic contests; for the
end at which boxers aim is pleasant—the crown and the
honours—but the blows they take are distressing to flesh
5 and blood, and painful, and so is their whole exertion; and
because the blows and the exertions are many the end,
which is but small, appears to have nothing pleasant in it.
And so, if the case of courage is similar, death and wounds
will be painful to the brave man and against his will, but
he will face them because it is noble to do so or because it
is base not to do so. And the more he is possessed of virtue
10 in its entirety and the happier he is, the more he will be
pained at the thought of death; for life is best worth living
for such a man, and he is knowingly losing the greatest
goods, and this is painful. But he is none the less brave, and
perhaps all the more so, because he chooses noble deeds of
15 war at that cost. It is not the case, then, with all the virtues
that the exercise of them is pleasant, except in so far as it
reaches its end. But it is quite possible that the best soldiers
may be not men of this sort but those who are less brave
but have no other good; for these are ready to face danger,
and they sell their life for trifling gains.
20   So much, then, for courage; it is not difficult to grasp its
nature in outline, at any rate, for what has been said.
     After courage let us speak of temperance; for these seem
to be the virtues of the irrational parts.

[20] 1115ᵇ 7–13.

10 We have said [21] that temperance is a mean with regard to pleasures (for it is less, and not in the same way, 25 concerned with pains); self-indulgence also is manifested in the same sphere. Now, therefore, let us determine with what sort of pleasures they are concerned. We may assume the distinction between bodily pleasures and those of the soul, such as love of honour and love of learning; for the lover of each of these delights in that of which he is a lover, 30 the body being in no way affected, but rather the mind; but men who are concerned with such pleasures are called neither temperate nor self-indulgent. Nor, again, are those who are concerned with the other pleasures that are not bodily; for those who are fond of hearing and telling stories and who spend their days on anything that turns up are 35 called gossips, but not self-indulgent, nor are those who are pained at the loss of money or of friends.

Temperance must be concerned with bodily pleasures, **1118ᵃ** but not all even of these; for those who delight in objects of vision, such as colours and shapes and painting, are called 5 neither temperate nor self-indulgent; yet it would seem possible to delight even in these either as one should or to excess or to a deficient degree.

And so too is it with objects of hearing; no one calls those who delight extravagantly in music or acting self-indulgent, nor those who do so as they ought temperate.

Nor do we apply these names to those who delight in odour, unless it be incidentally; we do not call those self-indulgent who delight in the odour of apples or roses or incense, but rather those who delight in the odour of un- 10 guents or of dainty dishes; for self-indulgent people delight in these because these remind them of the objects of their appetite. And one may see even other people, when they are hungry, delighting in the smell of food; but to delight in this kind of thing is the mark of the self-indulgent man; 15 for these are objects of appetite to him.

[21] 1107ᵇ 4–6.

Nor is there in animals other than man any pleasure connected with these senses, except incidentally. For dogs do not delight in the scent of hares, but in the eating of them, 20 but the scent told them the hares were there; nor does the lion delight in the lowing of the ox, but in eating it; but he perceived by the lowing that it was near, and therefore appears to delight in the lowing; and similarly he does not delight because he sees 'a stag or a wild goat',[22] but because he is going to make a meal of it. Temperance and self-indulgence, however, are concerned with the kind of pleas- 25 ures that the other animals share in, which therefore appear slavish and brutish; these are touch and taste. But even of taste they appear to make little or no use; for the business of taste is the discriminating of flavours, which is done by wine-tasters and people who season dishes; but they hardly take pleasure in making these discriminations, or at least 30 self-indulgent people do not, but in the actual enjoyment, which in all cases comes through touch, both in the case of food and in that of drink and in that of sexual intercourse. This is why a certain gourmand prayed that his throat might become longer than a crane's, implying that it was 1118ᵇ the contact that he took pleasure in. Thus the sense with which self-indulgence is connected is the most widely shared of the senses; and self-indulgence would seem to be justly a matter of reproach, because it attaches to us not as men but as animals. To delight in such things, then, and to love them above all others, is brutish. For even of the pleasures of touch the most liberal have been eliminated, e. g. those produced in the gymnasium by rubbing and by 5 the consequent heat; for the contact characteristic of the self-indulgent man does not affect the whole body but only certain parts.

11 Of the appetites some seem to be common, others to be peculiar to individuals and acquired; e. g. the ap- 10 petite for food is natural, since every one who is without it

[22] Il. iii. 24.

craves for food or drink, and sometimes for both, and for love also (as Homer says) [23] if he is young and lusty; but not every one craves for this or that kind of nourishment or love, nor for the same things. Hence such craving appears to be our very own. Yet it has of course something natural about it; for different things are pleasant to different kinds of people, and some things are more pleasant to every one 15 than chance objects. Now in the natural appetites few go wrong, and only in one direction, that of excess; for to eat or drink whatever offers itself till one is surfeited is to exceed the natural amount, since natural appetite is the replenishment of one's deficiency. Hence these people are called belly-gods, this implying that they fill their belly be- 20 yond what is right. It is people of entirely slavish character that become like this. But with regard to the pleasures peculiar to individuals many people go wrong and in many ways. For while the people who are 'fond of so and so' are so called because they delight either in the wrong things, or more than most people do, or in the wrong way, the self- 25 indulgent exceed in all three ways; they both delight in some things that they ought not to delight in (since they are hateful), and if one ought to delight in some of the things they delight in, they do so more than one ought and than most men do.

Plainly, then, excess with regard to pleasures is self-indulgence and is culpable; with regard to pains one is not, as in the case of courage, called temperate for facing them 30 or self-indulgent for not doing so, but the self-indulgent man is so called because he is pained more than he ought at not getting pleasant things (even his pain being caused by pleasure), and the temperate man is so called because he is not pained at the absence of what is pleasant and at his abstinence from it.

The self-indulgent man, then, craves for all pleasant 1119ᵃ things or those that are most pleasant, and is led by his appetite to choose these at the cost of everything else;

[23] *Il.* xxiv. 130.

hence he is pained both when he fails to get them and
when he is merely craving for them (for appetite involves
5 pain); but it seems absurd to be pained for the sake of
pleasure. People who fall short with regard to pleasures and
delight in them less than they should are hardly found; for
such insensibility is not human. Even the other animals
distinguish different kinds of food and enjoy some and not
others; and if there is any one who finds nothing pleasant
and nothing more attractive than anything else, he must be
10 something quite different from a man; this sort of person
has not received a name because he hardly occurs. The
temperate man occupies a middle position with regard to
these objects. For he neither enjoys the things that the self-
indulgent man enjoys most—but rather dislikes them—nor
in general the things that he should not, nor anything of
this sort to excess, nor does he feel pain or craving when
they are absent, or does so only to a moderate degree, and
15 not more than he should, nor when he should not, and so
on; but the things that, being pleasant, make for health or
for good condition, he will desire moderately and as he
should, and also other pleasant things if they are not hindrances to these ends, or contrary to what is noble, or beyond his means. For he who neglects these conditions loves
such pleasures more than they are worth, but the temperate
20 man is not that sort of person, but the sort of person that
the right rule prescribes.

12 Self-indulgence is more like a voluntary state than
cowardice. For the former is actuated by pleasure, the
latter by pain, of which the one is to be chosen and the
other to be avoided; and pain upsets and destroys the nature of the person who feels it, while pleasure does nothing
of the sort. Therefore self-indulgence is more voluntary.
25 Hence also it is more a matter of reproach; for it is easier
to become accustomed to its objects, since there are many
things of this sort in life, and the process of habituation to
them is free from danger, while with terrible objects the re-

verse is the case. But cowardice would seem to be voluntary in a different degree from its particular manifestations; for it is itself painless, but in these we are upset by pain, so that we even throw down our arms and disgrace ourselves in other ways; hence our acts are even thought to be done 30 under compulsion. For the self-indulgent man, on the other hand, the particular acts are voluntary (for he does them with craving and desire), but the whole state is less so; for no one craves to be self-indulgent.

The name self-indulgence is applied also to childish faults; for they bear a certain resemblance to what we have been considering. Which is called after which, makes no difference to our present purpose; plainly, however, the 1119 later is called after the earlier. The transference of the name seems not a bad one; for that which desires what is base and which develops quickly ought to be kept in a chastened condition, and these characteristics belong above all to appetite and to the child, since children in fact live at the beck and call of appetite, and it is in them that the desire 5 for what is pleasant is strongest. If, then, it is not going to be obedient and subject to the ruling principle, it will go to great lengths; for in an irrational being the desire for pleasure is insatiable even if it tries every source of gratification, and the exercise of appetite increases its innate force, and 10 if appetites are strong and violent they even expel the power of calculation. Hence they should be moderate and few, and should in no way oppose the rational principle— and this is what we call an obedient and chastened state— and as the child should live according to the direction of his tutor, so the appetitive element should live according to 15 rational principle. Hence the appetitive element in a temperate man should harmonize with the rational principle; for the noble is the mark at which both aim, and the temperate man craves for the things he ought, as he ought, and when he ought; and this is what rational principle directs.

Here we conclude our account of temperance.

1   Let us speak next of liberality. It seems to be the mean
with regard to wealth; for the liberal man is praised
not in respect of military matters, nor of those in respect
25 of which the temperate man is praised, nor of judicial decisions, but with regard to the giving and taking of wealth,
and especially in respect of giving. Now by 'wealth' we
mean all the things whose value is measured by money.
Further, prodigality and meanness are excesses and defects
30 with regard to wealth; and meanness we always impute to
those who care more than they ought for wealth, but we
sometimes apply the word 'prodigality' in a complex sense;
for we call those men prodigals who are incontinent and
spend money on self-indulgence. Hence also they are
thought the poorest characters; for they combine more
vices than one. Therefore the application of the word to
1120ª them is not its proper use; for a 'prodigal' means a man
who has a single evil quality, that of wasting his substance;
since a prodigal is one who is being ruined by his own fault,
and the wasting of substance is thought to be a sort of ruin-
ing of oneself, life being held to depend on possession of
substance.

This, then, is the sense in which we take the word 'prod-
5 igality'. Now the things that have a use may be used either
well or badly; and riches is a useful thing; and everything
is used best by the man who has the virtue concerned with
it; riches, therefore, will be used best by the man who has
the virtue concerned with wealth; and this is the liberal
man. Now spending and giving seem to be the using of
wealth; taking and keeping rather the possession of it.
10 Hence it is more the mark of the liberal man to give to the
right people than to take from the right sources and not to
take from the wrong. For it is more characteristic of virtue
to do good than to have good done to one, and more characteristic to do what is noble than not to do what is base;

and it is not hard to see that giving implies doing good and doing what is noble, and taking implies having good done to one or not acting basely. And gratitude is felt towards him who gives, not towards him who does not take, and praise also is bestowed more on him. It is easier, also, not to take than to give; for men are apter to give away their own too little than to take what is another's. Givers, too, are called liberal; but those who do not take are not praised for liberality but rather for justice; while those who take are hardly praised at all. And the liberal are almost the most loved of all virtuous characters, since they are useful; and this depends on their giving.

Now virtuous actions are noble and done for the sake of the noble. Therefore the liberal man, like other virtuous men, will give for the sake of the noble, and rightly; for he will give to the right people, the right amounts, and at the right time, with all the other qualifications that accompany right giving; and that too with pleasure or without pain; for that which is virtuous is pleasant or free from pain—least of all will it be painful. But he who gives to the wrong people or not for the sake of the noble but for some other cause, will be called not liberal but by some other name. Nor is he liberal who gives with pain; for he would prefer the wealth to the noble act, and this is not characteristic of a liberal man. But no more will the liberal man take from wrong sources; for such taking is not characteristic of the man who sets no store by wealth. Nor will he be a ready asker; for it is not characteristic of a man who confers benefits to accept them lightly. But he will take from the right sources, e. g. from his own possessions, not as something noble but as a necessity, that he may have something to give. Nor will he neglect his own property, since he wishes by means of this to help others. And he will refrain from giving to anybody and everybody, that he may have something to give to the right people, at the right time, and where it is noble to do so. It is highly characteristic of a liberal man also to go to excess in giving, so that he leaves

5 too little for himself; for it is the nature of a liberal man not to look to himself. The term 'liberality' is used relatively to a man's substance; for liberality resides not in the multitude of the gifts but in the state of character of the giver, and this is relative to the giver's substance. There is therefore nothing to prevent the man who gives less from being the more liberal man, if he has less to give. Those are thought 10 to be more liberal who have not made their wealth but inherited it; for in the first place they have no experience of want, and secondly all men are fonder of their own produc- 15 tions, as are parents and poets. It is not easy for the liberal man to be rich, since he is not apt either at taking or at keeping, but at giving away, and does not value wealth for its own sake but as a means to giving. Hence comes the charge that is brought against fortune, that those who deserve riches most get it least. But it is not unreasonable that it should turn out so; for he cannot have wealth, any more 20 than anything else, if he does not take pains to have it. Yet he will not give to the wrong people nor at the wrong time, and so on; for he would no longer be acting in accordance with liberality, and if he spent on these objects he would have nothing to spend on the right objects. For, as has been said, he is liberal who spends according to his sub- 25 stance and on the right objects; and he who exceeds is prodigal. Hence we do not call despots prodigal; for it is thought not easy for them to give and spend beyond the amount of their possessions. Liberality, then, being a mean with regard to giving and taking of wealth, the liberal man will both give and spend the right amounts and on the right 30 objects, alike in small things and in great, and that with pleasure; he will also take the right amounts and from the right sources. For, the virtue being a mean with regard to both, he will do both as he ought; since this sort of taking accompanies proper giving, and that which is not of this sort is contrary to it, and accordingly the giving and taking that accompany each other are present together in the same 1121ᵃ man, while the contrary kinds evidently are not. But if

he happens to spend in a manner contrary to what is right and noble, he will be pained, but moderately and as he ought; for it is the mark of virtue both to be pleased and to be pained at the right objects and in the right way. Further, 5 the liberal man is easy to deal with in money matters; for he can be got the better of, since he sets no store by money, and is more annoyed if he has not spent something that he ought than pained if he has spent something that he ought not, and does not agree with the saying of Simonides.

The prodigal errs in these respects also; for he is neither pleased nor pained at the right things or in the right way; this will be more evident as we go on. We have said [1] that 10 prodigality and meanness are excesses and deficiencies, and in two things, in giving and in taking; for we include spending under giving. Now prodigality exceeds in giving and not taking, and falls short in taking, while meanness falls short in giving, and exceeds in taking, except in small 15 things.

The characteristics of prodigality are not often combined; for it is not easy to give to all if you take from none; private persons soon exhaust their substance with giving, and it is to these that the name of prodigals is applied— though a man of this sort would seem to be in no small degree better than a mean man. For he is easily cured both 20 by age and by poverty, and thus he may move towards the middle state. For he has the characteristics of the liberal man, since he both gives and refrains from taking, though he does neither of these in the right manner or well. Therefore if he were brought to do so by habituation or in some other way, he would be liberal; for he will then give to the right people, and will not take from the wrong sources. This is why he is thought to have not a bad character; it is 25 not the mark of a wicked or ignoble man to go to excess in giving and not taking, but only of a foolish one. The man who is prodigal in this way is thought much better than the mean man both for the aforesaid reasons and because he

[1] 1119^b 27.

benefits many while the other benefits no one, not even himself.

But most prodigal people, as has been said,[2] also take
30 from the wrong sources, and are in this respect mean. They become apt to take because they wish to spend and cannot do this easily; for their possessions soon run short. Thus they are forced to provide means from some other source.
1121ᵇ At the same time, because they care nothing for honour, they take recklessly and from any source; for they have an appetite for giving, and they do not mind how or from what source. Hence also their giving is not liberal; for it is not noble, nor does it aim at nobility, nor is it done in the
5 right way; sometimes they make rich those who should be poor, and will give nothing to people of respectable character, and much to flatterers or those who provide them with some other pleasure. Hence also most of them are self-indulgent; for they spend lightly and waste money on their indulgences, and incline towards pleasures because
10 they do not live with a view to what is noble.

The prodigal man, then, turns into what we have described if he is left untutored, but if he is treated with care he will arrive at the intermediate and right state. But meanness is both incurable (for old age and every disability is
15 thought to make men mean) and more innate in men than prodigality; for most men are fonder of getting money than of giving. It also extends widely, and is multiform, since there seem to be many kinds of meanness.

For it consists in two things, deficiency in giving and excess is taking, and is not found complete in all men but is sometimes divided; some men go to excess in taking,
20 others fall short in giving. Those who are called by such names as 'miserly', 'close', 'stingy', all fall short in giving, but do not covet the possessions of others nor wish to get them. In some this is due to a sort of honesty and avoidance
25 of what is disgraceful (for some seem, or at least profess, to hoard their money for this reason, that they may not

[2] ll. 16–19.

some day be forced to do something disgraceful; to this class belong the cheeseparer and every one of the sort; he is so called from his excess of unwillingness to give anything); while others again keep their hands off the property of others from fear, on the ground that it is not easy, if one takes the property of others oneself, to avoid having one's own taken by them; they are therefore content neither to take nor to give.

Others again exceed in respect of taking by taking any- 30 thing and from any source, e. g. those who ply sordid trades, pimps and all such people, and those who lend small sums and at high rates. For all of these take more than they 1122ᵃ ought and from wrong sources. What is common to them is evidently sordid love of gain; they all put up with a bad name for the sake of gain, and little gain at that. For those who make great gains but from wrong sources, and not the right gains, e. g. despots when they sack cities and spoil 5 temples, we do not call mean but rather wicked, impious, and unjust. But the gamester and the footpad [and the highwayman] belong to the class of the mean, since they have a sordid love of gain. For it is for gain that both of them ply their craft and endure the disgrace of it, and the one faces the greatest dangers for the sake of the booty, while the other makes gain from his friends, to whom he 10 ought to be giving. Both, then, since they are willing to make gain from wrong sources, are sordid lovers of gain; therefore all such forms of taking are mean.

And it is natural that meanness is described as the contrary of liberality; for not only is it a greater evil than prodigality, but men err more often in this direction than 15 in the way of prodigality as we have described it.

So much, then, for liberality and the opposed vices.

2 It would seem proper to discuss magnificence next. For this also seems to be a virtue concerned with 20 wealth; but it does not like liberality extend to all the actions that are concerned with wealth, but only to those

that involve expenditure; and in these it surpasses liberality
in scale. For, as the name itself suggests, it is a fitting
expenditure involving largeness of scale. But the scale is
relative; for the expense of equipping a trireme is not the
25 same as that of heading a sacred embassy. It is what is
fitting, then, in relation to the agent, and to the circumstances and the object. The man who in small or middling
things spends according to the merits of the case is not
called magnificent (e. g. the man who can say 'many a
gift I gave the wanderer'),³ but only the man who does so
in great things. For the·magnificent man is liberal, but the
30 liberal man is not necessarily magnificent. The deficiency
of this state of character is called niggardliness, the excess
vulgarity, lack of taste, and the like, which do not go to
excess in the amount spent on right objects, but by showy
expenditure in the wrong circumstances and the wrong
manner; we shall speak of these vices later.⁴

The magnificent man is like an artist; for he can see what
is fitting and spend large sums tastefully. For, as we said
35 at the beginning,⁵ a state of character is determined by its
1122ᵇ activities and by its objects. Now the expenses of the
magnificent man are large and fitting. Such, therefore, are
also his results; for thus there will be a great expenditure
and one that is fitting to its result. Therefore the result
should be worthy of the expense, and the expense should
5 be worthy of the result, or should even exceed it. And the
magnificent man will spend such sums for honour's sake;
for this is common to the virtues. And further he will do so
gladly and lavishly; for nice calculation is a niggardly thing.
And he will consider how the result can be made most
beautiful and most becoming rather than for how much it
can be produced and how it can be produced most cheaply.
10 It is necessary, then, that the magnificent man be also
liberal. For the liberal man also will spend what he ought

³ *Od.* xvii. 420.
⁴ 1123ᵃ 19–33.
⁵ Not in so many words, but Cf. 1103ᵇ 21–23, 1104ᵃ 27–29.

and as he ought; and it is in these matters that the greatness implied in the name of the magnificent man—his
bigness, as it were—is manifested, since liberality is concerned with these matters; and at an equal expense he will
produce a more magnificent work of art. For a possession
and a work of art have not the same excellence. The most
valuable possession is that which is worth most, e. g. gold, 15
but the most valuable work of art is that which is great and
beautiful (for the contemplation of such a work inspires
admiration, and so does magnificence); and a work has an
excellence—viz. magnificence—which involves magnitude.
Magnificence is an attribute of expenditures of the kind
which we call honourable, e. g. those connected with the
gods—votive offerings, buildings, and sacrifices—and similarly with any form of religious worship, and all those that
are proper objects of public-spirited ambition, as when 20
people think they ought to equip a chorus or a trireme,
or entertain the city, in a brilliant way. But in all cases,
as has been said,[6] we have regard to the agent as well and
ask who he is and what means he has; for the expenditure 25
should be worthy of his means, and suit not only the
result but also the producer. Hence a poor man cannot be
magnificent, since he has not the means with which to
spend large sums fittingly; and he who tries is a fool, since
he spends beyond what can be expected of him and what is
proper, but it is *right* expenditure that is virtuous. But great
expenditure is becoming to those who have suitable means, 30
to start with, acquired by their own efforts or from ancestors or connexions, and to people of high birth or reputation, and so on; for all these things bring with them greatness and prestige. Primarily, then, the magnificent man is 35
of this sort, and magnificence is shown in expenditures of
this sort, as has been said;[7] for these are the greatest and
most honourable. Of *private* occasions of expenditure the
most suitable are those that take place once for all, e. g. a

6 a 24–26.
7 ll. 19–23.

1123ᵃ wedding or anything of the kind, or anything that interests
the whole city or the people of position in it, and also the
receiving of foreign guests and the sending of them on their
5 way, and gifts and counter-gifts; for the magnificent man
spends not on himself but on public objects, and gifts bear
some resemblance to votive offerings. A magnificent man
will also furnish his house suitably to his wealth (for even a
house is a sort of public ornament), and will spend by preference on those works that are lasting (for these are the most
beautiful), and on every class of things he will spend what
10 is becoming; for the same things are not suitable for gods
and for men, nor in a temple and in a tomb. And since
each expenditure may be great of its kind, and what is
most magnificent absolutely is great expenditure on a great
object, but what is magnificent *here* is what is great in
these circumstances, and greatness in the work differs from
15 greatness in the expense. (for the most beautiful ball or
bottle is magnificent as a gift to a child, but the price of
it is small and mean)—therefore it is characteristic of the
magnificent man, whatever kind of result he is producing,
to produce it magnificently (for such a result is not easily
surpassed) and to make it worthy of the expenditure.

Such, then, is the magnificent man; the man who goes
to excess and is vulgar exceeds, as has been said,[8] by spend-
20 ing beyond what is right. For on small objects of expenditure he spends much and displays a tasteless showiness; e. g.
he gives a club dinner on the scale of a wedding banquet,
and when he provides the chorus for a comedy he brings
them on to the stage in purple, as they do at Megara.
25 And all such things he will do not for honour's sake but
to show off his wealth, and because he thinks he is admired
for these things, and where he ought to spend much he
spends little and where little, much. The niggardly man on
the other hand will fall short in everything, and after spending the greatest sums will spoil the beauty of the result for
a trifle, and whatever he is doing he will hesitate and con-

[8] 1122ᵃ 31–33.

sider how he may spend least, and lament even that, and 30
think he is doing everything on a bigger scale than he
ought.

These states of character, then, are vices; yet they do not
bring disgrace because they are neither harmful to one's
neighbour nor very unseemly.

3 Pride seems even from its name [9] to be concerned with
    great things; what sort of great things, is the first ques-
tion we must try to answer. It makes no difference whether
we consider the state of character or the man characterized 35
by it. Now the man is thought to be proud who thinks
himself worthy of great things, being worthy of them; for 1123[b]
he who does so beyond his deserts is a fool, but no virtuous
man is foolish or silly. The proud man, then, is the man
we have described. For he who is worthy of little and thinks
himself worthy of little is temperate, but not proud; for 5
pride implies greatness, as beauty implies a good-sized
body, and little people may be neat and well-proportioned
but cannot be beautiful. On the other hand, he who thinks
himself worthy of great things, being unworthy of them, is
vain; though not every one who thinks himself worthy of
more than he really is worthy of is vain. The man who
thinks himself worthy of less than he is really worthy of is
unduly humble, whether his deserts be great or moderate,
or his deserts be small but his claims yet smaller. And the 10
man whose deserts are great would seem *most* unduly
humble; for what would he have done if they had been
less? The proud man, then, is an extreme in respect of the
greatness of his claims, but a mean in respect of the rightness of them; for he claims what is in accordance with his
merits, while the others go to excess or fall short.

If, then, he deserves and claims great things, and above
all the greatest things, he will be concerned with one thing 15
in particular. Desert is relative to external goods; and the

[9] 'Pride' of course has not the etymological associations of *megalo-
psychia*, but seems in other respects the best translation.

greatest of these, we should say, is that which we render
to the gods, and which people of position most aim at, and
20 which is the prize appointed for the noblest deeds; and this
is honour; that is surely the greatest of external goods. Honours and dishonours, therefore, are the objects with respect
to which the proud man is as he should be. And even apart
from argument it is with honour that proud men appear
to be concerned; for it is honour that they chiefly claim,
but in accordance with their deserts. The unduly humble
man falls short both in comparison with his own merits and
25 in comparison with the proud man's claims. The vain man
goes to excess in comparison with his own merits, but does
not exceed the proud man's claims.

Now the proud man, since he deserves most, must be
good in the highest degree; for the better man always
30 deserves more, and the best man most. Therefore the truly
proud man must be good. And greatness in every virtue
would seem to be characteristic of a proud man. And it
would be most unbecoming for a proud man to fly from
danger, swinging his arms by his sides, or to wrong another; for to what end should he do disgraceful acts, he to
whom nothing is great? If we consider him point by point,
we shall see the utter absurdity of a proud man who is not
35 good. Nor, again, would he be worthy of honour if he were
bad; for honour is the prize of virtue, and it is to the good
1124ª that it is rendered. Pride, then, seems to be a sort of crown
of the virtues; for it makes them greater, and it is not found
without them. Therefore it is hard to be truly proud; for it
is impossible without nobility and goodness of character.
5 It is chiefly with honours and dishonours, then, that the
proud man is concerned; and at honours that are great and
conferred by good men he will be moderately pleased,
thinking that he is coming by his own or even less than
his own; for there can be no honour that is worthy of per-
10 fect virtue, yet he will at any rate accept it since they have
nothing greater to bestow on him; but honour from casual
people and on trifling grounds he will utterly despise, since

it is not this that he deserves, and dishonour too, since in his case it cannot be just. In the first place, then, as has been said,[10] the proud man is concerned with honours; yet he will also bear himself with moderation towards wealth and power and all good or evil fortune, whatever may befall 15 him, and will be neither over-joyed by good fortune nor over-pained by evil. For not even towards honour does he bear himself as if it were a very great thing. Power and wealth are desirable for the sake of honour (at least those who have them wish to get honour by means of them); and for him to whom even honour is a little thing the others must be so too. Hence proud men are thought to be disdainful.

The goods of fortune also are thought to contribute to- 20 wards pride. For men who are well-born are thought worthy of honour, and so are those who enjoy power or wealth; for they are in a superior position, and everything that has a superiority in something good is held in greater honour. Hence even such things make men prouder; for they are honoured by some for having them; but in truth the good man alone is to be honoured; he, however, who has both 25 advantages is thought the more worthy of honour. But those who without virtue have such goods are neither justified in making great claims nor entitled to the name of 'proud'; for these things imply perfect virtue. Disdainful and insolent, however, even those who have such goods become. For without virtue it is not easy to bear gracefully the goods of fortune; and, being unable to bear them, and 30 thinking themselves superior to others, they despise others and themselves do what they please. They imitate the 1124ᵇ proud man without being like him, and this they do where they can; so they do not act virtuously, but they do despise others. For the proud man despises justly (since he thinks 5 truly), but the many do so at random.

He does not run into trifling dangers, nor is he fond of danger, because he honours few things; but he will face

[10] 1123ᵇ 15–22.

great dangers, and when he is in danger he is unsparing of his life, knowing that there are conditions on which life is not worth having. And he is the sort of man to confer benefits, but he is ashamed of receiving them; for the one 10 is the mark of a superior, the other of an inferior. And he is apt to confer greater benefits in return; for thus the original benefactor besides being paid will incur a debt to him, and will be the gainer by the transaction. They seem also to remember any service they have done, but not those they have received (for he who receives a service is inferior to him who has done it, but the proud man wishes to be superior), and to hear of the former with pleasure, of the 15 latter with displeasure; this, it seems, is why Thetis did not mention to Zeus the services she had done him,[11] and why the Spartans did not recount their services to the Athenians, but those they had received. It is a mark of the proud man also to ask for nothing or scarcely anything, but to give help readily, and to be dignified towards people who enjoy high position and good fortune, but unassuming towards 20 those of the middle class; for it is a difficult and lofty thing to be superior to the former, but easy to be so to the latter, and a lofty bearing over the former is no mark of ill-breeding, but among humble people it is as vulgar as a display of strength against the weak. Again, it is characteristic of the proud man not to aim at the things commonly held in honour, or the things in which others excel; to be sluggish 25 and to hold back except where great honour or a great work is at stake, and to be a man of few deeds, but of great and notable ones. He must also be open in his hate and in his love (for to conceal one's feelings, i. e. to care less for truth than for what people will think, is a coward's part), and must speak and act openly; for he is free of speech because 30 he is contemptuous, and he is given to telling the truth, except when he speaks in irony to the vulgar. He must be 1125ᵃ unable to make his life revolve round another, unless it be a friend; for this is slavish, and for this reason all flatterers are

[11] In fact she did, Il. i. 503.

servile and people lacking in self-respect are flatterers. Nor
is he given to admiration; for nothing to him is great. Nor
is he mindful of wrongs; for it is not the part of a proud man
to have a long memory, especially for wrongs, but rather to 5
overlook them. Nor is he a gossip; for he will speak neither
about himself nor about another, since he cares not to be
praised nor for others to be blamed; nor again is he given to
praise; and for the same reason he is not an evil-speaker,
even about his enemies, except from haughtiness. With
regard to necessary or small matters he is least of all men 10
given to lamentation or the asking of favours; for it is the
part of one who takes such matters seriously to behave
so with respect to them. He is one who will possess beautiful and profitless things rather than profitable and useful
ones; for this is more proper to a character that suffices to
itself.

Further, a slow step is thought proper to the proud
man, a deep voice, and a level utterance; for the man who
takes few things seriously is not likely to be hurried, nor the
man who thinks nothing great to be excited, while a shrill 15
voice and a rapid gait are the results of hurry and excitement.

Such, then, is the proud man; the man who falls short
of him is unduly humble, and the man who goes beyond
him is vain. Now even these are not thought to be bad (for
they are not malicious), but only mistaken. For the unduly humble man, being worthy of good things, robs him- 20
self of what he deserves, and seems to have something bad
about him from the fact that he does not think himself
worthy of good things, and seems also not to know himself;
else he would have desired the things he was worthy of,
since these were good. Yet such people are not thought to
be fools, but rather unduly retiring. Such a reputation, 25
however, seems actually to make them worse; for each class
of people aims at what corresponds to its worth, and these
people stand back even from noble actions and undertak-
ings, deeming themselves unworthy, and from external

goods no less. Vain people, on the other hand, are fools
and ignorant of themselves, and that manifestly; for, not
being worthy of them, they attempt honourable undertak-
30 ings, and then are found out; and they adorn themselves
with clothing and outward show and such things, and wish
their strokes of good fortune to be made public, and speak
about them as if they would be honoured for them. But
undue humility is more opposed to pride than vanity is; for
it is both commoner and worse.

Pride, then, is concerned with honour on the grand scale,
35 as has been said.[12]

4   There seems to be in the sphere of honour also, as
1125ᵇ   was said in our first remarks on the subject,[13] a virtue
which would appear to be related to pride as liberality is to
magnificence. For neither of these has anything to do with
5 the grand scale, but both dispose us as is right with regard
to middling and unimportant objects; as in getting and
giving of wealth there is a mean and an excess and defect,
so too honour may be desired more than is right, or less,
or from the right sources and in the right way. We blame
both the ambitious man as aiming at honour more than is
10 right and from wrong sources, and the unambitious man as
not willing to be honoured even for noble reasons. But
sometimes we praise the ambitious man as being manly and
a lover of what is noble, and the unambitious man as being
moderate and self-controlled, as we said in our first treatment of the subject.[14] Evidently, since 'fond of such and
such an object' has more than one meaning, we do not
assign the term 'ambition' or 'love of honour' always to the
same thing, but when we praise the quality we think of the
15 man who loves honour more than most people, and when
we blame it we think of him who loves it more than is
right. The mean being without a name, the extremes seem

¹² 1107ᵇ 26, 1123ᵃ 34.–ᵇ 22.
¹³ Ib. 24–27.
¹⁴ 1107ᵇ 33.

to dispute for its place as though that were vacant by de-
fault. But where there is excess and defect, there is also an
intermediate; now men desire honour both more than they
should and less; therefore it is possible also to do so as one
should; at all events this is the state of character that is 20
praised, being an unnamed mean in respect of honour. Relatively to ambition it seems to be unambitiousness, and
relatively to unambitiousness it seems to be ambition, while
relatively to both severally it seems in a sense to be both
together. This appears to be true of the other virtues also.
But in this case the extremes seem to be contradictories because the mean has not received a name. 25

5 Good temper is a mean with respect to anger; the
middle state being unnamed, and the extremes almost
without a name as well, we place good temper in the
middle position, though it inclines towards the deficiency,
which is without a name. The excess might be called a sort 30
of 'irascibility'. For the passion is anger, while its causes
are many and diverse.

The man who is angry at the right things and with the
right people, and, further, as he ought, when he ought, and
as long as he ought, is praised. This will be the good-tempered man, since good temper is praised. For the good-tempered man tends to be unperturbed and not to be led by 35
passion, but to be angry in the manner, at the things, and 1126ᵃ
for the length of time, that the rule dictates; but he is
thought to err rather in the direction of deficiency; for the
good-tempered man is not revengeful, but rather tends to
make allowances.

The deficiency, whether it is a sort of 'inirascibility' or
whatever it is, is blamed. For those who are not angry at
the things they should be angry at are thought to be fools, 5
and so are those who are not angry in the right way, at the
right time, or with the right persons; for such a man is
thought not to feel things nor to be pained by them, and,
since he does not get angry, he is thought unlikely to

defend himself; and to endure being insulted and put up
with insult to one's friends is slavish.

The excess can be manifested in all the points that have
been named (for one can be angry with the wrong persons,
10 at the wrong things, more than is right, too quickly, or too
long); yet *all* are not found in the same person. Indeed
they could not; for evil destroys even itself, and if it is complete becomes unbearable. Now *hot-tempered* people get
angry quickly and with the wrong persons and at the wrong
things and more than is right, but their anger ceases quickly
15 —which is the best point about them. This happens to
them because they do not restrain their anger but retaliate
openly owing to their quickness of temper, and then their
anger ceases. By reason of excess *choleric* people are quick-
tempered and ready to be angry with everything and on
every occasion; whence their name. *Sulky* people are hard
20 to appease, and retain their anger long; for they repress
their passion. But it ceases when they retaliate; for revenge
relieves them of their anger, producing in them pleasure
instead of pain. If this does not happen they retain their
burden; for owing to its not being obvious no one even rea-
25 sons with them, and to digest one's anger in oneself takes
time. Such people are most troublesome to themselves and
to their dearest friends. We call *bad-tempered* those who
are angry at the wrong things, more than is right, and
longer, and cannot be appeased until they inflict vengeance
or punishment.

To good temper we oppose the excess rather than the
defect; for not only is it commoner (since revenge is the
30 more human), but bad-tempered people are worse to live
with.

What we have said in our earlier treatment of the subject [15] is plain also from what we are now saying; viz. that
it is not easy to define how, with whom, at what, and how
long one should be angry, and at what point right action
35 ceases and wrong begins. For the man who strays a little

[15] 1109^b 14–26.

from the path, either towards the more or towards the less,
is not blamed; since sometimes we praise those who exhibit
the deficiency, and call them good-tempered, and sometimes we call angry people. manly, as being capable of rul- **1126**ᵇ
ing. How far, therefore, and how a man must stray before
he becomes blameworthy, it is not easy to state in words;
for the decision depends on the particular facts and on
perception. But so much at least is plain, that the middle
state is praiseworthy—that in virtue of which we are angry **5**
with the right people, at the right things, in the right way,
and so on, while the excesses and defects are blameworthy
—slightly so if they are present in a low degree, more if in
a higher degree, and very much if in a high degree. Evidently, then, we must cling to the middle state.—Enough
of the states relative to anger.   **10**

6   In gatherings of men, in social life and the interchange
        of words and deeds, some men are thought to be obse-
quious, viz. those who to give pleasure praise everything
and never oppose, but think it their duty 'to give no pain
to the people they meet'; while those who, on the contrary, **15**
oppose everything and care not a whit about giving pain
are called churlish and contentious. That the states we have
named are culpable is plain enough, and that the middle
state is laudable—that in virtue of which a man will put up
with, and will resent, the right things and in the right way;
but no name has been assigned to it, though it most resembles friendship. For the man who corresponds to this **20**
middle state is very much what, with affection added, we
call a good friend. But the state in question differs from
friendship in that it implies no passion or affection for one's
associates; since it is not by reason of loving or hating that
such a man takes everything in the right way, but by being
a man of a certain kind. For he will behave so alike towards **25**
those he knows and those he does not know, towards intimates and those who are not so, except that in each of
these cases he will behave as is befitting; for it is not proper

to have the same care for intimates and for strangers, nor
again is it the same conditions that make it right to give
pain to them. Now we have said generally that he will associate with people in the right way; but it is by reference to
what is honourable and expedient that he will aim at not
30 giving pain or at contributing pleasure. For he seems to be
concerned with the pleasures and pains of social life; and
wherever it is not honourable, or is harmful, for him to
contribute pleasure, he will refuse, and will choose rather
to give pain; also if his acquiescence in another's action
would bring disgrace, and that in a high degree, or injury,
35 on that other, while his opposition brings a little pain, he
will not acquiesce but will decline. He will associate
1127ᵃ differently with people in high station and with ordinary
people, with closer and more distant acquaintances, and so
too with regard to all other differences, rendering to each
class what is befitting, and while for its own sake he
chooses to contribute pleasure, and avoids the giving of
5 pain, he will be guided by the consequences, if these are
greater, i. e. honour and expediency. For the sake of a great
future pleasure, too, he will inflict small pains.

The man who attains the mean, then, is such as we have
described, but has not received a name; of those who contribute pleasure, the man who aims at being pleasant with
no ulterior object is obsequious, but the man who does so
10 in order that he may get some advantage in the direction of
money or the things that money buys is a flatterer; while
the man who quarrels with everything is, as has been said,[16]
churlish and contentious. And the extremes seem to be
contradictory to each other because the mean is without a
name.

7   The mean opposed to boastfulness is found in almost
the same sphere; and this also is without a name. It
15 will be no bad plan to describe these states as well; for we
shall both know the facts about character better if we go
through them in detail, and we shall be convinced that the

[16] 1125ᵇ 14–16.

virtues are means if we see this to be so in all cases. In the field of social life those who make the giving of pleasure or pain their object in associating with others have been described; [17] let us now describe those who pursue truth or falsehood alike in words and deeds and in the claims they 20 put forward. The boastful man, then, is thought to be apt to claim the things that bring glory, when he has not got them, or to claim more of them than he has, and the mock-modest man on the other hand to disclaim what he has or belittle it, while the man who observes the mean is one who calls a thing by its own name, being truthful both in life and in word, owning to what he has, and neither 25 more nor less. Now each of these courses may be adopted either with or without an object. But each man speaks and acts and lives in accordance with his character, if he is *not* acting for some ulterior object. And falsehood is *in itself* [18] mean and culpable, and truth noble and worthy of praise. Thus the truthful man is another case of a man who, being 30 in the mean, is worthy of praise, and both forms of untruthful man are culpable, and particularly the boastful man.

Let us discuss them both, but first of all the truthful man. We are not speaking of the man who keeps faith in his agreements, i. e. in the things that pertain to justice or injustice (for this would belong to another virtue), but the man who in the matters in which nothing of this sort is at **1127ᵇ** stake is true both in word and in life because his character is such. But such a man would seem to be as a matter of fact equitable. For the man who loves truth, and is truthful where nothing is at stake, will still more be truthful where something is at stake; he will avoid falsehood as 5 something base, seeing that he avoided it even for its own sake; and such a man is worthy of praise. He inclines rather to understate the truth; for this seems in better taste because exaggerations are wearisome.

He who claims more than he has with no ulterior object

---

[17] Ch. 6.
[18] i. e. apart from any ulterior object it may serve.

is a contemptible sort of fellow (otherwise he would not
10 have delighted in falsehood), but seems futile rather than
bad; but if he does it for an object, he who does it for the
sake of reputation or honour is (for a boaster) not very
much to be blamed, but he who does it for money, or the
things that lead to money, is an uglier character (it is not
the capacity that makes the boaster, but the purpose; for
it is in virtue of his state of character and by being a man
of a certain kind that he is a boaster); as one man is a liar
15 because he enjoys the lie itself, and another because he
desires reputation or gain. Now those who boast for the
sake of reputation claim such qualities as win praise or
congratulation, but those whose object is gain claim qualities which are of value to one's neighbours and one's lack
of which is not easily detected, e. g. the powers of a seer,
20 a sage, or a physician. For this reason it is such things as
these that most people claim and boast about; for in them
the above-mentioned qualities are found.

Mock-modest people, who understate things, seem more
attractive in character; for they are thought to speak not
for gain but to avoid parade; and here too it is qualities
25 which bring reputation that they disclaim, as Socrates used
to do. Those who disclaim trifling and obvious qualities
are called humbugs and are more contemptible; and sometimes this seems to be boastfulness, like the Spartan dress;
for both excess and great deficiency are boastful. But
30 those who use understatement with moderation and understate about matters that do not very much force themselves
on our notice seem attractive. And it is the boaster that
seems to be opposed to the truthful man; for he is the worse
character.

8 Since life includes rest as well as activity, and in this
is included leisure and amusement, there seems here
1128ᵃ also to be a kind of intercourse which is tasteful; there is
such a thing as saying—and again listening to—what one
should and as one should. The kind of people one is speak-

ing or listening to will also make a difference. Evidently here also there is both an excess and a deficiency as compared with the mean. Those who carry humour to excess 5 are thought to be vulgar buffoons, striving after humour at all costs, and aiming rather at raising a laugh than at saying what is becoming and at avoiding pain to the object of their fun; while those who can neither make a joke themselves nor put up with those who do are thought to be boorish and unpolished. But those who joke in a tasteful way are called ready-witted, which implies a sort of readiness to 10 turn this way and that; for such sallies are thought to be movements of the character, and as bodies are discriminated by their movements, so too are characters. The ridiculous side of things is not far to seek, however, and most people delight more than they should in amusement and in jesting, and so even buffoons are called ready-witted 15 because they are found attractive; but that they differ from the ready-witted man, and to no small extent, is clear from what has been said.

To the middle state belongs also tact; it is the mark of a tactful man to say and listen to such things as befit a good and well-bred man; for there are some things that it befits 20 such a man to say and to hear by way of jest, and the well-bred man's jesting differs from that of a vulgar man, and the joking of an educated man from that of an uneducated. One may see this even from the old and the new comedies; to the authors of the former indecency of language was amusing, to those of the latter innuendo is more so; and these differ in no small degree in respect of propriety. Now 25 should we define the man who jokes well by his saying what is not unbecoming to a well-bred man, or by his not giving pain, or even giving delight, to the hearer? Or is the latter definition, at any rate, itself indefinite, since different things are hateful or pleasant to different people? The kind of jokes he will listen to will be the same; for the kind he can put up with are also the kind he seems to make. There are, then, jokes he will not make; for the jest is a sort of

30 abuse, and there are things that lawgivers forbid us to abuse; and they should, perhaps, have forbidden us even to make a jest of such. The refined and well-bred man, therefore, will be as we have described, being as it were a law to himself.

Such, then, is the man who observes the mean, whether he be called tactful or ready-witted. The buffoon, on the other hand, is the slave of his sense of humour, and spares 35 neither himself nor others if he can raise a laugh, and says things none of which a man of refinement would say, and 1128ᵇ to some of which he would not even listen. The boor, again, is useless for such social intercourse; for he contributes nothing and finds fault with everything. But relaxation and amusement are thought to be a necessary element in life.

The means in life that have been described, then, are three in number, and are all concerned with an interchange 5 of words and deeds of some kind. They differ, however, in that one is concerned with truth, and the other two with pleasantness. Of those concerned with pleasure, one is displayed in jests, the other in the general social intercourse of life.

9   Shame should not be described as a virtue; for it is 10   more like a feeling than a state of character. It is defined, at any rate, as a kind of fear of dishonour, and produces an effect similar to that produced by fear of danger; for people who feel disgraced blush, and those who fear death turn pale. Both, therefore, seem to be in a sense bodily conditions, which is thought to be characteristic of feeling rather than of a state of character.

The feeling is not becoming to every age, but only to 15 youth. For we think young people should be prone to the feeling of shame because they live by feeling and therefore commit many errors, but are restrained by shame; and we praise young people who are prone to this feeling, but an older person no one would praise for being prone to the

sense of disgrace, since we think he should not do anything
that need cause this sense. For the sense of disgrace is not 20
even characteristic of a good man,[19] since it is consequent
on bad actions (for such actions should not be done; and
if some actions are disgraceful in very truth and others
only according to common opinion, this makes no difference; for neither class of actions should be done, so that no
disgrace should be felt); and it is a mark of a bad man 25
even to be such as to do any disgraceful action. To be so
constituted as to feel disgraced if one does such an action,
and for this reason to think oneself good, is absurd; for it is
for voluntary actions that shame is felt, and the good man
will never voluntarily do bad actions. But shame may be 30
said to be conditionally a good thing; *if* a good man does
such actions, he will feel disgraced; but the virtues are not
subject to such a qualification. And if shamelessness—not
to be ashamed of doing base actions—is bad, that does not
make it good to be ashamed of doing such actions. Continence too is not virtue, but a mixed sort of state; this will 35
be shown later.[20] Now, however, let us discuss justice.

BOOK V

1   With regard to justice and injustice we must consider 1129ᵃ
(1) what kind of actions they are concerned with, (2)
what sort of mean justice is, and (3) between what ex- 5
tremes the just act is intermediate. Our investigation
shall follow the same course as the preceding discussions.

We see that all men mean by justice that kind of state of
character which makes people disposed to do what is just
and makes them act justly and wish for what is just; and
similarly by injustice that state which makes them act un- 10
justly and wish for what is unjust. Let us too, then, lay this
down as a general basis. For the same is not true of the
sciences and the faculties as of states of character. A

---

[19] sc. still less is it itself a virtue.
[20] vii. 1–10.

faculty or a science which is one and the same is held to relate to contrary objects, but a state of character which is
15 one of two contraries does *not* produce the contrary results;
e. g. as a result of health we do not do what is the opposite
of healthy, but only what is healthy; for we say a man walks
healthily, when he walks as a healthy man would.

Now often one contrary state is recognized from its contrary, and often states are recognized from the subjects that
20 exhibit them; for (A) if good condition is known, bad condition also becomes known, and (B) good condition is
known from the things that are in good condition, and
they from it. If good condition is firmness of flesh, it is
necessary both that bad condition should be flabbiness of
flesh and that the wholesome should be that which causes
firmness in flesh. And it follows for the most part that if
25 one contrary is ambiguous the other also will be ambiguous; e. g. if 'just' is so, that 'unjust' will be so too.

Now 'justice' and 'injustice' seem to be ambiguous, but
because their different meanings approach near to one another the ambiguity escapes notice and is not obvious as
it is, comparatively, when the meanings are far apart, e. g.
(for here the difference in outward form is great) as the
30 ambiguity in the use of *kleis* for the collar-bone of an animal and for that with which we lock a door. Let us take
as a starting-point, then, the various meanings of 'an unjust man'. Both the lawless man and the grasping and unfair man are thought to be unjust, so that evidently both
the law-abiding and the fair man will be just. The just,
then, is the lawful and the fair, the unjust the unlawful and
the unfair.

Since the unjust man is grasping, he must be concerned
1129ᵇ with goods—not all goods, but those with which prosperity and adversity have to do, which taken absolutely are
always good, but for a particular person are not always
5 good. Now men pray for and pursue these things; but they
should not, but should pray that the things that are good
absolutely may also be good for them, and should choose

the things that are good for them. The unjust man does not always choose the greater, but also the less—in the case of things bad absolutely; but because the lesser evil is itself thought to be in a sense good, and graspingness is directed at the good, therefore he is thought to be grasping. 10 And he is unfair; for this contains and is common to both.

Since the lawless man was seen to be unjust and the law-abiding man just, evidently all lawful acts are in a sense just acts; for the acts laid down by the legislative art are lawful, and each of these, we say, is just. Now the laws in their enactments on all subjects aim at the common ad- 15 vantage either of all or of the best or of those who hold power, or something of the sort; so that in one sense we call those acts just that tend to produce and preserve happiness and its components for the political society. And the law bids us do both the acts of a brave man (e. g. not to 20 desert our post nor take to flight nor throw away our arms), and those of a temperate man (e. g. not to commit adultery nor to gratify one's lust), and those of a good-tempered man (e. g. not to strike another nor to speak evil), and similarly with regard to the other virtues and forms of wickedness, commanding some acts and forbidding others; and the rightly-framed law does this rightly, and the hastily conceived one less well.

This form of justice, then, is complete virtue, but not absolutely, but in relation to our neighbour. And there- 25 fore justice is often thought to be the greatest of virtues, and 'neither evening nor morning star' is so wonderful; and proverbially 'in justice is every virtue comprehended'. And it is complete virtue in its fullest sense, because it is the 30 actual exercise of complete virtue. It is complete because he who possesses it can exercise his virtue not only in himself but towards his neighbour also; for many men can exercise virtue in their own affairs, but not in their rela- **1130ᵃ** tions to their neighbour. This is why the saying of Bias is thought to be true, that 'rule will show the man'; for a ruler is necessarily in relation to other men and a member

of a society. For this same reason justice, alone of the virtues, is thought to be 'another's good',[1] because it is re-
5 lated to our neighbour; for it does what is advantageous to
another, either a ruler or a copartner. Now the worst man
is he who exercises his wickedness both towards himself and
towards his friends, and the best man is not he who exercises his virtue towards himself but he who exercises it
towards another; for this is a difficult task. Justice in this
10 sense, then, is not part of virtue but virtue entire, nor is the
contrary injustice a part of vice but vice entire. What the
difference is between virtue and justice in this sense is plain
from what we have said; they are the same but their essence is not the same; what, as a relation to one's neighbour,
is justice is, as a certain kind of state without qualification,
virtue.

2   But at all events what we are investigating is the
justice which is a part of virtue; for there is a justice
15 of this kind, as we maintain. Similarly it is with injustice
in the particular sense that we are concerned.

That there is such a thing is indicated by the fact that
while the man who exhibits in action the other forms of
wickedness acts wrongly indeed, but not graspingly (e. g.
the man who throws away his shield through cowardice or
speaks harshly through bad temper or fails to help a friend
with money through meanness), when a man acts grasp-
20 ingly he often exhibits none of these vices—no, nor all
together, but certainly wickedness of some kind (for we
blame him) and injustice. There is, then, another kind of
injustice which is a part of injustice in the wide sense, and
a use of the word 'unjust' which answers to a part of what
is unjust in the wide sense of 'contrary to the law'. Again,
if one man commits adultery for the sake of gain and
25 makes money by it, while another does so at the bidding of
appetite though he loses money and is penalized for it, the
latter would be held to be self-indulgent rather than grasp-

[1] Pl. Rep. 343 c.

ing, but the former is unjust, but not self-indulgent; evidently, therefore, he is unjust by reason of his making gain
by his act. Again, all other unjust acts are ascribed invariably to some particular kind of wickedness, e. g. adul- 30
tery to self-indulgence, the desertion of a comrade in battle
to cowardice, physical violence to anger; but if a man makes
gain, his action is ascribed to no form of wickedness but injustice. Evidently, therefore, there is apart from injustice in
the wide sense another, 'particular', injustice which shares
the name and nature of the first, because its definition falls
within the same genus; for the significance of both consists
in a relation to one's neighbour, but the one is concerned **1130ᵇ**
with honour or money or safety—or that which includes all
these, if we had a single name for it—and its motive is the
pleasure that arises from gain; while the other is concerned
with all the objects with which the good man is concerned. 5

It is clear, then, that there is more than one kind of
justice, and that there is one which is distinct from virtue
entire; we must try to grasp its genus and differentia.

The unjust has been divided into the unlawful and the
unfair, and the just into the lawful and the fair. To the
unlawful answers the afore-mentioned sense of injustice.
But since the unfair and the unlawful are not the same, but
are different as a part is from its whole (for all that is unfair 10
is unlawful, but not all that is unlawful is unfair), the unjust and injustice in the sense of the unfair are not the same
as but different from the former kind, as part from whole;
for injustice in this sense is a part of injustice in the wide
sense, and similarly justice in the one sense of justice in
the other. Therefore we must speak also about particular 15
justice and particular injustice, and similarly about the just
and the unjust. The justice, then, which answers to the
whole of virtue, and the corresponding injustice, one being
the exercise of virtue as a whole, and the other that of vice
as a whole, towards one's neighbour, we may leave on one
side. And how the meanings of 'just' and 'unjust' which an- 20
swer to these are to be distinguished is evident; for prac-

tically the majority of the acts commanded by the law are
those which are prescribed from the point of view of virtue
taken as a whole; for the law bids us practise every virtue
and forbids us to practise any vice. And the things that tend
25 to produce virtue taken as a whole are those of the acts
prescribed by the law which have been prescribed with a
view to education for the common good. But with regard to
the education of the individual as such, which makes him
without qualification a good man, we must determine
later [2] whether this is the function of the political art or of
another; for perhaps it is not the same to be a good man and
a good citizen of any state taken at random.

Of particular justice and that which is just in the cor-
30 responding sense, (A) one kind is that which is manifested
in distributions of honour or money or the other things that
fall to be divided among those who have a share in the
constitution (for in these it is possible for one man to have
a share either unequal or equal to that of another), and
(B) one is that which plays a rectifying part in trans-
1131ᵃ actions between man and man. Of this there are two divisions; of transactions (1) some are voluntary and (2)
others involuntary—voluntary such transactions as sale,
purchase, loan for consumption, pledging, loan for use, de-
positing, letting (they are called voluntary because the
5 origin of these transactions is voluntary), while of the involuntary (a) some are clandestine, such as theft, adultery,
poisoning, procuring, enticement of slaves, assassination,
false witness, and (b) others are violent, such as assault,
imprisonment, murder, robbery with violence, mutilation,
abuse, insult.

10 **3**   (A) We have shown that both the unjust man and
the unjust act are unfair or unequal; now it is clear
that there is also an intermediate between the two unequals involved in either case. And this is the equal; for

[2] 1179ᵇ 20–1181ᵇ 12. Pol. 1276ᵇ 16–1277ᵇ 32, 1278ᵃ 40–ᵇ5, 1288ᵃ
32–ᵇ2, 1333ᵃ 11–16, 1337ᵃ 11–14.

in any kind of action in which there is a more and a less there is also what is equal. If, then, the unjust is unequal, the just is equal, as all men suppose it to be, even apart from argument. And since the equal is intermediate, the just will be an intermediate. Now equality implies at least 15 two things. The just, then, must be both intermediate and equal and relative (i. e. for certain persons). And qua intermediate it must be between certain things (which are respectively greater and less); qua equal, it involves two things; qua just, it is for certain people. The just, therefore, involves at least four terms; for the persons for whom it is in fact just are two, and the things in which it is mani- 20 fested, the objects distributed, are two. And the same equality will exist between the persons and between the things concerned; for as the latter—the things concerned— are related, so are the former; if they are not equal, they will not have what is equal, but this is the origin of quarrels and complaints—when either equals have and are awarded unequal shares, or unequals equal shares. Further, this is plain from the fact that awards should be 'according to 25 merit'; for all men agree that what is just in distribution must be according to merit in some sense, though they do not all specify the same sort of merit, but democrats identify it with the status of freeman, supporters of oligarchy with wealth (or with noble birth), and supporters of aristocracy with excellence.

The just, then, is a species of the proportionate (propor- 30 tion being not a property only of the kind of number which consists of abstract units, but of number in general). For proportion is equality of ratios, and involves four terms at least (that discrete proportion involves four terms is plain, but so does continuous proportion, for it uses one term as two and mentions it twice; e. g. 'as the line A is to the line B, so is the line B to the line C'; the line B, then, has been **1131ᵇ** mentioned twice, so that if the line B be assumed twice, the proportional terms will be four); and the just, too, involves at least four terms, and the ratio between one pair is

the same as that between the other pair; for there is a similar distinction between the persons and between the
5 things. As the term A, then, is to B, so will C be to D, and therefore, *alternando*, as A is to C, B will be to D. Therefore also the whole is in the same ratio to the whole; [3] and this coupling the distribution effects, and, if the terms are so combined, effects justly. The conjunction, then, of the term A with C and of B with D is what is just in distribution,[4] and this species of the just is intermediate, and the
10 unjust is what violates the proportion; for the proportional is intermediate, and the just is proportional. (Mathematicians call this kind of proportion geometrical; for it is in geometrical proportion that it follows that the whole is to
15 the whole as either part is to the corresponding part.) This proportion is not continuous; for we cannot get a single term standing for a person and a thing.

This, then, is what the just is—the proportional; the unjust is what violates the proportion. Hence one term becomes too great, the other too small, as indeed happens in practice; for the man who acts unjustly has too much, and the man who is unjustly treated too little, of what is good.
20 In the case of evil the reverse is true; for the lesser evil is reckoned a good in comparison with the greater evil, since the lesser evil is rather to be chosen than the greater, and what is worthy of choice is good, and what is worthier of choice a greater good.

This, then, is one species of the just.

4   (B) The remaining one is the rectificatory, which
25   arises in connexion with transactions both voluntary

[3] Person A + thing C to person B + thing D.

[4] The problem of distributive justice is to divide the distributable honour or reward into parts which are to one another as are the merits of the persons who are to participate. If
A (first person) : B (second person) :: C (first portion) : D (second portion), then (*alternando*) A : C :: B : D,
and therefore (*componendo*) A + C : B + D :: A : B.
In other words the position established answers to the relative merits of the parties.

and involuntary. This form of the just has a different specific character from the former. For the justice which
distributes common possessions is always in accordance
with the kind of proportion mentioned above [5] (for in the
case also in which the distribution is made from the common funds of a partnership it will be according to the 30
same ratio which the funds put into the business by the
partners bear to one another); and the injustice opposed
to this kind of justice is that which violates the proportion.
But the justice in transactions between man and man is a 1132ᵃ
sort of equality indeed, and the injustice a sort of inequality; not according to that kind of proportion, however,
but according to arithmetical proportion.[6] For it makes no
difference whether a good man has defrauded a bad man or
a bad man a good one, nor whether it is a good or a bad man
that has committed adultery; the law looks only to the
distinctive character of the injury, and treats the parties as 5
equal, if one is in the wrong and the other is being wronged,
and if one inflicted injury and the other has received it.
Therefore, this kind of injustice being an inequality, the
judge tries to equalize it; for in the case also in which one
has received and the other has inflicted a wound, or one
has slain and the other been slain, the suffering and the
action have been unequally distributed; but the judge tries
to equalize things by means of the penalty, taking away 10
from the gain of the assailant. For the term 'gain' is applied generally to such cases, even if it be not a term ap-

[5] l. 12 f.

[6] The problem of 'rectificatory justice' has nothing to do with punishment proper but is only that of rectifying a wrong that has been
done, by awarding damages; i. e. rectificatory justice is that of
the civil, not that of the criminal courts. The parties are treated by the
court as equal (since a law court is not a court of morals), and the
wrongful act is reckoned as having brought equal gain to the wrongdoer and loss to his victim; it brings A to the position A + C, and B
to the position B − C. The judge's task is to find the arithmetical
mean between these, and this he does by transferring C from A to B.
Thus (A being treated as = B) we get the arithmetical 'proportion'

$$(A + C) - (A + C - C) = (A + C - C) - (B - C)$$
or $$(A + C) - (B - C + C) = (B - C + C) - (B - C).$$

propriate to certain cases, e. g. to the person who inflicts a
wound—and 'loss' to the sufferer; at all events when the
suffering has been estimated, the one is called loss and the
15 other gain. Therefore the equal is intermediate between
the greater and the less, but the gain and the loss are respectively greater and less in contrary ways; more of the
good and less of the evil are gain, and the contrary is loss;
intermediate between them is, as we saw,[7] the equal, which
we say is just; therefore corrective justice will be the inter-
20 mediate between loss and gain. This is why, when people
dispute, they take refuge in the judge; and to go to the
judge is to go to justice; for the nature of the judge is to be
a sort of animate justice; and they seek the judge as an
intermediate, and in some states they call judges mediators,
on the assumption that if they get what is intermediate
they will get what is just. The just, then, is an intermediate, since the judge is so. Now the judge restores equality;
it is as though there were a line divided into unequal
25 parts, and he took away that by which the greater segment
exceeds the half, and added it to the smaller segment. And
when the whole has been equally divided, then they say
they have 'their own'—i. e. when they have got what is
equal. The equal is intermediate between the greater and
the lesser line according to arithmetical proportion. It is
30 for this reason also that it is called just (dikaion), because
it is a division into two equal parts (dicha), just as if one
were to call it (dichaion); and the judge (dicastes) is one
who bisects (dichastes). For when something is subtracted
from one of two equals and added to the other, the other is
in excess by these two; since if what was taken from the
one had not been added to the other, the latter would have
been in excess by one only. It therefore exceeds the inter-
1132[b] mediate by one, and the intermediate exceeds by one that
from which something was taken. By this, then, we shall
recognize both what we must subtract from that which has
more, and what we must add to that which has less; we

[7] l. 14.

must add to the latter that by which the intermediate exceeds it, and subtract from the greatest that by which it 5
exceeds the intermediate. Let the lines AA', BB', CC' be
equal to one another; from the line AA' let the segment
AE have been subtracted, and to the line CC' let the segment CD [8] have been added, so that the whole line DCC'
exceeds the line EA' by the segment CD and the segment
CF; therefore it exceeds the line BB' by the segment CD.

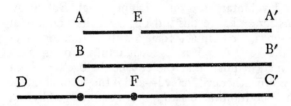

These names, both loss and gain, have come from voluntary
exchange; for to have more than one's own is called gain- 11
ing, and to have less than one's original share is called
losing, e. g. in buying and selling and in all other matters 15
in which the law has left people free to make their own
terms; but when they get neither more nor less but just
what belongs to themselves, they say that they have their
own and that they neither lose nor gain.

Therefore the just is intermediate between a sort of gain
and a sort of loss, viz. those which are involuntary; [9] it consists in having an equal amount before and after the trans- 20
action.

5   Some think that reciprocity is without qualification
just, as the Pythagoreans said; for they defined justice
without qualification as reciprocity. Now 'reciprocity' fits
neither distributive nor rectificatory justice—yet people 25
want even the justice of Rhadamanthus to mean this;

[8] sc. equal to AE.
[9] i. e. for the loser.

Should a man suffer what he did, right justice would
be done

—for in many cases reciprocity and rectificatory justice are
not in accord, e. g. (1) if an official has inflicted a wound,
he should not be wounded in return, and if some one has
30 wounded an official, he ought not to be wounded only but
punished in addition. Further (2) there is a great difference
between a voluntary and an involuntary act. But in associations for exchange this sort of justice does hold men
together—reciprocity in accordance with a proportion and
not on the basis of precisely equal return. For it is by
proportionate requital that the city holds together. Men
1133ª seek to return either evil for evil—and if they cannot do so,
think their position mere slavery—or good for good—and
if they cannot do so there is no exchange, but it is by exchange that they hold together. This is why they give a
prominent place to the temple of the Graces—to promote
the requital of services; for this is characteristic of grace—
we should serve in return one who has shown grace to us,
and should another time take the initiative in showing it.
5   Now proportionate return is secured by cross-conjunc-
tion. Let A be a builder, B a shoemaker, C a house, D a
shoe. The builder, then, must get from the shoemaker the
10 latter's work, and must himself give him in return his
own. If, then, first there is proportionate equality of goods,
and then reciprocal action takes place, the result we mention will be effected. If not, the bargain is not equal, and
does not hold; for there is nothing to prevent the work of
the one being better than that of the other; they must
15 therefore be equated. (And this is true of the other arts
also; for they would have been destroyed if what the patient suffered had not been just what the agent did, and of
the same amount and kind.) For it is not two doctors that
associate for exchange, but a doctor and a farmer, or in
general people who are different and unequal; but these
must be equated. This is why all things that are exchanged

must be somehow comparable. It is for this end that money has been introduced, and it becomes in a sense an intermediate; for it measures all things, and therefore the excess and the defect—how many shoes are equal to a 20 house or to a given amount of food. The number of shoes exchanged for a house [or for a given amount of food] must therefore correspond to the ratio of builder to shoemaker. For if this be not so, there will be no exchange and no intercourse. And this proportion will not be effected unless the goods are somehow equal. All goods must 25 therefore be measured by some one thing, as we said before. Now this unit is in truth demand, which holds all things together (for if men did not need one another's goods at all, or did not need them equally, there would be either no exchange or not the same exchange); but money has become by convention a sort of representative of demand; 30 and this is why it has the name 'money' (*nomisma*)—because it exists not by nature but by law (*nomos*) and it is in our power to change it and make it useless. There will, then, be reciprocity when the terms have been equated so that as farmer is to shoemaker, the amount of the shoemaker's work is to that of the farmer's work for which it exchanges. But we must not bring them into a figure of 1133ᵇ proportion when they have already exchanged (otherwise one extreme will have both excesses), but when they still have their own goods. Thus they are equals and associates just because this equality can be effected in their case. Let A be a farmer, C food, B a shoemaker, D his product 5 equated to C. If it had not been possible for reciprocity to be thus effected, there would have been no association of the parties. That demand holds things together as a single unit is shown by the fact that when men do not need one another, i. e. when neither needs the other or one does not need the other, they do not exchange, as we do when some one wants what one has oneself, e. g. when people permit the exportation of corn in exchange for wine. This equation therefore must be established. And for the future exchange 10

—that if we do not need a thing now we shall have it if ever we do need it—money is as it were our surety; for it must be possible for us to get what we want by bringing the money. Now the same thing happens to money itself as to goods—it is not always worth the same; yet it tends to be steadier. This is why all goods must have a price set on
15 them; for then there will always be exchange, and if so, association of man with man. Money, then, acting as a measure, makes goods commensurate and equates them; for neither would there have been association if there were not exchange, nor exchange if there were not equality, nor equality if there were not commensurability. Now in truth it is impossible that things differing so much should
20 become commensurate, but with reference to demand they may become so sufficiently. There must, then, be a unit, and that fixed by agreement (for which reason it is called money); for it is this that makes all things commensurate, since all things are measured by money. Let A be a house, B ten minae, C a bed. A is half of B, if the house is worth
25 five minae or equal to them; the bed, C, is a tenth of B; it is plain, then, how many beds are equal to a house, viz. five. That exchange took place thus before there was money is plain; for it makes no difference whether it is five beds that exchange for a house, or the money value of five beds.

30   We have now defined the unjust and the just. These having been marked off from each other, it is plain that just action is intermediate between acting unjustly and being unjustly treated; for the one is to have too much and the other to have too little. Justice is a kind of mean, but not in the same way as the other virtues, but because it relates to an intermediate amount, while injustice relates
1134ᵃ to the extremes. And justice is that in virtue of which the just man is said to be a doer, by choice, of that which is just, and one who will distribute either between himself and another or between two others not so as to give more of what is desirable to himself and less to his neighbour (and
5 conversely with what is harmful), but so as to give what is

equal in accordance with proportion; and similarly in dis-
tributing between two other persons. Injustice on the other
hand is similarly related to the unjust, which is excess and
defect, contrary to proportion, of the useful or hurtful. For
which reason injustice is excess and defect, viz. because it is
productive of excess and defect—in one's own case excess
of what is in its own nature useful and defect of what is 10
hurtful, while in the case of others it is as a whole like what
it is in one's own case, but proportion may be violated in
either direction. In the unjust act to have too little is to be
unjustly treated; to have too much is to act unjustly.

Let this be taken as our account of the nature of justice
and injustice, and similarly of the just and the unjust in 15
general.

6   Since acting unjustly does not necessarily imply being
    unjust, we must ask what sort of unjust acts imply that
the doer is unjust with respect to each type of injustice, e. g.
a thief, an adulterer, or a brigand. Surely the answer does
not turn on the difference between these types. For a man
might even lie with a woman knowing who she was, but the
origin of his act might be not deliberate choice but passion.
He acts unjustly, then, but is not unjust; e. g. a man is not 20
a thief, yet he stole, nor an adulterer, yet he committed
adultery; and similarly in all other cases.

Now we have previously stated how the reciprocal is related to the just; [10] but we must not forget that what we are
looking for is not only what is just without qualification 25
but also political justice. This is found among men who
share their life with a view to self-sufficiency, men who are
free and either proportionately or arithmetically equal,
so that between those who do not fulfil this condition
there is no political justice but justice in a special sense
and by analogy. For justice exists only between men whose
mutual relations are governed by law; and law exists for 30
men between whom there is injustice; for legal justice is

[10] 1132ᵇ 21–1133ᵇ 28.

the discrimination of the just and the unjust. And between men between whom there is injustice there is also unjust action (though there is not injustice between all between whom there is unjust action), and this is assigning too much to oneself of things good in themselves and too little of things evil in themselves. This is why we do not
35 allow a man to rule, but *rational principle*, because a man behaves thus in his own interests and becomes a tyrant.
1134ᵇ The magistrate on the other hand is the guardian of justice, and, if of justice, then of equality also. And since he is assumed to have no more than his share, if he is just (for he does not assign to himself more of what is good in itself, unless such a share is proportional to his merits—so that it is for others that he labours, and it is for this reason that
5 men, as we stated previously,[11] say that justice is 'another's good'), therefore a reward must be given him, and this is honour and privilege; but those for whom such things are not enough become tyrants.

The justice of a master and that of a father are not the same as the justice of citizens, though they are like it; for there can be no injustice in the unqualified sense towards things that are one's own, but a man's chattel,[12] and his
10 child until it reaches a certain age and sets up for itself, are as it were part of himself, and no one chooses to hurt himself (for which reason there can be no injustice towards oneself). Therefore the justice or injustice of citizens is not manifested in these relations; for it was as we saw[13] according to law, and between people naturally subject to law, and these as we saw[14] are people who have an equal
15 share in ruling and being ruled. Hence justice can more truly be manifested towards a wife than towards children and chattels, for the former is household justice; but even this is different from political justice.

---

[11] 1130ᵃ 3.
[12] i. e. his slave.
[13] ᵃ 30.
[14] ᵃ 26–8.

7   Of political justice part is natural, part legal—natural,
that which everywhere has the same force and does not
exist by people's thinking this or that; legal, that which is 20
originally indifferent, but when it has been laid down is not
indifferent, e. g. that a prisoner's ransom shall be a mina, or
that a goat and not two sheep shall be sacrificed, and
again all the laws that are passed for particular cases, e. g.
that sacrifice shall be made in honour of Brasidas, and
the provisions of decrees. Now some think that all justice 25
is of this sort, because that which is by nature is unchangeable and has everywhere the same force (as fire burns both
here and in Persia), while they see change in the things
recognized as just. This, however, is not true in this unqualified way, but is true in a sense; or rather, with the
gods it is perhaps not true at all, while with us there is
something that is just even by nature, yet all of it is
changeable; but still some is by nature, some not by nature. 30
It is evident which sort of thing, among things capable of
being otherwise, is by nature; and which is not but is legal
and conventional, assuming that both are equally changeable. And in all other things the same distinction will apply;
by nature the right hand is stronger, yet it is possible that all
men should come to be ambidextrous. The things which **1135ᵃ**
are just by virtue of convention and expediency are like
measures; for wine and corn measures are not everywhere
équal, but larger in wholesale and smaller in retail markets.
Similarly, the things which are just not by nature but by
human enactment are not everywhere the same, since
constitutions also are not the same, though there is but one
which is everywhere by nature the best.

Of things just and lawful each is related as the universal 5
to its particulars; for the things that are done are many,
but of them each is one, since it is universal.

There is a difference between the act of injustice and
what is unjust, and between the act of justice and what is
just; for a thing is unjust by nature or by enactment; and 10
this very thing, when it has been done, is an act of in-

justice, but before it is done is not yet that but is unjust.
So, too, with an act of justice (though the general term is
rather 'just action', and 'act of justice' is applied to the
correction of the act of injustice).

Each of these must later [15] be examined separately with
regard to the nature and number of its species and the
nature of the things with which it is concerned.

8   Acts just and unjust being as we have described them,
15   a man acts unjustly or justly whenever he does such
acts voluntarily; when involuntarily, he acts neither unjustly nor justly except in an incidental way; for he does
things which happen to be just or unjust. Whether an act
is or is not one of injustice (or of justice) is determined by
its voluntariness or involuntariness; for when it is volun-
20 tary it is blamed, and at the same time is then an act of
injustice; so that there will be things that are unjust but
not yet acts of injustice, if voluntariness be not present
as well. By the voluntary I mean, as has been said before,[16]
any of the things in a man's own power which he does with
knowledge, i. e. not in ignorance either of the person acted
on or of the instrument used or of the end that will be at-
25 tained (e. g. whom he is striking, with what, and to what
end), each such act being done not incidentally nor
under compulsion (e. g. if A takes B's hand and therewith strikes C, B does not act voluntarily; for the act was
not in his own power). The person struck may be the
striker's father, and the striker may know that it is a man
30 or one of the persons present, but not know that it is his
father; a similar distinction may be made in the case of the
end, and with regard to the whole action. Therefore that
which is done in ignorance, or though not done in ignorance is not in the agent's power, or is done under compulsion, is involuntary (for many natural processes, even,

[15] Possibly a reference to an intended (or now lost) book of the
Politics on laws.

[16] 1109ᵇ35–1111ᵃ24.

we knowingly both perform and experience, none of which
is either voluntary or involuntary; e. g. growing old or 1135ᵇ
dying). But in the case of unjust and just acts alike the
injustice or justice may be only incidental; for a man might
return a deposit unwillingly and from fear, and then he
must not be said either to do what is just or to act justly, 5
except in an incidental way. Similarly the man who under
compulsion and unwillingly fails to return the deposit must
be said to act unjustly, and to do what is unjust, only
incidentally. Of voluntary acts we do some by choice,
others not by choice; by choice those which we do after 10
deliberation, not by choice those which we do without
previous deliberation. Thus there are three kinds of injury
in transactions between man and man; those done in ignorance are mistakes when the person acted on, the act, the
instrument, or the end that will be attained is other than
the agent supposed; the agent thought either that he was
not hitting any one or that he was not hitting with this
missile or not hitting this person or to this end, but a result followed other than that which he thought likely (e. g. 15
he threw not with intent to wound but only to prick), or
the person hit or the missile was other than he supposed.
Now when (1) the injury takes place contrary to reasonable expectation, it is a misadventure. When (2) it is not
contrary to reasonable expectation, but does not imply vice,
it is a mistake (for a man makes a mistake when the fault
originates in him, but is the victim of accident when the
origin lies outside him). When (3) he acts with knowledge
but not after deliberation, it is an act of injustice—e. g. the 20
acts due to anger or to other passions necessary or natural to
man; for when men do such harmful and mistaken acts
they act unjustly, and the acts are acts of injustice, but this
does not imply that the doers are unjust or wicked; for the
injury is not due to vice. But when (4) a man acts from 25
choice, he is an unjust man and a vicious man.

Hence acts proceeding from anger are rightly judged not
to be done of malice aforethought; for it is not the man

who acts in anger but he who enraged him that starts the
mischief. Again, the matter in dispute is not whether the
thing happened or not, but its justice; for it is apparent
injustice that occasions rage. For they do not dispute about
30 the occurrence of the act—as in commercial transactions
where one of the two parties *must* be vicious [17]—unless
they do so owing to forgetfulness; but, agreeing about the
fact, they dispute on which side justice lies (whereas a man
who has deliberately injured another cannot help knowing
that he has done so), so that the one thinks he is being
treated unjustly and the other disagrees.

1136ᵃ But if a man harms another by choice, he acts unjustly;
and *these* are the acts of injustice which imply that the
doer is an unjust man, provided that the act violates proportion or equality. Similarly, a man *is just* when he acts
justly by choice; but he *acts justly* if he merely acts voluntarily.

5 Of involuntary acts some are excusable, others not. For
the mistakes which men make not only in ignorance but
also from ignorance are excusable, while those which men
do not from ignorance but (though they do them *in* ignorance) owing to a passion which is neither natural nor
such as man is liable to, are not excusable.

10 **9** Assuming that we have sufficiently defined the suffering and doing of injustice, it may be asked (1) whether
the truth is expressed in Euripides' paradoxical words:

> 'I slew my mother, that's my tale in brief.'
> 'Were you both willing, or unwilling both?'

Is it truly possible to be willingly treated unjustly, or is all
15 suffering of injustice on the contrary involuntary, as all unjust action is voluntary? And is all suffering of injustice of
the latter kind or else all of the former, or is it sometimes

---

[17] The plaintiff, if he brings a false accusation; the defendant, if he
denies a true one.

voluntary, sometimes involuntary? So, too, with the case
of being justly treated; all just action is voluntary, so that
it is reasonable that there should be a similar opposition
in either case—that both being unjustly and being justly
treated should be either alike voluntary or alike involun- 20
tary. But it would be thought paradoxical even in the case
of being justly treated, if it were always voluntary; for some
are unwillingly treated justly. (2) One might raise this
question also, whether every one who has suffered what is
unjust is being unjustly treated, or on the other hand it is
with suffering as with acting. In action and in passivity 25
alike it is possible to partake of justice incidentally, and
similarly (it is plain) of injustice; for to do what is unjust
is not the same as to act unjustly, nor to suffer what is unjust as to be treated unjustly, and similarly in the case of
acting justly and being justly treated; for it is impossible
to be unjustly treated if the other does not act unjustly,
or justly treated unless he acts justly. Now if to act un- 30
justly is simply to harm some one voluntarily, and 'voluntarily' means 'knowing the person acted on, the instrument,
and the manner of one's acting', and the incontinent man
voluntarily harms himself, not only will he voluntarily be
unjustly treated but it will be possible to treat oneself
unjustly. (This also is one of the questions in doubt,
whether a man can treat himself unjustly.) Again, a man
may voluntarily, owing to incontinence, be harmed by 1136ᵇ
another who acts voluntarily, so that it would be possible
to be voluntarily treated unjustly. Or is our definition incorrect; must we to 'harming another, with knowledge both
of the person acted on, of the instrument, and of the manner' add 'contrary to the wish of the person acted on'? Then
a man may be voluntarily harmed and voluntarily suffer 5
what is unjust, but no one is voluntarily treated unjustly;
for no one wishes to be unjustly treated, not even the incontinent man. He acts contrary to his wish; for no one
wishes for what he does not think to be good, but the incontinent man does *do* things that he does not think he

ought to do. Again, one who gives what is his own, as Homer says Glaucus gave Diomede

Armour of gold for brazen, the price of a hundred beeves
10 *for nine,*[18] is not unjustly treated; for though to give is in his power, to be unjustly treated is not, but there must be some one to treat him unjustly. It is plain, then, that being unjustly treated is not voluntary.

15   Of the questions we intended to discuss two still remain for discussion; (3) whether it is the man who has assigned to another more than his share that acts unjustly, or he who has the excessive share, and (4) whether it is possible to treat oneself unjustly. The questions are connected; for if the former alternative is possible and the distributor acts unjustly and not the man who has the excessive share, then if a man assigns more to another than
20 to himself, knowingly and voluntarily, he treats himself unjustly; which is what modest people seem to do, since the virtuous man tends to take less than his share. Or does this statement too need qualification? For (a) he perhaps gets more than his share of some other good, e. g. of honour or of intrinsic nobility. (b) The question is solved by applying the distinction we applied to unjust action;[19] for he suffers nothing contrary to his own wish, so that he is not unjustly treated as far as this goes, but at most only suffers harm.

25   It is plain too that the distributor acts unjustly, but not always the man who has the excessive share; for it is not he to whom what is unjust appertains that acts unjustly, but he to whom it appertains to do the unjust act voluntarily, i. e. the person in whom lies the origin of the action, and this lies in the distributor, not in the receiver. Again,
30 since the word 'do' is ambiguous, and there is a sense in which lifeless things, or a hand, or a servant who obeys an order, may be said to slay, he who gets an excessive share does not act unjustly, though he 'does' what is unjust.

[18] *Il.* vi. 236.
[19] ll. 3–5.

Again, if the distributor gave his judgment in ignorance, he does not act unjustly in respect of legal justice, and his judgment is not unjust in this sense, but in a sense it is unjust (for legal justice and primordial justice are differ-**1137ᵃ** ent); but if with knowledge he judged unjustly, he is himself aiming at an excessive share either of gratitude or of revenge. As much, then, as if he were to share in the plunder, the man who has judged unjustly for these reasons has got too much; the fact that what he gets is different from what he distributes makes no difference, for even if he awards land with a view to sharing in the plunder he gets not land but money.

Men think that acting unjustly is in their power, and 5 therefore that being just is easy. But it is not; to lie with one's neighbour's wife, to wound another, to deliver a bribe, is easy and in our power, but to do these things as a result of a certain state of character is neither easy nor in our power. Similarly to know what is just and what is unjust requires, men think, no great wisdom, because it is not hard to understand the matters dealt with by the laws 10 (though these are not the things that are just, except incidentally); but how actions must be done and distributions effected in order to be just, to know this is a greater achievement than knowing what is good for the health; though even there, while it is easy to know that honey, wine, hellebore, cautery, and the use of the knife are so, to know how, to whom, and when these should be applied with a 15 view to producing health, is no less an achievement than that of being a physician. Again, for this very reason ²⁰ men think that acting unjustly is characteristic of the just man no less than of the unjust, because he would be not less but even more capable of doing each of these unjust acts; ²¹ for he could lie with a woman or wound a neighbour; and the brave man could throw away his shield and turn to flight in this direction or in that. But to play the 20

²⁰ i. e. that stated in l. 4 f., that acting unjustly is in our own power.
²¹ Cf. ll. 6–8.

coward or to act unjustly consists not in doing these things, except incidentally, but in doing them as the result of a certain state of character, just as to practise medicine and healing consists not in applying or not applying the knife, in using or not using medicines, but in doing so in a certain 25 way.

Just acts occur between people who participate in things good in themselves and can have too much or too little of them; for some beings (e. g. presumably the gods) cannot have too much of them, and to others, those who are incurably bad, not even the smallest share in them is beneficial but all such goods are harmful, while to others they are beneficial up to a point; therefore justice is essentially 30 something human.

10 Our next subject is equity and the equitable (*to epieikes*), and their respective relations to justice and the just. For on examination they appear to be neither absolutely the same nor generically different; and while we 35 sometimes praise what is equitable and the equitable man (so that we apply the name by way of praise even to instances of the other virtues, instead of 'good,' meaning by 1137ᵇ *epieikesteron* that a thing is better), at other times, when we reason it out, it seems strange if the equitable, being something different from the just, is yet praiseworthy; for either the just or the equitable is not good, if they are different; or, if both are good, they are the same.

5 These, then, are pretty much the considerations that give rise to the problem about the equitable; they are all in a sense correct and not opposed to one another; for the equitable, though it is better than one kind of justice, yet is just, and it is not as being a different class of thing that it is better than the just. The same thing, then, is just and 10 equitable, and while both are good the equitable is superior. What creates the problem is that the equitable is just, but not the legally just but a correction of legal justice. The reason is that all law is universal but about some things it is not possible to make a universal statement which shall be

correct. In those cases, then, in which it is necessary to 15
speak universally, but not possible to do so correctly,
the law takes the usual case, though it is not ignorant of the
possibility of error. And it is none the less correct; for the
error is not in the law nor in the legislator but in the nature
of the thing, since the matter of practical affairs is of this
kind from the start. When the law speaks universally, then, 20
and a case arises on it which is not covered by the universal
statement, then it is right, where the legislator fails us and
has erred by over-simplicity, to correct the omission—to say
what the legislator himself would have said had he been
present, and would have put into his law if he had known.
Hence the equitable is just, and better than one kind of 25
justice—not better than absolute justice but better than the
error that arises from the absoluteness of the statement.
And this is the nature of the equitable, a correction of law
where it is defective owing to its universality. In fact this is
the reason why all things are not determined by law, viz.
that about some things it is impossible to lay down a law,
so that a decree is needed. For when the thing is indefinite
the rule also is indefinite, like the leaden rule used in mak- 30
ing the Lesbian moulding; the rule adapts itself to the
shape of the stone and is not rigid, and so too the decree is
adapted to the facts.

It is plain, then, what the equitable is, and that it is just
and is better than one kind of justice. It is evident also from
this who the equitable man is; the man who chooses and 35
does such acts, and is no stickler for his rights in a bad sense **1138ᵃ**
but tends to take less than his share though he has the law
on his side, is equitable, and this state of character is equity,
which is a sort of justice and not a different state of character.

11 Whether a man can treat himself unjustly or not, is
    evident from what has been said.[22] For (a) one class 5
of just acts are those acts in accordance with any virtue
which are prescribed by the law; e. g. the law does not ex-

[22] Cf. 1129ᵃ 32–ᵇ 1, 1136ᵃ 10–1137ᵃ 4.

pressly permit suicide, and what it does not expressly permit
it forbids. Again, when a man in violation of the law harms
another (otherwise than in retaliation) voluntarily, he acts
unjustly, and a voluntary agent is one who knows both the
person he is affecting by his action and the instrument he
is using; and he who through anger voluntarily stabs him-
10 self does this contrary to the right rule of life, and this the
law does not allow; therefore he is acting unjustly. But towards whom? Surely towards the state, not towards himself.
For he suffers voluntarily, but no one is voluntarily treated
unjustly. This is also the reason why the state punishes; a
certain loss of civil rights attaches to the man who destroys
himself, on the ground that he is treating the state unjustly.

Further (b) in that sense of 'acting unjustly' in which
the man who 'acts unjustly' is unjust only and not bad all
round, it is not possible to treat oneself unjustly (this is
15 different from the former sense; the unjust man in one
sense of the term is wicked in a particularized way just as
the coward is, not in the sense of being wicked all round,
so that his 'unjust act' does not manifest wickedness in
general). For (i) that would imply the possibility of the
same thing's having been subtracted from and added to
the same thing at the same time; but this is impossible—the
just and the unjust always involve more than one person.
20 Further, (ii) unjust action is voluntary and done by choice,
and takes the initiative (for the man who because he has
suffered does the same in return is not thought to act unjustly); but if a man harms himself he suffers and does the
same things at the same time. Further, (iii) if a man could
treat himself unjustly, he could be voluntarily treated unjustly. Besides, (iv) no one acts unjustly without committing particular acts of injustice; but no one can commit
25 adultery with his own wife or housebreaking on his own
house or theft on his own property.

In general, the question 'can a man treat himself unjustly?' is solved also by the distinction we applied to the
question 'can a man be voluntarily treated unjustly?' [23]

[23] Cf. 1136ª 31–ᵇ 5.

(It is evident too that both are bad, being unjustly treated and acting unjustly; for the one means having less and the other having more than the intermediate amount, which plays the part here that the healthy does in the 30 medical art, and that good condition does in the art of bodily training. But still acting unjustly is the worse, for it involves vice and is blameworthy—involves vice which is either of the complete and unqualified kind or almost so (we must admit the latter alternative, because not all voluntary unjust action implies injustice as a state of character), while being unjustly treated does not involve vice 35 and injustice in oneself. In itself, then, being unjustly treated is less bad, but there is nothing to prevent its being **1138ᵇ** incidentally a greater evil. But theory cares nothing for this; it calls pleurisy a more serious mischief than a stumble; yet the latter may become incidentally the more serious, if the fall due to it leads to your being taken prisoner or put to death by the enemy.)

Metaphorically and in virtue of a certain resemblance 5 there is a justice not indeed between a man and himself, but between certain parts of him; yet not every kind of justice but that of master and servant or that of husband and wife.²⁴ For these are the ratios in which the part of the soul that has a rational principle stands to the irrational part; and it is with a view to these parts that people also think a man can be unjust to himself, viz. because these 10 parts are liable to suffer something contrary to their respective desires; there is therefore thought to be a mutual justice between them as between ruler and ruled.

Let this be taken as our account of justice and the other, i. e. the other moral, virtues.

BOOK VI

1   Since we have previously said that one ought to choose that which is intermediate, not the excess nor the defect,¹ and that the intermediate is determined by the dic-

²⁴ Cf. 1134ᵇ 15–17.
¹ 1104ᵃ 11–27, 1106ᵃ 26–1107ᵃ 27.

20 tates of the right rule,[2] let us discuss the nature of these dictates. In all the states of character we have mentioned,[3] as in all other matters, there is a mark to which the man who has the rule looks, and heightens or relaxes his activity accordingly, and there is a standard which determines the mean states which we say are intermediate between excess 25 and defect, being in accordance with the right rule. But such a statement, though true, is by no means clear; for not only here but in all other pursuits which are objects of knowledge it is indeed true to say that we must not exert ourselves nor relax our efforts too much nor too little, but to an intermediate extent and as the right rule dictates; but if a man had only this knowledge he would be none the 30 wiser—e. g. we should not know what sort of medicines to apply to our body if some one were to say 'all those which the medical art prescribes, and which agree with the practice of one who possesses the art.' Hence it is necessary with regard to the states of the soul also not only that this true statement should be made, but also that it should be determined what is the right rule and what is the standard that fixes it.

We divided the virtues of the soul and said that some are 35 virtues of character and others of intellect.[4] Now we have 1139ᵃ discussed in detail the moral virtues;[3] with regard to the others let us express our view as follows, beginning with some remarks about the soul. We said before [5] that there are two parts of the soul—that which grasps a rule or ra- 5 tional principle, and the irrational; let us now draw a similar distinction within the part which grasps a rational principle. And let it be assumed that there are two parts which grasp a rational principle—one by which we contemplate the kind of things whose originative causes are invariable, and one by which we contemplate variable things; for where objects differ in kind the part of the soul answering to each

2 1107ᵃ 1, Cf. 1103ᵇ 31, 1114ᵇ 29.
3 In iii. 6–v. 11.
4 1103ᵃ 3–7.
5 1102ᵃ 26–8.

of the two is different in kind, since it is in virtue of a
certain likeness and kinship with their objects that they 10
have the knowledge they have. Let one of these parts be
called the scientific and the other the calculative; for to deliberate and to calculate are the same thing, but no one
deliberates about the invariable. Therefore the calculative
is one part of the faculty which grasps a rational principle.
We must, then, learn what is the best state of each of these
two parts; for this is the virtue of each.   15

2   The virtue of a thing is relative to its proper work.
        Now there are three things in the soul which control
action and truth—sensation, reason, desire.
        Of these sensation originates no action; this is plain from
the fact that the lower animals have sensation but no share
in action.   20
        What affirmation and negation are in thinking, pursuit
and avoidance are in desire; so that since moral virtue is a
state of character concerned with choice, and choice is deliberate desire, therefore both the reasoning must be true
and the desire right, if the choice is to be good, and the 25
latter must pursue just what the former asserts. Now this
kind of intellect and of truth is practical; of the intellect
which is contemplative, not practical nor productive, the
good and the bad state are truth and falsity respectively
(for this is the work of everything intellectual); while of 30
the part which is practical and intellectual the good state is
truth in agreement with right desire.
        The origin of action—its efficient, not its final cause—
is choice, and that of choice is desire and reasoning with a
view to an end. This is why choice cannot exist either without reason and intellect or without a moral state; for good
action and its opposite cannot exist without a combination 35
of intellect and character. Intellect itself, however, moves
nothing, but only the intellect which aims at an end and is
practical; for this rules the productive intellect as well, since **1139ᵇ**
every one who makes makes for an end, and that which is

made is not an end in the unqualified sense (but only an
end in a particular relation, and the end of a particular
operation)—only that which is done is that; for good action is an end, and desire aims at this. Hence choice is
either desiderative reason or ratiocinative desire, and such
5 an origin of action is a man. (It is to be noted that nothing
that is past is an object of choice, e. g. no one chooses to
have sacked Troy; for no one deliberates about the past, but
about what is future and capable of being otherwise, while
what is past is not capable of not having taken place; hence
Agathon is right in saying

10   For this alone is lacking even to God,
       To make undone things that have once been done.)

The work of both the intellectual parts, then, is truth.
Therefore the states that are most strictly those in respect
of which each of these parts will reach truth are the virtues
of the two parts.

3   Let us begin, then, from the beginning, and discuss
15   these states once more. Let it be assumed that the
states by virtue of which the soul possesses truth by way
of affirmation or denial are five in number, i. e. art, scientific
knowledge, practical wisdom, philosophic wisdom, intuitive
reason; we do not include judgement and opinion because
in these we may be mistaken.

Now what scientific knowledge is, if we are to speak exactly and not follow mere similarities, is plain from what
20 follows. We all suppose that what we know is not even
capable of being otherwise; of things capable of being
otherwise we do not know, when they have passed outside
our observation, whether they exist or not. Therefore the
object of scientific knowledge is of necessity. Therefore it is
eternal; for things that are of necessity in the unqualified
sense are all eternal; and things that are eternal are ungen-
erated and imperishable. Again, every science is thought to
25 be capable of being taught, and its object of being learned.

And all teaching starts from what is already known, as we maintain in the *Analytics* [6] also; for it proceeds sometimes through induction and sometimes by syllogism. Now induction is the starting-point which knowledge even of the universal presupposes, while syllogism proceeds *from* universals. There are therefore starting-points from which syllogism proceeds, which are not reached by syllogism; it is therefore by induction that they are acquired. Scientific 30 knowledge is, then, a state of capacity to demonstrate, and has the other limiting characteristics which we specify in the *Analytics;* [7] for it is when a man believes in a certain way and the starting-points are known to him that he has scientific knowledge, since if they are not better known to him than the conclusion, he will have his knowledge only incidentally.

Let this, then, be taken as our account of scientific knowledge. 35

4 In the variable are included both things made and things done; making and acting are different (for their **1140ª** nature we treat even the discussions outside our school as reliable); so that the reasoned state of capacity to act is different from the reasoned state of capacity to make. 5 Hence too they are not included one in the other; for neither is acting making nor is making acting. Now since architecture is an art and is essentially a reasoned state of capacity to make, and there is neither any art that is not such a state nor any such state that is not an art, *art* is identical with a state of capacity to make, involving a true course of reasoning. All art is concerned with coming into 10 being, i. e. with contriving and considering how something may come into being which is capable of either being or not being, and whose origin is in the maker and not in the thing made; for art is concerned neither with things that are, or come into being, by necessity, nor with things that

[6] *An. Post.* 71ª 1.
[7] Ib. ᵇ 9–23.

do so in accordance with nature (since these have their
15 origin in themselves). Making and acting being different,
art must be a matter of making, not of acting. And in a
sense chance and art are concerned with the same objects;
as Agathon says, 'art loves chance and chance loves art'
Art, then, as has been said,[8] is a state concerned with mak-
20 ing, involving a true course of reasoning, and lack of art on
the contrary is a state concerned with making, involving a
false course of reasoning; both are concerned with the variable.

5   Regarding *practical wisdom* we shall get at the truth
25   by considering who are the persons we credit with it.
Now it is thought to be the mark of a man of practical
wisdom to be able to deliberate well about what is good
and expedient for himself, not in some particular respect,
e. g. about what sorts of thing conduce to health or to
strength, but about what sorts of thing conduce to the
good life in general. This is shown by the fact that we credit
men with practical wisdom in some particular respect when
30 they have calculated well with a view to some good end
which is one of those that are not the object of any art.
It follows that in the general sense also the man who is
capable of deliberating has practical wisdom. Now no one
deliberates about things that are invariable, nor about
things that it is impossible for him to do. Therefore,
since scientific knowledge involves demonstration, but
there is no demonstration of things whose first principles
35 are variable (for all such things might actually be otherwise), and since it is impossible to deliberate about things
1140ᵇ that are of necessity, practical wisdom cannot be scientific
knowledge nor art; not science because that which can be
done is capable of being otherwise, not art because action
and making are different kinds of thing. The remaining
5 alternative, then, is that it is a true and reasoned state of
capacity to act with regard to the things that are good or
bad for man. For while making has an end other than itself,

[8] l. 9.

action cannot; for good action itself is its end. It is for this
reason that we think Pericles and men like him have practical wisdom, viz. because they can see what is good for
themselves and what is good for men in general; we con- 10
sider that those can do this who are good at managing
households or states. (This is why we call temperance
(*sophrosyne*) by this name; we imply that it preserves one's
practical wisdom (*sodsousa ten phronesin*). Now what it
preserves is a judgement of the kind we have described.
For it it not any and every judgement that pleasant and
painful objects destroy and pervert, e. g. the judgement
that the triangle has or has not its angles equal to two right 15
angles, but only judgements about what is to be done. For
the originating causes of the things that are done consist
in the end at which they are aimed; but the man who has
been ruined by pleasure or pain forthwith fails to see any
such originating cause—to see that for the sake of this or
because of this he ought to choose and do whatever he
chooses and does; for vice is destructive of the originating
cause of action.)

Practical wisdom, then, must be a reasoned and true
state of capacity to act with regard to human goods. But 20
further, while there is such a thing as excellence in art,
there is no such thing as excellence in practical wisdom;
and in art he who errs willingly is preferable, but in practical wisdom, as in the virtues, he is the reverse. Plainly,
then, practical wisdom is a virtue and not an art. There
being two parts of the soul that can follow a course of 25
reasoning, it must be the virtue of one of the two, i. e. of
that part which forms opinions; for opinion is about the
variable and so is practical wisdom. But yet it is not only
a reasoned state; this is shown by the fact that a state of
that sort may be forgotten but practical wisdom cannot. 30

6 Scientific knowledge is judgement about things that
are universal and necessary, and the conclusions of
demonstration, and all scientific knowledge, follow from
first principles (for scientific knowledge involves apprehen-

sion of a rational ground). This being so, the first principle from which what is scientifically known follows cannot be an object of scientific knowledge, of art, or of practical
35 wisdom; for that which can be scientifically known can be demonstrated, and art and practical wisdom deal with
1141ª things that are variable. Nor are these first principles the objects of philosophic wisdom, for it is a mark of the philosopher to have *demonstration* about some things. If, then, the states of mind by which we have truth and are never deceived about things invariable or even variable are scientific knowledge, practical wisdom, philosophic wis-
5 dom, and intuitive reason, and it cannot be any of the three (i. e. practical wisdom, scientific knowledge, or philo-sophic wisdom), the remaining alternative is that it is *intuitive reason* that grasps the first principles.

7 Wisdom (1) in the arts we ascribe to their most fin-ished exponents, e. g. to Phidias as a sculptor and to
10 Polyclitus as a maker of portrait-statues, and here we mean nothing by wisdom except excellence in art; but (2) we think that some people are wise in general, not in some particular field or in any other limited respect, as Homer says in the *Margites*,

Him did the gods make neither a digger nor yet a
15 ploughman
Nor wise in anything else.

Therefore wisdom must plainly be the most finished of the forms of knowledge. It follows that the wise man must not only know what follows from the first principles, but must also possess truth about the first principles. Therefore wisdom must be intuitive reason combined with scientific knowledge—scientific knowledge of the highest objects which has received as it were its proper completion.
20 Of the highest objects, we say; for it would be strange to think that the art of politics, or practical wisdom, is the best knowledge, since man is not the best thing in the

world. Now if what is healthy or good is different for men
and for fishes, but what is white or straight is always the 25
same, any one would say that what is wise is the same but
what is practically wise is different; for it is to that which
observes well the various matters concerning itself that one
ascribes practical wisdom, and it is to this that one will
entrust such matters. This is why we say that some even
of the lower animals have practical wisdom, viz. those
which are found to have a power of foresight with regard to
their own life. It is evident also that philosophic wisdom
and the art of politics cannot be the same; for if the state
of mind concerned with a man's own interests is to be 30
called philosophic wisdom, there will be many philosophic
wisdoms; there will not be one concerned with the good of
all animals (any more than there is one art of medicine for
all existing things), but a different philosophic wisdom
about the good of each species.

But if the argument be that man is the best of the animals, this makes no difference; for there are other things 1141ᵇ
much more divine in their nature even than man, e. g.,
most conspicuously, the bodies of which the heavens are
framed. From what has been said it is plain, then, that
philosophic wisdom is scientific knowledge, combined with
intuitive reason, of the things that are highest by nature.
This is why we say Anaxagoras, Thales, and men like them
have philosophic but not practical wisdom, when we see 5
them ignorant of what is to their own advantage, and why
we say that they know things that are remarkable, admirable, difficult, and divine, but useless; viz. because it is not
human goods that they seek.

Practical wisdom on the other hand is concerned with
things human and things about which it is possible to
deliberate; for we say this is above all the work of the man 10
of practical wisdom, to deliberate well, but no one deliberates about things invariable, nor about things which have
not an end, and that a good that can be brought about by
action. The man who is without qualification good at delib-

erating is the man who is capable of aiming in accordance
with calculation at the best for man of things attainable by
15 action. Nor is practical wisdom concerned with universals
only—it must also recognize the particulars; for it is practical, and practice is concerned with particulars. This is why
some who do not know, and especially those who have
experience, are more practical than others who know; for
if a man knew that light meats are digestible and wholesome, but did not know which sorts of meat are light, he
20 would not produce health, but the man who knows that
chicken is wholesome is more likely to produce health.

Now practical wisdom is concerned with action; therefore one should have both forms of it, or the latter in preference to the former. But of practical as of philosophic
wisdom there must be a controlling kind.

8   Political wisdom and practical wisdom are the same
state of mind, but their essence is not the same. Of the
wisdom concerned with the city, the practical wisdom
which plays a controlling part is legislative wisdom, while
25 that which is related to this as particulars to their universal
is known by the general name 'political wisdom'; this has to
do with action and deliberation, for a decree is a thing to
be carried out in the form of an individual act. This is why
the exponents of this art are alone said to 'take part in
politics'; for these alone 'do things' as manual labourers 'do
things'.

Practical wisdom also is identified especially with that
form of it which is concerned with a man himself—with
the individual; and this is known by the general name
30 'practical wisdom'; of the other kinds one is called household management, another legislation, the third politics,
and of the latter one part is called deliberative and the other
judicial. Now knowing what is good for oneself will be one
kind of knowledge, but it is very different from the other
1142ᵃ kinds; and the man who knows and concerns himself with
his own interests is thought to have practical wisdom,

while politicians are thought to be busybodies; hence the words of Euripides,

> But how could I be wise, who might at ease,
> Numbered among the army's multitude,
> Have had an equal share? . . .
> For those who aim too high and do too much   5

Those who think thus seek their own good, and consider that one ought to do so. From this opinion, then, has come the view that such men have practical wisdom; yet perhaps one's own good cannot exist without household management, nor without a form of government. Further, how 10 one should order one's own affairs is not clear and needs inquiry.

What has been said is confirmed by the fact that while young men become geometricians and mathematicians and wise in matters like these, it is thought that a young man of practical wisdom cannot be found. The cause is that such wisdom is concerned not only with universals but with particulars, which become familiar from experience, but a 15 young man has no experience, for it is length of time that gives experience; indeed one might ask this question too, why a boy may become a mathematician, but not á philosopher or a physicist. Is it because the objects of mathematics exist by abstraction, while the first principles of these other subjects come from experience, and because young men have no conviction about the latter but merely use the proper language, while the essence of mathematical objects is plain enough to them?

Further, error in deliberation may be either about the 20 universal or about the particular; we may fail to know either that all water that weighs heavy is bad, or that this particular water weighs heavy.

That practical wisdom is not scientific knowledge is evident; for it is, as has been said,[9] concerned with the ultimate particular fact, since the thing to be done is of this 25

[9] 1141ᵇ 14–22.

nature. It is opposed, then, to intuitive reason; for intuitive reason is of the limiting premisses, for which no reason can be given, while practical wisdom is concerned with the ultimate particular, which is the object not of scientific knowledge but of perception—not the perception of qualities peculiar to one sense but a perception akin to that by which we perceive that the particular figure before us is a triangle; for in that direction as well as in that of the major premiss there will be a limit. But this is rather perception 30 than practical wisdom, though it is another kind of perception than that of the qualities peculiar to each sense.

9   There is a difference between inquiry and deliberation; for deliberation is inquiry into a particular kind of thing. We must grasp the nature of excellence in deliberation as well—whether it is a form of scientific knowledge, or opinion, or skill in conjecture, or some other kind of thing. *Scientific knowledge* it is not; for men do not 1142ᵇ inquire about the things they know about, but good deliberation is a kind of deliberation, and he who deliberates inquires and calculates. Nor is it *skill in conjecture*; for this both involves no reasoning and is something that is quick in its operation, while men deliberate a long time, and they say that one should carry out quickly the con-5 clusions of one's deliberation, but should deliberate slowly. Again, *readiness of mind* is different from excellence in deliberation; it is a sort of skill in conjecture. Nor again is excellence in deliberation *opinion* of any sort. But since the man who deliberates badly makes a mistake, while he who deliberates well does so correctly, excellence in deliberation is clearly a kind of correctness, but neither of knowledge nor of opinion; for there is no such thing as 10 correctness of knowledge (since there is no such thing as error of knowledge), and correctness of opinion is truth; and at the same time everything that is an object of opinion is already determined. But again excellence in deliberation involves reasoning. The remaining alternative, then, is that it is correctness of thinking; for this is not yet assertion, since, while even opinion is not inquiry but has reached the stage of assertion, the man who is deliberating, whether he does so well or ill, is searching for something and calcu- 15 lating.

But excellence in deliberation is a certain correctness of deliberation; hence we must first inquire what deliberation is and what it is about. And, there being more than one kind of correctness, plainly excellence in deliberation is not any and every kind; for (1) the incontinent man and the bad man, if he is clever, will reach as a result of his calculation what he sets before himself, so that he will have deliberated correctly, but he will have got for himself a great evil. Now to have deliberated well is thought to be a good thing; for it is this kind of correctness of deliberation 20 that is excellence in deliberation, viz. that which tends to attain what is good. But (2) it is possible to attain even good by a false syllogism, and to attain what one ought to do but not by the right means, the middle term being false; so that this too is not yet excellence in deliberation —this state in virtue of which one attains what one ought 25 but not by the right means. Again (3) it is possible to attain it by long deliberation while another man attains it quickly. Therefore in the former case we have not yet got excellence in deliberation, which is rightness with re-gard to the expedient—rightness in respect both of the end, the manner, and the time. (4) Further it is possible to have deliberated well either in the unqualified sense or with reference to a particular end. Excellence in deliberation in the unqualified sense, then, is that which succeeds with ref-erence to what is the end in the unqualified sense, and excellence in deliberation in a particular sense is that which 30 succeeds relatively to a particular end. If, then, it is char-acteristic of men of practical wisdom to have deliberated well, excellence in deliberation will be correctness with regard to what conduces to the end of which practical wis-dom is the true apprehension.

10 Understanding, also, and goodness of understanding, in virtue of which men are said to be men of under-
1143ª standing or of good understanding, are neither entirely the same as opinion or scientific knowledge (for at that rate all men would have been men of understanding), nor are they one of the particular sciences, such as medicine, the science of things connected with health, or geometry,
5 the science of spatial magnitudes. For understanding is neither about things that are always and are unchangeable, nor about any and every one of the things that come into being, but about things which may become subjects of questioning and deliberation. Hence it is about the same objects as practical wisdom; but understanding and practical wisdom are not the same. For practical wisdom issues commands, since its end is what ought to be done or not to be done; but understanding only judges. (Un-
10 derstanding is identical with goodness of understanding, men of understanding with men of good understanding.) Now understanding is neither the having nor the acquiring of practical wisdom; but as learning is called understanding when it means the exercise of the faculty of knowledge, so 'understanding' is applicable to the exercise of the faculty of opinion for the purpose of judging of what some one else says about matters with which practical wis-
15 dom is concerned—and of judging soundly; for 'well' and 'soundly' are the same thing. And from this has come the use of the name 'understanding' in virtue of which men are said to be 'of good understanding', viz. from the application of the word to the grasping of scientific truth; for we often call such grasping understanding.

11 What is called judgement, in virtue of which men are
20   said to 'be sympathetic judges' and to 'have judgement', is the right discrimination of the equitable. This is shown by the fact that we say the equitable man is above all others a man of sympathetic judgement, and identify equity with sympathetic judgement about certain facts.

And sympathetic judgement is judgement which discriminates what is equitable and does so correctly; and correct
judgement is that which judges what is true.

Now all the states we have considered converge, as might 25
be expected, to the same point; for when we speak of
judgement and understanding and practical wisdom and
intuitive reason we credit the same people with possessing
judgement and having reached years of reason and with
having practical wisdom and understanding. For all these
faculties deal with ultimates, i. e. with particulars; and
being a man of understanding and of good or sympathetic
judgement consists in being able to judge about the things 30
with which practical wisdom is concerned; for the equities
are common to all good men in relation to other men. Now
all things which have to be done are included among
particulars or ultimates; for not only must the man of
practical wisdom know particular facts, but understanding
and judgement are also concerned with things to be done,
and these are ultimates. And intuitive reason is concerned
with the ultimates in both directions; for both the first 35
terms and the last are objects of intuitive reason and not
of argument, and the intuitive reason which is presupposed 1143^b
by demonstrations grasps the unchangeable and first terms,
while the intuitive reason involved in practical reasonings
grasps the last and variable fact, i. e. the minor premiss.
For these variable facts are the starting-points for the
apprehension of the end, since the universals are reached
from the particulars; of these therefore we must have per- 5
ception, and this perception is intuitive reason.

This is why these states are thought to be natural endow-
ments—why, while no one is thought to be a philosopher
by nature, people are thought to have by nature judgement,
understanding, and intuitive reason. This is shown by the
fact that we think our powers correspond to our time of
life, and that a particular age brings with it intuitive reason
and judgement; this implies that nature is the cause.
[Hence intuitive reason is both beginning and end; for

10 demonstrations are from these and about these.] Therefore
we ought to attend to the undemonstrated sayings and
opinions of experienced and older people or of people of
practical wisdom not less than to demonstrations; for because experience has given them an eye they see aright.

We have stated, then, what practical and philosophic
wisdom are, and with what each of them is concerned, and
15 we have said that each is the virtue of a different part of the
soul.

12 Difficulties might be raised as to the utility of these
qualities of mind. For (1) philosophic wisdom will
contemplate none of the things that will make a man
happy (for it is not concerned with any coming into be-
20 ing), and though practical wisdom has *this* merit, for what
purpose do we need it? Practical wisdom is the quality of
mind concerned with things just and noble and good for
man, but these are the things which it is the mark of a
good man to do, and we are none the more able to act for
knowing them if the virtues are states of *character*, just
25 as we are none the better able to act for knowing the things
that are healthy and sound, in the sense not of producing
but of issuing from the state of health; for we are none the
more able to act for having the art of medicine or of gymnastics. But (2) if we are to say that a man should have
practical wisdom not for the sake of knowing moral truths
30 but for the sake of becoming good, practical wisdom will be
of no use to those who are good; but again it is of no use
to those who have *not* virtue; for it will make no difference
whether they have practical wisdom themselves or obey
others who have it, and it would be enough for us to do
what we do in the case of health; though we wish to become healthy, yet we do not learn the art of medicine.
(3) Besides this, it would be thought strange if practical
wisdom, being inferior to philosophic wisdom, is to be put
in authority over it, as seems to be implied by the fact that

the art which produces anything rules and issues commands about that thing.

These, then, are the questions we must discuss; so far we 35 have only stated the difficulties.

(1) Now first let us say that in themselves these states 1144ᵃ must be worthy of choice because they are the virtues of the two parts of the soul respectively, even if neither of them produce anything.

(2) Secondly, they do produce something, not as the art of medicine produces health, however, but as health produces health; [10] so does philosophic wisdom produce happiness; for, being a part of virtue entire, by being possessed 5 and by actualizing itself it makes a man happy.

(3) Again, the work of man is achieved only in accordance with practical wisdom as well as with moral virtue; for virtue makes us aim at the right mark, and practical wisdom makes us take the right means. (Of the fourth part of the soul—the nutritive [11]—there is no such virtue; for 10 there is nothing which it is in its power to do or not to do.)

(4) With regard to our being none the more able to do because of our practical wisdom what is noble and just, let us begin a little further back, starting with the following principle. As we say that some people who do just acts are not necessarily just, i. e. those who do the acts ordained 15 by the laws either unwillingly or owing to ignorance or for some other reason and not for the sake of the acts themselves (though, to be sure, they do what they should and all the things that the good man ought), so is it, it seems, that in order to be good one must be in a certain state when one does the several acts, i. e. one must do them as a result 20 of choice and for the sake of the acts themselves. Now virtue makes the choice right, but the question of the things which should naturally be done to carry out our

[10] i. e. as health, as an inner state, produces the activities which we know as constituting health.

[11] The other three being the scientific, the calculative, and the desiderative.

choice belongs not to virtue but to another faculty. We
must devote our attention to these matters and give a
clearer statement about them. There is a faculty which is
25 called cleverness; and this is such as to be able to do the
things that tend towards the mark we have set before ourselves, and to hit it. Now if the mark be noble, the cleverness is laudable, but if the mark be bad, the cleverness is
mere smartness; hence we call even men of practical wisdom clever or smart. Practical wisdom is not the faculty,
but it does not exist without this faculty. And this eye of
30 the soul acquires its formed state not without the aid of
virtue, as has been said [12] and is plain; for the syllogisms
which deal with acts to be done are things which involve a
starting-point, viz. 'since the end, i. e. what is best, is of
such and such a nature', whatever it may be (let it for the
sake of argument be what we please); and this is not evi-.
dent except to the good man; for wickedness perverts us
35 and causes us to be deceived about the starting-points of
action. Therefore it is evident that it is impossible to be
practically wise without being good.

13 We must therefore consider virtue also once more;
1144ᵇ   for virtue too is similarly related; as practical wisdom
is to cleverness—not the same, but like it—so is natural
virtue to virtue in the strict sense. For all men think that
each type of character belongs to its possessors in some
sense by nature; for from the very moment of birth we are
5 just or fitted for self-control or brave or have the other
moral qualities; but yet we seek something else as that
which is good in the strict sense—we seek for the presence
of such qualities in another way. For both children and
brutes have the natural dispositions to these qualities, but
without reason these are evidently hurtful. Only we seem
10 to see this much, that, while one may be led astray by them,
as a strong body which moves without sight may stumble
badly because of its lack of sight, still, if a man once ac-

[12] ll. 6–26.

quires reason, that makes a difference in action; and his state, while still like what it was, will then be virtue in the strict sense. Therefore, as in the part of us which forms opinions there are two types, cleverness and practical wisdom, so too in the moral part there are two types, natural 15 virtue and virtue in the strict sense, and of these the latter involves practical wisdom. This is why some say that all the virtues are forms of practical wisdom, and why Socrates in one respect was on the right track while in another he went astray; in thinking that all the virtues were forms of practical wisdom he was wrong, but in saying they implied practical wisdom he was right. This is confirmed by the fact 20 that even now all men, when they define virtue, after naming the state of character and its objects add 'that (state) which is in accordance with the right rule'; now the right rule is that which is in accordance with practical wisdom. All men, then, seem somehow to divine that this kind of state is virtue, viz. that which is in accordance with practical 25 wisdom. But we must go a little further. For it is not merely the state in accordance with the right rule, but the state that implies the presence of the right rule, that is virtue; and practical wisdom is a right rule about such matters. Socrates, then, thought the virtues were rules or rational principles (for he thought they were, all of them, forms of scientific knowledge), while we think they *involve* a rational principle.

It is clear, then, from what has been said, that it is not 30 possible to be good in the strict sense without practical wisdom, nor practically wise without moral virtue. But in this way we may also refute the dialectical argument whereby it might be contended that the virtues exist in separation from each other; the same man, it might be said, is not best equipped by nature for all the virtues, so that he will have already acquired one when he has not yet acquired 35 another. This is possible in respect of the natural virtues, but not in respect of those in respect of which a man is 1145ᵃ called without qualification good; for with the presence of

the one quality, practical wisdom, will be given all the virtues. And it is plain that, even if it were of no practical value, we should have néeded it becáuse it is the virtue of the part of us in question; plain too that the choice will
5 not be right without practical wisdom any more than without virtue; for the one determines the end and the other makes us do the things that lead to the end.

But again it is not supreme over philosophic wisdom, i. e. over the superior part of us, any more than the art of medicine is over health; for it does not use it but provides
10 for its coming into being; it issues orders, then, for its sake, but not to it. Further, to maintain its supremacy would be like saying that the art of politics rules the gods because it issues orders about all the affairs of the state.

BOOK VII

15 **1**   Let us now make a fresh beginning and point out that of moral states to be avoided there are three kinds— vice, incontinence, brutishness. The contraries of two of these are evident—one we call virtue, the other continence;
20 to brutishness it would be most fitting to oppose super- human virtue, a heroic and divine kind of nature, as Homer has represented Priam saying of Hector that he was very good,

> For he seemed not, he,
> The child of a mortal man, but as one that of God's
>   seed came.[1]

Therefore if, as they say, men become gods by excess of virtue, of this kind must evidently be the state opposed to the brutish state; for as a brute has no vice or virtue, so
25 neither has a god; his state is higher than virtue, and that of a brute is a different kind of state from vice.

Now, since it is rarely that a godlike man is found—to use the epithet of the Spartans, who when they admire any one highly call him a 'godlike man'—so too the brutish

[1] *Il.* xxiv. 258 f.

type is rarely found among men; it is found chiefly among barbarians, but some brutish qualities are also produced 30 by disease or deformity; and we also call by this evil name those men who go beyond all ordinary standards by reason of vice. Of this kind of disposition, however, we must later make some mention,[2] while we have discussed vice before;[3] we must now discuss incontinence and softness (or effeminacy), and continence and endurance; for 35 we must treat each of the two neither as identical with virtue or wickedness, nor as a different genus. We must, as 1145ᵇ in all other cases, set the observed facts before us and, after first discussing the difficulties, go on to prove, if possible, the truth of all the common opinions about these affections of the mind, or, failing this, of the greater number and the most authoritative; for if we both refute the objections 5 and leave the common opinions undisturbed, we shall have proved the case sufficiently.

Now (1) both continence and endurance are thought to be included among things good and praiseworthy, and both incontinence and softness among things bad and blameworthy; and the same man is thought to be continent 10 and ready to abide by the result of his calculations, or incontinent and ready to abandon them. And (2) the incontinent man, knowing that what he does is bad, does it as a result of passion, while the continent man, knowing that his appetites are bad, refuses on account of his rational principle to follow them. (3) The temperate man all men call continent and disposed to endurance, while 15 the continent man some maintain to be always temperate but others do not; and some call the self-indulgent man incontinent and the incontinent man self-indulgent indiscriminately while others distinguish them. (4) The man of practical wisdom, they sometimes say, cannot be incontinent, while sometimes they say that some who are practically wise and clever are incontinent. Again (5) men

[2] Ch. 5.
[3] Bks. II–V.

are said to be incontinent even with respect to anger,
20 honour, and gain.—These, then, are the things that are
said.

2   Now we may ask (1) how a man who judges rightly can
behave incontinently. That he should behave so when
he has knowledge, some say is impossible; for it would be
strange—so Socrates [4] thought—if when knowledge was in
25 a man something else could master it and drag it about
like a slave. For Socrates was entirely opposed to the view
in question, holding that there is no such thing as incontinence; no one, he said, when he judges acts against
what he judges best—people act so only by reason of
ignorance. Now this view plainly contradicts the observed facts, and we must inquire about what happens to
such a man; if he acts by reason of ignorance, what is the
30 manner of his ignorance? For that the man who behaves
incontinently does not, before he gets into this state, *think*
he ought to act so, is evident. But there are *some* who con-
cede certain of Socrates' contentions but not others; that
nothing is stronger than knowledge they admit, but not
that no one acts contrary to what has seemed to him the
better course, and therefore they say that the incontinent
man has not knowledge when he is mastered by his
35 pleasures, but opinion. But *if* it is opinion and not knowl-
1146ᵃ edge, if it is not a strong conviction that resists but a weak
one, as in men who hesitate, we sympathize with their
failure to stand by such convictions against strong appetites; but we do not sympathize with wickedness, nor
with any of the other blameworthy states. Is it then
5 *practical wisdom* whose resistance is mastered? That is the
strongest of all states. But this is absurd; the same man will
be at once practically wise and incontinent, but *no one*
would say that it is the part of a practically wise man to do
willingly the basest acts. Besides, it has been shown before
that the man of practical wisdom is one who will *act* [5] (for

---

[4] Pl. *Prot.* 352 B, C.
[5] 1140ᵇ 4–6.

he is a man concerned with the individual facts) [6] and who
has the other virtues.[7]

(2) Further, if continence involves having strong and
bad appetites, the temperate man will not be continent 10
nor the continent man temperate; for a temperate man will
have neither excessive nor bad appetites. But the continent
man *must*; for if the appetites are good, the state of character that restrains us from following them is bad, so that 15
not all continence will be good; while if they are weak and
not bad, there is nothing admirable in resisting them, and
if they are weak and bad, there is nothing great in resisting
these either.

(3) Further, if continence makes a man ready to stand
by any and every opinion, it is bad, i. e. if it makes him
stand even by a false opinion; and if incontinence makes a
man apt to abandon any and every opinion, there will be a
good incontinence, of which Sophocles' Neoptolemus in
the *Philoctetes* [8] will be an instance; for he is to be praised 20
for not standing by what Odysseus persuaded him to do,
because he is pained at telling a lie.

(4) Further, the sophistic argument presents a difficulty;
the syllogism arising from men's wish to expose paradoxical
results arising from an opponent's view, in order that they
may be admired when they succeed, is one that puts us in a
difficulty (for thought is bound fast when it will not rest 25
because the conclusion does not satisfy it, and cannot
advance because it cannot refute the argument). There is
an argument from which it follows that folly coupled with
incontinence is virtue; for a man does the opposite of what
he judges, owing to incontinence, but judges what is good
to be evil and something that he should not do, and in
consequence he will do what is good and not what is evil. 30

(5) Further, he who on conviction does and pursues
and chooses what is pleasant would be thought to be better
than one who does so as a result not of calculation but of

---

[6] 1141ᵇ 16, 1142ᵃ 24.
[7] 1144ᵇ 30–1145ᵃ 2.
[8] ll. 895–916.

incontinence; for he is easier to cure since he may be persuaded to change his mind. But to the incontinent man
may be applied the proverb 'when water chokes, what is
one to wash it down with?' If he had been persuaded of
35 the rightness of what he does, he would have desisted when
1146ᵇ he was persuaded to change his mind; but now he acts in
spite of his being persuaded of something quite different.

(6) Further, if incontinence and continence are concerned with any and every kind of object, who is it that
is incontinent in the unqualified sense? No one has all the
forms of incontinence, but we say some people are in-
5 continent without qualification.

3   Of some such kind are the difficulties that arise;
some of these points must be refuted and the others
left in possession of the field; for the solution of the difficulty is the discovery of the truth. (1) We must consider
first, then, whether incontinent people act knowingly or
not, and in what sense knowingly; then (2) with what
sorts of object the incontinent and the continent man may
be said to be concerned (i. e. whether with any and every
10 pleasure and pain or with certain determinate kinds), and
whether the continent man and the man of endurance are
the same or different; and similarly with regard to the other
matters germane to this inquiry. The starting-point of our
investigation is (a) the question whether the continent
man and the incontinent are differentiated by their objects
15 or by their attitude, i. e. whether the incontinent man is incontinent simply by being concerned with such and such
objects, or, instead, by his attitude, or, instead of that, by
both these things; (b) the second question is whether incontinence and continence are concerned with any and
every object or not. The man who is incontinent in the unqualified sense is neither concerned with any and every
20 object, but with precisely those with which the self-indulgent man is concerned, nor is he characterized by being
simply related to these (for then his state would be the
same as self-indulgence), but by being related to them in a

certain way. For the one is led on in accordance with his own choice, thinking that he ought always to pursue the present pleasure; while the other does not think so, but yet pursues it.

(1) As for the suggestion that it is true opinion and not knowledge against which we act incontinently, that makes no difference to the argument; for some people when in a 25 state of opinion do not hesitate, but think they know exactly. If, then, the notion is that owing to their weak conviction those who have opinion are more likely to act against their judgement than those who know, we answer that there need be no difference between knowledge and opinion in this respect; for some men are no less convinced of what they think than others of what they know; as is 30 shown by the case of Heraclitus. But (a), since we use the word 'know' in two senses (for both the man who has knowledge but is not using it and he who is using it are said to know), it *will* make a difference whether, when a man does what he should not, he has the knowledge but is not exercising it, or *is* exercising it; for the latter seems strange, but not the former.

(b) Further, since there are two kinds of premisses, 35 there is nothing to prevent a man's having both premisses 1147ᵃ and acting against his knowledge, provided that he is using only the universal premiss and not the particular; for it is particular acts that have to be done. And there are also two kinds of universal term; one is predicable of the agent, 5 the other of the object; e. g. 'dry food is good for every man', and 'I am a man', or 'such and such food is dry'; but whether 'this food is such and such', of this the incontinent man either has not or is not exercising the knowledge.[9] There will, then, be, firstly, an enormous difference between these manners of knowing, so that to know

[9] i. e., if I am to be able to deduce from (a) 'dry food is good for all men' that 'this food is good for me', I must have (b) the premiss 'I am a man' and (c) the premisses (i) 'x food is dry', (ii) 'this food is x'. I cannot fail to know (b), and I may know (c i); but if I do not know (c ii), or know it only 'at the back of my mind', I shall not draw the conclusion.

in one way when we act incontinently would not seem anything strange, while to know in the other way would be extraordinary.

And further (c) the possession of knowledge in another
10 sense than those just named is something that happens to men; for within the case of having knowledge but not using it we see a difference of state, admitting of the possibility of having knowledge in a sense and yet not having it, as in the instance of a man asleep, mad, or drunk. But now this is just the condition of men under the influence of passion; for outbursts of anger and sexual ap-
15 petites and some other such passions, it is evident, actually alter our bodily condition, and in some men even produce fits of madness. It is plain, then, that incontinent people must be said to be in a similar condition to men asleep, mad, or drunk. The fact that men use the language that flows from knowledge proves nothing; for even men under
20 the influence of these passions utter scientific proofs and verses of Empedocles, and those who have just begun to learn a science can string together its phrases, but do not yet know it; for it has to become part of themselves, and that takes time; so that we must suppose that the use of language by men in an incontinent state means no more than its utterance by actors on the stage.

(d) Again, we may also view the cause as follows with
25 reference to the facts of human nature. The one opinion is universal, the other is concerned with the particular facts, and here we come to something within the sphere of perception; when a single opinion results from the two, the soul must in one type of case [10] affirm the conclusion, while in the case of opinions concerned with production it must immediately act (e. g. if 'everything sweet ought to be tasted', and 'this is sweet', in the sense of being one of the
30 particular sweet things, the man who can act and is not prevented must at the same time actually act accordingly). When, then, the universal opinion is present in us for-

[10] i. e. in scientific reasoning.

bidding us to taste, and there is also the opinion that
'everything sweet is pleasant', and that 'this is sweet' (now
this is the opinion that is active),[11] and when appetite happens to be present in us, the one opinion bids us avoid the
object, but appetite leads us towards it (for .it can move 35
each of our bodily parts); so that it turns out that a man
behaves incontinently under the influence (in a sense) of
a rule and an opinion, and of one not contrary in itself,
but only incidentally—for the appetite is contrary, not the 1147ᵇ
opinion—to the right rule. It also follows that this is the
reason why the lower animals are not incontinent, viz.
because they have no universal judgment but only imagina- 5
tion and memory of particulars.

The explanation of how the ignorance is dissolved and
the incontinent man regains his knowledge, is the same as
in the case of the man drunk or asleep and is not particular
to this condition; we must go to the students of natural
science for it. Now, the last premiss both being an opinion
about a perceptible object, and being what determines our 10
actions, this a man either has not when he is in the state of
passion, or has it in the sense in which having knowledge
did not mean knowing but only talking, as a drunken man
may mutter the verses of Empedocles.[12] And because the
last term is not universal nor equally an object of scientific
knowledge with the universal term, the position that 15
Socrates sought to establish [13] actually seems to result; for
it is not in the presence of what is thought to be knowledge
proper that the affection of incontinence arises (nor is it
this that is dragged about' as a result of the state of passion), but in that of perceptual knowledge.[14]

This must suffice as our answer to the question of action

---

[11] i. e. determines action (Cf. ᵇ10).
[12] Cf. ᵃ10–24.
[13] 1145ᵇ 22–24.
[14] Even before the minor premiss of the practical syllogism has been
obscured by passion, the incontinent man has not scientific knowledge
in the strict sense, since his minor premiss is not universal but has for
its subject a sensible particular, e. g. 'this glass of wine'.

with and without knowledge, and how it is possible to behave incontinently with knowledge.

20 **4**   (2) We must next discuss whether there is any one
who is incontinent without qualification, or all men
who are incontinent are so in a particular sense, and if there
is, with what sort of objects he is concerned. That both
continent persons and persons of endurance, and incontinent and soft persons, are concerned with pleasures and
pains, is evident.

   Now of the things that produce pleasure some are necessary, while others are worthy of choice in themselves
25 but admit of excess, the bodily causes of pleasure being
necessary (by such I mean both those concerned with food
and those concerned with sexual intercourse, i. e. the bodily
matters with which we defined [15] self-indulgence and temperance as being concerned), while the others are not
necessary but worthy of choice in themselves (e. g. victory,
30 honour, wealth, and good and pleasant things of this sort).
This being so, (a) those who go to excess with reference to
the latter, contrary to the right rule which is in themselves, are not called incontinent simply, but incontinent
with the qualification 'in respect of money, gain, honour,
or anger',—not simply incontinent, on the ground that they
are different from incontinent people and are called incontinent by reason of a resemblance. (Compare the case
35 of Anthropos (Man), who won a contest at the Olympic
1148ᵃ games; in his case the general definition of man differed
little from the definition peculiar to him, but yet it was
different.) [16] This is shown by the fact that incontinence
either without qualification or in respect of some particular
bodily pleasure is blamed not only as a fault but as a kind of
vice, while none of the people who are incontinent in these
other respects is so blamed.

[15] III. 10.
[16] i. e. the definition appropriate to him was not 'rational animal'
but 'rational animal who won the boxing contest at Olympia in 456
B. C.'

But (*b*) of the people who are incontinent with respect to bodily enjoyments, with which we say the temperate and the self-indulgent man are concerned, he who pursues 5 the excesses of things pleasant—and shuns those of things painful, of hunger and thirst and heat and cold and all the objects of touch and taste—not by choice but contrary to his choice and his judgment, is called incontinent, not with the qualification 'in respect of this or that', e. g. of anger, 10 but just simply. This is confirmed by the fact that men are called 'soft' with regard to these pleasures, but not with regard to any of the others. And for this reason we group together the incontinent and the self-indulgent, the continent and the temperate man—but not any of these other types—because they are concerned somehow with the same pleasures and pains; but though these are concerned with 15 the same objects, they are not similarly related to them, but some of them make a deliberate choice while the others do not.[17]

This is why we should describe as self-indulgent rather the man who without appetite or with but a slight appetite pursues the excesses of pleasure and avoids moderate pains, than the man who does so because of his strong appetites; for what would the former do, if he had in addition a 20 vigorous appetite, and a violent pain at the lack of the 'necessary' objects?

Now of appetites and pleasures some belong to the class of things generically noble and good—for some pleasant things are by nature worthy of choice, while others are contrary to these, and others are intermediate, to adopt our previous distinction [18]—e. g. wealth, gain, victory, honour. 25 And with reference to all objects whether of this or of the intermediate kind men are not blamed for being affected by them, for desiring and loving them, but for doing so in a certain way, i. e. for going to excess. (This is why all those

[17] i. e. the temperate and the self-indulgent, not the continent and the incontinent.

[18] 1147[b] 23–31, where, however, the 'contraries' are not mentioned.

who contrary to the rule either are mastered by or pursue
30 one of the objects which are naturally noble and good, e. g.
those who busy themselves more than they ought about
honour or about children and parents, [are not wicked]; for
these too are goods, and those who busy themselves about
them are praised; but yet there is an excess even in them—
if like Niobe one were to fight even against the gods, or
1148ᵇ were to be as much devoted to one's father as Satyrus
nicknamed 'the filial', who was thought to be very silly on
this point.¹⁹) There is no wickedness, then, with regard to
these objects, for the reason named, viz. because each of
them is by nature a thing worthy of choice for its own sake;
yet excesses in respect of them are bad and to be avoided.
5 Similarly there is no incontinence with regard to them; for
incontinence is not only to be avoided but is also a thing
worthy of blame; but owing to a similarity in the state of
feeling people apply the name incontinence, adding in
each case what it is in respect of, as we may describe as a
bad doctor or a bad actor one whom we should not call
bad, simply. As, then, in this case we do not apply the term
without qualification because each of these conditions is
10 not badness but only analogous to it, so it is clear that in
the other case also that alone must be taken to be incontinence and continence which is concerned with the same
objects as temperance and self-indulgence, but we apply
the term to anger by virtue of a resemblance; and this is
why we say with a qualification 'incontinent in respect of
anger' as we say 'incontinent in respect of honour, or of
gain'.

15 **5**   (1) Some things are pleasant by nature, and of these
        (a) some are so without qualification, and (b) others
are so with reference to particular classes either of animals
or of men; while (2) others are not pleasant by nature,

¹⁹ Nothing is really known about the Satyrus referred to, but Prof.
Burnet's suggestion that he was a king of Bosporus who deified his father seems probable.

but (*a*) some of them become so by reason of injuries to the system, and (*b*) others by reason of acquired habits, and (*c*) others by reason of originally bad natures. This being so, it is possible with regard to each of the latter kinds to discover similar states of character to those recognized with regard to the former; I mean (A) the brutish states,[20] as in the case of the female who, they say, rips open pregnant women and devours the infants, or of the things in which some of the tribes about the Black Sea that have gone savage are said to delight—in raw meat or in human flesh, or in lending their children to one another to feast upon—or of the story told of Phalaris.[21]

These states are brutish, but (B) others arise as a result of disease [22] (or, in some cases, of madness, as with the man who sacrificed and ate his mother, or with the slave who ate the liver of his fellow), and others are morbid states (C) resulting from custom,[23] e. g. the habit of plucking out the hair or of gnawing the nails, or even coals or earth, and in addition to these paederasty; for these arise in some by nature and in others, as in those who have been the victims of lust from childhood, from habit.

Now those in whom nature is the cause of such a state no one would call incontinent, any more than one would apply the epithet to women because of the passive part they play in copulation; nor would one apply it to those who are in a morbid condition as a result of habit. To have these various types of habit is beyond the limits of vice, as brutishness is too; for a man who has them to master or be 1149ᵃ mastered by them is not simple [continence or] incontinence but that which is so by analogy, as the man who is in this condition in respect of fits of anger is to be called incontinent in respect of that feeling, but not incontinent simply.

For every excessive state whether of folly, of cowardice,

---

[20] Answering to (2 c).
[21] sc. and the bull. But Cf. 1149ᵃ 14.
[22] Answering to (2 a).
[23] Answering to (2 b).

5 of self-indulgence, or of bad temper, is either brutish or
morbid; the man who is by nature apt to fear everything,
even the squeak of a mouse, is cowardly with a brutish
cowardice, while the man who feared a weasel did so in
consequence of disease; and of foolish people those who by
nature are thoughtless and live by their senses alone are
brutish, like some races of the distant barbarians, while
10 those who are so as a result of disease (e. g. of epilepsy) or
of madness are morbid. Of these characteristics it is possible to have some only at times, and not to be mastered
by them, e. g. Phalaris may have restrained a desire to eat
the flesh of a child or an appetite for unnatural sexual
pleasure; but it is also possible to be mastered, not merely
15 to have the feelings. Thus, as the wickedness which is on
the human level is called wickedness simply, while that
which is not is called wickedness not simply but with the
qualification 'brutish' or 'morbid', in the same way it is
plain that some incontinence is brutish and some morbid,
20 while only that which corresponds to human self-indulgence is incontinence simply.

That incontinence and continence, then, are concerned
only with the same objects as self-indulgence and temperance and that what is concerned with other objects is a type
distinct from incontinence, and called incontinence by a
metaphor and not simply, is plain.

6   That incontinence in respect of anger is less disgraceful than that in respect of the appetites is what we
25 will now proceed to see. (1) Anger seems to listen to argument to some extent, but to mishear it, as do hasty servants
who run out before they have heard the whole of what one
says, and then muddle the order, or as dogs bark if there
is but a knock at the door, before looking to see if it is a
30 friend; so anger by reason of the warmth and hastiness of
its nature, though it hears, does not hear an order, and
springs to take revenge. For argument or imagination in-
forms us that we have been insulted or slighted, and anger,

reasoning as it were that anything like this must be fought against, boils up straightway; while appetite, if argument or perception merely says that an object is pleasant, springs 35 to the enjoyment of it. Therefore anger obeys the argu-1149 ment in a sense, but appetite does not. It is therefore more disgraceful; for the man who is incontinent in respect of anger is in a sense conquered by argument, while the other is conquered by appetite and not by argument.

(2) Further, we pardon people more easily for follow-ing natural desires, since we pardon them more easily for 5 following such appetites as are common to all men, and in so far as they are common; now anger and bad temper are more natural than the appetites for excess, i. e. for un-necessary objects. Take for instance the man who de-fended himself on the charge of striking his father by say-ing 'yes, but *he* struck *his* father, and *he* struck *his*, and' 10 (pointing to his child) 'this boy will strike *me* when he is a man; it runs in the family'; or the man who when he was being dragged along by his son bade him stop at the doorway, since he himself had dragged his father only as far as that.

(3) Further, those who are more given to plotting against others are more criminal. Now a passionate man is not given to plotting, nor is anger itself—it is open; but 15 the nature of appetite is illustrated by what the poets call Aphrodite, 'guile-weaving daughter of Cyprus', and by Homer's words about her 'embroidered girdle':

> And the whisper of wooing is there,
> Whose subtlety stealeth the wits of the wise, how
>   prudent soe'er.[24]

Therefore if this form of incontinence is more criminal and disgraceful than that in respect of anger, it is both incontinence without qualification and in a sense vice.

(4) Further, no one commits wanton outrage with a feeling of pain, but every one who acts in anger acts with 20

[24] *Il.* xiv. 214, 217.

pain, while the man who commits outrage acts with pleasure. If, then, those acts at which it is most just to be angry are more criminal than others, the incontinence which is due to appetite is the more criminal; for there is no wanton outrage involved in anger.

Plainly, then, the incontinence concerned with appetite is more disgraceful than that concerned with anger, 25 and continence and incontinence are concerned with bodily appetites and pleasures; but we must grasp the differences among the latter themselves. For, as has been said at the beginning,[25] some are human and natural both in kind and in magnitude, others are brutish, and others are due to organic injuries and diseases. Only with the first 30 of these are temperance and self-indulgence concerned; this is why we call the lower animals neither temperate nor self-indulgent except by a metaphor, and only if some one race of animals exceeds another as a whole in wantonness, destructiveness, and omnivorous greed; these have no power of choice or calculation, but they are departures 35 from the natural norm,[26] as, among men, madmen are. Now 1150ᵃ brutishness is a less evil than vice, though more alarming; for it is not that the better part has been perverted, as in man—they have no better part. Thus it is like comparing a lifeless thing with a living in respect of badness; for the badness of that which has no originative source of movement is always less hurtful, and reason is an originative 5 source. Thus it is like comparing injustice in the abstract with an unjust man. Each is in some sense worse; for a bad man will do ten thousand times as much evil as a brute.

7   With regard to the pleasures and pains and appetites and aversions arising through touch and taste, to which 10 both self-indulgence and temperance were formerly narrowed down,[27] it is possible to be in such a state as to be

25 1148ᵇ 15–31.
26 And therefore cannot be called self-indulgent properly, but can be so called by a metaphor.
27 III. 10.

defeated even by those of them which most people master,
or to master even those by which most people are defeated;
among these possibilities, those relating to pleasures are
incontinence and continence, those relating to pains softness and endurance. The state of most people is intermediate, even if they lean more towards the worse states.   15

Now, since some pleasures are necessary while others are
not, and are necessary up to a point while the excesses of
them are not, nor the deficiencies, and this is equally true
of appetites and pains, the man who pursues the excesses
of things pleasant, or pursues to excess necessary objects, 20
and does so by choice, for their own sake and not at all for
the sake of any result distinct from them, is self-indulgent;
for such a man is of necessity unlikely to repent, and therefore incurable, since a man who cannot repent cannot be
cured. The man who is deficient in his pursuit of them is
the opposite of self-indulgent; the man who is intermediate
is temperate. Similarly, there is the man who avoids bodily
pains not because he is defeated by them but by choice.
(Of those who do not *choose* such acts, one kind of man is 25
led to them as a result of the pleasure involved, another
because he avoids the pain arising from the appetite, so
that these types differ from one another. Now any one
would think worse of a man if with no appetite or with
weak appetite he were to do something disgraceful, than if
he did it under the influence of powerful appetite, and
worse of him if he struck a blow not in anger than if he
did it in anger; for what would he have done if he *had* been 30
strongly affected? This is why the self-indulgent man is
worse than the incontinent.) Of the states named, then,[28]
the latter is rather a kind of softness; [29] the former is self-
indulgence. While to the incontinent man is opposed
the continent, to the soft is opposed the man of endurance;
for endurance consists in resisting, while continence con- 35

[28] In ll. 19–25.
[29] Not softness proper, which is non-deliberate avoidance of pain
(ll. 13–15).

sist in conquering, and resisting and conquering are different, as not being beaten is different from winning; this is
1150ᵇ why continence is also more worthy of choice than endurance. Now the man who is defective in respect of resistance
to the things which most men both resist and resist successfully is soft and effeminate; for effeminacy too is a kind
of softness; such a man trails his cloak to avoid the pain of
lifting it, and plays the invalid without thinking himself
wretched, though the man he imitates is a wretched man.

5   The case is similar with regard to continence and incontinence. For if a man is defeated by violent and excessive pleasures or pains, there is nothing wonderful in
that; indeed we are ready to pardon him if he has resisted,
as Theodectes' Philoctetes does when bitten by the snake,
10 or Carcinus' Cercyon in the *Alope*, and as people who try
to restrain their laughter burst out in a guffaw, as happened
to Xenophantus. But it is surprising if a man is defeated by
and cannot resist pleasures or pains which most men can
hold out against, when this is not due to heredity or disease, like the softness that is hereditary with the kings of
the Scythians, or that which distinguishes the female sex
15 from the male.

    The lover of amusement, too, is thought to be self-
indulgent, but is really soft. For amusement is a relaxation, since it is a rest from work; and the lover of amusement is one of the people who go to excess in this.

    Of incontinence one kind is impetuosity, another weak-
ness. For some men after deliberating fail, owing to their
20 emotion, to stand by the conclusions of their deliberation,
others because they have not deliberated are led by their
emotion; since some men (just as people who first tickle
others are not tickled themselves), if they have first perceived and seen what is coming and have first roused
themselves and their calculative faculty, are not defeated
by their emotion, whether it be pleasant or painful. It is
25 keen and excitable people that suffer especially from the
impetuous form of incontinence; for the former by reason

of their quickness and the latter by reason of the violence
of their passions do not await the argument, because they
are apt to follow their imagination.

8   The self-indulgent man, as was said,[30] is not apt to repent; for he stands by his choice; but any incontinent
man is likely to repent. This is why the position is not as it 30
was expressed in the formulation of the problem,[31] but the
self-indulgent man is incurable and the incontinent man
curable; for wickedness is like a disease such as dropsy or
consumption, while incontinence is like epilepsy; the
former is a permanent, the latter an intermittent badness.
And generally incontinence and vice are different in kind; 35
vice is unconscious of itself, incontinence is not (of incontinent men themselves, those who become temporarily be- **1151ᵃ**
side themselves are better than those who have the rational
principle but do not abide by it, since the latter are defeated
by a weaker passion, and do not act without previous deliberation like the others); for the incontinent man is like
the people who get drunk quickly and on little wine, i. e.
on less than most people.

Evidently, then, incontinence is not vice (though perhaps it is so in a qualified sense); for incontinence is con- 5
trary to choice while vice is in accordance with choice; not
but what they are similar in respect of the actions they lead
to; as in the saying of Demodocus about the Milesians, 'the
Milesians are not without sense, but they do the things
that senseless people do', so too incontinent people are not
criminal, but they will do criminal acts.   10

Now, since the incontinent man is apt to pursue, not on
conviction, bodily pleasures that are excessive and contrary
to the right rule, while the self-indulgent man is convinced
because he is the sort of man to pursue them, it is on the
contrary the former that is easily persuaded to change his 15
mind, while the latter is not. For virtue and vice respec-

[30] ᵃ 21.
[31] 1146ᵃ 31–ᵇ 2.

tively preserve and destroy the first principle, and in actions the final cause is the first principle, as the hypotheses [32] are in mathematics; neither in that case is it argument that teaches the first principles, nor is it so here—virtue either natural or produced by habituation is what teaches right opinion about the first principle. Such a man as this, then, is temperate; his contrary is the self-indulgent.

20   But there is a sort of man who is carried away as a result of passion and contrary to the right rule—a man whom passion masters so that he does not act according to the right rule, but does not master to the extent of making him ready to believe that he ought to pursue such pleasures without reserve; this is the incontinent man, who is better 25 than the self-indulgent man, and not bad without qualification; for the best thing in him, the first principle, is preserved. And contrary to him is another kind of man, he who abides by his convictions and is not carried away, at least as a result of passion. It is evident from these considerations that the latter is a good state and the former a bad one.

9   Is the man continent who abides by any and every rule and any and every choice, or the man who abides 30 by the right choice, and is he incontinent who abandons any and every choice and any and every rule, or he who abandons the rule that is not false and the choice that is right; this is how we put it before in our statement of the problem.[33] Or is it incidentally any and every choice but 35 per se the true rule and the right choice by which the one 1151ᵇ abides and the other does not? If any one chooses or pursues this for the sake of that, per se he pursues and chooses the latter, but incidentally the former. But when we speak without qualification we mean what is per se. Therefore in

---

[32] i. e. the assumptions of the existence of the primary objects of mathematics, such as the straight line or the unit.
[33] 1146ᵃ 16–31.

a sense the one abides by, and the other abandons, any and every opinion; but without qualification, the true opinion.

There are some who are apt to abide by their opinion, who are called strong-headed, viz. those who are hard to 5 persuade in the first instance and are not easily persuaded to change; these have in them something like the continent man, as the prodigal is in a way like the liberal man and the rash man like the confident man; but they are different in many respects. For it is to passion and appetite that the one will not yield, since on occasion the continent man will be easy to persuade; but it is to argument that the others refuse to yield, for they do form appetites and many 10 of them are led by their pleasures. Now the people who are strong-headed are the opinionated, the ignorant, and the boorish—the opinionated being influenced by pleasure and pain; for they delight in the victory they gain if they are not persuaded to change, and are pained if their decisions become null and void as decrees sometimes do; so that they 15 are liker the incontinent than the continent man.

But there are some who fail to abide by their resolutions, not as a result of incontinence, e. g. Neoptolemus in Sophocles' *Philoctetes*; yet it was for the sake of pleasure that he did not stand fast—but a noble pleasure; for telling the truth was noble to him, but he had been persuaded by 20 Odysseus to tell the lie. For not every one who does anything for the sake of pleasure is either self-indulgent or bad or incontinent, but he who does it for a disgraceful pleasure.

Since there is also a sort of man who takes less delight than he should in bodily things, and does not abide by the rule, he who is intermediate between him and the incontinent man is the continent man; for the incontinent man 25 fails to abide by the rule because he delights too much in them, and this man because he delights in them too little; while the continent man abides by the rule and does not change on either account. Now if continence is good, both the contrary states must be bad, as they actually appear to

30 be; but because the other extreme is seen in few people and seldom, as temperance is thought to be contrary only to self-indulgence, so is continence to incontinence.

Since many names are applied analogically, it is by analogy that we have come to speak of the 'continence' of the temperate man; for both the continent man and the 35 temperate man are such as to do nothing contrary to the 1152ᵃ rule for the sake of the bodily pleasures, but the former has and the latter has not bad appetites, and the latter is such as not to feel pleasure contrary to the rule, while the former is such as to feel pleasure but not to be led by it. And the incontinent and the self-indulgent man are also like an-5 other; they are different, but both pursue bodily pleasures —the latter, however, also thinking that he ought to do so, while the former does not think this.

10 Nor can the same man have practical wisdom and be incontinent; for it has been shown [34] that a man is at the same time practically wise, and good in respect of character. Further, a man has practical wisdom not by knowing only but by being able to act; but the incontinent man is unable to act—there is, however, nothing to prevent a 10 clever man from being incontinent; this is why it is sometimes actually thought that some people have practical wisdom but are incontinent, viz. because cleverness and practical wisdom differ in the way we have described in our first discussions,[35] and are near together in respect of their reasoning, but differ in respect of their purpose—nor yet is the incontinent man like the man who knows and is con-15 templating a truth, but like the man who is asleep or drunk. And he acts willingly (for he acts in a sense with knowledge both of what he does and of the end to which he does it), but is not wicked, since his purpose is good; so that he is half-wicked. And he is not a criminal; for he does not act of malice aforethought; of the two types of in-

34 1144ᵃ 11–ᵇ 32.
35 1144ᵃ 23–ᵇ4.

continent man the one does not abide by the conclusions
of his deliberation, while the excitable man does not de- 20
liberate at all. And thus the incontinent man is like a city
which passes all the right decrees and has good laws, but
makes no use of them, as in Anaxandrides' jesting remark,

'The city willed it, that cares nought for laws';

but the wicked man is like a city that uses its laws, but has
wicked laws to use.

Now incontinence and continence are concerned with 25
that which is in excess of the state characteristic of most
men; for the continent man abides by his resolutions more
and the incontinent man less than most men can.

Of the forms of incontinence, that of excitable people is
more curable than that of those who deliberate but do not
abide by their decisions, and those who are incontinent
through habituation are more curable than those in whom
incontinence is innate; for it is easier to change a habit 30
than to change one's nature; even habit is hard to change
just because it is like nature, as Evenus says:

I say that habit's but long practice, friend,
And this becomes men's nature in the end.

We have now stated what continence, incontinence, endurance, and softness are, and how these states are related 35
to each other.

11   The study of pleasure and pain belongs to the province 1152ᵇ
of the political philosopher; for he is the architect of
the end, with a view to which we call one thing bad and
another good without qualification. Further, it is one of
our necessary tasks to consider them; for not only did we
lay it down that moral virtue and vice are concerned with 5
pains and pleasures,³⁶ but most people say that happiness

³⁶ 1104ᵇ 8–1105ᵃ 13.

involves pleasure; this is why the blessed man is called by
a name derived from a word meaning enjoyment.[37]

Now (1) some people think that no pleasure is a good,
either in itself or incidentally, since the good and pleasure
are not the same; (2) others think that some pleasures are
10 good but that most are bad. (3) Again there is a third view,
that even if all pleasures are goods, yet the best thing in the
world cannot be pleasure. (1) The reasons given for the
view that pleasure is not a good at all are (a) that every
pleasure is a perceptible process to a natural state, and that
no process is of the same kind as its end, e. g. no process of
15 building of the same kind as a house. (b) A temperate man
avoids pleasures. (c) A man of practical wisdom pursues
what is free from pain, not what is pleasant. (d) The
pleasures are a hindrance to thought, and the more so the
more one delights in them, e. g. in sexual pleasure; for no
one could think of anything while absorbed in this. (e)
There is no art of pleasure; but every good is the product of
some art. (f) Children and the brutes pursue pleasures.
20 (2) The reasons for the view that not all pleasures are good
are that (a) there are pleasures that are actually base and
objects of reproach, and (b) there are harmful pleasures;
for some pleasant things are unhealthy. (3) The reason
for the view that the best thing in the world is not pleasure
is that pleasure is not an end but a process.

12   These are pretty much the things that are said. That
25   it does not follow from these grounds that pleasure is
not a good, or even the chief good, is plain from the following considerations. (A) [38] (a) First, since that which is
good may be so in either of two senses (one thing good
simply and another good for a particular person), natural
constitutions and states of being, and therefore also the
corresponding movements and processes, will be correspondingly divisible. Of those which are thought to be bad

[37] makarios from mala chairein!
[38] (A) is the answer to (1 a) and (3).

some will be bad if taken without qualification but not bad
for a particular person, but worthy of his choice, and
some will not be worthy of choice even for a particular 30
person, but only at a particular time and for a short period,
though not without qualification; while others are not even
pleasures, but seem to be so, viz. all those which involve
pain and whose end is curative, e. g. the processes that go
on in sick persons.

(b) Further, one kind of good being activity and another being state, the processes that restore us to our natural
state are only incidentally pleasant; for that matter the 35
activity at work in the appetites for them is the activity of
so much of our state and nature as has remained unim-
paired; for there are actually pleasures that involve *no* pain 1153ᵃ
or appetite (e. g. those of contemplation), the nature in
such a case not being defective at all. That the others are
incidental is indicated by the fact that men do not enjoy
the same pleasant objects when their nature is in its settled
state as they do when it is being replenished, but in the
former case they enjoy the things that are pleasant without
qualification, in the latter the contraries of these as well; for
then they enjoy even sharp and bitter things, none of 5
which is pleasant either by nature or without qualification.
The states they produce, therefore, are not pleasures
naturally or without qualification; for as pleasant things
differ, so do the pleasures arising from them.

(c) Again, it is not necessary that there should be something else better than pleasure, as some say the end is better
than the process; for pleasures are not processes nor do 10
they all involve process—they are activities and ends;
nor do they arise when we are becoming something, but
when we are exercising some faculty; and not all pleasures
have an end different from themselves, but only the
pleasures of persons who are being led to the perfecting of
their nature. This is why it is not right to say that pleasure
is perceptible process, but it should rather be called activity 15
of the natural state, and instead of 'perceptible' 'unim-

peded'. It is thought by some people to be process just because they think it is in the strict sense good; for they think that activity is process, which it is not.

(B) [39] The view that pleasures are bad because some pleasant things are unhealthy is like saying that healthy things are bad because some healthy things are bad for 20 money-making; both are bad in the respect mentioned, but they are not *bad* for *that* reason—indeed, thinking itself is sometimes injurious to health.

Neither practical wisdom nor any state of being is impeded by the pleasure arising from it; it is foreign pleasures that impede, for the pleasures arising from thinking and learning will make us think and learn all the more.

(C) [40] The fact that no pleasure is the product of any 25 art arises naturally enough; there is no art of any other activity either, but only of the corresponding faculty; though for that matter the arts of the perfumer and the cook are thought to be arts of pleasure.

(D) [41] The arguments based on the grounds that the temperate man avoids pleasure and that the man of practical wisdom pursues the painless life, and that children and the brutes pursue pleasure, are all refuted by the some consideration. We have pointed out [42] in what sense pleasures are good without qualification and in what sense some are not good; now both the brutes and children pur- 30 sue pleasures of the latter kind (and the man of practical wisdom pursues tranquil freedom from that kind), viz. those which imply appetite and pain, i. e. the bodily pleasures (for it is these that are of this nature) and the excesses of them, in respect of which the self-indulgent man is self-indulgent. This is why the temperate man 35 avoids these pleasures; for even he *has* pleasures of his own.

---

[39] Answer to (2 b) and (1 d).
[40] Answer to (1 e).
[41] Answer to (1 b), (1 c), (1 f).
[42] 1152^b 26–1153^a 7.

13 But further (E) it is agreed that pain is bad and to
be avoided; for some pain is without qualification 1153ᵇ
bad, and other pain is bad because it is in some respect an
impediment to us. Now the contrary of that which is to
be avoided, qua something to be avoided and bad, is
good. Pleasure, then, is necessarily a good. For the answer
of Speusippus, that pleasure is contrary both to pain and
to good, as the greater is contrary both to the less and to the 5
equal, is not successful; since he would not say that
pleasure is essentially just a species of evil.

And (F) ⁴³ if certain pleasures are bad, that does not
prevent the chief good from being some pleasure, just as
the chief good may be some form of knowledge though
certain kinds of knowledge are bad. Perhaps it is even
necessary, if each disposition has unimpeded activities, that, 10
whether the activity (if unimpeded) of all our dispositions
or that of some one of them is happiness, this should be the
thing most worthy of our choice; and this activity is
pleasure. Thus the chief good would be some pleasure,
though most pleasures might perhaps be bad without
qualification. And for this reason all men think that the
happy life is pleasant and weave pleasure into their ideal
of happiness—and reasonably too; for no activity is perfect 15
when it is impeded, and happiness is a perfect thing; this is
why the happy man needs the goods of the body and external goods, i. e. those of fortune, viz. in order that he
may not be impeded in these ways. Those who say that the
victim on the rack or the man who falls into great misfortunes is happy if he is good, are, whether they mean to
or not, talking nonsense. Now because we need fortune as 20
well as other things, some people think good fortune the
same thing as happiness; but it is not that, for even good
fortune itself when in excess is an impediment, and perhaps should then be no longer called good fortune; for its
limit is fixed by reference to happiness.

⁴³ Answer to (2 a).

25   And indeed the fact that all things, both brutes and
men, pursue pleasure is an indication of its being somehow the chief good:

No voice is wholly lost that many peoples . . .

But since no one nature or state either is or is thought the
30 best for all, neither do all pursue the same pleasure; yet all
pursue pleasure. And perhaps they actually pursue not the
pleasure they think they pursue nor that which they would
say they pursue, but the same pleasure; for all things have
by nature something divine in them. But the bodily
pleasures have appropriated the name both because we
oftenest steer our course for them and because all men
35 share in them; thus because they alone are familiar, men
think there are no others.

1154ᵃ   It is evident also that if pleasure, i. e. the activity of our
faculties, is not a good, it will not be the case that the happy
man lives a pleasant life; for to what end should he need
pleasure, if it is not a good but the happy man may even
5 live a painful life? For pain is neither an evil nor a good,
if pleasure is not; why then should he avoid it? Therefore,
too, the life of the good man will not be pleasanter than
that of any one else, if his activities are not more pleasant.

14   (G) ⁴⁴ With regard to the bodily pleasures, those
who say that some pleasures are very much to be
10 chosen, viz. the noble pleasures, but not the bodily pleasures, i. e. those with which the self-indulgent man is concerned, must consider why, then, the contrary things are
bad. For the contrary of bad is good. Are the necessary
pleasures good in the sense in which even that which is
not bad is good? Or are they good up to a point? Is it that
where you have states and processes of which there cannot
be too much, there cannot be too much of the corresponding pleasure, and that where there can be too much of the
15 one there can be too much of the other also? Now there
can be too much of bodily goods, and the bad man is bad

⁴⁴ Answer to (2).

by virtue of pursuing the excess, not by virtue of pursuing the necessary pleasures (for *all* men enjoy in some way or other both dainty foods and wines and sexual intercourse, but not all men do so as they ought). The contrary is the case with pain; for he does not avoid the excess of it, he avoids it altogether; and this is peculiar to him, for the 20 alternative to excess of pleasure is not pain, except to the man who pursues this excess.

Since we should state not only the truth, but also the cause of error—for this contributes towards producing conviction, since when a reasonable explanation is given of why the false view appears true, this tends to produce belief in the true view—therefore we must state why the 25 bodily pleasures appear the more worthy of choice. (a) Firstly, then, it is because they expel pain; owing to the excesses of pain that men experience, they pursue excessive and in general bodily pleasure as being a cure for the pain. Now curative agencies produce intense feeling— 30 which is the reason why they are pursued—because they show up against the contrary pain. (Indeed pleasure is thought not to be good for these two reasons, as has been said,[45] viz. that (α) some of them are activities belonging to a bad nature—either congenital, as in the case of a brute, or due to habit, i. e. those of bad men; while (β) others are meant to cure a defective nature, and it is better to be in a healthy state than to be getting into it, but these arise during the process of being made perfect and are 1154ᵃ therefore only incidentally good.) (b) Further, they are pursued because of their violence by those who cannot enjoy other pleasures. (At all events they go out of their way to manufacture thirsts somehow for themselves. When these are harmless, the practice is irreproachable; when they are hurtful, it is bad.) For they have nothing else to enjoy, and, besides, a neutral state is painful to many 5 people because of their nature. For the animal nature is always in travail, as the students of natural science also

[45] 1152ᵇ 26–33.

testify, saying that sight and hearing are painful; but we have become used to this, as they maintain. Similarly, while, in youth, people are, owing to the growth that is going on, in a situation like that of drunken men, and 10 youth is pleasant,[46] on the other hand people of excitable nature [47] always need relief; for even their body is ever in torment owing to its special composition, and they are always under the influence of violent desire; but pain is driven out both by the contrary pleasure, and by any chance pleasure if it be strong; and for these reasons they become 15 self-indulgent and bad. But the pleasures that do not involve pains do not admit of excess; and these are among the things pleasant by nature and not incidentally. By things pleasant incidentally I mean those that act as cures (for because as a result people are cured, through some action of the part that remains healthy, for this reason the process is thought pleasant); by things naturally pleasant I mean those that stimulate the action of the healthy nature.

20   There is no one thing that is always pleasant, because our nature is not simple but there is another element in us as well, inasmuch as we are perishable creatures, so that if the one element does something, this is unnatural to the other nature, and when the two elements are evenly balanced, what is done seems neither painful nor pleasant; for 25 if the nature of anything were simple, the same action would always be most pleasant to it. This is why God always enjoys a single and simple pleasure; for there is not only an activity of movement but an activity of immobility, and pleasure is found more in rest than in movement. But 'change in all things is sweet', as the poet says, because of some vice; for as it is the vicious man that is changeable, 30 so the nature that needs change is vicious; for it is not simple nor good.

---

[46] i. e. the growth or replenishment that is going on produces exhilaration and pleasure.

[47] Lit., melancholic people, those characterized by an excess of black bile.

We have now discussed continence and incontinence, and pleasure and pain, both what each is and in what sense some of them are good and others bad; it remains to speak of friendship.

BOOK VIII

1   After what we have said, a discussion of friendship 1155ᵃ
would naturally follow, since it is a virtue or implies virtue, and is besides most necessary with a view to living. 5 For without friends no one would choose to live, though he had all other goods; even rich men and those in possession of office and of dominating power are thought to need friends most of all; for what is the use of such prosperity without the opportunity of beneficence, which is exercised chiefly and in its most laudable form towards friends? Or how can prosperity be guarded and preserved 10 without friends? The greater it is, the more exposed is it to risk. And in poverty and in other misfortunes men think friends are the only refuge. It helps the young, too, to keep from error; it aids older people by ministering to their needs and supplementing the activities that are failing from weakness; those in the prime of life it stimulates to noble 15 actions—'two going together' ¹—for with friends men are more able both to think and to act. Again, parent seems by nature to feel it for offspring and offspring for parent, not only among men but among birds and among most animals; it is felt mutually by members of the same race, 20 and especially by men, whence we praise lovers of their fellowmen. We may see even in our travels how near and dear every man is to every other. Friendship seems too to hold states together, and lawgivers to care more for it than for justice; for unanimity seems to be something like friendship, and this they aim at most of all, and expel faction as their worst enemy; and when men are friends they have 25 no need of justice, while when they are just they need

¹ *Il.* x. 224.

friendship as well, and the truest form of justice is thought
to be a friendly quality.

But it is not only necessary but also noble; for we praise
those who love their friends, and it is thought to be a fine
30 thing to have many friends; and again we think it is the
same people that are good men and are friends.

Not a few things about friendship are matters of debate.
Some define it as a kind of likeness and say like people are
friends, whence come the sayings 'like to like', 'birds of a
35 feather flock together', and so on; others on the contrary
1155ᵇ say 'two of a trade never agree'. On this very question they
inquire for deeper and more physical causes, Euripides saying that 'parched earth loves the rain, and stately heaven
when filled with rain loves to fall to earth', and Heraclitus
that 'it is what opposes that helps' and 'from different tones
5 comes the fairest tune' and 'all things are produced through
strife'; while Empedocles, as well as others, expresses the
opposite view that like aims at like. The physical problems
we may leave alone (for they do not belong to the present
inquiry); let us examine those which are human and involve character and feeling, e. g. whether friendship can
10 arise between any two people or people cannot be friends
if they are wicked, and whether there is one species of
friendship or more than one. Those who think there is only
one because it admits of degrees have relied on an inadequate indication; for even things different in species
15 admit of degree. We have discussed this matter previously.

2   The kinds of friendship may perhaps be cleared up if
we first come to know the object of love. For not
everything seems to be loved but only the lovable, and this
is good, pleasant, or useful; but it would seem to be that
by which some good or pleasure is produced that is useful,
so that it is the good and the useful that are lovable as ends.
20 Do men love, then, the good, or what is good for them?
These sometimes clash. So too with regard to the pleasant.

Now it is thought that each loves what is good for himself,
and that the good is without qualification lovable, and what
is good for each man is lovable for him; but each man loves
not what is good for him but what seems good. This how- 25
ever will make no difference; we shall just have to say that
this *is* 'that which seems lovable'. Now there are three
grounds on which people love; of the love of lifeless objects
we do not use the word 'friendship'; for it is not mutual
love, nor is there a wishing of good to the other (for it
would surely be ridiculous to wish wine well; if one wishes 30
anything for it, it is that it may keep, so that one may have
it oneself); but to a friend we say we ought to wish what
is good for his sake. But to those who thus wish good we
ascribe only goodwill, if the wish is not reciprocated; goodwill when it *is* reciprocal being friendship. Or must we add
'when it is recognized'? For many people have goodwill to 35
those whom they have not seen but judge to be good or 1156ᵃ
useful; and one of these might return this feeling. These
people seem to bear goodwill to each other; but how could
one call them friends when they do not know their mutual
feelings? To be friends, then, they must be mutually recognized as bearing goodwill and wishing well to each other 5
for one of the aforesaid reasons.

3   Now these reasons differ from each other in kind; so,
      therefore, do the corresponding forms of love and
friendship. There are therefore three kinds of friendship,
equal in number to the things that are lovable; for with
respect to each there is a mutual and recognized love, and
those who love each other wish well to each other in that
respect in which they love one another. Now those who 10
love each other for their utility do not love each other
for themselves but in virtue of some good which they get
from each other. So too with those who love for the sake
of pleasure; it is not for their character that men love ready-
witted people, but because they find them pleasant. There-

15 fore those who love for the sake of utility love for the
sake of what is good for *themselves*, and those who love
for the sake of pleasure do so for the sake of what is pleasant
to *themselves*, and not in so far as the other is the person
loved but in so far as he is useful or pleasant. And thus
these friendships are only incidental; for it is not as being
the man he is that the loved person is loved, but as provid-
20 ing some good or pleasure. Such friendships, then, are
easily dissolved, if the parties do not remain like themselves; for if the one party is no longer pleasant or useful
the other ceases to love him.

Now the useful is not permanent but is always changing.
Thus when the motive of the friendship is done away, the
friendship is dissolved, inasmuch as it existed only for the
25 ends in question. This kind of friendship seems to exist
chiefly between old people (for at that age people pursue
not the pleasant but the useful) and, of those who are in
their prime or young, between those who pursue utility.
And such people do not live much with each other either;
for sometimes they do not even find each other pleasant;
therefore they do not need such companionship unless
they are useful to each other; for they are pleasant to each
other only in so far as they rouse in each other hopes of
30 something good to come. Among such friendships people
also class the friendship of host and guest. On the other
hand the friendship of young people seems to aim at
pleasure; for they live under the guidance of emotion,
and pursue above all what is pleasant to themselves and
what is immediately before them; but with increasing age
their pleasures become different. This is why they quickly
35 become friends and quickly cease to be so; their friendship
changes with the object that is found pleasant, and such
pleasure alters quickly.

1156ᵇ Young people are amorous too; for the greater part of the
friendship of love depends on emotion and aims at pleasure; this is why they fall in love and quickly fall out of love,
changing often within a single day. But these people do

wish to spend their days and lives together; for it is thus
that they attain the purpose of their friendship. 5

Perfect friendship is the friendship of men who are good,
and alike in virtue; for these wish well alike to each other
qua good, and they are good in themselves. Now those
who wish well to their friends for their sake are most
truly friends; for they do this by reason of their own nature 10
and not incidentally; therefore their friendship lasts as long
as they are good—and goodness is an enduring thing.
And each is good without qualification and to his friend,
for the good are both good without qualification and useful to each other. So too they are pleasant; for the good are 15
pleasant both without qualification and to each other, since
to each his own activities and others like them are pleasurable, and the actions of the good are the same or like.
And such a friendship is as might be expected permanent,
since there meet in it all the qualities that friends should
have. For all friendship is for the sake of good or of pleasure
—good or pleasure either in the abstract or such as will be 20
enjoyed by him who has the friendly feeling—and is based
on a certain resemblance; and to a friendship of good
men all the qualities we have named belong in virtue of the
nature of the friends themselves; for in the case of this kind
of friendship the other qualities also [2] are alike in both
friends, and that which is good without qualification is
also without qualification pleasant, and these are the most
lovable qualities. Love and friendship therefore are found
most and in their best form between such men.

But it is natural that such friendships should be infre-
quent; for such men are rare. Further, such friendship
requires time and familiarity; as the proverb says, men can- 25
not know each other till they have 'eaten salt together';
nor can they admit each other to friendship or be friends
till each has been found lovable and been trusted by each.
Those who quickly show the marks of friendship to each

[2] i. e. absolute pleasantness, relative goodness, and relative pleasantness, as well as absolute goodness.

30 other wish to be friends, but are not friends unless they both are lovable and know the fact; for a wish for friendship may arise quickly, but friendship does not.

4 This kind of friendship, then, is perfect both in respect of duration and in all other respects, and in it each gets from each in all respects the same as, or some-
35 thing like what, he gives; which is what ought to happen
1157ᵃ between friends. Friendship for the sake of pleasure bears a resemblance to this kind; for good people too are pleasant to each other. So too does friendship for the sake of utility; for the good are also useful to each other. Among men of these inferior sorts too, friendships are most permanent
5 when the friends get the same thing from each other (e. g. pleasure), and not only that but also from the same source, as happens between ready-witted people, not as happens between lover and beloved. For these do not take pleasure in the same things, but the one in seeing the beloved and the other in receiving attentions from his lover; and when the bloom of youth is passing the friendship sometimes passes too (for the one finds no pleasure in the sight of the
10 other, and the other gets no attentions from the first); but many lovers on the other hand are constant, if familiarity has led them to love each other's characters, these being alike. But those who exchange not pleasure but utility in their amour are both less truly friends and less constant.
15 Those who are friends for the sake of utility part when the advantage is at an end; for they were lovers not of each other but of profit.

For the sake of pleasure or utility, then, even bad men may be friends of each other, or good men of bad, or one who is neither good nor bad may be a friend to any sort of person, but for their own sake clearly only good men can be friends; for bad men do not delight in each other unless some advantage come of the relation.
20 The friendship of the good too and this alone is proof

against slander; for it is not easy to trust any one's talk about a man who has long been tested by oneself; and it is among good men that trust and the feeling that 'he would never wrong me' and all the other things that are demanded in true friendship are found. In the other kinds of friendship, however, there is nothing to prevent these evils arising.

For men apply the name of friends even to those whose 25 motive is utility, in which sense states are said to be friendly (for the alliances of states seem to aim at advantage), and to those who love each other for the sake of pleasure, in which sense children are called friends. Therefore we too ought perhaps to call such people friends, and say that 30 there are several kinds of friendship—firstly and in the proper sense that of good men qua good, and by analogy the other kinds; for it is in virtue of something good and something akin to what is found in true friendship that they are friends, since even the pleasant is good for the lovers of pleasure. But these two kinds of friendship are not often united, nor do the same people become friends for the sake of utility and of pleasure; for things that are only incidentally connected are not often coupled to- 35 gether.

Friendship being divided into these kinds, bad men will be friends for the sake of pleasure or of utility, being in this 1157ᵇ respect like each other, but good men will be friends for their own sake, i. e. in virtue of their goodness. These, then, are friends without qualification; the others are friends incidentally and through a resemblance to these.

5   As in regard to the virtues some men are called good in respect of a state of character, others in respect of 5 an activity, so too in the case of friendship; for those who live together delight in each other and confer benefits on each other, but those who are asleep or locally separated are not performing, but are disposed to perform, the activi-

ties of friendship; distance does not break off the friend-
10 ship absolutely, but only the activity of it. But if the absence is lasting, it seems actually to make men forget their
friendship; hence the saying 'out of sight, out of mind'.
Neither old people nor sour people seem to make friends
easily; for there is little that is pleasant in them, and no
15 one can spend his days with one whose company is painful, or not pleasant, since nature seems above all to avoid
the painful and to aim at the pleasant. Those, however,
who approve of each other but do not live together seem to
be well-disposed rather than actual friends. For there is
nothing so characteristic of friends as living together (since
20 while it is people who are in need that desire benefits, even
those who are supremely happy desire to spend their days
together; for solitude suits such people least of all); but
people cannot live together if they are not pleasant and do
not enjoy the same things, as friends who are companions
seem to do.

The truest friendship, then, is that of the good, as we
25 have frequently said; [3] for that which is without qualification good or pleasant seems to be lovable and desirable,
and for each person that which is good or pleasant to him;
and the good man is lovable and desirable to the good man
for both these reasons. Now it looks as if love were a feel-
30 ing, friendship a state of character; for love may be felt just
as much towards lifeless things, but mutual love involves
choice and choice springs from a state of character; and
men wish well to those whom they love, for their sake, not
as a result of feeling but as a result of a state of character.
And in loving a friend men love what is good for themselves; for the good man in becoming a friend becomes a
35 good to his friend. Each, then, both loves what is good for
himself, and makes an equal return in goodwill and in
pleasantness; for friendship is said to be equality, and both
of these are found most in the friendship of the good.

[3] 1156^b 7, 23, 33, 1157^a 30, ^{b}4.

6   Between sour and elderly people friendship arises less **1158ᵃ** readily, inasmuch as they are less good-tempered and enjoy companionship less; for these are thought to be the greatest marks of friendship and most productive of it. This is why, while young men become friends quickly, old 5 men do not; it is because men do not become friends with those in whom they do not delight; and similarly sour people do not quickly make friends either. But such men may bear goodwill to each other; for they wish one another well and aid one another in need; but they are hardly *friends* because they do not spend their days together nor delight in each other, and these are thought the greatest marks of friendship.

One cannot be a friend to many people in the sense of 10 having friendship of the perfect type with them, just as one cannot be in love with many people at once (for love is a sort of excess of feeling, and it is the nature of such only to be felt towards one person); and it is not easy for many people at the same time to please the same person very greatly, or perhaps even to be good in his eyes. One must, too, acquire some experience of the other person and become familiar with him, and that is very hard. But with a 15 view to utility or pleasure it is possible that many people should please one; for many people are useful or pleasant, and these services take little time.

Of these two kinds that which is for the sake of pleasure is the more like friendship, when both parties get the same things from each other and delight in each other or in the same things, as in the friendships of the young; for 20 generosity is more found in such friendships. Friendship based on utility is for the commercially minded. People who are supremely happy, too, have no need of useful friends, but do need pleasant friends: for they wish to live with some one and, though they can endure for a short time what is painful, no one could put up with it continuously, nor even with the Good itself if it were painful

to him; this is why they look out for friends who are
25 pleasant. Perhaps they should look out for friends who,
being pleasant, are also good, and good for them, too; for
so they will have all the characteristics that friends should
have.

People in positions of authority seem to have friends
who fall into distinct classes; some people are useful to
them and others are pleasant, but the same people are rarely
both; for they seek neither those whose pleasantness is ac-
30 companied by virtue nor those whose utility is with a view
to noble objects, but in their desire for pleasure they seek
for ready-witted people, and their other friends they
choose as being clever at doing what they are told, and
these characteristics are rarely combined. Now we have
said that the *good* man *is* at the same time pleasant and
useful; [4] but such a man does not become the friend of one
who surpasses him in station, unless he is surpassed also
35 in virtue; if this is not so, he does not establish equality
by being proportionally exceeded in both respects. But
people who surpass him in both respects are not so easy
to find.

However that may be, the aforesaid friendships involve
1158[b] equality; for the friends get the same things from one another and wish the same things for one another,
or exchange one thing for another, e. g. pleasure for
utility; we have said,[5] however, that they are both less truly
friendships and less permanent. But it is from their like-
5 ness and their unlikeness to the same thing that they are
thought both to be and not to be friendships. It is by their
likeness to the friendship of virtue that they seem to be
friendships (for one of them involves pleasure and the
other utility, and these characteristics belong to the friendship of virtue as well); while it is because the friendship
of virtue is proof against slander and permanent, while
these quickly change (besides differing from the former

---

[4] 1156[b] 13–15, 1157[a] 1–3.
[5] 1156[a] 16–24, 1157[a] 20–33.

in many other respects), that they appear *not* to be
friendships; i. e. it is because of their unlikeness to the 10
friendship of virtue.

7 But there is another kind of friendship, viz. that which
involves an inequality between the parties, e. g. that
of father to son and in general of elder to younger, that
of man to wife and in general that of ruler to subject. And
these friendships differ also from each other; for it is not 15
the same that exists between parents and children and between rulers and subjects, nor is even that of father to son
the same as that of son to father, nor that of husband to
wife the same as that of wife to husband. For the virtue
and the function of each of these is different, and so are
the reasons for which they love; the love and the friendship 20
are therefore different also. Each party, then, neither gets
the same from the other, nor ought to seek it; but when
children render to parents what they ought to render to
those who brought them into the world, and parents
render what they should to their children, the friendship
of such persons will be abiding and excellent. In all friendships implying inequality the love also should be propor- 25
tional, i. e. the better should be more loved than he loves,
and so should the more useful, and similarly in each of the
other cases; for when the love is in proportion to the merit
of the parties, then in a sense arises equality, which is
'certainly held to be characteristic of friendship.

But equality does not seem to take the same form in acts
of justice and in friendship; for in acts of justice what is 30
equal in the primary sense is that which is in proportion
to merit, while quantitative equality is secondary, but in
friendship quantitative equality is primary and proportion
to merit secondary. This becomes clear if there is a great
interval in respect of virtue or vice or wealth or anything
else between the parties; for then they are no longer
friends, and do not even expect to be so. And this is most 35
manifest in the case of the gods; for they surpass us most

1159ª decisively in all good things. But it is clear also in the
case of kings; for with them, too, men who are much their
inferiors do not expect to be friends; nor do men of no
account expect to be friends with the best or wisest men. In
such cases it is not possible to define exactly up to what
point friends can remain friends; for much can be taken
away and friendship remain, but when one party is re-
5 moved to a great distance, as God is, the possibility of
friendship ceases. This is in fact the origin of the question
whether friends really wish for their friends the greatest
goods, e. g. that of being gods; since in that case their
friends will no longer be friends to them, and therefore
will not be good things for them (for friends are good
things). The answer is that if we were right in saying that
friend wishes good to friend for his sake,[6] his friend must
10 remain the sort of being he is, whatever that may be; therefore it is for him only so long as he remains a man that he
will wish the greatest goods. But perhaps not all the greatest
goods; for it is for himself most of all that each man wishes
what is good.

8   Most people seem, owing to ambition, to wish to be
loved rather than to love; which is why most men love
flattery; for the flatterer is a friend in an inferior position,
or pretends to be such and to love more than he is loved;
15 and being loved seems to be akin to being honoured, and
this is what most people aim at. But it seems to be not for
its own sake that people choose honour, but incidentally.
For most people enjoy being honoured by those in positions of authority because of their hopes (for they think
20 that if they want anything they will get it from them;
and therefore they delight in honour as a token of favour to
come); while those who desire honour from good men, and
men who know, are aiming at confirming their own opinion
of themselves; they delight in honour, therefore, because
they believe in their own goodness on the strength of the

[6] 1155ᵇ 31.

judgement of those who speak about them. In being loved, on the other hand, people delight for its own sake; whence it would seem to be better than being honoured, and 25 friendship to be desirable in itself. But it seems to lie in loving rather than in being loved, as is indicated by the delight mothers take in loving; for some mothers hand over their children to be brought up, and so long as they know their fate they love them and do not seek to be loved 30 in return (if they cannot have both), but seem to be satisfied if they see them prospering; and they themselves love their children even if these owing to their ignorance give them nothing of a mother's due. Now since friendship depends more on loving, and it is those who love their friends that are praised, loving seems to be the characteristic virtue of friends, so that it is only those in whom this is 35 found in due measure that are lasting friends, and only their friendship that endures.

It is in this way more than any other that even unequals can be friends; they can be equalized. Now equality and 1159ᵇ likeness are friendship, and especially the likeness of those who are like in virtue; for being steadfast in themselves they hold fast to each other, and neither ask nor give base serv- 5 ices, but (one may say) even prevent them; for it is characteristic of good men neither to go wrong themselves nor to let their friends do so. But wicked men have no steadfastness (for they do not remain even like to themselves), but become friends for a short time because they delight in each other's wickedness. Friends who are useful 10 or pleasant last longer; i. e. as long as they provide each other with enjoyments or advantages. Friendship for utility's sake seems to be that which most easily exists between contraries, e. g. between poor and rich, between ignorant and learned; for what a man actually lacks he aims at, and one gives something else in return. But under this head, 15 too, we might bring lover and beloved, beautiful and ugly. This is why lovers sometimes seem ridiculous, when they demand to be loved as they love; if they are equally lovable

their claim can perhaps be justified, but when they have
nothing lovable about them it is ridiculous. Perhaps, how-
20 ever, contrary does not even aim at contrary by its own
nature, but only incidentally, the desire being for what is
intermediate; for that is what is good, e. g. it is good for
the dry not to become wet [7] but to come to the intermediate state, and similarly with the hot and in all other
cases. These subjects we may dismiss; for they are indeed
somewhat foreign to our inquiry.

25 **9**   Friendship and justice seem, as we have said at the
outset·of our discussion,[8] to be concerned with the
same objects and exhibited between the same persons. For
in every community there is thought to be some form of
justice, and friendship too; at least men address as friends
their fellow-voyagers and fellow-soldiers, and so too those
associated with them in any other kind of community. And
the extent of their association is the extent of their friend-
30 ship, as it is the extent to which justice exists between
them. And the proverb 'what friends have is common
property' expresses the truth; for friendship depends on
community. Now brothers and comrades have all things
in common, but the others to whom we have referred have
definite things in common—some more things, others
35 fewer; for of friendships, too, some are more and others less
1160ª truly friendships. And the claims of justice differ too; the
duties of parents to children and those of brothers to each
·other are not the same nor those of comrades and those of
fellow-citizens, and so, too, with the other kinds of friendship. There iş a difference, therefore, also between the acts
that are unjust towards each of these classes of associates,
and the injustice increases by being exhibited towards
those who are friends in a fuller sense; e. g. it is a more
terrible thing to defraud a comrade than a fellow-citizen,
5 more terrible not to help a brother than a stranger, and

[7] Cf. 1155ᵇ 3.
[8] 1155ª 22–28.

more terrible to wound a father than any one else. And the demands of justice also seem to increase with the intensity of the friendship, which implies that friendship and justice exist between the same persons and have an equal extension.

Now all forms of community are like parts of the political community; for men journey together with a view to some particular advantage, and to provide something that they 10 need for the purposes of life; and it is for the sake of advantage that the political community too seems both to have come together originally and to endure, for this is what legislators aim at, and they call just that which is to the common advantage. Now the other communities aim at advantage bit by bit, e. g. sailors at what is advantageous on a voyage with a view to making money or something of 15 the kind, fellow-soldiers at what is advantageous in war, whether it is wealth or victory or the taking of a city that they seek, and members of tribes and demes act similarly [Some communities seem to arise for the sake of pleasure, viz. religious guilds and social clubs; for these exist respectively for the sake of offering sacrifice and of com- 20 panionship. But all these seem to fall under the political community; for it aims not at present advantage but at what is advantageous for life as a whole], offering sacrifices and arranging gatherings for the purpose, and assigning honours to the gods, and providing pleasant relaxations for themselves. For the ancient sacrifices and gatherings seem to take place after the harvest as a sort of firstfruits, 25 because it was at these seasons that people had most leisure. All the communities, then, seem to be parts of the political community; and the particular kinds of friendship will correspond to the particular kinds of community.   30

10   There are three kinds of constitution, and an equal number of deviation-forms—perversions, as it were, of them. The constitutions are monarchy, aristocracy, and thirdly that which is based on a property qualification,

which it seems appropriate to call timocratic, though most
people are wont to call it polity. The best of these is
35 monarchy, the worst timocracy. The deviation from monarchy is tyranny; for both are forms of one-man rule, but
1160ᵇ there is the greatest difference between them; the tyrant
looks to his own advantage, the king to that of his subjects.
For a man is not a king unless he is sufficient to himself
and excels his subjects in all good things; and such a man
needs nothing further; therefore he will not look to his own
5 interests but to those of his subjects; for a king who is not
like that would be a mere titular king. Now tyranny is the
very contrary of this; the tyrant pursues his own good.
And it is clearer in the case of tyranny that it is the worst
deviation-form; ⁹ but it is the contrary of the best that is
worst.¹⁰ Monarchy passes over into tyranny, for tyranny is
10 the evil form of one-man rule and the bad king becomes
a tyrant. Aristocracy passes over into oligarchy by the badness of the rulers, who distribute contrary to equity what
belongs to the city—all or most of the good things to
15 themselves, and office always to the same people, paying
most regard to wealth; thus the rulers are few and are bad
men instead of the most worthy. Timocracy passes over
into democracy; for these are coterminous, since it is the
ideal even of timocracy to be the rule of the majority, and
all who have the property qualification count as equal.
20 Democracy is the least bad of the deviations; for in its case
the form of constitution is but a slight deviation. These
then are the changes to which constitutions are most subject; for these are the smallest and easiest transitions.

One may find resemblances to the constitutions and,
as it were, patterns of them even in households. For the as-
25 sociation of a father with his sons bears the form of
monarchy, since the father cares for his children; and this
is why Homer calls Zeus 'father'; it is the ideal of monarchy
to be paternal rule. But among the Persians the rule of the
father is tyrannical; they use their sons as slaves. Tyrannical

⁹ Than it is that monarchy is the best genuine form (ᵃ 35).
¹⁰ Therefore monarchy must be the best.

too is the rule of a master over slaves; for it is the advantage
of the master that is brought about in it. Now this seems to 30
be a correct form of government, but the Persian type is
perverted; for the modes of rule appropriate to different
relations are diverse. The association of man and wife seems
to be aristocratic; for the man rules in accordance with his
worth, and in those matters in which a man should rule,
but the matters that befit a woman he hands over to her. 35
If the man rules in everything the relation passes over into
oligarchy; for in doing so he is not acting in accordance
with their respective worth, and not ruling in virtue of his
superiority. Sometimes, however, women rule, because 1161ᵃ
they are heiresses; so their rule is not in virtue of excellence
but due to wealth and power, as in oligarchies. The association of brothers is like timocracy; for they are equal, except 5
in so far as they differ in age; hence if they differ much in
age, the friendship is no longer of the fraternal type. Democracy is found chiefly in masterless dwellings (for here
every one is on an equality), and in those in which the
ruler is weak and every one has license to do as he pleases.

11 Each of the constitutions may be seen to involve 10
friendship just in so far as it involves justice. The
friendship between a king and his subjects depends on an
excess of benefits conferred; for he confers benefits on his
subjects if being a good man he cares for them with a view
to their well-being, as a shepherd does for his sheep
(whence Homer called Agamemnon 'shepherd of the peo- 15
ples'). Such too is the friendship of a father, though this
exceeds the other in the greatness of the benefits conferred;
for he is responsible for the existence of his children, which
is thought the greatest good, and for their nurture and upbringing. These things are ascribed to ancestors as well.
Further, by nature a father tends to rule over his sons,
ancestors over descendants, a king over his subjects. These
friendships imply superiority of one party over the other,
which is why ancestors are honoured. The justice there- 20
fore that exists between persons so related is not the same

on both sides but is in every case proportioned to merit;
for that is true of the friendship as well. The friendship of
man and wife, again, is the same that is found in an
aristocracy; for it is in accordance with virtue—the better
gets more of what is good, and each gets what befits him;
and so, too, with the justice in these relations. The friendship of brothers is like that of comrades; for they are
25 equal and of like age, and such persons are for the most
part like in their feelings and their character. Like this,
too, is the friendship appropriate to timocratic government;
for in such a constitution the ideal is for the citizens to be
equal and fair; therefore rule is taken in turn, and on equal
terms; and the friendship appropriate here will correspond.

But in the deviation-forms, as justice hardly exists, so
30 too does friendship. It exists least in the worst form; in
tyranny there is little or no friendship. For where there is
nothing common to ruler and ruled, there is not friendship
either, since there is not justice; e.g. between craftsman and
35 tool, soul and body, master and slave; the latter in each
1161ᵇ case· is benefited by that which uses it, but there is no
friendship nor justice towards lifeless things. But neither is
there friendship towards a horse or an ox, nor to a slave
qua slave. For there is nothing common to the two parties;
the slave is a living tool and the tool a lifeless slave. Qua
5 slave then, one cannot be friends with him. But qua man
one can; for there seems to be some justice between any
man and any other who can share in a system of law or be a
party to an agreement; therefore there can also be friendship with him in so far as he is a man. Therefore while in
tyrannies friendship and justice hardly exist, in democracies they exist more fully; for where the citizens are equal
10 they have much in common.

12 Every form of friendship, then, involves association,
as has been said.[11] One might, however, mark off from
the rest both the friendship of kindred and that of comrades. Those of fellow-citizens, fellow-tribesmen, fellow-

[11] 1159ᵇ 29–32.

voyagers, and the like are more like mere friendships of association; for they seem to rest on a sort of compact. With 15
them we might class the friendship of host and guest.

The friendship of kinsmen itself, while it seems to be of
many kinds, appears to depend in every case on parental
friendship; for parents love their children as being a part
of themselves, and children their parents as being something originating from them. Now (1) parents know their 20
offspring better than their children know that they are
their children, and (2) the originator feels his offspring to
be his own more than the offspring do their begetter; for
the product belongs to the producer (e. g. a tooth or hair
or anything else to him whose it is), but the producer does
not belong to the product, or belongs in a less degree. And
(3) the length of time produces the same result; parents 25
love their children as soon as these are born, but children
love their parents only after time has elapsed and they have
acquired understanding or the power of discrimination
by the senses. From these considerations it is also plain
why mothers love more than fathers do. Parents, then,
love their children as themselves (for their issue are by
virtue of their separate existence a sort of other selves),
while children love their parents as being born of them, and
brothers love each other as being born of the same parents; 30
for their identity with them makes them identical with each
other (which is the reason why people talk of 'the same
blood', 'the same stock', and so on). They are, therefore,
in a sense the same thing, though in separate individuals.
Two things that contribute greatly to friendship are a common upbringing and similarity of age; for 'two of an age
take to each other', and people brought up together tend to 35
be comrades; whence the friendship of brothers is akin to 1162ᵃ
that of comrades. And cousins and other kinsmen are
bound up together by derivation from brothers, viz. by
being derived from the same parents. They come to be
closer together or farther apart by virtue of the nearness
or distance of the original ancestor.

The friendship of children to parents, and of men to

5 gods, is a relation to them as to something good and superior; for they have conferred the greatest benefits, since they are the causes of their being and of their nourishment, and of their education from their birth; and this kind of friendship possesses pleasantness and utility also, more than that of strangers, inasmuch as their life is lived more in common. The friendship of brothers has the character-
10 istics found in that of comrades (and especially when these are good), and in general between people who are like each other, inasmuch as they belong more to each other and start with a love for each other from their very birth, and inasmuch as those born of the same parents and brought up together and similarly educated are more akin in character; and the test of time has been applied most fully and convincingly in their case.

Between other kinsmen friendly relations are found in
15 due proportion. Between man and wife friendship seems to exist by nature; for man is naturally inclined to form couples—even more than to form cities, inasmuch as the household is earlier and more necessary than the city, and reproduction is more common to man with the animals. With the other animals the union extends only to this point, but human beings live together not only for
20 the sake of reproduction but also for the various purposes of life; for from the start the functions are divided, and those of man and woman are different; so they help each other by throwing their peculiar gifts into the common
25 stock. It is for these reasons that both utility and pleasure seem to be found in this kind of friendship. But this friendship may be based also on virtue, if the parties are good; for each has its own virtue and they will delight in the fact. And children seem to be a bond of union (which is the reason why childless people part more easily); for children are a good common to both and what is common holds them together.

How man and wife and in general friend and friend ought mutually to behave seems to be the same question

as how it is just for them to behave; for a man does not 30
seem to have the same duties to a friend, a stranger, a comrade, and a schoolfellow.

13 There are three kinds of friendship, as we said at the
    outset of our inquiry,[12] and in respect of each some
are friends on an equality and others by virtue of a superior- 35
ity (for not only can equally good men become friends but
a better man can make friends with a worse, and similarly 1162ᵇ
in friendships of pleasure or utility the friends may be equal
or unequal in the benefits they confer). This being so,
equals must effect the required equalization on a basis of
equality in love and in all other respects, while unequals
must render what is in proportion to their superiority or inferiority.

Complaints and reproaches arise either only or chiefly in
the friendship of utility, and this is only to be expected. 5
For those who are friends on the ground of virtue are
anxious to do well by each other (since that is a mark of
virtue and of friendship), and between men who are
emulating each other in this there cannot be complaints
or quarrels; no one is offended by a man who loves him
and does well by him—if he is a person of nice feeling he
takes his revenge by doing well by the other. And the man 10
who excels the other in the services he renders will not
complain of his friend, since he gets what he aims at;
for each man desires what is good. Nor do complaints arise
much even in friendships of pleasure; for both get at the
same time what they desire, if they enjoy spending their
time together; and even a man who complained of an- 15
other for not affording him pleasure would seem ridiculous,
since it is in his power not to spend his days with him.

But the friendship of utility is full of complaints; for
as they use each other for their own interests they always
want to get the better of the bargain, and think they have
got less than they should, and blame their partners be-

[12] 1156ᵃ 7.

20 cause they do not get all they 'want and deserve'; and those
who do well by others cannot help them as much as those
whom they benefit want.

Now it seems that, as justice is of two kinds, one unwritten and the other legal, one kind of friendship of utility is moral and the other legal. And so complaints arise
most of all when men do not dissolve the relation in the
25 spirit of the same type of friendship in which they contracted it. The *legal* type is that which is on fixed terms; its
purely commercial variety is on the basis of immediate payment, while the more liberal variety allows time but stipu-
lates for a definite *quid pro quo*. In this variety the debt
is clear and not ambiguous, but in the postponement it con-
30 tains an element of friendliness; and so some states do not
allow suits arising out of such agreements, but think men
who have bargained on a basis of credit ought to accept the
consequences. The *moral* type is not on fixed terms; it
makes a gift, or does whatever it does, as to a friend; but
one expects to receive as much or more, as having not
given but lent; and if a man is worse off when the relation
35 is dissolved than he was when it was contracted he will
complain. This happens because all or most men, while
they wish for what is noble, choose what is advantageous;
now it is noble to do well by another without a view to re-
payment, but it is the receiving of benefits that is advantageous.

1163ᵃ   Therefore if we can we should return the equivalent of
what we have received (for we must not make a man our
friend against his will; we must recognize that we were mistaken at the first and took a benefit from a person we
should not have taken it from—since it was not from a
friend, nor from one who did it just for the sake of acting
5 so—and we must settle up just as if we had been benefited
on fixed terms). Indeed, one would agree to repay if one
could (if one could not, even the giver would not have
expected one to do so); therefore if it is possible we must
repay. But at the outset we must consider the man by

whom we are being benefited and on what terms he is acting, in order that we may accept the benefit on these terms,
or else decline it.

It is disputable whether we ought to measure a service
by its utility to the receiver and make the return with a 10
view to that, or by the benevolence of the giver. For those
who have received say they have received from their benefactors what meant little to the latter and what they might
have got from others—minimizing the service; while the
givers, on the contrary, say it was the biggest thing they
had, and what could not have been got from others, and
that it was given in times of danger or similar need. Now if 15
the friendship is one that aims at *utility*, surely the advantage to the receiver is the measure. For it is he that asks
for the service, and the other man helps him on the assumption that he will receive the equivalent; so the assistance has been precisely as great as the advantage to the
receiver, and therefore he must return as much as he has
received, or even more (for that would be nobler). In 20
friendships based on *virtue* on the other hand, complaints
do not arise, but the purpose of the doer is a sort of measure; for in purpose lies the essential element of virtue
and character.

14 Differences arise also in friendships based on superiority; for each expects to get more out of them, but
when this happens the friendship is dissolved. Not only 25
does the better man think he ought to get more, since more
should be assigned to a good man, but the more useful
similarly expects this; they say a useless man should not get
as much as they should, since it becomes an act of public
service and not a friendship if the proceeds of the friendship do not answer to the worth of the benefits conferred.
For they think that, as in a commercial partnership those 30
who put more in get more out, so it should be in friendship.
But the man who is in a state of need and inferiority makes
the opposite claim; they think it is the part of a good friend

to help those who are in need; what, they say, is the use of being the friend of a good man or a powerful man, if one is 35 to get nothing out of it?

At all events it seems that each party is justified in his 1163ᵇ claim, and that each should get more out of the friendship than the other—not more of the same thing, however, but the superior more honour and the inferior more gain; for honour is the prize of virtue and of beneficence, while gain is the assistance required by inferiority.

It seems to be so in constitutional arrangements also; the 5 man who contributes nothing good to the common stock is not honoured; for what belongs to the public is given to the man who benefits the public, and honour does belong to the public. It is not possible to get wealth from the 10 common stock and at the same time honour. For no one puts up with the smaller share in *all* things; therefore to the man who loses in wealth they assign honour and to the man who is willing to be paid, wealth, since the proportion to merit equalizes the parties and preserves the friendship, as we have said.[13]

This then is also the way in which we should associate with unequals; the man who is benefited in respect of wealth or virtue must give honour in return, repaying what he can. For friendship asks a man to do what he can, not 15 what is proportional to the merits of the case; since that cannot always be done, e. g. in honours paid to the gods or to parents; for no one could ever return to them the equivalent of what he gets, but the man who serves them to the utmost of his power is thought to be a good man.

This is why it would not seem open to a man to disown 20 his father (though a father may disown his son; being in debt, he should repay, but there is nothing by doing which a son will have done the equivalent of what he has received, so that he is always in debt. But creditors can remit a debt; and a father can therefore do so too. At the same time it is thought that presumably no one would repudiate a son

¹³ 1162ᵃ 34–ᵇ 4, Cf. 1158ᵇ 27, 1159ᵃ 35–ᵇ 3.

who was not far gone in˙wickedness; for apart from the
natural friendship of father and son it is human nature not
to reject a son's assistance. But the son, if he *is* wicked, will 25
naturally avoid aiding his father, or not be zealous about
it; for most people wish to get benefits, but avoid doing
them, as a thing unprofitable.—So much for these questions.

BOOK IX

1 In all friendships between dissimilars it is, as we have
said,[1] proportion that equalizes the parties and preserves the friendship; e. g. in the political form of friendship the shoemaker gets a return for his shoes in proportion 35
to his worth, and the weaver and all other craftsmen do the 1164ᵃ
same. Now here a common measure has been provided in
the form of money, and therefore everything is referred
to this and measured by this; but in the friendship of lovers
sometimes the lover complains that his excess of love is not
met by love in return (though perhaps there is nothing 5
lovable about him), while often the beloved complains
that the lover who formerly promised everything now per-
forms nothing. Such incidents happen when the lover loves
the beloved for the sake of pleasure while the beloved loves
the lover for the sake of utility, and they do not both
possess the qualities expected of them. If these be the objects of the friendship it is dissolved when they do not
get the things that formed the motives of their love; for 10
each did not love the other person himself but the qualities he had, and these were not enduring; that is why the
friendships also are transient. But the love of characters,
as has been said, endures because it is self-dependent.[2] Differences arise when what they get is something different
and not what they desire; for it is like getting nothing at all

[1] This has not been said precisely of friendship between dissimilars,
but Cf. 1132ᵇ 31–33, 1158ᵇ 27, 1159ᵃ 35–ᵇ 3, 1162ᵃ 34–ᵇ 4, 1163ᵇ
11.

[2] 1156ᵇ 9–12.

15 when we do not get what we aim at; compare the story
of the person who made promises to a lyre-player, prom-
ising him the more, the better he sang, but in the morning,
when the other demanded the fulfilment of his promises,
said that he had given pleasure [3] for pleasure. Now if this
had been what each wanted, all would have been well; but
if the one wanted enjoyment but the other gain, and the
one has what he wants while the other has not, the terms
of the association will not have been properly fulfilled; for
20 what each in fact wants is what he attends to, and it is for
the sake of that that he will give what he has.

But who is to fix the worth of the service; he who makes
the sacrifice or he who has got the advantage? At any rate
the other seems to leave it to him. This is what they say
25 Protagoras used to do; [4] whenever he taught anything
whatsoever, he bade the learner assess the value of the
knowledge, and accepted the amount so fixed. But in such
matters some men approve of the saying 'let a man have
his fixed reward'.

Those who get the money first and then do none of the
things they said they would, owing to the extravagance of
their promises, naturally find themselves the objects of
complaint; for they do not fulfil what they agreed to. The
30 sophists are perhaps compelled to do this because no one
would give money for the things they do know. These
people then, if they do not do what they have been paid
for, are naturally made the objects of complaint.

But where there is no contract of service, those who give
up something for the sake of the other party cannot (as we
have said [5]) be complained of (for that is the nature of the
35 friendship of virtue), and the return to them must be made
1164ᵇ on the basis of their purpose (for it is purpose that is the
characteristic thing in a friend and in virtue). And so too, it
seems, should one make a return to those with whom one

---

[3] i. e. the pleasure of expectation.
[4] Cf. Pl. Prot. 328 B, C.
[5] 1162ᵇ 6–13.

has studied philosophy; for their worth cannot be measured against money, and they can get no honour which
will balance their services, but still it is perhaps enough, 5
as it is with the gods and with one's parents, to give them
what one can.

If the gift was not of this sort, but was made with a view
to a return, it is no doubt preferable that the return made
should be one that seems fair to both parties, but if this
cannot be achieved, it would seem not only necessary that
the person who gets the first service should fix the reward, 10
but also just; for if the other gets in return the equivalent of
the advantage the beneficiary has received, or the price he
would have paid for the pleasure, he will have got what is
fair as from the other.

We see this happening too with things put up for sale,
and in some places there are laws providing that no actions
shall arise out of voluntary contracts, on the assumption
that one should settle with a person to whom one has given 15
credit, in the spirit in which one bargained with him. The
law holds that it is more just that the person to whom
credit was given should fix the terms than that the person
who gave a credit should do so. For most things are not
assessed at the same value by those who have them and
those who want them; each class values highly what is its
own and what it is offering; yet the return is made on the 20
terms fixed by the receiver. But no doubt the receiver
should assess a thing not at what it seems worth when he
has it, but at what he assessed it at before he had it.

2   A further problem is set by such questions as, whether
    one should in all things give the preference to one's
father and obey him, or whether when one is ill one should
trust a doctor, and when one has to elect a general should 25
elect a man of military skill; and similarly whether one
should render a service by preference to a friend or to a
good man, and should show gratitude to a benefactor or
oblige a friend, if one cannot do both.

All such questions are hard, are they not, to decide with precision? For they admit of many variations of all sorts in 30 respect both of the magnitude of the service and of its nobility and necessity. But that we should not give the preference in all things to the same person is plain enough; and we must for the most part return benefits rather than oblige friends, as we must pay back a loan to a creditor rather than make one to a friend. But perhaps even this is not always true; e. g. should a man who has been ransomed 35 out of the hands of brigands ransom his ransomer in re-1165ᵃ turn, whoever he may be (or pay him if he has not been captured but demands payment), or should he ransom his father? It would seem that he should ransom his father in preference even to himself. As we have said,⁶ then, generally the debt should be paid, but if the gift is exceedingly noble or exceedingly necessary, one should defer to these 5 considerations. For sometimes it is not even fair to return the equivalent of what one has received, when the one man has done a service to one whom he knows to be good, while the other makes a return to one whom he believes to be bad. For that matter, one should sometimes not lend in return to one who has lent to oneself; for the one person lent to a good man, expecting to recover his loan, while the other has no hope of recovering from one who is believed 10 to be bad. Therefore if the facts really are so, the demand is not fair; and if they are not, but people think they are, they would be held to be doing nothing strange in refusing. As we have often pointed out,⁷ then, discussions about feelings and actions have just as much definiteness as their subject-matter.

That we should not make the same return to everyone, nor give a father the preference in everything, as one does 15 not sacrifice everything to Zeus,⁸ is plain enough; but since we ought to render different things to parents, brothers,

⁶ 1164ᵇ 31–1165ᵃ 2.
⁷ 1094ᵇ 11–27, 1098ᵃ 26–29, 1103ᵇ 34–1104ᵃ 5.
⁸ Cf. 1134ᵇ 18–24.

comrades, and benefactors, we ought to render to each class what is appropriate and becoming. And this is what people seem in fact to do; to marriages they invite their kinsfolk; for these have a part in the family and therefore in the doings that affect the family; and at funerals also they think that kinsfolk, before all others, should meet, 20 for the same reason. And it would be thought that in the matter of food we should help our parents before all others, since we owe our own nourishment to them, and it is more honourable to help in this respect the authors of our being even before ourselves; and honour too one should give to one's parents as one does to the gods, but not any and every honour; for that matter one should not give the 25 same honour to one's father and one's mother, nor again should one give them the honour due to a philosopher or to a general, but the honour due to a father, or again to a mother. To all older persons, too, one should give honour appropriate to their age, by rising to receive them and finding seats for them and so on; while to comrades and brothers one should allow freedom of speech and common use 30 of all things. To kinsmen, too, and fellow-tribesmen and fellow-citizens and to every other class one should always try to assign what is appropriate, and to compare the claims of each class with respect to nearness of relation and to virtue or usefulness. The comparison is easier when the persons belong to the same class, and more laborious when they are different. Yet we must not on *that* account 35 shrink from the task, but decide the question as best we can.

3 Another question that arises is whether friendships should or should not be broken off when the other party does not remain the same. Perhaps we may say that **1165ᵇ** there is nothing strange in breaking off a friendship based on utility or pleasure, when our friends no longer have these attributes. For it was of these attributes that we were the friends; and when these have failed it is reasonable to

5 love no longer. But one might complain of another if,
when he loved us for our usefulness or pleasantness, he pre-
tended to love us for our character. For, as we said at the
outset,[9] most differences arise between friends when they
are not friends in the spirit in which they think they are.
So when a man has deceived himself and has thought he
was being loved for his character, when the other person
10 was doing nothing of the kind, he must blame himself; but
when he has been deceived by the pretences of the other
person, it is just that he should complain against his de-
ceiver; he will complain with more justice than one does
against people who counterfeit the currency, inasmuch as
the wrongdoing is concerned with something more valuable.

But if one accepts another man as good, and he turns
out badly and is seen to do so, must one still love him?
Surely it is impossible, since not everything can be loved,
15 but only what is good. What is evil neither can nor should
be loved; for it is not one's duty to be a lover of evil, nor to
become like what is bad; and we have said [10] that like is
dear to like. Must the friendship, then, be forthwith
broken off? Or is this not so in all cases, but only when
one's friends are incurable in their wickedness? If they are
capable of being reformed one should rather come to the
20 assistance of their character or their property, inasmuch as
this is better and more characteristic of friendship. But a
man who breaks off such a friendship would seem to be doing nothing strange; for it was not to a man of this sort
that he was a friend; when his friend has changed, therefore, and he is unable to save him, he gives him up.

But if one friend remained the same while the other
became better and far outstripped him in virtue, should
25 the latter treat the former as a friend? Surely he cannot.
When the interval is great this becomes most plain, e. g.
in the case of childish friendships; if one friend remained a

child in intellect while the other became a fully developed
man, how could they be friends when they neither approved of the same things nor delighted in and 'were pained
by the same things? For not even with regard to each other
will their tastes agree, and without this (as we saw [11]) they
cannot be friends; for they cannot live together. But we 30
have discussed these matters.[12]

Should he, then, behave no otherwise towards him than
he would if he had never been his friend? Surely he should
keep a remembrance of their former intimacy, and as we
think we ought to oblige friends rather than strangers, so
to those who have been our friends we ought to make 35
some allowance for our former friendship, when the
breach has not been due to excess of wickedness.

4 Friendly relations with one's neighbours, and the
marks by which friendships are defined, seem to have 1166ᵃ
proceeded from a man's relations to himself. For (1) we define a friend as one who wishes and does what is good, or
seems so, for the sake of his friend, or (2) as one who
wishes his friend to exist and live, for his sake; which
mothers do to their children, and friends do who have 5
come into conflict. And (3) others define him as one who
lives with and (4) has the same tastes as another, or (5)
one who grieves and rejoices with his friend; and this too
is found in mothers most of all. It is by some one of these
characteristics that friendship too is defined.

Now each of these is true of the good man's relation to
himself (and of all other men in so far as they think them- 10
selves good; virtue and the good man seem, as has been
said,[13] to be the measure of every class of things). For [14]
his opinions are harmonious, and he desires the same things
with all his soul; and therefore [15] he wishes for himself what

---

[11] 1157ᵇ 22–24.
[12] ib. 17–24, 1158ᵇ 33–35.
[13] 1113ᵃ 22–33, Cf. 1099ᵃ 13.
[14] (4) above.
[15] (1) above.

is good and what seems so, and does it (for it is character-
15 istic of the good man to work out the good), and does so
for his own sake (for he does it for the sake of the intellectual element in him, which is thought to be the man
himself); and [16] he wishes himself to live and be preserved,
and especially the element by virtue of which he thinks.
For existence is good to the virtuous man, and each man
wishes himself what is good, while no one chooses to
20 possess the whole world if he has first to become some one
else (for that matter, even now God possesses the good [17]);
he wishes for this only on condition of being whatever he is;
and the element that thinks would seem to be the individual man, or to be so more than any other element in
him. And [18] such a man wishes to live with himself; for he
does so with pleasure, since the memories of his past acts
25 are delightful and his hopes for the future are good, and
therefore pleasant. His mind is well stored too with subjects of contemplation. And [19] he grieves and rejoices, more
than any other, with himself; for the same thing is always
painful, and the same thing always pleasant, and not one
thing at one time and another at another; he has, so to
speak, nothing to repent of.

Therefore, since each of these characteristics belongs
30 to the good man in relation to himself, and he is related to
his friend as to himself (for his friend is another self),
friendship too is thought to be one of these attributes,
and those who have these attributes to be friends. Whether
there is or is not friendship between a man and himself
is a question we may dismiss for the present; [20] there would
35 seem to be friendship in so far as he is two or more, to
1166[b] judge from the aforementioned attributes of friendship,

---

[16] (2) above.
[17] sc. but as no one gains by God's now having the good, he would
not gain if a new person which was no longer himself were to possess
it. Cf. 1159[a] 5–11.
[18] (3) above.
[19] (5) above.
[20] Cf. 1168[a] 28–1169[b] 2.

and from the fact that the extreme of friendship is likened to one's love for oneself.

But the attributes named seem to belong even to the majority of men, poor creatures though they may be. Are we to say then that in so far as they are satisfied with themselves and think they are good, they share in these attributes? Certainly no one who is thoroughly bad and impious has these attributes, or even seems to do so. They hardly belong even to inferior people; for they [21] are at variance with themselves, and have appetites for some things and rational desires for others. This is true, for instance, of incontinent people; for they choose, instead of the things they themselves think good, things that are pleasant but hurtful; while others again, through cowardice and laziness, shrink from doing what they think best for themselves. And [22] those who have done many terrible deeds and are hated for their wickedness even shrink from life and destroy themselves. And [23] wicked men seek for people with whom to spend their days, and shun themselves; for they remember many a grievous deed, and anticipate others like them, when they are by themselves, but when they are with others they forget. And [24] having nothing lovable in them they have no feeling of love to themselves. Therefore [25] also such men do not rejoice or grieve with themselves; for their soul is rent by faction, and one element in it by reason of its wickedness grieves when it abstains from certain acts, while the other part is pleased, and one draws them this way and the other that, as if they were pulling them in pieces. If a man cannot at the same time be pained and pleased, at all events after a short time he is pained *because* he was pleased, and he could have wished that these things had not been pleasant to him; for bad men are laden with repentance.

[21] (4) above.
[22] (2) above.
[23] (3) above.
[24] (1) above.
[25] (5) above.

Therefore the bad man does not seem to be amicably
25 disposed even to himself, because there is nothing in him
to love; so that if to be thus is the height of wretchedness,
we should strain every nerve to avoid wickedness and
should endeavour to be good; for so and only so can one
be either friendly to oneself or a friend to another.

5   Goodwill is a friendly sort of relation, but is not
30   *identical* with friendship; for one may have goodwill
both towards people whom one does not know, and without their knowing it, but not friendship. This has indeed
been said already.[26] But goodwill is not even friendly feeling. For it does not involve intensity or desire, whereas
these accompany friendly feeling; and friendly feeling implies intimacy while goodwill may arise of a sudden, as it
35 does towards competitors in a contest; we come to feel
1167ᵃ goodwill for them and to share in their wishes, but we
would not *do* anything with them; for, as we said, we feel
goodwill suddenly and love them only superficially.

Goodwill seems, then, to be a beginning of friendship,
as the pleasure of the eye is the beginning of love. For no
one loves if he has not first been delighted by the form
5 of the beloved, but he who delights in the form of another
does not, for all that, love him, but only does so when he
also longs for him when absent and craves for his presence;
so too it is not possible for people to be friends if they
have not come to feel goodwill for each other, but those
who feel goodwill are not for all that friends; for they only
wish well to those for whom they feel goodwill, and would
not do anything with them nor take trouble for them. And
10 so one might by an extension of the term friendship say
that goodwill is inactive friendship, though when it is pro-
longed and reaches the point of intimacy it becomes friendship—not the friendship based on utility nor that based on
pleasure; for goodwill too does not arise on those terms.
The man who has received a benefit bestows goodwill in

[26] 1155ᵇ 32–1156ᵃ 5.

return for what has been done to him, but in doing so is only doing what is just; while he who wishes some one to prosper because he hopes for enrichment through him 15 seems to have goodwill not to him but rather to himself, just as a man is not a friend to another if he cherishes him for the sake of some use to be made of him. In general, goodwill arises on account of some excellence and worth, when one man seems to another beautiful or brave or something of the sort, as we pointed out in the case of competitors in a contest. 20

6 Unanimity also seems to be a friendly relation. For this reason it is not identity of opinion; for that might occur even with people who do not know each other; nor do we say that people who have the same views on any and every subject are unanimous, e. g. those who agree about 25 the heavenly bodies (for unanimity about these is not a friendly relation), but we do say that a city is unanimous when men have the same opinion about what is to their interest, and choose the same actions, and do what they have resolved in common. It is about things to be done, therefore, that people are said to be unanimous, and, among these, about matters of consequence and in which it is possible for both or all parties to get what they want; e. g. a city is unanimous when all its citizens think that 30 the offices in it should be elective, or that they should form an alliance with Sparta, or that Pittacus should be their ruler—at a time when he himself was also willing to rule. But when each of two people wishes himself to have the thing in question, like the captains in the *Phoenissae*,[27] they are in a state of faction; for it is not 35 unanimity when each of two parties thinks of the same thing, whatever that may be, but only when they think of the same thing in the same hands, e. g. when both the common people and those of the better class wish the best **1167ᵇ** men to rule; for thus and thus alone do all get what they

[27] Eteocles and Polynices (Eur. *Phoen.* 588 ff.).

aim at. Unanimity seems, then, to be political friendship,
as indeed it is commonly said to be; for it is concerned
with things that are to our interest and have an influence
on our life.

5   Now such unanimity is found among good men; for they
are unanimous both in themselves and with one another,
being, so to say, of one mind (for the wishes of such men
are constant and not at the mercy of opposing currents
like a strait of the sea), and they wish for what is just
and what is advantageous, and these are the objects of
their common endeavour as well. But bad men cannot be
unanimous except to a small extent, any more than they
10 can be friends, since they aim at getting more than their
share of advantages, while in labour and public service
they fall short of their share; and each man wishing for advantage to himself criticizes his neighbour and stands in his
way; for if people do not watch it carefully the common
weal is soon destroyed. The result is that they are in a state
15 of faction, putting compulsion on each other but unwill-
ing themselves to do what is just.

7   Benefactors are thought to love those they have benefited, more than those who have been well treated
love·those that have treated them well, and this is discussed as though it were paradoxical. Most people think it
is because the latter are in the position of debtors and the
former of creditors; and therefore as, in the case of loans,
20 debtors wish their creditors did not exist, while creditors
actually take care of the safety of their debtors, so it is
thought that benefactors wish the objects of their action to
exist since they will then get their gratitude, while the
25 beneficiaries take no interest in making this return. Epicharmus would perhaps declare that they say this because
they 'look at things on their bad side', but it is quite like
human nature; for most people are forgetful, and are more
anxious to be well treated than to treat others well. But the

cause would seem to be more deeply rooted in the nature
of things; the case of those who have lent money is not
even analogous. For they have no friendly feeling to their
debtors, but only a wish that they may be kept safe with 30
a view to what is to be got from them; while those who have
done a service to others feel friendship and love for those
they have served even if these are not of any use to them
and never will be. This is what happens with craftsmen
too; every man loves his own handiwork better than he 35
would be loved by it if it came alive; and this happens perhaps most of all with poets; for they have an excessive love 1168ᵃ
for their own poems, doting on them as if they were their
children. This is what the position of benefactors is like;
for that which they have treated well is their handiwork,
and therefore they love this more than the handiwork does
its maker. The cause of this is that existence is to all men a 5
thing to be chosen and loved, and that we exist by virtue
of activity (i. e. by living and acting), and that the handiwork *is* in a sense, the producer in activity; he loves his
handiwork, therefore, because he loves existence. And this
is rooted in the nature of things; for what he is in potentiality, his handiwork manifests in activity.

At the same time to the benefactor that is noble which
depends on his action, so that he delights in the object of
his action, whereas to the patient there is nothing noble 10
in the agent, but at most something advantageous, and this
is less pleasant and lovable. What *is* pleasant is the activity
of the present, the hope of the future, the memory of the
past; but most pleasant is that which depends on activity,
and similarly this is most lovable. Now for a man who has
made something his work remains (for the noble is last- 15
ing), but for the person acted on the utility passes away.
And the memory of noble things is pleasant, but that of
useful things is not likely to be pleasant, or is less so; though
the reverse seems true of expectation.

Further, love is like activity, being loved like passivity;

and loving and its concomitants are attributes of those who
20 are the more active.[28]

Again, all men love more what they have won by labour;
e. g. those who have made their money love it more than
those who have inherited it; and to be well treated seems
to involve no labour, while to treat others well is a laborious
25 task. These are the reasons, too, why mothers are fonder
of their children than fathers; bringing them into the world
costs them more pains, and they know better that the children are their own. This last point, too, would seem to
apply to benefactors.

8   The question is also debated, whether a man should
love himself most, or some one else. People criticize
those who love themselves most, and call them self-lovers,
30 using this as an epithet of disgrace, and a bad man seems
to do everything for his own sake, and the more so the more
wicked he is—and so men reproach him, for instance, with
doing nothing of his own accord—while the good man acts
for honour's sake, and the more so the better he is, and acts
for his friend's sake, and sacrifices his own interest.

35   But the facts clash with these arguments, and this is not
1168b surprising. For men say that one ought to love best one's
best friend, and a man's best friend is one who wishes well
to the object of his wish for his sake, even if no one is to
know of it; and these attributes are found most of all in a
man's attitude towards himself, and so are all the other
5 attributes by which a friend is defined; for, as we have
said,[29] it is from this relation that all the characteristics of
friendship have extended to our neighbours. All the proverbs, too, agree with this, e. g. 'a single soul', and 'what
friends have is common property', and 'friendship is equality', and 'charity begins at home'; for all these marks will
be found most in a man's relation to himself; he is his own
best friend and therefore ought to love himself best. It is

[28] i. e. benefactors.
[29] Ch. 4.

therefore a reasonable question, which of the two views 10 we should follow; for both are plausible.

Perhaps we ought to mark off such arguments from each other and determine how far and in what respects each view is right: Now if we grasp the sense in which each school uses the phrase 'lover of self', the truth may become 15 evident. Those who use the term as one of reproach ascribe self-love to people who assign to themselves the greater share of wealth, honours, and bodily pleasures; for these are what most people desire, and busy themselves about as though they were the best of all things, which is the reason, too, why they become objects of competition. So those who are grasping with regard to these things gratify their ap- 20 petites and in general their feelings and the irrational element of the soul; and most men are of this nature (which is the reason why the epithet has come to be used as it is— it takes its meaning from the prevailing type of self-love, which is a bad one); it is just, therefore, that men who are lovers of self in this way are reproached for being so. That it is those who give themselves the preference in regard to objects of this sort that most people usually call lovers of self is plain; for if a man were always anxious that he him- 25 self, above all things, should act justly, temperately, or in accordance with any other of the virtues, and in general were always to try to secure for himself the honourable course, no one will call such a man a lover of self or blame him.

But such a man would seem more than the other a lover of self; at all events he assigns to himself the things that are noblest and best, and gratifies the most authoritative element in himself and in all things obeys this; and just as a 30 city or any other systematic whole is most properly identified with the most authoritative element in it, so is a man; and therefore the man who loves this and gratifies it is most of all a lover of self. Besides, a man is said to have or not to have self-control according as his reason has or has not the control, on the assumption that this is the man himself;

35 and the things men have done on a rational principle are
1169ᵃ thought most properly their own acts and voluntary acts.
That this is the man himself, then, or is so more than anything else, is plain, and also that the good man loves most
this part of him. Whence it follows that he is most truly a
lover of self, of another type than that which is a matter
of reproach, and as different from that as living according
to a rational principle is from living as passion dictates, and
5 desiring what is noble from desiring what seems advantageous. Those, then, who busy themselves in an exceptional
degree with noble actions all men approve and praise; and if
all were to strive towards what is noble and strain every
nerve to do the noblest deeds, everything would be as it
should be for the common weal, and every one would
10 secure for himself the goods that are greatest, since virtue is
the greatest of goods.

   Therefore the good man should be a lover of self (for he
will both himself profit by doing noble acts, and will
benefit his fellows), but the wicked man should not; for he
will hurt both himself and his neighbours, following as he
15 does evil passions. For the wicked man, what he does
clashes with what he ought to do, but what the good man
ought to do he does; for reason in each of its possessors
chooses what is best for itself, and the good man obeys his
reason. It is true of the good man too that he does many
acts for the sake of his friends and his country, and if neces-
20 sary dies for them; for he will throw away both wealth and
honours and in general the goods that are objects of competition, gaining for himself nobility; since he would prefer
a short period of intense pleasure to a long one of mild enjoyment, a twelve-month of noble life to many years of
25 humdrum existence, and one great and noble action to
many trivial ones. Now those who die for others doubtless
attain this result; it is therefore a great prize that they
choose for themselves. They will throw away wealth too on
condition that their friends will gain more; for while a
man's friend gains wealth he himself achieves nobility; he

is therefore assigning the greater good to himself. The same 30 too is true of honour and office; all these things he will sacrifice to his friend; for this is noble and laudable for himself. Rightly then is he thought to be good, since he chooses nobility before all else. But he may even give up actions to his friend; it may be nobler to become the cause of his friend's acting than to act himself. In all the actions, there- 35 fore, that men are praised for, the good man is seen to assign to himself the greater share in what is noble. In this sense, then, as has been said, a man should be a lover of 1169ᵇ self; but in the sense in which most men are so, he ought not.

9 It is also disputed whether the happy man will need friends or not. It is said that those who are supremely happy and self-sufficient have no need of friends; for they 5 have the things that are good, and therefore being self-sufficient they need nothing further, while a friend, being another self, furnishes what a man cannot provide by his own effort; whence the saying 'when fortune is kind, what need of friends?' But it seems strange, when one assigns all good things to the happy man, not to assign friends, who 10 are thought the greatest of external goods. And if it is more characteristic of a friend to do well by another than to be well done by, and to confer benefits is characteristic of the good man and of virtue, and it is nobler to do well by friends than by strangers, the good man will need people to do well by. This is why the question is asked whether we 15 need friends more in prosperity or in adversity, on the assumption that not only does a man in adversity need people to confer benefits on him, but also those who are prospering need people to do well by. Surely it is strange, too, to make the supremely happy man a solitary; for no one would choose the whole world on condition of being alone, since man is a political creature and one whose nature is to live with others. Therefore even the happy man lives with others; for he has the things that are by nature good. And

20 plainly it is better to spend his days with friends and good men than with strangers or any chance persons. Therefore the happy man needs friends.

What then is it that the first school means, and in what respect is it right? Is it that most men identify friends with useful people? Of such friends indeed the supremely happy man will have no need, since he already has the things that 25 are good; nor will he need those whom one makes one's friends because of their pleasantness, or he will need them only to a small extent (for his life, being pleasant, has no need of adventitious pleasure); and because he does not need such friends he is thought not to need friends.

But that is surely not true. For we have said at the outset [30] that happiness is an activity; and activity plainly comes into being and is not present at the start like a piece 30 of property. If (1) happiness lies in living and being active, and the good man's activity is virtuous and pleasant in itself, as we have said at the outset,[31] and (2) a thing's being one's own is one of the attributes that make it pleasant, and (3) we can contemplate our neighbours better than ourselves and their actions better than our own, and if the 35 actions of virtuous men who are their friends are pleasant to 1170ᵃ good men (since these have both the attributes that are naturally pleasant [32])—if this be so, the supremely happy man will need friends of this sort, since his purpose is to contemplate worthy actions and actions that are his own, and the actions of a good man who is his friend have both these qualities.

Further, men think that the happy man ought to live pleasantly. Now if he were a solitary, life would be hard for 5 him; for by oneself it is not easy to be continuously active; but with others and towards others it is easier. With others therefore his activity will be more continuous, and it is in itself pleasant, as it ought to be for the man who is su-

---

[30] 1098ᵃ 16ᵇ, 31–1099ᵃ 7.
[31] 1099ᵃ 14, 21.
[32] i. e. the attribute of goodness and that of being their own.

premely happy; for a good man qua good delights in virtuous actions and is vexed at vicious ones, as a musical man enjoys beautiful tunes but is pained at bad ones. A certain 10 training in virtue arises also from the company of the good, as Theognis has said before us.

If we look deeper into the nature of things, a virtuous friend seems to be naturally desirable for a virtuous man. For that which is good by nature, we have said,[33] is for the virtuous man good and pleasant in itself. Now life is de- 15 fined in the case of animals by the power of perception, in that of man by the power of perception or thought; and a power is defined by reference to the corresponding activity, which is the essential thing; therefore life seems to be essentially the act of perceiving or thinking. And life is among the things that are good and pleasant in themselves, 20 since it is determinate and the determinate is of the nature of the good; and that which is good by nature is also good for the virtuous man (which is the reason why life seems pleasant to all men); but we must not apply this to a wicked and corrupt life nor to a life spent in pain; for such a life is indeterminate, as are its attributes. The nature of 25 pain will become plainer in what follows.[34] But if life itself is good and pleasant (which it seems to be, from the very fact that all men desire it, and particularly those who are good and supremely happy; for to such men life is most desirable, and their existence is the most supremely happy); and if he who sees perceives that he sees, and he who hears, that he hears, and he who walks, that he walks, and in the 30 case of all other activities similarly there is something which perceives that we are active, so that if we perceive, we perceive that we perceive, and if we think, that we think; and if to perceive that we perceive or think is to perceive that we exist (for existence was defined as perceiv- **1170'** ing or thinking); and if perceiving that one lives is in itself one of the things that are pleasant (for life is by nature

<hr />

[33] 1099[a] 7–11, 1113[a] 25–33.
[34] x. 1–5.

good, and to perceive what is good present in oneself is
pleasant); and if life is desirable, and particularly so for
good men, because to them existence is good and pleasant
5 (for they are pleased at the consciousness of the presence
in them of what is in itself good); and if as the virtuous
man is to himself, he is to his friend also (for his friend is
another self):—if all this be true, as his own being is desirable for each man, so, or almost so, is that of his friend.
Now his being was seen to be desirable because he per-
10 ceived his own goodness, and such perception is pleasant
in itself. He needs, therefore, to be conscious of the existence of his friend as well, and this will be realized in their
living together and sharing in discussion and thought; for
this is what living together would seem to mean in the case
of man, and not, as in the case of cattle, feeding in the same
place.

If, then, being is in itself desirable for the supremely
15 happy man (since it is by its nature good and pleasant),
and that of his friend is very much the same, a friend will
be one of the things that are desirable. Now that which is
desirable for him he must have, or he will be deficient in
this respect. The man who is to be happy will therefore
need virtuous friends.

20 **10** Should we, then, make as many friends as possible,
or—as in the case of hospitality it is thought to be
suitable advice, that one should be 'neither a man of many
guests nor a man with none'—will that apply to friendship
as well; should a man neither be friendless nor have an
excessive number of friends?

To friends made with a view to utility this saying would
seem thoroughly applicable; for to do services to many
people in return is a laborious task and life is not long
25 enough for its performance. Therefore friends in excess of
those who are sufficient for our own life are superfluous,
and hindrances to the noble life; so that we have no need

of them. Of friends made with a view to *pleasure*, also, few are enough, as a little seasoning in food is enough.

But as regards good friends, should we have as many as possible, or is there a limit to the number of one's friends, as there is to the size of a city? You cannot make a city of 30 ten men, and if there are a hundred thousand it is a city no longer. But the proper number is presumably not a single number, but anything that falls between certain fixed points. So for friends too there is a fixed number—perhaps **1171ᵃ** the largest number with whom one can live together (for that, we found,[85] is thought to be very characteristic of friendship); and that one cannot live with many people and divide oneself up among them is plain. Further, they too must be friends of one another, if they are all to spend their days together; and it is a hard business for this condition to be fulfilled with a large number. It is found difficult, 5 too, to rejoice and to grieve in an intimate way with many people, for it may likely happen that one has at once to be happy with one friend and to mourn with another. Presumably, then, it is well not to seek to have as many friends as possible, but as many as are enough for the purpose of living together; for it would seem actually impossible to be a great friend to many people. This is why one cannot love 10 several people; love is ideally a sort of excess of friendship, and that can only be felt towards one person; therefore great friendship too can only be felt towards a few people. This seems to be confirmed in practice; for we do not find many people who are friends in the comradely way of friendship, and the famous friendships of this sort are always between two people. Those who have many friends 15 and mix intimately with them all are thought to be no one's friend, except in the way proper to fellow-citizens, and such people are also called obsequious. In the way proper to fellow-citizens, indeed, it is possible to be the friend of many and yet not be obsequious but a genuinely good man;

[85] 1157ᵇ 19, 1158ᵃ 3, 10.

but one cannot have with many people the friendship based
20 on virtue and on the character of our friends themselves,
and we must be content if we find even a few such.

11 Do we need friends more in good fortune or in bad?
They are sought after in both; for while men in adversity need help, in prosperity they need people to live with
and to make the objects of their beneficence; for they wish
to do well by others. Friendship, then, is more necessary in
25 bad fortune, and so it is useful friends that one wants in
this case; but it is more noble in good fortune, and so we
also seek for good men as our friends, since it is more desirable to confer benefits on these and to live with these.
For the very presence of friends is pleasant both in good
30 fortune and also in bad, since grief is lightened when
friends sorrow with us. Hence one might ask whether they
share as it were our burden, or—without that happening—
their presence by its pleasantness, and the thought of their
grieving with us, make our pain less. Whether it is for these
reasons or for some other that our grief is lightened, is a
question that may be dismissed; at all events what we have
described appears to take place.

But their presence seems to contain a mixture of various
35 factors. The very seeing of one's friends is pleasant, espe-
1171ᵇ cially if one is in adversity, and becomes a safeguard against
grief (for a friend tends to comfort us both by the sight of
him and by his words, if he is tactful, since he knows our
5 character and the things that please or pain us); but to see
him pained at our misfortunes is painful; for every one
shuns being a cause of pain to his friends. For this reason
people of a manly nature guard against making their friends
grieve with them, and, unless he be exceptionally insensible
to pain, such a man cannot stand the pain that ensues for
his friends, and in general does not admit fellow-mourners
10 because he is not himself given to mourning; but women
and womanly men enjoy sympathisers in their grief, and
love them as friends and companions in sorrow. But in all

things one obviously ought to imitate the better type of person.

On the other hand, the presence of friends in our prosperity implies both a pleasant passing of our time and the pleasant thought of their pleasure at our own good fortune. For this cause it would seem that we ought to summon our friends readily to share our good fortunes (for the beneficent character is a noble one), but summon them to our bad fortunes with hesitation; for we ought to give them as little a share as possible in our evils—whence the saying 'enough is my misfortune'. We should summon friends to us most of all when they are likely by suffering a few inconveniences to do us a great service.

Conversely, it is fitting to go unasked and readily to the aid of those in adversity (for it is characteristic of a friend to render services, and especially to those who are in need and have not demanded them; such action is nobler and pleasanter for both persons); but when our friends are prosperous we should join readily in their activities (for they need friends for these too), but be tardy in coming forward to be the objects of their kindness; for it is not noble to be keen to receive benefits. Still, we must no doubt avoid getting the reputation of kill-joys by repulsing them; for that sometimes happens.

The presence of friends, then, seems desirable in all circumstances.

12 Does it not follow, then, that, as for lovers the sight of the beloved is the thing they love most, and they prefer this sense to the others because on it love depends most for its being and for its origin, so for friends the most desirable thing is living together? For friendship is a partnership, and as a man is to himself, so is he to his friend; now in his own case the consciousness of his being is desirable, and so therefore is the consciousness of his friend's being, and the activity of this consciousness is produced when they live together, so that it is natural that they aim 1172ᵃ

at this. And whatever existence means for each class of
men, whatever it is for whose sake they value life, in *that*
they wish to occupy themselves with their friends; and so
some drink together, others dice together, others join in
athletic exercises and hunting, or in the study of philoso-
5 phy, each class spending their days together in whatever
they love most in life; for since they wish to live with their
friends, they do and share in those things which give them
the sense of living together. Thus the friendship of bad
men turns out an evil thing (for because of their instability
10 they unite in bad pursuits, and besides they become evil by
becoming like each other), while the friendship of good
men is good, being augmented by their companionship;
and they are thought to become better too by their activities and by improving each other; for from each other they
take the mould of the characteristics they approve—whence
the saying 'noble deeds from noble men'.—So much, then,
15 for friendship; our next task must be to discuss pleasure.

BOOK X

1   After these matters we ought perhaps next to discuss
      pleasure. For it is thought to be most intimately con-
nected with our human nature, which is the reason why
20 in educating the young we steer them by the rudders of
pleasure and pain; it is thought, too, that to enjoy the
things we ought and to hate the things we ought has the
greatest bearing on virtue of character. For these things
extend right through life, with a weight and power of their
25 own in respect both to virtue and to the happy life, since
men choose what is pleasant and avoid what is painful;
and such things, it will be thought, we should least of all
omit to discuss, especially since they admit of much dispute. For some [1] say pleasure is the good, while others,[2] on

---

[1] The school of Eudoxus, Cf. ᵇ9. Aristippus is perhaps also referred
to.

[2] The school of Speusippus, Cf. 1153ᵇ 5.

the contrary, say it is thoroughly bad—some no doubt being persuaded that the facts are so, and others thinking it
has a better effect on our life to exhibit pleasure as a bad 30
thing even if it is not; for most people (they think) incline
towards it and are the slaves of their pleasures, for which
reason they ought to lead them in the opposite direction,
since thus they will reach the middle state. But surely this
is not correct. For arguments about matters concerned with
feelings and actions are less reliable than facts: and so when 35
they clash with the facts of perception they are despised,
and discredit the truth as well; if a man who runs down 1172ᵇ
pleasure is once seen to be aiming at it, his inclining towards it is thought to imply that it is all worthy of being
aimed at; for most people are not good at drawing distinctions. True arguments seem, then, most useful, not only
with a view to knowledge, but with a view to life also; 5
for since they harmonize with the facts they are believed,
and so they stimulate those who understand them to live
according to them.—Enough of such questions; let us proceed to review the opinions that have been expressed about
pleasure.

2   Eudoxus thought pleasure was the good because he
      saw all things, both rational and irrational, aiming at 10
it, and because in all things that which is the object of
choice is what is excellent, and that which is most the object of choice the greatest good; thus the fact that all things
moved towards the same object indicated that this was for
all things the chief good (for each thing, he argued, finds
its own good, as it finds its own nourishment); and that
which is good for all things and at which all aim was the 15
good. His arguments were credited more because of the
excellence of his character than for their own sake; he was
thought to be remarkably self-controlled, and therefore it
was thought that he was not saying what he did say as a
friend of pleasure, but that the facts really were so. He
believed that the same conclusion followed no less plainly

from a study of the contrary of pleasure; pain was in itself
an object of aversion to all things, and therefore its contrary
20 must be similarly an object of choice. And again that is
most an object of choice which we choose not because or
for the sake of something else, and pleasure is admittedly of
this nature; for no one asks to what end he is pleased, thus
implying that pleasure is in itself an object of choice. Further, he argued that pleasure when added to any good, e. g.
to just or temperate action, makes it more worthy of choice,
25 and that it is only by itself that the good can be increased.

This argument seems to show it to be one of the goods,
and no more a good than any other; for every good is more
worthy of choice along with another good than taken alone.
And so it is by an argument of this kind that Plato [3] proves
the good not to be pleasure; he argues that the pleasant life
30 is more desirable with wisdom than without, and that if the
mixture is better, pleasure is not the good; for the good cannot become more desirable by the addition of anything to
it. Now it is clear that nothing else, any more than pleasure,
can be the good if it is made more desirable by the addition
of any of the things that are good in themselves. What,
then, is there that satisfies this criterion, which at the same
time we can participate in? It is something of this sort that
we are looking for.

Those who object that that at which all things aim is not
35 necessarily good are, we may surmise, talking nonsense.
For we say that that which every one thinks really is so;
1173ᵃ and the man who attacks this belief will hardly have anything more credible to maintain instead. If it is senseless
creatures that desire the things in question, there might be
something in what they say; but if intelligent creatures do
so as well, what sense can there be in this view? But perhaps even in inferior creatures there is some natural good
stronger than themselves which aims at their proper good.

Nor does the argument about the contrary of pleasure
5 seem to be correct. They say that if pain is an evil it does

[3] *Phil.* 60 B–E.

not follow that pleasure is a good; for evil is opposed to evil and at the same time both are opposed to the neutral state —which is correct enough but does not apply to the things in question. For if both pleasure and pain belonged to the 10 class of evils they ought both to be objects of aversion, while if they belonged to the class of neutrals neither should be an object of aversion or they should both be equally so; but in fact people evidently avoid the one as evil and choose the other as good; that then must be the nature of the opposition between them.

3   Nor again, if pleasure is not a quality, does it follow that it is not a good; for the activities of virtue are not qualities either, nor is happiness.

They say,[4] however, that the good is determinate, while 15 pleasure is indeterminate, because it admits of degrees. Now if it is from the feeling of pleasure that they judge thus, the same will be true of justice and the other virtues, in respect of which we plainly say that people of a certain character are so more or less, and act more or less in accord- 20 ance with these virtues; for people may be more just or brave, and it is possible also to act justly or temperately more or less. But if their judgement is based on the various pleasures, surely they are not stating the real cause,[5] if in fact some pleasures are unmixed and others mixed. Again, just as health admits of degrees without being indetermi- 25 nate, why should not pleasure? The same proportion is not found in all things, nor a single proportion always in the same thing, but it may be relaxed and yet persist up to a point, and it may differ in degree. The case of pleasure also may therefore be of this kind.

Again, they assume [6] that the good is perfect while movements and comings into being are imperfect, and try to 30 exhibit pleasure as being a movement and a coming into

[4] Ib. 24 E–25 A, 31 A.
[5] sc., of the badness of (some) pleasures.
[6] Pl. *Phil.* 53 C–54 D.

being. But they do not seem to be right even in saying that it is a movement. For speed and slowness are thought to be proper to every movement, and if a movement, e. g. that of the heavens, has not speed or slowness in itself, it has it in relation to something else; but of pleasure neither of these things is true. For while we may *become* pleased **1173ᵇ** quickly as we may become angry quickly, we cannot *be* pleased quickly, not even in relation to some one else, while we *can* walk, or grow, or the like, quickly. While, then, we can change quickly or slowly into a state of pleasure, we cannot quickly exhibit the activity of pleasure, i. e. be pleased. Again, how can it be a coming into being? It is not thought that any chance thing can come out of any chance 5 thing, but that a thing is dissolved into that out of which it comes into being; and pain would be the destruction of that of which pleasure is the coming into being.

They say, too,⁷ that pain is the lack of that which is according to nature, and pleasure is replenishment. But these experiences are bodily. If then pleasure is replenishment with that which is according to nature, that which feels pleasure will be that in which the replenishment takes 10 place, i. e. the body; but that is not thought to be the case; therefore the replenishment is not pleasure, though one would be pleased when replenishment was taking place, just as one would be pained if one was being operated on.⁸ This opinion seems to be based on the pains and pleasures connected with nutrition; on the fact that when people have been short of food and have felt pain beforehand they are pleased by the replenishment. But this does not happen 15 with all pleasures; for the pleasures of learning and, among the sensuous pleasures, those of smell, and also many sounds and sights, and memories and hopes, do not pre-

---

⁷ Ib. 31 E–32 B, 42 C, D.
⁸ The point being that the being replenished no more *is* pleasure than the being operated on *is* pain. For the instance, Cf. Pl. *Tim.* 65 B.

suppose pain. Of what then will these be the coming into being? There has not been lack of anything of which they could be the supplying anew.

In reply to those who bring forward the disgraceful pleasures one may say that these are not pleasant; if things 20 are pleasant to people of vicious constitution, we must not suppose that they are also pleasant to others than these, just as we do not reason so about the things that are wholesome or sweet or bitter to sick people, or ascribe whiteness to the things that seem white to those suffering from a disease of the eye. Or one might answer thus—that the pleasures are desirable, but not from *these* sources, as 25 wealth is desirable, but not as the reward of betrayal, and health, but not at the cost of eating anything and everything. Or perhaps pleasures differ in kind; for those derived from noble sources are different from those derived from base sources, and one cannot get the pleasure of the just man without being just, nor that of the musical man without being musical, and so on. 30

The fact, too, that a friend is different from a flatterer seems to make it plain that pleasure is not a good or that pleasures are different in kind; for the one is thought to consort with us with a view to the good, the other with a view to our pleasure, and the one is reproached for his conduct while the other is praised on the ground that he consorts with us for different ends. And no one would choose to live with the intellect of a child throughout his **1174ᵃ** life, however much he were to be pleased at the things that children are pleased at, nor to get enjoyment by doing some most disgraceful deed, though he were never to feel any pain in consequence. And there are many things we should be keen about even if they brought no pleasure, e. g. 5 seeing, remembering, knowing, possessing the virtues. If pleasures necessarily do accompany these, that makes no odds; we should choose these even if no pleasure resulted. It seems to be clear, then, that neither is pleasure the good

10 nor is all pleasure desirable, and that some pleasures are
desirable in kind or in their sources from the others. So
much for the things that are said about pleasure and pain.

4   What pleasure is, or what kind of thing it is, will
become plainer if we take up the question again from
15 the beginning. Seeing seems to be at any moment complete, for it does not lack anything which coming into
being later will complete its form; and pleasure also seems
to be of this nature. For it is a whole, and at no time can
one find a pleasure whose form will be completed if the
pleasure lasts longer. For this reason, too, it is not a movement. For every movement (e. g. that of building) takes
20 time and is for the sake of an end, and is complete when
it has made what it aims at. It is complete, therefore, only
in the whole time or at that final moment. In their parts
and during the time they occupy, all movements are incomplete, and are different in kind from the whole movement and from each other. For the fitting together of the
stones is different from the fluting of the column, and
25 these are both different from the making of the temple;
and the making of the temple is complete (for it lacks
nothing with a view to the end proposed), but the making
of the base or of the triglyph is incomplete; for each is the
making of only a part. They differ in kind, then, and it is
not possible to find at any and every time a movement
complete in form, but if at all, only in the whole time.
So, too, in the case of walking and all other movements.
30 For if locomotion is a movement from here to there, it, too,
has differences in kind—flying, walking, leaping, and so on.
And not only so, but in walking itself there are such differences; for the whence and whither are not the same in
the whole racecourse and in a part of it, nor in one part
1174ᵇ and in another, nor is it the same thing to traverse this line
and that; for one traverses not only a line but one which
is in a place, and this one is in a different place from that.
We have discussed movement with precision in another

work,[9] but it seems that it is not complete at any and every time, but that the many movements are incomplete and different in kind, since the whence and whither give them 5 their form. But of pleasure the form is complete at any and every time. Plainly, then, pleasure and movement must be different from each other, and pleasure must be one of the things that are whole and complete. This would seem to be the case, too, from the fact that it is not possible to move otherwise than in time, but it *is* possible to be pleased; for that which takes place in a moment is a whole.

From these considerations it is clear, too, that these thinkers are not right in saying there is a movement or a coming into being of pleasure. For these cannot be ascribed to all things, but only to those that are divisible and not 10 wholes; there is no coming into being of seeing nor of a point nor of a unit, nor is any of these a movement or coming into being; therefore there is no movement or coming into being of pleasure either; for it is a whole.

Since every sense is active in relation to its object, and a sense which is in good condition acts perfectly in relation 15 to the most beautiful of its objects (for perfect activity seems to be ideally of this nature; whether we say that *it* is active, or the organ in which it resides, may be assumed to be immaterial), it follows that in the case of each sense the best activity is that of the best-conditioned organ in relation to the finest of its objects. And this activity will be the most complete and pleasant. For, while there is pleasure in respect of any sense, and in respect of thought 20 and contemplation no less, the most complete is pleasantest, and that of a well-conditioned organ in relation to the worthiest of its objects is the most complete; and the pleasure completes the activity. But the pleasure does not complete it in the same way as the combination of object and sense, both good, just as health and the doctor are not 25 in the same way the cause of a man's being healthy. (That pleasure is produced in respect to each sense is plain; for

[9] *Phys.* vi–viii.

we speak of sights and sounds as pleasant. It is also plain that it arises most of all when both the sense is at its best and it is active in reference to an object which corresponds; when both object and perceiver are of the best there will 30 always be pleasure, since the requisite agent and patient are both present.) Pleasure completes the activity not as the corresponding permanent state does, by its immanence, but as an end which supervenes as the bloom of youth does on those in the flower of their age. So long, then, as both the intelligible or sensible object and the discriminating or contemplative faculty are as they should be, the pleasure will be involved in the activity; for when both the 1175ᵃ passive and the active factor are unchanged and are related to each other in the same way, the same result naturally follows.

How, then, is it that no one is continuously pleased? Is it that we grow weary? Certainly all human things are incapable of continuous activity. Therefore pleasure also is 5 not continuous; for it accompanies activity. Some things delight us when they are new, but later do so less, for the same reason; for at first the mind is in a state of stimulation and intensely active about them, as people are with respect to their vision when they look hard at a thing, but afterwards our activity is not of this kind, but has grown relaxed; for which reason the pleasure also is dulled.

10   One might think that all men desire pleasure because they all aim at life; life is an activity, and each man is active about those things and with those faculties that he loves most; e. g. the musician is active with his hearing in ref- 15 erence to tunes, the student with his mind in reference to theoretical questions, and so on in each case; now pleasure completes the activities, and therefore life, which they desire. It is with good reason, then, that they aim at pleasure too, since for every one it completes life, which is desirable. But whether we choose life for the sake of pleasure or pleasure for the sake of life is a question we may dismiss 20 for the present. For they seem to be bound up together and

not to admit of separation, since without activity pleasure does not arise, and every activity is completed by the attendant pleasure.

5 For this reason pleasures seem, too, to differ in kind.

For things different in kind are, we think, completed by different things (we see this to be true both of natural objects and of things produced by art, e. g. animals, trees, 25 a painting, a sculpture, a house, an implement); and, similarly, we think that activities differing in kind are completed by things differing in kind. Now the activities of thought differ from those of the senses, and both differ among themselves, in kind; so, therefore, do the pleasures that complete them.

This may be seen, too, from the fact that each of the pleasures is bound up with the activity it completes. For an activity is intensified by its proper pleasure, since each 30 class of things is better judged of and brought to precision by those who engage in the activity with pleasure; e. g. it is those who enjoy geometrical thinking that become geometers and grasp the various propositions better, and, similarly, those who are fond of music or of building, and so on, make progress in their proper function by enjoying it; so 35 the pleasures intensify the activities, and what intensifies a thing is proper to it, but things different in kind have properties different in kind.

This will be even more apparent from the fact that ac- 1175ᵇ tivities are hindered by pleasures arising from other sources. For people who are fond of playing the flute are incapable of attending to arguments if they overhear some one playing the flute, since they enjoy flute-playing more than the 5 activity in hand; so the pleasure connected with flute-playing destroys the activity concerned with argument. This happens, similarly, in all other cases, when one is active about two things at once; the more pleasant activity drives out the other, and if it is much more pleasant does so all the more, so that one even ceases from the other. This is

10 why when we enjoy anything very much we do not throw
ourselves into anything else, and do one thing only when
we are not much pleased by another; e. g. in the theatre the
people who eat sweets do so most when the actors are poor.
Now since activities are made precise and more enduring
and better by their proper pleasure, and injured by alien
15 pleasures, evidently the two kinds of pleasure are far apart.
For alien pleasures do pretty much what proper pains do,
since activities are destroyed by their proper pains; e. g. if
a man finds writing or doing sums unpleasant and painful,
he does not write, or does not do sums, because the activity
20 is painful. So an activity suffers contrary effects from its
proper pleasures and pains, i. e. from those that supervene
on it in virtue of its own nature. And alien pleasures have
been stated to do much the same as pain; they destroy
the activity, only not to the same degree.

Now since activities differ in respect of goodness and
badness, and some are worthy to be chosen, others to be
25 avoided, and others neutral, so, too, are the pleasures; for to
each activity there is a proper pleasure. The pleasure proper
to a worthy activity is good and that proper to an unworthy
activity bad; just as the appetites for noble objects are
laudable, those for base objects culpable. But the pleasures
30 involved in activities are more proper to them than the
desires; for the latter are separated both in time and in
nature, while the former are close to the activities, and so
hard to distinguish from them that it admits of dispute
whether the activity is not the same as the pleasure. (Still,
pleasure does not seem to be thought or perception—that
would be strange; but because they are not found apart they
35 appear to some people the same.) As activities are different,
then, so are the corresponding pleasures. Now sight is su-
1176ᵃ perior to touch in purity, and hearing and smell to taste;
the pleasures, therefore, are similarly superior, and those
of thought superior to these, and within each of the two
kinds some are superior to others.

Each animal is thought to have a proper pleasure, as it

has a proper function; viz. that which corresponds to its activity. If we survey them species by species, too, this will be evident; horse, dog, and man have different pleasures, 5 as Heraclitus says 'asses would prefer sweepings to gold'; for food is pleasanter than gold to asses. So the pleasures of creatures different in kind differ in kind, and it is plausible to suppose that those of a single species do not differ. But they vary to no small extent, in the case of men at least; 10 the same things delight some people and pain others, and are painful and odious to some, and pleasant to and liked by others. This happens, too, in the case of sweet things; the same things do not seem sweet to a man in a fever and a healthy man—nor hot to a weak man and one in good condition. The same happens in other cases. But in all such 15 matters that which appears to the good man is thought to be really so. If this is correct, as it seems to be, and virtue and the good man as such are the measure of each thing, those also will be pleasures which appear so to him, and those things pleasant which he enjoys. If the things he finds tiresome seem pleasant to some one, that is nothing surpris- 20 ing; for men may be ruined and spoilt in many ways; but the things are not pleasant, but only pleasant to these people and to people in this condition. Those which are admittedly disgraceful plainly should not be said to be pleasures, except to a perverted taste; but of those that are thought to be good what kind of pleasure or what pleasure should be said to be that proper to man? Is it not 25 plain from the corresponding activities? The pleasures follow these. Whether, then, the perfect and supremely happy man has one or more activities, the pleasures that perfect these will be said in the strict sense to be pleasures proper to man, and the rest will be so in a secondary and fractional way, as are the activities.

6 Now that we have spoken of the virtues, the forms of 30 friendship, and the varieties of pleasure, what remains is to discuss in outline the nature of happiness, since this

is what we state the end of human nature to be. Our discussion will be the more concise if we first sum up what we
have said already. We said,[10] then, that it is not a disposition; for if it were it might belong to some one who was
35 asleep throughout his life, living the life of a plant, or,
1176ᵇ again, to some one who was suffering the greatest misfortunes. If these implications are unacceptable, and we must
rather class happiness as an activity, as we have said before,[11] and if some activities are necessary, and desirable
for the sake of something else, while others are so in themselves, evidently happiness must be placed among those
5 desirable in themselves, not among those desirable for
the sake of something else; for happiness does not lack
anything, but is self-sufficient. Now those activities are
desirable in themselves from which nothing is sought beyond the activity. And of this nature virtuous actions are
thought to be; for to do noble and good deeds is a thing
desirable for its own sake.

Pleasant amusements also are thought to be of this nature, we choose them not for the sake of other things; for
we are injured rather than benefited by them, since we are
10 led to neglect our bodies and our property. But most of the
. people who are deemed happy take refuge in such pastimes,
which is the reason why those who are ready-witted at them
are highly esteemed at the courts of tyrants; they make
themselves pleasant companions in the tyrants' favourite
15 pursuits, and that is the sort of man they want. Now these
things are thought to be of the nature of happiness because
people in despotic positions spend their leisure in them,
but perhaps such people prove nothing; for virtue and reason, from which good activities flow, do not depend on
despotic position; nor, if these people, who have never
tasted pure and generous pleasure, take refuge in the bodily
20 pleasures, should these for that reason be thought more

---

[10] 1095ᵇ 31–1096ᵃ 2, 1098ᵇ 31–1099ᵃ 7.
[11] 1098ᵃ 5–7

desirable; for boys, too, think the things that are valued among themselves are the best. It is to be expected, then, that, as different things seem valuable to boys and to men, so they should to bad men and to good. Now, as we have often maintained,[12] those things are both valuable and 25 pleasant which are such to the good man; and to each man the activity in accordance with his own disposition is most desirable, and, therefore, to the good man that which is in accordance with virtue. Happiness, therefore, does not lie in amusement; it would, indeed, be strange if the end were amusement, and one were to take trouble and suffer hardship all one's life in order to amuse oneself. For, in a word, 30 everything that we choose we choose for the sake of something else—except happiness, which is an end. Now to exert oneself and work for the sake of amusement seems silly and utterly childish. But to amuse oneself in order that one may exert oneself, as Anacharsis puts it, seems right; for amusement is a sort of relaxation, and we need relaxation because we cannot work continuously. Relaxa- 35 tion, then, is not an end; for it is taken for the sake of activity.

The happy life is thought to be virtuous; now a virtuous life requires exertion, and does not consist in amusement. 1177ᵃ And we say that serious things are better than laughable things and those connected with amusement, and that the activity of the better of any two things—whether it be two elements of our being or two men—is the more serious; but the activity of the better is *ipso facto* superior and more of 5 the nature of happiness. And any chance person—even a slave—can enjoy the bodily pleasures no less than the best man; but no one assigns to a slave a share in happiness— unless he assigns to him also a share in human life. For 10 happiness does not lie in such occupations, but, as we have said before,[13] in virtuous activities.

---

[12] 1099ᵃ 13, 1113ᵃ 22–33, 1166ᵃ 12, 1170ᵃ 14–16, 1176ᵃ 15–22.
[13] 1098ᵃ 16, 1176ᵃ 35–ᵇ9.

7 If happiness is activity in accordance with virtue, it is reasonable that it should be in accordance with the highest virtue; and this will be that of the best thing in us. Whether it be reason or something else that is this element 15 which is thought to be our natural ruler and guide and to take thought of things noble and divine, whether it be itself also divine or only the most divine element in us, the activity of this in accordance with its proper virtue will be perfect happiness. That this activity is contemplative we have already said.[14]

Now this would seem to be in agreement both with what 20 we said before [15] and with the truth. For, firstly, this activity is the best (since not only is reason the best thing in us, but the objects of reason are the best of knowable objects); and, secondly, it is the most continuous, since we can contemplate truth more continuously than we can do anything. And we think happiness has pleasure mingled with it, but the activity of philosophic wisdom is admit- 25 tedly the pleasantest of virtuous activities; at all events the pursuit of it is thought to offer pleasures marvellous for their purity and their enduringness, and it is to be expected that those who know will pass their time more pleasantly than those who inquire. And the self-sufficiency that is spoken of must belong most to the contemplative activity. For while a philosopher, as well as a just man or one pos- 30 sessing any other virtue, needs the necessaries of life, when they are sufficiently equipped with things of that sort the just man needs people towards whom and with whom he shall act justly, and the temperate man, the brave man, and each of the others is in the same case, but the philos- opher, even when by himself, can contemplate truth, and the better the wiser he is; he can perhaps do so better if 177ᵇ he has fellow-workers, but still he is the most self-sufficient. And this activity alone would seem to be loved for its own

[14] This has not been said, but Cf. 1095ᵇ 14–1096ᵃ 5, 1141ᵃ 18–ᵇ 3, 1143ᵇ 33–1144ᵃ 6, 1145ᵃ 6–11.
[15] 1097ᵃ 25–ᵇ 21, 1099ᵃ 7–21, 1173ᵇ 15–19, 1174ᵇ 20–23, 1175ᵇ 36–1176ᵃ 3.

sake; for nothing arises from it apart from the contemplating, while from practical activities we gain more or less
apart from the action. And happiness is thought to depend 5
on leisure; for we are busy that we may have leisure, and
make war that we may live in peace. Now the activity of
the practical virtues is exhibited in political or military
affairs, but the actions concerned with these seem to be unleisurely. Warlike actions are completely so (for no one
chooses to be at war, or provokes war, for the sake of being
at war; any one would seem absolutely murderous if he 10
were to make enemies of his friends in order to bring about
battle and slaughter); but the action of the statesman is
also unleisurely, and—apart from the political action itself
—aims at despotic power and honours, or at all events
happiness, for him and his fellow citizens—a happiness
different from political action, and evidently sought as be- 15
ing different. So if among virtuous actions political and
military actions are distinguished by nobility and greatness,
and these are unleisurely and aim at an end and are not
desirable for their own sake, but the activity of reason,
which is contemplative, seems both to be superior in serious worth and to aim at no end beyond itself, and to have
its pleasure proper to itself (and this augments the 20
activity), and the self-sufficiency, leisureliness, unwearied-
ness (so far as this is possible for man), and all the other
attributes ascribed to the supremely happy man are evidently those connected with this activity, it follows that
this will be the complete happiness of man, if it be allowed
a complete term of life (for none of the attributes of happiness is incomplete).   25

But such a life would be too high for man; for it is
not in so far as he is man that he will live so, but in so
far as something divine is present in him; and by so much
as this is superior to our composite nature is its activity superior to that which is the exercise of the other kind of
virtue. If reason is divine, then, in comparison with man,
the life according to it is divine in comparison with human 30

life. But we must not follow those who advise us, being
men, to think of human things, and, being mortal, of mortal things, but must, so far as we can, make ourselves
immortal, and strain every nerve to live in accordance with
1178ᵃ the best thing in us; for even if it be small in bulk, much
more does it in power and worth surpass everything. This
would seem, too, to be each man himself, since it is the
authoritative and better part of him. It would be strange,
then, if he were to choose not the life of his self but that of
something else. And what we said before [16] will apply now;
5 that which is proper to each thing is by nature best and
most pleasant for each thing; for man, therefore, the life
according to reason is best and pleasantest, since reason
more than anything else *is* man. This life therefore is also
the happiest.

8   But in a secondary degree the life in accordance with
the other kind of virtue is happy; for the activities in
10 accordance with this befit our human estate. Just and brave
acts, and other virtuous acts, we do in relation to each
other, observing our respective duties with regard to contracts and services and all manner of actions and with regard
to passions; and all of these seem to be typically human.
15 Some of them seem even to arise from the body, and virtue
of character to be in many ways bound up with the passions. Practical wisdom, too, is linked to virtue of character,
and this to practical wisdom, since the principles of practical wisdom are in accordance with the moral virtues and
rightness in morals is in accordance with practical wisdom.
Being connected with the passions also, the moral virtues
must belong to our composite nature; and the virtues of
20 our composite nature are human; so, therefore, are the life
and the happiness which correspond to these. The excellence of the reason is a thing apart; we must be content
to say this much about it, for to describe it precisely is a
task greater than our purpose requires. It would seem,

[16] 1169ᵇ 33, 1176ᵇ 26.

however, also to need external equipment but little, or less 25 than moral virtue does. Grant that both need the neces- saries, and do so equally, even if the statesman's work is the more concerned with the body and things of that sort; for there will be little difference there; but in what they need for the exercise of their activities there will be much difference. The liberal man will need money for the doing of his liberal deeds, and the just man too will need it for 30 the returning of services (for wishes are hard to discern, and even people who are not just pretend to wish to act justly); and the brave man will need power if he is to accomplish any of the acts that correspond to his virtue, and the tem- perate man will need opportunity; for how else is either he or any of the others to be recognized? It is debated, too, whether the will or the deed is more essential to virtue, 35 which is assumed to involve both; it is surely clear that its 1178^b perfection involves both; but for deeds many things are needed, and more, the greater and nobler the deeds are. But the man who is contemplating the truth needs no such thing, at least with a view to the exercise of his activity; indeed they are, one may say, even hindrances, at all events 5 to his contemplation; but in so far as he is a man and lives with a number of people, he chooses to do virtuous acts; he will therefore need such aids to living a human life.

But that perfect happiness is a contemplative activity will appear from the following consideration as well. We assume the gods to be above all other beings blessed and happy; but what sort of actions must we assign to them? Acts of justice? Will not the gods seem absurd if they make 10 contracts and return deposits, and so on? Acts of a brave man, then, confronting dangers and running risks because it is noble to do so? Or liberal acts? To whom will they give? It will be strange if they are really to have money or anything of the kind. And what would their temperate acts be? Is not such praise tasteless, since they have no bad 15 appetites? If we were to run through them all, the circum- stances of action would be found trivial and unworthy of

gods. Still, every one supposes that they live and therefore
that they are active; we cannot suppose them to sleep like
20 Endymion. Now if you take away from a living being
action, and still more production, what is left but contemplation? Therefore the activity of God, which surpasses all
others in blessedness, must be contemplative; and of human activities, therefore, that which is most akin to this
must be most of the nature of happiness.

This is indicated, too, by the fact that the other animals
have no share in happiness, being completely deprived of
such activity. For while the whole life of the gods is
25 blessed, and that of men too in so far as some likeness of
such activity belongs to them, none of the other animals
is happy, since they in no way share in contemplation.
Happiness extends, then, just so far as contemplation does,
and those to whom contemplation more fully belongs are
more truly happy, not as a mere concomitant but in virtue
30 of the contemplation; for this is in itself precious. Happiness, therefore, must be some form of contemplation.

But, being a man, one will also need external prosperity;
for our nature is not self-sufficient for the purpose of contemplation, but our body also must be healthy and must
35 have food and other attention. Still, we must not think
1179ᵃ that the man who is to be happy will need many things or
great things, merely because he cannot be supremely happy
without external goods; for self-sufficiency and action do
not involve excess, and we can do noble acts without ruling
5 earth and sea; for even with moderate advantages one can
act virtuously (this is manifest enough; for private persons
are thought to do worthy acts no less than despots—indeed
even more); and it is enough that we should have so
much as that; for the life of the man who is active in accordance with virtue will be happy. Solon, too, was perhaps
10 sketching well the happy man when he described him as
moderately furnished with externals but as having done
(as Solon thought) the noblest acts, and lived temperately;
for one can with but moderate possessions do what one

ought. Anaxagoras also seems to have supposed the happy
man not to be rich nor a despot, when he said that he
would not be surprised if the happy man were to seem to
most people a strange person; for they judge by externals, 15
since these are all they perceive. The opinions of the wise
seem, then, to harmonize with our arguments. But while
even such things carry some conviction, the truth in practical matters is discerned from the facts of life; for these are 20
the decisive factor. We must therefore survey what we have
already said, bringing it to the test of the facts of life, and if
it harmonizes with the facts we must accept it, but if it
clashes with them we must suppose it to be mere theory.
Now he who exercises his reason and cultivates it seems
to be both in the best state of mind and most dear to the
gods. For if the gods have any care for human affairs, as 25
they are thought to have, it would be reasonable both that
they should delight in that which was best and most akin
to them (i. e. reason) and that they should reward those
who love and honour this most, as caring for the things
that are dear to them and acting both rightly and nobly.
And that all these attributes belong most of all to the 30
philosopher is manifest. He, therefore, is the dearest to the
gods. And he who is that will presumably be also the happiest; so that in this way too the philosopher will more
than any other be happy.

9   If these matters and the virtues, and also friendship
        and pleasure, have been dealt with sufficiently in out-
line, are we to suppose that our programme has reached 35
its end? Surely, as the saying goes, where there are things
to be done the end is not to survey and recognize the vari- 1179ᵇ
ous things, but rather to do them; with regard to virtue,
then, it is not enough to know, but we must try to have
and use it, or try any other way there may be of becoming
good. Now if arguments were in themselves enough to
make men good, they would justly, as Theognis says, have 5
won very great rewards, and such rewards should have been

provided; but as things are, while they seem to have power
to encourage and stimulate the generous-minded among
our youth, and to make a character which is gently born,
10 and a true lover of what is noble, ready to be possessed by
virtue, they are not able to encourage the many to nobility
and goodness. For these do not by nature obey the sense of
shame, but only fear, and do not abstain from bad acts
because of their baseness but through fear of punishment;
living by passion they pursue their own pleasures and the
15 means to them, and avoid the opposite pains, and have not
even a conception of what is noble and truly pleasant,
since they have never tasted it. What argument would re-
mould such people? It is hard, if not impossible, to remove
by argument the traits that have long since been incorporated in the character; and perhaps we must be content
if, when all the influences by which we are thought to become good are present, we get some tincture of virtue.

Now some think that we are made good by nature, others
20 by habituation, others by teaching. Nature's part evidently
does not depend on us, but as a result of some divine causes
is present in those who are truly fortunate; while argument
and teaching, we may suspect, are not powerful with all
men, but the soul of the student must first have been
25 cultivated by means of habits for noble joy and noble hatred, like earth which is to nourish the seed. For he who
lives as passion directs will not hear argument that dis-
suades him, nor understand it if he does; and how can we
persuade one in such a state to change his ways? And in
general passion seems to yield not to argument but to
force. The character, then, must somehow be there already
30 with a kinship to virtue, loving what is noble and hating
what is base.

But it is difficult to get from youth up a right training
for virtue if one has not been brought up under right laws;
for to live temperately and hardily is not pleasant to most
people, especially when they are young. For this reason
35 their nurture and occupations should be fixed by law; for

they will not be painful when they have become customary. But it is surely not enough that when they are young 1180ᵃ they should get the right nurture and attention; since they must, even when they are grown up, practise and be habituated to them, we shall need laws for this as well, and generally speaking to cover the whole of life; for most people obey necessity rather then argument, and punishments rather than the sense of what is noble.

This is why some think [17] that legislators ought to stimulate men to virtue and urge them forward by the motive 5 of the noble, on the assumption that those who have been well advanced by the formation of habits will attend to such influences; and that punishments and penalties should be imposed on those who disobey and are of inferior nature, while the incurably bad should be completely banished.[18] A good man (they think), since he lives with his mind fixed on what is noble, will submit to argument, while a bad man, whose desire is for pleasure, is corrected 10 by pain like a beast of burden. This is, too, why they say the pains inflicted should be those that are most opposed to the pleasures such men love.

However that may be, if (as we have said) [19] the man who is to be good must be well trained and habituated, 15 and go on to spend his time in worthy occupations and neither willingly nor unwillingly do bad actions, and if this can be brought about if men live in accordance with a sort of reason and right order, provided this has force—if this be so, the paternal command indeed has not the required force or compulsive power (nor in general has the 20 command of one man, unless he be a king or something similar), but the law *has* compulsive power, while it is at the same time a rule proceeding from a sort of practical wisdom and reason. And while people hate men who oppose their impulses, even if they oppose them rightly, the

[17] Pl. *Laws* 722 D ff.
[18] Pl. *Prot.* 325 A.
[19] 1179ᵇ 31–1180ᵃ 5.

law in its ordaining of what is good is not burdensome.
25 In the Spartan state alone, or almost alone, the legislator
seems to have paid attention to questions of nurture and
occupations; in most states such matters have been neglected, and each man lives as he pleases, Cyclops-fashion,
'to his own wife and children·dealing law'.[20] Now it is
30 best that there should be a public and proper care for such
matters; but if they are neglected by the community it
would seem right for each man to help his children and
friends towards virtue, and that they should have the
power, or at least the will, to do this.

It would seem from what has been said that he can do
this better if he makes himself capable of legislating. For
public control is plainly effected by laws, and good con-
35 trol by good laws; whether written or unwritten would
1180ᵇ seem to make no difference, nor whether they are laws
providing for the education of individuals or of groups—
any more than it does in the case of music or gymnastics
and other such pursuits. For as in cities laws and prevailing
types of character have force, so in households do the in-
5 junctions and the habits of the father, and these have even
more because of the tie of blood and the benefits he confers; for the children start with a natural affection and
disposition to obey. Further, private education has an advantage over public, as private medical treatment has; for
while in general rest and abstinence from food are good
10 for a man in a fever, for a particular man they may not be;
and a boxer presumably does not prescribe the same style
of fighting to all his pupils. It would seem, then, that the
detail is worked out with more precision if the control is
private; for each person is more likely to get what suits his
case.

But the details can be best looked after, one by one, by
a doctor or gymnastic instructor or any one else who has
the general knowledge of what is good for every one or
for people of a certain kind (for the sciences both are

[20] *Od.* ix. 114 f.

said to be, and are, concerned with what is universal); not 15 but what some particular detail may perhaps be well looked after by an unscientific person, if he has studied accurately in the light of experience what happens in each case, just as some people seem to be their own best doctors, though they could give no help to any one else. None the less, it will perhaps be agreed that if a man does wish to become 20 master of an art or science he must go to the universal, and come to know it as well as possible; for, as we have said, it is with this that the sciences are concerned.

And surely he who wants to make men, whether many or few, better by his care must try to become capable of legislating, if it is through laws that we can become good. For to get any one whatever—any one who is put before 25 us—into the right condition is not for the first chance comer; if any one can do it, it is the man who knows, just as in medicine and all other matters which give scope for care and prudence.

Must we not, then, next examine whence or how one can learn how to legislate? Is it, as in all other cases, from statesmen? Certainly it was thought to be a part of states-manship.[21] Or is a difference apparent between states- 30 manship and the other sciences and arts? In the others the same people are found offering to teach the arts and practising them, e. g. doctors or painters; but while the sophists profess to teach politics, it is practised not by any 35 of them but by the politicians, who would seem to do so 1181ᵃ by dint of a certain skill and experience rather than of thought; for they are not found either writing or speaking about such matters (though it were a nobler occupation perhaps than composing speeches for the law-courts and the assembly), nor again are they found to have made statesmen of their own sons or any other of their friends. 5 But it was to be expected that they should if they could; for there is nothing better than such a skill that they could have left to their cities, or could prefer to have for them-

[21] 1141ᵇ 24.

selves, or, therefore, for those dearest to them. Still, experience seems to contribute not a little; else they could
10 not have become politicians by familiarity with politics;
and so it seems that those who aim at knowing about the·
art of politics need experience as well.

But those of the sophists who profess the art seem to be
very far from teaching it. For, to put the matter generally,
they do not even know what kind of thing it is nor what
kinds of things it is about; otherwise they would not have
15 classed it as identical with rhetoric or even inferior to it,[22]
nor have thought it easy to legislate by collecting the laws
that are thought well of; [23] they say it is possible to select
the best laws, as though even the selection did not demand
intelligence and as though right judgement were not the
greatest thing, as in matters of music. For while people
20 experienced in any department judge rightly the works produced in it, and understand by what means or how they
are achieved, and what harmonizes with what, the inexperienced must be content if they do not fail to see whether
the work has been well or ill made—as in the case of painting. Now laws are as it were the 'works' of the political art;
1181ᵇ how then can one learn from them to be a legislator, or
judge which are best? Even medical men do not seem to be
made by a study of text-books. Yet people try, at any rate,
to state not only the treatments, but also how particular
5 classes of people can be cured and should be treated—
distinguishing the various habits of body; but while this
seems useful to experienced people, to the inexperienced it
is valueless. Surely, then, while collections of laws, and of
constitutions also, may be serviceable to those who can
study them and judge what is good or bad and what enact-
10 ments suit what circumstances, those who go through such
collections without a practised faculty will not have right
judgement (unless it be as a spontaneous gift of nature),

----

[22] Isoc. *Antid.* § 80.
[23] Ib. §§ 82, 83.

though they may perhaps become more intelligent in such matters.

Now our predecessors have left the subject of legislation to us unexamined; it is perhaps best, therefore, that we should ourselves study it, and in general study the question of the constitution, in order to complete to the best of our 15 ability our philosophy of human nature. First, then, if anything has been said well in detail by earlier thinkers, let us try to review it; then in the light of the constitutions we have collected let us study what sorts of influence preserve and destroy states, and what sorts preserve or destroy the particular kinds of constitution, and to what causes it is due that some are well and others ill administered. When 20 these have been studied we shall perhaps be more likely to see with a comprehensive view, which constitution is best, and how each must be ordered, and what laws and customs it must use, if it is to be at its best.[24] Let us make a beginning of our discussion.

[24] 1181ᵇ 12–23 is a programme for the *Politics,* agreeing to a large extent with the existing contents of that work.

Politics

INTRODUCTION

Every community, like every action, is aimed at some good. Good in individual actions is traced back to virtues which are sources of action and have a natural basis in the psychological faculties of man. Good in states is based on the good of the communities or associations of which they are formed, "for the state or political community, which is the highest of all, and which embraces all the rest, aims at good in a higher degree than any other, and at the highest good." Aristotle criticizes philosophers like Plato, who think that the functions and qualifications of a statesman, king, householder, and master are the same, and that they differ not in kind but only in the number of their subjects. Centuries later Locke was to make a like criticism of Filmer, in the opening pages of the second treatise on *Civil Government*, for making a similar reduction in his *Patriarcha*. As in other sciences, so in politics, the compound should be resolved into the simple elements or least parts of the whole, and the method of inquiry is therefore to look at the elements of which the state is composed in order to "see in what the different kinds of rule differ from one another, and whether any scientific result can be attained about each one of them."

The first book of the *Politics*, which is included in this collection, like the first book of the *Nicomachean Ethics*, is devoted to the preparatory investigation. The primary association for the necessities of life is the family (*oikia*, the subject of the science later to be called "economics") which is based on three *natural* relations, man and wife, parents and children, masters and instruments, both animate and inanimate, that is, slaves and property. Families are associated in villages, and villages in states. The end of lesser associations is living. The end of the state is living well. Although the beginnings of the distinction between economics and politics are in this differentiation, the distinction between living and living well is different from what it was to become when Adam Smith invented political economy. For Aristotle, a state is possible only when there is a sufficiency, autonomy, of material goods to make the pursuit of other goods possible. "Welfare" today is limited to the material goods of economics—food, clothing, housing, health services, security for oneself and one's family, work, and training for work. Welfare in the sense of faring-well in life, insofar as governments function to affect it, is either reduced to material welfare or elevated to something extraneous called "culture." The state is a creation of nature, and man is by nature a political animal. The state is by nature prior both to the family, a natural association, and to the individual man, a natural existent being.

The second book of the *Politics*, like the first books of the *Physics*, the *Metaphysics*, and *De Anima*, reviews and criticizes earlier theories. It is a short history, since political thought began with Socrates and Plato, to whom jointly are attributed doctrines not only from the *Republic* but also from the *Laws*, in which Socrates does not appear. Phaleas and Hippodamas are added as political thinkers, and since politics is a practical science and political theories are embodied in constitutions as well as formulated in treatises, the best existent states—Sparta, Crete, and Carthage—and the Greek lawgivers are added as further doctrinal variants.

The third book, which is included in this collection, is devoted to defining the state and to differentiating kinds of governments. Aristotle uses his familiar regressive method, discovering that to define the state (*polis*) it is necessary first to define the constitution (*politeia*), and that the definition of the citizen (*polites*) is needed in defining constitution. A citizen is one who participates in the processes of ruling and being ruled. Aristotle remarks that this definition is best suited to a democracy, but an element of self-rule or acceptance is essential to the being and efficacy of any kind of state. The definition of the citizen orders the relations of ruler and ruled, of ruling and being ruled, by providing a reflexive first principle, self-rule; the kinds of states are differentiated by their aim: true constitutions—monarchies, aristocracies, and polities or constitutions—are designed to achieve the common welfare, or common interest, or common good; perverted constitutions—tyrannies, oligarchies, and democracies—are directed to partial or private interests. A tyranny is the rule of one, the rule of a master, but the difference between the oligarchy and the democracy is not a question of the rule of a few or of many, but of the rule of the rich or of the poor. The two constitutions differ in their objectives—wealth and freedom—and political qualifications to rule are determined by inequalities proportionate to wealth or equalities of freedom. Both miss the true object of the state, which is virtue. Aristotle is sometimes said to have taken an unfavorable view of democracy. On the other hand, what he calls 'democracy' is a perversion of the form of government to which he gives the generic name 'constitution' or 'polity,' the constitutional form of government, in which the ruled participate in ruling. Moreover, after he has refuted the views that the supreme power or sovereignty should be the multitude, or the wealthy, or the good, he observes that the principle that the multitude rather than the few best ought to be supreme seems to contain an element of truth, for the many may very likely be better than the few good, if regarded not individually but collectively. The many are better judges of music and poetry than a single man, and for like reasons they should be assigned some deliberative and judicial functions in the state. Laws, when good, should be supreme, however, and magistrates should regulate those matters only on which the laws are unable to determine precisely, because of the difficulty of any general principle embracing all particulars. Laws vary, in turn, since they are adapted to constitutions.

In all sciences and arts the end is a good. It is the greatest good, and in the highest degree a good, in the most authoritative or architectonic science. Like metaphysics, political science is an 'architectonic' science: metaphysics orders and organizes arts and sciences as forms of knowledge according to their principles; political science orders them as forms of activity in the common life, and in pursuit of the common good, among the activities and pursuits of the community. The good of political science is justice, which all men think to be a sort of equality. The kinds of justice and equality are not only the ends of particular forms of government; they also provide reasons advanced by men who seek office in a state—the noble, or freeborn, or rich. Wealth and freedom are necessary elements without which the state cannot exist at all; justice and valour are elements without which it cannot exist well. None of the principles on which men claim to rule, however, is strictly right. 'What is just and right' is to be interpreted in the sense of 'what is equal' in the advantage of the state and in the common good of the citizens. "And a citizen is one who shares in governing and being governed. He differs under different forms of government, but in the best state he is one who is able and willing to be governed and to govern with a view to the life of virtue." The third book closes with an examination of the various forms of monarchy and aristocracy, the rule of one and the rule of the best.

Political science is a single science. Investigation of its subject-matter, government, includes determining what government is best and how it is adapted to the realization of our aspirations. The fourth book begins, consequently, by differentiating four senses of best': (1) the best in the abstract or absolutely (and then political problems are conceived largely in terms of the education of citizens as a means of improving political institutions and their functionings), (2) the best under particular circumstances or assumed conditions (and then political problems are conceived in terms of existing power blocs and the operation and modification of political institutions and political operators), (3) the best in the modification or preservation of original forms of government or *ex hypothesi* (and then political problems are conceived in terms of the prevention or furtherance of revolutions), and (4) the best in general or most suited to all states (and then political problems are conceived in terms of functions and powers operating in the solution of problems as they occur without prior anticipation or prearranged legal preparation).

The four senses of best have had a long and varied history in political thought, and they are prominent in contemporary theories and controversies concerning established states, concerning newly liberated peoples aspiring to self-government, and concerning minority groups aspiring to liberty and self-rule. Since the state is defined in terms of the citizen and the citizen in terms of his participation in the operations of the state, the good man will be the same as the good citizen only in the perfect state. The "best absolutely" is still envisaged in planning to educate the masses in existing states, to form new states by giving liberated people know-how and an operative sense of dignity, and to integrate minority groups by improving their education and relating their values to the common values of the community. But the best is also sought "in particular circumstances," in the oppositions and confrontations of parties and pressure groups by establishing policy and winning elections by presentation to and persuasion of the people, or by resolving opposition by spying on, bugging, and destroying opponents. The best is also sought by instituting separations of powers and functions to provide means for the solution of problems never encountered before by rules and prerogatives suited to achieve the "best in general," and modern constitutional thinking has profited by the tradition of thought in which

Aristotle's differentiation of the legislative, executive, and judicial functions has been elaborated. The best, finally, is still sought in the hypothetically best in revolutions by which real or alleged inequalities are to be remedied and removed; and Machiavelli, in drawing up programs by which princes may acquire and maintain power, as well as later theorists, projecting revolutions or foreseeing and seeking to thwart totalitarians, might have found many of their devices in Aristotle's treatment of power and persuasion.

Since monarchical and aristocratic governments have been examined in the third book to test the claim that they provide, in some of their forms, instances of the "best absolutely," the remainder of the fourth book is devoted to examining the other kinds of states and the other kinds of best. Aristotle criticizes the view that democracy and oligarchy are the main types of constitution and also the view that the difference between them is the proportion of rulers to ruled. In democracies the many are also the poor and in oligarchies the few are also the rich, a class distinction that exists in all states. There are various kinds of democracy and of oligarchy, but only one form of aristocracy, the rule of the best. Polity or constitutional government is a compromise between democracy and oligarchy, inclining to the democratic side, but many so-called aristocracies are really polities. The "best under particular circumstances" is examined by considering what constitutions are best and what constitutions are possible in the average Greek city-state. The best constitution for the average city-state is rule of the middle-class, a mean between the rule of rich and poor; but it is adapted to large states, and in the small Greek city-states it has rarely succeeded. Democracy and oligarchy are the only constitutions possible in some states. The "best in general" is provided for by writing into the law of the constitution the functions and modes of selection of the deliberative assembly, the executive, and the courts of law. The fifth book is concerned with the fourth kind of best, the "best ex hypothesi," or revolutions. The language in which Aristotle discusses revolutions has other suggestive paradoxical overtones besides its designation as the hypothetically best: the word for faction, *stasis*, also signifies status, a fixed position as well as a position of dissent, and the word for revolution, *metabole*, is the word for change in the *Physics* applied to constitutions in the *Politics*. The causes of revolution are injustice and inequality. Revolutions may effect two kinds of changes in governments, a change in the constitution or a change in the administration without affecting the form of government. The sixth book returns to the consideration of the best under particular circumstances to determine the proper organization of democracies and oligarchies, as the most likely forms of government of the average city-state. It is harder to preserve than to found a democracy; its preservation depends on preventing the poor from plundering the rich. Oligarchies are best preserved by careful organization, and much depends on an army in which subjects do not acquire too powerful a role. The last two books, Books VII and VIII, turn from the practicalities and manoeuvres of the best under particular circumstances to education under the ideal conditions of the best absolutely.

POLITICA

CONTENTS

BOOK I

BOOK III

Chapters 1–5. The Citizen, civic virtue, and the civic body.

tion of political power; when the mode of distribution is changed a new state comes into existence/623

4. The good citizen may not be a good man; the good citizen is one who does good service to his state, and this state may be bad in principle. In a constitutional state the good citizen knows both how to rule and how to obey. The good man is one who is fitted to rule. But the citizen in a constitutional state learns to rule by obeying orders. Therefore citizenship in such a state is a moral training/625

5. Mechanics will not be citizens in the best state. Extreme democracies, and some oligarchies, neglect this rule. But circumstances oblige them to do this. They have no choice/629

Chapters 6–13. The Classification of Constitutions; Democracy and Oligarchy; Kingship.

6. The aims of the state are two: to satisfy man's social instinct, and to fit him for the good life. Political rule differs from that over slaves in aiming primarily at the good of those who are ruled/630

7. Constitutions are bad or good according as the common welfare is, or is not, their aim. Of good Constitutions there are three: Monarchy, Aristocracy, and Polity. Of bad there are also three: Tyranny, Oligarchy, Extreme Democracy. The bad are perversions of the good/632

8. Democracies and Oligarchies are not made by the numerical proportion of the rulers to the ruled. Democracy is the rule of the poor; oligarchy is that of the rich/633

9. Democrats take Equality for their motto; oligarchs believe that political rights should be unequal and proportionate to wealth. But both sides miss the true object of the state, which is virtue. Those who do most to promote virtue deserve the greatest share of power/635

10. On the same principle, Justice is not the will of the majority or of the wealthier, but that course of action which the moral aim of the state requires/638

11. But are the Many or the Few likely to be the better rulers? It would be unreasonable to give the highest offices to the Many. But they have a faculty of criticism which fits them for deliberative and judicial power. The good

critic need not be an expert; experts are sometimes bad
judges. Moreover, the Many have a greater stake in the
city than the Few. But the governing body, whether Few
or Many, must be held in check by the laws/639

12. On what principle should political power be distributed?
Granted that equals deserve equal shares; who are these
equals? Obviously those who are equally able to be of service to the state/642

13. Hence there is something in the claims advanced by the
wealthy, the free born, the noble, the highly gifted. But
no one of these classes should be allowed to rule the rest.
A state should consist of men who are equal, or nearly so,
in wealth, in birth, in moral and intellectual excellence.
The principle which underlies Ostracism is plausible. But
in the ideal state, if a pre-eminent individual be found, he
should be made a king/644

Chapters 14–18. The Forms of Monarchy.

14. Of Monarchy there are five kinds, (1) the Spartan, (2)
the Barbarian, (3) the elective dictatorship, (4) the Heroic, (5) Absolute Kingship/648

15. The last of these forms might appear the best polity to
some; that is, if the king acts as the embodiment of law.
For he will dispense from the law in the spirit of the law.
But this power would be less abused if reserved for the
Many. Monarchy arose to meet the needs of primitive society; it is now obsolete and on various grounds objection-
able/651

16. It tends to become hereditary; it subjects equals to the
rule of an equal. The individual monarch may be misled
by his passions, and no single man can attend to all the
duties of government/654

17. One case alone can be imagined in which Absolute Kingship would be just/657

18. Let us consider the origin and nature of the best polity,
now that we have agreed not to call Absolute Kingship
the best/658

Politica

Politics

Translated by Benjamin Jowett

ЦЦЦ

BOOK I

Every state is a community of some kind, and every community is established with a view to some good; **1252ᵃ** for mankind always act in order to obtain that which they think good. But, if all communities aim at some good, the state or political community, which is the highest of all, and which embraces all the rest, aims at good in a 5 greater degree than any other, and at the highest good.

Some people think¹ that the qualifications of a statesman, king, householder, and master are the same, and that they differ, not in kind, but only in the number of their subjects. For example, the ruler over a few is called a mas- 10 ter; over more, the manager of a household; over a still larger number, a statesman or king, as if there were no difference between a great household and a small state. The distinction which is made between the king and the statesman is as follows: When the government is personal, the ruler is a king; when, according to the rules of the political 15 science, the citizens rule and are ruled in turn, then he is called a statesman.

But all this is a mistake; for governments differ in kind, as will be evident to any one who considers the matter ac-

---

¹ Cp. Plato, *Politicus*, 258 ᴇ–259 ᴅ.

cording to the method [2] which has hitherto guided us. As
20 in other departments of science, so in politics, the compound should always be resolved into the simple elements
or least parts of the whole. We must therefore look at the
elements of which the state is composed, in order that we
may see in what the different kinds of rule differ from one
another, and whether any scientific result can be attained
about each one of them.

2   He who thus considers things in their first growth and
origin, whether a state or anything else, will obtain the
25 clearest view of them. In the first place there must be a
union of those who cannot exist without each other;
namely, of male and female, that the race may continue
(and this is a union which is formed, not of deliberate
purpose, but because, in common with other animals and
30 with plants, mankind have a natural desire to leave behind
them an image of themselves), and of natural ruler and
subject, that both may be preserved. For that which can
foresee by the exercise of mind is by nature intended to be
lord and master, and that which can with its body give
effect to such foresight is a subject, and by nature a slave;
1252[b] hence master and slave have the same interest. Now nature
has distinguished between the female and the slave. For
she is not niggardly, like the smith who fashions the
Delphian knife for many uses; she makes each thing for a
single use, and every instrument is best made when in-
5 tended for one and not for many uses. But among barbarians no distinction is made between women and slaves, because there is no natural ruler among them: they are a
community of slaves, male and female. Wherefore the
poets say—

'It is meet that Hellenes should rule over barbarians';

as if they thought that the barbarian and the slave were by
nature one.

[2] Cp. 1256[a]2.

Out of these two relationships between man and woman, master and slave, the first thing to arise is the family, and Hesiod is right when he says— [10]

'First house and wife and an ox for the plough',

for the ox is the poor man's slave. The family is the association established by nature for the supply of men's everyday wants, and the members of it are called by Charondas 'companions of the cupboard', and by Epimenides the Cretan, 'companions of the manger.' But when several families are united, and the association aims at [15] something more than the supply of daily needs, the first society to be formed is the village. And the most natural form of the village appears to be that of a colony from the family, composed of the children and grandchildren, who are said to be 'suckled with the same milk'. And this is the [20] reason why Hellenic states were originally governed by kings; because the Hellenes were under royal rule before they came together, as the barbarians still are. Every family is ruled by the eldest, and therefore in the colonies of the family the kingly form of government prevailed because they were of the same blood. As Homer says: [3]

'Each one gives law to his children and to his wives.'

For they lived dispersedly, as was the manner in ancient times. Wherefore men say that the Gods have a king, because they themselves either are or were in ancient times under the rule of a king. For they imagine, not only the [25] forms of the Gods, but their ways of life to be like their own.

When several villages are united in a single complete community, large enough to be nearly or quite self-sufficing, the state comes into existence, originating in the bare needs of life, and continuing in existence for the sake of a good life. And therefore, if the earlier forms of society are [30]

[3] *Od.* ix. 114, quoted by Plato, *Laws,* iii. 680 B, and in *N. Eth. x.* 1180ᵃ 28.

natural, so is the state, for it is the end of them, and the nature of a thing is its end. For what each thing is when fully developed, we call its nature, whether we are speaking of a man, a horse, or a family. Besides, the final cause and end of a thing is the best, and to be self-sufficing is the **1253ᵃ** end and the best.

Hence it is evident that the state is a creation of nature, and that man is by nature a political animal. And he who by nature and not by mere accident is without a state, is either a bad man or above humanity; he is like the

'Tribeless, lawless, heartless one,'

whom Homer[4] denounces—the natural outcast is forthwith a lover of war; he may be compared to an isolated piece at draughts.

Now, that man is more of a political animal than bees or any other gregarious animals is evident. Nature, as we often say, makes nothing in vain,[5] and man is the only animal whom she has endowed with the gift of speech.[6]
10 And whereas mere voice is but an indication of pleasure or pain, and is therefore found in other animals (for their nature attains to the perception of pleasure and pain and the intimation of them to one another, and no further), the power of speech is intended to set forth the expedient and inexpedient, and therefore likewise the just and the un-
15 just. And it is a characteristic of man that he alone has any sense of good and evil, of just and unjust, and the like, and the association of living beings who have this sense makes a family and a state.

Further, the state is by nature clearly prior to the family and to the individual, since the whole is of necessity prior
20 to the part; for example, if the whole body be destroyed, there will be no foot or hand, except in an equivocal

[4] *Il.* ix. 63.
[5] Cp. 1256ᵇ 20.
[6] Cp. vii. 1332ᵇ 5.

sense, as we might speak of a stone hand; for when de-stroyed the hand will be no better than that. But things are defined by their working and power; and we ought not to say that they are the same when they no longer have their proper quality, but only that they have the same 25 name. The proof that the state is a creation of nature and prior to the individual is that the individual, when isolated, is not self-sufficing; and therefore he is like a part in rela-tion to the whole. But he who is unable to live in society, or who has no need because he is sufficient for himself, must be either a beast or a god: he is no part of a state. A social instinct is implanted in all men by nature, and yet he 30 who first founded the state was the greatest of benefactors. For man, when perfected, is the best of animals, but, when separated from law and justice, he is the worst of all; since armed injustice is the more dangerous, and he is equipped at birth with arms, meant to be used by intelligence and virtue, which he may use for the worst ends. Wherefore, if 35 he have not virtue, he is the most unholy and the most savage of animals, and the most full of lust and gluttony. But justice is the bond of men in states, for the administra-tion of justice, which is the determination of what is just,[7] is the principle of order in political society.

3　Seeing then that the state is made up of households, before speaking of the state we must speak of the management of the household. The parts of household 1253^b management correspond to the persons who compose the household, and a complete household consists of slaves and freemen. Now we should begin by examining everything in its fewest possible elements; and the first and fewest possi- 5 ble parts of a family are master and slave, husband and wife, father and children. We have therefore to consider what each of these three relations is and ought to be:—I mean the relation of master and servant, the marriage relation 10

[7] Cp. *N. Eth.* v. 1134ᵃ 31.

(the conjunction of man and wife has no name of its own),
and thirdly, the procreative relation (this also has no proper
name). And there is another element of a household, the
so-called art of getting wealth, which, according to some, is
identical with household management, according to others,
a principal part of it; the nature of this art will also have to
be considered by us.

15 Let us first speak of master and slave, looking to the
needs of practical life and also seeking to attain some better
theory of their relation than exists at present. For some are
of opinion that the rule of a master is a science, and that
the management of a household, and the mastership of
20 slaves, and the political and royal rule, as I was saying at
the outset,[8] are all the same. Others affirm that the rule of
a master over slaves is contrary to nature, and that the distinction between slave and freeman exists by law only, and
not by nature; and being an interference with nature is
therefore unjust.

4   Property is a part of the household, and the art of
      acquiring property is a part of the art of managing the
household; for no man can live well, or indeed live at all,
25 unless he be provided with necessaries. And as in the arts
which have a definite sphere the workers must have their
own proper instruments for the accomplishment of their
work, so it is in the management of a household. Now
instruments are of various sorts; some are living, others
lifeless; in the rudder, the pilot of a ship has a lifeless, in
the look-out man, a living instrument; for in the arts the
servant is a kind of instrument. Thus, too, a possession
30 is an instrument for maintaining life. And so, in the arrangement of the family, a slave is a living possession, and
property a number of such instruments; and the servant is
himself an instrument which takes precedence of all other
instruments. For if every instrument could accomplish its
own work, obeying or anticipating the will of others, like

[8] Plato in *Pol.* 258 E–259 D, referred to already in 1252ª 7–16.

the statues of Daedalus, or the tripods of Hephaestus, 35 which, says the poet,[9]

'of their own accord entered the assembly of the Gods';

if, in like manner, the shuttle would weave and the plectrum touch the lyre without a hand to guide them, chief work-men would not want servants, nor masters slaves. Here, however, another distinction must be drawn; the instru- 1254ᵃ ments commonly so called are instruments of production, whilst a possession is an instrument of action. The shuttle, for example, is not only of use; but something else is made by it, whereas of a garment or of a bed there is only the use. Further, as production and action are different in kind, and both require instruments, the instruments which 5 they employ must likewise differ in kind. But life is action and not production, and therefore the slave is the minister of action. Again, a possession is spoken of as a part is spoken of; for the part is not only a part of something else, but wholly belongs to it; and this is also true of a possession. 10 The master is only the master of the slave; he does not be-long to him, whereas the slave is not only the slave of his master, but wholly belongs to him. Hence we see what is the nature and office of a slave; he who is by nature not his own but another's man, is by nature a slave; and he 15 may be said to be another's man who, being a human being, is also a possession. And a possession may be defined as an instrument of action, separable from the possessor.

5   But is there any one thus intended by nature to be a slave, and for whom such a condition is expedient and right, or rather is not all slavery a violation of nature?

There is no difficulty in answering this question, on 20 grounds both of reason and of fact. For that some should rule and others be ruled is a thing not only necessary, but expedient; from the hour of their birth, some are marked out for subjection, others for rule.

[9] Hom. *Il.* xviii. 376.

And there are many kinds both of rulers and subjects
25 (and that rule is the better which is exercised over better
subjects—for example, to rule over men is better than to
rule over wild beasts; for the work is better which is executed by better workmen, and where one man rules and
another is ruled, they may be said to have a work); for in
all things which form a composite whole and which are
30 made up of parts, whether continuous or discrete, a distinction between the ruling and the subject element comes to
light. Such a duality exists in living creatures, but not in
them only; it originates in the constitution of the universe;
even in things which have no life there is a ruling principle,
as in a musical mode. But we are wandering from the subject. We will therefore restrict ourselves to the living crea-
35 ture, which, in the first place, consists of soul and body: and
of these two, the one is by nature the ruler, and the other
the subject. But then we must look for the intentions of
nature in things which retain their nature, and not in
things which are corrupted. And therefore we must study
the man who is in the most perfect state both of body and
soul, for in him we shall see the true relation of the two;
1254ᵇ although in bad or corrupted natures the body will often
appear to rule over the soul, because they are in an evil
and unnatural condition. At all events we may firstly observe in living creatures both a despotical and a constitutional rule; for the soul rules the body with a despotical
rule, whereas the intellect rules the appetites with a
5 constitutional and royal rule. And it is clear that the rule of
the soul over the body, and of the mind and the rational
element over the passionate, is natural and expedient;
whereas the equality of the two or the rule of the inferior
is always hurtful. The same holds good of animals in rela-
10 tion to men; for tame animals have a better nature than
wild, and all tame animals are better off when they are
ruled by man; for then they are preserved. Again, the male
is by nature superior, and the female inferior; and the
one rules, and the other is ruled; this principle, of neces-

sity, extends to all mankind. Where then there is such a 15
difference as that between soul and body, or between men
and animals (as in the case of those whose business is to
use their body, and who can do nothing better), the lower
sort are by nature slaves, and it is better for them as for all
inferiors that they should be under the rule of a master.
For he who can be, and therefore is, another's, and he who
participates in rational principle enough to apprehend, but 20
not to have, such a principle, is a slave by nature. Whereas
the lower animals cannot even apprehend a principle; they
obey their instincts. And indeed the use made of slaves
and of tame animals is not very different; for both with
their bodies minister to the needs of life. Nature would
like to distinguish between the bodies of freemen and 25
slaves, making the one strong for servile labour, the other
upright, and although useless for such services, useful for
political life in the arts both of war and peace. But the op- 30
posite often happens—that some have the souls and others
have the bodies of freemen. And doubtless if men differed
from one another in the mere forms of their bodies as
much as the statues of the Gods do from men, all would
acknowledge that the inferior class should be slaves of the 35
superior. And if this is true of the body, how much more
just that a similar distinction should exist in the soul? but
the beauty of the body is seen, whereas the beauty of the
soul is not seen. It is clear, then, that some men are by 1255ᵃ
nature free, and others slaves, and that for these latter
slavery is both expedient and right.

6 But that those who take the opposite view have in a
certain way right on their side, may be easily seen. For
the words slavery and slave are used in two senses. There
is a slave or slavery by law as well as by nature. The law of 5
which I speak is a sort of convention—the law by which
whatever is taken in war is supposed to belong to the vic-
tors. But this right many jurists impeach, as they would
an orator who brought forward an unconstitutional meas-

ure: they detest the notion that, because one man has the
power of doing violence and is superior in brute strength,
10 another shall be his slave and subject. Even among philosophers there is a difference of opinion. The origin of the
dispute, and what makes the views invade each other's ter-
ritory, is as follows: in some sense virtue, when furnished
with means, has actually the greatest power of exercising
force: and as superior power is only found where there is
superior excellence of some kind, power seems to imply
virtue, and the dispute to be simply one about justice.(for
15 it is due to one party identifying justice with goodwill,[10]
while the other identifies it with the mere rule of
the stronger). If these views are thus set out separately, the
20 other views [11] have no force or plausibility against the
view that the superior in virtue ought to rule, or be master.
Others, clinging, as they think, simply to a principle of
justice (for law and custom are a sort of justice), assume
that slavery in accordance with the custom of war is justified by law, but at the same moment they deny this. For
25 what if the cause of the war be unjust? And again, no one
would ever say that he is a slave who is unworthy to be a
slave. Were this the case, men of the highest rank would
be slaves and the children of slaves if they or their parents
chance to have been taken captive and sold. Wherefore
Hellenes do not like to call Hellenes slaves, but confine the
30 term to barbarians. Yet, in using this language, they really
mean the natural slave of whom we spoke at first; [12] for it
must be admitted that some are slaves everywhere, others
nowhere. The same principle applies to nobility. Hellenes
regard themselves as noble everywhere, and not only in
35 their own country, but they deem the barbarians noble

[10] i. e. mutual goodwill, which is held to be incompatible with the
relation of master and slave.

[11] i. e. those stated in ll. 5–12, that the stronger always has, and that
he never has, a right to enslave the weaker. Aristotle finds that these
views cannot maintain themselves against his intermediate view, that
the superior in *virtue* should rule.

[12] Chap. 5.

only when at home, thereby implying that there are two sorts of nobility and freedom, the one absolute, the other relative. The Helen of Theodectes says:

'Who would presume to call me servant who am on both sides sprung from the stem of the Gods?'

What does this mean but that they distinguish freedom and slavery, noble and humble birth, by the two principles 40 of good and evil? They think that as men and animals beget **1255ᵇ** men and animals, so from good men a good man springs. But this is what nature, though she may intend it, cannot always accomplish.

We see then that there is some foundation for this difference of opinion, and that all are not either slaves by 5 nature or freemen by nature, and also that there is in some cases a marked distinction between the two classes, rendering it expedient and right for the one to be slaves and the others to be masters: the one practising obedience, the others exercising the authority and lordship which nature intended them to have. The abuse of this authority is injurious to both; for the interests of part and whole,[13] of 10 body and soul, are the same, and the slave is a part of the master, a living but separated part of his bodily frame. Hence, where the relation of master and slave between them is natural they are friends and have a common interest, but where it rests merely on law and force the reverse is true. 15

7   The previous remarks are quite enough to show that the rule of a master is not a constitutional rule, and that all the different kinds of rule are not, as some affirm, the same with each other.[14] For there is one rule exercised over subjects who are by nature free, another over subjects who are by nature slaves. The rule of a household is a mon-

---

[13] Cp. 1254ᵃ 8.
[14] Plato, *Polit.* 258 ᴇ–259 ᴅ, referred to already in 1252ᵃ 7–16, 1253ᵇ 18–20.

archy, for every house is under one head: whereas constitutional rule is a government of freemen and equals. The
20 master is not called a master because he has science,[15] but
because he is of a certain character, and the same remark
applies to the slave and the freeman. Still there may be a
science for the master and a science for the slave. The
science of the slave would be such as the man of Syracuse
taught, who made money by instructing slaves in their
25 ordinary duties. And such a knowledge may be carried
further, so as to include cookery and similar menial arts.
For some duties are of the more necessary, others of the
more honourable sort; as the proverb says, 'slave before
slave, master before master'. But all such branches of
30 knowledge are servile. There is likewise a science of the
master, which teaches the use of slaves; for the master as
such is concerned, not with the acquisition, but with the
use of them. Yet this so-called science is not anything great
or wonderful; for the master need only know how to order
that which the slave must know how to execute. Hence
35 those who are in a position which places them above toil
have stewards who attend to their households while they
occupy themselves with philosophy or with politics. But
the art of acquiring slaves, I mean of justly acquiring them,
differs both from the art of the master and the art of the
slave, being a species of hunting or war.[16] Enough of the
40 distinction between master and slave.

8 Let us now inquire into property generally, and into
1256ᵃ the art of getting wealth, in accordance with our usual
method,[17] for a slave has been shown [18] to be a part of
property. The first question is whether the art of getting
wealth is the same with the art of managing a household
or a part of it, or instrumental to it; and if the last, whether
in the way that the art of making shuttles is instrumental

[15] *Polit.* 259 c, 293 c.
[16] Cp. vii. 1333ᵇ 38.
[17] Of understanding the whole by the part, Cp. 1252ᵃ 17.
[18] Chap. 4.

to the art of weaving, or in the way that the casting of
bronze is instrumental to the art of the statuary, for they 5
are not instrumental in the same way, but the one provides
tools and the other material; and by material I mean the
substratum out of which any work is made; thus wool is 10
the material of the weaver, bronze of the statuary. Now it is
easy to see that the art of household management is not
identical with the art of getting wealth, for the one uses
the material which the other provides. For the art which
uses household stores can be no other than the art of household management. There is, however, a doubt whether the
art of getting wealth is a part of household management or
a distinct art. If the getter of wealth has to consider whence 15
wealth and property can be procured, but there are many
sorts of property and riches, then are husbandry, and the
care and provision of food in general, parts of the wealth-
getting art or distinct arts? Again, there are many sorts of
food, and therefore there are many kinds of lives both of 20
animals and men; they must all have food, and the differences in their food have made differences in their ways of
life. For beasts, some are gregarious, others are solitary;
they live in the way which is best adapted to sustain them,
accordingly as they are carnivorous or herbivorous or om- 25
nivorous: and their habits are determined for them by nature in such a manner that they may obtain with greater
facility the food of their choice. But, as different species
have different tastes, the same things are not naturally
pleasant to all of them; and therefore the lives of carnivorous or herbivorous animals further differ among them- 30
selves. In the lives of men too there is a great difference.
The laziest are shepherds, who lead an idle life, and get
their subsistence without trouble from tame animals; their
flocks having to wander from place to place in search of
pasture, they are compelled to follow them, cultivating a 35
sort of living farm. Others support themselves by hunting,
which is of different kinds. Some, for example, are brigands,
others, who dwell near lakes or marshes or rivers or a sea in

which there are fish, are fishermen, and others live by the
pursuit of birds or wild beasts. The greater number obtain
40 a living from the cultivated fruits of the soil. Such are the
modes of subsistence which prevail among those whose
1256ᵇ industry springs up of itself, and whose food is not acquired
by exchange and retail trade—there is the shepherd, the
husbandman, the brigand, the fisherman, the hunter. Some
gain a comfortable maintenance out of two employments,
eking out the deficiencies of one of them by another: thus
5 the life of a shepherd may be combined with that of a
brigand, the life of a farmer with that of a hunter. Other
modes of life are similarly combined in any way which the
needs of men may require. Property, in the sense of a bare
livelihood, seems to be given by nature herself to all, both
when they are first born, and when they are grown up. For
10 some animals bring forth, together with their offspring, so
much food as will last until they are able to supply themselves; of this the vermiparous or oviparous animals are
an instance; and the viviparous animals have up to a certain time a supply of food for their young in themselves,
which is called milk. In like manner we may infer that, after
15 the birth of animals, plants exist for their sake, and that
the other animals exist for the sake of man, the tame for
use and food, the wild, if not all, at least the greater part
of them, for food, and for the provision of clothing and
various instruments. Now if nature makes nothing incom-
20 plete, and nothing in vain, the inference must be that she
has made all animals for the sake of man. And so, in one
point of view, the art of war is a natural art of acquisition,
for the art of acquisition includes hunting, an art which we
ought to practise against wild beasts, and against men who,
25 though intended by nature to be governed, will not submit;
for war of such a kind is naturally just.[19]

Of the art of acquisition then there is one kind which by
nature is a part of the management of a household, in so
far as the art of household management must either find

[19] Cp. 1255ᵇ 38, 1333ᵇ 38.

ready to hand, or itself provide, such things necessary to
life, and useful for the community of the family or state, 30
as can be stored. They are the elements of true riches; for
the amount of property which is needed for a good life is
not unlimited, although Solon in one of his poems says that

'No bound to riches has been fixed for man'.

But there is a boundary fixed, just as there is in the other
arts; for the instruments of any art are never unlimited,
either in number or size, and riches may be defined as a 35
number of instruments to be used in a household or in a
state. And so we see that there is a natural art of acquisition
which is practised by managers of households and by statesmen, and what is the reason of this.

9 There is another variety of the art of acquisition which
is commonly and rightly called an art of wealth-getting, 40
and has in fact suggested the notion that riches and property have no limit. Being nearly connected with the pre- **1257ᵃ**
ceding, it is often identified with it. But though they are
not very different, neither are they the same. The kind already described is given by nature, the other is gained by
experience and art.

Let us begin our discussion of the question with the
following considerations: 5
Of everything which we possess there are two uses: both
belong to the thing as such, but not in the same manner,
for one is the proper, and the other the improper or
secondary use of it. For example, a shoe is used for wear,
and is used for exchange; both are uses of the shoe. He who 10
gives a shoe in exchange for money or food to him who
wants one, does indeed use the shoe as a shoe, but this is
not its proper or primary purpose, for a shoe is not made to
be an object of barter. The same may be said of all possessions, for the art of exchange extends to all of them, and 15
it arises at first from what is natural, from the circumstance

that some have too little, others too much. Hence we may
infer that retail trade is not a natural part of the art of
getting wealth; had it been so, men would have ceased to
exchange when they had enough. In the first community,
20 indeed, which is the family, this art is obviously of no use,
but it begins to be useful when the society increases. For
the members of the family originally had all things in common; later, when the family divided into parts, the parts
shared in many things, and different parts in different
things, which they had to give in exchange for what they
25 wanted, a kind of barter which is still practised among
barbarous nations who exchange with one another the
necessaries of life and nothing more; giving and receiving
wine, for example, in exchange for corn, and the like.
This sort of barter is not part of the wealth-getting art and
30 is not contrary to nature, but is needed for the satisfaction
of men's natural wants. The other or more complex form
of exchange grew, as might have been inferred, out of the
simpler. When the inhabitants of one country became
more dependent on those of another, and they imported
what they needed, and exported what they had too much
35 of, money necessarily came into use. For the various necessaries of life are not easily carried about, and hence men
agreed to employ in their dealings with each other something which was intrinsically useful and easily applicable
to the purposes of life, for example, iron, silver, and the like.
Of this the value was at first measured simply by size and
40 weight, but in process of time they put a stamp upon it, to
save the trouble of weighing and to mark the value.
1257ᵇ   When the use of coin had once been discovered, out of
the barter of necessary articles arose the other art of wealth-
getting, namely, retail trade; which was at first probably
a simple matter, but became more complicated as soon as
men learned by experience whence and by what exchanges
5 the greatest profit might be made. Originating in the use
of coin, the art of getting wealth is generally thought to be

chiefly concerned with it, and to be the art which produces riches and wealth; having to consider how they may
be accumulated. Indeed, riches is assumed by many to be
only a quantity of coin, because the arts of getting wealth
and retail trade are concerned with coin. Others maintain 10
that coined money is a mere sham, a thing not natural, but
conventional only, because, if the users substitute another
commodity for it, it is worthless, and because it is not useful
as a means to any of the necessities of life, and, indeed, he
who is rich in coin may often be in want of necessary food.
But how can that be wealth of which a man may have a
great abundance and yet perish with hunger, like Midas in 15
the fable, whose insatiable prayer turned everything that
was set before him into gold?

Hence men seek after a better notion of riches and of
the art of getting wealth than the mere acquisition of coin,
and they are right. For natural riches and the natural art of
wealth-getting are a different thing; in their true form they
are part of the management of a household; whereas retail 20
trade is the art of producing wealth, not in every way, but
by exchange. And it is thought to be concerned with coin;
for coin is the unit of exchange and the measure or limit of
it. And there is no bound to the riches which spring from
this art of wealth-getting.[20] As in the art of medicine there
is no limit to the pursuit of health, and as in the other arts 25
there is no limit to the pursuit of their several ends, for they
aim at accomplishing their ends to the uttermost (but of
the means there is a limit, for the end is always the limit),
so, too, in this art of wealth-getting there is no limit of the
end, which is riches of the spurious kind, and the acquisition of wealth. But the art of wealth-getting which consists 30
in household management, on the other hand, has a limit;
the unlimited acquisition of wealth is not its business.
And, therefore, in one point of view, all riches must have a
limit; nevertheless, as a matter of fact, we find the opposite

[20] Cp. 1256^b 32.

to be the case; for all getters of wealth increase their hoard of coin without limit. The source of the confusion is the near connexion between the two kinds of wealth-getting; 35 in either, the instrument is the same, although the use is different, and so they pass into one another; for each is a use of the same property, but with a difference: accumulation is the end in the one case, but there is a further end in the other. Hence some persons are led to believe that getting wealth is the object of household management, and the whole idea of their lives is that they ought either to in-40 crease their money without limit, or at any rate not to lose it. The origin of this disposition in men is that they are intent upon living only, and not upon living well; and, as 1258ª their desires are unlimited, they also desire that the means of gratifying them should be without limit. Those who do 5 aim at a good life seek the means of obtaining bodily pleasures; and, since the enjoyment of these appears to depend on property, they are absorbed in getting wealth: and so there arises the second species of wealth-getting. For, as their enjoyment is in excess, they seek an art which produces the excess of enjoyment; and, if they are not able to supply their pleasures by the art of getting wealth, they try 10 other arts, using in turn every faculty in a manner contrary to nature. The quality of courage, for example, is not intended to make wealth, but to inspire confidence; neither is this the aim of the general's or of the physician's art; but the one aims at victory and the other at health. Nevertheless, some men turn every quality or art into a means of getting wealth; this they conceive to be the end, and to the promotion of the end they think all things must contribute.

Thus, then, we have considered the art of wealth-getting 15 which is unnecessary, and why men want it; and also the necessary art of wealth-getting, which we have seen to be different from the other, and to be a natural part of the art of managing a household, concerned with the provision of food, not, however, like the former kind, unlimited, but having a limit.

10　And we have found the answer to our original question,[21] Whether the art of getting wealth is the business of the manager of a household and of the statesman 20
or not their business?—viz. that wealth is presupposed by
them. For as political science does not make men, but
takes them from nature and uses them, so too nature provides them with earth or sea or the like as a source of food.
At this stage begins the duty of the manager of a household, who has to order the things which nature supplies;— 25
he may be compared to the weaver who has not to make
but to use wool, and to know, too, what sort of wool is
good and serviceable or bad and unserviceable. Were this
otherwise, it would be difficult to see why the art of getting
wealth is a part of the management of a household and the
art of medicine not; for surely the members of a household
must have health just as they must have life or any other 30
necessary. The answer is that as from one point of view the
master of the house and the ruler of the state have to consider about health, from another point of view not they but
the physician; so in one way the art of household management, in another way the subordinate art, has to consider
about wealth. But, strictly speaking, as I have already said,
the means of life must be provided beforehand by nature;
for the business of nature is to furnish food to that which is 35
born; and the food of the offspring is always what remains
over of that from which it is produced.[22] Wherefore the
art of getting wealth out of fruits and animals is always
natural.

There are two sorts of wealth-getting, as I have said [23];
one is a part of household management, the other is retail
trade: the former necessary and honourable, while that
which consists in exchange is justly censured; for it is un- 40
natural, and a mode by which men gain from one another. **1258ᵇ**
The most hated sort, and with the greatest reason, is usury,

---

[21] 1256ᵃ 3.
[22] Cp. 1256ᵇ 10.
[23] 1256ᵃ 15–1258ᵃ 18.

which makes a gain out of money itself, and not from the natural object of it. For money was intended to be used in exchange, but not to increase at interest. And this term in-
5 terest,[24] which means the birth of money from money, is applied to the breeding of money because the offspring resembles the parent. Wherefore of all modes of getting wealth this is the most unnatural.

11 Enough has been said about the theory of wealth-getting; we will now proceed to the practical part. The
10 discussion of such matters is not unworthy of philosophy, but to be engaged in them practically is illiberal and irksome. The useful parts of wealth-getting are, first, the knowledge of live-stock—which are most profitable, and where, and how—as, for example, what sort of horses or sheep or oxen or any other animals are most likely to give a
15 return. A man ought to know which of these pay better than others, and which pay best in particular places, for some do better in one place and some in another. Secondly, husbandry, which may be either tillage or planting, and the keeping of bees and of fish, or fowl, or of any animals which may be useful to man. These are the divisions of the
20 true or proper art of wealth-getting and come first. Of the other, which consists in exchange, the first and most important division is commerce (of which there are three kinds—the provision of a ship, the conveyance of goods, exposure for sale—these again differing as they are safer or more profitable), the second is usury, the third, service for
25 hire—of this, one kind is employed in the mechanical arts, the other in unskilled and bodily labour. There is still a third sort of wealth-getting intermediate between this and the first or natural mode which is partly natural, but is also concerned with exchange, viz. the industries that make their profit from the earth, and from things growing from
30 the earth which, although they bear no fruit, are nevertheless profitable; for example, the cutting of timber and

[24] *tokos*, lit. 'offspring'.

all mining. The art of mining, by which minerals are obtained, itself has many branches, for there are various kinds of things dug out of the earth. Of the several divisions of wealth-getting I now speak generally; a minute consideration of them might be useful in practice, but it would be tiresome to dwell upon them at greater length now.

Those occupations are most truly arts in which there is 35 the least element of chance; they are the meanest in which the body is most deteriorated, the most servile in which there is the greatest use of the body, and the most illiberal in which there is the least need of excellence.

Works have been written upon these subjects by various persons; for example, by Chares the Parian, and Apol- 40 lodorus the Lemnian, who have treated of Tillage and 1259ᵃ Planting, while others have treated of other branches; any one who cares for such matters may refer to their writings. It would be well also to collect the scattered stories of the ways in which individuals have succeeded in amassing a fortune; for all this is useful to persons who value the art of 5 getting wealth. There is the anecdote of Thales the Milesian and his financial device, which involves a principle of universal application, but is attributed to him on account of his reputation for wisdom. He was reproached for his poverty, which was supposed to show that philosophy was 10 of no use. According to the story, he knew by his skill in the stars while it was yet winter that there would be a great harvest of olives in the coming year; so, having a little money, he gave deposits for the use of all the olive-presses in Chios and Miletus, which he hired at a low price because no one bid against him. When the harvest-time came, and many were wanted all at once and of a sudden, he let them 15 out at any rate which he pleased, and made a quantity of money. Thus he showed the world that philosophers can easily be rich if they like, but that their ambition is of another sort. He is supposed to have given a striking proof of his wisdom, but, as I was saying, his device for getting 20 wealth is of universal application, and is nothing but the creation of a monopoly. It is an art often practised by cities when they are in want of money; they make a monopoly of provisions.

There was a man of Sicily, who, having money deposited with him, bought up all the iron from the iron mines; 25 afterwards, when the merchants from their various markets came to buy, he was the only seller, and without much increasing the price he gained 200 per cent. Which when Dionysius heard, he told him that he might take away his money, but that he must not remain at Syracuse, for he 30 thought that the man had discovered a way of making money which was injurious to his own interests. He made the same discovery as Thales; they both contrived to create a monopoly for themselves. And statesmen as well ought to know these things; for a state is often as much in want of money and of such devices for obtaining it as a household, or even more so; hence some public men devote 35 themselves entirely to finance.

12 Of household management we have seen [25] that there are three parts—one is the rule of a master over slaves, which has been discussed already,[26] another of a father, and the third of a husband. A husband and father, we saw, 40 rules over wife and children, both free, but the rule differs, the rule over his children being a royal, over his wife a constitutional rule. For although there may be exceptions 1259ᵇ to the order of nature, the male is by nature fitter for command than the female, just as the elder and full-grown is superior to the younger and more immature. But in most 5 constitutional states the citizens rule and are ruled by turns, for the idea of a constitutional state implies that the natures of the citizens are equal, and do not differ at all.[27] Nevertheless, when one rules and the other is ruled we endeavour to create a difference of outward forms and names

---

[25] 1253 ᵇ 3–11.
[26] 1253ᵇ 14–1255ᵇ 39.
[27] Cp. ii. 1261ᵃ 39, iii. 1288ᵃ 12.

and titles of respect, which may be illustrated by the saying
of Amasis about his foot-pan.[28] The relation of the male to
the female is of this kind, but there the inequality is permanent. The rule of a father over his children is royal, for 10
he rules by virtue both of love and of the respect due to
age, exercising a kind of royal power. And therefore Homer
has appropriately called Zeus 'father of Gods and men', because he is the king of them all. For a king is the natural
superior of his subjects, but he should be of the same kin
or kind with them, and such is the relation of elder and 15
younger, of father and son.

13   Thus it is clear that household management attends
more to men than to the acquisition of inanimate
things, and to human excellence more than to the excellence of property which we call wealth, and to the virtue 20
of freemen more than to the virtue of slaves. A question
may indeed be raised, whether there is any excellence at
all in a slave beyond and higher than merely instrumental
and ministerial qualities—whether he can have the virtues
of temperance, courage, justice, and the like; or whether
slaves possess only bodily and ministerial qualities. And, 25
whichever way we answer the question, a difficulty arises;
for, if they have virtue, in what will they differ from freemen? On the other hand, since they are men and share in
rational principle, it seems absurd to say that they have no
virtue. A similar question may be raised about women and
children, whether they too have virtues: ought a woman to 30
be temperate and brave and just, and is a child to be called
temperate, and intemperate, or not? So in general we may
ask about the natural ruler, and the natural subject, whether
they have the same or different virtues. For if a noble
nature is equally required in both, why should one of them 35
always rule, and the other always be ruled? Nor can we say
that this is a question of degree, for the difference between
ruler and subject is a difference of kind, which the differ-

[28] Herod. ii. 172.

ence of more and less never is. Yet how strange is the supposition that the one ought, and that the other ought not,
40 to have virtue! For if the ruler is intemperate and unjust,
1260ª how can he rule well? if the subject, how can he obey well?
If he be licentious and cowardly, he will certainly not do his duty. It is evident, therefore, that both of them must have a share of virtue, but varying as natural subjects also vary
5 among themselves. Here the very constitution of the soul has shown us the way; in it one part naturally rules, and the other is subject, and the virtue of the ruler we maintain to be different from that of the subject;—the one being the virtue of the rational, and the other of the irrational part. Now, it is obvious that the same principle applies generally, and therefore almost all things rule and are ruled according to nature. But the kind of rule differs;—the freeman rules over the slave after another manner from
10 that in which the male rules over the female, or the man over the child; although the parts of the soul are present in all of them, they are present in different degrees. For the slave has no deliberative faculty at all; the woman has, but it
15 is without authority, and the child has, but it is immature. So it must necessarily be supposed to be with the moral virtues also; all should partake of them, but only in such manner and degree as is required by each for the fulfillment of his duty. Hence the ruler ought to have moral virtue in perfection, for his function, taken absolutely, demands a master artificer, and rational principle is such an artificer; the sub-
20 jects, on the other hand, require only that measure of virtue which is proper to each of them. Clearly, then, moral virtue belongs to all of them; but the temperance of a man and of a woman, or the courage and justice of a man and of a woman, are not, as Socrates maintained,[29] the same; the courage of a man is shown in commanding, of a woman in
25 obeying. And this holds of all other virtues, as will be more clearly seen if we look at them in detail, for those who say generally that virtue consists in a good disposition of the

[29] Plato, Meno, 72 A–73 C.

soul, or in doing rightly, or the like, only deceive themselves. Far better than such definitions is their mode of
speaking, who, like Gorgias,[30] enumerate the virtues. All
classes must be deemed to have their special attributes; as
the poet says of women,

> 'Silence is a woman's glory',　　30

but this is not equally the glory of man. The child is imperfect, and therefore obviously his virtue is not relative to
himself alone, but to the perfect man and to his teacher,
and in like manner the virtue of the slave is relative to a
master. Now we determined [31] that a slave is useful for the
wants of life, and therefore he will obviously require only
so much virtue as will prevent him from failing in his duty 35
through cowardice or lack of self-control. Some one will
ask whether, if what we are saying is true, virtue will not
be required also in the artisans, for they often fail in their
work through the lack of self-control? But is there not a
great difference in the two cases? For the slave shares in his
master's life; the artisan is less closely connected with him, 40
and only attains excellence in proportion as he becomes a
slave. The meaner sort of mechanic has a special and
separate slavery; and whereas the slave exists by nature, not 1260ᵇ
so the shoemaker or other artisan. It is manifest, then,
that the master ought to be the source of such excellence in
the slave, and not a mere possessor of the art of mastership
which trains the slave in his duties.[32] Wherefore they are 5
mistaken who forbid us to converse with slaves and say
that we should employ command only,[33] for slaves stand
even more in need of admonition than children.

So much for this subject; the relations of husband and
wife, parent and child, their several virtues, what in their
intercourse with one another is good, and what is evil,
and how we may pursue the good and escape the evil, 10

[30] *Meno*, 71 E, 72 A.
[31] 1254ᵇ 16–39. Cf. 1259ᵇ 25 sq.
[32] Cp. 1255ᵇ 23, 31–35.
[33] Plato, *Laws*, vi. 777 E.

will have to be discussed when we speak of the different forms of government.[34] For, inasmuch as every family is a part of a state, and these relationships are the parts of a family, and the virtue of the part must have regard to the virtue of the whole, women and children must be trained 15 by education with an eye to the constitution,[35] if the virtues of either of them are supposed to make any difference in the virtues of the state. And they must make a difference: for the children grow up to be citizens, and half the free persons in a state are women.[36]

Of these matters, enough has been said; of what remains, 20 let us speak at another time. Regarding, then, our present inquiry as complete, we will make a new beginning. And, first, let us examine the various theories of a perfect state.

BOOK III

1274[b] 1 He who would inquire into the essence and attributes of various kinds of governments must first of all determine 'What is a state?' At present this is a disputed ques-35 tion. Some say that the state has done a certain act; others, no, not the state,[1] but the oligarchy or the tyrant. And the legislator or statesman is concerned entirely with the state; a constitution or government being an arrangement of the inhabitants of a state. But a state is composite, like any 40 other whole made up of many parts;—these are the citizens, 1275[a] who compose it. It is evident, therefore, that we must begin by asking, Who is the citizen, and what is the meaning of the term? For here again there may be a difference of opinion. He who is a citizen in a democracy will often not 5 be a citizen in an oligarchy. Leaving out of consideration those who have been made citizens, or who have obtained the name of citizen in any other accidental manner, we may say, first, that a citizen is not a citizen because he lives in

[34] The question is not actually discussed in the *Politics*.
[35] Cp. v. 1310[a] 12–36, viii. 1337[a] 11–18.
[36] Plato, *Laws*, vi. 781 A.
[1] Cp. 1276[a] 8.

a certain place, for resident aliens and slaves share in the place; nor is he a citizen who has no legal right except that of suing and being sued; for this right may be enjoyed 10 under the provisions of a treaty. Nay, resident aliens in many places do not possess even such rights completely, for they are obliged to have a patron, so that they do but imperfectly participate in citizenship, and we call them citizens only in a qualified sense, as we might apply the term to children who are too young to be on the register, 15 or to old men who have been relieved from state duties. Of these we do not say quite simply that they are citizens, but add in the one case that they are not of age, and in the other, that they are past the age, or something of that sort; 20 the precise expression is immaterial, for our meaning is clear. Similar difficulties to those which I have mentioned may be raised and answered about deprived citizens and about exiles. But the citizen whom we are seeking to define is a citizen in the strictest sense, against whom no such exception can be taken, and his special characteristic is that he shares in the administration of justice, and in offices. Now of offices some are discontinuous, and the same persons are not allowed to hold them twice, or can only hold them after a fixed interval; others have no limit of time— 25 for example, the office of dicast or ecclesiast.[2] It may, indeed, be argued that these are not magistrates at all, and that their functions give them no share in the government. But surely it is ridiculous to say that those who have the supreme power do not govern. Let us not dwell further upon this, which is a purely verbal question; what we want is a common term including both dicast and ecclesiast. Let 30 us, for the sake of distinction, call it 'indefinite office', and we will assume that those who share in such office are citizens. This is the most comprehensive definition of a citizen, and best suits all those who are generally so called.

But we must not forget that things of which the under-

___

[2] 'Dicast' = juryman and judge in one: 'ecclesiast' = member of the ecclesia or assembly of the citizens.

35 lying principles differ in kind, one of them being first,
another second, another third, have, when regarded in this
relation, nothing, or hardly anything, worth mentioning in
common. Now we see that governments differ in kind,
and that some of them are prior and that others are posterior; those which are faulty or perverted are necessarily
1275ᵇ posterior to those which are perfect. (What we mean by
perversion will be hereafter explained.[3]) The citizen then
of necessity differs under each form of government; and our
5 definition is best adapted to the citizen of a democracy;
but not necessarily to other states. For in some states the
people are not acknowledged, nor have they any regular
assembly, but only extraordinary ones; and suits are distributed by sections among the magistrates. At Lacedaemon, for instance, the Ephors determine suits about con-
10 tracts, which they distribute among themselves, while the
elders are judges of homicide, and other causes are decided
by other magistrates. A similar principle prevails at Carthage; [4] there certain magistrates decide all causes. We may,
indeed, modify our definition of the citizen so as to include
these states. In them it is the holder of a definite, not of
15 an indefinite office, who legislates and judges, and to some
or all such holders of definite offices is reserved the right of
deliberating or judging about some things or about all
things. The conception of the citizen now begins to clear
up.

He who has the power to take part in the deliberative or
judicial administration of any state is said by us to be a
20 citizen of that state; and, speaking generally, a state is a
body of citizens sufficing for the purposes of life.

2   But in practice a citizen is defined to be one of whom
both the parents are citizens; other insist on going
25 further back; say to two or three or more ancestors. This
is a short and practical definition; but there are some who

[3] Cp. 1279ᵃ 19.
[4] Cp. ii. 1273ᵃ 19.

raise the further question: How this third or fourth ancestor came to be a citizen? Gorgias of Leontini, partly because he was in a difficulty, partly in irony, said—'Mortars
are what is made by the mortar-makers, and the citizens of
Larissa are those who are made by the magistrates; [5] for it is
their trade to make Larissaeans.' Yet the question is really 30
simple, for, if according to the definition just given they
shared in the government, they were citizens. This is a
better definition than the other. For the words, 'born of a
father or mother who is a citizen', cannot possibly apply to
the first inhabitants or founders of a state.

There is a greater difficulty in the case of those who have
been made citizens after a revolution, as by Cleisthenes at 35
Athens after the expulsion of the tyrants, for he enrolled
in tribes many metics, both strangers and slaves. The doubt
in these cases is, not who is, but whether he who is ought 1276ᵃ
to be a citizen; and there will still be a further doubt,
whether he who ought not to be a citizen, is one in fact, for
what ought not to be is what is false. Now, there are some
who hold office, and yet ought not to hold office, whom we
describe as ruling, but ruling unjustly. And the citizen was
defined [6] by the fact of his holding some kind of rule or
office—he who holds a judicial or legislative office fulfils 5
our definition of a citizen. It is evident, therefore, that the
citizens about whom the doubt has arisen must be called
citizens

3 Whether they ought to be so or not is a question
which is bound up with the previous inquiry.[7] For a
parallel question is raised respecting the state, whether a
certain act is or is not an act of the state; for example,
in the transition from an oligarchy or a tyranny to a democracy. In such cases persons refuse to fulfil their contracts 10

---

[5] An untranslatable play upon the word *demiourgos*, which means
either 'a magistrate' or 'an artisan'.
    [6] 1275ᵃ 22 sqq.
    [7] Cp. 1274ᵇ 34.

or any other obligations, on the ground that the tyrant, and
not the state, contracted them; they argue that some constitutions are established by force, and not for the sake of
the common good. But this would apply equally to democ-
15 racies, for they too may be founded on violence, and then
the acts of the democracy will be neither more nor less acts
of the state in question than those of an oligarchy or of a
tyranny. This question runs up into another:—on what
principle shall we ever say that the state is the same, or
different? It would be a very superficial view which considered only the place and the inhabitants (for the soil and
the population may be separated, and some of the inhabit-
20 ants may live in one place and some in another). This,
however, is not a very serious difficulty; we need only remark that the word 'state' is ambiguous.[8]

It is further asked: When are men, living in the same
25 place, to be regarded as a single city—what is the limit?
Certainly not the wall of the city, for you might surround
all Peloponnesus with a wall. Like this, we may say, is
Babylon,[9] and every city that has the compass of a nation
rather than a city; Babylon, they say, had been taken for
three days before some part of the inhabitants became
30 aware of the fact. This difficulty may, however, with advantage be deferred [10] to another occasion; the statesman has
to consider the size of the state, and whether it should consist of more than one nation or not.

Again, shall we say that while the race of inhabitants,
35 as well as their place of abode, remain the same, the city
is also the same, although the citizens are always dying and
being born, as we call rivers and fountains the same, although the water is always flowing away and coming again?
Or shall we say that the generations of men, like the rivers,
40 are the same, but that the state changes? For, since the state

---

[8] i. e. *Polis* means both 'state' and 'city'.
[9] Cp. ii. 1265[a] 14.
[10] The size of the state is discussed in vii. 1326[a] 8–1327[a] 3; the
question whether it should consist of more than one nation is barely
touched upon, in v. 1303[a] 25–[b] 3.

is a partnership, and is a partnership of citizens in a consti- **1276ᵇ**
tution, when the form of the government changes, and becomes different, then it may be supposed that the state is
no longer the same, just as a tragic differs from a comic
chorus, although the members of both may be identical. 5
And in this manner we speak of every union or composition
of elements as different when the form of their composition
alters; for example, a scale containing the same sounds is
said to be different, accordingly as the Dorian or the Phryg-
ian mode is employed. And if this is true it is evident that 10
the sameness of the state consists chiefly in the sameness of
the constitution, and it may be called or not called by the
same name, whether the inhabitants are the same or entirely different. It is quite another question, whether a state
ought or ought not to fulfil engagements when the form of 15
government changes.

4 There is a point nearly allied to the preceding:
Whether the virtue of a good man and a good citizen
is the same or not.[11] But, before entering on this discussion, we must certainly first obtain some general notion of 20
the virtue of the citizen. Like the sailor, the citizen is a
member of a community. Now, sailors have different functions, for one of them is a rower, another a pilot, and a
third a look-out man, a fourth is described by some similar
term; and while the precise definition of each individual's 25
virtue applies exclusively to him, there is, at the same time,
a common definition applicable to them all. For they have
all of them a common object, which is safety in navigation.
Similarly, one citizen differs from another, but the salvation
of the community is the common business of them all. This
community is the constitution; the virtue of the citizen 30
must therefore be relative to the constitution of which he
is a member. If, then, there are many forms of government,
it is evident that there is not one single virtue of the good
citizen which is perfect virtue. But we say that the good

[11] Cp. *N. Eth.* v. 1130ᵇ 28.

man is he who has one single virtue which is perfect virtue.
Hence it is evident that the good citizen need not of neces-
35 sity possess the virtue which makes a good man.

The same question may also be approached by another
road, from a consideration of the best constitution. If the
state cannot be entirely composed of good men, and yet
40 each citizen is expected to do his own business well, and
1277ᵃ must therefore have virtue, still, inasmuch as all the citizens
cannot be alike, the virtue of the citizen and of the good
man cannot coincide. All must have the virtue of the good
citizen—thus, and thus only, can the state be perfect; but
they will not have the virtue of a good man, unless we assume that in the good state all the citizens must be good.

5 Again, the state, as composed of unlikes, may be compared to the living being: as the first elements into which a
living being is resolved are soul and body, as soul is made up
of rational principle and appetite, the family of husband
and wife, property of master and slave, so of all these, as
well as other dissimilar elements, the state is composed;
10 and, therefore, the virtue of all the citizens cannot possibly
be the same, any more than the excellence of the leader
of a chorus is the same as that of the performer who stands
by his side. I have said enough to show why the two kinds
of virtue cannot be absolutely and always the same.

But will there then be no case in which the virtue of the
15 good citizen and the virtue of the good man coincide? To
this we answer that the good ruler is a good and wise man,
and that he who would be a statesman must be a wise man.
And some persons say that even the education of the ruler
should be of a special kind; for are not the children of kings
instructed in riding and military exercises? As Euripides
says:

'No subtle arts for me, but what the state requires.'

As though there were a special education needed by a ruler.
If then the virtue of a good ruler is the same as that of a

good man, and we assume further that the subject is a 20 citizen as well as the ruler, the virtue of the good citizen and the virtue of the good man cannot be absolutely the same, although in some cases they may; for the virtue of a ruler differs from that of a citizen. It was the sense of this difference which made Jason say that 'he felt hungry when he was not a tyrant', meaning that he could not endure to live in a private station. But, on the other hand, it may be argued that men are praised for knowing both how to rule 25 and how to obey, and he is said to be a citizen of approved virtue who is able to do both. Now if we suppose the virtue of a good man to be that which rules, and the virtue of the citizen to include ruling and obeying, it cannot be said that they are equally worthy of praise. Since, then, it is sometimes thought that the ruler and the ruled must learn 30 different things and not the same, but that the citizen must know and share in them both, the inference is obvious. There is, indeed, the rule of a master, which is concerned with menial offices [12]—the master need not know how to perform these, but may employ others in the execution of them: the other would be degrading; and by the other I 35 mean the power actually to do menial duties, which vary much in character and are executed by various classes of slaves, such, for example, as handicraftsmen, who, as their name signifies, live by the labour of their hands:—under these the mechanic is included. Hence in ancient times, 1277ᵇ and among some nations, the working classes had no share in the government—a privilege which they only acquired under the extreme democracy. Certainly the good man and the statesman and the good citizen ought not to learn the crafts of inferiors except for their own occasional use; [13] if they habitually practise them, there will cease to be a dis- 5 tinction between master and slave.

This is not the rule of which we are speaking; but there is

[12] Cp. i. 1255ᵇ 20–37.
[13] Cp. viii. 1337ᵇ 15.

a rule of another kind, which is exercised over freemen and
equals by birth—a constitutional rule, which the ruler must
10 learn by obeying, as he would learn the duties of a general
of cavalry by being under the orders of a general of cavalry,
or the duties of a general of infantry by being under the
orders of a general of infantry, and by having had the command of a regiment and of a company. It has been well said
that 'he who has never learned to obey cannot be a good
commander'. The two are not the same, but the good
citizen ought to be capable of both; he should know how
15 to govern like a freeman, and how to obey like a freeman—
these are the virtues of a citizen. And, although the temperance and justice of a ruler are distinct from those of a subject, the virtue of a good man will include both; for the
virtue of the good man who is free and also a subject,
e. g. his justice, will not be one but will comprise distinct
kinds, the one qualifying him to rule, the other to obey,
20 and differing as the temperance and courage of men and
women differ.[14] For a man would be thought a coward if
he had no more courage than a courageous woman, and a
woman would be thought loquacious if she imposed no
more restraint on her conversation than the good man; and
indeed their part in the management of the household is
25 different, for the duty of the one is to acquire, and of the
other to preserve. Practical wisdom only is characteristic of
the ruler: [15] it would seem that all other virtues must
equally belong to ruler and subject. The virtue of the subject is certainly not wisdom, but only true opinion; he may
be compared to the maker of the flute, while his master is
the flute-player or user of the flute.[16]

30   From these considerations may be gathered the answer
to the question, whether the virtue of the good man is the
same as that of the good citizen, or different, and how far
the same, and how far different.[17]

[14] Cp. i. 1260^a 20.
[15] Cp. Rep. iv. 428.
[16] Cp. Rep. x. 601 D, E.
[17] Cp. 1278^a 40, 1288^a 39, iv. 1293^b 5, vii. 1333^a 11.

5   There still remains one more question about the citizen: Is he only a true citizen who has a share of office, 35 or is the mechanic to be included? If they who hold no office are to be deemed citizens, not every citizen can have this virtue of ruling and obeying; for this man is a citizen. And if none of the lower class are citizens, in which part of the state are they to be placed? For they are not resident aliens, and they are not foreigners. May we not reply, that **1278ᵃ** as far as this objection goes there is no more absurdity in excluding them than in excluding slaves and freedmen from any of the above-mentioned classes? It must be admitted that we cannot consider all those to be citizens who are necessary to the existence of the state; for example, children are not citizens equally with grown-up men, who are citizens absolutely, but children, not being grown up, 5 are only citizens on a certain assumption.[18] Nay, in ancient times, and among some nations, the artisan class were slaves or foreigners, and therefore the majority of them are so now. The best form of state will not admit them to citizenship; but if they are admitted, then our definition of the virtue of a citizen will not apply to every citizen, nor to every free man as such, but only to those who are freed from necessary services. The necessary people are either 10 slaves who minister to the wants of individuals, or mechanics and labourers who are the servants of the community. These reflections carried a little further will explain their position; and indeed what has been said already [19] is of itself, when understood, explanation enough.

Since there are many forms of government there must be many varieties of citizens, and especially of citizens who are 15 subjects; so that under some governments the mechanic and the labourer will be citizens, but not in others, as, for example, in aristocracy or the so-called government of the best (if there be such an one), in which honours are given according to virtue and merit; for no man can practise 20

---

[18] sc. that they grow up to be men.
[19] 1275ᵃ 38 sqq.

virtue who is living the life of a mechanic or labourer. In oligarchies the qualification for office is high, and therefore no labourer can ever be a citizen; but a mechanic may, for an actual majority of them are rich. At Thebes [20] there was
25 a law that no man could hold office who had not retired from business for ten years. But in many states the law goes to the length of admitting aliens; for in some democracies a man is a citizen though his mother only be a citizen; and a similar principle is applied to illegitimate children; the law is relaxed when there is a dearth of population. But
30 when the number of citizens increases, first the children of a male or a female slave are excluded; then those whose mothers only are citizens; and at last the right of citizenship is confined to those whose fathers and mothers are both citizens.

Hence, as is evident, there are different kinds of citizens;
35 and he is a citizen in the highest sense who shares in the honours of the state. Compare Homer's words 'like some dishonoured stranger'; [21] he who is excluded from the honours of the state is no better than an alien. But when this exclusion is concealed, then the object is that the privileged class may deceive their fellow inhabitants.

As to the question whether the virtue of the good man
40 is the same as that of the good citizen, the considerations
1278ᵇ already adduced prove that in some states the good man and the good citizen are the same, and in others different. When they are the same it is not every citizen who is a good
5 man, but only the statesman and those who have or may have, alone or in conjunction with others, the conduct of public affairs.

6 Having determined these questions, we have next to consider whether there is only one form of government or many, and if many, what they are, and how many, and what are the differences between them.

²⁰ Cp. vi. 1321ᵃ 28.
²¹ Achilles complains of Agamemnon's so treating him, Il. ix. 648, xvi. 59.

A constitution is the arrangement of magistracies in a 10 state,[22] especially of the highest of all. The government is everywhere sovereign in the state, and the constitution is in fact the government. For example, in democracies the people are supreme, but in oligarchies, the few; and, therefore, we say that these two forms of government also are different: and so in other cases.

First, let us consider what is the purpose of a state, and 15 how many forms of government there are by which human society is regulated. We have already said, in the first part of this treatise,[23] when discussing household management and the rule of a master, that man is by nature a political 20 animal. And therefore, men, even when they do not require one another's help, desire to live together; not but that they are also brought together by their common interests in proportion as they severally attain to any measure of well-being. This is certainly the chief end, both of individuals and of states. And also for the sake of mere life 25 (in which there is possibly some noble element so long as the evils of existence do not greatly overbalance the good) mankind meet together and maintain the political community. And we all see that men cling to life even at the cost of enduring great misfortune, seeming to find in life a natural sweetness and happiness.

There is no difficulty in distinguishing the various kinds 30 of authority; they have been often defined already in discussions outside the school. The rule of a master, although the slave by nature and the master by nature have in reality the same interests, is nevertheless exercised primarily with a 35 view to the interest of the master, but accidentally considers the slave, since, if the slave perish, the rule of the master perishes with him. On the other hand, the government of a wife and children and of a household, which we have called household management, is exercised in the first instance for the good of the governed or for the common

[22] Cp. 1274^b 38, iv. 1289^a 15.
[23] Cp. i. 1253^a 2.

40 good of both parties, but essentially for the good of the
governed, as we see to be the case in medicine, gymnastic,
1279ᵃ and the arts in general, which are only accidentally concerned with the good of the artists themselves.[24] For there
is no reason why the trainer may not sometimes practise
gymnastics, and the helmsman is always one of the crew.
The trainer or the helmsman considers the good of those
committed to his care. But, when he is one of the persons
5 taken care of, he accidentally participates in the advantage,
for the helmsman is also a sailor, and the trainer becomes
one of those in training. And so in politics: when the state
is framed upon the principle of equality and likeness, the
citizens think that they ought to hold office by turns.
10 Formerly, as is natural, every one would take his turn of
service; and then again, somebody else would look after his
interest, just as he, while in office, had looked after theirs.[25]
But nowadays, for the sake of the advantage which is to be
gained from the public revenues and from office, men want
to be always in office. One might imagine that the rulers,
being sickly, were only kept in health while they continued
15 in office; in that case we may be sure that they would be
hunting after places. The conclusion is evident: that governments which have a regard to the common interest are
constituted in accordance with strict principles of justice,
and are therefore true forms; but those which regard only
20 the interest of the rulers are all defective and perverted
forms, for they are despotic, whereas a state is a community
of freemen.

7   Having determined these points, we have next to consider how many forms of government there are, and
what they are; and in the first place what are the true forms,
for when they are determined the perversions of them will
25 at once be apparent. The words constitution and government have the 'same meaning, and the government, which

[24] Cp. Pl. Rep. i. 341 D.
[25] Cp. ii. 1261ᵃ 37–ᵇ 6.

is the supreme authority in states, must be in the hands of one, or of a few, or of the many. The true forms of government, therefore, are those in which the one, or the few, or the many, govern with a view to the common interest; but governments which rule with a view to the private interest, 30 whether of the one, or of the few, or of the many, are perversions.[26] For the members of a state, if they are truly citizens, ought to participate in its advantages. Of forms of government in which one rules, we call that which regards the common interests, kingship or royalty; that in which more than one, but not many, rule, aristocracy; and it is so 35 called, either because the rulers are the best men, or because they have at heart the best interests of the state and of the citizens. But when the citizens at large administer the state for the common interest, the government is called by the generic name—a constitution. And there is a reason for this use of language. One man or a few may excel in 40 virtue; but as the number increases it becomes more diffi- **1279ᵇ** cult for them to attain perfection in every kind of virtue, though they may in military virtue, for this is found in the masses. Hence in a constitutional government the fighting-men have the supreme power, and those who possess arms are the citizens.

Of the above-mentioned forms, the perversions are as follows:—of royalty, tyranny; of aristocracy, oligarchy; of 5 constitutional government, democracy. For tyranny is a kind of monarchy which has in view the interest of the monarch only; oligarchy has in view the interest of the wealthy; democracy, of the needy: none of them the com- 10 mon good of all.

8 But there are difficulties about these forms of government, and it will therefore be necessary to state a little more at length the nature of each of them. For he who would make a philosophical study of the various sciences,

[26] Cp. N. *Eth.* viii. 10.

15 and does not regard practice only, ought not to overlook or omit anything, but to set forth the truth in every particular. Tyranny, as I was saying, is monarchy exercising the rule of a master over the political society; oligarchy is when men of property have the government in their hands; democracy, the opposite, when the indigent, and not the men of property, are the rulers. And here arises the first of our 20 difficulties, and it relates to the distinction just drawn. For democracy is said to be the government of the many. But what if the many are men of property and have the power in their hands? In like manner oligarchy is said to be the government of the few; but what if the poor are fewer than 25 the rich, and have the power in their hands because they are stronger? In these cases the distinction which we have drawn between these different forms of government would no longer hold good.

Suppose, once more, that we add wealth to the few and poverty to the many, and name the governments accordingly—an oligarchy is said to be that in which the few and 30 the wealthy, and a democracy that in which the many and the poor are the rulers—there will still be a difficulty. For, if the only forms of government are the ones already mentioned, how shall we describe those other governments also just mentioned by us, in which the rich are the more numerous and the poor are the fewer, and both govern in their respective states?

35   The argument seems to show that, whether in oligarchies or in democracies, the number of the governing body, whether the greater number, as in a democracy, or the smaller number, as in an oligarchy, is an accident due to the fact that the rich everywhere are few, and the poor numerous. But if so, there is a misapprehension of the causes of the difference between them. For the real difference be-40 tween democracy and oligarchy is poverty and wealth. 1280ᵃ Wherever men rule by reason of their wealth, whether they be few or many, that is an oligarchy, and where the poor rule, that is a democracy. But as a fact the rich are few

and the poor many; for few are well-to-do, whereas freedom is enjoyed by all, and wealth and freedom are the grounds on which the oligarchical and democratical parties respec- 5 tively claim power in the state.

9 Let us begin by considering the common definitions of oligarchy and democracy, and what is justice oligarchical and democratical. For all men cling to justice of some kind, but their conceptions are imperfect and they 10 do not express the whole idea. For example, justice is thought by them to be, and is, equality, not, however, for all, but only for equals. And inequality is thought to be, and is, justice; neither is this for all, but only for unequals. When the persons are omitted, then men judge errone- ously. The reason is that they are passing judgement on themselves, and most people are bad judges in their own 15 case. And whereas justice implies a relation to persons as well as to things, and a just distribution, as I have already said in the *Ethics*,[27] implies the same ratio between the per- sons and between the things, they agree about the equality of the things, but dispute about the equality of the persons, chiefly for the reason which I have just given—because they 20 are bad judges in their own affairs; and secondly, because both the parties to the argument are speaking of a limited and partial justice, but imagine themselves to be speak- ing of absolute justice. For the one party, if they are unequal in one respect, for example wealth, consider themselves to be unequal in all; and the other party, if they are equal in one respect, for example free birth, con- sider themselves to be equal in all. But they leave out the 25 capital point. For if men met and associated out of regard to wealth only, their share in the state would be propor- tioned to their property, and the oligarchical doctrine would then seem to carry the day. It would not be just that he who paid one mina should have the same share of a hundred minae, whether of the principal or of the

[27] v. 1131ᵃ 15.

30 profits, as he who paid the remaining ninety-nine. But a
state exists for the sake of a good life, and not for the sake
of life only: if life only were the object, slaves and brute
animals might form a state, but they cannot, for they have
35 no share in happiness or in a life of free choice. Nor does
a state exist for the sake of alliance and security from injustice, nor yet for the sake of exchange and mutual intercourse; for then the Tyrrhenians and the Carthaginians, and
all who have commercial treaties with one another,[28] would
be the citizens of one state. True, they have agreements
40 about imports, and engagements that they will do no wrong
1280[b] to one another, and written articles of alliance. But there
are no magistracies common to the contracting parties who
will enforce their engagements; different states have each
their own magistracies. Nor does one state take care that
the citizens of the other are such as they ought to be,
nor see that those who come under the terms of the treaty
do no wrong or wickedness at all, but only that they do no
5 injustice to one another. Whereas, those who care for good
government take into consideration virtue and vice in
states. Whence it may be further inferred that virtue must
be the care of a state which is truly so called, and not merely
enjoys the name: for without this end the community becomes a mere alliance which differs only in place from
alliances of which the members live apart; and law is
10 only a convention, 'a surety to one another of justice,' as
the sophist Lycophron says, and has no real power to make
the citizens good and just.

This is obvious; for suppose distinct places, such as
Corinth and Megara, to be brought together so that their
walls touched, still they would not be one city, not even if
15 the citizens had the right to intermarry, which is one of
the rights peculiarly characteristic of states. Again, if men
dwelt at a distance from one another, but not so far off as
to have no intercourse, and there were laws among them

[28] Cp. 1275[a] 10.

that they should not wrong each other in their exchanges, neither would this be a state. Let us suppose that one 20 man is a carpenter, another a husbandman, another a shoe-maker, and so on, and that their number is ten thousand: nevertheless, if they have nothing in common but exchange, alliance, and the like, that would not constitute a 25 state. Why is this? Surely not because they are at a distance from one another: for even supposing that such a community were to meet in one place, but that each man had a house of his own, which was in a manner his state, and that they made alliance with one another, but only against evil-doers; still an accurate thinker would not deem this to be a state, if their intercourse with one another was of the 30 same character after as before their union. It is clear then that a state is not a mere society, having a common place, established for the prevention of mutual crime and for the sake of exchange.[29] These are conditions without which a state cannot exist; but all of them together do not constitute a state, which is a community of families and aggregations of families in well-being, for the sake of a perfect and self-sufficing life. Such a community can only be estab- 35 lished among those who live in the same place and inter-marry. Hence arise in cities family connexions, brotherhoods, common sacrifices, amusements which draw men together. But these are created by friendship, for the will to live together is friendship. The end of the state is the good life, and these are the means towards it. And the state is 40 the union of families and villages in a perfect and self-sufficing life, by which we mean a happy and honourable 1281ᵃ life.[30]

Our conclusion, then, is that political society exists for the sake of noble actions, and not of mere companionship. Hence they who contribute most to such a society have a greater share in it than those who have the same 5

[29] Cp. *Protag.* 322 в.
[30] Cp. i. 1252ᵇ 27; *N. Eth.* i. 1097ᵇ 6.

or a greater freedom or nobility of birth but are inferior to them in political virtue; or than those who exceed them in wealth but are surpassed by them in virtue.

From what has been said it will be clearly seen that all the partisans of different forms of government speak of a
10 part of justice only.

10 There is also a doubt as to what is to be the supreme power in the state:—Is it the multitude? Or the wealthy? Or the good? Or the one best man? Or a tyrant? Any of these alternatives seems to involve disagreeable consequences. If the poor, for example, because they are more in number, divide among themselves the property of the rich—is not this unjust? No, by heaven (will be the reply),
15 for the supreme authority justly willed it. But if this is not injustice, pray what is? Again, when in the first division all has been taken, and the majority divide anew the property of the minority, is it not evident, if this goes on, that they will ruin the state? Yet surely, virtue is not the ruin of those who possess her, nor is justice destructive of a state; and therefore this law of confiscation clearly cannot be just.
20 If it were, all the acts of a tyrant must of necessity be just; for he only coerces other men by superior power, just as the multitude coerce the rich. But is it just then that the
25 few and the wealthy should be the rulers? And what if they, in like manner, rob and plunder the people—is this just? If so, the other case will likewise be just. But there can be no doubt that all these things are wrong and unjust.

Then ought the good to rule and have supreme power?
30 But in that case everybody else, being excluded from power, will be dishonoured. For the offices of a state are posts of honour; and if one set of men always hold them, the rest must be deprived of them. Then will it be well that the one best man should rule? Nay, that is still more oligarchical, for the number of those who are dishonoured is thereby increased. Some one may say that it is bad in any
35 case for a man, subject as he is to all the accidents of human

passion, to have the supreme power, rather than the law. But what if the law itself be democratical or oligarchical, how will that help us out of our difficulties? [31] Not at all; the same consequences [32] will follow.

11 Most of these questions may be reserved for another occasion.[33] The principle that the multitude ought to 40 be supreme rather than the few best is one that is maintained, and, though not free from difficulty, yet seems to contain an element of truth. For the many, of whom each **1281**[b] individual is but an ordinary person, when they meet together may very likely be better than the few good, if regarded not individually but collectively, just as a feast to which many contribute is better than a dinner provided out of a single purse. For each individual among the many has a share of virtue and prudence, and when they meet 5 together, they become in a manner one man, who has many feet, and hands, and senses; that is a figure of their mind and disposition. Hence the many are better judges than a single man of music and poetry; for some understand one part, and some another, and among them they understand 10 the whole. There is a similar combination of qualities in good men, who differ from any individual of the many, as the beautiful are said to differ from those who are not beautiful, and works of art from realities, because in them the scattered elements are combined, although, if taken separately, the eye of one person or some other feature in another person would be fairer than in the picture. 15 Whether this principle can apply to every democracy, and to all bodies of men, is not clear. Or rather, by heaven, in some cases it is impossible of application; for the argument would equally hold about brutes; and wherein, it will be asked, do some men differ from brutes? But there may 20 be bodies of men about whom our statement is nevertheless

[31] Cp. 1282[b] 6.
[32] Cp. ll. 11–34.
[33] cc. 12–17, iv., vi.

true. And if so, the difficulty which has been already
raised,[34] and also another which is akin to it—viz. what
power should be assigned to the mass of freemen and
25 citizens, who are not rich and have no personal merit—
are both solved. There is still a danger in allowing them to
share the great offices of state, for their folly will lead them
into error, and their dishonesty into crime. But there is a
danger also in not letting them share, for a state in which
30 many poor men are excluded from office will necessarily be
full of enemies. The only way of escape is to assign to them
some deliberative and judicial functions. For this reason
Solon [35] and certain other legislators give them the power
of electing to offices, and of calling the magistrates to account, but they do not allow them to hold office singly.
When they meet together their perceptions are quite good
35 enough, and combined with the better class they are useful
to the state (just as impure food when mixed with what
is pure sometimes makes the entire mass more wholesome
than a small quantity of the pure would be), but each
individual, left to himself, forms an imperfect judgement.
On the other hand, the popular form of government involves certain difficulties. In the first place, it might be
40 objected that he who can judge of the healing of a sick
man would be one who could himself heal his disease, and
make him whole—that is, in other words, the physician;
1282ª and so in all professions and arts. As, then, the physician
ought to be called to account by physicians, so ought men
in general to be called to account by their peers. But
physicians are of three kinds:—there is the ordinary practi-
tioner, and there is the physician of the higher class, and
thirdly the intelligent man who has studied the art: in all
arts there is such a class; and we attribute the power of
5 judging to them quite as much as to professors of the art.
Secondly, does not the same principle apply to elections?
For a right election can only be made by those who have

[34] c. 10.
[35] Cp. ii. 1274ª 15.

knowledge; those who know geometry, for example, will choose a geometrician rightly, and those who know how to steer, a pilot; and, even if there be some occupations and arts in which private persons share in the ability to choose, they certainly cannot choose better than those who know. So that, according to this argument, neither the election of magistrates, nor the calling of them to account, should be entrusted to the many. Yet possibly these objections are to a great extent met by our old answer,[36] that if the people are not utterly degraded, although individually they may be worse judges than those who have special knowledge—as a body they are as good or better. Moreover, there are some arts whose products are not judged of solely, or best, by the artists themselves, namely those arts whose products are recognized even by those who do not possess the art; for example, the knowledge of the house is not limited to the builder only; the user, or, in other words, the master, of the house will even be a better judge than the builder, just as the pilot will judge better of a rudder than the carpenter, and the guest will judge better of a feast than the cook.

This difficulty seems now to be sufficiently answered, but there is another akin to it. That inferior persons should have authority in greater matters than the good would appear to be a strange thing, yet the election and calling to account of the magistrates is the greatest of all. And these, as I was saying,[37] are functions which in some states are assigned to the people, for the assembly is supreme in all such matters. Yet persons of any age, and having but a small property qualification, sit in the assembly and deliberate and judge, although for the great officers of state, such as treasurers and generals, a high qualification is required. This difficulty may be solved in the same manner as the preceding, and the present practice of democracies may be really defensible. For the power does not reside in the dicast, or senator, or ecclesiast, but in the court, and the

---

[36] 1281ᵃ 40–ᵇ 21.
[37] 1281ᵇ 32.

senate, and the assembly, of which individual senators, or ecclesiasts, or dicasts, are only parts or members. And for this reason the many may claim to have a higher authority than the few; for the people, and the senate, and the courts 40 consist of many persons, and their property collectively is greater than the property of one or of a few individuals holding great offices. But enough of this.

1282ᵇ The discussion of the first question [38] shows nothing so clearly as that laws, when good, should be supreme; and that the magistrate or magistrates should regulate those 5 matters only on which the laws are unable to speak with precision owing to the difficulty of any general principle embracing all particulars.[39] But what are good laws has not yet been clearly explained; the old difficulty remains.[40] The goodness or badness, justice or injustice, of laws varies of 10 necessity with the constitutions of states. This, however, is clear, that the laws must be adapted to the constitutions. But if so, true forms of government will of necessity have just laws, and perverted forms of government will have unjust laws.

15 **12** In all sciences and arts the end is a good, and the greatest good and in the highest degree a good in the most authoritative of all [41]—this is the political science of which the good is justice, in other words, the common interest. All men think justice to be a sort of equality; and to a certain extent [42] they agree in the philosophical distinc- 20 tions which have been laid down by us about Ethics.[43] For they admit that justice is a thing and has a relation to persons, and that equals ought to have equality. But there still remains a question: equality or inequality of what? here is a difficulty which calls for political speculation.

[38] c. 10.
[39] Cp. N. Eth. v. 1137ᵇ 19.
[40] Cp. 1281ᵃ 36.
[41] Cp. i. 1252ᵃ 2; N. Eth. i. 1094ᵃ 1.
[42] Cp. 1280ᵃ 9.
[43] Cp. N. Eth. v. 3.

For very likely some persons will say that offices of state ought to be unequally distributed according to superior excellence, in whatever respect, of the citizen, although there is no other difference between him and the rest of the 25 community; for that those who differ in any one respect have different rights and claims. But, surely, if this is true, the complexion or height of a man, or any other advantage, will be a reason for his obtaining a greater share of political 30 rights. The error here lies upon the surface, and may be illustrated from the other arts and sciences. When a number of flute-players are equal in their art, there is no reason why those of them who are better born should have better flutes given to them; for they will not play any better on the flute, and the superior instrument should be reserved for him who is the superior artist. If what I am saying is still obscure, it will be made clearer as we proceed. For if there were a superior flute-player who was far inferior in 35 birth and beauty, although either of these may be a greater good than the art of flute-playing, and may excel flute-playing in a greater ratio than he excels the others in his 40 art, still he ought to have the best flutes given to him, unless the advantages of wealth and birth contribute to excel-1283ᵃ lence in flute-playing, which they do not. Moreover, upon this principle any good may be compared with any other. For if a given height may be measured against wealth and against freedom, height in general may be so measured. 5 Thus if A excels in height more than B in virtue, even if virtue in general excels height still more, all goods will be commensurable; for if a certain amount is better than some other, it is clear that some other will be equal. But since no such comparison can be made, it is evident that there is 10 good reason why in politics men do not ground their claim to office on every sort of inequality any more than in the arts. For if some be slow, and others swift, that is no reason why the one should have little and the others much; it is in gymnastic contests that such excellence is rewarded. Whereas the rival claims of candidates for office can only

15 be based on the possession of elements which enter into the composition of a state. And therefore the noble, or free-born, or rich, may with good reason claim office; for holders of offices must be freemen and tax-payers: a state can be no more composed entirely of poor men than entirely of slaves. But if wealth and freedom are necessary elements, justice and valour are equally so; [44] for without the former quali-
20 ties a state cannot exist at all, without the latter not well.

13 If the existence of the state is alone to be considered, then it would seem that all, or some at least, of these
25 claims are just; but, if we take into account a good life, then, as I have already said,[45] education and virtue have superior claims. As, however, those who are equal in one thing ought not to have an equal share in all, nor those who are unequal in one thing to have an unequal share in all, it is certain that all forms of government which rest on either of these principles are perversions. All men have
30 a claim in a certain sense, as I have already admitted,[46] but all have not an absolute claim. The rich claim because they have a greater share in the land, and land is the common element of the state; also they are generally more trust-worthy in contracts. The free claim under the same title as the noble; for they are nearly akin. For the noble are citizens in a truer sense than the ignoble, and good birth is
35 always valued in a man's own home and country.[47] Another reason is, that those who are sprung from better ancestors are likely to be better men, for nobility is excellence of race. Virtue, too, may be truly said to have a claim, for justice has been acknowledged by us to be a social [48] virtue,
40 and it implies all others.[49] Again, the many may urge their claim against the few; for, when taken collectively, and

[44] Cp. iv. 1291ᵃ 19–33.
[45] Cp. 1281ᵃ 4.
[46] 1280ᵃ 9 sqq.
[47] Cp. i. 1255ᵃ 32.
[48] Cp. i. 1253ᵃ 37.
[49] Cp. N. Eth. v. 1129ᵇ 25.

compared with the few, they are stronger and richer and **1283ᵇ** better. But, what if the good, the rich, the noble, and the other classes who make up a state, are all living together in the same city, will there, or will there not, be any doubt who shall rule?—No doubt at all in determining who ought to rule in each of the above-mentioned forms of 5 government. For states are characterized by differences in their governing bodies—one of them has a government of the rich, another of the virtuous, and so on. But a difficulty arises when all these elements coexist. How are we to decide? Suppose the virtuous to be very few in number: may 10 we consider their numbers in relation to their duties, and ask whether they are enough to administer the state, or so many as will make up a state? Objections may be urged against all the aspirants to political power. For those who 15 found their claims on wealth or family might be thought to have no basis of justice; on this principle, if any one person were richer than all the rest, it is clear that he ought to be ruler of them. In like manner he who is very distinguished by his birth ought to have the superiority over all those who claim on the ground that they are freeborn. In an aristocracy, or government of the best, a like difficulty 20 occurs about virtue; for if one citizen be better than the other members of the government, however good they may be, he too, upon the same principle of justice, should rule over them. And if the people are to be supreme because they are stronger than the few, then if one man, or more than one, but not a majority, is stronger than the many, 25 they ought to rule, and not the many.

All these considerations appear to show that none of the principles on which men claim to rule and to hold all other men in subjection to them are strictly right. To those who claim to be masters of the government on the ground 30 of their virtue or their wealth, the many might fairly answer that they themselves are often better and richer than the few—I do not say individually, but collectively. And another ingenious objection which is sometimes put forward

35 may be met in a similar manner. Some persons doubt
whether the legislator who desires to make the justest laws
ought to legislate with a view to the good of the higher
classes or of the many, when the case which we have
40 mentioned occurs.[50] Now what is just or right is to be interpreted in the sense of 'what is equal'; and that which is right
in the sense of being equal is to be considered with reference to the advantage of the state, and the common good
of the citizens. And a citizen is one who shares in governing
and being governed. He differs under different forms of
1284ᵃ government, but in the best state he is one who is able and
willing to be governed and to govern with a view to the life
of virtue.

If, however, there be some one person, or more than one,
although not enough to make up the full complement of a
state, whose virtue is so pre-eminent that the virtues or the
5 political capacity of all the rest admit of no comparison
with his or theirs, he or they can be no longer regarded as
part of a state; for justice will not be done to the superior,
if he is reckoned only as the equal of those who are so far
inferior to him in virtue and in political capacity. Such
10 an one may truly be deemed a God among men. Hence we
see that legislation is necessarily concerned only with those
who are equal in birth and in capacity; and that for men of
pre-eminent virtue there is no law—they are themselves a
law. Any one would be ridiculous who attempted to make
15 laws for them: they would probably retort what, in the
fable of Antisthenes, the lions said to the hares,[51] when in
the council of the beasts the latter began haranguing and
claiming equality for all. And for this reason democratic
20 states have instituted ostracism; equality is above all things
their aim, and therefore they ostracized and banished from
the city for a time those who seemed to predominate too
much through their wealth, or the number of their friends,
or through any other political influence. Mythology tells us

---

[50] i. e. when the many collectively are better than the few.
[51] i. e. 'where are your claws and teeth?'

that the Argonauts left Heracles behind for a similar reason; the ship Argo would not take him because she feared that 25 he would have been too much for the rest of the crew. Wherefore those who denounce tyranny and blame the counsel which Periander gave to Thrasybulus cannot be held altogether just in their censure. The story is that Periander, when the herald was sent to ask counsel of him, said nothing, but only cut off the tallest ears of corn till 30 he had brought the field to a level. The herald did not know the meaning of the action, but came and reported what he had seen to Thrasybulus, who understood that he was to cut off the principal men in the state; [52] and this is a 35 policy not only expedient for tyrants or in practice confined to them, but equally necessary in oligarchies and democracies. Ostracism [53] is a measure of the same kind, which acts by disabling and banishing the most prominent citizens. Great powers do the same to whole cities and nations, as the Athenians did to the Samians, Chians, and Lesbians; 40 no sooner had they obtained a firm grasp of the empire, 1284ᵇ than they humbled their allies contrary to treaty; and the Persian king has repeatedly crushed the Medes, Babylonians, and other nations, when their spirt has been stirred by the recollection of their former greatness.

The problem is a universal one, and equally concerns all forms of government, true as well as false; for, although perverted forms with a view to their own interests may 5 adopt this policy, those which seek the common interest do so likewise. The same thing may be observed in the arts and sciences; [54] for the painter will not allow the figure to have a foot which, however beautiful, is not in proportion, nor will the ship-builder allow the stern or any other part 10 of the vessel to be unduly large, any more than the chorusmaster will allow any one who sings louder or better than all the rest to sing in the choir. Monarchs, too, may practise

[52] Cp. v. 1311ᵃ 20.
[53] Cp. v. 1302ᵇ 18.
[54] Cp. v. 1302ᵇ 34, 1309ᵇ 21; vii. 1326ᵃ 35; *Rep.* iv. 420.

15 compulsion and still live in harmony with their cities, if
their own government is for the interest of the state. Hence
where there is an acknowledged superiority the argument
in favour of ostracism is based upon a kind of political
justice. It would certainly be better that the legislator
should from the first so order his state as to have no need
of such a remedy. But if the need arises, the next best thing
is that he should endeavour to correct the evil by this or
20 some similar measure. The principle, however, has not been
fairly applied in states; for, instead of looking to the good
of their own constitution, they have used ostracism for
factious purposes. It is true that under perverted forms of
government, and from their special point of view, such a
measure is just and expedient, but it is also clear that it
25 is not absolutely just. In the perfect state there would be
great doubts about the use of it, not when applied to
excess in strength, wealth, popularity, or the like, but when
used against some one who is pre-eminent in virtue—what
is to be done with him? Mankind will not say that such an
one is to be expelled and exiled; on the other hand, he
30 ought not to be a subject—that would be as if mankind
should claim to rule over Zeus, dividing his offices among
them. The only alternative is that all should joyfully obey
such a ruler, according to what seems to be the order of
nature, and that men like him should be kings in their
state for life.

14   The preceding discussion, by a natural transition, leads
35   to the consideration of royalty, which we admit to be
one of the true forms of government. Let us see whether
in order to be well governed a state or country should be
under the rule of a king or under some other form of government; and whether monarchy, although good for some,
40 may not be bad for others. But first we must determine
whether there is one species of royalty or many. It is easy
1285ᵃ to see that there are many, and that the manner of government is not the same in all of them.

Of royalties according to law, (1) the Lacedaemonian is thought to answer best to the true pattern; but there the royal power is not absolute, except when the kings go on an expedition, and then they take the command. Matters of 5 religion are likewise committed to them. The kingly office is in truth a kind of generalship, irresponsible and perpetual. The king has not the power of life and death, except in a specified case, as for instance, in ancient times, he had it when upon a campaign, by right of force. This custom is described in Homer. For Agamemnon is patient when he 10 is attacked in the assembly, but when the army goes out to battle he has the power even of life and death. Does he not say?—'When I find a man skulking apart from the battle, nothing shall save him from the dogs and vultures, for in my hands is death.' [55]

This, then, is one form of royalty—a generalship for life: 15 and of such royalties some are hereditary and others elective.

(2) There is another sort of monarchy not uncommon among the barbarians, which nearly resembles tyranny. But this is both legal and hereditary. For barbarians, being 20 more servile in character than Hellenes, and Asiatics than Europeans, do not rebel against a despotic government. Such royalties have the nature of tyrannies because the people are by nature slaves; [56] but there is no danger of their being overthrown, for they are hereditary and legal. Wherefore also their guards are such as a king and not such 25 as a tyrant would employ, that is to say, they are composed of citizens, whereas the guards of tyrants are mercenaries. [57] For kings rule according to law over voluntary subjects, but tyrants over involuntary; and the one are guarded by their fellow-citizens, the others are guarded against them.

These are two forms of monarchy, and there was a third 30 (3) which existed in ancient Hellas, called an Aesymnetia

---

[55] *Il.* ii. 391–393. The last clause is not found in our Homer.
[56] Cp. i. 1252^b 7.
[57] Cp. v. 1311^a 7.

or dictatorship. This may be defined generally as an elective tyranny, which, like the barbarian monarchy, is legal, but differs from it in not being hereditary. Sometimes the office 35 was held for life, sometimes for a term of years, or until certain duties had been performed. For example, the Mytilenaeans elected Pittacus leader against the exiles, who were headed by Antimenides and Alcaeus the poet. And Alcaeus himself shows in one of his banquet odes that they chose Pittacus tyrant, for he reproaches his fellow-citizens for 'having made the low-born Pittacus tyrant of **1285ᵇ** the spiritless and ill-fated city, with one voice shouting his praises'.

These forms of government have always had the character of tyrannies, because they possess despotic power; but inasmuch as they are elective and acquiesced in by their subjects, they are kingly.

(4) There is a fourth species of kingly rule—that of the heroic times—which was hereditary and legal, and was 5 exercised over willing subjects. For the first chiefs were benefactors of the people [58] in arts or arms; they either gathered them into a community, or procured land for them; and thus they became kings of voluntary subjects, and their power was inherited by their descendants. They 10 took the command in war and presided over the sacrifices, except those which required a priest. They also decided causes either with or without an oath; and when they swore, the form of the oath was the stretching out of their sceptre. In ancient times their power extended continuously to 15 all things whatsoever, in city and country, as well as in foreign parts; but at a later date they relinquished several of these privileges, and others the people took from them, until in some states nothing was left to them but the sacrifices; and where they retained more of the reality they had only the right of leadership in war beyond the border.

These, then, are the four kinds of royalty. First the 20 monarchy of the heroic ages; this was exercised over volun-

[58] Cp. v. 1310ᵇ 10.

tary subjects, but limited to certain functions; the king was
a general and a judge, and had the control of religion. The
second is that of the barbarians, which is an hereditary
despotic government in accordance with law. A third is
the power of the so-called Aesymnete or Dictator; this is
an elective tyranny. The fourth is the Lacedaemonian, 25
which is in fact a generalship, hereditary and perpetual.
These four forms differ from one another in the manner
which I have described.

(5) There is a fifth form of kingly rule in which one
has the disposal of all, just as each nation or each state has
the disposal of public matters; this form corresponds to 30
the control of a household. For as household management
is the kingly rule of a house, so kingly rule is the household
management of a city, or of a nation, or of many nations.

15 Of these forms we need only consider two, the Lacedaemonian and the absolute royalty; for most of the
others lie in a region between them, having less power than 35
the last, and more than the first. Thus the inquiry is reduced to two points: first, is it advantageous to the state
that there should be a perpetual general, and if so, should
the office be confined to one family, or open to the citizens
in turn? Secondly, is it well that a single man should have 1286ᵃ
the supreme power in all things? The first question falls
under the head of laws rather than of constitutions; for
perpetual generalship might equally exist under any form
of government, so that this matter may be dismissed for
the present.[59] The other kind of royalty is a sort of constitution; this we have now to consider, and briefly to run 5
over the difficulties involved in it. We will begin by inquiring whether it is more advantageous to be ruled by the best
man or by the best laws.[60]

The advocates of royalty maintain that the laws speak
only in general terms, and cannot provide for circum- 10

[59] It is not discussed later.
[60] Cp. Plato, *Polit.* 294 ᴀ–295 ᴄ.

stances; and that for any science to abide by written rules
is absurd. In Egypt the physician is allowed to alter his
treatment after the fourth day, but if sooner, he takes the
15 risk. Hence it is clear that a government acting according
to written laws is plainly not the best. Yet surely the ruler
cannot dispense with the general principle which exists in
law; and that is a better ruler which is free from passion
than that in which it is innate. Whereas the law is passion-
20 less, passion must ever sway the heart of man. Yes, it may
be replied, but then on the other hand an individual will
be better able to deliberate in particular cases.

The best man, then, must legislate, and laws must be
passed, but these laws will have no authority when they
25 miss the mark, though in all other cases retaining their
authority. But when the law cannot determine a point at
all, or not well, should the one best man or should all decide? According to our present practice assemblies meet, sit
in judgement, deliberate, and decide, and their judgements
all relate to individual cases. Now any member of the assembly, taken separately, is certainly inferior to the wise
man. But the state is made up of many individuals. And
as a feast to which all the guests contribute is better than
30 a banquet furnished by a single man,[61] so a multitude is a
better judge of many things than any individual.

Again, the many are more incorruptible than the few;
they are like the greater quantity of water which is less
easily corrupted than a little. The individual is liable to be
35 overcome by anger or by some other passion, and then his
judgement is necessarily perverted; but it is hardly to be
supposed that a great number of persons would all get into
a passion and go wrong at the same moment. Let us assume that they are the freemen, and that they never act
in violation of the law, but fill up the gaps which the law
is obliged to leave. Or, if such virtue is scarcely attainable
by the multitude, we need only suppose that the majority
40 are good men and good citizens, and ask which will be the

[61] Cp. 1281ᵃ 42.

more incorruptible, the one good ruler, or the many who **1286ᵇ** are all good? Will not the many? But, you will say, there may be parties among them, whereas the one man is not divided against himself. To which we may answer that their character is as good as his. If we call the rule of many 5 men, who are all of them good, aristocracy, and the rule of one man royalty, then aristocracy will be better for states than royalty, whether the government is supported by force or not,[62] provided only that a number of men equal in virtue can be found.

The first governments were kingships, probably for this reason, because of old, when cities were small, men of eminent virtue were few. Further, they were made kings be- 10 cause they were benefactors,[63] and benefits can only be bestowed by good men. But when many persons equal in merit arose, no longer enduring the pre-eminence of one, they desired to have a commonwealth, and set up a constitution. The ruling class soon deteriorated and enriched themselves out of the public treasury; riches became the path to honour, and so oligarchies naturally grew up. These 15 passed into tyrannies and tyrannies into democracies; for love of gain in the ruling classes was always tending to diminish their number, and so to strengthen the masses, who in the end set upon their masters and established democracies. Since cities have increased in size, no other form 20 of government appears to be any longer even easy to establish.[64]

Even supposing the principle to be maintained that kingly power is the best thing for states, how about the family of the king? Are his children to succeed him? If they are no better than anybody else, that will be mischievous But, says the lover of royalty, the king, though 25 he might, will not hand on his power to his children. That, however, is hardly to be expected, and is too much to

---

[62] Cp. l. 27.
[63] Cp. 1285ᵇ 6.
[64] Cp. iv. 1293ᵃ 1, 1297ᵇ 22.

ask of human nature. There is also a difficulty about the
force which he is to employ; should a king have guards
about him by whose aid he may be able to coerce the
30 refractory? if not, how will he administer his kingdom?
Even if he be the lawful sovereign who does nothing ar-
bitrarily or contrary to law, still he must have some force
wherewith to maintain the law. In the case of a limited
monarchy there is not much difficulty in answering this
35 question; the king must have such force as will be more
than a match for one or more individuals, but not so
great as that of the people. The ancients observe this principle when they have guards to any one whom they appointed dictator or tyrant. Thus, when Dionysius asked the
Syracusans to allow him guards, somebody advised that
40 they should give him only such a number.

16 At this place in the discussion there impends the in-
1287ª   quiry respecting the king who acts solely according
to his own will; he has now to be considered. The so-called
limited monarchy, or kingship according to law, as I have
already remarked,[65] is not a distinct form of government,
5 for under all governments, as, for example, in a democracy
or aristocracy, there may be a general holding office for
life, and one person is often made supreme over the administration of a state. A magistracy of this kind exists at
Epidamnus,[66] and also at Opus, but in the latter city has a
10 more limited power. Now, absolute monarchy, or the arbitrary rule of a sovereign over all the citizens, in a city
which consists of equals, is thought by some to be quite
contrary to nature; it is argued that those who are by
nature equals must have the same natural right and worth,
and that for unequals to have an equal share, or for equals
15 to have an unequal share, in the offices of state, is as bad
as for different bodily constitutions to have the same food
and clothing. Wherefore it is thought to be just that

[65] 1286ª 2.
[66] Cp. v. 1301ᵇ 21.

among equals every one be ruled as well as rule, and
therefore that all should have their turn. We thus arrive
at law; for an order of succession implies law. And the rule
of the law, it is argued, is preferable to that of any indi- 20
vidual. On the same principle, even if it be better for
certain individuals to govern, they should be made only
guardians and ministers of the law. For magistrates there
must be—this is admitted; but then men say that to give
authority to any one man when all are equal is unjust.
Nay, there may indeed be cases which the law seems unable to determine, but in such cases can a man? Nay, it 25
will be replied, the law trains officers for this express purpose, and appoints them to determine matters which are
left undecided by it, to the best of their judgement.
Further, it permits them to make any amendment of the
existing laws which experience suggests. Therefore he who
bids the law rule may be deemed to bid God and Reason
alone rule, but he who bids man rule adds an element of 30
the beast; for desire is a wild beast, and passion perverts
the minds of rulers, even when they are the best of men.
The law is reason unaffected by desire. We are told [67] that
a patient should call in a physician; he will not get better
if he is doctored out of a book. But the parallel of the arts
is clearly not in point; for the physician does nothing con- 35
trary to rule from motives of friendship; he only cures a
patient and takes a fee; whereas magistrates do many
things from spite and partiality. And, indeed, if a man
suspected the physician of being in league with his enemies
to destroy him for a bribe, he would rather have recourse 40
to the book. But certainly physicians, when they are sick,
call in other physicians, and training-masters, when they 1287ᵇ
are in training, other training-masters, as if they could not
judge truly about their own case and might be influenced
by their feelings. Hence it is evident that in seeking for
justice men seek for the mean or neutral,[68] for the law is 5

[67] Cp. 1286ᵃ 12–14, *Polit.* 296 B.
[68] Cp. *N. Eth.* v. 1132ᵃ 22.

the mean. Again, customary laws have more weight, and relate to more important matters, than written laws, and a
man may be a safer ruler than the written law, but not
safer than the customary law.

Again, it is by no means easy for one man to superintend
many things; he will have to appoint a number of subordinates, and what difference does it make whether these
10 subordinates always existed or were appointed by him be
cause he needed them? If, as I said before,[69] the good man
has a right to rule because he is better, still two good men
are better than one: this is the old saying—

'two going together',[70]

and the prayer of Agamemnon—

'would that I had ten such counsellors!' [71]

And at this day there are magistrates, for example judges,
15 who have authority to decide some matters which the law
is unable to determine, since no one doubts that the law
would command and decide in the best manner whatever
it could. But some things can, and other things cannot, be
20 comprehended under the law, and this is the origin of the
vexed question whether the best law or the best man should
rule. For matters of detail about which men deliberate
cannot be included in legislation. Nor does any one deny
that the decision of such matters must be left to man, but
it is argued that there should be many judges, and not one
25 only. For every ruler who has been trained by the law
judges well; and it would surely seem strange that a person
should see better with two eyes, or hear better with two
ears, or act better with two hands or feet, than many with
many; indeed, it is already the practice of kings to make to
themselves many eyes and ears and hands and feet. For
30 they make colleagues of those who are the friends of them-

[69] 1283^b 21, 1284^b 32.
[70] *Il*. x. 224.
[71] *Il*. ii. 372.

selves and their governments. They must be friends of the
monarch and of his government; if not his friends, they
will not do what he wants; but friendship implies likeness
and equality; and, therefore, if he thinks that his friends
ought to rule, he must think that those who are equal to
himself and like himself ought to rule equally with him- 35
self. These are the principal controversies relating to monarchy.

17 But may not all this be true in some cases and not in
others? for there is by nature both a justice and an
advantage appropriate to the rule of a master, another to
kingly rule, another to constitutional rule; but there is
none naturally appropriate to tyranny, or to any other perverted form of government; for these come into being
contrary to nature. Now, to judge at least from what has
been said, it is manifest that, where men are alike and 40
equal, it is neither expedient nor just that one man should **1288ª**
be lord of all, whether there are laws, or whether there are
no laws, but he himself is in the place of law. Neither
should a good man be lord over good men, nor a bad man
over bad; nor, even if he excels in virtue, should he have a
right to rule, unless in a particular case, at which I have
already hinted, and to which I will once more recur.[72] But 5
first of all, I must determine what natures are suited for
government by a king, and what for an aristocracy, and
what for a constitutional government.

A people who are by nature capable of producing a race
superior in the virtue needed for political rule are fitted
for kingly government; and a people submitting to be ruled 10
as freemen by men whose virtue renders them capable of
political command are adapted for an aristocracy: while
the people who are suited for constitutional freedom are
those among whom there naturally exists a warlike multitude [73] able to rule and to obey in turn by a law which

[72] 1284ª 3, and 1288ª 15.
[73] Cp. 1279ᵇ 2.

15 gives office to the well-to-do according to their desert.
But when a whole family, or some individual, happens to
be so pre-eminent in virtue as to surpass all others, then
it is just that they should be the royal family and supreme
over all, or that this one citizen should be king of the whole
20 nation. For, as I said before,[74] to give them authority is not
only agreeable to that ground of right which the founders
of all states, whether aristocratical, or oligarchical, or again
democratical, are accustomed to put forward (for these
25 all recognize the claim of excellence, although not the
same excellence), but accords with the principle already
laid down. For surely it would not be right to kill, or ostra-
cize, or exile such a person, or require that he should take
his turn in being governed. The whole is naturally superior
to the part, and he who has this pre-eminence is in the
relation of a whole to a part. But if so, the only alternative is that he should have the supreme power, and that
30 mankind should obey him, not in turn, but always. These
are the conclusions at which we arrive respecting royalty
and its various forms, and this is the answer to the question,
whether it is or is not advantageous to states, and to which,
and how.

18 We maintain [75] that the true forms of government
35   are three, and that the best must be that which is
administered by the best, and in which there is one man,
or a whole family, or many persons, excelling all the others
together in virtue, and both rulers and subjects are fitted,
the one to rule, the others to be ruled, in such a manner
as to attain the most eligible life. We showed at the com-
mencement of our inquiry [76] that the virtue of the good
man is necessarily the same as the virtue of the citizen of
the perfect state. Clearly then in the same manner, and by
40 the same means through which a man becomes truly

[74] 1283[b] 20, 1284[a] 3–17, [b]25.
[75] Cp. 1279[a] 22–[b]4.
[76] cc. 4, 5.

good, he will frame a state that is to be ruled by an aristocracy or by a king, and the same education and the 1288^{b}
same habits will be found to make a good man and a man
fit to be a statesman or king.

Having arrived at these conclusions, we must proceed
to speak of the perfect state, and describe how it comes
into being and is established.   5

Poetics

⊔⊓⊔⊓⊔⊓⊔⊓⊔⊓⊔⊓⊔⊓⊔⊓⊔⊓⊔⊓⊔⊓⊔⊓

INTRODUCTION

Poetics is the science of making, as politics is the science of doing. Neither is theoretic or a science of knowing. Yet virtues, associations, and arts have analogies with natural objects and bases in natural powers or faculties. The distinction between moral and intellectual virtues is based on the difference between two faculties of "living things," appetition and thought; the distinction between lesser, or "natural," communities and the state is based on two senses of 'living,' mere living and living well; art has its basis as a faculty in a natural human tendency to imitate and to take delight in imitations, and as an object it is an imitation of nature. Art has been encountered as a subject in the discussions of the theoretic and practical sciences. Art is adduced as a kind of cause in the definition of nature in the *Physics*, an external principle of motion and change contrasted to nature, an internal principle. The processes of nature and of art are the same. Objects of art are produced as nature would have produced them. Art imitates nature and completes nature. Art is a stage in the evolution of thought from sense-perception to wisdom, sketched in the *Metaphysics*, a step beyond experience because of the use of causes in art. Art, like prudence, is an intellectual virtue in the *Ethics*, and the arts are employed in the education of citizens in the *Politics*. Art is like virtue in its mode of acquisition, since both are produced by performing the same actions which they will in turn cause, but they differ in that virtues are judged by the state of character from which the actions proceed while art is judged by the qualities of the objects produced by the making. In the poetic science the art object is examined as a composite object, not as a nature or a substance, created of its proper parts and with its characteristic unity by the artist. The pleasure proper to art is aesthetic, not moral or practical.

The opening chapter of the *Poetics* lays out the method of the treatise. As inquiry concerning the soul was carried out by investigating the nature and operation of different faculties, so inquiry concerning poetic must investigate the various forms of poetic and their capacities (Aristotle's word *dunamis* is translated in turn 'faculty' and 'capacity') and must determine how each poetic form is well constructed and of what parts. The inquiry must take its beginning "in accordance with nature," first from those things that are first.

These preparations preliminary to focussing on one poetic form, tragedy, are completed in the first five chapters. Since the first things in a poetic inquiry are the various poetic forms, the first three chapters order arts in turn according to their means, objects, and manners of imitation. Tragedy is found to share its means of imitation with epic, comedy, and dithyrambic poetry, its object of imitation with epic, and its manner of imitation with comedy. The fourth chapter relates imitation to its basis in human nature, and traces two lines of development which take their origins from the character of individual poets (but with Homer originating in both lines) and which were to lead to tragedy and comedy. Earlier forms of making in the development of the arts are examined, as earlier theories were examined in the theoretic sciences and earlier theories and practices in the practical sciences. The brief histories of comedy and tragedy in the fourth chapter concentrate on the successive appearance of constituent parts, and the movement of tragedy terminates when it attains its "natural form." In the fifth chapter tragedy is contrasted to comedy and compared with epic. Epic and tragedy are found to have the same parts and the judgment of good and bad in tragedy and epic is referred to the same faculty or ability.

The sixth chapter begins the discussion of tragedy by gathering the definition of tragedy from the preceding discussion. Like the definition of moral virtue, it is not a "natural" definition by genus and differentia, but a dialectically assembled definition combining four aspects of imitation, as the definition of moral virtue assembles four aspects of habituation. A tragedy is the imitation (1) of an action that is serious and also, having magnitude, complete in itself; (2) in language with pleasurable accessories, each kind brought in separately in the parts of the work; (3) in a dramatic, not a narrative form; (4) with incidents arousing pity and fear, wherewith to accomplish its catharsis of such emotions. (1) The object of imitation is a serious and complete action; (2) the means is language (*logos*) with the pleasurable accessories of rhythm and melody; (3) the manner is imitation by actors, not by the words of a narrator; (4) unity is achieved by the purgation of pity and fear reflexively by pity and fear. The definition of tragedy permits the differentiation of six parts in every tragedy: plot or myth, character, and thought, arising from what is imitated; and diction (*lexis*) and melody, from that by which it is imitated; and spectacle, from how it is imitated. The myth or plot is the principle and soul of tragedy. Character comes second in importance and thought third. Diction is expression in words, which has the same power or faculty in prose and verse, melody is the most pleasurable accessory of diction, and spectacle or visible appearance, though attractive, is the least artistic and has the least to do with poetic.

The next five chapters examine the myth or the "putting together of things done," its magnitude, its unity, its use of probability and necessity, the difference between simple and complex plots, reversal and discovery (the means joining beginning and end in a complex plot) and suffering (action of a destructive or painful nature on the stage). The probability and necessity of poetry is distinct from the probability and necessity found in statements of actual occurrences or in philosophical or scientific statements. It is not the poet's task to write of things that have happened but of things that can happen, the possible, according to probability or necessity. The difference between the historian and the poet is not a difference in diction, between prose and verse (Herodotus's history in verse would still be history), but a difference between saying what has been and what might be. Poetry is more philosophical and serious than history, since its statements are of universals while those of history are singulars. Philosophy or science makes universal statements concerning necessities and probabilities of human action by consideration of the psychological or natural powers or faculties of man. Poetic statements are universal concerning what such and such a kind of man will probably or necessarily say or do. Poetry may use names of historical persons, like Alcibiades, but history consists of statements of what Alcibiades did or had done to him. After this treatment of the formative elements of tragedy, its quantitative parts, the sections or sequences into which it is divided, like the acts and scenes of modern drama, are reviewed briefly.

Once the parts have been distinguished, the questions concerning the organization or structure of the tragedy are treated as questions of "why" and "how"—what should be aimed at in the construction of the story and from what the work of tragedy comes—in the thirteenth to sixteenth chapters: the sequence of action from good to bad fortune, in single and double plots; the operation of pity and fear and the kinds of discovery relative to action. In the seventeenth chapter the structure of the plot is examined as something perceived or put before the eyes, and in the eighteenth it is examined as a sequence of parts in complication and denouement.

The sequences and interconnections which constitute the structure (*sustasis*) of things and of myths make the consideration of character an essential part of the investigation of plot, for actions follow from characters and characters are known from actions. Diction and thought are joined in like fashion in the nineteenth chapter. They have similar reflexive relations to each other which extend to character and action: thoughts are expressed in diction, and what is said reveals character, arouses emotion, and leads to action. The functions of thought are discussed in the *Rhetoric*, and therefore Aristotle adds no further treatment of thought in the *Poetics*, and the poetic aspects of diction are distinguished from other aspects proper to other disciplines such as elocution or rhetoric, the architectonic art, which treats spoken language and examines the "turns" by which an expression may be a command or a prayer, a statement or a threat, a question or an answer. A like distinction is made between propositions, which are true or false, and other sentences in the *On Interpretation*. The twentieth chapter develops a schema of eight poetic "parts of speech" (as distinct from grammatical, rhetorical, or logical parts of speech since they are the "elements" of language used in poetic "compositions") ranging from letter and syllable through noun and verb to speech (*logos*); and the twenty-first chapter concentrates on one part of speech, the noun, particularly in one of its eight uses, as a metaphor. The twenty-second chapter turns to the perfection of diction, which is to be at once clear and not mean, and to the difference between the clarity of prosaic diction and the nonprosaic uses of words in distinguished diction. The metaphor has a prominent place among these uses of words. "But the greatest thing by far is to be a master of metaphor. It is the one thing that cannot be learned from others; and it is also a sign of genius, since a good metaphor implies an intuitive perception of the similarity in dissimilars." The heroic verse of epics may use all kinds of words, but in the iambic verse of drama, which is modeled on spoken language, only those kinds of words are in place which are also allowable in talking or in oration: the ordinary word, the metaphor, and the ornamental equivalent.

After the analysis of tragedy as imitation in action has

been completed, the last four chapters of the *Poetics* are devoted to a comparison and contrast of that art with the art of imitation by narrative and in verse of the epic. Their likenesses are such that common questions may be raised about them and a common art or faculty of judgement and criticism may be developed. Their construction of plots and their use of stories are similar. They are divided into the same kinds and have the same parts. The problems and the poetic solution of those problems are similar and lead to like criticism of the poet's art, his descriptions, and his language. Since they are similar in source, matter, and form, quesions of their relative value and ends may be raised.

DE POETICA

CONTENTS

De Poetica

Poetics

Translated by Ingram Bywater

ⅎⅎⅎ

1 Our subject being Poetry, I propose to speak not only
1447ᵃ of the art in general but also of its species and their
respective capacities; of the structure of plot required for a
good poem; of the number and nature of the constituent
10 parts of a poem; and likewise of any other matters in the
same line of inquiry. Let us follow the natural order and
begin with the primary facts.

Epic poetry and Tragedy, as also Comedy, Dithyrambic
poetry, and most flute-playing and lyre-playing, are all,
15 viewed as a whole, modes of imitation. But at the same
time they differ from one another in three ways, either by
a difference of kind in their means, or by differences in
the objects, or in the manner of their imitations.

I. Just as colour and form are used as means by some,
who (whether by art or constant practice) imitate and
portray many things by their aid, and the voice is used by
20 others; so also in the above-mentioned group of arts, the
means with them as a whole are rhythm, language, and
harmony—used, however, either singly or in certain combinations. A combination of harmony and rhythm alone is
the means in flute-playing and lyre-playing, and any other
arts there may be of the same description, e. g. imitative
25 piping. Rhythm alone, without harmony, is the means in
the dancer's imitations; for even he, by the rhythms of his

attitudes, may represent men's characters, as well as what
they do and suffer. There is further an art which imitates
by language alone, without harmony, in prose or in verse,
and if in verse, either in some one or in a plurality of
metres. This form of imitation is to this day without a 1447ᵇ
name. We have no common name for a mime of Sophron
or Xenarchus and a Socratic Conversation; and we should 10
still be without one even if the imitation in the two instances were in trimeters or elegiacs or some other kind of
verse—though it is the way with people to tack on 'poet'
to the name of a metre, and talk of elegiac-poets and epic-
poets, thinking that they call them poets not by reason of
the imitative nature of their work, but indiscriminately by 15
reason of the metre they write in. Even if a theory of
medicine or physical philosophy be put forth in a metrical
form, it is usual to describe the writer in this way; Homer
and Empedocles, however, have really nothing in common
apart from their metre; so that, if the one is to be called a
poet, the other should be termed a physicist rather than 20
a poet. We should be in the same position also, if the
imitation in these instances were in all the metres, like
the *Centaur* (a rhapsody in a medley of all metres) of
Chaeremon; and Chaeremon one has to recognize as a
poet. So much, then, as to these arts. There are, lastly,
certain other arts, which combine all the means enu- 25
merated, rhythm, melody, and verse, e. g. Dithyrambic
and Nomic poetry, Tragedy and Comedy; with this difference, however, that the three kinds of means are in some
of them all employed together, and in others brought in
separately, one after the other. These elements of difference in the above arts I term the means of their imitation.

2   II. The objects the imitator represents are actions, 1448ˣ
         with agents who are necessarily either good men or
bad—the diversities of human character being nearly always derivative from this primary distinction, since the line
between virtue and vice is one dividing the whole of man-

kind. It follows, therefore, that the agents represented
must be either above our own level of goodness, or be-
5 neath it, or just such as we are; in the same way as, with
the painters, the personages of Polygnotus are better than
we are, those of Pauson worse, and those of Dionysius just
like ourselves. It is clear that each of the above-mentioned
arts will admit of these differences, and that it will become
a separate art by representing objects with this point of difference. Even in dancing, flute-playing, and lyre-playing
10 such diversities are possible; and they are also possible in
the nameless art that uses language, prose or verse without
harmony, as its means; Homer's personages, for instance, are
better than we are; Cleophon's are on our own level; and
those of Hegemon of Thasos, the first writer of parodies,
15 and Nicochares, the author of the Diliad, are beneath it.
The same is true of the Dithyramb and the Nome: the personages may be presented in them with the difference exemplified in the . . . of . . . and Argas, and in the Cy-
clopses of Timotheus and Philoxenus. This difference it is
that distinguishes Tragedy and Comedy also; the one
would make its personages worse, and the other better,
than the men of the present day.

3   III. A third difference in these arts is in the manner in
20   which each kind of object is represented. Given both
the same means and the same kind of object for imitation,
one may either (1) speak at one moment in narrative and at
another in an assumed character, as Homer does; or (2)
one may remain the same throughout, without any such
change; or (3) the imitators may represent the whole story
dramatically, as though they were actually doing the
things described.

As we said at the beginning, therefore, the differences in
the imitation of these arts come under three heads, their
means, their objects, and their manner.

So that as an imitator Sophocles will be on one side
25 akin to Homer, both portraying good men; and on another

to Aristophanes, since both present their personages as acting and doing. This in fact, according to some, is the reason for plays being termed dramas, because in a play the personages act the story. Hence too both Tragedy and Comedy are claimed by the Dorians as their discoveries; 30 Comedy by the Megarians—by those in Greece as having arisen when Megara became a democracy, and by the Sicilian Megarians on the ground that the poet Epicharmus was of their country, and a good deal earlier than Chionides and Magnes; even Tragedy also is claimed by certain of the Peloponnesian Dorians. In support of this claim they point to the words 'comedy' and 'drama'. Their word for the outlying hamlets, they say, is *comae*, whereas 35 Athenians call them *demes*—thus assuming that comedians got the name not from their *comoe* or revels, but from their strolling from hamlet to hamlet, lack of appreciation keeping them out of the city. Their word also for 'to act', they 1448ᵇ say, is *dran*, whereas Athenians use *prattein*.

So much, then, as to the number and nature of the points of difference in the imitation of these arts.

4   It is clear that the general origin of poetry was due to two causes, each of them part of human nature. Imitation is natural to man from childhood, one of his ad- 5 vantages over the lower animals being this, that he is the most imitative creature in the world, and learns at first by imitation. And it is also natural for all to delight in works of imitation. The truth of this second point is shown by experience: though the objects themselves may be painful 10 to see, we delight to view the most realistic representations of them in art, the forms for example of the lowest animals and of dead bodies. The explanation is to be found in a further fact: to be learning something is the greatest of pleasures not only to the philosopher but also to the rest of mankind, however small their capacity for it; the reason 15 of the delight in seeing the picture is that one is at the same time learning—gathering the meaning of things, e. g.

that the man there is so-and-so; for if one has not seen the
thing before, one's pleasure will not be in the picture as an
20 imitation of it, but will be due to the execution or colour-
ing or some similar cause. Imitation, then, being natural
to us—as also the sense of harmony and rhythm, the metres
being obviously species of rhythms—it was through their
original aptitude, and by a series of improvements for the
most part gradual on their first efforts, that they created
poetry out of their improvisations.

Poetry, however, soon broke up into two kinds according
25 to the differences of character in the individual poets; for
the graver among them would represent noble actions, and
those of noble personages; and the meaner sort the actions
of the ignoble. The latter class produced invectives at first,
just as others did hymns and panegyrics. We know of no
such poem by any of the pre-Homeric poets, though there
were probably many such writers among them; instances,
however, may be found from Homer downwards, e. g. his
30 *Margites*, and the similar poems of others. In this poetry
of invective its natural fitness brought an iambic metre into
use; hence our present term 'iambic', because it was the
metre of their 'iambs' or invectives against one another.
The result was that the old poets became some of them
writers of heroic and others of iambic verse. Homer's position, however, is peculiar: just as he was in the serious style
35 the poet of poets, standing alone not only through the
literary excellence, but also through the dramatic character
of his imitations, so too he was the first to outline for us
the general forms of Comedy by producing not a dramatic
invective, but a dramatic picture of the Ridiculous; his
Margites in fact stands in the same relation to our come-
1449ᵃ dies as the *Iliad* and *Odyssey* to our tragedies. As soon, however, as Tragedy and Comedy appeared in the field, those
naturally drawn to the one line of poetry became writers
5 of comedies instead of iambs, and those naturally drawn
to the other, writers of tragedies instead of epics, because

these new modes of art were grander and of more esteem than the old.

If it be asked whether Tragedy is now all that it need be in its formative elements, to consider that, and decide it theoretically and in relation to the theatres, is a matter for another inquiry.

It certainly began in improvisations—as did also Com- 10 edy; the one originating with the authors of the Dithyramb, the other with those of the phallic songs, which still survive as institutions in many of our cities. And its advance after that was little by little, through their improving on whatever they had before them at each stage. It was in fact only after a long series of changes that the movement of Tragedy stopped on its attaining to its natural form. (1) 15 The number of actors was first increased to two by Aeschylus, who curtailed the business of the Chorus, and made the dialogue, or spoken portion, take the leading part in the play. (2) A third actor and scenery were due to Sophocles. (3) Tragedy acquired also its magnitude. Discarding short stories and a ludicrous diction through its 20 passing out of its satyric stage, it assumed, though only at a late point in its progress, a tone of dignity; and its metre changed then from trochaic to iambic. The reason for their original use of the trochaic tetrameter was that their poetry was satyric and more connected with dancing than it now is. As soon, however, as a spoken part came in, nature herself found the appropriate metre. The iambic, we know, is the most speakable of metres, as is shown by the fact that we very often fall into it in conversation, 25 whereas we rarely talk hexameters, and only when we depart from the speaking tone of voice. (4) Another change was a plurality of episodes or acts. As for the remaining matters, the superadded embellishments and the account of their introduction, these must be taken as said, as it would probably be a long piece of work to go through the details.   30

5   As for Comedy, it is (as has been observed [1] an imitation of men worse than the average; worse, however,
not as regards any and every sort of fault, but only as regards one particular kind, the Ridiculous, which is a species of the Ugly. The Ridiculous may be defined as a
35 mistake or deformity not productive of pain or harm to
others; the mask, for instance, that excites laughter, is something ugly and distorted without causing pain.

Though the successive changes in Tragedy and their authors are not unknown, we cannot say the same of Comedy;
its early stages passed unnoticed, because it was not as yet
1449ᵇ taken up in a serious way. It was only at a late point in its
progress that a chorus of comedians was officially granted
by the archon; they used to be mere volunteers. It had also
already certain definite forms at the time when the record
of those termed comic poets begins. Who it was who supplied it with masks, or prologues, or a plurality of actors
and the like, has remained unknown. The invented Fable,
5 or Plot, however, originated in Sicily with Epicharmus
and Phormis; of Athenian poets Crates was the first to drop
the Comedy of invective and frame stories of a general and
non-personal nature, in other words, Fables or Plots.

Epic poetry, then, has been seen to agree with Tragedy
to this extent, that of being an imitation of serious subjects
10 in a grand kind of verse. It differs from it, however, (1) in
that it is in one kind of verse and in narrative form; and
(2) in its length—which is due to its action having no
fixed limit of time, whereas Tragedy endeavours to keep
as far as possible within a single circuit of the sun, or something near that. This, I say, is another point of difference
15 between them, though at first the practice in this respect
was just the same in tragedies as in epic poems. They differ
also (3) in their constituents, some being common to both
and others peculiar to Tragedy—hence a judge of good and
bad in Tragedy is a judge of that in epic poetry also. All the

[1] 1448ᵃ 17; 1448ᵇ 37.

parts of an epic are included in Tragedy; but those of Tragedy are not all 'of them to be found in the Epic.

6   Reserving hexameter poetry and Comedy for con- 20
sideration hereafter,[2] let us proceed now to the discussion of Tragedy; before doing so, however, we must gather up the definition resulting from what has been said. A tragedy, then, is the imitation of an action that is serious 25 and also, as having magnitude, complete in itself; in language with pleasurable accessories, each kind brought in separately in the parts of the work; in a dramatic, not in a narrative form; with incidents arousing pity and fear, wherewith to accomplish its catharsis of such emotions. Here by 'language with pleasurable accessories' I mean that with rhythm and harmony or song superadded; and by 'the kinds 30 separately' I mean that some portions are worked out with verse only, and others in turn with song.

I. As they act the stories, it follows that in the first place the Spectacle (or stage-appearance of the actors) must be some part of the whole; and in the second Melody and Diction, these two being the means of their imitation. Here by 'Diction' I mean merely this, the composition of 35 the verses; and by 'Melody', what is too completely understood to require explanation. But further: the subject represented also is an action; and the action involves agents, who must necessarily have their distinctive qualities both of character and thought, since it is from these that we ascribe 1450 certain qualities to their actions. There are in the natural order of things, therefore, two causes, Thought and Character, of their actions, and consequently of their success or failure in their lives. Now the action (that which was done) is represented in the play by the Fable or Plot. The Fable, in our present sense of the term, is simply this, the combination of the incidents, or things done in the story;

[2] For hexameter poetry cf. chap. 23 f.; comedy was treated of in the lost Second Book.

5 whereas Character is what makes us ascribe certain moral qualities to the agents; and Thought is shown in all they say when proving a particular point or, it may be, enunciating a general truth. There are six parts consequently of every tragedy, as a whole (that is) of such or such quality, viz. a Fable or Plot, Characters, Diction, Thought, Spectacle, and Melody; two of them arising from the means, 10 one from the manner, and three from the objects of the dramatic imitation; and there is nothing else besides these six. Of these, its formative elements, then, not a few of the dramatists have made due use, as every play, one may say, admits of Spectacle, Character, Fable, Diction, Melody, and Thought.

II. The most important of the six is the combination of 15 the incidents of the story. Tragedy is essentially an imitation not of persons but of action and life, of happiness and misery. All human happiness or misery takes the form of action; the end for which we live is a certain kind of activity, not a quality. Character gives us qualities, but it is in our actions—what we do—that we are happy or the reverse. In a play accordingly they do not act in order to 20 portray the Characters; they include the Characters for the sake of the action. So that it is the action in it, i. e. its Fable or Plot, that is the end and purpose of the tragedy; and the end is everywhere the chief thing. Besides this, a tragedy is impossible without action, but there may be one without Character. The tragedies of most of the moderns 25 are characterless—a defect common among poets of all kinds, and with its counterpart in painting in Zeuxis as compared with Polygnotus; for whereas the latter is strong in character, the work of Zeuxis is devoid of it. And again: one may string together a series of characteristic speeches of the utmost finish as regards Diction and Thought, and 30 yet fail to produce the true tragic effect; but one will have much better success with a tragedy which, however inferior in these respects, has a Plot, a combination of incidents, in it. And again: the most powerful elements of attraction in

Tragedy, the Peripeties and Discoveries, are parts of the Plot. A further proof is in the fact that beginners succeed 35 earlier with the Diction and Characters than with the construction of a story; and the same may be said of nearly all the early dramatists. We maintain, therefore, that the first essential, the life and soul, so to speak, of Tragedy is the Plot; and that the Characters come second—compare the parallel in painting, where the most beautiful colours laid 1450ᵇ on without order will not give one the same pleasure as a simple black-and-white sketch of a portrait. We maintain that Tragedy is primarily an imitation of action, and that it is mainly for the sake of the action that it imitates the personal agents. Third comes the element of Thought, i. e. the power of saying whatever can be said, or what is appropriate 5 to the occasion. This is what, in the speeches in Tragedy, falls under the arts of Politics and Rhetoric; for the older poets make their personages discourse like statesmen, and the modern like rhetoricians. One must not confuse it with Character. Character in a play is that which reveals the moral purpose of the agents, i. e. the sort of thing they seek or avoid, where that is not obvious—hence there is no room for Character in a speech on a purely indifferent subject. Thought, on the other hand, is shown in all they say when 10 proving or disproving some particular point, or enunciating some universal proposition. Fourth among the literary elements is the Diction of the personages, i. e., as before explained,[3] the expression of their thoughts in words, which is practically the same thing with verse as with prose. As 15 for the two remaining parts, the Melody is the greatest of the pleasurable accessories of Tragedy. The Spectacle, though an attraction, is the least artistic of all the parts, and has least to do with the art of poetry. The tragic effect is quite possible without a public performance and actors; and besides, the getting-up of the Spectacle is more a matter for the costumier than the poet. 20

[3] 1449ᵇ 34.

7 Having thus distinguished the parts, let us now consider the proper construction of the Fable or Plot, as
that is at once the first and the most important thing in
Tragedy. We have laid it down that a tragedy is an imitation of an action that is complete in itself, as a whole of
25 some magnitude; for a whole may be of no magnitude to
speak of. Now a whole is that which has beginning, middle, and end. A beginning is that which is not itself necessarily after anything else, and which has naturally some-
30 thing else after it; an end is that which is naturally after
something itself, either as its necessary or usual consequent,
and with nothing else after it; and a middle, that which is
by nature after one thing and has also another after it. A
well-constructed Plot, therefore, cannot either begin or end
at any point one likes; beginning and end in it must be of
the forms just described. Again: to be beautiful, a living
35 creature, and every whole made up of parts, must not only
present a certain order in its arrangement of parts, but also
be of a certain definite magnitude. Beauty is a matter of
size and order, and therefore impossible either (1) in a very
minute creature, since our perception becomes indistinct as
it approaches instantaneity; or (2) in a creature of vast size
—one, say, 1,000 miles long—as in that case, instead of the
1451ᵃ object being seen all at once, the unity and wholeness of
it is lost to the beholder. Just in the same way, then, as a
beautiful whole made up of parts, or a beautiful living
creature, must be of some size, but a size to be taken in by
5 the eye, so a story or Plot must be of some length, but of a
length to be taken in by the memory. As for the limit of its
length, so far as that is relative to public performances and
spectators, it does not fall within the theory of poetry. If
they had to perform a hundred tragedies, they would be
timed by water-clocks, as they are said to have been at one
period. The limit, however, set by the actual nature of the
10 thing is this: the longer the story, consistently with its
being comprehensible as a whole, the finer it is by reason
of its magnitude. As a rough general formula, 'a length
which allows of the hero passing by a series of probable or

necessary stages from misfortune to happiness, or from happiness to misfortune', may suffice as a limit for the magnitude of the story.   15

8   The Unity of a Plot does not consist, as some suppose,
        in its having one man as its subject. An infinity of
things befall that one man, some of which it is impossible
to reduce to unity; and in like manner there are many
actions of one man which cannot be made to form one action. One sees, therefore, the mistake of all the poets who
have written a *Heracleid*, a *Theseid*, or similar poems; they 20
suppose that, because Heracles was one man, the story also
of Heracles must be one story. Homer, however, evidently
understood this point quite well, whether by art or instinct,
just in the same way as he excels the rest in every other
respect. In writing an *Odyssey*, he did not make the poem
cover all that ever befell his hero—it befell him, for in-   25
stance, to get wounded on Parnassus and also to feign madness at the time of the call to arms, but the two incidents
had no necessary or probable connexion with one another
—instead of doing that, he took as the subject of the *Odyssey*, as also of the *Iliad*, an action with a Unity of the kind
we are describing. The truth is that, just as in the other 30
imitative arts one imitation is always of one thing, so in
poetry the story, as an imitation of action, must represent
one action, a complete whole, with its several incidents so
closely connected that the transposal or withdrawal of any
one of them will disjoin and dislocate the whole. For that
which makes no perceptible difference by its presence or
absence is no real part of the whole.   35

9   From what we have said it will be seen that the poet's
        function is to describe, not the thing that has hap-
pened, but a kind of thing that might happen, i. e. what is
possible as being probable or necessary. The distinction between historian and poet is not in the one writing prose **1451**ᵇ
and the other verse—you might put the work of Herodotus
into verse, and it would still be a species of history; it con-

sists really in this, that the one describes the thing that has
been, and the other a kind of thing that might be. Hence
poetry is something more philosophic and of graver import
than history, since its statements are of the nature rather of
universals, whereas those of history are singulars. By a universal statement I mean one as to what such or such a kind
of man will probably or necessarily say or do—which is the
aim of poetry, though it affixes proper names to the characters; by a singular statement, one as to what, say, Alcibiades
did or had done to him. In Comedy this has become clear
by this time; it is only when their plot is already made up
of probable incidents that they give it a basis of proper
names, choosing for the purpose any names that may occur
to them, instead of writing like the old iambic poets about
particular persons. In Tragedy, however, they still adhere to
the historic names; and for this reason: what convinces is
the possible; now whereas we are not yet sure as to the
possibility of that which has not happened, that which has
happened is manifestly possible, else it would not have
come to pass. Nevertheless even in Tragedy there are some
plays with but one or two known names in them, the rest
being inventions; and there are some without a single
known name, e. g. Agathon's *Antheus*, in which both incidents and names are of the poet's invention; and it is no
less delightful on that account. So that one must not aim
at a rigid adherence to the traditional stories on which
tragedies are based. It would be absurd, in fact, to do so, as
even the known stories are only known to a few, though
they are a delight none the less to all.

It is evident from the above that the poet must be more
the poet of his stories or Plots than of his verses, inasmuch
as he is a poet by virtue of the imitative element in his
work, and it is actions that he imitates. And if he should
come to take a subject from actual history, he is none the
less a poet for that; since some historic occurrences may
very well be in the probable and possible order of things;
and it is in that aspect of them that he is their poet.

Of simple Plots and actions the episodic are the worst.

I call a Plot episodic when there is neither probability nor necessity in the sequence of its episodes. Actions of this sort 35 bad poets construct through their own fault, and good ones on account of the players. His work being for public performance, a good poet often stretches out a Plot beyond its capabilities, and is thus obliged to twist the sequence of incident.

Tragedy, however, is an imitation not only of a complete 1452ᵃ action, but also of incidents arousing pity and fear. Such incidents have the very greatest effect on the mind when they occur unexpectedly and at the same time in consequence of one another; there is more of the marvellous in them then than if they happened of themselves or by mere 5 chance. Even matters of chance seem most marvellous if there is an appearance of design as it were in them; as for instance the statue of Mitys at Argos killed the author of Mitys' death by falling down on him when a looker-on at a public spectacle; for incidents like that we think to be not without a meaning. A Plot therefore, of this sort is neces- 10 sarily finer than others.

10 Plots are either simple or complex, since the actions they represent are naturally of this twofold description. The action, proceeding in the way defined, as one continuous whole, I call simple, when the change in the hero's 15 fortunes takes place without Peripety or Discovery; and complex, when it involves one or the other, or both. These should each of them arise out of the structure of the Plot itself, so as to be the consequence, necessary or probable, of the antecedents. There is a great difference between a thing happening *propter hoc* and *post hoc*. 20

11 A Peripety is the change of the kind described from one state of things within the play to its opposite, and that too in the way we are saying, in the probable or necessary sequence of events; as it is for instance in *Oedipus*: here the opposite state of things is produced by the 25 Messenger, who, coming to gladden Oedipus and to re-

move his fears as to his mother, reveals the secret of his birth.[4] And in *Lynceus*:[5] just as he is being led off for execution, with Danaus at his side to put him to death, the incidents preceding this bring it about that he is saved and
30 Danaus put to death. A Discovery is, as the very word implies, a change from ignorance to knowledge, and thus to either love or hate, in the personages marked for good or evil fortune. The finest form of Discovery is one attended by Peripeties, like that which goes with the Discovery in *Oedipus*. There are no doubt other forms of it; what we have said may happen in a way in reference to inanimate
35 things, even things of a very casual kind; and it is also possible to discover whether some one has done or not done something. But the form most directly connected with the Plot and the action of the piece is the first-mentioned.
1452ᵇ This, with a Peripety, will arouse either pity or fear—actions of that nature being what Tragedy is assumed to represent; and it will also serve to bring about the happy or unhappy ending. The Discovery, then, being of persons, it may be that of one party only to the other, the latter being
5 already known; or both the parties may have to discover themselves. Iphigenia, for instance, was discovered to Orestes by sending the letter;[6] and another Discovery was required to reveal him to Iphigenia.

Two parts of the Plot, then, Peripety and Discovery, are
10 on matters of this sort. A third part is Suffering; which we may define as an action of a destructive or painful nature, such as murders on the stage, tortures, woundings, and the like. The other two have been already explained.

12   The parts of Tragedy to be treated as formative elements
15   in the whole were mentioned in a previous Chapter.[7] From the point of view, however, of its quantity, i. e. the separate sections into which it is divided, a tragedy

[4] *O. T.* 911–1085.
[5] By Theodectes.
[6] *Iph. Taur.* 727 ff.
[7] Ch. 6.

has the following parts: Prologue, Episode, Exode, and a choral portion, distinguished into Parode and Stasimon; these two are common to all tragedies, whereas songs from the stage and Commoe are only found in some. The Pro- 20 logue is all that precedes the Parode of the chorus; an Episode all that comes in between two whole choral songs; the Exode all that follows after the last choral song. In the choral portion the Parode is the whole first statement of the chorus; a Stasimon, a song of the chorus without anapaests or trochees; a Commos, a lamentation sung by chorus and actor in concert. The parts of Tragedy to be used as forma- 25 tive elements in the whole we have already mentioned; the above are its parts from the point of view of its quantity, or the separate sections into which it is divided.

13   The next points after what we have said above will be these: (1) What is the poet to aim at, and what is he to avoid, in constructing his Plots? and (2) What are the conditions on which the tragic effect depends?

We assume that, for the finest form of Tragedy, the Plot 30 must be not simple but complex; and further, that it must imitate actions arousing fear and pity, since that is the distinctive function of this kind of imitation. It follows, therefore, that there are three forms of Plot to be avoided. (1) A good man must not be seen passing from happiness to misery, or (2) a bad man from misery to happiness. The 35 first situation is not fear-inspiring or piteous, but simply odious to us. The second is the most untragic that can be; it has no one of the requisites of Tragedy; it does not appeal either to the human feeling in us, or to our pity, or to our fears. Nor, on the other hand, should (3) an extremely 1453 bad man be seen falling from happiness into misery. Such a story may arouse the human feeling in us, but it will not move us to either pity or fear; pity is occasioned by un- 5 deserved misfortune, and fear by that of one like ourselves; so that there will be nothing either piteous or fear-inspiring in the situation. There remains, then, the intermediate

kind of personage, a man not pre-eminently virtuous and
just, whose misfortune, however, is brought upon him not
by vice and depravity but by some error of judgement, of
the number of those in the enjoyment of great reputation
10 and prosperity; e. g. Oedipus, Thyestes, and the men of
note of similar families. The perfect Plot, accordingly, must
have a single, and not (as some tell us) a double issue; the
change in the hero's fortunes must be not from misery to
happiness, but on the contrary from happiness to misery;
and the cause of it must lie not in any depravity, but in
15 some great error on his part; the man himself being either
such as we have described, or better, not worse, than that.
Fact also confirms our theory. Though the poets began by
accepting any tragic story that came to hand, in these days
the finest tragedies are always on the story of some few
20 houses, on that of Alcmeon, Oedipus, Orestes, Meleager,
Thyestes, Telephus, or any others that may have been involved, as either agents or sufferers, in some deed of horror.
The theoretically best tragedy, then, has a Plot of this description. The critics, therefore, are wrong who blame
Euripides for taking this line in his tragedies, and giving
25 many of them an unhappy ending. It is, as we have said,
the right line to take. The best proof is this: on the stage,
and in the public performances, such plays, properly
worked out, are seen to be the most truly tragic; and Euripides, even if his execution be faulty in every other point, is
seen to be nevertheless the most tragic certainly of the
30 dramatists. After this comes the construction of Plot which
some rank first, one with a double story (like the Odyssey)
and an opposite issue for the good and the bad personages.
It is ranked as first only through the weakness of the audiences; the poets merely follow their public, writing as its
35 wishes dictate. But the pleasure here is not that of Tragedy.
It belongs rather to Comedy, where the bitterest enemies in
the piece (e. g. Orestes and Aegisthus) walk off good
friends at the end, with no slaying of any one by any one.

14 The tragic fear and pity may be aroused by the Spectacle; but they may also be aroused by the very struc- 1453ᵇ
ture and incidents of the play—which is the better way and
shows the better poet. The Plot in fact should be so framed
that, even without seeing the things take place, he who 5
simply hears the account of them shall be filled with horror
and pity at the incidents; which is just the effect that the
mere recital of the story in *Oedipus* would have on one. To
produce this same effect by means of the Spectacle is less
artistic, and requires extraneous aid. Those, however, who
make use of the Spectacle to put before us that which is
merely monstrous and not productive of fear, are wholly 10
out of touch with Tragedy; not every kind of pleasure
should be required of a tragedy, but only its own proper
pleasure.

The tragic pleasure is that of pity and fear, and the poet
has to produce it by a work of imitation; it is clear, therefore, that the causes should be included in the incidents of
his story. Let us see, then, what kinds of incident strike 15
one as horrible, or rather as piteous. In a deed of this description the parties must necessarily be either friends, or
enemies, or indifferent to one another. Now when enemy
does it on enemy, there is nothing to move us to pity either
in his doing or in his meditating the deed, except so far as
the actual pain of the sufferer is concerned; and the same is
true when the parties are indifferent to one another. Whenever the tragic deed, however, is done within the family— 20
when murder or the like is done or meditated by brother on
brother, by son on father, by mother on son, or son on
mother—these are the situations the poet should seek after.
The traditional stories, accordingly, must be kept as they
are, e. g. the murder of Clytaemnestra by Orestes and of
Eriphyle by Alcmeon. At the same time even with these 25
there is something left to the poet himself; it is for him to
devise the right way of treating them. Let us explain more
clearly what we mean by 'the right way'. The deed of horror

may be done by the doer knowingly and consciously, as in
the old poets, and in Medea's murder of her children in
30 Euripides.[8] Or he may do it, but in ignorance of his relationship, and discover that afterwards, as does the Oedipus
in Sophocles. Here the deed is outside the play; but it may
be within it, like the act of the Alcmeon in Astydamas, or
that of the Telegonus in *Ulysses Wounded*.[9] A third pos-
35 sibility is for one meditating some deadly injury to another,
in ignorance of his relationship, to make the discovery in
time to draw back. These exhaust the possibilities, since the
deed must necessarily be either done or not done, and
either knowingly or unknowingly.

The worst situation is when the personage is with full
knowledge on the point of doing the deed, and leaves it
undone. It is odious and also (through the absence of suffering) untragic; hence it is that no one is made to act thus
1454ᵃ except in some few instances, e. g. Haemon and Creon in
Antigone.[10] Next after this comes the actual perpetration of
the deed meditated. A better situation than that, however,
is for the deed to be done in ignorance, and the relationship
discovered afterwards, since there is nothing odious in it,
and the Discovery will serve to astound us. But the best of
5 all is the last; what we have in *Cresphontes*,[11] for example,
where Merope, on the point of slaying her son, recognizes
him in time; in *Iphigenia*, where sister and brother are in a
like position; and in *Helle*,[12] where the son recognizes his
mother, when on the point of giving her up to her enemy.

This will explain why our tragedies are restricted (as we
said just now) [13] to such a small number of families. It was
10 accident rather than art that led the poets in quest of subjects to embody this kind of incident in their Plots. They

[8] *Med.* 1236.
[9] Perhaps by Sophocles.
[10] l. 1231.
[11] By Euripides.
[12] Authorship unknown.
[13] 1453ᵃ 19.

are still obliged, accordingly, to have recourse to the families in which such horrors have occurred.

On the construction of the Plot, and the kind of Plot required for Tragedy, enough has now been said.   15

15 In the Characters there are four points to aim at. First
and foremost, that they shall be good. There will be an element of character in the play, if (as has been observed) [14] what a personage says or does reveals a certain moral purpose; and a good element of character, if the purpose so revealed is good. Such goodness is possible in every type of personage, even in a woman or a slave, though the one is 20 perhaps an inferior, and the other a wholly worthless being. The second point is to make them appropriate. The Character before us may be, say, manly; but it is not appropriate in a female Character to be manly, or clever. The third is to make them like the reality, which is not the same as their being good and appropriate, in our sense of the term. The 25 fourth is to make them consistent and the same throughout; even if inconsistency be part of the man before one for imitation as presenting that form of character, he should still be consistently inconsistent. We have an instance of baseness of character, not required for the story, in the Menelaus in *Orestes*; of the incongruous and unbefitting in the lamentation of Ulysses in *Scylla*,[15] and in the (clever) 30 speech of Melanippe;[16] and of inconsistency in *Iphigenia at Aulis*,[17] where Iphigenia the suppliant is utterly unlike the later Iphigenia. The right thing, however, is in the Characters just as in the incidents of the play to endeavour always after the necessary or the probable; so that whenever 35 such-and-such a personage says or does such-and-such a thing, it shall be the necessary or probable outcome of his

[14] 1450ᵇ 8.
[15] A dithyramb by Timotheus.
[16] (Euripides).
[17] ll. 1211 ff., 1368 ff.

character; and whenever this incident follows on that, it
shall be either the necessary or the probable consequence of
it. From this one sees (to digress for a moment) that the
1454ᵇ Dénouement also should arise out of the plot itself, and
not depend on a stage-artifice, as in *Medea*,[18] or in the story
of the (arrested) departure of the Greeks in the *Iliad*.[19] The
artifice must be reserved for matters outside the play—for
5 past events beyond human knowledge, or events yet to
come, which require to be foretold or announced; since it
is the privilege of the Gods to know everything. There
should be nothing improbable among the actual incidents.
If it be unavoidable, however, it should be outside the
tragedy, like the improbability in the *Oedipus* of Sophocles.
But to return to the Characters. As Tragedy is an imitation
of personages better than the ordinary man, we in our way
10 should follow the example of good portrait-painters, who
reproduce the distinctive features of a man, and at the same
time, without losing the likeness, make him handsomer
than he is. The poet in like manner, in portraying men
quick or slow to anger, or with similar infirmities of character, must know how to represent them as such, and at the
same time as good men, as Agathon and Homer have represented Achilles.

15   All these rules one must keep in mind throughout, and,
further, those also for such points of stage-effect as directly
depend on the art of the poet, since in these too one may
often make mistakes. Enough, however, has been said on
the subject in one of our published writings.[20]

16   Discovery in general has been explained already.[21] As
20   for the species of Discovery, the first to be noted is (1)
the least artistic form of it, of which the poets make most
use through mere lack of invention, Discovery by signs
or marks. Of these signs some are congenital, like the

[18] l. 1317.
[19] ii. 155.
[20] In the lost dialogue *On Poets*.
[21] 1452ᵃ 29.

'lance-head which the Earth-born have on them',[22] or 'stars',
such as Carcinus brings in his *Thyestes*; others acquired
after birth—these latter being either marks on the body,
e. g. scars, or external tokens, like necklaces, or (to take
another sort of instance) the ark in the Discovery in *Tyro*.[23] 25
Even these, however, admit of two uses, a better and a
worse; the scar of Ulysses is an instance; the Discovery of
him through it is made in one way by the nurse [24] and in
another by the swineherds.[25] A Discovery using signs as a
means of assurance is less artistic, as indeed are all such as
imply reflection; whereas one bringing them in all of a
sudden, as in the *Bath-story*,[26] is of a better order. Next 30
after these are (2) Discoveries made directly by the poet;
which are inartistic for that very reason; e. g. Orestes' Discovery of himself in *Iphigenia*: whereas his sister reveals
who she is by the letter,[27] Orestes is made to say himself
what the poet rather than the story demands.[28] This, there- 35
fore, is not far removed from the first-mentioned fault,
since he might have presented certain tokens as well. Another instance is the 'shuttle's voice' in the *Tereus* of
Sophocles. (3) A third species is Discovery through memory, from a man's consciousness being awakened by something seen. Thus in *The Cyprioe* of Dicaeogenes, the sight **1455ᵃ**
of the picture makes the man burst into tears; and in the
Tale of Alcinous,[29] hearing the harper Ulysses is reminded
of the past and weeps; the Discovery of them being the
result. (4) A fourth kind is Discovery through reasoning;
e. g. in *The Choephoroe*; [30] 'One like me is here; there is no
one like me but Orestes; he, therefore, must be here.' Or 5
that which Polyidus the Sophist suggested for *Iphigenia*;

[22] Authorship unknown.
[23] By Euripides.
[24] *Od.* xix. 386–475.
[25] *Od.* xxi. 205–25.
[26] *Od.* xix. 392.
[27] *Iph. Taur.* 727 ff.
[28] Ib., 800 ff.
[29] *Od.* viii. 521 ff. (Cf. viii, 83 ff.).
[30] ll. 168–234.

since it was natural for Orestes to reflect: 'My sister was
sacrificed, and I am to be sacrificed like her.' Or that in
the Tydeus of Theodectes: 'I came to find a son, and am to
10 die myself.' Or that in The Phinidae: [81] on seeing the place
the women inferred their fate, that they were to die there,
since they had also been exposed there. (5) There is, too,
a composite Discovery arising from bad reasoning on the
side of the other party. An instance of it is in Ulysses the
False Messenger: [81] he said he should know the bow—
15 which he had not seen; but to suppose from that that he
would know it again (as though he had once seen it) was
bad reasoning. (6) The best of all Discoveries, however, is
that arising from the incidents themselves, when the great
surprise comes about through a probable incident, like that
in the Oedipus of Sophocles; and also in Iphigenia; [82] for it
was not improbable that she should wish to have a letter
taken home. These last are the only Discoveries independ-
20 ent of the artifice of signs and necklaces. Next after them
come Discoveries through reasoning.

17   At the time when he is constructing his Plots, and
engaged on the Diction in which they are worked out,
the poet should remember (1) to put the actual scenes
25 as far as possible before his eyes. In this way, seeing everything with the vividness of an eye-witness as it were, he
will devise what is appropriate, and be least likely to overlook incongruities. This is shown by what was censured in
Carcinus, the return of Amphiaraus from the sanctuary; it
would have passed unnoticed, if it had not been actually
seen by the audience; but on the stage his play failed, the incongruity of the incident offending the spectators. (2) As
far as may be, too, the poet should even act his story with
30 the very gestures of his personages. Given the same natural
qualifications, he who feels the emotions to be described
will be the most convincing; distress and anger, for in-

[81] Authorship unknown.
[82] Iph. Taur. 582.

stance, are portrayed most truthfully by one who is feeling
them at the moment. Hence it is that poetry demands a
man with a special gift for it, or else one with a touch of
madness in him; the former can easily assume the required
mood, and the latter may be actually beside himself with
emotion. (3) His story, again, whether already made or of
his own making, he should first simplify and reduce to a **1455ᵇ**
universal form, before proceeding to lengthen it out by the
insertion of episodes. The following will show how the
universal element in *Iphigenia*, for instance, may be
viewed: A certain maiden having been offered in sacrifice,
and spirited away from her sacrifices into another land,
where the custom was to sacrifice all strangers to the 5
Goddess, she was made there the priestess of this rite. Long
after that the brother of the priestess happened to come;
the fact, however, of the oracle having for a certain reason
bidden him go thither, and his object in going, are outside the Plot of the play. On his coming he was arrested,
and about to be sacrificed, when he revealed who he was—
either as Euripides puts it, or (as suggested by Polyidus) 10
by the not improbable exclamation, 'So I too am doomed
to be sacrificed, as my sister was'; and the disclosure led to
his salvation. This done, the next thing, after the proper
names have been fixed as a basis for the story, is to work
in episodes or accessory incidents. One must mind, however, that the episodes are appropriate, like the fit of madness [33] in Orestes, which led to his arrest, and the purify- 15
ing,[34] which brought about his salvation. In plays, then,
the episodes are short; in epic poetry they serve to lengthen
out the poem. The argument of the *Odyssey* is not a long
one. A certain man has been abroad many years; Poseidon
is ever on the watch for him, and he is all alone. Matters at
home too have come to this, that his substance is being 20
wasted and his son's death plotted by suitors to his wife.
Then he arrives there himself after his grievous sufferings;

[33] *Iph. Taur.* 281 ff.
[34] Ib., 1163 ff.

reveals himself, and falls on his enemies; and the end is his
salvation and their death. This being all that is proper to
the Odyssey, everything else in it is episode.

18　(4) There is a further point to be borne in mind.
Every tragedy is in part Complication and in part
Dénouement; the incidents before the opening scene, and
often certain also of those within the play, forming the
25 Complication; and the rest the Dénouement. By Complication I mean all from the beginning of the story to
the point just before the change in the hero's fortunes; by
Dénouement, all from the beginning of the change to the
end. In the Lynceus of Theodectes, for instance, the Com-
30 plication includes, together with the presupposed incidents,
the seizure of the child and that in turn of the parents; and
1456ᵃ7 the Dénouement all from the indictment for the murder
to the end. Now it is right, when one speaks of a tragedy as
the same or not the same as another, to do so on the
ground before all else of their Plot, i. e. as having the same
or not the same Complication and Dénouement. Yet there
are many dramatists who, after a good Complication, fail
in the Dénouement. But it is necessary for both points of
construction to be always duly mastered. (5) There are
1455ᵇ32   1
four distinct species of Tragedy—that being the number
of the constituents also that have been mentioned: [35] first,
the complex Tragedy, which is all Peripety and Discovery;
second, the Tragedy of suffering, e. g the Ajaxes and Ixions;
1456ᵃ third, the Tragedy of character, e. g. The Phthiotides [36]
and Peleus. [37] The fourth constituent is that of 'Spectacle',
exemplified in The Phorcides, [38] in Prometheus, [39] and in
all plays with the scene laid in the nether world. The poet's
aim, then, should be to combine every element of interest,

[35] This does not agree with anything actually said before.
[36] By Sophocles.
[37] Probably Sophocles' Peleus is inc rrect.
[38] By Aeschylus.
[39] Probably a satyric drama by Aeschylus.

if possible, or else the more important and the major part
of them. This is now especially necessary owing to the
unfair criticism to which the poet is subjected in these
days. Just because there have been poets before him strong 5
in the several species of tragedy, the critics now expect
the one man to surpass that which was the strong point
of each one of his predecessors. (6) One should also remember what has been said more than once,[40] and not 10
write a tragedy on an epic body of incident (i. e. one with a
plurality of stories in it), by attempting to dramatize, for
instance, the entire story of the *Iliad*. In the epic owing
to its scale every part is treated at proper length; with a
drama, however, on the same story the result is very dis-
appointing. This is shown by the fact that all who have 15
dramatized the fall of Ilium in its entirety, and not part by
part, like Euripides, of the whole of the Niobe story, instead of a portion, like Aeschylus, either fail utterly or
have but ill success on the stage; for that and that alone
was enough to ruin even a play by Agathon. Yet in their
Peripeties, as also in their simple plots, the poets I mean 20
show wonderful skill in aiming at the kind of effect they
desire—a tragic situation that arouses the human feeling in
one, like the clever villain (e. g. Sisyphus) deceived, or the
brave wrongdoer worsted. This is probable, however, only
in Agathon's sense, when he speaks of the probability of
even improbabilities coming to pass. (7) The Chorus too 25
should be regarded as one of the actors; it should be an
integral part of the whole, and take a share in the action—
that which it has in Sophocles, rather than in Euripides.
With the later poets, however, the songs in a play of theirs
have no more to do with the Plot of that than of any other
tragedy. Hence it is that they are now singing intercalary
pieces, a practice first introduced by Agathon. And yet 30
what real difference is there between singing such intercalary pieces, and attempting to fit in a speech, or even
a whole act, from one play into another?

[40] A loose reference to 1449[b] 12, 1455[b] 15.

19 The Plot and Characters having been discussed, it remains to consider the Diction and Thought. As for
35 the Thought, we may assume what is said of it in our Art
of Rhetoric,[41] as it belongs more properly to that department of inquiry. The Thought of the personages is shown
in everything to be effected by their language—in every
effort to prove or disprove, to arouse emotion (pity, fear,
1456ᵇ anger, and the like), or to maximize or minimize things.
It is clear, also, that heir mental procedure must be on
the same lines n heir actions likewise, whenever they wish
5 them to arouse pity or horror, or to have a look of importance or probability. The only difference is that with the
act the impression has to be made without explanation;
whereas with the spoken word it has to be produced by the
speaker, and result from his language. What, indeed, would
be the good of the speaker, if things appeared in the required light even apart from anything he says?

As regards the Diction, one subject for inquiry under this
head is the turns given to the language when spoken; e. g.
10 the difference between command and prayer, simple statement and threat, question and answer, and so forth. The
theory of such matters, however, belongs to Elocution and
the professors of that art. Whether the poet knows these
15 things or not, his art as a poet is never seriously criticized on
that account. What fault can one see in Homer's 'Sing of
the wrath, Goddess'?—which Protagoras has criticized as
being a command where a prayer was meant, since to bid
one do or not do, he tells us, is a command. Let us pass
over this, then, as appertaining to another art, and not to
that of poetry.

20 The Diction viewed as a whole is made up of the
40   following parts: the Letter (or ultimate element), the
Syllable, the Conjunction, the Article, the Noun, the Verb,
the Case, and the Speech. (1) The Letter is an indivisible
sound of a particular kind, one that may become a factor in

[41] Cf. especially *Rhet.* 1356ᵃ 1.

an intelligible sound. Indivisible sounds are uttered by the brutes also, but no one of these is a Letter in our sense of the term. These elementary sounds are either vowels, semi-vowels, or mutes. A vowel is a Letter having an audible 25 sound without the addition of another Letter. A semi-vowel, one having an audible sound by the addition of an-other Letter; e. g. S and R. A mute, one having no sound at all by itself, but becoming audible by an addition, that of one of the Letters which have a sound of some sort of their own; e. g. G and D. The Letters differ ın various 30 ways: as produced by different conformations or in dif-ferent regions of the mouth; as aspirated, not aspirated, or sometimes one and sometimes the other; as long, short, or of variable quantity; and further as having an acute, grave, or intermediate accent. The details of these matters we must leave to the metricians. (2) A Syllable is a non-significant composite sound, made up of a mute and a 35 Letter having a sound (a vowel or semi-vowel); for GR, without an A, is just as much a Syllable as GRA, with an A. The various forms of the Syllable also belong to the theory of metre. (3) A Conjunction is (a) a non-significant sound which, when one significant sound is formable out of several, neither hinders nor aids the union, and which, if **1457ᵃ** the Speech thus formed stands by itself (apart from other Speeches), must not be inserted at the beginning of it; e. g. μέυ, δή, τοι, δέ. Or (b) a non-significant sound capable of combining two or more significant sounds into one; e. g. 5 ἀμφί, περί &c. (4) An Article is a non-significant sound marking the beginning, end, or dividing-point of a Speech, its natural place being either at the extremities or in the middle. (5) A Noun or name is a composite significant 10 sound not involving the idea of time, with parts which have no significance by themselves in it. It is to be remembered that in a compound we do not think of the parts as having a significance also by themselves; in the name 'Theodorus', for instance, the δῶρον means nothing to us. (6) A Verb is a composite significant sound involving the idea of time,

with parts which (just as in the Noun) have no significance
15 by themselves in it. Whereas the word 'man' or 'white'
does not imply when, 'walks' and 'has walked,' involve in
addition to the idea of walking that of time present or time
past. (7) A Case of a Noun or Verb is when the word
20 means 'of' or 'to' a thing, and so forth, or for one or many
(e. g. 'man' and 'men'); or it may consist merely in the
mode of utterance, e. g. in question, command, &c.
'Walked?' and 'Walk!' are Cases of the verb 'to walk'
of this last kind. (8) A Speech is a composite significant
sound, some of the parts of which have a certain signifi-
25 cance by themselves. It may be observed that a Speech is
not always made up of Noun and Verb; it may be without
a Verb, like the definition of man; but it will always have
some part with a certain significance by itself. In the
Speech 'Cleon walks', 'Cleon' is an instance of such a part.
A Speech is said to be one in two ways, either as signifying
one thing, or as a union of several Speeches made into one
30 by conjunction. Thus the *Iliad* is one Speech by conjunction of several; and the definition of man is one through its
signifying one thing.

21 Nouns are of two kinds, either (1) simple, i. e. made
up of non-significant parts, like the word γῆ, or (2)
double; in the latter case the word may be made up either
of a significant and a non-significant part (a distinction
35 which disappears in the compound), or of two significant
parts. It is possible also to have triple, quadruple, or higher
compounds, like most of our amplified names; e. g. 'Hermo-
caïcoxanthus' and the like.
1457ᵇ Whatever its structure, a Noun must always be either
(1) the ordinary word for the thing, or (2) a strange word,
or (3) a metaphor, or (4) an ornamental word, or (5) a
coined word, or (6) a word lengthened out, or (7) curtailed, or (8) altered in form. By the ordinary word I mean
that in general use in a country; and by a strange word,
one in use elsewhere. So that the same word may obviously

be at once strange and ordinary, though not in reference to 5
the same people; σίγυνον, for instance, is an ordinary word
in Cyprus, and a strange word with us. Metaphor consists
in giving the thing a name that belongs to something else;
the transference being either from genus to species, or
from species to genus, or from species to species, or on
grounds of analogy. That from genus to species is ex- 10
emplified in 'Here stands my ship'; [42] for lying at anchor
is the 'standing' of a particular kind of thing. That from
species to genus in 'Truly ten thousand good deeds has
Ulysses wrought',[43] where 'ten thousand', which is a particular large number, is put in place of the generic 'a large
number'. That from species to species in 'Drawing the life
with the bronze',[44] and in 'Severing with the enduring
bronze'; [44] where the poet uses 'draw' in the sense of 15
'sever' and 'sever' in that of 'draw', both words meaning to 'take away' something. That from analogy is possible whenever there are four terms so related that the
second (B) is to the first (A), as the fourth (D) to
the third (C); for one may then metaphorically put D in
lieu of B, and B in lieu of D. Now and then, too, they
qualify the metaphor by adding on to it that to which the
word it supplants is relative. Thus a cup (B) is in relation 20
to Dionysus (A) what a shield (D) is to Ares (C). The
cup accordingly will be metaphorically described as the
'shield of Dionysus' (D + A), and the shield as the 'cup of
Ares' [45] (B + C). Or to take another instance: As old age
(D) is to life (C), so is evening (B) to day (A). One will
accordingly describe evening (B) as the 'old age of the day'
(D + A)—or by the Empedoclean equivalent; and old age
(D) as the 'evening' [46] or 'sunset of life' [47] (B + C). It may
be that some of the terms thus related have no special 25

---

[42] *Od.* i. 185, xxiv. 308.
[43] *Il.* ii. 272.
[44] Empedocles.
[45] Timotheus.
[46] Alexis.
[47] Pl., *Laws* 770 A.

name of their own, but for all that they will be metaphorically described in just the same way. Thus to cast forth
seed-corn is called 'sowing'; but to cast forth its flame, as
said of the sun, has no special name. This nameless act
(B), however, stands in just the same relation to its object,
sunlight (A), as sowing (D) to the seed-corn (C). Hence
the expression in the poet, 'sowing around a god-created
30 flame' [48] (D + A). There is also another form of qualified
metaphor. Having given the thing the alien name, one may
by a negative addition deny of it one of the attributes
naturally associated with its new name. An instance of this
would be to call the shield not the 'cup *of Ares*', as in the
former case, but a 'cup *that holds no wine*'. . . . A coined
word is a name which, being quite unknown among a
people, is given by the poet himself; e. g. (for there are some
words that seem to be of this origin) ἔρνυγες for horns,
and ἀρητήρ for priest.[49] A word is said to be lengthened
35 out, when it has a short vowel made long, or an extra
1458ᵃ syllable inserted; e. g. πόληος for πόλεως, Πηληιάδεω for
Πηλείδου. It is said to be curtailed, when it has lost a part;
5 e. g. κρῖ, δῶ, and ὄψ in μία γίνεται ἀμφοτέρων ὄψ.[50] It is an
altered word, when part is left as it was and part is of the
poet's making; e. g. δεξιτερόν for δεξιόν, in δεξιτερὸν κατὰ
μαζόν.[51]

The Nouns themselves (to whatever class they may belong) are either masculines, feminines, or intermediates
(neuter). All ending in N, P, Σ, or in the two compounds
10 of this last, Ψ and Ξ, are masculines. All ending in the invariably long vowels, H and Ω, and in A among the vowels
that may be long, are feminines. So that there is an equal
number of masculine and feminine terminations, as Ψ and
Ξ are the same as Σ, and need not be counted. There is no
15 Noun, however, ending in a mute or in either of the two

---

[48] Authorship unknown.
[49] *Il.* i. 11.
[50] Empedocles.
[51] *Il.* v. 393.

short vowels, E and O. Only three (μέλι, κόμμι, πέπερι)
end in I and five in Υ. The intermediates, or neuters, end
in the variable vowels or in N, P, Σ.

22 The perfection of Diction is for it to be at once clear
and not mean. The clearest indeed is that made up of
the ordinary words for things, but it is mean, as is shown 20
by the poetry of Cleophon and Sthenelus. On the other
hand the Diction becomes distinguished and non-prosaic
by the use of unfamiliar terms, i. e. strange words, metaphors, lengthened forms, and everything that deviates
from the ordinary modes of speech.—But a whole statement in such terms will be either a riddle or a barbarism, 25
a riddle, if made up of metaphors, a barbarism, if made up
of strange words. The very nature indeed of a riddle is this,
to describe a fact in an impossible combination of words
(which cannot be done with the real names for things, but
can be with their metaphorical substitutes); e. g. 'I saw a
man glue brass on another with fire',[52] and the like. The 30
corresponding use of strange words results in a barbarism.
—A certain admixture, accordingly, of unfamiliar terms is
necessary. These, the strange word, the metaphor, the ornamental equivalent, &c., will save the language from seeming
mean and prosaic, while the ordinary words in it will secure the requisite clearness. What helps most, however, to 1458ᵇ
render the Diction at once clear and non-prosaic is the use
of the lengthened, curtailed, and altered forms of words.
Their deviation from the ordinary words will, by making
the language unlike that in general use, give it a non-
prosaic appearance; and their having much in common
with the words in general use will give it the quality of 5
clearness. It is not right, then, to condemn these modes of
speech, and ridicule the poet for using them, as some have
doné; e. g. the elder Euclid, who said it was easy to make
poetry if one were to be allowed to lengthen the words in
the statement itself as much as one likes—a procedure

[52] Cleobulina.

10 he caricatured by reading Ἐπιχάρην εἶδον Μαραθῶνάδε βαδίζοντα, and οὐκ ἄν γ' ἐράμενος τὸν ἐκείνου ἐλλέβορον as verses. A too apparent use of these licences has certainly a ludicrous effect, but they are not alone in that; the rule of moderation applies to all the constituents of the poetic vocabulary; even with metaphors, strange words, and the rest, the effect will be the same, if one uses them improperly and with a view to provoking laughter. The proper

15 use of them is a very different thing. To realize the difference one should take an epic verse and see how it reads when the normal words are introduced. The same should be done too with the strange word, the metaphor, and the rest; for one has only to put the ordinary words in their place to see the truth of what we are saying. The same iambic, for instance, is found in Aeschylus and Euripides, and as it stands in the former it is a poor line; whereas

20 Euripides, by the change of a single word, the substitution of a strange for what is by usage the ordinary word, has made it seem a fine one. Aeschylus having said in his *Philoctetes*:

φαγέδαινα ἥ μου σάρκας ἐσθίει ποδός

Euripides has merely altered the ἐσθίει here into ηοινᾶται. Or suppose

25   νῦν δέ μ' ἐὼν ὀλίγος τε καὶ οὐτιδανὸς καὶ ἀεικής [53]

to be altered, by the substitution of the ordinary words, into

νῦν δέ μ' ἐὼν μικρός τε καὶ ἀσθενικὸς καὶ ἀειδής.

Or the line

δίφρον ἀεικέλιον καταθεὶς ὀλίγην τε τράπεζαν [54]

into

30   δίφρον μοχθηρὸν καταθεὶς μικράν τε τράπεζαν,

[53] Od. ix. 515.
[54] Od. xx. 259.

Or ἠιόνες βοόωσιν[55] into ἠιόνες κράζουσιν. Add to this that Ariphrades used to ridicule the tragedians for introducing expressions unknown in the language of common life, δωμάτων ἄπο (for ἀπὸ δωμάτων), σέθεν, ἐγὼ δέ νιν,[56] 'Αχιλλέως πέρι (for περὶ 'Αχιλλέως), and the like. The mere fact of their not being in ordinary speech gives the 1459a
Diction a non-prosaic character; but Ariphrades was unaware of that. It is a great thing, indeed, to make a proper use of these poetical forms, as also of compounds and strange words. But the greatest thing by far is to be a master of metaphor. It is the one thing that cannot be learnt from others; and it is also a sign of genius, since a good metaphor implies an intuitive perception of the similarity in dissimilars.

Of the kinds of words we have enumerated it may be observed that compounds are most in place in the dithyramb, strange words in heroic, and metaphors in iambic poetry. Heroic poetry, indeed, may avail itself of them all. But in iambic verse, which models itself as far as possible on the spoken language, only those kinds of words are in place which are allowable also in an oration, i. e. the ordinary word, the metaphor, and the ornamental equivalent.

Let this, then, suffice as an account of Tragedy, the art imitating by means of action on the stage.

23 As for the poetry which merely narrates, or imitates by means of versified language (without action), it is evident that it has several points in common with Tragedy.

I. The construction of its stories should clearly be like that in a drama; they should be based on a single action, one that is a complete whole in itself, with a beginning, middle, and end, so as to enable the work to produce its own proper pleasure with all the organic unity of a living creature. Nor should one suppose that there is anything like them in our usual histories. A history has to deal not

55 *Il.* xvii. 265.
56 Soph., *O. C.*, 986.

with one action, but with one period and all that happened in that to one or more persons, however discon-
25 nected the several events may have been. Just as two events
may take place at the same time, e. g. the sea-fight off
Salamis and the battle with the Carthaginians in Sicily,
without converging to the same end, so too of two consecutive events one may sometimes come after the other
with no one end as their common issue. Nevertheless most
of our epic poets, one may say, ignore the distinction.
30 · Herein, then, to repeat what we have said before,[57] we
have a further proof of Homer's marvellous superiority to
the rest. He did not attempt to deal even with the Trojan
war in its entirety, though it was a whole with a definite
beginning and end—through a feeling apparently that it
35 was too long a story to be taken in in one view, or if not
that, too complicated from the variety of incident in it. As
it is, he has singled out one section of the whole; many of
the other incidents, however, he brings in as episodes,
using the Catalogue of the Ships, for instance, and other
episodes to relieve the uniformity of his narrative. As for
the other epic poets, they treat of one man, or one period;
1459ᵇ or else of an action which, although one, has a multiplicity of parts in it. This last is what the authors of the
Cypria [58] and Little Iliad [58] have done. And the result is
that, whereas the Iliad or Odyssey supplies materials for
only one, or at most two tragedies, the Cypria does that for
several and the Little Iliad for more than eight: for an
5 Adjudgment of Arms, a Philoctetes, a Neoptolemus, a Eu-
rypylus, a Ulysses as Beggar, a Laconian Women, a Fall of
Ilium, and a Departure of the Fleet; as also a Sinon, and a
Women of Troy.

24 II. Besides this, Epic poetry must divide into the same
species as Tragedy; it must be either simple or complex, a story of character or one of suffering. Its parts, too,

[57] 1451ᵃ 23 ff.
[58] Authorship unknown.

with the exception of Song and Spectacle, must be the same, as it requires Peripeties, Discoveries, and scenes of suffering just like Tragedy. Lastly, the Thought and Diction in it must be good in their way. All these elements appear in Homer first; and he has made due use of them. His two poems are each examples of construction, the *Iliad* simple and a story of suffering, the *Odyssey* complex (there is Discovery throughout it) and a story of character. And they are more than this, since in Diction and Thought too they surpass all other poems.

There is, however, a difference in the Epic as compared with Tragedy, (1) in its length, and (2) in its metre. (1) As to its length, the limit already suggested [59] will suffice: it must be possible for the beginning and end of the work to be taken in in one view—a condition which will be fulfilled if the poem be shorter than the old epics, and about as long as the series of tragedies offered for one hearing. For the extension of its length epic poetry has a special advantage, of which it makes large use. In a play one cannot represent an action with a number of parts going on simultaneously; one is limited to the part on the stage and connected with the actors. Whereas in epic poetry the narrative form makes it possible for one to describe a number of simultaneous incidents; and these, if germane to the subject, increase the body of the poem. This then is a gain to the Epic, tending to give it grandeur, and also variety of interest and room for episodes of diverse kinds. Uniformity of incident by the satiety it soon creates is apt to ruin tragedies on the stage. (2) As for its metre, the heroic has been assigned it from experience; were any one to attempt a narrative poem in some one, or in several, of the other metres, the incongruity of the thing would be apparent. The heroic in fact is the gravest and weightiest of metres —which is what makes it more tolerant than the rest of strange words and metaphors, that also being a point in which the narrative form of poetry goes beyond all others.

[59] 1451[a] 3.

The iambic and trochaic, on the other hand, are metres of 1460ª movement, the one representing that of life and action, the other that of the dance. Still more unnatural would it appear, if one were to write an epic in a medley of metres, as Chaeremon did.[60] Hence it is that no one has ever written a long story in any but heroic verse; nature herself, as we have said,[61] teaches us to select the metre appropriate to such a story.

5   Homer, admirable as he is in every other respect, is especially so in this, that he alone among epic poets is not unaware of the part to be played by the poet himself in the poem. The poet should say very little *in propria persona*, as he is no imitator when doing that. Whereas the other poets are perpetually coming forward in person, and say but little, and that only here and there, as imitators, 10 Homer after a brief preface brings in forthwith a man, a a woman, or some other Character—no one of them characterless, but each with distinctive characteristics.

The marvellous is certainly required in Tragedy. The Epic, however, affords more opening for the improbable, the chief factor in the marvellous, because in it the agents 15 are not visibly before one. The scene of the pursuit of Hector would be ridiculous on the stage—the Greeks halting instead of pursuing him, and Achilles shaking his head to stop them; [62] but in the poem the absurdity is overlooked. The marvellous, however, is a cause of pleasure, as is shown by the fact that we all tell a story with additions, in the belief that we are doing our hearers a pleasure.

Homer more than any other has taught the rest of us 20 the art of framing lies in the right way. I mean the use of paralogism. Whenever, if A is or happens, a consequent, B, is or happens, men's notion is that, if the B is, the A also is—but that is a false conclusion. Accordingly, if A is untrue, but there is something else, B, that on the assump-

[60] Centaur, cf. 1447ᵇ 21.
[61] 1449ª 24.
[62] *Il.* xxii. 205.

tion of its truth follows as its consequent, the right thing then is to add on the B. Just because we know the truth of the consequent, we are in our own minds led on to the erroneous inference of the truth of the antecedent. Here is 25 an instance, from the *Bath*-story in the *Odyssey*.[63]

A likely impossibility is always preferable to an unconvincing possibility. The story should never be made up of improbable incidents; there should be nothing of the sort in it. If, however, such incidents are unavoidable, they should be outside the piece, like the hero's ignorance in 30 *Oedipus* of the circumstances of Laius' death; not within it, like the report of the Pythian games in *Electra*,[64] or the man's having come to Mysia from Tegea without uttering a word on the way, in *The Mysians*.[65] So that it is ridiculous to say that one's Plot would have been spoilt without them, since it is fundamentally wrong to make up such Plots. If the poet has taken such a Plot, however, and one sees that he might have put it in a more probable form, he is guilty of absurdity as well as a fault of art. Even in 35 the *Odyssey* the improbabilities in the setting-ashore of Ulysses [66] would be clearly intolerable in the hands of an inferior poet. As it is, the poet conceals them, his other 1460ᵛ excellences veiling their absurdity. Elaborate Diction, however, is required only in places where there is no action, and no Character or Thought to be revealed. Where there is Character or Thought, on the other hand, an over-ornate 5 Diction tends to obscure them.

25 As regards Problems and their Solutions, one may see the number and nature of the assumptions on which they proceed by viewing the matter in the following way. (1) The poet being an imitator just like the painter or other maker of likenesses, he must necessarily in all instances represent things in one or other of three aspects,

[63] xix. 164–260.
[64] Soph. *El.* 660 ff.
[65] Probably by Aeschylus.
[66] xiii. 116 ff.

10 either as they were or are, or as they are said or thought to
be or to have been, or as they ought to be. (2) All this he
does in language, with an admixture, it may be, of strange
words and metaphors, as also of the various modified forms
of words, since the use of these is conceded in poetry.
(3) It is to be remembered, too, that there is not the same
kind of correctness in poetry as in politics, or indeed any
other art. There is, however, within the limits of poetry
15 itself a possibility of two kinds of error, the one directly,
the other only accidentally connected with the art. If the
poet meant to describe the thing correctly, and failed
through lack of power of expression, his art itself is at
fault. But if it was through his having meant to describe it
in some incorrect way (e. g. to make the horse in movement have both right legs thrown forward) that the
technical error (one in a matter of, say, medicine or some
20 other special science), or impossibilities of whatever kind
they may be, have got into his description, his error in that
case is not in the essentials of the poetic art. These, therefore, must be the premisses of the Solutions in answer to
the criticisms involved in the Problems.

I. As to the criticisms relating to the poet's art itself. Any
impossibilities there may be in his descriptions of things
are faults. But from another point of view they are justi-
25 fiable, if they serve the end of poetry itself—if (to assume
what we have said of that end) [67] they make the effect of
either that very portion of the work or some other portion
more astounding. The Pursuit of Hector is an instance in
point. If, however, the poetic end might have been as well
or better attained without sacrifice of technical correctness
in such matters, the impossibility is not to be justified,
since the description should be, if it can, entirely free from
30 error. One may ask, too, whether the error is in a matter
directly or only accidentally connected with the poetic
art; since it is a lesser error in an artist not to know, for

[67] 1452ᵃ 4, 1454ᵃ 4, 1455ᵃ 17, 1460ᵃ 11.

instance, that the hind has no horns, than to produce an
unrecognizable picture of one.

II. If the poet's description be criticized as not true to
fact, one may urge perhaps that the object ought to be as
described—an answer like that of Sophocles, who said that
he drew men as they ought to be, and Euripides as they 35
were. If the description, however, be neither true nor of
the thing as it ought to be, the answer must be then, that it
is in accordance with opinion. The tales about Gods, for
instance, may be as wrong as Xenophanes thinks, neither
true nor the better thing to say; but they are certainly in
accordance with opinion. Of other statements in poetry 1461ᵉ
one may perhaps say, not that they are better than the
truth, but that the fact was so at the time; e. g. the description of the arms: 'their spears stood upright, butt-end upon
the ground'; [68] for that was·the usual way of fixing them
then, as it is still with the Illyrians. As for the question
whether something said or done in a poem is morally right
or not, in dealing with that one should consider not only 5
the intrinsic quality of the actual word or deed, but also
the person who says or does it, the person to whom he
says or does it, the time, the means, and the motive of
the agent—whether he does it to attain a greater good, or
to avoid a greater evil.

III. Other criticisms one must meet by considering a
language of the poet: (1) by the assumption of a strange 10
word in a passage like οὐρῆας μὲν πρῶτον,[69] where by
οὐρῆας Homer may perhaps mean not mules but sentinels.
And in saying of Dolon,ὅς ῥ' ἦ τοι εἶδος μὲν ἔην κακός,[70]
his meaning may perhaps be, not that Dolon's body was de-
formed, but that his face was ugly, as εὐειδής is the Cretan
word for handsome-faced. So, too, ζωρότερον δὲ κέραιε [71] 15

[68] Il. x. 152.
[69] Il. i. 50.
[70] Il. x. 316.
[71] Il. ix. 202.

may mean not 'mix the wine stronger', as though for
topers, but 'mix it quicker', (2) Other expressions in Homer
may be explained as metaphorical; e. g. in ἄλλοι μέν ῥα θεοί
τε καὶ ἀνέρες εὖδον <ἅπαντες> παννύχιοι,[72] as compared
with what he tells us at the same time, ἦ τοι ὅτ᾽ ἐς πεδίον τὸ
Τρωικον ἀθρήσειεν, αὐλῶν συρίγγων †τε ὁμαδόν†,[73] the word
ἅπαντες, 'all', is metaphorically put for 'many', since 'all'
is a species of 'many'. So also his οἴη δ᾽ ἄμμορος[74] is meta-
20 phorical, the best known standing 'alone'. (3) A change,
as Hippias of Thasos suggested, in the mode of reading a
word will solve the difficulty in δίδομεν δέ οἱ,[75] and in τὸ μὲν
οὗ καταπύθεται ὄμβρῳ[76] (4) Other difficulties may be solved
by another punctuation; e. g. in Empedocles, αἶψα δὲ θνήτ᾽
25 ἐφύοντο, τὰ πρὶν μάθον ἀθάνατα ζωρά τε πρὶν κέκρητο. Or
(5) by the assumption of an equivocal term, as in
παρῴχηκεν δὲ πλέω νύξ,[77] where πλέω is equivocal. Or (6)
by an appeal to the custom of language. Wine-and-water we
call 'wine'; and it is on the same principle that Homer
speaks of a κνημὶς νεοτεύκτου κασσιτέροιο[78] a 'greave of new-
wrought tin'. A worker in iron we call a 'brazier'; and it is
on the same principle that Ganymede is described as the
'wine-server' of Zeus,[79] though the Gods do not drink
30 wine. This latter, however, may be an instance of metaphor. But whenever also a word seems to imply some contradiction, it is necessary to reflect how many ways there
may be of understanding it in the passage in question;
e. g. in Homer's τῇ ῥ᾽ ἔσχετο χάλκεον ἔγχος[80] one should
consider the possible senses of 'was stopped there'—
whether by taking it in this sense or in that one will best

[72] Cf. Il. x. 1, ii. 1.
[73] Il. x. 11–13.
[74] Il. xviii. 489 = Od. v. 275.
[75] Cf. Soph. El. 166ᵇ 1; Il. ii. 15.
[76] Il. xxiii. 327.
[77] Il. x. 251.
[78] Il. xxi. 592.
[79] Il. xx. 234.
[80] Il. xx. 267.

avoid the fault of which Glaucon speaks: 'They start with 35
some improbable presumption; and having so decreed it 1461ᵇ
themselves, proceed to draw inferences, and censure the
poet as though he had actually said whatever they happen
to believe, if his statement conflicts with their own notion
of things.' This is how Homer's silence about Icarius has
been treated. Starting with the notion of his having been a
Lacedaemonian, the critics think it strange for Telemachus
not to have met him when he went to Lacedaemon. 5
Whereas the fact may have been as the Cephallenians say,
that the wife of Ulysses was of a Cephallenian family, and
that her father's name was Icadius, not Icarius. So that it
is probably a mistake of the critics that has given rise to the
Problem.

Speaking generally, one has to justify (1) the Impossible
by reference to the requirements of poetry, or to the better,
or to opinion. For the purposes of poetry a convincing im- 10
possibility is preferable to an unconvincing possibility; and
if men such as Zeuxis depicted be impossible, the answer
is that it is better they should be like that, as the artist
ought to improve on his model. (2) The Improbable one
has to justify either by showing it to be in accordance with
opinion, or by urging that at times it is not improbable; for
there is a probability of things happening also against 15
probability. (3) The contradictions found in the poet's
language one should first test as one does an opponent's
confutation in a dialectical argument, so as to see whether
he means the same thing, in the same relation, and in the
same sense, before admitting that he has contradicted
either something he has said himself or what a man of
sound sense assumes as true. But there is no possible apol-
ogy for improbability of Plot or depravity of character,
when they are not necessary and no use is made of them, 20
like the improbability in the appearance of Aegeus in
Medea [81] and the baseness of Menelaus in *Orestes*.

The objections, then, of critics start with faults of five

[81] l. 663.

kinds: the allegation is always that something is either (1)
impossible, (2) improbable, (3) corrupting, (4) contradictory, or (5) against technical correctness. The answers
25 to these objections must be sought under one or other of
the above-mentioned heads, which are twelve in number.

26   The question may be raised whether the epic or the
tragic is the higher form of imitation. It may be argued that, if the less vulgar is the higher, and the less
vulgar is always that which addresses the better public, an
art addressing any and every one is of a very vulgar order.
It is a belief that their public cannot see the meaning, un-
30 less they add something themselves, that causes the perpetual movements of the performers—bad flute-players,
for instance, rolling about, if quoit-throwing is to be represented, and pulling at the conductor, if Scylla is the subject
of the piece. Tragedy, then, is said to be an art of this order
—to be in fact just what the later actors were in the eyes of
their predecessors; for Mynniscus used to call Callippides
35 'the ape', because he thought he so overacted his parts;
1462ᵃ and a similar view was taken of Pindarus also. All Tragedy,
however, is said to stand to the Epic as the newer to the
older school of actors. The one, accordingly, is said to address a cultivated audience, which does not need the accompaniment of gesture; the other, an uncultivated one.
5 If, therefore, Tragedy is a vulgar art, it must clearly be lower
than the Epic.
     The answer to this is twofold. In the first place, one may
urge (1) that the censure does not touch the art of the
dramatic poet, but only that of his interpreter; for it is
quite possible to overdo the gesturing even in an epic
recital, as did Sosistratus, and in a singing contest, as
did Mnasitheus of Opus. (2) That one should not condemn all movement, unless one means to condemn even
the dance, but only that of ignoble people—which is the
point of the criticism passed on Callippides and in the
10 present day on others, that their women are not like
gentlewomen. (3) That Tragedy may produce its effect

even without movement or action in just the same way as Epic poetry; for from the mere reading of a play its quality may be seen. So that, if it be superior in all other respects, this element of inferiority is no necessary part of it.

In the second place, one must remember (1) that Tragedy has everything that the Epic has (even the epic metre being admissible), together with a not inconsiderable addition in the shape of the Music (a very real factor in the pleasure of the drama) and the Spectacle. (2) That its reality of presentation is felt in the play as read, as well as in the play as acted. (3) That the tragic imitation requires less space for the attainment of its end; which is a great advantage, since the more concentrated effect is more 1462ᵇ pleasurable than one with a large admixture of time to dilute it—consider the *Oedipus* of Sophocles, for instance, and the effect of expanding it into the number of lines of the *Iliad*. (4) That there is less unity in the imitation of the epic poets, as is proved by the fact that any one work of theirs supplies matter for several tragedies; the result being that, if they take what is really a single story, it seems curt when briefly told, and thin and waterish when on the scale of length usual with their verse. In saying that there is less unity in an epic, I mean an epic made up of a plurality of actions, in the same way as the *Iliad* and *Odyssey* have many such parts, each one of them in itself of some magnitude; yet the structure of the two Homeric poems is as perfect as can be, and the action in them is as nearly as possible one action. If, then, Tragedy is superior in these respects, and also, besides these, in its poetic effect (since the two forms of poetry should give us, not any or every pleasure, but the very special kind we have mentioned), it is clear that, as attaining the poetic effect better than the Epic, it will be the higher form of art.

So much for Tragedy and Epic poetry—for these two arts in general and their species; the number and nature of their constituent parts; the causes of success and failure in them; the Objections of the critics, and the Solutions in answer to them.

Rhetoric

⊔⊔⊔⊔⊔⊔⊔⊔⊔⊔⊔⊔⊔⊔⊔⊔⊔⊔⊔⊔⊔⊔⊔

INTRODUCTION

All the formulations of science, art, and communication are arguments, and the term "argument" (*logos*) undergoes systematic transformations of meaning to bind together what men say, and do, and think, and are. Argument or logos is the statement of a scientific truth, and it is the essence of things signified by a true scientific proposition. Scientific *method* constructs arguments for discovery of truths about the unknown and for teaching truths already known. Arguments are about changing physical things, abstract mathematical things, and eternal metaphysical things. In addition to its use in arguments concerning things "known" in theoretic sciences, scientific method is applicable to the construction of practical arguments to guide and to judge things "done," and poetic arguments to construct and to judge things "made," which include things made of language, like tragedy, of which the argument or logos is the form or the soul.

In the sciences, method is addressed to the discovery of things, and logic to the formulation and validation of scientific discoveries. Rhetoric and its counterpart, dialectic, are universal arts addressed to the opinions of men about things which are known, more or less, by all men, and which are the subject of no science. The examination of arguments applicable to all things and to no particular things presents problems distinct from those of scientific arguments yet inseparably connected with them, since sciences are formed from the opinions of men concerning things. Dialectic is used to establish or falsify opinions concerning definitions, kinds, properties, and accidents of things. These were later called the four predicables (and were developed into five and then six predicables). They are formulated in dialectical propositions and dialectical syllogisms which provide logical means of proceeding from dialectical to demonstrative proof, from opinons to knowledge Rhetoric is used to support or refute opinons about particular matters which are not subject to scientific or dialectical proof, and its arguments relate particular speakers to particular hearers in "persuasions" or "beliefs." The meanings of Aristotle's word *pistis* include reference to the process of communication, the disposition of mind, and the formulation of statement of conveyed convictions which is not carried by any one of the words used in translating it. His criticism of other treatises on rhetoric is that they omit this essential part of the art. The sciences use methods adapted to things; dialectic and rhetoric make methods of their arts by finding "things" in the process of affecting opinions to take the place of the "things" uncovered by the methods of science. Aristotle uses the ingenious and untranslatable expression *entechnos methodos*, "in-arted method" (*Rhetoric* 1355ᵃ4), to convey that reorientation.

In the first chapter of the first book of the *Rhetoric*, Aristotle presents rhetoric as a method constituted by the structure of art concerned with persuasions, and argues that it is a kind of "demonstration," that is, a "showing forth." The dialectical examination of rhetorical argument or persuasion is by comparison of dialectic and rhetoric and of political and forensic rhetoric. After these preliminary considerations, the second chapter makes a "fresh start" with a definition of rhetoric: it is the faculty or power (*dunamis*) of perceiving in any given subject the possible means of persuasion. There are means of persuasion that fall outside art as well as means subject to art—"atechnical" means like witnesses, tortures, contracts which may be used when available, and "technical" or "artful" means which must be invented. Among the artful means of persuasion are those devised by speech (*logos*), which are of three kinds, since speech is communication between speaker and hearer: (1) the influence of the character of the speaker, (2) the frame of mind induced in the hearer, and (3) the speech (*logos*) itself insofar as it proves or seems to prove. The equivalents of induction, syllogism, and apparent syllogism in dialectic are example, enthymeme, and apparent enthymeme in rhetoric. What is persuasive and credible is so, either at once and in and by itself, or because it appears to be proved by propositions which are convincing. The subjects for rhetoric are matters of deliberation which seem to present us with alternative possibilities. The enthymeme and the example deal with what is in the main contingent.

An *enthymeme* is constructed of probabilities and signs, as a syllogism is constructed of propositions which are generally true and propositions which are necessarily true. Aristotle's analysis of kinds of "probability" and "signs" in the *Rhetoric* supplements his analysis of kinds of "being" in the *Metaphysics*. In the case of "being" the problem is to proceed from statements *about being* to the perception of *being in itself* as a subject without predicates. In the case of "probability" and "signs" the problem is to proceed from statements of opinions about connections to the recognition of connections which are probable or necessary. The metaphysical problem is a question of subject and predicate focussing on the subject; the rhetorical problem is a question of particular and universal focussing on the particular. The two analyses may be arranged in the same four steps. (1) An instance of "accidental being" is expressed, when it is opined, by use of the kind of sign in which a particular occurrence is used as warrant for a universal conclusion: "The fact that Socrates was wise and just is a sign that the wise are just." Even if the statement about Socrates is true, a syllogism cannot be formed from it, and the argument is therefore refutable. (2) An instance of "assertoric being" is expressed, when it is opined, by use of an instance of the kind of sign in which a universal law is used as warrant for a particular conclusion: "The fact that he breathes fast is a sign that he has a fever." Even if the statement is true, the argument is refutable because there are other causes of fast breathing than fever. (3) An instance of "predicational being" is expressed, when it is opined, by use of probability. A probability is "a thing that usually happens": it has the same relation to probable occurrences that a universal has to particulars. It is usually warmer in summer than in winter, but the inference that it will be warmer next August than last February may be refuted by the occurrence. (4) An instance of "ontic being" is expressed, when it is opined, by use of an infallible sign, a *tekmerion*, which is in itself a complete proof and irrefutable. "The fact that he has a fever is a sign that he is ill." An *example* is a kind of induction and is related to the proposition it supports not as part to whole, nor as whole to part, nor as whole to whole, but as part to part, or like to like.

Rhetorical enthymemes and dialectical syllogisms differ from the enthymemes and syllogisms used in other arts and faculties in that they are not about any particular subject matters. The more discourse conforms to a particular subject the more it departs from rhetoric and dialectic. Dialectical and rhetorical syllogisms are concerned with empty "places," or "topics" or "lines of argument." Common places, like "the more and the less" are used in otherwise unrelated subject matters like law, physics, or politics, and specific places, or proper places, or special lines of argument are based on propositions which apply to particular groups or classes of things. The organization of the *Rhetoric*, after these two chapters of preparation, is based on the use of the three means of persuasion—speaker, hearer, and speech—and of the common places and proper places. The first book treats and arranges subject-matters according to the proper places of audiences. The second book arranges arguments according to the common and proper places of speakers and hearers. The third book arranges speeches according to style and content.

The third chapter of the first book divides rhetoric into three kinds according to three kinds of listeners. For a speech is put together of three parts: the speaker, what he speaks about, and the hearer to whom he speaks; and the last, the hearer, determines the end of the speech. The hearers are observers or judges of things—past, present, and future. Political oratory in the legislative assembly is hortatory or dissuasive; the time under consideration is the future; and the end is the expedient or the harmful. Forensic oratory in the courtroom is accusatory or defensive; the time of the actions under consideration is the past; and its end is the just or the unjust. Epideictic oratory in the marketplace is laudatory or censorious; its time is the present; and its end is the honorable or the disgraceful. The remainder of the first book fills out the subject-matter proper to the three kinds of rhetoric by means of topics, like good and bad, virtue and vice, noble and base, and wrongdoing, and ends with a chapter on the atechnical means of persuasion.

The second book begins with an analysis of how a speaker can present his character as trustworthy, by leading his hearers to feel that he possesses prudence, virtue, and good will, and how he can put his hearers in the right frame of mind; and succeeding chapters distinguish the relevant emotions and types of human character. The eighteenth chapter turns from the means of investing speeches with moral character to the *topics* common to all oratory, like possible and impossible and differences of size or degree, the topic of amplification being most appropriate to epideictic oratory, the topic of past to forensic oratory, and the topic of possibility and the future to political oratory. In like fashion the twentieth chapter turns to the *persuasions* common to all kinds of oratory. The *example*, as a form of induction, has two varieties: the statement of actual historical facts, or the invention of

imagined facts, which takes two forms, illustrative parallels or parables and fables. The enthymeme, as a syllogism dealing with practical subjects, is related to maxims which are roughly the premisses or conclusions of
syllogisms, and the kinds and uses of maxims and enthymemes are examined. Enthymeme provides a selection
of arguments about questions that may arise. The remainder of the second book is a detailed treatment of
topics for enthymemes.

The third book begins with a summary of what has
been done and a restatement of what remains to be done.
There are three things to consider in making a speech,
the means of producing persuasion, the style or the
language to be used, and the proper arrangement of the
parts of the speech. The first two books have been devoted to a consideration of "that from which" or the matter of the speech or the sources of persuasion. They are
three: all persuasion must be effected by working on the
emotions of the judges, by giving them the right impression of the speaker's character, and by proving the truth
of the statements made. The style and the organization
of the speech are treated in the third book.

Aristotle recognized the affinity of rhetoric with politics, poetic, and logic, but he was also insistent on the
importance of keeping them distinct and the danger of
merging or confusing them. He speaks scornfully, in the
second chapter of the first book of the Rhetoric, of the
rhetoric that masquerades as political science and the
professors of rhetoric that pass themselves off as political
experts. In the last chapter of the Nicomachean Ethics,
he prepares for the transition from ethics to politics by
discussing legislation, and he criticizes the sophists who
profess to teach politics and reduce it to rhetoric and who
study bodies of law to select the best laws as if they were
works of art. One of the paradoxes of the influence of
Aristotle is that the Rhetoric has had more obvious and
noteworty effects in the development of aesthetics, polit-

ical science, history, and logic than in rhetoric itself. The *Poetics* have had little direct or undistorted effect on literature or literary criticism, but discussions of the arguments of history, parable, and fable, and analyses of the maxim viewed as expression of thought and judgment of value and of the enthymeme viewed as applied argument or personalized essay—not to mention Theophrastus's transformation of "characters"—were stimulating causes of the development of literary genres which did not exist when Aristot'e wrote the *Poetics*. The kinds of rhetoric have been generalized from their original practical forms —political, forensic, and epideictic—to become general forms of discourse—deliberative, judicial, and demonstrative—applicable in the classification of the genres of literature. We have no Greek commentaries on the *Poetics*; Arabic poetry is so unlike Greek poetry that Arabic commentaries on the *Poetics*, like Alfarabi's, are scrupulous in their concern with only the first three chapters of Aristotle's text; the first Latin translation of the *Poetics* appeared in the thirteenth century, and thereafter the numerous Renaissance commentaries adjust Aristotle's poetic science to Horace's rhetorical art. Early modern rhetoricians made rhetoric an organon for the study of literature and a program for the teaching of composition. John Bodin gave strong impulse to the formation of modern theories of history and political science by reformulating both on the basis of the study of law. Francis Bacon and earlier Renaissance speculators on the new method of science and the method of discovery found part of their inspiration in the common places of rhetoric. The topics of rhetoric are empty places to be used for the discovery of arguments and things, but they have been so filled since Aristotle delineated them, with the matters of related arts and sciences that, despite their contribution to the development of those disciplines, they have been degraded to schematized *topics* and banal *common places* unsuited for the detection or rediscovery of common places and topics as devices of invention and discovery.

RHETORICA

CONTENTS

BOOK I

1. Rhetoric is the counterpart of Dialectic. It is a subject that can be treated systematically. The argumentative modes of persuasion are the essence of the art of rhetoric: appeals to the emotions warp the judgement. The writers of current text-books on rhetoric give too much attention to the forensic branch (in which chicanery is easier) and too little to the political (where the issues are larger). Argumentative persuasion is a sort of demonstration; and the rhetorical form of demonstration is the enthymeme. Four uses of rhetoric. Its possible abuse is no argument against its proper use on the side of truth and justice. The honest rhetorician has no separate name to distinguish him from the dishonest/726

2. Definition of rhetoric as 'the faculty of observing in any given case the available means of persuasion'. Of the modes of persuasion some belong strictly to the art of rhetoric, and some do not. The rhetorician finds the latter kind (viz. witnesses, contracts, and the like) ready to his hand. The former kind he must provide himself; and it has three divisions—(1) the speaker's power of evincing a personal character which will make his speech credible; (2) his power of stirring the emotions of his hearers; (3) his power of proving a truth, or an apparent truth, by means of persuasive arguments. Hence rhetoric may be regarded as an offshoot of dialectic, and also of ethical (or, political) studies. The persuasive arguments are (a) the example, corresponding to induction in dialectic; (b) the enthymeme, corresponding to the syllogism; (c) the apparent Enthymeme, corresponding to the apparent syllogism. The Enthymeme is a rhetorical syllogism, and the example a rhetorical induction. Rhetoric has regard to classes of men, not to individual men; its subjects, and the premises from which it argues, are in the main such as present alternative possibilities in the sphere of human action; and it must

adapt itself to an audience of untrained thinkers who cannot follow a long train of reasoning. The premisses from which enthymemes are formed are 'probabilities' and 'signs'; and signs are either fallible or infallible, in which latter case they are termed *tekmeria*. The lines of argument, or topics, which Enthymemes follow may be distinguished as common (or, general) and special (i. e. special to a single study, such as natural science or ethics). The special lines should be used discreetly, if the rhetorician is not to find himself deserting his own field for another/731

3. There are three kinds of rhetoric: A. political (deliberative), B. forensic (legal), and C. epideictic (the ceremonial oratory of display). Their (a) divisions, (b) times, and (c) ends are as follows: A. Political (a) exhortation and dehortation, (b) future, (c) expediency and inexpediency; B. Forensic (a) accusation and defence, (b) past, (c) justice and injustice; C. Epideictic (a) praise and censure, (b) present, (c) honour and dishonour/739

4. (A) The subjects of Political Oratory fall under five main heads: (1) ways and means, (2) war and peace, (3) national defence, (4) imports and exports, (5) legislation. The scope of each of these divisions/742

BOOK II

18. Retrospect, and glance forward. The forms of argument common to all oratory will next be discussed/745

19. The four general lines (common-places) of argument are: (1) The Possible and Impossible; (2) Fact Past; (3) Fact Future; (4) Degree/746

20. The two general modes of persuasion are: (1) the example, (2) the Enthymeme; the maxim being part of the Enthymeme. Examples are either (a) historical parallels, or (b) invented parallels, viz. either (i) illustrations, or (ii) fables, such as those of Aesop. Fables are suitable for popular addresses; and they have this advantage, that they are comparatively easy to invent, whereas it is hard to find parallels among actual past events/750

21. Use of maxims. A maxim is a general statement about questions of practical conduct. It is an incomplete Enthymeme. Four kinds of maxims. Maxims should be used

(a) by elderly men, and (b) to controvert popular sayings. Advantages of maxims: (a) they enable a speaker to gratify his commonplace hearers by expressing as a universal truth the opinions which they themselves hold about particular cases; (b) they invest a speech with moral character/752

22. **Enthymemes.** In Enthymemes we must not carry our reasoning too far back, nor must we put in all the steps that lead to our conclusion. There are two kinds of Enthymemes: (a) the demonstrative, formed by the conjunction of compatible propositions; (b) the refutative, formed by the conjunction of incompatible propositions/756

Rhetorica

(Rhetoric)

Translated by W. Rhys Roberts

⊔⊔⊔

BOOK I

1354ª 1   Rhetoric is the counterpart of Dialectic.[1] Both alike
are concerned with such things as come, more or less,
within the general ken of all men and belong to no definite science. Accordingly all men make use, more or less,
of both; for to a certain extent all men attempt to discuss
5 statements and to maintain them, to defend themselves
and to attack others. Ordinary people do this either at
random or through practice and from acquired habit.
Both ways being possible, the subject can plainly be
handled systematically, for it is possible to inquire the
10 reason why some speakers succeed through practice and
others spontaneously, and every one will at once agree
that such an inquiry is the function of an art.

   Now, the framers of the current treatises on rhetoric
have constructed but a small portion of that art. The
modes of persuasion are the only true constituents of the
art: everything else is merely accessory. These writers,
however, say nothing about Enthymemes, which are the
15 substance of rhetorical persuasion, but deal mainly with
non-essentials. The arousing of prejudice, pity, anger, and

---

   [1] 'Rhetoric' and 'Dialectic' may be roughly Englished as 'the art
of speaking' and 'the art of logical discussion.' Aristotle's philosophical definition of 'Rhetoric' is given at the beginning of c. 2.

similar emotions has nothing to do with the essential
facts, but is merely a personal appeal to the man who is
judging the case. Consequently if the rules for trials
which are now laid down in some states—especially in 20
well-governed states—were applied everywhere, such people would have nothing to say. All men, no doubt, *think*
that the laws should prescribe such rules, but some, as in
the court of Areopagus, give practical effect to their
thoughts and forbid talk about non-essentials. This is
sound law and custom. It is not right to pervert the judge [2]
by moving him to anger or envy or pity—one might as 25
well warp a carpenter's rule before using it. Again, a lita-
gant has clearly nothing to do but to show that the alleged
fact is so or is not so, that it has or has not happened. As
to whether a thing is important or unimportant, just or
unjust, the judge must surely refuse to take his instruc-
tions from the litigants: he must decide for himself all 30
such points as the law-giver has not already defined for
him.

Now, it is of great moment that well-drawn laws should
themselves define all the points they possibly can and
leave as few as may be to the decision of the judges; and
this for several reasons. First, to find one man, or a few
men, who are sensible persons and capable of legislating 1354ᵇ
and administering justice is easier than to find a large
number. Next, laws are made after long consideration,
whereas decisions in the courts are given at short notice,
which makes it hard for those who try the case to satisfy
the claims of justice and expediency. The weightiest reason of all is that the decision of the lawgiver is not particu- 5
lar but prospective and general, whereas members of the
assembly and the jury find it *their* duty to decide on definite cases brought before them. They will often have
allowed themselves to be so much influenced by feelings
of friendship or hatred or self-interest that they lose any

[2] Here and in what follows, the English reader should understand
'judge' in a broad sense, including 'jurymen' and others who 'judge.'

10 clear vision of the truth and have their judgement obscured by considerations of personal pleasure or pain. In
general, then, the judge should, we say, be allowed to
decide as few things as possible. But questions as to
whether something has happened or has not happened,
will be or will not be, is or is not, must of necessity be left
15 to the judge, since the lawgiver cannot foresee them. If
this is so, it is evident that any one who lays down rules
about other matters, such as what must be the contents of
the 'introduction' or the 'narration' or any of the other
divisions of a speech, is theorizing about non-essentials as
if they belonged to the art. The only question with which
these writers here deal is how to put the judge into a given
20 frame of mind. About the orator's proper modes of persuasion they have nothing to tell us; nothing, that is, about
how to gain skill in Enthymemes.

Hence it comes that, although the same systematic
principles apply to political as to forensic oratory,[3] and
25 although the former is a nobler business, and fitter for a
citizen, than that which concerns the relations of private
individuals, these authors say nothing about political oratory, but try, one and all, to write treatises on the way to
plead in court. The reason for this is that in political
oratory there is less inducement to talk about non-essentials. Political oratory is less given to unscrupulous practices than forensic, because it treats of wider issues. In a
30 political debate the man who is forming a judgement is
making a decision about his own vital interests. There is
no need, therefore, to prove anything except that the facts
are what the supporter of a measure maintains they are.
In forensic oratory this is not enough; to conciliate the
listener is what pays here. It is other people's affairs that
35 are to be decided, so that the judges, intent on their own

[3] The words 'orator' and 'oratory' have the advantages of brevity,
but the reader will bear in mind that 'public speaker' and 'public
speaking' are in some ways nearer the Greek conception of 'rhetor'
and 'rhetoric.'

satisfaction and listening with partiality, surrender themselves to the disputants instead of judging between them.1355ᵃ
Hence in many places, as we have said already,⁴ irrelevant
speaking is forbidden in the law-courts: in the public assembly those who have to form a judgement are themselves well able to guard against that.

It is clear, then, that rhetorical study, in its strict sense,
is concerned with the modes of persuasion. Persuasion is 5
clearly a sort of demonstration, since we are most fully
persuaded when we consider a thing to have been demonstrated. The orator's demonstration is an Enthymeme, and
this is, in general, the most effective of the modes of persuasion. The Enthymeme is a sort of syllogism, and the
consideration of syllogisms of all kinds, without distinction, is the business of dialectic, either of dialectic as a
whole or of one of its branches. It follows plainly, there- 10
fore, that he who is best able to see how and from what
elements a syllogism is produced will also be best skilled
in the Enthymeme, when he has further learnt what its
subject-matter is and in what respects it differs from the
syllogism of strict logic. The true and the approximately
true are apprehended by the same faculty; it may also be
noted that men have a sufficient natural instinct for what 15
is true, and usually do arrive at the truth. Hence the man
who makes a good guess at truth is likely to make a good
guess at probabilities.

It has now been shown that the ordinary writers on
rhetoric treat of non-essentials; it has also been shown
why they have inclined more towards the forensic branch
of oratory. 20

Rhetoric is useful (1) because things that are true and
things that are just have a natural tendency to prevail over
their opposites, so that if the decisions of judges are not
what they ought to be, the defeat must be due to the
speakers themselves, and they must be blamed accordingly. Moreover (2) before some audiences not even the

⁴ 1354ᵃ 22.

25 possession of the exactest knowledge will make it easy for
what we say to produce conviction. For argument based
on knowledge implies instruction, and there are people
whom one cannot instruct. Here, then, we must use, as
our modes of persuasion and argument, notions possessed
by everybody, as we observed in the *Topics* [5] when dealing
with the way to handle a popular audience. Further, (3)
we must be able to employ persuasion, just as strict rea-
30 soning can be employed, on opposite sides of a question,
not in order that we may in practice employ it in both
ways (for we must not make people believe what is
wrong), but in order that we may see clearly what the
facts are, and that, if another man argues unfairly, we on
our part may be able to confute him. No other of the arts
35 draws opposite conclusions: dialectic and rhetoric alone
do this. Both these arts draw opposite conclusions impartially. Nevertheless, the underlying facts do not lend
themselves equally well to the contrary views. No; things
that are true and things that are better are, by their nature,
practically always easier to prove and easier to believe in.
1355b Again, (4) it is absurd to hold that a man ought to be
ashamed of being unable to defend himself with his limbs,
but not of being unable to defend himself with speech and
reason, when the use of rational speech is more distinctive
of a human being than the use of his limbs. And if it be
objected that one who uses such power of speech unjustly
might do great harm, *that* is a charge which may be made
in common against all good things except virtue, and
5 above all against the things that are most useful, as
strength, health, wealth, generalship. A man can confer
the greatest of benefits by a right use of these, and inflict
the greatest of injuries by using them wrongly.

It is clear, then, that rhetoric is not bound up with a
single definite class of subjects, but is as universal as dialectic; it is clear, also, that it is useful. It is clear, further, that
10 its function is not simply to succeed in persuading, but

[5] *Topics*, i. 2, 101a 30–4.

rather to discover the means of coming as near such success as the circumstances of each particular case allow. In
this it resembles all other arts. For example, it is not the
function of medicine simply to make a man quite healthy,
but to put him as far as may be on the road to health; it is
possible to give excellent treatment even to those who can
never enjoy sound health. Furthermore, it is plain that it
is the function of one and the same art to discern the real
and the apparent means of persuasion, just as it is the 15
function of dialectic to discern the real and the apparent
syllogism. What makes a man a 'sophist' is not his faculty,
but his moral purpose. In rhetoric, however, the term
'rhetorician' may describe either the speaker's knowledge
of the art, or his moral purpose. In dialectic it is different: 20
a man is a 'sophist' because he has a certain kind of moral
purpose, a 'dialectician' in respect, not of his moral purpose, but of his faculty.

Let us now try to give some account of the systematic
principles of Rhetoric itself—of the right method and
means of succeeding in the object we set before us. We
must make as it were a fresh start, and before going further
define what rhetoric is.   25

2 Rhetoric may be defined as the faculty of observing
in any given case the available means of persuasion. This
is not a function of any other art. Every other art can instruct or persuade about its own particular subject-matter;
for instance, medicine about what is healthy and unhealthy, geometry about the properties of magnitudes, 30
arithmetic about numbers, and the same is true of the
other arts and sciences. But rhetoric we look upon as the
power of observing the means of persuasion on almost any
subject presented to us; and that is why we say that, in its
technical character, it is not concerned with any special 35
or definite class of subjects.

Of the modes of persuasion some belong strictly to the
art of rhetoric and some do not. By the latter I mean such

things as are not supplied by the speaker but are there at the outset—witnesses, evidence given under torture, written contracts, and so on. By the former I mean such as we can ourselves construct by means of the principles of rhetoric. The one kind has merely to be used, the other has to be invented.

1356ᵃ Of the modes of persuasion furnished by the spoken word there are three kinds. The first kind depends on the personal character of the speaker; the second on putting the audience into a certain ⁶ frame of mind; the third on the proof, or apparent proof, provided by the words of the speech itself. Persuasion is achieved by the speaker's per-
5 sonal character when the speech is so spoken as to make us think him credible. We believe good men more fully and more readily than others: this is true generally whatever the question is, and absolutely true where exact certainty is impossible and opinions are divided. This kind of persuasion, like the others, should be achieved by what the speaker says, not by what people think of his character
10 before he begins to speak. It is not true, as some writers assume in their treatises on rhetoric, that the personal goodness revealed by the speaker contributes nothing to his power of persuasion; on the contrary, his character may almost be called the most effective means of persuasion he possesses. Secondly, persuasion may come through the hearers, when the speech stirs their emotions. Our judge-
15 ments when we are pleased and friendly are not the same as when we are pained and hostile. It is towards producing these effects, as we maintain, that present-day writers on rhetoric direct the whole of their efforts. This subject shall be treated in detail when we come to speak of the emotions.⁷ Thirdly, persuasion is effected through the speech
20 itself when we have proved a truth or an apparent truth by means of the persuasive arguments suitable to the case in question.

There are, then, these three means of effecting persua-

⁶ i. e. the right, fit, required frame of mind.
⁷ ii, cc. 2–11.

sion. The man who is to be in command of them must, it is clear, be able (1) to reason logically, (2) to understand human character and goodness in their various forms, and (3) to understand the emotions—that is, to name them and describe them, to know their causes and the way in which they are excited. It thus appears that rhetoric is an 25 offshoot of dialectic and also of ethical studies. Ethical studies may fairly be called political; and for this reason rhetoric masquerades as political science, and the professors of it as political experts—sometimes from want of education, sometimes from ostentation, sometimes owing to other human failings. As a matter of fact, it is a branch 30 of dialectic and similar to it, as we said at the outset.[8] Neither rhetoric nor dialectic is the scientific study of any one separate subject: both are faculties for providing arguments. This is perhaps a sufficient account of their scope and of how they are related to each other.   35

With regard to the persuasion achieved by proof or apparent proof: just as in dialectic there is induction on the 1356[b] one hand and syllogism or apparent syllogism on the other, so it is in rhetoric. The example is an induction, the Enthymeme is a syllogism, and the apparent Enthymeme is an apparent syllogism. I call the Enthymeme a rhetorical syllogism, and the example a rhetorical induction. Every 5 one who effects persuasion through proof does in fact use either Enthymemes or examples; there is no other way. And since every one who proves anything at all is bound to use either syllogisms or inductions (and this is clear to us from the *Analytics* [9]), it must follow that Enthymemes are syllogisms and examples are inductions. The difference 10 between example and Enthymeme is made plain by the passages in the *Topics* [10] where induction and syllogism have already been discussed. When we base the proof of a proposition on a number of similar cases, this is induction in dialectic, example in rhetoric; when it is shown that,

[8] i. 1. 1354[a] 1.
[9] *Anal. Pr.* ii 23, 24; *Anal. Post.* i 1. Cp. 68[b] 13.
[10] *Top.* i. 1 and 12.

15 certain propositions being true, a further and quite distinct proposition must also be true in consequence, whether invariably or usually, this is called syllogism in dialectic, Enthymeme in rhetoric. It is plain also that each of these types of oratory has its advantages. Types of oratory, I say: for what has been said in the *Methodics* [11] applies equally well here; in some oratorical styles exam-
20 ples prevail, in others Enthymemes; and in like manner, some orators are better at the former and some at the latter. Speeches that rely on examples are as persuasive as the other kind, but those which rely on Enthymemes excite the louder applause. The sources of examples and Enthymemes, and their proper uses, we will discuss later.[12] Our next step is to define the processes themselves more
25 clearly.

A statement is persuasive and credible either because it is directly self-evident or because it appears to be proved from other statements that are so. In either case it is persuasive because there is somebody whom it persuades. But none of the arts theorize about individual cases. Medicine, for instance, does not theorize about what will help to
30 cure Socrates or Callias, but only about what will help to cure any or all of a given class of patients: this alone is its business: individual cases are so infinitely various that no systematic knowledge of them is possible. In the same way the theory of rhetoric is concerned not with what seems probable to a given individual like Socrates or Hippias, but with what seems probable to men of a given type; and this is true of dialectic also. Dialectic does not construct its
35 syllogisms out of any haphazard materials, such as the fancies of crazy people, but out of materials that call for discussion; and rhetoric, too, draws upon the regular sub-
1357ᵃ jects of debate. The duty of rhetoric is to deal with such matters as we deliberate upon without arts or systems to guide us, in the hearing of persons who cannot take in at a glance a complicated argument, or follow a long chain of

[11] A lost logical treatise of Aristotle.
[12] ii, cc. 20–4.

reasoning. The subjects of our deliberation are such as seem to present us with alternative possibilities: about things that could not have been, and cannot now or in the future be, other than they are, nobody who takes them to be of this nature wastes his time in deliberation.

It is possible to form syllogisms and draw conclusions from the results of previous syllogisms; or, on the other hand, from premisses which have not been thus proved, and at the same time are so little accepted that they call for proof. Reasonings of the former kind will necessarily be hard to follow owing to their length, for we assume an audience of untrained thinkers; those of the latter kind will fail to win assent, because they are based on premisses that are not generally admitted or believed.

The Enthymeme and the example must, then, deal with what is in the main contingent, the example being an induction, and the Enthymeme a syllogism, about such matters. The Enthymeme must consist of a few propositions, fewer often than those which make up the normal syllogism. For if any of these propositions is a familiar fact, there is no need even to mention it; the hearer adds it himself. Thus, to show that Dorieus has been victor in a contest for which the prize is a crown, it is enough to say 'For he has been victor in the Olympic games,' without adding 'And in the Olympic games the prize is a crown,' a fact which everybody knows.

There are few facts of the 'necessary' type that can form the basis of rhetorical syllogisms. Most of the things about which we make decisions, and into which therefore we inquire, present us with alternative possibilities. For it is about our actions that we deliberate and inquire, and all our actions have a contingent character; hardly any of them are determined by necessity. Again, conclusions that state what is merely usual or possible must be drawn from premisses that do the same, just as 'necessary' conclusions must be drawn from 'necessary' premisses; this too is clear to us from the *Analytics*.[13] It is evident, therefore, that the

[13] *An. Pr.* i. 8, 12–14, 27.

propositions forming the basis of Enthymemes, though some of them may be 'necessary,' will most of them be only usually true. Now the materials of Enthymemes are Probabilities and Signs, which we can see must correspond respectively with the propositions that are generally and 35 those that are necessarily true. A Probability is a thing that usually happens; not, however, as some definitions would suggest, anything whatever that usually happens, but only if it belongs to the class of the 'contingent' or 'variable.' It bears the same relation to that in respect of which it is probable as the universal bears to the particular. 1357ᵇ Of Signs, one kind bears the same relation to the statement it supports as the particular bears to the universal, the other the same as the universal bears to the particular. The infallible kind is a 'complete proof'; the fallible kind 5 has no specific name. By infallible signs I mean those on which syllogisms proper may be based: and this shows us why this kind of Sign is called 'complete proof': when people think that what they have said cannot be refuted, they then think that they are bringing forward a 'complete proof,' meaning that the matter has now been demonstrated and completed; for the word peras has the same 10 meaning (of 'end' or 'boundary') as the word tekmar in the ancient tongue. Now the one kind of Sign (that which bears to the proposition it supports the relation of particlar to universal) may be illustrated thus. Suppose it were said, 'The fact that Socrates was wise and just is a sign that the wise are just.' Here we certainly have a Sign; but even though the proposition be true, the argument is refutable, since it does not form a syllogism. Suppose, on the other hand, it were said, 'The fact that he has a fever is a sign 15 that he is ill,' or, 'The fact that she is giving milk is a sign that she has lately borne a child.' Here we have the infallible kind of Sign, the only kind that constitutes a complete proof, since it is the only kind that, if the particular statement is true, is irrefutable. The other kind of Sign, that which bears to the proposition it supports the rela-

tion of universal to particular, might be illustrated by
saying, 'The fact that he breathes fast is a sign that he has
a fever.' This argument also is refutable, even if the statement about the fast breathing be true, since a man may
breathe hard without having a fever.   20

It has, then, been stated above what is the nature of a
Probability, of a Sign, and of a complete proof, and what
are the differences between them. In the *Analytics* [14] a
more explicit description has been given of these points;
it is there shown why some of these reasonings can be put
into syllogisms and some cannot.

The 'example' has already been described as one kind 25
of induction; and the special nature of the subject-matter
that distinguishes it from the other kinds has also been
stated above. Its relation to the proposition it supports is
not that of part to whole, nor whole to part, nor whole to
whole, but of part to part, or like to like. When two statements are of the same order, but one is more familiar than
the other, the former is an 'example.' The argument may, 30
for instance, be that Dionysius, in asking as he does for a
bodyguard, is scheming to make himself a despot. For in
the past Peisistratus kept asking for a bodyguard in order
to carry out such a scheme, and did make himself a despot
as soon as he got it; and so did Theagenes at Megara; and
in the same way all other instances known to the speaker
are made into examples, in order to show what is not yet
known, that Dionysius has the same purpose in making 35
the same request: all these being instances of the one general principle, that a man who asks for a bodyguard is
scheming to make himself a despot. We have now de-1358ᵃ
scribed the sources of those means of persuasion which
are popularly supposed to be demonstrative.

There is an important distinction between two sorts of
enthymemes that has been wholly overlooked by almost
everybody—one that also subsists between the syllogisms
treated of in dialectic. One sort of Enthymeme really

[14] An. Pr. ii. 27.

5 belongs to rhetoric, as one sort of syllogism really belongs to dialectic; but the other sort really belongs to other arts and faculties, whether to those we already exercise or to those we have not yet acquired. Missing this distinction, people fail to notice that the more correctly they handle their particular subject the further they are getting away from pure rhetoric or dialectic. This statement will be 10 clearer if expressed more fully. I mean that the proper subjects of dialectical and rhetorical syllogisms are the things with which we say the regular or universal Lines of Argument [15] are concerned, that is to say those lines of argument that apply equally to questions of right conduct, natural science, politics, and many other things that have nothing to do with one another. Take, for instance, the line of argument concerned with 'the more or less.' [16] On 15 this line of argument it is equally easy to base a syllogism or Enthymeme about any of what nevertheless are essentially disconnected subjects—right conduct, natural science, or anything else whatever. But there are also those special Lines of Argument which are based on such propositions as apply only to particular groups or classes of things. Thus there are propositions about natural science on which it is impossible to base any Enthymeme or syllogism about ethics, and other propositions about ethics on which nothing can be based about natural science. The 20 same principle applies throughout. The general Lines of Argument have no special subject-matter, and therefore will not increase our understanding of any particular class of things. On the other hand, the better the selection one makes of propositions suitable for special Lines of Argument, the nearer one comes, unconsciously, to setting up a science that is distinct from dialectic and rhetoric. One may succeed in stating the required principles, but one's 25 science will be no longer dialectic or rhetoric, but the science to which the principles thus discovered belong. Most Enthymemes are in fact based upon these particular

[15] Or Topics, Commonplaces.
[16] i.e. the topic of degree.

or special Lines of Argument; comparatively few on the common or general kind. As in the *Topics*,[17] therefore, so in this work, we must distinguish, in dealing with Enthy- 30 memes, the special and the general Lines of Argument on which they are to be founded. By special Lines of Argument I mean the propositions peculiar to each several class of things, by general those common to all classes alike. We may begin with the special Lines of Argument. But, first of all, let us classify rhetoric into its varieties. Having distinguished these we may deal with them one by one, and try to discover the elements of which each is composed, and the propositions each must employ.   35

3 Rhetoric falls into three divisions, determined by the three classes of listeners to speeches. For of the three elements in speech-making—speaker, subject, and person addressed—it is the last one, the hearer, that determines the speech's end and object. The hearer must be either a 1358ᵇ judge, with a decision to make about things past or future, or an observer. A member of the assembly decides about future events, a juryman about past events: while those who merely decide on the orator's skill are observers. From 5 this it follows that there are three divisions of oratory— (1) political, (2) forensic, and (3) the ceremonial oratory of display.[18]

Political speaking urges us either to do or not to do something: one of these two courses is always taken by private counsellors, as well as by men who address public assemblies. Forensic speaking either attacks or defends 10 somebody: one or other of these two things must always be one by the parties in a case. The ceremonial oratory of display either praises or censures somebody. These three

---

[17] Cp. *Top.* 1. 10, 14; iii. 5; *Soph. El.* 9.

[18] Or; deliberative (advisory), legal, and epideictic—the oratory respectively of parliamentary assemblies, of law-courts, and of ceremonial occasions when there is an element of 'display,' 'show,' 'declamation,' and the result is a 'set speech' or 'harangue.'

kinds of rhetoric refer to three different kinds of time. The
political orator is concerned with the future: it is about
things to be done hereafter that he advises, for or against.
15 The party in a case at law is concerned with the past: one
man accuses the other, and the other defends himself with
reference to things already done. The ceremonial orator
is, properly speaking, concerned with the present, since all
men praise or blame in view of the state of things existing
at the time, though they often find it useful also to recall
20 the past and to make guesses at the future.

Rhetoric has three distinct ends in view, one for each
of its three kinds. The political orator aims at establishing
the expediency or the harmfulness of a proposed course
of action; if he urges its acceptance, he does so on the
ground that it will do good; if he urges its rejection, he
does so on the ground that it will do harm; and all other
points, such as whether the proposal is just or unjust, hon-
25 ourable or dishonourable, he brings in as subsidiary and
relative to this main consideration. Parties in a law-case
aim at establishing the justice or injustice of some action,
and they too bring in all other points as subsidiary and
relative to this one. Those who praise or attack a man aim
at proving him worthy of honour or the reverse, and they
too treat all other considerations with reference to this
one.

That the three kinds of rhetoric do aim respectively at
30 the three ends we have mentioned is shown by the fact
that speakers will sometimes not try to establish anything
else. Thus, the litigant will sometimes not deny that a
thing has happened or that he has done harm. But that he
is guilty of injustice he will never admit; otherwise there
would be no need of a trial. So too, political orators often
make any concession short of admitting that they are rec-
ommending their hearers to take an inexpedient course or
35 not to take an expedient one. The question whether it is
not *unjust* for a city to enslave its innocent neighbours
often does not trouble them at all. In like manner those

who praise or censure a man do not consider whether his 1359ᵃ
acts have been expedient or not, but often make it a
ground of actual praise that he has neglected his own
interest to do what was honourable. Thus, they praise
Achilles because he championed his fallen friend Patro-
clus, though he knew that this meant death, and that
otherwise he need not die: yet while to die thus was the
nobler thing for him to do, the expedient thing was to
live on.   5

It is evident from what has been said that it is these
three subjects, more than any others, about which the
orator must be able to have propositions at his command.
Now the propositions of Rhetoric are Complete Proofs,
Probabilities, and Signs. Every kind of syllogism is composed of propositions, and the enthymeme is a particular 10
kind of syllogism composed of the aforesaid propositions.[19]

Since only possible actions, and not impossible ones, can
ever have been done in the past or the present, and since
things which have not occurred, or will not occur, also
cannot have been done or be going to be done, it is necessary for the political, the forensic, and the ceremonial 15
speaker alike to be able to have at their command propositions about the possible and the impossible, and about
whether a thing has or has not occurred, will or will not
occur. Further, all men, in giving praise or blame, in urging us to accept or reject proposals for action, in accusing
others or defending themselves, attempt not only to
prove the points mentioned but also to show that the 20
good or the harm, the honour or disgrace, the justice or
injustice, is great or small, either absolutely or relatively;
and therefore it is plain that we must also have at our
command propositions about greatness or smallness and
the greater or the lesser—proposition both universal and
particular. Thus, we must be able to say which is the
greater or lesser good, the greater or lesser act of justice or
injustice; and so on.

Such, then, are the subjects regarding which we are

[19] i.e. of Complete Proofs, Probabilities, and Signs relating to the
three subjects of the expedient, the just, and the noble.

inevitably bound to master the propositions relevant to them. We must now discuss each particular class of these subjects in turn, namely those dealt with in political, in ceremonial, and lastly in legal, oratory.

30 **4**   First, then, we must ascertain what are the kinds of things, good or bad, about which the political orator offers counsel. For he does not deal with all things, but only with such as may or may not take place. Concerning things which exist or will exist inevitably, or which cannot possibly exist or take place, no counsel can be given. Nor, again, can counsel be given about the whole class of things which may or may not take place; for this class includes some good things that occur naturally, and some that 35 occur by accident; and about these it is useless to offer counsel. Clearly counsel can only be given on matters about which people deliberate; matters, namely, that ultimately depend on ourselves, and which we have it in our power to set going. For we turn a thing over in our mind until we have reached the point of seeing whether we can 1359ᵇ do it or not.

Now to enumerate and classify accurately the usual subjects of public business, and further to frame, as far as possible, true definitions of them, is a task which we mu.t 5 not attempt on the present occasion. For it does not belong to the art of rhetoric, but to a more instructive art and a more real branch of knowledge; and as it is, rhetoric has been given a far wider subject-matter than strictly belongs to it. The truth is, as indeed we ha ʼe said already,[20] that rhetoric is a combination of the science of 10 logic and of the ethical branch of politics; and it is partly like dialectic, partly like sophistical reasoning. But the more we try to make either dialectic or rhetoric not, what they really are, practical faculties, but sciences, the more 15 we shall inadvertently be destroying their true nature; for we shall be re-fashioning them and shall be passing into

[20] i. 2. 1356ᵃ 25 ff.

the region of sciences dealing with definite subjects rather than simply with words and forms of reasoning. Even here, however, we will mention those points which it is of practical importance to distinguish, their fuller treatment falling naturally to political science.

The main matters on which all men deliberate and on which political speakers make speeches are some five in number: ways and means, war and peace, national de- 20 fence, imports and exports, and legislation.

As to Ways and Means, then, the intending speaker will need to know the number and extent of the country's sources of revenue, so that, if any is being overlooked, it may be added, and, if any is defective, it may be increased. 25 Further, he should know all the expenditure of the country, in order that, if any part of it is superfluous, it may be abolished, or, if any is too large, it may be reduced. For men become richer not only by increasing their existing wealth but also by reducting their expenditure. A comprehensive view of these questions cannot be gained 30 solely from experience in home affairs; in order to advise on such matters a man must be keenly interested in the methods worked out in other lands.

As to Peace and War, he must know the extent of the military strength of his country, both actual and potential, 35 and also the nature of that actual and potential strength; and further, what wars his country has waged, and how it has waged them. He must know these facts not only about his own country, but also about neighbouring countries; and also about countries with which war is likely, in order that peace may be maintained with those stronger than his own, and that his own may have power to make war or not against those that are weaker. He should know, too, 1360ᵃ whether the military power of another country is like or unlike that of his own; for this is a matter that may affect their relative strength. With the same end in view he must, besides, have studied the wars of other countries as well as those of his own, and the way they ended; similar

5 causes are likely to have similar results.

With regard to National Defence: he ought to know all about the methods of defence in actual use, such as the strength and character of the defensive force and the positions of the forts—this last means that he must be well acquainted with the lie of the country—in order that a 10 garrison may be increased if it is too small or removed if it is not wanted, and that the strategic points may be guarded with special care.

With regard to the Food Supply: he must know what outlay will meet the needs of his country; what kinds of food are produced at home and what imported; and what articles must be exported or imported. This last he must 15 know in order that agreements and commercial treaties may be made with the countries concerned. There are, indeed, two sorts of state to which he must see that his countrymen give no cause for offence, states stronger than his own, and states with which it is advantageous to trade.

But while he must, for security's sake, be able to take all this into account, he must before all things understand 20 the subject of legislation; for it is on a country's laws that its whole welfare depends. He must, therefore, know how many different forms of constitution there are; under what conditions each of these will prosper and by what internal developments or external attacks each of them tends to be destroyed. When I speak of destruction through internal developments I refer to the fact that all constitutions, except the best one of all, are destroyed both by not being pushed far enough and by being pushed too far. Thus, 25 democracy loses its vigour, and finally passes into oligarchy, not only when it is not pushed far enough, but also when it is pushed a great deal too far; just as the aquiline and the snub nose not only turn into normal noses by not being aquiline or snub enough, but also by being too violently aquiline or snub arrive at a condition in which they no longer look like noses at all.

30　It is useful, in framing laws, not only to study the past

history of one's own country, in order to understand
which constitution is desirable for it now, but also to have
a knowledge of the constitutions of other nations, and so
to learn for what kinds of nation the various kinds of constitution are suited. From this we can see that books of
travel are useful aids to legislation, since from these we
may learn the laws and customs of different races. The
political speaker will also find the researches of historians 35
useful. But all this is the business of political science and
not of rhetoric.

These, then, are the most important kinds of information which the political speaker must possess. Let us now 1360ᵇ
go back and state the premises from which he will have
to argue in favour of adopting or rejecting measures regarding these and other matters. . . .

BOOK II

18 The use of persuasive speech is to lead to decisions.
(When we know a thing, and have decided about it, there
is no further use in speaking about it.) This is so even if
one is addressing a single person and urging him to do or
not to do something, as when we scold a man for his con- 10
duct or try to change his views: the single person is as
much your 'judge' as if he were one of many; we may say,
without qualification, that any one is your judge whom you
have to persuade. Nor does it matter whether we are arguing against an actual opponent or against a mere proposition; in the latter case we still have to use speech and
overthrow the opposing arguments, and we attack these as 15
we should attack an actual opponent. Our principle holds
good of ceremonial speeches also; the 'onlookers' for
whom such a speech is put together are treated as the
judges of it. Broadly speaking, however, the only sort of
person who can strictly be called a judge is the man who
decides the issue in some matter of public controversy;
that is, in law suits and in political debates, in both of

which there are issues to be decided. In the section on
political oratory an account has already been given of the
20 types of character that mark the different constitutions.[21]

The manner and means of investing speeches with
moral character may now be regarded as fully set forth.

Each of the main divisions of oratory has, we have
seen,[22] its own distinct purpose. With regard to each division, we have noted the accepted views and propositions
upon which we may base our arguments—for political,[23]
25 for ceremonial,[24] and for forensic speaking.[25] We have
further determined completely by what means speeches
may be invested with the required moral character. We
are now to proceed to discuss the arguments common to
all oratory. All orators, besides their special lines of argument, are bound to use, for instance, the topic of the Possible and Impossible; and to try to show that a thing has
30 happened, or will happen in future. Again, the topic of
Size is common to all oratory; all of us have to argue that
things are bigger or smaller than they seem, whether we are
making political speeches, speeches of eulogy or attack, or
prosecuting or defending in the law-courts. Having ana-
1392a lysed these subjects, we will try to say what we can about
the general principles of arguing by 'enthymeme' and 'example,' by the addition of which we may hope to complete the project with which we set out. Of the above-
mentioned general lines of argument, that concerned with
5 Amplification is—as has been already said [26]—most appropriate to ceremonial speeches; that concerned with the
Past, to forensic speeches, where the required decision is
always about the past; that concerned with Possibility and
the Future, to political speeches.

19   Let us first speak of the Possible and Impossible. It
may plausibly be argued: That if it is possible for one of a
pair of contraries to be or happen, then it is possible for

[21] i, c. 8.   [22] i, c. 3.   [23] i, cc. 4–8.
[24] i, c. 9.   [25] i, cc. 10–14.   [26] i, c. 9.

the other: e.g. if a man can be cured, he can also fall ill; 10
for any two contraries are equally possible, in so far as they
are contraries. That if of two similar things one is possible,
so is the other. That if the harder of two things is possible,
so is the easier. That if a thing can come into existence in
a good and beautiful form, then it can come into existence
generally; thus a house can exist more easily than a beauti- 15
ful house. That if the beginning of a thing can occur, so
can the end; for nothing impossible occurs or begins to
occur; thus the commensurability of the diagonal of a
square with its side neither occurs nor can begin to occur.
That if the end is possible, so is the beginning; for all 20
things that occur have a beginning. That if that which is
posterior in essence or in order of generation can come
into being, so can that which is prior: thus if a man can
come into being, so can a boy, since the boy comes first in
order of generation; and if a boy can, so can a man, for the
man also is first. That those things are possible of which
the love or desire is natural; for no one, as a rule, loves or 25
desires impossibilities. That things which are the object
of any kind of science or art are possible and exist or come
into existence. That anything is possible the first step in
whose production depends on men or things which we
can compel or persuade to produce it, by our greater
strength, our control of them, or our friendship with them.
That where the parts are possible, the whole is possible;
and where the whole is possible, the parts are usually possible. For if the slit in front, the toe-piece, and the upper 30
leather can be made, then shoes can be made; and if shoes,
then also the front slit and toe-piece. That if a whole1392ᵇ
genus is a thing that can occur, so can the species; and if
the species can occur, so can the genus: thus, if a sailing
vessel can be made, so also can a trireme; and if a trireme,
then a sailing vessel also. That if one of two things whose
existence depends on each other is possible, so is the other;
for instance, if 'double', then 'half', and if 'half', then 5
'double'. That if a thing can be produced without art or

preparation, it can be produced still more certainly by the careful application of art to it. Hence Agathon has said:

> To some things we by art must needs attain,
> Others by destiny or luck we gain.

10 That if anything is possible to inferior, weaker, and stupider people, it is more so for their opposites; thus Isocrates said that it would be a strange thing if he could not discover a thing that Euthynus had found out.[27] As for Impossibility, we can clearly get what we want by taking the contraries of the arguments stated above.

Questions of Past Fact may be looked at in the follow-
15 ing ways: First, that if the less likely of two things has occurred, the more likely must have occurred also. That if one thing that usually follows another has happened, then that other thing has happened; that, for instance, if a man has forgotten a thing, he has also once learnt it. That if a man had the power and the wish to do a thing, he has done it; for every one does do whatever he intends to do whenever he can do it, there being nothing to stop
20 him. That, further, he has done the thing in question either if he intended it and nothing external prevented him; or if he had the power to do it and was angry at the time; or if he had the power to do it and his heart was set upon it—for people as a rule do what they long to do, if they can; bad people through lack of self-control; good people, because their hearts are set upon good things.
25 Again, that if a thing was 'going to happen', it has happened; if a man was 'going to do something', he has done it, for it is likely that the intention was carried out. That if one thing has happened which naturally happens before another or with a view to it, the other has happened; for instance, if it has lightened, it has also thundered; and if an action has been attempted, it has been done. That if one thing has happened which naturally happens after another, or with a view to which that other happens, then that other (that which happens first, or happens with a

[27] CD ᴵsocr. xviii. 15.

view to this thing) has also happened; thus, if it has thundered it has also lightened, and if an action has been done it has been attempted. Of all these sequences some are inevitable and some merely usual. The arguments for the non-occurrence of anything can obviously be found by considering the opposite of those that have been mentioned.

How questions of Future Fact should be argued is clear 1393ᵃ from the same considerations: That a thing will be done if there is both the power and the wish to do it; or if along with the power to do it there is a craving for the result, or anger, or calculation, prompting it. That the thing will be done, in these cases, if the man is actually setting about it, or even if he means to do it later—for usually what we mean to do happens rather than what we do not mean to do. That a thing will happen if another thing which naturally happens before it has already happened; thus, if it is clouding over, it is likely to rain. That if the means to an end have occurred, then the end is likely to occur; thus, if there is a foundation, there will be a house.

For arguments about the Greatness and Smallness of things, the greater and the lesser, and generally great things and small, what we have already said will show the line to take. In discussing deliberative oratory we have spoken about the relative greatness of various goods, and about the greater and lesser in general.[28] Since therefore in each type of oratory the object under discussion is some kind of good—whether it is utility, nobleness, or justice—it is clear that every orator must obtain the materials of amplification through these channels.[29] To go further than this, and try to establish abstract laws of greatness and superiority, is to argue without an object; in practical life, particular facts count more than generalizations.

Enough has now been said about these questions of possibility and the reverse, of past or future fact, and of the relative greatness or smallness of things.

[28] i, c. 7.
[29] i.e. some kind of good.

20   The special forms of oratorical argument having
now been discussed, we have next to treat of those which
are common to all kinds of oratory. These are of two
main kinds, 'Example' and 'Enthymeme'; for the 'Maxim'
is part of an Enthymeme.

25   We will first treat of argument by Example, for it has
the nature of induction, which is the foundation of reasoning. This form or argument has two varieties; one
consisting in the mention of actual past facts, the other
in the invention of facts by the speaker. Of the latter,
again, here are two varieties, the illustrative parallel and
30 the fable (e.g. the fables of Aesop, or those from Libya).
As an instance of the mention of actual facts, take the
following. The speaker may argue thus: 'We must prepare
for war against the king of Persia and not let him subdue
Egypt. For Darius of old did not cross the Aegean until
1393ᵇ he had seized Egypt; but once he had seized it, he did
cross. And Xerxes, again, did not attack us until he had
seized Egypt; but once he had seized it, he did cross. If
therefore the present king seizes Egypt, he also will cross,
and therefore we must not let him.'

The illustrative parallel is the sort of argument Socrates
used: e.g. 'Public officials ought not to be selected by lot.
5 That is like using the lot to select athletes, instead of
choosing those who are fit for the contest; or using the
lot to select a steersman from among a ship's crew, as if
we ought to take the man on whom the lot falls, and not
the man who knows most about it.'

Instances of the fable are that of Stesichorus about
Phalaris, and that of Aesop in defence of the popular
10 leader. When the people of Himera had made Phalaris
military dictator, and were going to give him a bodyguard,
Stesichorus wound up a long talk by telling them the
fable of the horse who had a field all to himself. Presently
there came a stag and began to spoil his pasturage. The
horse, wishing to revenge himself on the stag, asked a man
15 if he could help him to do so. The man said, 'Yes, if you

will let me bridle you and get on your back with javelins in my hand'. The horse agreed, and the man mounted; but instead of getting his revenge on the stag, the horse found himself the slave of the man. 'You too', said Stesichorus, 'take care lest, in your desire for revenge on your enemies, you meet the same fate as the horse. By making Phalaris 20 military dictator, you have already let yourselves be bridled. If you let him get on to your backs by giving him a bodyguard, from that moment you will be his slaves.'

Aesop, defending before the assembly at Samos a popular leader who was being tried for his life, told this story: A fox, in crossing a river, was swept into a hole in the rocks; and, not being able to get out, suffered miseries for 25 a long time through the swarms of fleas that fastened on her. A hedgehog, while roaming around, noticed the fox; and feeling sorry for her asked if he might remove the fleas. But the fox declined the offer; and when the hedgehog asked why, she replied, 'These fleas are by this time full of me and not sucking much blood; if you take them away, others will come with fresh appetites and drink up 30 all the blood I have left.' 'So, men of Samos,' said Aesop, 'my client will do you no further harm; he is wealthy already. But if you put him to death, others will come along who are not rich, and their peculations will empty your treasury completely.'   1394ᵃ

Fables are suitable for addresses to popular assemblies; and they have one advantage—they are comparatively easy to invent, whereas it is hard to find parallels among actual past events. You will in fact frame them just as you frame illustrative parallels: all you require is the power of think- 5 ing out your analogy, a power developed by intellectual training. But while it is easier to supply parallels by inventing fables, it is more valuable for the political speaker to supply them by quoting what has actually happened, since in most respects the future will be like what the past has been.

Where we are unable to argue by Enthymeme, we

must try to demonstrate our point by this method of
10 Example, and to convince our hearers thereby. If we can
argue by Enthymeme, we should use our Examples as
subsequent supplementary evidence. They should not
precede the Enthymemes: that will give the argument an
inductive air, which only rarely suits the conditions of
speech-making. If they follow the Enthymemes, they
have the effect of witnesses giving evidence, and this al-
15 ways tells. For the same reason, if you put your examples
first you must give a large number of them; if you put
them last, a single one is sufficient; even a single witness
will serve if he is a good one. It has now been stated how
many varieties of argument by Example there are, and
how and when they are to be employed.

21   We now turn to the use of maxims, in order to
see upon what subjects and occasions, and for what kind
20 of speaker, they will appropriately form part of a speech.
This will appear most clearly when we have defined a
maxim. It is a statement; not about a particular fact, such
as the character of Iphicrates, but of a general kind; nor
is it about any and every subject—e.g. 'straight is the contrary of curved' is not a maxim—but only about questions
of practical conduct, courses of conduct to be chosen or
25 avoided. Now an Enthymeme is a syllogism dealing with
such practical subjects. It is therefore roughly true that
the premisses or conclusions of Enthymemes, considered
apart from the rest of the argument, are maxims: e.g.

Never should any man whose wits are sound
30 Have his sons taught more wisdom than their fellows.[30]

Here we have a maxim; add the reason or explanation,
and the whole thing is an Enthymeme; thus—

It makes them idle; and therewith they earn
Ill-will and jealousy throughout the city.[31]

Again,

[30] Euripides, *Medea*, 295.   [31] ib. 297.

> There is no man in all things prosperous,[32]   1394^b

and

> There is no man among us all is free.

are maxims; but the latter, taken with what follows it, is 5 an Enthymeme—

> For all are slaves of money or of chance.[33]

From this definition of a maxim it follows that there are four kinds of maxims. In the first place, the maxim may or may not have a supplement. Proof is needed where the statement is paradoxical or disputable; no supplement is 10 wanted where the statement contains nothing paradoxical, either because the view expressed is already a known truth, e.g.

> Chiefest of blessing is health for a man, as it seemeth to me,[34]

this being the general opinion: or because, as soon as the view is stated, it is clear at a glance, e.g.   15

> No love is true save that which loves for ever.[35]

Of the maxims that do have a supplement attached, some are part of an Enthymeme, e.g.

> Never should any man whose wits are sound, &c.[36]

Others have the essential character of Enthymemes, but are not stated as parts of Enthymemes; these latter are reckoned the best; they are those in which the reason for the view expressed is simply implied, e.g.   20

> O mortal man, nurse not immortal wrath.

[32] Euripides, fragm.
[33] Euripides, *Hecuba*, 864 f.
[34] Possibly a fragment of Epicharmus.
[35] Euripides, *Troades*, 1051.
[36] Euripides, *Medea*, 295.

To say 'it is not right to nurse immortal wrath' is a maxim; the added words 'O mortal man' give the reason. Similarly, with the words

Mortal creatures ought to cherish mortal, not immortal thoughts.[37]

25   What has been said has shown us how many kinds of maxims there are, and to what subjects the various kinds are appropriate. They must not be given without supplement if they express disputed or paradoxical views: we must, in that case, either put the supplement first and make a maxim of the conclusion, e.g. you might say, 'For 30 my part, since both unpopularity and idleness are undesirable, I hold that it is better not be be educated'; or you may say this first, and then add the previous clause. Where a statement, without being paradoxical, is not obviously true, the reason should be added as concisely as possible. In such cases both laconic and enigmatic sayings are suit-1395ᵃ able; thus one might say what Stesichorus said to the Locrians, 'Insolence is better avoided, lest the cicalas chirp on the ground.' [38]

The use of maxims is appropriate only to elderly men, and in handling subjects in which the speaker is experienced. For a young man to use them is—like telling stories —unbecoming; to use them in handling things in which 5 one has no experience is silly and ill-bred: a fact sufficiently proved by the special fondness of country fellows for striking out maxims, and their readiness to air them.

To declare a thing to be universally true when it is not is most appropriate when working up feelings of horror and indignation in our hearers; especially by way of pref-10 ace, or after the facts have been proved. Even hackneyed and commonplace maxims are to be used, if they suit one's purpose: just because they are commonplace, every one seems to agree with them, and therefore they are

[37] Epicharmus?
[38] The cicalas would have to chirp on the ground if an enemy cut down the trees.

taken for truth. Thus, any one who is calling on his men to risk an engagement without obtaining favourable omens may quote

One omen of all is best, that we fight for our fatherland.[39]

Or, if he is calling on them to attack a stronger force—

The War-God showeth no favour.[40]   15

Or, if he is urging people to destroy the innocent children of their enemies—

Fool, who slayeth the father and leaveth his sons to avenge him.[41]

Some proverbs are also maxims, e.g. the proverb 'An Attic neighbour'. You are not to avoid uttering maxims that contradict such sayings as have become public property (I mean such sayings as 'know thyself' and 'nothing in 20 excess'), if doing so will raise your hearers' opinion of your character, or convey an effect of strong emotion— e.g. an angry speaker might well say, 'It is not true that we ought to know ourselves: anyhow, if this man had known himself, he would never have thought himself fit for any army command.' It will raise people's opinion of our character to say, for instance, 'We ought not to fol- 25 low the saying that bids us treat our friends as future enemies: much better to treat our enemies as future friends.' [42] The moral purpose should be implied partly by the very wording of our maxim. Failing this, we should add our reason: e.g. having said 'We should treat our friends, not as the saying advises, but as if they were going to be our friends always,' we should add 'for the other be- haviour is that of a traitor': or we might put it, 'I disapprove 30 of that saying. A true friend will treat his friend as if he were going to be his friend for ever'; and again, 'Nor do I ap-

[39] *Iliad.* xii. 243.   [40] Ibid. xviii. 309.
[41] Cp. i, c. 15, 1376ᵃ 7   [42] Cp. ii, c. 13, 1389ᵇ 23–5.

prove of the saying "nothing in excess": we are bound to
hate bad men excessively.'

1395ᵇ   One great advantage of maxims to a speaker is due to
the want of intelligence in his hearers, who love to hear
him succeed in expressing as a universal truth the opinions which they hold themselves about particular cases.
I will explain what I mean by this, indicating at the same
time how we are to hunt down the maxims required. The
5 maxim, as has been already said,[43] is a general statement
and people love to hear stated in general terms what they
already believe in some particular connexion: e.g. if a man
happens to have bad neighbours or bad children, he will
agree with any one who tells him, 'Nothing is more an-
noying than having neighbours', or, 'Nothing is more foolish than to be the parent of children.' The orator has
10 therefore to guess the subjects on which his hearers really
hold views already, and what those views are, and then
must express, as general truths, these same views on these
same subjects. This is one advantage of using maxims.
There is another which is more important—it invests a
speech with moral character. There is moral character in
every speech in which the moral purpose is conspicuous:
and maxims always produce this effect, because the utter-
15 ance of them amounts to a general declaration of moral
principles: so that, if the maxims are sound, they display
the speaker as a man of sound moral character. So much
for the maxim—its nature, varieties, proper use, and advantages.

20 **22**   We now come to the Enthymemes, and will begin
the subject with some general consideration of the proper
way of looking for them, and then proceed to what is a
distinct question, the lines of argument to be embodied
in them. It has already [44] been pointed out that the Enthymeme is a syllogism, and in what sense it is so. We have
also noted the differences between it and the syllogism of

[43] 1394ᵃ 23.   [44] i, c. 2, 1356ᵇ 3, 1357ᵃ 16.

dialectic. Thus we must not carry its reasoning too far
back, or the length of our argument will cause obscurity: 25
nor must we put in all the steps that lead to our conclusion, or we shall waste words in saying what is manifest.
It is this simplicity that makes the uneducated more effective than the educated when addressing popular audiences—makes them, as the poets [45] tell us, 'charm the
crowd's ears more finely'. Educated men lay down broad
general principles; uneducated men argue from common 30
knowledge and draw obvious conclusions. We must not,
therefore, start from any and every accepted opinion, but
only from those we have defined—those accepted by our
judges or by those whose authority they recognize: and
there must, moreover, be no doubt in the minds of most, 1396ª
if not all, of our judges that the opinions put forward
really are of this sort. We should also base our arguments
upon probabilities as well as upon certainties.

The first thing we have to remember is this. Whether
our argument concerns public affairs or some other sub- 5
jects, we must know some, if not all, of the facts about the
subject on which we are to speak and argue. Otherwise we
can have no materials out of which to construct arguments. I mean, for instance, how could we advise the
Athenians whether they should go to war or not, if we
did not know their strength, whether it was naval or military or both, and how great it is; what their revenues 10
amount to; who their friends and enemies are; what wars,
too, they have waged, and with what success; and so on?
Or how could we eulogize them if we knew nothing about
the sea-fight at Salamis, or the battle of Marathon, or
what they did for the Heracleidae, or any other facts like
that? All eulogy is based upon the noble deeds—real or
imaginary—that stand to the credit of those eulogized. On 15
the same principle, invectives are based on facts of the
opposite kind: the orator looks to see what base deeds—
real or imaginary—stand to the discredit of those he is

[45] Cp. Euripides, *Hippolytus*, 989.

attacking, such as treachery to the cause of Hellenic freedom, or the enslavement of their gallant allies against the
20 barbarians (Aegina,[46] Potidaea,[47] &c.), or any other mis-
deeds of this kind that are recorded against them. So, too,
in a court of law: whether we are prosecuting or defending,
we must pay attention to the existing facts of the case.
It makes no difference whether the subject is the Lacedae-
monians or the Athenians, a man or a god; we must do the
same thing. Suppose it to be Achilles whom we are to ad-
25 vise, to praise or blame, to accuse or defend; here too we
must take the facts, real or imaginary; these must be our
material, whether we are to praise or blame him for the
noble or base deeds he has done, to accuse or defend him
for his just or unjust treatment of others, or to advise him
30 about what is or is not to his interest. The same thing
applies to any subject whatever. Thus, in handling the
question whether justice is or is not a good, we must start
with the real facts about justice and goodness. We see,
then, that this is the only way in which any one ever
1396ᵇ proves anything, whether his arguments are strictly cogent
or not: not all facts can form his basis, but only those that
bear on the matter in hand: nor, plainly, can proof be
effected otherwise by means of the speech. Consequently,
as appears in the *Topics*,[48] we must first of all have by
5 us a selection of arguments about questions that may arise
and are suitable for us to handle; and then we must try
to think out arguments of the same type for special needs
as they emerge; not vaguely and indefinitely, but by keeping our eyes on the actual facts of the subject we have to
speak on, and gathering in as many of them as we can
that bear closely upon it: for the more actual facts we
10 have at our command, the more easily we prove our case;
and the more closely they bear on the subject, the more
they will seem to belong to that speech only instead of
being commonplaces. By 'commonplaces' I mean, for example, eulogy of Achilles because he is a human being, or
a demi-god, or because he joined the expedition against

---

46 Cp. Thucyd. ii. 27; iv. 57.   47 Cp. Thucyd. ii. 70.
48 Cp. *Top.* i, c. 14.

Troy: these things are true of many others, so that this kind of eulogy applies no better to Achilles than to Diomede. The special facts here needed are those that are true of Achilles alone; such facts as that he slew Hector, the bravest of the Trojans, and Cycnus the invulnerable, who prevented all the Greeks from landing, and again that he was the youngest man who joined the expedition, and was not bound by oath to join it, and so on.

Here, then, we have our first principle of selection of Enthymemes—that which refers to the lines of argument selected. We will now consider the various elementary classes of Enthymemes. (By an 'elementary class' of Enthymeme I mean the same thing as a 'line of argument'.) We will begin, as we must begin, by observing that there are two kinds of Enthymemes. One kind proves some affirmative or negative proposition; the other kind disproves one. The difference between the two kinds is the same as that between syllogistic proof and disproof in dialectic. The demonstrative Enthymeme is formed by the conjunction of compatible propositions; the refutative, by the conjunction of incompatible propositions.

We may now be said to have in our hands the lines of argument for the various *special* subjects that it is useful or necessary to handle, having selected the propositions suitable in various cases. We have, in fact, already ascertained the lines of argument applicable to Enthymemes about good and evil, the noble and the base, justice and injustice, and also to those about types of character, emotions, and moral qualities.[49] Let us now lay hold of certain facts about the whole subject, considered from a different and more general point of view. In the course of our discussion we will take note of the distinction between lines of proof and lines of disproof:[50] and also of those lines of argument used in what seem to be Enthymemes, but are not, since they do not represent valid syllogisms.[51] Having made all this clear, we will proceed to classify Objections and Refutations, showing how they can be brought to bear upon Enthymemes.[52]

1397ᵃ

---

[49] i, cc. 4–14; ii, cc. 1–18.   [51] ii, c. 24.
[50] ii, c. 23.   [52] ii, c. 25.